BHB
Baylor Handbook on the Hebrew Bible

General Editor

W. Dennis Tucker Jr.

DEUTERONOMY 1–11
A Handbook on the Hebrew Text

James E. Robson

BAYLOR UNIVERSITY PRESS

© 2016 by Baylor University Press
Waco, Texas 76798

All Rights Reserved. No part of this publication may be reproduced, stored in a retrieval system, or transmitted, in any form or by any means, electronic, mechanical, photocopying, recording, or otherwise, without the prior permission in writing of Baylor University Press.

Cover Design by Pamela Poll
Cover photograph by Bruce and Kenneth Zuckerman, West Semitic Research, in collaboration with the Ancient Biblical Manuscript Center. Courtesy Russian National Library (Saltykov-Shchedrin).

Library of Congress Cataloging-in-Publication Data

Names: Robson, James (James E.), author.
Title: Deuteronomy 1–11 : a handbook on the Hebrew text / James E. Robson.
Description: Waco, Texas : Baylor University Press, [2016] | ©2016 | Series: Baylor handbook on the Hebrew Bible | Includes bibliographical references and index.
Identifiers: LCCN 2016003893 (print) | LCCN 2016007324 (ebook) | ISBN 9781602585737 (pbk. : alk. paper) | ISBN 9781481305617 (ebook-Mobi/Kindle) | ISBN 9781481305624 (web PDF)
Subjects: LCSH: Bible. Deuteronomy I-XI—Criticism, interpretation, etc.
Classification: LCC BS1275.52 .R63 2016 (print) | LCC BS1275.52 (ebook) | DDC 222/.15077—dc23
LC record available at http://lccn.loc.gov/2016003893

Printed in the United States of America on acid-free paper with a minimum of 30 percent post-consumer waste recycled content.

TABLE OF CONTENTS

Acknowledgments	ix
Abbreviations	xi
Introduction	1

Moses' First Address: 1:1–4:49

Deuteronomy 1:1-5	11
Deuteronomy 1:6-8	22
Deuteronomy 1:9-18	26
Deuteronomy 1:19-25	38
Deuteronomy 1:26-33	45
Deuteronomy 1:34-40	53
Deuteronomy 1:41–2:1	60
Deuteronomy 2:2-8a	67
Deuteronomy 2:8b-15	73
Deuteronomy 2:16-25	79
Deuteronomy 2:26-37	88
Deuteronomy 3:1-7	99
Deuteronomy 3:8-17	105
Deuteronomy 3:18-22	115
Deuteronomy 3:23-29	121
Deuteronomy 4:1-8	128

Deuteronomy 4:9-14	137
Deuteronomy 4:15-22	144
Deuteronomy 4:23-31	152
Deuteronomy 4:32-40	161
Deuteronomy 4:41-43	171
Deuteronomy 4:44-49	174

Moses' Second Address: 5:1–11:32(26:19)

Deuteronomy 5:1-5	178
Deuteronomy 5:6-21	182
Deuteronomy 5:22-33	197
Deuteronomy 6:1-3	210
Deuteronomy 6:4-9	213
Deuteronomy 6:10-19	217
Deuteronomy 6:20-25	225
Deuteronomy 7:1-6a	231
Deuteronomy 7:6b-11	237
Deuteronomy 7:12-16	243
Deuteronomy 7:17-24	248
Deuteronomy 7:25-26	256
Deuteronomy 8:1-10	259
Deuteronomy 8:11-20	270
Deuteronomy 9:1-6	279
Deuteronomy 9:7-24	286
Deuteronomy 9:25-29	302
Deuteronomy 10:1-11	306
Deuteronomy 10:12–11:1	316
Deuteronomy 11:2-9	326
Deuteronomy 11:10-12	334

Deuteronomy 11:13-17	338
Deuteronomy 11:18-21	342
Deuteronomy 11:22-25	344
Deuteronomy 11:26-32	348
Glossary	355
Works Cited	359
Author Index	366
Subject Index	369

ACKNOWLEDGMENTS

This has been a most enjoyable project, although demanding in ways that I had not expected. It could not have happened without the assistance of others. I am grateful to Dr. W. Dennis Tucker, the editor of this series, and Dr. Carey C. Newman, director of Baylor University Press, for the commission to write it. Students past and present have taught me much, and continue to do so. Their probing questions lie directly behind some of the annotations I have made. But, far more than that, they have demonstrated to me the need for a teacher to enter their world. It is with that spirit that I have written this book. On the one hand, I have imagined an inquisitive student sitting with me and asking, "But what about . . . ?" On the other hand, I have imagined standing behind a student as they work, asking them, "Have you thought about . . . ?"

The bulk of this book has been written during research leave from Wycliffe Hall, Oxford. I am grateful to my colleagues for carrying my load during that time.

Finally, I want to pay tribute to my wife, Bridget, and to our daughters, Anna and Naomi. Without their support, encouragement, and love, this project would be much less, to say nothing of the author.

ABBREVIATIONS

AC Arnold, Bill T., and John H. Choi. *A Guide to Biblical Hebrew Syntax*. Cambridge: Cambridge University Press, 2003.

ANE Ancient Near-East

BDB Brown, F. S., S. R. Driver, and C. A. Briggs. *A Hebrew and English Lexicon of the Old Testament*. Oxford: Clarendon, 190.7

BHL Dotan, Aron, ed. *Biblia Hebraica Leningradensia: Prepared According to the Vocalization, Accents, and Masora of Aaron Ben Moses Ben Asher in the Leningrad Codex*. Peabody, Mass.: Hendrickson, 2001.

BHQ McCarthy, Carmel. *Deuteronomy*. Biblia Hebraica Quinta 5. Stuttgart: Deutsche Bibelgesellschaft, 2007.

BHS Elliger, K., and W. Rudolph. *Biblia Hebraica Stuttgartensia*. 1967. Repr. Stuttgart: Deutsche Bibelgesellschaft, 1990.

CDCH Clines, David J. A., ed. *The Concise Dictionary of Classical Hebrew*. Sheffield: Sheffield Phoenix Press, 2009.

CV Consonant Vowel (Open Syllable)

CVC Consonant Vowel Consonant (Closed Syllable)

DHS Davidson, A. B. *Introductory Hebrew Grammar: Hebrew Syntax*. Edinburgh: T&T Clark, 1896.

ED expository discourse (see §4)

ET English Translation

GKC Kautzsch, E., ed. *Gesenius' Hebrew Grammar*. 2nd ed. Translated by A. E. Cowley. Oxford: Clarendon, 1910.

HALOT Koehler, Ludwig, Walter Baumgartner, and Johann J. Stamm. *The Hebrew and Aramaic Lexicon of the Old Testament*. Study ed. Leiden: Brill, 2001.

HD	hortatory discourse (see §4)
ID	interrogative discourse (see §4)
JM	Joüon, Paul, and Takamitsu Muraoka. *A Grammar of Biblical Hebrew*. Rev. ed. Subsidia Biblica 27. Rome: Pontificio Istituto Biblico, 2006.
LXX	Septuagint
MNK	van der Merwe, Christo H. J., J. A. Naudé, and Jan H. Kroeze. *A Biblical Hebrew Reference Grammar*. Biblical Languages: Hebrew 3. Sheffield: Sheffield Academic, 1999.
MT	Masoretic text
ND	narrative discourse (see §4)
NJPS	New Jewish Publication Society of America Tanakh
NP	noun phrase
OT	Old Testament
PD	predictive discourse (see §4)
PP	prepositional phrase
Smr	Samaritan Pentateuch
s.v.	*sub verbo* ("under the word")
WHS	Williams, Ronald J. *Hebrew Syntax*. 3rd ed. Revised and expanded by John C. Beckman. Toronto: University of Toronto Press, 2007.
WO	Waltke, Bruce K., and M. P. O'Connor. *An Introduction to Biblical Hebrew Syntax*. Winona Lake, Ind.: Eisenbrauns, 1990.
WS	Williams, Ronald J. *Hebrew Syntax: An Outline*. 2nd ed. Toronto: University of Toronto Press, 1976.

INTRODUCTION

The aim of this handbook is to assist a student working on the Hebrew text of Deuteronomy 1–11. The student may be an undergraduate studying intermediate Hebrew or an advanced researcher, although the series starts with the former. Throughout, I have tried to think chiefly of what students have asked or would ask. The advantage of a narrow focus is twofold: (1) there is scope to address questions that commentaries do not have the space (or inclination) to cover; and (2) there is a more comprehensive and Deuteronomy-focused approach than grammars can adopt. I am conscious that a work like this is often picked up and put down, rather than read. So this opening section helps to orient one to the structure, layout, and content, assuming that he/she will have limited time and will need to navigate quickly to the relevant content. Thus this introduction is divided into five parts, all of which relate directly to the handbook itself rather than being of general interest:

1. orientation to the book of Deuteronomy (§1);
2. explanation of the layout of the handbook (§2);
3. explanation of embedded direct discourse (§3);
4. guide to different types of discourse (§4); and
5. linguistic background: some key pairs of opposites (§5).

§1 The Book of Deuteronomy

Deuteronomy is a book of pivotal importance for both Judaism and Christianity. In it Yhwh through Moses confronts Israel on the edge of the promised land with a word that is demanding, insistent, contemporary, and urgent. The book of Deuteronomy confronts its readers with that same word. Deuteronomy sets out a vision for life in a land that remains to be possessed, a vision that comes close to a full-orbed political theology. It demands uncompromising obedience to that vision. It also tells a story that reaches back into the past and looks forward to the future. The story of the past is one of promises made to the patriarchs, rescue from slavery in Egypt, revelation at Horeb, and wilderness wanderings. The story of the future is one of life (in the land), apostasy, death (exile from the land), and restoration. The book marshals story and demands to challenge readers of Deuteronomy to "Choose life" (30:19) "today." That challenge is always present and remains ever relevant. It recognizes the reality of life lived on the threshold, on the boundary. Behind lies a past made up of human failure and rebellion; of Yhwh's faithfulness in history. Ahead lies a future shaped by promise that needs to be claimed. And every day is a day of choice, a day of demand, a day of dignity and significance—to choose life and live in conformity with that vision. And the choice that is made affects the future.

Deuteronomy is dominated by the speeches of Moses. In the introduction (1:1-5), the narrator introduces Moses in the third person. Moses' first speech then runs from 1:6 through 4:40. The narrator's voice is heard again in 4:41–5:1a, followed by Moses' second speech continuing from 5:1b through the end of chapter 26. There is a natural break at the end of chapter 11, and so this handbook ends there. Deuteronomy 12:1 shifts from Moses' more general exhortation to the specific "statutes and judgments" (הַחֻקִּים וְהַמִּשְׁפָּטִים).

§2 Layout of the Handbook

This handbook breaks down the text of Deuteronomy into six levels. Alongside the desire to preserve something of Deuteronomy's logic and flow is the need to work with manageable chunks of text.

1. *Major sections*: two major speeches of Moses and surrounding material (1:1–4:49; 5:1–11:32).
2. *Minor sections*: larger subsections that sometimes cross chapter boundaries. I provide brief comments on the minor section as a whole, indicating where knowledge of the Hebrew provides guidance on structure.
3. *Units*: smaller more manageable units within a minor section. Sometimes there may be connections *across* units, such as subordinating conjunctions starting a unit, but there is something discrete and manageable about the units chosen. I make a few introductory comments on the unit, and then provide

my own translation of the Hebrew text, in italics, based on the conclusions reached in the more detailed discussion.

The core of the book is to be found in levels 4–6.

4. *Verses*: After each Hebrew verse, there are brief comments about the verse as a whole, chiefly from the perspective of how knowledge of the Hebrew contributes to understanding the text. Following these comments, I identify the domain of discourse and type of discourse (see below).
5. *Divisions of the verse*: This largely follows a predictable pattern: the main components in text order (often these will be main clauses), parsing of verb form (often with morphological and/or syntactical comments), clausal issues (often with comments on constituents, though not exhaustive).
6. *Key words or phrases* (including some subordinate clauses).

Within parts 4–6, there are some points to note:

* D1–D5: domains of discourse (see §3);
* ND/PD/HD/ED/ID: types of discourse (see §4);
* Verb conjugations: I have mostly chosen theory-neutral titles (*wayyiqtol* / *yiqtol* / *qatal*) for the different verb conjugations, not least because debates still continue (e.g., Cook 2012; Joosten; Robar), although I have called *weqatal* "*qatal* (modal)" following Cook 2012.
* Cases: I follow many grammar books in using traditional grammatical categories associated with Latin: accusative (= object of the verb, usually direct); genitive (= "of"; the absolute in a construct chain); dative (= "to," "for"; ל preposition). While Hebrew does not have cases as such, there is still the value of simplicity and consistency in working with these terms.
* References: all references are to Deuteronomy, unless indicated; all verse references are to the same chapter under discussion, unless indicated.
* Words in **bold**: these are terms that appear in the glossary at the back of the book, and serve as illustrated examples of that term found in the text.

* More common syntactical and linguistic terms, which can be seen as paired opposites, receive their own treatment below in the section on linguistic orientation (§5).
* Because there are repeated or stereotypical phrases in Deuteronomy, I simply refer the reader to the first occurrence where there is a full discussion of the phrase. There are occasions, however, in which I summarize the original analysis.

§3 Embedded Direct Discourse

Deuteronomy is dominated by speech. In chapters 1–11, the reader/hearer encounters different voices or perspectives. At the most basic level, or "domain," there is the narrator's perspective (D1) (cf. de Regt 1988: 1:43–47; DeRouchie 2007: 82). Beyond the shape and contents of Deuteronomy itself, the perspective of the narrator of the book is heard where Moses is spoken of in the third person (1:1-5; 4:41–5:1a) and in historical notes or parenthetical comments (2:10-12, 20-23; 3:9, 11, 13b-14; 4:38b; 10:6-7). Whenever the narrator relates the words of other speakers, it move from the primary domain (D1) to a subdomain (D2). Since the decision on what is included or excluded from D2 is dependent on the narrator (D1), D2 is appropriately termed a "subdomain" (cf. de Regt 1988: 1:43). In chapters 1–11, the only speaker in D2 is Moses (Yhwh's voice is not heard, unmediated by Moses, until 31:14. Furthermore, sometimes Moses cites the words of others, such as Yhwh, the people, the spies, or even his own words from another occasion (D3). In turn, these voices may convey the words of yet others (D4). This embedding of subdomains of discourse, which is a major feature of Deuteronomy's rhetoric, is well illustrated in Deuteronomy 5.

D1 Narrator (v. 1a)
   D2 Moses (vv. 1b-5)
      D3 Yhwh (vv. 6-21)
   D2 Moses (vv. 22-24aα)
      D3 Israel's leaders (vv. 24aβ-27)
   D2 Moses (v. 28a)
      D3 Yhwh (vv. 28b-30a)
         D4 Moses (v. 30b)
      D3 Yhwh (v. 31)
   D2 Moses (vv. 32-33)

Almost always a further subdomain of direct discourse is introduced by √אמר. Exceptions are: (1) after narratorial interruptions, when Moses' (3:9, 11, 13b-14; 4:38b; 10:6-7) or Yhwh's (2:10-12, 20-23) speech simply continues (cf. de Regt 1988: 1:45); (2) in 9:2, where Moses reminds his hearers of the Anakites' reputation of which they have heard (√שמע). Further, √אמר almost always introduces direct discourse. An exception is in 1:39 (s.v.), where it introduces indirect speech.

The embedding of discourse aligns the different voices and makes their words as present to the hearers *of* Deuteronomy as the hearers *in* Deuteronomy.

§4 Types of Discourse

When a character is speaking, they may be recounting history, asking a question, giving an instruction, or making a statement. In Hebrew each of these purposes has different constellations of verb forms and syntactical structures (Heller). Attention to one can give insight into another. It is important to consider not just what the text is *saying*, but what the character is *doing, in saying* something.

Assigning discourse to categories is not straightforward. The more finely calibrated the categories, the more "accurate" but the less manageable and accessible. As an example of the possible complexity, see Callaham who discusses up to twenty subcategories (20–21). For this handbook, however, I have chosen to work with the five main categories outlined in Heller (26), who in turn built his study on the work of Longacre (80–136). Here is a list, with their abbreviations, of these five types of discourse:

Narrative discourse (ND)—"in which a character reports an event or series of events that have occurred prior, from the character's point of view, to that moment"; e.g., יְהוָה אֱלֹהֵינוּ דִּבֶּר אֵלֵינוּ בְּחֹרֵב, "Yhwh our God spoke to us at Horeb" (1:6).

Expository discourse (ED)—"in which a character explains or describes general or present facts or actions"; e.g., וְהִנְּכֶם הַיּוֹם כְּכוֹכְבֵי הַשָּׁמַיִם לָרֹב, "See, you are today like the stars of heaven in abundance" (1:10).

Predictive discourse (PD)—"in which a character proposes or plans for events that will occur or may occur in the future"; e.g., גַּם־אַתָּה לֹא־תָבֹא שָׁם, "you too will not enter there" (1:37).

Hortatory discourse (HD)—"in which a character attempts to elicit a response from another character or other characters"; e.g., בֹּאוּ וּרְשׁוּ אֶת־הָאָרֶץ, "enter and possess the land" (1:8).
Interrogative discourse (ID)—"in which a character attempts to elicit a verbal response from the hearer(s)"; e.g., אָנָה ׀ אֲנַחְנוּ עֹלִים, "to where are we going up?" (1:28).

§5 Linguistic Framework: Paired Opposites

There are characteristics of this book that are my own, but there are others that are indebted to previous volumes in this handbook series. In particular, the linguistic framework that characterized Holmstedt on Ruth is one that I find both persuasive and helpful (2010). Below are pairs of terms that you will find in the handbook with examples. In every case, these are "opposites" in the sense that both cannot be true at the same time for a particular phrase.

1. Coordinate vs subordinate

Clauses are in **coordinate** relationship if more than one stands in sequence, at the same level; e.g., וּשְׁמַרְתֶּם וַעֲשִׂיתֶם, "and keep and do" (4:6). The main coordinating conjunction is ו. Phrases can also be coordinated or conjoined, if a ו-conjunction connects them. **Subordinate** clauses are those that are dependent on, or subordinate to, another clause; e.g., כַּאֲשֶׁר דִּבֶּר יְהוָה אֵלָי, "just as Yhwh said to me" (2:1). A subordinating conjunction (e.g., כאשר) usually introduces a subordinate clause.

2. Disjunctive vs conjunctive

These terms relate both to clauses and to accentuation. A clause is said to be **conjunctive** if ו-conjunction is joined directly to a finite verb form, where there is a certain *continuity* between this clause and the one preceding; e.g., וַיִּפְנוּ וַיַּעֲלוּ הָהָרָה וַיָּבֹאוּ עַד־נַחַל אֶשְׁכֹּל, "and they turned and went up to the hill country and came to Wadi Eshcol" (1:24). A clause is said to be **disjunctive** if a constituent occurs between the conjunction and the verb, where there is a certain *discontinuity* (e.g., temporal, logical) between this clause and the one preceding; e.g., וְלֹא אֲבִיתֶם לַעֲלֹת, "*but* you were not willing to go up" (1:26). An accent is **conjunctive** if the word is to be taken with what follows (e.g., in 5:6 יְהוָה), and **disjunctive** if the word is to be taken with what precedes (e.g., in 1:15 וְשֹׁטְרִים).

3. Syndesis (syndetic) vs asyndesis (asyndetic)

Coordinate clauses (and phrases) can be joined to the previous clause (or phrase) **syndetically** (with ו) or **asyndetically** (Ø). The latter (**asyndesis**) almost always does one of two things (cf. DeRouchie 2007: 225):

1. gives an explanatory or parenthetical phrase, clause or section; e.g., אֶעְבְּרָה בְאַרְצֶךָ בַּדֶּרֶךְ בַּדֶּרֶךְ אֵלֵךְ, "Let me pass through your land. *I will travel on the road, and only on the road . . .*" (2:27); or
2. starts a new section; e.g., הִשָּׁמְרוּ לָכֶם, "Watch yourselves . . .", (4:23).

4. Covert vs overt

Constituents are **overt** when they are present in the text. When the constituent is overt for reasons other than for narrative cohesion, the reader needs to ask why that constituent is present: e.g., וְהֵם יִירָשׁוּהָ, "and *they* will possess it" (1:39). Constituents are **covert** (or **null**) when they are not explicit in the text, but are effectively present from the point of view of syntax and semantics; e.g., כַּאֲשֶׁר נִסִּיתֶם בַּמַּסָּה, "just as you tested [Yhwh] at Massah" (6:16). A common instance is the **null-copula** clause, where the copula (the verb "to be") is **covert**.

5. Complement/argument vs adjunct

A clause is minimally made up of a subject and a predicate. From one perspective, that of **argument** structure, a clause comprises a predicate (P) and at least one argument (A). The predicate (P) denotes attributes of or relations between arguments (A). **Arguments** are necessary constituents (e.g., noun phrases, pronouns, certain adverbial phrases, different kinds of subordinate clauses). A predicate can be considered one-, two-, or three-place (i.e., with one, two, or three arguments). The verb √נתן is usually a three-place predicate; e.g., יְהוָה אֱלֹהֵיכֶם נָתַן לָכֶם אֶת־הָאָרֶץ הַזֹּאת, "Yhwh your God has given this land to you . . ." (3:18). There are three arguments: subject (יהוה אלהיכם, NP), object (את־הארץ הזאת, NP), and indirect object (לכם, PP).

Another way of considering a clause is by using **complements** and **adjuncts**. **Complements** are constituents that are *necessary* for a clause to be grammatical; for example, in the clause above, את־הארץ הזאת is the accusative complement, while לכם is the oblique complement (i.e., introduced by a preposition). **Adjuncts** are *optional* constituents;

e.g., כִּי אִתָּנוּ אֲנַחְנוּ אֵלֶּה פֹה הַיּוֹם כֻּלָּנוּ חַיִּים, "but with us, yes us, these ones here today, all of us [who are] alive." The only *syntactically necessary* phrase is the opening PP, "but with us" ("it was not with our fathers that Yhwh made this covenant . . . but with us . . ."). All the other phrases are **adjuncts**. Given that an **adjunct** is not *necessary*, a reader needs to ask why it is present at all.

6. Restrictive vs non-restrictive

A relative clause is **restrictive** if it identifies more closely a noun's referent; e.g., אֶת־הַדְּבָרִים אֲשֶׁר־רָאוּ עֵינֶיךָ, "the things *that/which your eyes saw*" (4:9). In English, no comma precedes the relative clause. A reader needs to ask why the noun is identified in *this* way. A relative clause is **non-restrictive** if it provides additional information and is not necessary for identifying the noun; e.g., סִיחֹן מֶלֶךְ הָאֱמֹרִי אֲשֶׁר יוֹשֵׁב בְּחֶשְׁבּוֹן, "Sihon, king of the Amorites, *who reigned in Heshbon*" (1:4). In English, a comma precedes the relative clause. A reader needs to ask why it is present at all.

7. Protasis vs apodosis

A **protasis** is a subordinate clause that is resumed by the **apodosis**, or main clause. Such clauses may be temporal, "When . . ., then . . ."; conditional, "If . . ., then . . ."; or causal, "Because . . ., therefore . . ."; e.g., אִם־יֹסְפִים ׀ אֲנַחְנוּ לִשְׁמֹעַ . . . וָמָתְנוּ, "if we hear again . . ., then we will die" (5:25).

8. Indicative (realis) vs modal (irrealis)

A verb is **indicative** if it expresses something factual; e.g., יְהוָה אֱלֹהֵינוּ דִּבֶּר אֵלֵינוּ, "Yhwh our God spoke to us . . ." (1:6). A verb is **modal** if it is concerned with whether something is possible, desirable, or necessary; e.g., הִשָּׁמְרוּ לָכֶם פֶּן־תִּשְׁכְּחוּ, "Watch yourselves *lest you forget . . .*" (4:23).

9. Unmarked vs marked

"Given two similar constructions, the one occurring more often and in a greater number of environments is **unmarked** while the one the [*sic*] occurs less often and in restricted environments is **marked**" (Holmstedt 2011: 8–9). The unmarked word order for **null-copula** clauses is Subject-Predicate (Buth); e.g., אֵלֶּה הַדְּבָרִים, "these are the words . . ." (1:1). Clauses with a finite verb also have a Subject-Predicate unmarked order (Holmstedt 2011); e.g., יְהוָה אֱלֹהֵיכֶם הִרְבָּה אֶתְכֶם, "Yhwh your God has multiplied you" (1:10). Often, though, the verb will come first for syntactical reasons, due to **triggered inversion** (e.g., after subordinating conjunctions; the verb form *wayyiqtol*).

10. Topic and focus

Beyond the world of semantics and syntax lies "pragmatics." This is about the users of language, and how more is communicated than simply what is said (cf. Yule). Two key concepts of pragmatics are **topic** and **focus**. Constituents can move around a clause not just for syntactical reasons, but also for pragmatic ones. A constituent may be "fronted" or "preposed" (i.e., in the preverbal field) as:

1. **topic**: "the entity that the utterance is primarily about" (Levinsohn and Dooley, §11.2). Most utterances are about someone or something that is already **discourse active** (i.e., the hearer knows this is what is being talked about). Either a *time frame* or a *participant* can be **topicalized** to help anchor the discourse for the hearer; e.g., זֶה | אַרְבָּעִים שָׁנָה יְהוָה אֱלֹהֶיךָ עִמָּךְ, "*these forty years* Yhwh your God has been with you" (2:7).
2. **focus**: "that part which indicates what the speaker intends as the most important or salient change to be made in the hearer's mental representation . . . " (Levinsohn and Dooley, §11.2), whether by giving *new information* or by creating a *contrast* between this item and an imaginary domain of other possible entities that could occupy that slot; e.g., אֶת־יְהוָה אֱלֹהֶיךָ תִּירָא וְאֹתוֹ תַעֲבֹד וּבִשְׁמוֹ תִּשָּׁבֵעַ, "It is *Yhwh your God* that you should fear, and it is *he* that you should serve, and it is *in his name* that you should swear" (6:13).

An example where both **topic** and **focus** are present—a distinctive example because the **topic** is **extraposed** (in this case outside the confines of the clause itself)—is found in 1:17: כִּי הַמִּשְׁפָּט לֵאלֹהִים הוּא, "for *as for judgment* (**topic**; extraposed), it *belongs to God* (**focus**)."

MOSES' FIRST ADDRESS
DEUTERONOMY 1:1–4:49

Moses' first speech to Israel in the plains of Moab dominates the opening four chapters. After the narratorial introduction (1:1-5), Moses recounts Israel's history since Horeb (1:6–3:29; ND). Chapter 1 relates Israel's flagrant rejection of Yhwh's word and the deadly consequences. Chapters 2–3 give a paradigm for the impending crossing of the Jordan, one dependent on Yhwh's initiative and obedience to his commands. In 4:1 Moses returns to the present to address directly those in Moab (ועתה; שמע [HD]). With powerful rhetoric, Moses confronts Israel to heed the commands he is giving them "today" in Moab, and to watch out for idolatry.

General Introduction: Deuteronomy 1:1-5

In the prologue, the narrator specifies the time and place of Moses' speaking. The temporal and geographical references serve to provide a contrast between failure and success. This contrast previews the rest of chapters 1–3 and sets up the two choices lying before Moses and the book's subsequent hearers (see 30:15). The structure is carefully balanced (see McConville, 60–61; Nelson, 16; Christensen 9):

a   "These are the words Moses spoke" (v. 1a)
  b   Place "in the Jordan region" (v. 1b)
    c   Time "eleven days journey" (v. 2)
      d   "Moses spoke . . . according to all which Yhwh commanded" (v. 3)
    c´   Time "after he had defeated Sihon . . ." (v. 4)
  b´   Place "in the Jordan region" (v. 5a)
a´   "Moses undertook to expound this law" (v. 5b)

The subtly shifting characterization of Moses' speaking in vv. 1, 3, and 5 serves to match Moses' words (v. 1) with Yhwh's command (v. 3) and with torah (v. 5) (McConville, 60).

¹These are the words that Moses spoke to all Israel across the Jordan, in the wilderness, in the Arabah, opposite Suph, between Paran and Tophel, Laban, Hazeroth, and Di-Zahab. ²It is eleven days from Horeb by the Mount Seir way to Kadesh Barnea. ³It was in the fortieth year in the eleventh month on the first day of the month that Moses spoke to all the Israelites according to all that Yhwh had commanded him for them, ⁴after he had struck down Sihon, king of the Amorites, who reigned in Heshbon, and Og, king of Bashan, who reigned in Ashtaroth at Edrei. ⁵Across the Jordan, in the land of Moab, Moses undertook to expound this torah, saying,

1:1 אֵ֣לֶּה הַדְּבָרִ֗ים אֲשֶׁ֨ר דִּבֶּ֤ר מֹשֶׁה֙ אֶל־כָּל־יִשְׂרָאֵ֔ל
בְּעֵ֖בֶר הַיַּרְדֵּ֑ן בַּמִּדְבָּ֡ר בָּֽעֲרָבָה֩ מ֨וֹל ס֜וּף בֵּֽין־פָּארָ֧ן
וּבֵֽין־תֹּ֛פֶל וְלָבָ֥ן וַחֲצֵרֹ֖ת וְדִ֥י זָהָֽב׃

D1. ED. With a prophetic flavor, the narrator introduces the words that the rest of the book of Deuteronomy will contain (cf. Jer 1:1).

אֵ֣לֶּה הַדְּבָרִ֗ים. The opening **null-copula** clause has the customary S–P word order, as the narrator speaks (ED). The demonstrative pronoun (אלה), a **deictic** word, points to something "near" within the mental map of the speaker. Here it introduces what will follow and is characteristic of the structural markers that give definition to the book (4:44 [and 4:45]; 6:1; 12:1; 29:1; 33:1). הדברים is the **head** of the following restrictive relative clause that serves to identify "the words." Without the subsequent relative clause, the **head**, הדברים, remains underspecified.

אֲשֶׁ֨ר דִּבֶּ֤ר מֹשֶׁה֙ אֶל־כָּל־יִשְׂרָאֵ֔ל בְּעֵ֖בֶר הַיַּרְדֵּ֑ן בַּמִּדְבָּ֡ר בָּֽעֲרָבָה֩ מ֨וֹל ס֜וּף בֵּֽין־פָּארָ֧ן וּבֵֽין־תֹּ֛פֶל וְלָבָ֥ן וַחֲצֵרֹ֖ת וְדִ֥י זָהָֽב. This restrictive relative clause, serving to specify further the **head**, הדברים, has the standard P–S order because of **triggered inversion** after the relative word אשר (אשר is not strictly a *pronoun* since its morphology does not change in order to agree, and it does not appear in the same syntactic settings; see Holmstedt 2006: 9 n. 2). After the predicate דבר and the subject, there follows a succession of prepositional phrases. The first PP (אל־כל־ישראל) is an oblique complement. The second PP (בעבר הירדן) is a spatial adjunct. Verse 1b (במדבר . . . ודי זהב) is joined asyndetically to v. 1a. It should probably be taken as appositional to בעבר הירדן. This provides further specification of the location of Moses' speaking, but with a purposeful merging of past event (itinerary; exodus/wilderness wanderings) into the present (location of Moses speaking in the plains of Moab) (Nelson, 17). The alternative, that v. 1b should be taken with v. 2 as part of the itinerary (so Weinfeld, 125; NJPS), does not account adequately for a number of factors: (1) the classic Deuteronomic **asyndesis** which serves to expand on or explain what has preceded; (2) the abrupt transition from v. 1a to v. 1b, (3) the LXX, which regards במדבר בערבה as locations for Moses' speaking; (4) סוף, which does not fit within the itinerary of v. 2, whether it speaks of the Sea of Reeds (so LXX: πλησίον τῆς ἐρυθρᾶς) or Suphah (סוּפָה; cf. Num 21:14).

דִּבֶּר. *Qatal* 3ms Piel √דבר. One of three verbs that have *segol* as the theme vowel in Piel 3ms (JM §52c). The verb does not normally introduce direct speech without the addition of √אמר. Examining the verb דבר from the perspective of argument structure, it is either a one-, two-, or three-place predicate. There is a subject doing the speaking (sometimes, as here, overt; at other times, contained within the verb). Then there may be none, one or both of a PP indicating the recipient of the speech and a direct object indicating what has been spoken (here, the relative word אשר). The recipient of the speech, the oblique complement, is designated either by אל, "to" or by ב, "with." Here, דבר is a three-place predicate.

אֶל־כָּל־יִשְׂרָאֵל. The PP oblique complement of דבר consists of the preposition אל followed by a construct (כל) and absolute (ישראל). It is a characteristically Deuteronomic phrase (Driver, lxxxii, 1), conceiving of Israel as "an integer" (Hawk, xxix).

בְּעֵבֶר הַיַּרְדֵּן. This (spatial) PP adjunct to דבר consists of the preposition ב followed by a construct (עבר) and absolute (הירדן). The whole phrase is definite because the absolute is definite. The precise referent of the phrase has been much discussed. Either it refers to a specific geographical region and serves as a name for that region (cf. NIV), or it is a term designating the region "beyond the Jordan" relative to the narrator (so NRSV). The narrator consistently uses the phrase for the land east of the Jordan (1:1, 5; 4:41, 46, 47, 49), making it impossible to determine whether relative or specific location is preferable. Moses' usage, though, gives evidence for acknowledging both views. Moses uses this term in 3:8 for the same side of the Jordan as he is standing, suggesting that it cannot simply be a relative term. However, more commonly in Moses' speeches, it refers to the land beyond the Jordan—that is, Canaan (3:20, 25; 11:30). This duality accords with elsewhere in the OT, where the phrase can be used *either* relatively *or* specifically around the river Jordan (Gemser). The phrase should not be marshalled as determinative evidence for establishing the location of the narrator.

הַיַּרְדֵּן. The presence of the article with ירדן indicates that it was not originally a proper noun, but the name of a place ("the watering-place"?) that has become a proper name (GKC §125d, e; WO §13.6a; JM §137b).

בַּמִּדְבָּר. This PP adjunct is appositional to בעבר הירדן, explaining the location of Moses' speaking. Being somewhat generic, it is further specified by the following PPs, but separate from them (cf. the disjunctive accent *pazer*).

בָּעֲרָבָה מוֹל סוּף. These two PP adjuncts are appositional to במדבר, giving further specification. They are marked as a unit by the conjunctive accent, *telisha qetanna*, on בערבה and the disjunctive *geresh* on סוף. The form מוֹל is a variant of מוּל, "facing," "opposite," "in front of," apparently pointed like this to avoid repetition of the vowels (GKC §27w; Weinfeld, 125–26). It is the only instance of מול being pointed like this (GKC §101a).

בֵּין־פָּארָן וּבֵין־תֹּפֶל וְלָבָן וַחֲצֵרֹת וְדִי זָהָב. This is the next PP unit, again an adjunct in apposition to the PPs that have preceded. בין ... בין ... either "distinguishes different parties ... that are each actively involved in a process" or "indicates localization in a space: between two or more points" (MNK §39.7). The latter is clearly the case here.

וְלָבָן וַחֲצֵרֹת וְדִי זָהָב. These place names further expand the second of the two points between which Moses spoke. The alternative, that it continues the list of places where Moses spoke picking up from בערבה, would require the repetition of the preposition ב (Driver, 1).

1:2 אַחַד עָשָׂר יוֹם מֵחֹרֵב דֶּרֶךְ הַר־שֵׂעִיר עַד קָדֵשׁ בַּרְנֵעַ:

D1. ED. **Null-copula** clause. A parenthetical statement indicates how long a journey from Horeb to Kadesh Barnea *should* take. There are three possible ways of construing the syntax of the verse. First, אחד עשׂר יום is the predicate, "[The journey] From Horeb . . . to Kadesh Barnea [is] eleven days"; second, "Eleven days [is] [the journey] from Horeb . . . to Kadesh Barnea"; thirdly, "It is eleven days from Horeb . . . to Kadesh Barnea." The third rendering, with the pronoun omitted, is possible in Hebrew, but almost always occurs in a participial clause or when the clause is introduced by הִנֵּה (cf. JM §154c, §146h). It is unlikely here. The second rendering is also unlikely. Normally in **null-copula** clauses the more well-known term (to the hearer) is the subject, and the less well-known, with the copula ("to be") supplied, the predicate. Here, the geographical references are more well known given the terms that appear in v. 1. The first rendering has P–S ordering, pointing to pragmatic inversion, with "eleven days" being highlighted, possibly as **focus**, giving a contrast with the temporal reference in v. 4. The translation "It is eleven days . . ." reflects this, yielding a rendition that is the same as the third version above via a different route.

אַחַ֣ד עָשָׂ֣ר יוֹם֩. אחד עשׂר is a variant way of expressing "eleven" (the other way is in v. 3) (cf. WO §15.2.3b). After numerals 11–19, typically the plural noun is used, except in the case of some common nouns, including יום (GKC §134f; JM §142e).

מֵחֹרֵ֗ב. PP. Part of the subject in the verbless clause. חרב is Deuteronomy's word for Sinai (1:2, 6, 19; 4:10, 15; 5:2; 9:8; 18:16; 29:1). The only exception is in Moses' blessing (33:2, 16). The inseparable preposition מן is attached with compensatory lengthening before the guttural, ח.

דֶּ֚רֶךְ הַר־שֵׂעִ֔יר. This adjunct construct phrase is a loose "accusative." It does not indicate the person or object that the verb affects. Instead, it indicates the particular circumstance—in this case, place—that modifies further the proposition made (GKC §118a, d, g). The phrase could designate either the route that goes over/past Mount Seir or one that leads to Mount Seir. The absolute, שׂעיר, specifies the name of the construct (cf. GKC §128k).

עַ֖ד קָדֵ֥שׁ בַּרְנֵֽעַ. PP. Part of the compound subject in the verbless clause. עד indicates extent, whether temporal or spatial.

Deuteronomy 1:3

וַיְהִי֙ בְּאַרְבָּעִ֣ים שָׁנָ֔ה בְּעַשְׁתֵּֽי־עָשָׂ֥ר חֹ֖דֶשׁ בְּאֶחָ֣ד 1:3
לַחֹ֑דֶשׁ דִּבֶּ֤ר מֹשֶׁה֙ אֶל־בְּנֵ֣י יִשְׂרָאֵ֔ל כְּ֠כֹל אֲשֶׁ֨ר צִוָּ֧ה
יְהוָ֛ה אֹת֖וֹ אֲלֵהֶֽם׃

D1. ND. The juxtaposition of eleven days and fortieth year highlights sharply the difference between how long it should have taken the Israelites to make the journey and how long it did. The reason for this extraordinary delay is recounted in the speech that follows: Israel's failure to trust and obey Yhwh. The narrator did not need to tell us these facts. The point is clear—"they should not squander the opportunity this time" (Wright, 22). Within the wilderness narrative as a whole, only three years are mentioned in the wilderness (van Goudoever, 145): the first year (Exod 12:2); the second year, in the desert (Exod 40:17; Num 1:1; 10:11); the fortieth year (1:3).

In Numbers 14:33-34, forty years was declared as the length of the penalty for being unwilling to go in and take possession of the land. That we are in the eleventh month in the fortieth year here says that the crossing will be very soon—the people are to be on tenterhooks. The fortieth year marks the end of the wilderness generation, symbolized by the death of three key figures: Miriam in the first month (Num 20:1), Aaron on the first day of the fifth month (Num 20:22-29; 33:38), and Moses. At the outset of the book, these words have the feel of Moses' last words. Moses' impending death dominates the book (Olson 1994).

וַיְהִי֙ בְּאַרְבָּעִ֣ים שָׁנָ֔ה בְּעַשְׁתֵּֽי־עָשָׂ֥ר חֹ֖דֶשׁ בְּאֶחָ֣ד לַחֹ֑דֶשׁ. After the ED of vv. 1-2, the *wayyiqtol* ויהי marks the shift to ND. ויהי followed by a temporal phrase (or a preposition with the infinitive construct) is a standard way of expressing the time in which subsequent events happen (Cook 2012: 309). Typically it begins a new section of the narrative (GKC §111f–g; Heller, 55). The syntax makes this the main clause, "It happened in the fortieth year . . ." with the following noun clause giving the contents of the "It."

וַיְהִי֙. *Wayyiqtol* 3ms √היה. III-ה verbs characteristically **apocopate** (lose the ה) in the jussive and in *wayyiqtol*. The absence of *dagesh forte* in the י is characteristic of a number of letters (mnemonic SQiN eM LeVY, where S indicates sibilants) when they occur with a vocal *sheva* (GKC §20m; JM §18m).

בְּאַרְבָּעִים שָׁנָה. PP adjunct. The *dagesh lene* in the ב, although it follows an open syllable (CV; the final syllable of וַיְהִי), is due to the disjunctive *pashtah* assigned to וַיְהִי. For numbers 1–10, ordinals have a distinct form. Beyond the number 10, Hebrew uses cardinal numbers for ordinals (GKC §134o; WO §15.3.1a), as here. The singular noun occurs with tens (GKC §134h; JM §142f; cf. on 1:2).

בְּעַשְׁתֵּי־עָשָׂר חֹדֶשׁ. PP adjunct. The other form of "eleven" עשתי עשר (GKC §97e n. 1), acting as an ordinal.

בְּאֶחָד לַחֹדֶשׁ. In addition to the ordinal ראשון, the cardinal אחד is sometimes used as the ordinal "first"; the noun it modifies is sometimes omitted if it has been used recently (WO §15.2.1b, 15.3.1a). Here, יום has not been used within this temporal phrase, but is implicit.

דִּבֶּר מֹשֶׁה אֶל־בְּנֵי יִשְׂרָאֵל. *Qatal* 3ms Piel √דבר (see on v. 1). This noun clause serves as the subject of ויהי (cf. WS §484). Often with a clause beginning with ויהי and specifying time, the following clause will be joined syndetically, either with a *wayyiqtol* or with ו + non-verb + *qatal*. Here, the noun clause follows asyndetically. דבר is a two-place predicate, with a subject (משה) and an oblique complement (אל־בני ישראל).

כְּכֹל אֲשֶׁר צִוָּה יְהוָה אֹתוֹ אֲלֵהֶם. This PP is not an oblique complement of דבר because דבר normally takes a direct object of what is spoken (though that is not usually reported direct speech). The phrase is thus a PP adjunct of manner, declaring that Moses spoke according to all that Yhwh had commanded him. כל, typically Deuteronomic, shows that Moses left nothing unsaid. It may be the **head** of the subsequent restrictive relative clause. Alternatively, the relative clause may be **null-head**, with the antecedent covert, rather than overt.

צִוָּה. *Qatal* 3ms Piel √צוה. III-ה verbs in 3ms *qatal* end in ־ָה in every *binyan*.

אֲלֵהֶם. PP adjunct. Written defectively for אֲלֵיהֶם. The preposition could = על, in which case it means, "concerning them" (Weinfeld, 125) or "in regard to them" (Nelson, 13). Alternatively, it means "for them," as a kind of **ellipsis** for "to speak to them" (cf. Nelson, 14). The latter is perhaps preferable because, in picking up אל־בני ישראל with אלהם, the narrator reinforces the notion that Moses' words come with the authority of Yhwh.

אַחֲרֵי הַכֹּתוֹ אֵת סִיחֹן מֶלֶךְ הָאֱמֹרִי אֲשֶׁר יוֹשֵׁב 1:4
בְּחֶשְׁבּוֹן וְאֵת עוֹג מֶלֶךְ הַבָּשָׁן אֲשֶׁר־יוֹשֵׁב
בְּעַשְׁתָּרֹת בְּאֶדְרֶעִי:

After the temporal reference fixing the absolute time of Moses' speaking in v. 3, there is a further, relative, temporal reference. We noted above how the first way of specifying is downbeat, emphasizing failure ("eleven days ... fortieth year"). This time reference is much more optimistic. Despite the failures, especially of the first generation, there have been recent successes. Just as the oblique reference to past failures in this opening anticipates the narrative that follows in chapter 1, so, too, the mention of Sihon and Og and the past victories anticipates chapters 2–3. Strikingly, by mentioning the military victory alongside both the time reference that speaks of failure and Moses expounding "this law" (v. 5) to "all Israel" (v. 1), the point is made: "Success in possessing the promised land lay not in military prowess and strength, but in an unbroken relationship with the Lord, who alone could bring further victories like those over Sihon and Og" (Craigie, 92).

אַחֲרֵי הַכֹּתוֹ ... בְּאֶדְרֶעִי. This PP is a temporal adjunct, functioning as an infinitival temporal clause (WO §36.2.2b). This is probably an adjunct to דִּבֶּר (v. 3), although it could also be an adjunct to הוֹאִיל and בֵּאֵר (v. 5). If the latter, this would lead to the parallel structuring of the *time* of speaking (vv. 3a, 4) and the *fact* of speaking (vv. 3b, 5). On this reading, there is an extended temporal reference that in each case precedes Moses speaking, one highlighting past failure, the other highlighting past success. There are two main pieces of evidence against this. First, if v. 4 were a fresh start, with a break after v. 3, then it is likely that Moses would have been overt as the subject of √נכה (אחרי הכת משה) rather than being referred to by a pronoun (הכתו). Second, it spoils the chiastic structure that is present in these opening verses. Further, taking it as adjunct to דבר still maintains the temporal contrast, such that one of the main reasons for proposing the link to v. 5 evaporates.

הַכֹּתוֹ. Inf constr Hiph √נכה with 3ms suffix. The initial נ assimilates, the evidence being the *dagesh forte* in the כ. III-ה verbs in every *binyan* have infinitive construct ending in -וֹת (here written defectively). The suffix is the subject of the verb. The accusative complement continues until the penultimate word of the verse, בעשתרת.

Deuteronomy 1:4

אֶת סִיחֹן מֶלֶךְ הָאֱמֹרִי. Part of the accusative complement of הכתו. מלך האמרי is in apposition to the proper name, סיחן. אמרי is a gentilic adjective, indicating the origin of the king. Gentilic adjectives characteristically end in ־ִי (JM §88Mg). Here it is used substantivally, as the absolute after the construct מלך. The presence of the article with the adjective signifies the referent as the entire group (WO §13.5.1g; cf. GKC §126m).

אֲשֶׁר יוֹשֵׁב בְּחֶשְׁבּוֹן. Non-restrictive relative clause, giving further, but not essential, information about the **head** סיחן.

יוֹשֵׁב. Ptcp ms Qal √ישׁב, written *plene*. The participle in Hebrew has similar syntax and function as the Hebrew adjective. Here it functions predicatively, with a **null-copula** (cf. Cook 2008). Although the root ישׁב means "sit" or "live" (hence ESV's "lived"), here it almost certainly means "reigned" (NRSV, NIV, TNIV), "sat [on the throne]." This specialized sense is apparent for three reasons: (1) from the parallel references to Og in Joshua 12:4 (ישׁב) and Joshua 13:12 (מלך), they appear synonymous; (2) from the use of ישׁב elsewhere in the OT with a similar meaning (Amos 1:8; cf. Amos 2:3); (3) finally, in a Ugaritic text, "El sits (*yšb* 'is enthroned') in Ashtaroth and rules (*tpṭ*) in Edrei" (Weinfeld, 128). For a participle speaking of a past state in a relative clause—Sihon is now dead—see GKC §116o.

בְּחֶשְׁבּוֹן. PP oblique complement of יושב.

וְאֵת עוֹג מֶלֶךְ הַבָּשָׁן. The other part of the accusative complement of הכתו. מלך הבשן is in apposition to the proper name, עוג. The presence of the article with בשן indicates that it was not originally a proper noun, but the name of a place ("the fertile plain"?) that has become a proper name (cf. GKC §125d, e; JM §137b).

אֲשֶׁר־יוֹשֵׁב בְּעַשְׁתָּרֹת. Non-restrictive relative clause, giving further, but not essential, information about the **head** עוג. See further above.

בְּאֶדְרֶעִי. PP adjunct. Without a conjunction on the front, "in Edrei" (slightly awkwardly) seems to indicate the location of the battle (cf. Num 3:1; 21:33), going with הכתו אחרי, "after he smote" (*BHQ: Deuteronomy*, 49*; cf. Weinfeld, 128). This is the reading of MT, Smr, 4QDeut[h], and the Targumim. Interestingly, in the book of Joshua, Og rules (12:4, ישׁב; 13:12, מלך) "in Ashtaroth *and* in Edrei." The reading *with* the conjunction is found in the LXX, Vulgate, and Syriac of 1:4, and may be an assimilation to Joshua in order to avoid awkward syntax. Nelson (14

n. d) suggests a further possibility, that "in Edrei" be taken with the start of v. 5: "In Edrei on the other side of the Jordan."

1:5 בְּעֵ֤בֶר הַיַּרְדֵּן֙ בְּאֶ֣רֶץ מוֹאָ֔ב הוֹאִ֣יל מֹשֶׁ֔ה בֵּאֵ֛ר אֶת־הַתּוֹרָ֥ה הַזֹּ֖את לֵאמֹֽר׃

Just as the *time* of Moses' speaking is overspecified (vv. 2-4), so also is the *place*. The location has already been articulated in v. 1. Here בעבר הירדן is repeated from v. 1, as are other clear indications that the location is outside the promised land. Together, the references form an *inclusio*, bracketing off the extended introduction and marking the geographical problem: they are in the "wrong" place, not yet in the land. The verse is a **quotative frame**.

בְּעֵ֤בֶר הַיַּרְדֵּן֙ בְּאֶ֣רֶץ מוֹאָ֔ב הוֹאִ֣יל מֹשֶׁ֔ה. The word order is PP–P–S. The fronting of the PP adjunct specifying location could be for **focus**, giving a contrast between the possible locations of Moses' speaking (within the mental maps of narrator and hearers) and the actual one, east of the Jordan. That they are in the wrong place is further emphasized. More likely, it is the **topic**, anchoring the discourse in a location.

בְּעֵ֤בֶר הַיַּרְדֵּן֙. PP adjunct, expressing the location of Moses' speaking. See on 1:1 for the referent and for the article on ירדן.

בְּאֶ֣רֶץ מוֹאָ֔ב. PP adjunct, in apposition to בעבר הירדן, further elucidating the location. This geographical referent would give some contrast with 1:1b if the intention there was to give a straightforward geographical location of the speeches that follow. The precise location is specified as "in the valley opposite Beth-Peor" in 3:29 and 4:46 (see Weinfeld, 128).

הוֹאִ֣יל. *Qatal* 3ms Hiph √יאל. The relationship between הואיל and באר is slightly unusual, in that they are asyndetically joined *qatals* (see GKC §120g, h; JM §177d; Weinfeld, 126). GKC renders הואיל as an activity done with the "idea of *willingly* or *gladly*," and notes that this construction sees the second verb (in this case באר) as the "principal idea."

בֵּאֵ֛ר אֶת־הַתּוֹרָ֥ה הַזֹּ֖את. *Qatal* 3ms Piel √באר. This phrase is pivotal for the interpretation of Deuteronomy, since it indicates what the narrator believes Moses is doing. The verb באר only occurs in two other places in the OT: Deut 27:8 and Hab 2:2. In the other two places, it speaks of writing something down plainly and clearly so that it is legible. Here it must introduce an oral event, because what happens subsequently is Moses' speaking. It is only in 31:9 that Moses is said to write down what he has spoken. The precise nature of the activity depends on the referent of את־התורה הזאת, the accusative complement of באר. Apart from 17:11, where תורה refers to an individual ruling of the priests and judge in office (cf. parallel with 17:10), תורה in Deuteronomy refers to all of Moses' preaching. This is clear partly from the presence of the demonstrative, זאת, in nineteen of the twenty-two occurrences in the book (not 17:11; 33:4, 10), partly from the accompanying constructs ("all the words of this תורה" [17:19; 27:3, 8, 26; 28:58; 29:28; 31:12, 24; 32:46] or "the book of this תורה" [28:61; 29:20; 30:10; 31:26]), and partly from the wider scope of the term evident in the other occurrences (1:5; 4:8, 44; 31:9, 11; 33:4, 10). Thus, what is seen in this phrase is not the bringing out of the meaning implicit in the revelation at Horeb, nor the reapplication of old laws for a new situation, rather, the articulation of the laws and commands that Yhwh has given to Moses, accompanied by explanation, motivation, and exhortation.

לֵאמֹר. Inf constr Qal √אמר with preposition ל. For the contraction from לֶאֱמֹר because of the quiescent א, see JM §24e. לאמר is often, but not always, found at the end of a **quotative frame**. When occurring in such a frame, it signals the end of the frame and the start of the complement (the quotation itself). It is best regarded as a **complementizer** or "particle" (Meier, 135) introducing a direct speech complement, and should not be translated. Since the root אמר is almost always followed by direct speech (an exception is Jonah 2:11), it is a reliable indicator of a switch from the **quotative frame** to the next subdomain of embedded discourse.

Historical Review of Failure and Success
Deuteronomy 1:6–3:29

As Moses begins speaking, he recounts the journey from Horeb to the plains of Moab. There are two parts to the journey, as evident from the repeated phrase רב־לכם ("enough of you ..."; 1:6; 2:2). The first part spells out the failure to enter the land (1:6–2:1), expanding on what 1:2-3 hinted at. Israel ends up heading back toward Egypt. The second part (2:2–3:29) recounts the taking of the Transjordan through heeding the voice of Yhwh (cf. 1:4). Together they expound in historical retrospect the two choices with which Moses will confront the people in the plains of Moab.

The command to leave (1:6-8)

The impetus for the exodus generation to leave Horeb was the prospect of inheriting the promised land. That same promised land lay before Moses' hearers in Moab, and before subsequent generations who would hear the book read after the exile.

> *⁶"Yhwh our God spoke to us at Horeb, 'Enough of your staying at this mountain! ⁷Turn, set out and enter the hill country of the Amorites and [come] to all their neighboring territories in the Arabah, in the hill country, in the Shephelah, in the Negev, and on the sea coast—the land of the Canaanites—and the Lebanon as far as the great river, the river Euphrates. ⁸See! I hereby put the land at your disposal. Enter and possess the land which Yhwh swore to your ancestors—to Abraham, to Isaac, and to Jacob—to give to them and to their offspring after them.'"*

1:6 יְהוָה אֱלֹהֵינוּ דִּבֶּר אֵלֵינוּ בְּחֹרֵב לֵאמֹר רַב־לָכֶם
שֶׁבֶת בָּהָר הַזֶּה:

ND then ED. Moses begins his speech, the first subdomain of embedded discourse (D2), by quoting the words of Yhwh (D3). Yhwh's words provide the narrative momentum for 1:6–2:1. They do not need to stay at Horeb because they are taking Yhwh's word with them as they journey to the land promised to them.

יְהוָה אֱלֹהֵינוּ דִּבֶּר אֵלֵינוּ בְּחֹרֵב לֵאמֹר. *Qatal* 3ms Piel √דבר (see on 1:1 for the form). ND. The unmarked order is S–P, as here. Embedded narrative discourse never begins with *wayyiqtol*, unlike narrative proper. The whole phrase provides new information, without attention being directed to any individual constituent.

יְהוָה אֱלֹהֵינוּ. NP, acting as the subject of דִּבֶּר. This occurs twenty-one times in Deuteronomy, nineteen of which are in chapters 1–11. אלהינו stands in apposition to the proper noun יהוה. The 1cp pronominal suffix may not be added to the proper noun.

אֵלֵינוּ. PP. Oblique complement. Along with the 1cp pronominal suffix on אלהינו, Moses' solidarity with the people is emphasized.

Further, the Moab generation is in solidarity with those who stood around Horeb, though they were not there (cf. 1:35; 2:14).

רַב־לָכֶם שֶׁבֶת בָּהָר הַזֶּה. ED. **Null-copula** clause, with P–S subject order. Lit. "staying at this mountain [is] much for you." Rather than this order being a rule when the subject is an infinitive (WO §8.4.2a), there is **focus** on the predicate. There are a number of similar ways of expressing that someone has done something for too long. Sometimes רב occurs absolutely, whether alone (2 Sam 24:16; 1 Kgs 19:4) or with ל (3:26; cf. Num 16:3, 7; Ezek 45:9); sometimes מן governs the noun of which there is enough (e.g., Exod 9:28; 1 Kgs 12:28; Ezek 44:6). The translation above reflects the focus on רב לכם and its exclamatory nature.

רַב־לָכֶם. The predicate of the **null-copula** clause. Although the inf constr √ישׁב has acquired the feminine ת (see below), the predicate is masculine (WO §36.2.1b).

שֶׁבֶת. Inf constr Qal √ישׁב. An original I-ו verb, the ו has disappeared (**aphaeresis**; see JM §17d) and a feminine ת has been added (JM §72d, §75a). It now has the form of a segholate noun. It stands here as the subject of the **null-copula** clause and should be translated as a verbal noun, or **gerund**, "staying" (WO §36.2.1b).

בָּהָר הַזֶּה. PP adjunct with verb שׁבת.

1:7 פְּנוּ ׀ וּסְעוּ לָכֶם וּבֹאוּ הַר הָאֱמֹרִי וְאֶל־כָּל־שְׁכֵנָיו בָּעֲרָבָה בָהָר וּבַשְּׁפֵלָה וּבַנֶּגֶב וּבְחוֹף הַיָּם אֶרֶץ הַכְּנַעֲנִי וְהַלְּבָנוֹן עַד־הַנָּהָר הַגָּדֹל נְהַר־פְּרָת:

With a succession of imperatives, Yhwh directs Israel to set out to enter the land (HD, D3). The abrupt shift from ED (v. 6) to HD is matched by the asyndetic opening. The relationship of the different geographical phrases to each other is not straightforward, and is discussed below.

פְּנוּ ׀ וּסְעוּ לָכֶם. Impv mp Qal √פנה and impv mp Qal √נסע. The two verbs recur in 2:1 (also 1:40). The opening failure is spanned by the command "Turn and journey (פנו וסעו)" and the somber reality that they "turned (פנה)" and "journeyed (נסע)" *to the desert* (2:1). פנה can have the sense of "turn" in the sense of "turn back," but it can also, as here, have the sense of "turn and go on" (HALOT 938).

לָכֶֽם. The preposition ל, when attached to a pronoun that has the same referent as the subject of the verb (as with לכם here), indicates reflexive nuance. It occurs especially with intransitive verbs and verbs of motion. It isolates and focuses attention on the subject (JM §133d; GKC §119s; WHS §272).

וּבֹאוּ הַר הָאֱמֹרִי. Impv mp Qal √בוא. בוא can be transitive with an accusative complement, "enter"; it can also be intransitive, with a PP as the oblique complement, "come to." In this phrase, הר האמרי is the accusative complement NP of the transitive verb. הר is in the construct state and need not indicate a specific mountain, but can designate "hill country." It governs the gentilic adjective אמרי with the article, which functions as the absolute (cf. on 1:4). This territory was the entry point for the Israelites, not the whole land (1:19-20, 44; though see below).

וְאֶל־כָּל־שְׁכֵנָיו. Adjunct construct PP. Construct plural of noun שָׁכֵן, with 3ms suffix which could refer back either to הר or to האמרי. The noun can designate people, whether inhabitants (e.g., Hos 10:5) or neighboring populations (e.g., Jer 49:10), and places (e.g., Jer 49:18). If it refers to the inhabitants, then the suffix refers back to הר and the phrase-initial ו is explanatory with the PP expanding further on what is meant by "the hill country of the Amorites" (so Mayes 1979: 120). On this reading, הר האמרי is a way of speaking of the whole land (cf. 1:19). However, although a possible reading, it is unlikely: the subsequent geographical references suggest a move beyond the "hill country of the Amorites"; the land promised on oath to Abraham (1:8) is never elsewhere explicitly designated הר האמרי (though note 3:25); the introduction of the preposition אל after the ו suggests that equivalence is not in view. Three other ways of reading are possible. שכניו could speak of (1) neighboring people, with the suffix referring back to האמרי, "to all their [the Amorites'] neighbours . . ."; (2) neighboring places, with the suffix referring back to הר, "to all its [the hill country of the Amorites'] neighboring places"; (3) neighboring places, with the suffix referring back to האמרי, "to all their [the Amorites'] neighboring territories." Given that Moses continues by listing place names, it is more likely that places are in view; the translation given above follows (3), but (2) is also possible.

בָּעֲרָבָה בָהָר וּבַשְּׁפֵלָה וּבַנֶּגֶב וּבְחוֹף הַיָּם. A succession of adjunct PPs, specifying further the location of the neighboring places. בהר is the only PP without a ו-conjunction. It does not explain further the Arabah, but refers to a different region, "the hill country." The Masoretes have assigned a conjunctive accent, *mereka'*, to the previous word, so the final open syllable (הֹ-) means there is no *dagesh lene* in the ב (cp. on בארבעים in 1:3; cf. GKC §21a, b; JM §19c). שפלה is the name of a territory, entitled thus because it is "lowland." בהוף הים has הוף, "shore" in construct relationship with the absolute הים.

אֶרֶץ הַכְּנַעֲנִי. The same syntax as in the phrase הר האמרי, with a noun in the construct state governing a gentilic adjective with the article designating a whole class (cf. on 1:4). The whole phrase is definite because the absolute is definite. The phrase is probably in apposition to all the previous places (so MT accentuation), which together comprise "the land of the Canaanites." Alternatively it is just in apposition to בהוף הים, in which case it further explains "the sea coast" (cf. Num 13:29; Josh 5:1).

וְהַלְּבָנוֹן עַד־הַנָּהָר הַגָּדֹל נְהַר־פְּרָת. The final place to enter (note the absence of the preposition ב) is "the Lebanon" (for the article, see on הירדן in 1:1), with the further specification of the northern boundary in the following PP.

נְהַר־פְּרָת. Construct phrase in apposition to הנהר הגדל, equating the two referents. The absolute specifies the name of the river (GKC §128k).

1:8 רְאֵה נָתַתִּי לִפְנֵיכֶם אֶת־הָאָרֶץ בֹּאוּ וּרְשׁוּ אֶת־הָאָרֶץ אֲשֶׁר נִשְׁבַּע יְהוָה לַאֲבֹתֵיכֶם לְאַבְרָהָם לְיִצְחָק וּלְיַעֲקֹב לָתֵת לָהֶם וּלְזַרְעָם אַחֲרֵיהֶם:

D3. A further command to enter the promised land follows (HD), but not before Yhwh speaks to hand over the land (ED—commissive).

רְאֵה. Impv ms Qal √ראה. HD. As an interjection (GKC §105b; JM §105d), it is singular despite the plural verb and pronoun forms reflecting an address to many. For observations about the "rare" ראה in the context of a discussion of "presentative exclamations" that speak of "immediacy" and of "fuller exclamations of perception, cause, circumstance etc.," see WO §40.2.1a n. 4.

נָתַתִּי לִפְנֵיכֶם אֶת־הָאָרֶץ. ED. *Qatal* 1cs Qal √נתן. To נתן something לפני someone is to lay something out before someone with a view to them acting appropriately (cf. 2:33; 30:15). This is a "commissive" *qatal*, an "extension" of the performative *qatal*. In a performative *qatal*, the action of the verb, in this case giving, is performed *in* the saying of these words (cf. WO §30.5.1d). In a "commissive," there is a gap between the declaration and the action (Cook 2012: 213), but the purpose of a "commissive" is "to commit a speaker to a certain course of action" (Austin, 156).

אֶת־הָאָרֶץ בֹּ֚אוּ וּרְשׁ֣וּ אֶת־הָאָ֔רֶץ. HD. Impv mp Qal √בוא and √ירש. הארץ functions as the accusative complement of both verbs. הארץ is the **head** of the following relative clause.

אֲשֶׁ֣ר נִשְׁבַּ֣ע יְ֠הוָה לַאֲבֹ֨תֵיכֶ֜ם לְאַבְרָהָ֨ם לְיִצְחָ֤ק וּֽלְיַעֲקֹב֙ לָתֵ֣ת לָהֶ֔ם וּלְזַרְעָ֖ם אַחֲרֵיהֶֽם. Restrictive relative clause that serves to identify "the land."

נִשְׁבַּע. *Qatal* 3ms Niph √שבע. The verb here is a three-place predicate, with subject יהוה, the action of giving the land as what is sworn, and the oblique complement, לאבתיכם, indicating the recipients of the oath.

לְאַבְרָהָ֤ם לְיִצְחָ֖ק וּֽלְיַעֲקֹב֙. Three PPs in apposition to לאבתיכם.

לָתֵ֣ת לָהֶ֔ם וּלְזַרְעָ֖ם אַחֲרֵיהֶֽם. Inf constr Qal √נתן with ל preposition. The form is difficult. Many I-נ verbs lose the נ in the imperative and infinitive construct (**aphaeresis**; JM §17d, §72c) and gain the compensating feminine ת (JM §72d). The hypothetical תנת becomes תֵּת due to the lack of vowel with נ (JM §72i). Before monosyllabic infinitives, the preposition ל usually has *qamets* (JM §103c). Infinitive phrase complement, describing what was sworn. The accusative complement is הארץ, represented in the relative clause by אשר.

לָהֶ֔ם וּלְזַרְעָ֖ם. PP complements, giving the recipients of the gift. ולזרעם comprises the segholate noun זֶרַע with 3mp suffix, with inseparable preposition ל and ו-conjunction pointed as *sureq* before vocal *sheva*. When pronominal suffixes attach to segholates, the original primitive form usually appears (JM §96c, e, g).

The appointing of judges (1:9-18)

Moses breaks off the narrative about travelling from Horeb to talk about the appointing of judges. The gap between "turn and journey (פנו וסעו)" and "so we set out (ונסע)" (vv. 7, 19) and the ***inclusio*** of "at that time" (בעת ההוא, vv. 9-18) indicate the unit's extent. The narrative effect is to show that entering and possessing the land, indeed the stability of the covenant community, depends on the quality and nature of leadership.

⁹*I said to you at that time, "I am not able to bear you alone.* ¹⁰*Yhwh your God has multiplied you and see, you are today like the stars of heaven in abundance.* ¹¹*May Yhwh the God of your ancestors increase you a thousand times what you are and may he bless you just as he promised you.* ¹²*How can I bear alone your burden, your load and your cases?* ¹³*Choose for yourselves wise, discerning, and knowledgeable men for your tribes that I may place them as your leaders."* ¹⁴*You answered me and said, "What you have proposed to do is good."* ¹⁵*So I took the leaders of your tribes, wise and knowledgeable men, and I appointed them as leaders over you, commanders of thousands, commanders of hundreds, commanders of fifties, commanders of tens, and officials, for your tribes.* ¹⁶*I commanded your judges at that time, "Listen to both sides of your brothers' [case] and judge justly between a man and his brother or his resident alien* ¹⁷*—do not show favoritism in judgment, you should hear the smallest just like the greatest, do not fear anyone—for judgment really belongs to God. And as for the case that is too hard for you, you should bring to me and I will hear it."* ¹⁸*So I commanded you at that time all the things that you should do.*

1:9 וָאֹמַ֣ר אֲלֵכֶ֔ם בָּעֵ֥ת הַהִ֖וא לֵאמֹ֑ר לֹא־אוּכַ֥ל לְבַדִּ֖י שְׂאֵ֥ת אֶתְכֶֽם׃

ND then ED. Having just finished recounting Yhwh's speech, Moses then recalls his own words "at that time" (D2). Moses reminds them of the problem that he could not bear the Israelites alone (D3).

וָאֹמַ֣ר אֲלֵכֶ֔ם בָּעֵ֥ת הַהִ֖וא לֵאמֹ֑ר. *Wayyiqtol* 1cs Qal √אמר. ND. The *yiqtol* and *wayyiqtol* 1cs Qal of I-א verbs have one א. The repeated root, "and I said (√אמר) ... saying (√אמר)" illustrates לאמר as a **complementizer** which can hardly be translated (cf. 1:5).

אֲלֵכֶ֔ם. Adjunct PP indicating addressees, written defectively without י (also 1:20, 29; cf. 1:43 etc.).

בָּעֵ֥ת הַהִ֖וא. Adjunct PP giving more general indication of the time of speaking. This is the first occurrence in Deuteronomy of the anomalously written 3fs personal pronoun subject, הוא, rather than היא. It is a *qere perpetuum*—that is, it is read differently from the way it is written (*ketiv*), but its frequency means that marginal notes are omitted (JM §16f2). The reason for the form has taxed grammarians for a long time (GKC §32l; JM §39c). The Samaritan Pentateuch regularly has היא while the MT has הוא. A plausible explanation is that the MT form is "derived from a certain late recension of the Pentateuch" (JM §39c). The phrase occurs also in vv. 16 and 18 and serves to mark off this section.

לֹא־אוּכַל לְבַדִּי שְׂאֵת אֶתְכֶם. *Yiqtol* 1cs Hoph √יכל. ED. The *yiqtol* form יוּכַל has long exercised grammarians. It looks like a Hophal, but the *qatal* is יָכֹל, which is clearly Qal. The most plausible explanation is that the verb is defective, with a Qal *qatal* and a Hophal *yiqtol*, with the causative meaning "he will be enabled" giving way to "he will be able" (JM §75i). The *yiqtol* here is used because it speaks of a repeated general or habitual situation (cf. WO §31.3e).

לְבַדִּי. PP adjunct. It comprises the noun בַּד and the preposition לְ, together with the 1cs pronominal suffix, "I alone." Often in Hebrew a preposition and noun together function adverbially, as with לְבַד here (JM §102d).

שְׂאֵת. Inf constr Qal √נשא. For the awkward form, see GKC §76b, 93t. Together with its direct object, אתכם, the phrase forms an infinitive phrase complement after אוכל.

1:10 יְהוָה אֱלֹהֵיכֶם הִרְבָּה אֶתְכֶם וְהִנְּכֶם הַיּוֹם כְּכוֹכְבֵי הַשָּׁמַיִם לָרֹב:

D3. ND, then ED. With echoes of the promises to the patriarchs (e.g., Gen 26:4), Moses shows that the inadequacies he feels in the previous verse are the outcome of Yhwh's faithfulness.

יְהוָה אֱלֹהֵיכֶם הִרְבָּה אֶתְכֶם. *Qatal* 3ms Hiph √רבה. ND. The S–P word order is basic and unmarked.

וְהִנְּכֶם הַיּוֹם כְּכוֹכְבֵי הַשָּׁמַיִם לָרֹב. **Null-copula** clause with the subject, "you," as a pronominal suffix on הנה. The PP predicate is ככוכבי השמים. It is not straightforward to capture the force and function of הנה, still less to translate it. Traditionally it has been translated with "behold." It is a **deictic** particle that draws particular attention to what follows (Miller-Naudé and van der Merwe). The ו connects this clause to the preceding proposition. Moses highlights to the people the truth of the first clause by pointing them to the present reality.

הַיּוֹם. Adverbial time adjunct NP. The article attached to יום and some other words designating time retains an original weak demonstrative sense, here "this day," hence "today" (GKC §126b; JM §137f). It is the first of 104 occurrences of היום in Deuteronomy. Although usually "today" in the plains of Moab, and occasionally the narrator's "today" (e.g., 2:22), here it is the "today" of Horeb. The different "todays" merge in Deuteronomy's rhetoric (Robson, 16–17).

כְּכוֹכְבֵי הַשָּׁמַיִם. Constr PP. This comparative phrase is the predicate of the **null-copula** clause.

לָרֹב. Adjunct PP, closely modifying ככוכבי השמים. The preposition ל, pointed with a *qamets* before the tone syllable, has the sense of "with regard to" (WO §11.2.10d) or "in respect of" (Driver, 15). The noun רב is "abundance."

1:11 יְהוָ֞ה אֱלֹהֵ֣י אֲבֽוֹתֵכֶ֗ם יֹסֵ֧ף עֲלֵיכֶ֛ם כָּכֶ֖ם אֶ֣לֶף פְּעָמִ֑ים וִיבָרֵ֣ךְ אֶתְכֶ֔ם כַּאֲשֶׁ֖ר דִּבֶּ֥ר לָכֶֽם׃

D3. HD. Two clauses with jussive verbs express Moses' wishes. Far from resenting the problems of growth resulting from Yhwh's faithfulness to his promises, Moses desires greater growth. The Israelites should have every expectation of Yhwh keeping his promise of future growth given his past faithfulness (v. 10).

יְהוָ֞ה אֱלֹהֵ֣י אֲבֽוֹתֵכֶ֗ם יֹסֵ֧ף עֲלֵיכֶ֛ם כָּכֶ֖ם אֶ֣לֶף פְּעָמִ֑ים. HD. Modal clauses, including the jussive, have VS ordering. Here the NP יהוה אלהי אבותכם is fronted as the **topic**, drawing attention to the agent who will need to act to implement Moses' wish. אלהי אבותכם is a construct NP, appositional to יהוה. The reference here reinforces the echo of the promises to the patriarchs.

יֹסֵף. Jussive 3ms Hiphil √יסף, indicating a wish (cf. GKC §109b). The verb √יסף is "quasi-defective"—that is, different parts of the conjugation come from different *binyanim* (JM §75f, §85b). For this verb, *qatal* is almost always Qal (יָסַף), while *yiqtol* has acquired a Hiphil-like form (יוֹסִיף). The Hiphil of יסף followed by על means "add" or "increase" (HALOT 418).

עֲלֵיכֶם. Oblique complement.

כָּכֶם. Adjunct PP. The preposition כ indicates agreement in quantity or measure, "as you are" (WO §11.2.9b).

אֶלֶף פְּעָמִים. Adverbial adjunct NP. The multiplicative idea in Hebrew is usually constructed using the cardinal number and, though sometimes omitted but implied, the plural of the feminine noun פַּעַם, "step," "occurrence" (GKC §134r; JM §142q).

וַיְבָרֵךְ אֶתְכֶם. Jussive 3ms Piel √ברך. There is no particular jussive form, but its occurrence in clause-initial position and its continuation of the jussive יֹסֵף indicate its modality, continuing the wish.

כַּאֲשֶׁר דִּבֶּר לָכֶם. Qatal 3ms Piel √דבר. For דִּבֶּר, see on 1:1. לכם is oblique complement. Comparative clause introduced by כאשר. After כאשר, there is usually **triggered inversion**, with P–S word order. Here it indicates a correspondence between the blessing anticipated and Yhwh's promise.

1:12 אֵיכָה אֶשָּׂא לְבַדִּי טָרְחֲכֶם וּמַשַּׂאֲכֶם וְרִיבְכֶם:

D3. ID. With a rhetorical question, Moses reprises his statement of v. 9 that he is unable to bear his people, though here the precise problems are now specified.

אֵיכָה. The interrogative particle, איכה, "how," occurs more rarely than its synonym, אֵיךְ.

אֶשָּׂא. Yiqtol (modal) 1cs Qal √נשא. The verb has a modal nuance, dealing with the subject's capability to perform the action of the verb, "how can I bear" as the link with 1:9 demonstrates (WO §31.4c; MNK §19.3.5[i]; JM §113l).

טָרְחֲכֶם וּמַשַּׂאֲכֶם וְרִיבְכֶם. These three nouns together form the accusative complement of אשא. טֹרַח is a rare noun (only here and Isa 1:14) meaning "burden"; מַשָּׂא is a "load" or "burden"; רִיב is a collective noun, here, speaking of the legal cases.

1:13 הָבוּ לָכֶם אֲנָשִׁים חֲכָמִים וּנְבֹנִים וִידֻעִים
לְשִׁבְטֵיכֶם וַאֲשִׂימֵם בְּרָאשֵׁיכֶם:

D3. HD. Moses takes decisive action because of his incapacity and instructs the people to find suitable leaders to step into the breach.

הָבוּ לָכֶם אֲנָשִׁים חֲכָמִים וּנְבֹנִים וִידֻעִים לְשִׁבְטֵיכֶם.

הָבוּ לָכֶם. Impv mp Qal √יהב. The expected form would be הֲבוּ (cf. רְשׁוּ in 1:8), but the imperative always has a *qamets* (GKC §69o; JM §75k). The verb only occurs in the imperative in the Hebrew Bible. Its lexical meaning is "give," though when followed by לכם, there is a reflexive nuance (see on 1:7), and the meaning of the phrase is "get" or "choose."

חֲכָמִים וּנְבֹנִים וִידֻעִים. A chain of three attributive adjectives modifying אנשים. ונבנים is Niphal participle from בִּין with ו-conjunction, functioning adjectivally, meaning here "discerning," "understanding." וידעים is the Qal passive participle √ידע with ו-conjunction. The form occurs only here, in v. 15, and at Isa 53:3. There are three possible ways of understanding it. The first is to take it with the following PP, לשבטיכם, "well known to your judges." The second is similar to the first, taking it in a passive sense, without it being connected to the PP: "known," "reputable." The third is to take it in a more active sense, "experienced," "knowledgeable" (JM §50e). The latter is most likely for several reasons: the three adjectives occur together in Eccl 9:11 (though note there that the participle of ידע is active); the other two adjectives are clearly active; when ידעים occurs in v. 15, it is unqualified; the disjunctive Masoretic accent, *tiphah*, separates לשבטיכם from וידעים, indicating that "for your tribes" further elucidates לכם ("choose for yourselves . . . for your tribes") rather than modifying closely וידעים ("well known to your tribes"); in Isa 53:3, the sense is similarly active, "familiar with sickness."

וַאֲשִׂימֵם בְּרָאשֵׁיכֶם. Cohortative 1cs Qal √שׂים with 3mp pronominal suffix. The cohortative is 1st person volitive, expressing the will of those speaking. Although not morphologically marked, its position at the start of the clause and the sequence of verbs of which it is a part indicates it is an **indirect volitive** (cf. JM §116b). The clause is syntactically coordinated with the previous clause, "choose . . . and I will place," but semantically subordinate, providing the purpose of the choosing, "choose . . . *that* I *may* place."

בְּרָאשֵׁיכֶם. The preposition ב is the so-called *beth essentiae*, "*in the capacity of* being your leaders" (cf. WO §11.2.5e). The irregular plural of רֹאשׁ, רָאשִׁים, has a *qamets* under the ר and the א quiesces. When א stands in the middle of a word and follows a vocal *sheva*, sometimes the long vowel replaces the *sheva* and the א remains to show etymology (GKC §23c).

1:14   וַתַּעֲנוּ אֹתִי וַתֹּאמְרוּ טוֹב־הַדָּבָר אֲשֶׁר־דִּבַּרְתָּ לַעֲשׂוֹת׃

Moses recounts (D2, ND) the assembly's positive response to his suggestion (D3, ED).

וַתַּעֲנוּ אֹתִי. *Wayyiqtol* 2mp Qal √ענה.

וַתֹּאמְרוּ. *Wayyiqtol* 2mp Qal √אמר. The accusative complement is the direct speech that follows.

טוֹב־הַדָּבָר. A **null-copula** clause with P–S word order. The P–S order is often taken as an indication that the clause's purpose is to classify, answering the question "What is the subject like?" (Andersen; WO §8.4.2a); this is in contrast to the S–P order, which is used for identifying, "Who/what is the subject?" A preferable way of understanding the order is to see pragmatically neutral **null-copula** clauses having word order S–P (Buth); variations from that order, whether X–S–P or P–S are marked. This analysis is in some ways related to the traditional approach, but is more comprehensive in its accounting for the data. The inverted order gives **focus** to טוב. Of the domain of possible responses to Moses' words, the people's verdict was "good." As a predicative adjective, there is no article.

אֲשֶׁר־דִּבַּרְתָּ לַעֲשׂוֹת. *Qatal* 2ms Piel √דבר. This restrictive relative clause further identifies the דבר that was good.

לַעֲשׂוֹת. Inf constr Qal √עשׂה with preposition ל. It is an infinitive phrase complement after דברת.

1:15 וָאֶקַּח אֶת־רָאשֵׁי שִׁבְטֵיכֶם אֲנָשִׁים חֲכָמִים
וִידֻעִים וָאֶתֵּן אוֹתָם רָאשִׁים עֲלֵיכֶם שָׂרֵי אֲלָפִים
וְשָׂרֵי מֵאוֹת וְשָׂרֵי חֲמִשִּׁים וְשָׂרֵי עֲשָׂרֹת וְשֹׁטְרִים
לְשִׁבְטֵיכֶם׃

D2. ND. With two *wayyiqtol* clauses, Moses recounts his actions in the light of the people's verdict on his suggestion.

וָאֶקַּח אֶת־רָאשֵׁי שִׁבְטֵיכֶם אֲנָשִׁים חֲכָמִים וִידֻעִים. *Wayyiqtol* 1cs Qal √לקח. The verb לקח behaves like a I-נ verb, hence the *dagesh forte* in the ק (JM §72j).

אֶת־רָאשֵׁי שִׁבְטֵיכֶם. The direct object of ואקח is a construct chain.

אֲנָשִׁים חֲכָמִים וִידֻעִים. NP in apposition to את־ראשי שבטיכם, further describing the "heads" or "leaders," echoing the qualities Moses identified in v. 13.

וָאֶתֵּן אוֹתָם רָאשִׁים עֲלֵיכֶם. *Wayyiqtol* 1cs Qal √נתן. When נתן has the sense of "turn someone into something" or "appoint," it has two accusatives, here אתם and ראשים (WO §10.2.3c). There is some awkwardness in how Moses appoints as "heads" those who already seem to be "heads" (15aα). Presumably Moses' appointment conforms with and ratifies existing tribal organization (Tigay 1996: 12). עליכם is adjunct PP.

שָׂרֵי אֲלָפִים וְשָׂרֵי מֵאוֹת וְשָׂרֵי חֲמִשִּׁים וְשָׂרֵי עֲשָׂרֹת וְשֹׁטְרִים לְשִׁבְטֵיכֶם. This extended NP is in apposition to רָאשִׁים עֲלֵיכֶם.

שָׂרֵי אֲלָפִים. Elsewhere the phrase can designate judicial or military roles (Exod 18:21, 25; Num 32:14, 48). The full spectrum from "officers of thousands" to "officers of tens" only occurs in Exodus 18, in a legal context.

וְשֹׁטְרִים. These "officials" may also appear in judicial or military contexts (16:18; 20:5). Their role in both cases is administrative.

לְשִׁבְטֵיכֶם. Adjunct PP, indicating the beneficiaries of the appointment (cf. on לנו in 1:22). The disjunctive Masoretic accent, *tiphah*, on ושטרים indicates that "for/throughout your tribes" further elucidates the setting as heads over them ("I set them as heads over your . . . for your tribes"; cf. NRSV, ESV) rather than modifying closely שטרים ("officials for your tribes/tribal officials"; cf. NASB, NIV).

1:16 וָאֲצַוֶּה אֶת־שֹׁפְטֵיכֶם בָּעֵת הַהִוא לֵאמֹר שָׁמֹעַ בֵּין־אֲחֵיכֶם וּשְׁפַטְתֶּם צֶדֶק בֵּין־אִישׁ וּבֵין־אָחִיו וּבֵין גֵּרוֹ׃

ND, then HD. Moses recalls (ND, D2) his instructions to those whom he has appointed (HD, D3). The themes of justice and "brotherhood" or familial community membership appear for the first time. Both will be significant throughout the book.

וָאֲצַוֶּה אֶת־שֹׁפְטֵיכֶם בָּעֵת הַהִוא לֵאמֹר. *Wayyiqtol* 1cs Piel √צוה. Often there is **apocopation** of the ה ֶ- with *wayyiqtol* of III-ה verbs (e.g., 3:18, וָאֲצַו), but sometimes the form occurs in full, especially in 1cs (GKC §75t). ND. בעת ההוא is adjunct PP (see on 1:9).

שָׁמֹעַ בֵּין־אֲחֵיכֶם וּשְׁפַטְתֶּם צֶדֶק בֵּין־אִישׁ וּבֵין־אָחִיו וּבֵין גֵּרוֹ. HD.

שָׁמֹעַ. Inf abs Qal √שמע. It functions here as a command (WO §35.5.1a), an older usage that gave way later to the imperative (the imperative plural שמעו is found in the Samaritan Pentateuch). Sometimes the standalone infinitive absolute is said to give an injunction or obligation, "you shall (must) do,'" rather than an imperative, "do" (JM §123v). There are some features that set the infinitive absolute apart from the imperative: it never is found with the particle נָא-, unlike the imperative; it is only used of someone socially superior to a subordinate; and it usually requires long-term obedience rather than an immediate response. Other evidence points toward an imperative modality (Callaham, 138–39): for example, it may be syntactically parallel to an imperative or to a negative command; it may, as here, be followed by the modal *qatal* that elsewhere can continue an imperative. These latter observations show that in terms of semantics, the infinitive absolute may be just like an imperative (cf. GKC §113bb). But usage in real life may be more restricted. This is the area of linguistics known as pragmatics. Given the breadth of nuance of the English imperative, translating with an imperative is preferable.

בֵּין־אֲחֵיכֶם. Adjunct P.P. בֵּין indicates giving both sides a hearing. This is the first time that אָח occurs in Deuteronomy. All are equal members of the familial community. That it is not necessarily a gendered term denoting a male is clear from 15:12, where it is used of a female slave. Translation is difficult. "Fellow Israelite" loses the familial connotation; "Kin(dred)" loses the closeness of familial tie; "sibling" lacks wider connotations, implying exclusively blood relative. With some hesitation I stick with "brother" (cf. French, *Liberté! Égalité! Fraternité!*).

וּשְׁפַטְתֶּם. *Qatal* (modal, sometimes termed *weqataltí*) 2mp Qal √שׁפט. An infinitive absolute functioning as an imperative can be continued by this verb form (GKC §112u; JM §119p). Many grammarians have seen this form (*wĕqatal* or *weqataltí*) as a distinctive conjugation in its own right, but that has recently been questioned (Cook 2012: 208–11).

צֶדֶק. The noun is an adjunct, functioning as an adverbial accusative of manner, describing the way in which the verb, in this case "judge," is to be performed (cf. WO §10.2.2e). The character of Yhwh and the egalitarian nature of the community make justice foundational in Deuteronomy.

בֵּין־אִישׁ וּבֵין־אָחִיו וּבֵין גֵּרוֹ. The preposition בֵּין is characteristically used before both parties, "between X and *between* Y"; here the second party may be one of two kinds: אחיו, "his brother," and גרו, "his resident alien." What is in view here is not a three-way judgment, but a judgment between a man and either a fellow Israelite or a resident alien. The pronominal suffix on גֵּר demonstrates the relational obligation between Israelite and alien.

1:17 לֹא־תַכִּירוּ פָנִים בַּמִּשְׁפָּט כַּקָּטֹן כַּגָּדֹל תִּשְׁמָעוּן
לֹא תָגוּרוּ מִפְּנֵי־אִישׁ כִּי הַמִּשְׁפָּט לֵאלֹהִים הוּא
וְהַדָּבָר אֲשֶׁר יִקְשֶׁה מִכֶּם תַּקְרִבוּן אֵלַי וּשְׁמַעְתִּיו:

HD. Three clauses follow asyndetically from the main command, in the previous verse, to judge justly (D3). Each clause explains further what is meant, first negatively, then positively, then negatively again. All three are grounded in the subsequent explanatory clause that connects justice with God. The second half of the verse, after the ʾatnakh, continues the theme of justice, prescribing what to do when the judges cannot resolve a case and establishing a two-tiered system. This is not for appeals, but for difficult cases.

לֹא־תַכִּירוּ פָנִים בַּמִּשְׁפָּט. *Yiqtol* 2mp Hiph √נכר. Prohibitions in Hebrew do not use the imperative, but either אַל + jussive or, as here, לֹא + *yiqtol*. The difference between them has been disputed (WO §34.2.2 n. 6; JM §113m). לֹא + *yiqtol* may be "more solemn" (JM §113m) or "more emphatic" (GKC §107o). It typically speaks of a permanent prohibition, while אַל + jussive pertains to the present moment, but the distinction is not always present (cf. 1:42). The idiom, rendered literally "do not recognize faces," only occurs in Deuteronomy and Proverbs; it forbids partiality or favoritism.

בַּמִּשְׁפָּט. Adjunct PP, indicating the sphere where favoritism is forbidden.

כַּקָּטֹן כַּגָּדֹל תִּשְׁמָעוּן. *Yiqtol* (modal) 2mp Qal √שמע with a **paragogic** ן. The final ן, as a relic of an older paradigm, occurs on *yiqtol* and *wayyiqtol* verb forms with vocalic subject suffixes (3mp; more rarely 2mp and 2fs) and is found in other Semitic languages (GKC §47m; WO §31.7.1; JM §44e, f). It often is found in pause and occurs most frequently in Deuteronomy (56×), although it is found elsewhere. Hoftijzer (55–56) has argued that it may mark "contrastivity." JM §44e observe that its presence may either be evidence of an older text, deliberate archaizing, or "a preference for a fuller and more emphatic or expressive form." The deontic modality, indicating obligation, "*should*," is apparent from the modality of the adjacent clauses, both of which are prohibitions.

כַּקָּטֹן כַּגָּדֹל. The double occurrence of כ marks a comparison indicating correspondence between the two items: they are like each other (GKC §161c; WO §11.2.9; JM §174i). The two adjectives (קטן, גדל) are used substantivally; together they form a standard **merism** indicating totality. The presence of the article is a way of expressing the "relative" or "comparative" superlative (for which, see on 10:14; cf. 1 Sam 30:19; WO §14.5c; JM §141j). The double PP acts as the oblique complement of the verb. It is **focus**-fronted, highlighting the contrast between different modes of hearing. They should hear "the smallest *just like* the greatest," rather than privileging the smallest over the greatest or the greatest over the smallest.

לֹא תָגוּרוּ מִפְּנֵי־אִישׁ. *Yiqtol* (modal) 2mp Qal √גור, "to fear." The root is a **homonym** of the more common verb, "to dwell as resident alien." It takes a PP introduced by either מן or מפני as its oblique complement (here מפני איש). See comment on לא תכירו in this verse for Hebrew prohibitions.

כִּי הַמִּשְׁפָּט לֵאלֹהִים הוּא. This explanatory clause, with subordinating conjunction כי, grounds the previous injunctions in God's concern for justice. This is the first of a number of examples in Deuteronomy of what is sometimes termed a **tripartite** nominal (Muraoka 1999; JM §154i, j) or verbless clause (Holmstedt and Jones). There are two main ways of reading such clauses. The first is to regard the first noun, here המשפט, as **extraposed** or dislocated—a noun outside the confines of the clause (traditionally called *casus pendens*)—in which case הוא is a resumptive pronoun, referring to the **extraposed** noun, and לאלהים is a PP acting as the predicate "[is/belongs] to God." It may then be translated as a **cleft** sentence, with the **extraposed** noun established as the **topic**: "as for the judgment, it belongs to God." The second is to regard the pronoun in such clauses as a pronominal copula "is." The presence of the pronoun in similarly constructed verbal clauses favors the former (e.g., Gen 3:12; Mal 1:7; cf. JM §154i n. 40). Instances such as 2 Kgs 19:15 (הָאֱלֹהִים), where the **extraposed** element (אתה) is a different person from the resumptive pronoun (הוא), favor the latter. Given that both are possible, each case should be examined on its own merits. On balance I favor the former here with המשפט **extraposed**, given the subsequent P–S word order and the pragmatic sense of such a reading (also Holmstedt and Jones, 77). The word order highlights המשפט as the **topic** and לאלהים as the **focus**. When it comes to matters of judgment and justice, of all the possible sources and owners, God is in fact the owner (cf. Prov 16:33; 2 Chr 19:6).

וְהַדָּבָר֙ אֲשֶׁ֤ר יִקְשֶׁה֙ מִכֶּ֔ם תַּקְרִב֖וּן אֵלַ֑י. *Yiqtol* (modal) 2mp Hiph √קרב with **paragogic** ן. HD. The *yiqtol* has the nuance of obligation (cf. JM §113m): the Israelites "*should* bring. . . ." Normally vocalic suffixes on the Hiphil *yiqtol* do not attract the tone, but וּן- always has the tone (GKC §53r). אלי is the oblique complement.

וְהַדָּבָר֙. הדבר is the accusative complement of the verb תקריבון and is the **head** of the following restrictive relative clause. A definite noun before the verb has no need for את marking the direct object (JM §125f). The phrase as a whole is fronted. Probably this is to establish it as the **topic** rather than the **focus**, "now the case that is too hard for you, you shall bring . . . ," because what is at stake is not so much what should be brought to Moses—of the domain of all things you *could* bring to me, bring only the hard cases—but how to handle different cases.

אֲשֶׁ֤ר יִקְשֶׁה֙ מִכֶּ֔ם. *Yiqtol* 3ms Qal √קשה. A variant on the use of מן to express comparison is when "the quality is *too little* or *too much* in force for the attainment of a particular aim or object" (GKC §133c).

וּשְׁמַעְתִּֽיו. *Qatal* (used modally) 1cs Qal √שמע, with 3ms object suffix, referring back to והדבר. Often modal *qatal* gives the consequence of the previous clause (JM §119a, c, e; WO §32.2.1).

1:18 וָאֲצַוֶּ֥ה אֶתְכֶ֖ם בָּעֵ֣ת הַהִ֑וא אֵ֥ת כָּל־הַדְּבָרִ֖ים אֲשֶׁ֥ר תַּעֲשֽׂוּן׃

ND. The section on appointing judges ends with Moses summarizing (D2) how he commanded the Israelites to do everything at that time.

וָאֲצַוֶּ֥ה. *Wayyiqtol* 1cs Piel √צוה. For the form, see on 1:16. It is followed by two direct objects as complements (GKC §117gg; AC §2.3.1e), indicating the recipients of Moses' command (אתכם) and what Moses commanded (את כל־הדברים).

בָּעֵ֣ת הַהִ֑וא. Adjunct PP giving more general indication of the time of speaking and concluding the section (see on 1:9).

אֲשֶׁ֥ר תַּעֲשֽׂוּן. *Yiqtol* (modal) 2mp Qal √עשה with **paragogic** ן. For the modal nuance of "must" or "should" here, see JM §113m. Restrictive relative clause, further identifying the **head** הדברים.

The sending of the spies (1:19-25)

Moses resumes the narrative of the journey to the plains of Moab (ונסע, cf. סעו in 1:7). From 1:19–2:1, Moses recalls the failed invasion. In this section he quickly covers the journey from Horeb to Kadesh Barnea, before recounting his injunction to them to possess the land and the people's suggestion of sending spies ahead. The spies' trip is covered with a sequence of nine breathless *wayyiqtol* clauses, from Moses' selection (ואקח, v. 23b) to their speech (ויאמרו, v. 25b) when they deliver their positive verdict on the land. The harmonious cooperation of Moses and the people and the upbeat summary leave the unsuspecting reader wholly unprepared for what follows.

> [19] Then we set out from Horeb and went through all of that great, dreadful desert which you saw, by the way of the Amorite hill country, just as Yhwh our God commanded us, and we came to Kadesh Barnea. [20] Then I said to you, "You have come to the Amorite hill country, which Yhwh our God is giving to us. [21] See! Yhwh your God has put the land at your disposal. Go up! Take possession, just as Yhwh the God of your ancestors promised you! Do not fear and do not be afraid!" [22] Then you approached me, all of you, and you said, "Let us send men ahead of us so they may spy out the land for us and bring us back a report of the route by which we should go up and of the cities into which we should come." [23] The suggestion pleased me, so I selected from you twelve men, one man per tribe, [24] and they turned and went up to the hill country and came to Wadi Eshcol and they spied it out. [25] They took some of the fruit of the land in their hand and brought [it] down to us, and they brought us back a report and said, "The land that Yhwh our God is giving to us is good."

1:19 וַנִּסַּע מֵחֹרֵב וַנֵּלֶךְ אֵת כָּל־הַמִּדְבָּר הַגָּדוֹל וְהַנּוֹרָא הַהוּא אֲשֶׁר רְאִיתֶם דֶּרֶךְ הַר הָאֱמֹרִי כַּאֲשֶׁר צִוָּה יְהוָה אֱלֹהֵינוּ אֹתָנוּ וַנָּבֹא עַד קָדֵשׁ בַּרְנֵעַ:

ND. Moses covers the journey from Horeb to Kadesh Barnea with minimum detail, the three *wayyiqtols* highlighting departure, journey, and arrival (D2). He emphasizes the solidarity of his addressees in Moab with himself ("*we . . .*") and with the Israelites at Horeb ("*we* set out *from Horeb*"). See on 1:6.

וַנִּסַּע מֵחֹרֵב. *Wayyiqtol* 1cp Qal √נסע. מֵחֹרֵב is PP adjunct.

וַנֵּ֡לֶךְ אֵ֣ת כָּל־הַמִּדְבָּ֣ר הַגָּדוֹל֩ וְהַנּוֹרָ֨א הַה֜וּא אֲשֶׁ֣ר רְאִיתֶ֗ם דֶּ֚רֶךְ הַ֣ר הָאֱמֹרִ֔י. *Wayyiqtol* 1cp Qal √הלך. ND. Rarely does an accusative complement follow הלך. Here, the NP complement gives further precision to the place *through* which they went (GKC §118d, h). The noun is modified by three attributive adjectives. The first is descriptive, גדול; the second is ptcp ms Niph √ירא, having what WO §23.3d term the "**gerundive**" use of the Niphal, indicating what is proper or possible (here "dread*ful*" or "terri*ble*"); the third is the weak (or quasi-)demonstrative, the personal pronoun הוא with the article (WO §17.5a; JM §143j). In such a chain, all three characteristically have the article, with the demonstrative placed last (GKC §126v).

אֲשֶׁ֣ר רְאִיתֶ֗ם. *Qatal* 2mp Qal √ראה. Restrictive relative clause, with **head** המדבר.

דֶּ֚רֶךְ הַ֣ר הָאֱמֹרִ֔י. Adjunct construct chain specifying the route travelled. For הר האמרי, see on 1:7. For the syntax of the whole phrase, see on דרך הר־שעיר in 1:2.

כַּאֲשֶׁ֥ר צִוָּ֛ה יְהוָ֥ה אֱלֹהֵ֖ינוּ אֹתָ֑נוּ. *Qatal* 3ms Piel √צוה. Comparative clause, introduced by כאשר, emphasizing the people's obedience. After כאשר, there is usually **triggered inversion**, with P–S word order. For the double accusative following the verb of commanding, see on 1:18.

וַנָּבֹ֕א עַ֖ד קָדֵ֥שׁ בַּרְנֵֽעַ. *Wayyiqtol* 1cp Qal √בוא. עד קדש ברנע is the oblique complement.

1:20 וָאֹמַ֖ר אֲלֵכֶ֑ם בָּאתֶם֙ עַד־הַ֣ר הָאֱמֹרִ֔י אֲשֶׁר־יְהוָ֥ה אֱלֹהֵ֖ינוּ נֹתֵ֥ן לָֽנוּ׃

ND, in which Moses reverts to first singular after the solidarity of v. 19. Within this ND (D2), Moses quotes words he had previously said to them (D3), recounting their arrival in the Amorite hill country (ND).

וָאֹמַ֖ר אֲלֵכֶ֑ם. *Wayyiqtol* 1cs Qal √אמר, followed by adjunct PP indicating addressees. See on 1:9.

בָּאתֶם֙ עַד־הַ֣ר הָאֱמֹרִ֔י. *Qatal* 2mp Qal √בוא. ND in direct discourse never begins with *wayyiqtol*, only with *qatal*. It is followed by an oblique complement. For הר האמרי, see on 1:7.

אֲשֶׁר־יְהוָ֥ה אֱלֹהֵ֖ינוּ נֹתֵ֥ן לָֽנוּ. Ptcp ms Qal √נתן. The participle here indicates a future action that is already in progress (JM §121e).

Non-restrictive relative clause, giving further, but not essential, specification of the **head** הר האמרי. While relative clauses with *yiqtol* or *qatal* verb forms have typical P–S word order with **triggered inversion**, **null-copula** relative clauses with the participle have S–P word order, as here. It is a standard Deuteronomic phrase, "which Yhwh (y)our God is giving you/us," occurring thirty-five times in Deuteronomy. Only here, 1:25, and 2:29 is it 1cp.

1:21 רְאֵה נָתַן יְהוָה אֱלֹהֶיךָ לְפָנֶיךָ אֶת־הָאָרֶץ עֲלֵה
רֵשׁ כַּאֲשֶׁר דִּבֶּר יְהוָה אֱלֹהֵי אֲבֹתֶיךָ לָךְ אַל־תִּירָא
וְאַל־תֵּחָת:

D3. An initial HD interjection, ראה, asks them to take note of what Yhwh has done (ND). In the light of that, there are four further HD clauses, two commands, and two prohibitions. The injunctions are rooted in Yhwh's prior action of giving (נתן). Moses' highlighting of Yhwh's generous action removes any legitimate grounds for dissent. The gift is now to "you" (v. 21) not to "us" (v. 20). This draws attention to the gap between Moses and the Israelites.

רְאֵה. Impv ms Qal √ראה. HD. An interjection. See on 1:8.

נָתַן יְהוָה אֱלֹהֶיךָ לְפָנֶיךָ אֶת־הָאָרֶץ. Qatal 3ms Qal √נתן. ND. For the meaning of the phrase לפני . . . נתן, see on 1:8.

עֲלֵה רֵשׁ. Impv ms Qal √עלה and √ירש. Two imperatives frequently occur asyndetically, especially where the first involves movement (JM §177e). This coordination is an alternative mode of expression to subordination, and the second verb expresses the main idea (cf. GKC §120d, g). It is a mark of elevated or rhetorical style (cf. GKC §120h). Although the Qal *yiqtol* is יִירַשׁ, the imperative always drops the י. The pointing here, with *tsere*, is characteristic of I-ו verbs that have two *tseres* in their *yiqtol*, such as יֵצֵא. The expected a-class vowel is also somtimes found in the Qal imperative of ירש, though רָשׁ rather than רַשׁ because it is in pause (2:24, 31; cf. GKC §69f).

כַּאֲשֶׁר דִּבֶּר יְהוָה אֱלֹהֵי אֲבֹתֶיךָ לָךְ. Qatal 3ms Piel √דבר. Comparative clause, introduced by כאשר, after which there is usually **triggered inversion**, with P–S word order. For דִּבֶּר, see on 1:1. Often in Deuteronomy, כאשר is followed by a verb with יהוה as the subject. When the verb is צוה, Yhwh's command is in view (e.g., 1:19); when, as here, it is דבר, Yhwh's promise is usually envisaged (e.g., 1:11). Here, then, although Yhwh's command is intended, the use of דבר, along with the echoes of v. 11 and "God of your ancestors," evokes memories of Yhwh's *promise* of possessing the land.

לָךְ. The pointing of the preposition ל with 2ms pronominal suffix, normally לְךָ, as לָךְ is due to it being in pause (cf. GKC §103f; JM §103f).

אַל־תִּירָא וְאַל־תֵּחָת. Jussive 2ms Qal √ירא followed by jussive 2ms Niph √חתת. Two prohibitions, unlike two imperatives, almost always are joined syndetically. Although the form is that of a prohibition, the function is that of assurance, given that absence of fear is hardly within the control of those so commanded (GKC §110c; Tigay 1996: 15, 346 n. 79).

1:22 וַתִּקְרְב֣וּן אֵלַי֮ כֻּלְּכֶם֒ וַתֹּאמְר֗וּ נִשְׁלְחָ֤ה אֲנָשִׁים֙ לְפָנֵ֔ינוּ וְיַחְפְּרוּ־לָ֖נוּ אֶת־הָאָ֑רֶץ וְיָשִׁ֤בוּ אֹתָ֙נוּ֙ דָּבָ֔ר אֶת־הַדֶּ֙רֶךְ֙ אֲשֶׁ֣ר נַעֲלֶה־בָּ֔הּ וְאֵת֙ הֶֽעָרִ֔ים אֲשֶׁ֥ר נָבֹ֖א אֲלֵיהֶֽן׃

Two ND clauses (D2) are followed by Moses quoting what the Israelites said to him (D3). The people propose the sending of men ahead of them to spy out the land and bring back a report (HD).

וַתִּקְרְב֣וּן אֵלַי֮ כֻּלְּכֶם֒. *Wayyiqtol* 2mp Qal √קרב with **paragogic** ן (see on 1:17). On only nine occasions in more than three hundred occurrences is **paragogic** ן with *wayyiqtol* (Cook 2012: 240 n. 9; JM §44e omits Judg 11:18). אלי is the oblique complement. כלכם is not the syntactic subject of the verb, which is 2mp, but an adjunct, "you came near . . ., all of you." This is not literally everyone, but all represented through the leaders (Weinfeld, 323; cf. 5:23; 29:9).

וַתֹּאמְר֗וּ. *Wayyiqtol* 2mp Qal √אמר.

נִשְׁלְחָ֤ה אֲנָשִׁים֙ לְפָנֵ֔ינוּ. Cohortative 1cp Qal √שלח. לפנינו is an adjunct PP used spatially, "before" in the sense of "ahead of." When used temporally, it governs an event (e.g., Amos 1:1).

וְיַחְפְּרוּ־לָ֖נוּ אֶת־הָאָ֑רֶץ. Jussive 3mp Qal √חפר. The verb's literal meaning is "dig" (e.g., Gen 21:30). It is also used metaphorically, as here, of "spying out" (cf. Josh 2:2, 4; Job 39:29). Although there is no distinct form for 3mp jussive, its position as first in the clause and the volitional form in the previous clause (נשלחה) indicate it is jussive. The sequence of cohortative then ו + jussive may have one of two senses. First, the ו may be a simple conjunction, "and": "Let us send . . . *and* let them spy out. . . ." This then, with וישבו, would be a sequence of direct volitives. The alternative is that the jussive ויחפרו is an **indirect volitive**, syntactically coordinate but logically subordinate to the cohortative, indicating purpose: "Let us send . . . *that they may* spy out." Although JM §116d doubts whether there are any sure examples of an indirect jussive after a cohortative, it is hard to deny the sense of purpose in the people's request here, and there *are* other instances (e.g., Exod 8:3; see GKC §109f; cf. Lambdin, 119). לנו is an adjunct PP, with the ל introducing what is sometimes called "the dative of advantage" giving the beneficiary of the action of the verb (cf. JM §133d; GKC §119s).

וְיָשִׁ֤בוּ אֹתָ֙נוּ֙ דָּבָ֔ר אֶת־הַדֶּ֗רֶךְ אֲשֶׁ֤ר נַעֲלֶה־בָּ֔הּ וְאֵת֙ הֶעָרִ֔ים אֲשֶׁ֥ר נָבֹ֖א אֲלֵיהֶֽן. Jussive 3mp Hiph √שוב. See previous comment for classification as jussive. The Hiphil of שוב followed by דבר is a common phrase, "to bring back a word," "to report." The verb takes a second direct object for the recipient of the דבר, here אתנו. This raises the question of how to interpret the conjoined NPs את־הדרך . . . אליהן. (1) It is loosely attached to וישבו . . . דבר, a kind of apposition indicating the content of the report (Tigay 1996: 16). (2) It is a further direct object of ויחפרו, given that שוב . . . דבר does not usually have another direct object dnoyeb the recipient (Weinfeld, 143, though see JM §125y). (3) It is not a further direct object of ויחפרו, but appositional to את־הארץ, elucidating what precisely the men should spy out. (1) is more likely. First, the flow in (2) and (3) would be awkward, resuming after וישבו . . . דבר with a second object, whether appositional or not. Second, the inclusion of the content of the report after שוב Hiph + דבר + accusative of recipients is found elsewhere, after the **complementizer** לאמר (e.g., 1 Kgs 2:30) or in the form of an interrogative pronoun (2 Sam 24:13).

אֲשֶׁ֥ר נַעֲלֶה־בָּ֔הּ. Restrictive relative clause, identifying further the **head** of the clause, הדרך. נעלה is *yiqtol* 1cp Qal √עלה. בה is PP oblique complement. The 3fs resumptive pronoun -ָהּ picks up the **head** of the relative clause.

אֲשֶׁ֥ר נָבֹ֖א אֲלֵיהֶֽן. Restrictive relative clause, identifying further the **head** of the clause, הערים. נבא is *yiqtol* 1cp Qal √בוא. אליהן is PP oblique complement. The 3fp resumptive pronoun -ֵיהֶן refers back to the **head** of the relative clause.

1:23 וַיִּיטַ֥ב בְּעֵינַ֖י הַדָּבָ֑ר וָאֶקַּ֤ח מִכֶּם֙ שְׁנֵ֣ים עָשָׂ֣ר אֲנָשִׁ֔ים אִ֥ישׁ אֶחָ֖ד לַשָּֽׁבֶט׃

D2. Moses outlines his response to the people's suggestion with two *wayyiqtol* clauses (ND). This is one of the rare occasions when the people's words are commended (cf. 5:28).

וַיִּיטַ֥ב בְּעֵינַ֖י הַדָּבָ֑ר. *Wayyiqtol* 3ms Qal √יטב. With the oblique complement בעיני, the verb means "be pleasing to"; the subject is usually impersonal, often הדבר. For more on the verb, see on 4:40.

וָאֶקַּ֤ח מִכֶּם֙ שְׁנֵ֣ים עָשָׂ֣ר אֲנָשִׁ֔ים אִ֥ישׁ אֶחָ֖ד לַשָּֽׁבֶט. *Wayyiqtol* 1cs Qal √לקח. The verb לקח behaves like a I-נ verb, hence the *dagesh forte* in the ק (JM §72j). מכם is adjunct PP, giving the source of the choice.

שְׁנֵ֣ים עָשָׂ֣ר אֲנָשִׁ֔ים. Numerals between 11 and 19 tend to take the singular form of certain nouns, including איש, but there are exceptions, as here with אנשים (GKC §134f).

אִ֥ישׁ אֶחָ֖ד לַשָּֽׁבֶט. Adjunct appositional NP, further explaining Moses' approach to selection. לשבט is PP, with ל expressing the distributive idea, "per" (WO §15.6b; JM §142p; GKC §134q).

1:24 וַיִּפְנוּ֙ וַיַּעֲל֣וּ הָהָ֔רָה וַיָּבֹ֖אוּ עַד־נַ֣חַל אֶשְׁכֹּ֑ל וַֽיְרַגְּל֖וּ אֹתָֽהּ׃

D2. Four terse *wayyiqtol* main clauses give a sense of momentum to the men's exploring (ND).

וַיִּפְנוּ֙. *Wayyiqtol* 3mp Qal √פנה. For the sense of "turn and go on," see on 1:7.

וַיַּעֲל֣וּ הָהָ֔רָה. *Wayyiqtol* 3mp Qal √עלה. ההרה is the directional adjunct. The **paragogic** ה on ההר indicates motion toward, the so-called *he locale* or locative ה (WO §10.5a, b; JM §93c). The accent does not shift when ה is added.

וַיָּבֹ֖אוּ עַד־נַ֣חַל אֶשְׁכֹּ֑ל. *Wayyiqtol* 3mp Qal √בוא. עד־נחל אשכל is oblique complement NP of verb ויבאו. אשכל is so-called because the Israelites cut a "cluster" of grapes there (Num 13:23-24). This kind of construct phrase has been termed "genitive of association" (WO §9.5.3h) where the absolute (אשכל) belongs to the class of the construct (נחל, "wadi").

וַיְרַגְּלוּ אֹתָהּ. *Wayyiqtol* 3mp Piel √רגל. A **denominative** verb (cf. רֶגֶל, "foot"). אתה, the accusative complement of וירגלו, is awkward because the 3fs suffix has no obvious antecedent, as נחל and הר are both masculine and דרך (v. 22) is too far removed. Presumably, as it stands, the land, הארץ (f), is in view. For discussion/explanations, see Tigay 1996: 346 n. 89; McConville, 57; *BHQ: Deuteronomy*, 51*.

1:25 וַיִּקְחוּ בְיָדָם מִפְּרִי הָאָרֶץ וַיּוֹרִדוּ אֵלֵינוּ וַיָּשִׁבוּ
אֹתָנוּ דָבָר וַיֹּאמְרוּ טוֹבָה הָאָרֶץ
אֲשֶׁר־יְהוָה אֱלֹהֵינוּ נֹתֵן לָנוּ׃

Four further succinct *wayyiqtol* main clauses (ND, D2) are followed by Moses recounting the spies' report that describes the land (ED, D3). The land has not only been sworn to them (1:8), but it is a good land. Yhwh's beneficence is not in doubt.

וַיִּקְחוּ בְיָדָם מִפְּרִי הָאָרֶץ. *Wayyiqtol* 3mp Qal √לקח. The absence of *dagesh forte* in the ק is characteristic of a number of letters when they occur with a vocal *sheva* (see on ויהי in 1:3). בידם is an adjunct PP to the verb ויקחו. מפרי הארץ is oblique complement construct PP. The preposition מן is partitive, used when taking a part from the whole (cf. WHS §324).

וַיּוֹרִדוּ אֵלֵינוּ. *Wayyiqtol* 3mp Hiph √ירד. Going up (עלה) to spy out the land is matched by "bringing down" (ירד) its produce. The accusative complement is covert, but easily recoverable from the context. אלינו is adjunct PP to the verb ויורדו.

וַיָּשִׁבוּ אֹתָנוּ דָבָר. *Wayyiqtol* 3mp Hiph √שוב. For the syntax and idiom, see on 1:22.

וַיֹּאמְרוּ. *Wayyiqtol* 3mp Qal √אמר. The root introduces the next level of embedded discourse (D3).

טוֹבָה הָאָרֶץ. P–S **null-copula** clause. Here, טובה is fronted for **focus**: of all the possible ways the land might be described, it is "good" (cf. on 1:14).

אֲשֶׁר־יְהוָה אֱלֹהֵינוּ נֹתֵן לָנוּ. Restrictive relative clause, further identifying the **head** הארץ. For the phrase, see on 1:20.

The people's refusal to enter (1:26-33)

After recounting succinctly the spies' mission and positive report, Moses reminds the Israelites of "their" (strictly, their fathers') response. Their unwillingness to go up was rebellious, rooted in the attribution of nefarious motives to Yhwh. The event of the exodus was not in doubt, but the interpretation was. While Moses selectively recalled the glowing report of the spies (v. 25), the people's hearts melted over the spies' words about the opposition that they would face. Moses recalls how he addressed their anxieties directly. He rooted the call not to fear in the future in a more accurate interpretation of Yhwh's activity on their behalf on the past (vv. 29-31). Even then, it was to no avail. The irrational and culpable nature of their unbelief is further emphasized by Moses in v. 33. But now Moses expands on Yhwh's activity for the benefit of his hearers today in Moab. There is a certain blurring of Moses' words to Israel at Kadesh forty years earlier and Moses' words to Israel in Moab, just as there is a coalescing of Israel then and Israel "today" in Moab. Yhwh's gracious activity is ever-present, while Israel's unbelief looms large as a present possibility.

²⁶But you were not willing to go up and you defied the word of Yhwh your God. ²⁷You cast accusations in your tents and said, "It is because of Yhwh's hatred of us that he brought us out from the land of Egypt to give us into the hand of the Amorites to destroy us. ²⁸To where are we going up? Our brothers made our hearts melt, saying 'A people greater and taller than us, cities that are great and fortified to the heavens, and even the Anakites we saw there.'" ²⁹Then I said to you, "Do not be terrified or afraid of them. ³⁰Yhwh your God who goes before you, he will fight for you just as he did for you in Egypt before your eyes, ³¹and in the wilderness where you saw that Yhwh your God carried you, just as a man carries his son, on the entire route you went until you came to this place." ³²But in spite of this word, you did not believe Yhwh your God, ³³who goes before you on the way to reconnoitre for you a place for you to camp—in the fire by night to show you the way you should go and in the cloud by day.

1:26 וְלֹא אֲבִיתֶם לַעֲלֹת וַתַּמְרוּ אֶת־פִּי יְהוָה אֱלֹהֵיכֶם:

D2. ND. After the sequence of nine *wayyiqtols* documenting smooth progress, there is an abrupt change of key. The initial disjunctive clause, the shift from 1cp (v. 25) to 2mp (v. 26) that distances the people from

Moses and links them to the rebellious first generation, and the damning indictment of their unwarranted behavior all shock hearers and readers.

וְלֹא אֲבִיתֶם לַעֲלֹת. *Qatal* 2mp Qal √אבה. The disjunctive clause (לא + *qatal*) stands in sharp contrast with the smooth sequence of *wayyiqtols*. לַעֲלֹת is inf constr Qal √עלה with preposition ל, functioning as the complement of אביתם.

וַתַּמְרוּ אֶת־פִּי יְהוָה אֱלֹהֵיכֶם. *Wayyiqtol* 2mp Hiph √מרה. מרה Hiphil can be intransitive, "to be defiant," or, as here, transitive, "to defy." פי יהוה (lit. "the mouth of Yhwh") is a common metonymy for what Yhwh's mouth has uttered. The NP את־פי יהוה אלהיכם is the accusative complement, denoting what the Israelites have defied. Their lack of willingness was not in response to a choice, but to a command.

1:27 וַתֵּרָגְנוּ בְאָהֳלֵיכֶם וַתֹּאמְרוּ בְּשִׂנְאַת יְהוָה אֹתָנוּ הוֹצִיאָנוּ מֵאֶרֶץ מִצְרָיִם לָתֵת אֹתָנוּ בְּיַד הָאֱמֹרִי לְהַשְׁמִידֵנוּ:

ND (D2), followed by embedded ND (D3). Slowing down the retelling by quoting the people's words enables exploration of the anatomy of unwillingness and rebellion. Moses' reframing of the events highlights the irrationality of the reaction in preparation for the rest of the book's exhortation.

וַתֵּרָגְנוּ בְאָהֳלֵיכֶם. *Wayyiqtol* 2mp Niph √רגן. ND. D2. The root's use in Proverbs (e.g., Prov 16:28; 18:8), in particular where it is associated with words that are like tasty morsels, suggests that neither demeanor, "appeared sullen" (Nelson, 22) nor "grumbling" (NRSV, NIV) is in view, but rather "slandering" or "casting accusations." באהליכם is adjunct PP, indicating the location of their slander.

וַתֹּאמְרוּ. *Wayyiqtol* 2mp Qal √אמר. The root אמר introduces embedded direct discourse as its complement, here D3.

בְּשִׂנְאַת יְהוָה אֹתָנוּ הוֹצִיאָנוּ מֵאֶרֶץ מִצְרָיִם לָתֵת אֹתָנוּ בְּיַד הָאֱמֹרִי לְהַשְׁמִידֵנוּ. *Qatal* 3ms Hiph √יצא with 1cp pronominal suffix. ND. מארץ מצרים is oblique complement, indicating from where Yhwh had brought them out. Within direct speech, the initial finite verb (הוציאנו) may not be *wayyiqtol*, only *qatal*.

בְּשִׂנְאַ֤ת יְהוָה֙ אֹתָ֔נוּ. Inf constr Qal √שׂנא with preposition בּ. The feminine form ending in ־ָה is found in the infinitive construct of some stative verbs; for שׂנא it is only here and 9:28 (JM §49d). The infinitive construct as a *verbal* noun still retains the ability to govern an accusative complement (אתנו) and to require a subject (יהוה). In such cases, the subject follows the infinitive construct directly (GKC §115h). At the same time, as a verbal *noun* it has as its subject יהוה in the genitive (absolute) following a clearly construct form, ־ַת (JM §124g). In the so-called "genitive of agency," the genitive performs the action of the construct (WO §9.5.1a, b; WHS §37). The preposition בּ attached to the infinitive construct often introduces temporal expressions, but here it is causal (WO §36.2.2b). The phrase as a whole is an adjunct infinitive phrase to the verb הוציאנו, fronted for **focus**. Out of all the reasons why Yhwh might have brought them out, it was because of his hatred of them. They are not denying Yhwh's action, but questioning Yhwh's motives.

לָתֵ֥ת אֹתָ֛נוּ בְּיַ֥ד הָאֱמֹרִ֖י. Inf constr Qal √נתן with preposition ל (see on 1:8). Adjunct infinitive phrase to הוציאנו, indicating purpose. The phrase נתן ביד is a common idiom for delivering someone into the hand of another. ביד האמרי is oblique complement construct phrase. For the gentilic adjective, האמרי, and the use of the article for the whole group, see on 1:4.

לְהַשְׁמִידֵֽנוּ. Inf constr Hiph √שמד with 1cp pronominal object suffix and with preposition ל. Adjunct infinitive phrase indicating purpose. According to the people, this is the final goal of Yhwh's hatred—their destruction.

1:28 אָנָ֣ה ׀ אֲנַ֣חְנוּ עֹלִ֗ים אַחֵינוּ֩ הֵמַ֨סּוּ אֶת־לְבָבֵ֜נוּ לֵאמֹ֗ר
עַ֣ם גָּד֤וֹל וָרָם֙ מִמֶּ֔נּוּ עָרִ֛ים גְּדֹלֹ֥ת וּבְצוּרֹ֖ת בַּשָּׁמָ֑יִם
וְגַם־בְּנֵ֥י עֲנָקִ֖ים רָאִ֥ינוּ שָֽׁם׃

Moses continues to report the people's rebellious words (D3). ID, followed by ND. There is further embedded discourse (D4) as the people then recount the spies' words to them (ND). Moses recounted only the positive side of the spies' report ("the land is good," v. 25) while his retelling puts on the people's lips only the negative (paraphrase: "everything we have seen is intimidating"). The selective narration graphically illustrates the gap between the people and him. Moses' addressees in Moab are clearly to align with him (cf. 1:35).

אָ֫נָה ׀ אֲנַ֫חְנוּ עֹלִ֫ים. Ptcp mp Qal √עלה. ID, introduced by interrogative particle, אנה, "to where" (WO §18.4f). Unmarked S–P word order in **null-copula** participial clause.

אַחֵ֫ינוּ הֵמַ֫סּוּ אֶת־לְבָבֵ֫נוּ לֵאמֹ֫ר. *Qatal* 3cp Hiph √מסס. Unmarked S–P word order. The people express solidarity with the men who had spied out the land ("our brothers") and attribute a certain responsibility to them, with √מסס Hiphil suggesting causation.

עַ֣ם גָּד֤וֹל וָרָם֙ מִמֶּ֔נּוּ עָרִ֛ים גְּדֹלֹ֥ת וּבְצוּרֹ֖ת בַּשָּׁמָ֑יִם וְגַם־בְּנֵ֥י עֲנָקִ֖ים רָאִ֥ינוּ שָֽׁם. *Qatal* 1cp Qal √ראה. ND. Notwithstanding many translations, there is one clause here with three accusative complement NPs fronted for **focus**. The lengthy preverbal field shows only too clearly what has consumed the spies, at least in the memory of the people. In a series of nouns or NPs, ו-conjunction may join each item, or just occur as here before the last one (JM §177o).

עַ֣ם גָּד֤וֹל וָרָם֙ מִמֶּ֫נּוּ. Ptcp ms Qal √רום. Accusative complement NP to the verb ראיתם. גדול and רם are attributive adjectives, modifying עם. If they were predicative, we would expect הָעָם. The ו-conjunction is often pointed with *qamets* before the tone syllable, especially when the words are closely paired (GKC §104g; JM §104d). Lacking particular forms for the comparative, Hebrew uses the preposition מן attached to the noun that is excelled (AC §4.1.13h), here represented by the pronominal suffix.

עָרִ֛ים גְּדֹלֹ֥ת וּבְצוּרֹ֖ת בַּשָּׁמָ֑יִם. Accusative complement NP to the verb ראיתם. בצורת is Qal passive participle from √בצר, functioning as an attributive adjective. בשמים is adjunct PP, indicating the extent of the fortifications.

וְגַם־בְּנֵ֥י עֲנָקִ֖ים. Accusative complement construct NP to the verb ראיתם. There are different ways of expressing a compound idea (construct + absolute) in the plural. Often this is done by making just the construct plural (cf. בני ענק, Num 13:33). Here, both nouns are plural (GKC §124q). גם is an "additive" particle, indicating that what follows is in addition to what has preceded (Muraoka 1985: 143–46). It can modify a word, a constituent of a clause, or the clause itself (MNK §41.4.5.1). Here, it is an "item adverb" (for which, see WO §39.3.1)—that is, it does not modify the clause, "also we saw the Anakites there," since there is no predicate associated with the previous NPs. Rather, it modifies an item within a clause. Given its position, it modifies בני ענקים, "and *also/ even the Anakites* we saw there."

שָׁם. Locative adverbial adjunct.

1:29 וַיֹּ֥אמֶר אֲלֵכֶ֖ם לֹא־תַֽעַרְצ֥וּן וְלֹא־תִֽירְא֖וּן מֵהֶֽם׃

D2, ND (v. 29a), followed by embedded discourse (D3), in which Moses urges the people not to fear (HD).

וָאֹמַ֖ר אֲלֵכֶ֑ם. *Wayyiqtol* 1cs Qal √אמר. ND. See on 1:9 for the identical phrase.

לֹא־תַֽעַרְצ֥וּן וְלֹא־תִֽירְא֖וּן מֵהֶֽם. *Yiqtol* (modal) 2mp Qal √ערץ and √ירא, both with **paragogic** ן. HD. See on 1:17 for **paragogic** ן and for prohibitions. Qal ערץ may either be intransitive, "be terrified," or transitive, "terrify." The former is the case here. מהם is probably the oblique complement of both ערץ and ירא, since elsewhere in Deuteronomy ערץ is followed by מפני (e.g., 7:21).

1:30 יְהוָ֤ה אֱלֹֽהֵיכֶם֙ הַהֹלֵ֣ךְ לִפְנֵיכֶ֔ם ה֖וּא יִלָּחֵ֣ם לָכֶ֑ם כְּכֹ֗ל אֲשֶׁ֨ר עָשָׂ֧ה אִתְּכֶ֛ם בְּמִצְרַ֖יִם לְעֵינֵיכֶֽם׃

D3. PD. There is no formal syntactic connection that links v. 30 with v. 29, but the **asyndesis** at the start of v. 30 indicates Moses is giving grounds for his injunction not to fear. Both he and the people are agreed about Yhwh's involvement in deliverance from Egypt. Moses counters their interpretation—Yhwh's hatred and destructive purpose—by making them consider Yhwh's constant fatherly care. Ability to trust Yhwh for the future depends on a right understanding of the past.

יְהוָ֤ה אֱלֹֽהֵיכֶם֙ הַהֹלֵ֣ךְ לִפְנֵיכֶ֔ם ה֖וּא יִלָּחֵ֣ם לָכֶ֑ם. ההלך is Ptcp ms Qal √הלך, with the article. There are two choices for how to take the opening phrase, יהוה אלהיכם ההלך לפניכם. The first is to see it as an **extraposed** NP (see further on 1:17), dislocated as the **topic**, with the resumptive subject pronoun הוא signalling **focus**. If so, the basic clause is הוא ילחם לכם, which, in contrast to v. 17, is a verbal clause. In this case, הוא can only be the resumptive pronoun picking up the **extraposed** NP. ההלך is then akin to an attributive adjective (for which, see WO §13.5.2d), although recent study suggests that the article ה is better characterized as introducing a relative clause with the adjectival participle functioning predicatively in a **null-copula** clause (Barr, 322–25; Holmstedt 2002: 83–90; cp. WO §19.7): "Yhwh your God, *who goes before you,* he [and no one else] will fight for you" (cf. NJPS, "None other than the Lord your God, who goes before you, will fight for you"). The other way is to regard יהוה אלהיכם ההלך לפניכם as a **null-copula** clause, with the predicate ההלך לפניכם (for which, see WO §13.5.2d). ההלך would then be akin to a substantive, although again it is better analyzed as a **null-head** restrictive relative clause, "[the one] who goes . . .": "Yhwh your God [is] [*the one*] *who goes* before you; he will fight for you." The difference is subtle. In the former, the key question is who will fight for them. In the latter, it is who goes before them. In favor of the latter is the use of ההלך in the very similar 20:4 (cf. 31:6, 8). There, ההלך עמכם can only be the predicate in a **null-copula** clause, "[is] [*the one*] *who goes*" (cf. ESV, NIV, NASB). On balance, though, I favor the former, for three reasons: (1) ההלך also occurs in 1:33, where יהוה אלהיכם (v. 32) is the **head** of the relative clause begun by ה at the start of v. 33 in similar fashion to the first rendering above; (2) the identical syntax in 1:38 only makes sense when understood along similar lines to the former rendering; and (3) it is not Yhwh's presence that is disputed, but the nature of Yhwh's activity. It would have little rhetorical force, since the people had impugned Yhwh's character (v. 27), for Moses to begin his response by a declaration that Yhwh was the one who would go with them.

הוּא יִלָּחֵם לָכֶם. *Yiqtol* 3ms Niph √לחם. The root לחם almost always occurs in the Niphal and is intransitive. לכם is adjunct PP, indicating for whom Yhwh will fight.

כְּכֹל אֲשֶׁר עָשָׂה אִתְּכֶם בְּמִצְרַיִם לְעֵינֵיכֶם. PP adjunct of manner, comparing Yhwh's future fighting for them with his past actions. כל shows that Yhwh will act "*just as*" he had done (JM §139e n. 3). It (כל) may be the **head** of the subsequent restrictive relative clause. Alternatively, the relative clause may be **null-head**, with the antecedent covert, rather than overt.

עָשָׂה אִתְּכֶם. *Qatal* 3ms Qal √עשׂה. אתכם is adjunct PP, indicating for whose advantage Yhwh acted (WHS §341) or with whom the verb's subject has dealt (MNK §39.5.2). The parallel with 4:34 and 10:21 makes the former preferable.

בְּמִצְרַיִם לְעֵינֵיכֶם. Adjunct PPs to the verb עשׂה, specifying where Yhwh acted and who saw it. Moses consistently addresses the new generation in Moab as if they had personally experienced the exodus (1:35; 2:14). This is part of his rhetoric whereby the past (cf. 5:2-4) and the future (cf. 29:13-14) are brought into "today" in Moab (Robson, 16–17).

וּבַמִּדְבָּר֙ אֲשֶׁ֣ר רָאִ֔יתָ אֲשֶׁ֤ר נְשָׂאֲךָ֙ יְהוָ֣ה אֱלֹהֶ֔יךָ 1:31
כַּאֲשֶׁ֥ר יִשָּׂא־אִ֖ישׁ אֶת־בְּנ֑וֹ בְּכָל־הַדֶּ֙רֶךְ֙ אֲשֶׁ֣ר
הֲלַכְתֶּ֔ם עַד־בֹּאֲכֶ֖ם עַד־הַמָּק֥וֹם הַזֶּֽה׃

PD (*cont.*). Moses continues his recollection of his speech outlining the grounds for the people not to be afraid (D3). Yhwh will fight for them in the future because he has done so in the past. Not only did Yhwh fight for them in Egypt (v. 30), but he also did so "in the wilderness," seen in the protective care as of a father for a son. All of Yhwh's providential protection in the past should be grounds for future confidence that Yhwh will fight for them.

וּבַמִּדְבָּר֙ אֲשֶׁ֣ר רָאִ֔יתָ. *Qatal* 2ms Qal √ראה. במדבר is a further adjunct PP, corresponding to במצרים in v. 30. מדבר is the **head** of the non-restrictive relative clause that follows. Although there is no resumptive adverb in the relative clause, there is a gap where one (שָׁם) would fit (cf. 4:5, אשר . . . שמה).

אֲשֶׁ֤ר נְשָׂאֲךָ֙ יְהוָ֣ה אֱלֹהֶ֔יךָ. *Qatal* 3ms Qal √נשא with 2ms suffix. אשר functions here as an accusative complement clause **complementizer**, "saw *that* Yhwh your God carried you" (Holmstedt 2006: 10; cf. JM §157c). It cannot be a relative marker since there is no position within the clause that would correspond to the **head** of the relative clause. In a relative clause, this position will have a resumptive pronoun or adverb, or will have a gap where that resumptive word could fit (Holmstedt 2002: 294–95).

כַּאֲשֶׁ֥ר יִשָּׂא־אִ֖ישׁ אֶת־בְּנ֑וֹ. *Yiqtol* 3ms Qal √נשא. Comparative clause, comparing Yhwh's carrying of Israel in the wilderness with a father carrying his son (cf. 8:5, of Yhwh's fatherly discipline; 32:11, of Yhwh carrying them [נשא] like an eagle). The *yiqtol* here speaks of habitual repeated action in the present (JM §113c n. 7). Note the P–S word order due to **triggered inversion**.

בְּכָל־הַדֶּ֙רֶךְ֙ אֲשֶׁ֣ר הֲלַכְתֶּ֔ם. *Qatal* 2mp Qal √הלך. Adjunct PP to the verb נשא. דרך is the **head** of the restrictive relative clause. There is no preposition with resumptive pronoun within the clause (בָּהּ, cf. 1:22), but the gap is clear. Yhwh did not merely "go (הלך) before them" (v. 30). The characteristically Deuteronomic כל shows that Yhwh *carried* them the entire route they "went" (הלך).

עַד־בֹּאֲכֶם עַד־הַמָּקוֹם הַזֶּה. Inf constr Qal √בוא with 2mp subject suffix. Temporal adjunct PP, within which is a spatial oblique complement, עַד־הַמקום הזה, for the verb באכם. The action of the main clause has continued *until* the time of the event specified by the infinitive construct (MNK §20.1.5[iii]).

1:32 וּבַדָּבָר הַזֶּה אֵינְכֶם מַאֲמִינִם בַּיהוָה אֱלֹהֵיכֶם:

ND. Moses breaks off from his retelling to address his hearers in Moab again (D2). By retaining "you" for D2 (Moses speaking in Moab) as well as for D3 (Moses speaking in Kadesh, some forty years before), he highlights the solidarity and continuity, blurring the distinction. Consistent with Deuteronomy's emphasis on the significance of words, Moses highlights their unbelieving response to his word back then.

וּבַדָּבָר הַזֶּה. Adjunct PP. The preposition ב can have the sense of "in spite of" (AC §4.1.5d), a sense derived either metaphorically from the "ב of price" (WO §11.2.5d n. 28) or from adversative ב (WHS §242; cf. Num 14:11). Alternatively, the phrase could mean "regarding this matter" (Rashi). The phrase is fronted for **focus**.

אֵינְכֶם מַאֲמִינִם. Ptcp mp Hiph √אמן. אין is an adverb of nonexistence (JM §154k, §160g). When the subject of a clause with אין is a personal pronoun, the pronoun is joined as a suffix to אין, -כם. The verb that follows is a participle, because אין always introduces a **null-copula** clause (GKC §152m). Given these syntactical constraints, the identification of this clause as ND depends on the time frame set by adjacent clauses.

בַּיהוָה אֱלֹהֵיכֶם. Oblique complement of ptcp מאמינם. אמן Hiph + ב often has Yhwh as the object of the preposition. The phrase does not have to mean "believe *in*," with the object of the preposition being the content of the belief. It may simply mean "believe" or "trust" (Walton, 53–54; cf. Num 20:12; Jonah 3:5). What matters here is not so much the content of their belief but whether they took Yhwh at his word, or "believed Yhwh."

1:33 הַהֹלֵךְ לִפְנֵיכֶם בַּדֶּרֶךְ לָתוּר לָכֶם מָקוֹם לַחֲנֹתְכֶם בָּאֵשׁ ׀ לַיְלָה לַרְאֹתְכֶם בַּדֶּרֶךְ אֲשֶׁר תֵּלְכוּ־בָהּ וּבֶעָנָן יוֹמָם:

ND (*cont.*). D2. The whole verse is a relative clause with a number of adjuncts. Yhwh's going before in v. 30 was with a view to fighting. Here it is to guide. The Israelites' construal of Yhwh's motives and purpose becomes more implausible, their unbelief more culpable.

הַהֹלֵךְ לִפְנֵיכֶם בַּדֶּרֶךְ לָתוּר לָכֶם מָקוֹם לַחֲנֹתְכֶם. Ptcp ms Qal √הלך, with what is sometimes termed the relative use of the article (see on 1:30). יהוה אלהיכם (v. 32) is the **head** of the relative clause begun by ה at the start of v. 33. לפניכם and בדרך are adjunct PPs.

לָתוּר לָכֶם מָקוֹם. Inf constr Qal √תור with preposition ל, "to spy out, reconnoitre." Adjunct infinitive phrase expressing purpose. מקום is the accusative complement. לכם is adjunct PP, expressing the beneficiary (cf. JM §133d).

לַחֲנֹתְכֶם. Inf constr Qal √חנה with 2mp subject suffix. Adjunct infinitive phrase functioning adverbially after מקום (cf. WO §36.2.3b; Gen 24:25; Jer 19:11).

בָּאֵשׁ ׀ לַיְלָה לַרְאֹתְכֶם בַּדֶּרֶךְ . . . וּבֶעָנָן יוֹמָם. Inf constr Hiph √ראה with ל preposition and with 2mp object suffix. Normally the Hiphil infinitive construct with an inseparable preposition retains the ה, so this is an exception (GKC §53q). באש and (ו)בענן are adjunct PPs that balance each other, expressing the mode of Yhwh's presence going before them to reconnoitre. לילה and יומם are temporal adjuncts, closely associated with their respective preceding PPs. לראתכם is an adjunct infinitive phrase to the participle הלך. Often ראה Hiphil has two accusative complements, "to show X Y"; here, however, there is only one, the object suffix of לראתכם, -כם; בדרך is adjunct PP. The phrase לראתכם . . . בה only relates to the pillar of fire by night, so the purpose is less to guide than to help them see: "so you can see *on the route*" (Weinfeld, 146; HALOT 1161).

אֲשֶׁר תֵּלְכוּ־בָהּ. *Yiqtol* 2mp Qal √הלך. Restrictive relative clause, identifying further the **head** of the clause, דרך. בה is oblique complement. The 3fs resumptive pronoun -ָהּ picks up the **head** of the relative clause.

Yhwh's anger with the rebellious generation (1:34-40)

In response to the people's rebellious unbelief, Yhwh in his anger declares that none but Caleb and Joshua will enter (D3). Moses himself is caught up in that verdict, so he is to exhort Joshua. Only a new generation, still children now, will do so. Resentment of the exodus and refusal to take the land leads Yhwh to give them what they have asked for: an anti-exodus back the way they have come (v. 40) and exclusion from the land.

³⁴*Yhwh heard your words and was angry and swore,* ³⁵*"For sure not one of these men—this evil generation—shall see the good land which I swore to give to your ancestors* ³⁶*except Caleb son of Jephunneh—he will see it—and it is to him that I shall give the land on which he has trodden, and to his sons, precisely because he has followed fully after Yhwh."* ³⁷*(With me, too, Yhwh was angry because of you, "You too shall not enter there. As for Joshua son of Nun, who stands before you, he will enter there. It is to him that you should say 'Be strong!' for it is he who will cause Israel to inherit it.")* ³⁹*"And as for your little ones, whom you said would be for plunder, and your children, who today do not know good and evil—they will enter there and to them I will give it and they will possess it. But as for you, turn and set out to the desert by the Sea of Reeds route."*

1:34 וַיִּשְׁמַע יְהוָה אֶת־קוֹל דִּבְרֵיכֶם וַיִּקְצֹף וַיִּשָּׁבַע לֵאמֹר:

ND. D2. While the people did not believe Moses' word (v. 32), Yhwh heard the people's words. He utters the "counter-oath" of 1:8.

וַיִּשְׁמַע יְהוָה אֶת־קוֹל דִּבְרֵיכֶם. *Wayyiqtol* 3ms Qal √שמע. ND. את־קול דברים is accusative complement construct NP. Given that often שמע takes דבר as accusative complement, קול highlights that Yhwh heard something not addressed or reported to him, in this case words spoken in tents (1:27; cf. 5:28). Audibility is in view, although the contrast is not between sound and silence (cf. 4:12). Clearly Yhwh heard the content, too.

וַיִּקְצֹף וַיִּשָּׁבַע לֵאמֹר. *Wayyiqtol* 3ms Qal √קצף and *wayyiqtol* 3ms Niph √שבע. לאמר is a **complementizer** (see on 1:5).

1:35 אִם־יִרְאֶה אִישׁ בָּאֲנָשִׁים הָאֵלֶּה הַדּוֹר הָרָע הַזֶּה אֵת הָאָרֶץ הַטּוֹבָה אֲשֶׁר נִשְׁבַּעְתִּי לָתֵת לַאֲבֹתֵיכֶם:

PD. D3. Yhwh swears an oath that none of the evil generation will inherit the land sworn to their ancestors. Yhwh's mention of the "good land" echoes and implicitly endorses Moses' recollection of the spies' report (1:25).

אִם־יִרְאֶה אִישׁ בָּאֲנָשִׁים הָאֵלֶּה הַדּוֹר הָרָע הַזֶּה אֵת הָאָרֶץ הַטּוֹבָה.
Yiqtol 3ms Qal √ראה. Hebrew oaths have a two-part structure, with an authenticating element (e.g., invoking witnesses) followed by the content (Conklin). In oaths of denial, the clause introduced by אם functions as the protasis in an incomplete condition: "[may god do X (the authenticating element),] *if* I do Y," meaning "I surely will *not* do Y." Although in origin and perhaps in use אם introduced the content element of a curse, it probably came to be used simply as an affirmative oath (GKC §149b, c; JM §165h); it is hard to imagine Yhwh uttering a self-imprecation.

אִישׁ בָּאֲנָשִׁים הָאֵלֶּה. NP. The adjunct PP באנשים האלה goes closely with איש, the preposition ב being partitive, giving the whole out of which the individual is taken (WHS §251).

הַדּוֹר הָרָע הַזֶּה. Appositional NP to איש באנשים האלה, making clear that "these men" are not just the spies but the whole generation who grumbled.

אֵת הָאָרֶץ הַטּוֹבָה. Accusative complement of verb ראה.

אֲשֶׁר נִשְׁבַּעְתִּי לָתֵת לַאֲבֹתֵיכֶם: *Qatal* 1cs Niph √שבע. Restrictive relative clause, identifying further the **head** הארץ הטובה.

לָתֵת לַאֲבֹתֵיכֶם. Inf constr Qal √נתן with ל preposition. לתת is infinitive complement (cf. on 1:8). לאבתיכם is the oblique complement of לתת.

1:36 זוּלָתִי כָּלֵב בֶּן־יְפֻנֶּה הוּא יִרְאֶנָּה וְלוֹ־אֶתֵּן אֶת־הָאָרֶץ אֲשֶׁר דָּרַךְ־בָּהּ וּלְבָנָיו יַעַן אֲשֶׁר מִלֵּא אַחֲרֵי יְהוָה:

PD. D3. Yhwh highlights an exception to the exclusion, Caleb, the nature of that exception and the grounds for it.

זוּלָתִי כָּלֵב בֶּן־יְפֻנֶּה. PP adjunct of verb ראה. זולתי introduces an exception after a negation. For the **paragogic** (word-extending) ־י, see JM §93q. בן יפנה is in apposition to Caleb.

הוּא יִרְאֶנָּה. *Yiqtol* 3ms Qal √ראה with 3fs suffix. The clause is joined asyndetically to the one that precedes, and is coordinated with two further clauses that follow. Together these explain what the exclusion of the opening PP looks like. The resumptive subject pronoun, הוא, signals **focus**. There is a contrast with v. 35, where Yhwh swears that no one will see (√ראה).

וְלוֹ־אֶתֵּן אֶת־הָאָרֶץ אֲשֶׁר דָּרַךְ־בָּהּ וּלְבָנָיו. *Yiqtol* 1cs Qal √נתן. לוֹ is oblique complement of the verb אתן. It is fronted for **focus**. It is "to him (Caleb)" and not to others that Yhwh will give the land. Because לוֹ is fronted, the other oblique complement of אתן—that is, לבניו—stands somewhat awkwardly after the restrictive relative clause. The resolution of the apparent contradiction between Yhwh's oath to their ancestors to give the land and Yhwh's oath to exclude everyone from the land lies in the gift to Caleb and to his sons (cf. Josh 14:14).

אֲשֶׁר דָּרַךְ־בָּהּ. *Qatal* 3ms Qal √דרך. Restrictive relative clause. בה is oblique complement of the verb דרך. The 3fs resumptive pronoun -הּ picks up the **head** of the relative clause, הארץ. It could be land that Caleb *has* (already) "trodden" (√דרך) and that others will (11:24, 25). Or it could be that the *qatal* here speaks of future time, but anterior relative to the action of the main verb, a future perfect, "will have trodden" (cf. 8:10; Craigie, 104; JM §112i; WO §30.3b).

יַעַן אֲשֶׁר מִלֵּא אַחֲרֵי יְהוָה. *Qatal* 3ms Piel √מלא. יען אשר, only here in Deuteronomy, gives the notion of "precisely because" (JM §170f). אחרי יהוה is an oblique complement of the verb מלא. אחרי after מלא Piel has the sense of "remaining true to," "following fully after."

1:37 גַּם־בִּי הִתְאַנַּף יְהוָה בִּגְלַלְכֶם לֵאמֹר גַּם־אַתָּה לֹא־תָבֹא שָׁם׃

ND, then PD. Verses 37-38 seem to be a parenthetical, though nonetheless important, aside from Moses, given (1) that Yhwh was addressing Israel (cf. the suffix on אבתיכם, v. 35), which address is resumed unannounced to Israel in v. 39 (טפכם); (2) the clausal **asyndesis** at the start of v. 37. Moses again picks up his recollection (D2), before citing Yhwh's words again (D3), this time to him. Yhwh's words are not just a prediction but a declaration that, in the very act of being made, sentences him to exclusion.

גַּם־בִּי הִתְאַנַּף יְהוָה בִּגְלַלְכֶם לֵאמֹר. *Qatal* 3ms Hitp √אנף. For the *patakh*, התאנף, see GKC §54k; WO §26.1.1c; Blau, 233.

בִּי is oblique complement of the verb הִתְאַנַּף. It is fronted for **focus** and is qualified by the item adverb, גַּם (see on 1:28). Out of the domain of those with whom Yhwh was angry, Moses is included rather than excluded. Until now, Moses' place in Yhwh's plans for the future has not been specified. Now it is clear. בִּגְלַלְכֶם is adjunct PP, giving the grounds for Yhwh's anger with Moses.

גַּם־אַתָּה לֹא־תָבֹא שָׁם. *Yiqtol* 2ms Qal √בוא. Although לֹא + *yiqtol* can indicate a prohibition (HD; see 1:17), here it is PD. Yhwh declares what will not be the case. The overt subject, אַתָּה, is not necessary, given the subject implicit in the finite verb. It, along with the item adverb גַּם (see on 1:28), is thus fronted for **focus**. As Moses has declared that "with me, too" Yhwh was angry, so now Yhwh declares, "you too will not enter." שָׁם is a locative adverb, functioning as the oblique complement. More commonly שָׁמָּה is found after בוא, the -הָ indicating motion toward (cf. v. 38), but שָׁם is also found.

1:38 יְהוֹשֻׁעַ בִּן־נוּן הָעֹמֵד לְפָנֶיךָ הוּא יָבֹא שָׁמָּה אֹתוֹ חַזֵּק כִּי־הוּא יַנְחִלֶנָּה אֶת־יִשְׂרָאֵל׃

PD then HD. Yhwh continues to address Moses in this aside (see on v. 37; D3). Alongside Caleb, Joshua will cross over and cause Israel to inherit the land. So Moses should give him encouragement.

יְהוֹשֻׁעַ בִּן־נוּן הָעֹמֵד לְפָנֶיךָ הוּא יָבֹא שָׁמָּה. The main clause is הוא יבא שמה. The opening NP, יהושע בן נון העמד לפניך, is **extraposed** (see on 1:17) and resumed by the pronoun הוּא. Extraposition of a NP followed by a resumptive subject pronoun with the predicate usually serves to mark the **extraposed** noun as the **topic** and the resumptive pronoun as the **focus**: it is Joshua [and not Moses] who will enter.

יְהוֹשֻׁעַ בִּן־נוּן הָעֹמֵד לְפָנֶיךָ. Ptcp ms Qal √עמד. העמד is the participle with the relative use of the article (see on 1:30); the resultant clause is non-restrictive. The construct of בֵּן is usually בֶּן־. With נון and one or two other nouns, however, it is always בִּן־ (JM §98c). The phrase בן־נון is in apposition to Joshua. לפניך is the oblique complement. The phrase עמד לפני is often idiomatic, indicating "serve," since servants "stand before" their master.

הוּא יָבֹא שָׁמָּה. *Yiqtol* 3ms Qal √בוא. שמה is a locative adverb, functioning as the oblique complement.

אֹתוֹ חַזֵּק. Impv ms Piel √חזק. אתו is the accusative complement, fronted for **focus**. Of those whom Moses should encourage, Yhwh singles out Joshua in particular, going on to explain why. The Piel is what has been termed "delocutive" (Hillers; cf. WO §24.2f, g)—that is, a command for Moses to *say* to Joshua, "be strong": "say to him, 'be strong'" (cf. 31:7).

כִּי־הוּא יַנְחִלֶנָּה אֶת־יִשְׂרָאֵל. *Yiqtol* 3ms Hiph √נחל with 3fs suffix. Explanatory clause, giving the reason why Moses should encourage Joshua. The initial subject pronoun, הוא, is not necessary syntactically. Further, after כי a *yiqtol* verb form normally follows directly, due to **triggered inversion**. The presence of the subject pronoun, when Joshua is already **discourse active**, is for **focus**. Of all those who will cause Israel to inherit, it is "*he* (Joshua)" who will do it (and not Moses). The verb ינחלנה, as a Hiphil, takes two accusative complements. The antecedent of the 3fs pronominal suffix is ארץ (v. 36), kept **discourse active** by שם / שמה.

1:39 וְטַפְּכֶם אֲשֶׁר אֲמַרְתֶּם לָבַז יִהְיֶה וּבְנֵיכֶם אֲשֶׁר
לֹא־יָדְעוּ הַיּוֹם טוֹב וָרָע הֵמָּה יָבֹאוּ שָׁמָּה וְלָהֶם
אֶתְּנֶנָּה וְהֵם יִירָשׁוּהָ:

Yhwh resumes the oath that has sworn in vv. 35-36 (see on v. 37). D3. None of the adults will enter except Caleb (vv. 35-36). Now, after two **extraposed** NPs, in three terse clauses (המה ... יירשוה), Yhwh declares that the people's little ones and children will enter and possess the land (PD).

וְטַפְּכֶם אֲשֶׁר אֲמַרְתֶּם לָבַז יִהְיֶה. **Extraposed** NP, established as the **topic** (see further on 1:17). The noun טף has a collective meaning, but has a singular verb (GCK §145f).

אֲשֶׁר אֲמַרְתֶּם. *Qatal* 2mp Qal √אמר. Non-restrictive relative clause.

לָבַז יִהְיֶה. *Yiqtol* 3ms Qal √היה. Although אמר usually introduces direct speech, the absence of an overt subject of יהיה suggests that this is indirect, "whom you said *would be for plunder*" rather than a direct quotation, "[about] whom you said, '*They will be for plunder.*'" The preposition ל is pointed with *qamets* (לָבַז) before the tone syllable. It is fronted for **focus**, calling to mind the set of other possible destinies for the children, and reminding them that they had said it was "for plunder."

וּבְנֵיכֶ֞ם אֲשֶׁ֨ר לֹא־יָדְע֥וּ הַיּוֹם֙ ט֣וֹב וָרָ֔ע. A second **extraposed** NP. *Qatal* 3cp Qal √ידע. Sometimes active or fientive verbs are like stative verbs, whereby *qatal* has a stative sense, here ידעו = "do [not] know" (JM §111h, §112a). Non-restrictive relative clause. היום is adverbial time adjunct NP. This is the "today" of Kadesh (see also on 1:10). ידע ... טוב ורע indicates they have not reached the age of responsibility (cf. Isa 7:15). For the ו-conjunction with *qamets* (וָרָע), see on 1:28.

הֵ֖מָּה יָבֹ֣אוּ שָׁ֑מָּה. *Yiqtol* 3mp Qal √בוא. PD. המה is resumptive independent personal pronoun, referring to the two **extraposed** NPs, וטפכם ... ובניכם. Given the syntactically unnecessary pronouns in the next two clauses, probably this one, too, is overt as the **focus**. **Extraposition** of a NP followed by a resumptive subject pronoun with the predicate usually serves to mark the **extraposed** noun as the **topic** and the resumptive pronoun as the **focus**. שמה is a locative adverb, functioning as the oblique complement. The phrase mirrors that describing Joshua (1:38). What is true of Joshua will be true of the little ones and children.

וְלָהֶ֥ם אֶתְּנֶ֖נָּה. *Yiqtol* 1cs Qal √נתן with 3fs pronominal suffix. PD. The antecedent of the 3fs pronominal suffix is ארץ (v. 36), kept **discourse active** by שם / שמה. להם is fronted for **focus**. With a threefold **focused** pronoun, v. 38 highlighted Joshua not Moses as the one to enter the land and to cause Israel to inherit it. Similarly, with a threefold **focused** pronoun, v. 39 highlights their little ones and children and not the adults as those who will enter and possess the land (cf. איש באנשים, v. 35).

וְהֵ֥ם יִֽירָשֽׁוּהָ. *Yiqtol* 3mp Qal √ירש with 3fs pronominal suffix (see above). PD. Although הם is in the **topic** position, since the little ones and children are already a **discourse active topic**, הם cannot be marking the **topic**. Further, as a finite verb, an overt pronominal subject is not necessary. הם, therefore, is marked for **focus**: "and *they* [and no one else] will possess it."

1:40 וְאַתֶּ֗ם פְּנ֤וּ לָכֶם֙ וּסְע֣וּ הַמִּדְבָּ֔רָה דֶּ֖רֶךְ יַם־סֽוּף׃

HD. D3. Yhwh, having finished the oath outlining the future begun in v. 35, instructs the people to turn back to the wilderness, echoing the initial call to leave Horeb (1:7).

וְאַתֶּ֗ם פְּנ֥וּ לָכֶ֛ם. Impv mp Qal √פנה. HD. אתם, the subject pronoun, is in the **topic** position and indicates a change of agent. It is not marked for **focus**, since there is no alternative against which to contrast לכם. אתם is adjunct PP with reflexive nuance (see on 1:7).

וּסְע֣וּ הַמִּדְבָּ֔רָה דֶּ֖רֶךְ יַם־סֽוּף. Impv mp Qal √נסע. HD. המדברה is a directional adjunct (cf. on ההרה in 1:24). דרך ים סוף is adverbial adjunct construct chain NP specifying the route to be travelled. For the syntax of the whole phrase, see on דרך הר־שעיר in 1:2.

The Israelites' failed attempt to enter (1:41–2:1)

Moses outlines the Israelites' response to Yhwh's words (D2). Before doing as Yhwh had instructed and setting off to the wilderness (2:1; cf. 1:40), the Israelites acknowledged their sin and insisted they would go up and fight. But Yhwh warned them that he was not in their midst. They did not listen to Yhwh's voice and pressed on regardless. Their attack ended in defeat and in tears, but now Yhwh did not listen to their voice. Only then did they set off.

⁴¹*Then you replied and said to me, "We have sinned against Yhwh. We will go up and fight just as Yhwh our God has commanded us." So you girded yourselves, each putting on his own weapons of war, and got yourselves ready to go up to the hill country.* ⁴²*Then Yhwh said to me, "Say to them, 'Do not go up and do not fight, for I am not in your midst. Otherwise you will be struck down before your enemies.'"* ⁴³*So I told you but you did not listen. You defied the word of Yhwh, acted presumptuously and went up to the hill country.* ⁴⁴*Then the Amorites who live in that hill country came out to meet you and they pursued you just as bees do, and they smashed you to pieces in the region of Seir as far as Hormah.* ⁴⁵*Then you returned and wept before Yhwh but Yhwh did not listen to your voice or give ear to you.* ⁴⁶*So you stayed in Kadesh as many days as the days you stayed.* ^{2:1}*Then we turned and set out to the desert by the Sea of Reeds route, just as Yhwh spoke to me, and circled the hill country of Seir for many days.*

1:41 וַתַּעֲנ֣וּ ׀ וַתֹּאמְר֣וּ אֵלַ֗י חָטָ֙אנוּ֙ לַֽיהוָ֔ה אֲנַ֥חְנוּ נַעֲלֶ֖ה
וְנִלְחַ֑מְנוּ כְּכֹ֥ל אֲשֶׁר־צִוָּ֖נוּ יְהוָ֣ה אֱלֹהֵ֑ינוּ וַֽתַּחְגְּר֗וּ
אִ֚ישׁ אֶת־כְּלֵ֣י מִלְחַמְתּ֔וֹ וַתָּהִ֖ינוּ לַעֲלֹ֥ת הָהָֽרָה׃

ND. Moses (D2) reminds the Israelites in Moab of their response (D3). They acknowledged their sin (ND) and declared their intent (HD). Moses then recounts their battle preparations with two *wayyiqtol* clauses (D2).

וַתַּעֲנוּ ׀ וַתֹּאמְרוּ אֵלַי. *Wayyiqtol* 2mp Qal √ענה and √אמר. ND. The content of the people's response comes only after ותאמרו, not after ותענו. For the different configurations of introducing direct speech, see Miller 1996.

חָטָאנוּ לַיהוָה. *Qatal* 1cp Qal √חטא. ND. ליהוה is oblique complement, specifying against whom the sin has been committed.

אֲנַחְנוּ נַעֲלֶה וְנִלְחָמְנוּ. *Yiqtol* (modal) 1cp Qal √עלה, followed by *qatal* (modal; see on 1:16) 1cp Niph √לחם. HD. Often modal *qatal* gives action subsequent to the previous clause (JM §119a, c, e; WO §32.2.1). The people declare their intention to do what Yhwh has said and go up and fight after all. Although אנחנו is in the topic position, it cannot be marking the **topic**, since "we" is already the **discourse active** topic ("we have sinned"). אנחנו, therefore, is marked for **focus**: "*we* [and not our children] will go up and fight. . . ."

כְּכֹל אֲשֶׁר־צִוָּנוּ יְהוָה אֱלֹהֵינוּ. PP adjunct of manner. כל may be the **head** of the subsequent restrictive relative clause. Alternatively, the relative clause may be **null-head**, with the antecedent covert, rather than overt. צונו is *qatal* 3ms Piel √צוה with 1cp pronominal suffix.

וַתַּחְגְּרוּ. *Wayyiqtol* 2mp Qal √חגר. ND. The accusative complement is **null**, but can straightforwardly be supplied from the following distributive clause (see below).

אִישׁ אֶת־כְּלֵי מִלְחַמְתּוֹ. This is a distributive clause in its own right, adjunct to ותחגרו. איש cannot be the subject of ויחגרו, because it is singular and is picked up by a 3ms pronoun, ‑ו, while the verb is 2mp. Instead, איש is used in the sense of "each," with the 3ms suffix on the noun (cf. JM §147d). את כלי מלחמתו is the accusative complement of the **null**, gapped verb, which would replicate ותחגרו but be syntactically appropriate in person and number (i.e., חָגַר). In this construct phrase, there is such a close union between absolute and construct that the pronominal suffix on the absolute affects not just the absolute but the whole phrase (JM §129kb, §140b; GKC §135n; WO §16.4e). As is usually the case when forming the plural of a construct chain, the first noun only is plural (JM §136m). The construct of מִלְחָמָה behaves like a segholate [presumably מִמְלֶכֶת, on the analogy with מִלְחֶמֶת], and, with suffixes, מִלְחַמְתּוֹ (cf. Blau, 4.4.2.4).

וַתָּהִינוּ לַעֲלֹת הָהָרָה. *Wayyiqtol* 2mp Hiph √הון. ND. The root is an OT *hapax*. Two main meanings have been proposed. The first is to connect it with the Arabic, *h-w-n*, and regard it as "to risk" (HALOT 242). On such a reading, the recklessness of the people is in view, moving from unjustified fear to unwarranted abandon. The second is to connect it with the occurrence of הִנֶּנּוּ in the parallel account in Num 14:40, and to regard it as a corresponding verbal form with the sense of "to be prepared" (Rashi; see Carasik 2015: 14). Ancient translators clearly struggled with it, judging by the different renderings in the versions. See further Tigay 1996: 348 n. 118; Nelson, 23; Weinfeld, 151. The translation given reflects the second of these.

לַעֲלֹת הָהָרָה. Inf constr Qal √עלה with preposition ל. It is an infinitive phrase complement after ותהינו. ההרה is the directional adjunct (see on 1:24).

1:42 וַיֹּאמֶר יְהוָה אֵלַי אֱמֹר לָהֶם לֹא תַעֲלוּ וְלֹא־תִלָּחֲמוּ כִּי אֵינֶנִּי בְּקִרְבְּכֶם וְלֹא תִּנָּגְפוּ לִפְנֵי אֹיְבֵיכֶם:

Moses recalls (D2, ND) Yhwh's instruction to him (HD, D3) to direct the people (HD, D4) not to go up or fight, for Yhwh would not be with them and they would be defeated if they did so. Moses as mediator and Yhwh's word as vital to heed are both prominent ideas.

וַיֹּאמֶר יְהוָה אֵלַי. *Wayyiqtol* 3ms Qal √אמר. ND. D2. יהוה is the subject, overt as the new **discourse active** agent. אלי is adjunct PP indicating addressee.

אֱמֹר לָהֶם. Impv ms Qal √אמר. HD. D3. להם is adjunct PP indicating addressee.

לֹא תַעֲלוּ וְלֹא־תִלָּחֲמוּ. *Yiqtol* (modal) 2mp Qal √עלה and *yiqtol* (modal) 2mp Niph √לחם. HD. D4. For prohibitions more generally, see on 1:17. For לא with a specific prohibition here, see JM §113m (in Num 14:42, it is אל־תעלו).

כִּי אֵינֶנִּי בְּקִרְבְּכֶם. Causal **null-copula** clause, giving the reason why they should not go up (AC §4.3.4a). When the subject in a **null-copula** clause is a personal pronoun (־ני, "I"), the pronoun is joined as a suffix to אֵין (GKC §152m). אֵין is an adverb of non-existence (JM §154k, §160g). בקרבכם is PP predicate.

וְלֹא תִּנָּגְפוּ לִפְנֵי אֹיְבֵיכֶם. *Yiqtol* 2mp Niph √נגף. PD. Although syntactically coordinate with לא תעלו ולא תלחמו, context indicates that this clause is not a further prohibition. Rather, it is semantically subordinate: לא + *yiqtol* is the main way of introducing a negative purpose clause, "so that . . . not . . ." (GKC §109g). There is a question to what the clause most closely relates. It could relate directly to the preceding causal clause, "for I am not in your midst *so that* you should not be defeated . . ." (Nelson, 22). Although a negative purpose clause usually follows a modal verb of volition, it may follow an indicative (JM §116j; GKC §109g), but this is rare. Alternatively, it follows from לא תעלו ולא תלחמו: "do not go up and do not fight . . ., *otherwise* you will be defeated" (NRSV). Given that these negative final clauses tend to follow modal verbs of volition, including לא + modal *yiqtol* (see, e.g., Lev 10:6; 18:21; Num 18:32), the latter is preferable.

לִפְנֵי אֹיְבֵיכֶם. Adjunct PP to the verb תנגפו.

1:43 וָאֲדַבֵּר אֲלֵיכֶם וְלֹא שְׁמַעְתֶּם וַתַּמְרוּ אֶת־פִּי יְהוָה וַתָּזִדוּ וַתַּעֲלוּ הָהָרָה׃

ND. With a succession of terse clauses, Moses recalls his telling the people and their rebellious response, going up regardless (D2). The embedded discourse that has characterized the previous verses (D3, D4) gives way to a condensed account of Israel's doomed attempt to enter. Narrative time becomes much shorter than narrated time.

וָאֲדַבֵּר אֲלֵיכֶם. *Wayyiqtol* 1cs Piel √דבר. ND. Unlike אמר, דבר does not usually take reported direct speech as its complement. It can be either a two- or three-place predicate (see on 1:1). If it is a three-place predicate here, there is a **null** accusative complement, easily supplied from the context as the words Yhwh has just said, "I told you" (NRSV). If it is a two-place predicate, then the content of what is spoken is less in view, "I spoke to you" (NASB).

וְלֹא שְׁמַעְתֶּם. *Qatal* 2mp Qal √שמע. ND. Throughout Moses' speech until now, *wayyiqtols* have dominated his recollections, advancing the storyline (D2). This second לא + *qatal* disjunctive clause (cf. לא אביתם,

1:26) stands in sharp contrast, breaking the flow, highlighting the people's culpability. שמע here is used absolutely, in the sense of "listen."

וַתַּמְרוּ אֶת־פִּי יְהוָה. *Wayyiqtol* 2mp Hiph √מרה. ND. For the phrase, see on 1:26. Their lack of listening is further explained. It was not an encouragement that was ignored, but a command that was defied.

וַתָּזִדוּ. *Wayyiqtol* 2mp Hiph √זיד. ND. The root is associated with bubbling or seething (cf. Ps 124:5), hence in the Hiphil of "cooking" (Gen 25:29). It speaks figuratively of the impetuous, presumptuous crossing of a boundary. The manifestation of their arrogance is evident in the following verb.

וַתַּעֲלוּ הָהָרָה:. *Wayyiqtol* 2mp Qal √עלה. ND. ההרה is the directional adjunct (see on 1:24). Temporal sequentiality is not a semantic property of the *wayyiqtol* form, though often there is a strong correlation between the two (Cook 2004). Rather, it is a pragmatic implication (i.e., a natural reading) of such bound forms occurring consecutively in narrative. But other contextual factors can override this, as here. Their going up is not subsequent to their rebellion and arrogant action, but the instantiation of it.

1:44 וַיֵּצֵא הָאֱמֹרִי הַיֹּשֵׁב בָּהָר הַהוּא לִקְרַאתְכֶם
וַיִּרְדְּפוּ אֶתְכֶם כַּאֲשֶׁר תַּעֲשֶׂינָה הַדְּבֹרִים וַיַּכְּתוּ
אֶתְכֶם בְּשֵׂעִיר עַד־חָרְמָה:

ND. D2. Three *wayyiqtol* clauses outline the action of the Amorites. No battle is mentioned. No sooner had they come out than they pursued and beat Israel back.

וַיֵּצֵא הָאֱמֹרִי הַיֹּשֵׁב בָּהָר הַהוּא לִקְרַאתְכֶם. ND.

וַיֵּצֵא הָאֱמֹרִי. *Wayyiqtol* 3ms Qal √יצא. ND. The presence of the article on the gentilic adjective indicates the whole group is meant (האמרי, see also on 1:4). It takes a singular verb here.

הַיֹּשֵׁב בָּהָר הַהוּא. Ptcp ms Qal √ישב, with the relative use of the article (see on 1:30). בהר ההוא is oblique complement PP with verb ישב.

לִקְרַאתְכֶם. Inf constr Qal √קרא, with ל preposition and with 2mp suffix. Adjunct PP, expressing purpose. The root קרא is a **homonym** of the more common verb, "to call." It is a **by-form** of קרה (JM §78k). In the infinitive construct, it adds ־ָה, but it only appears in construct form,

לִקְרַאת (JM §49d). Although acquiring a prepositional force on some occasions, "before," "in front of," the verbal idea remains here: "to meet you."

וַיִּרְדְּפוּ אֶתְכֶם. *Wayyiqtol* 3mp Qal √רדף. ND. Although the syntactical antecedent is singular, האמרי, the referent is plural when described by a pronoun, hence the plural verb. אתכם is accusative complement; רדף can also take an oblique complement with אַחֲרֵי.

כַּאֲשֶׁר תַּעֲשֶׂינָה הַדְּבֹרִים. Comparative clause, with *yiqtol* 3fp Qal √עשׂה. The *yiqtol* here indicates what bees characteristically or repeatedly do (GKC §107g; WHS §168; JM §113c). Note the P–S word order due to **triggered inversion** after כאשר.

וַיַּכְּתוּ אֶתְכֶם בְּשֵׂעִיר עַד־חָרְמָה׃. *Wayyiqtol* 3mp Hiph √כתת. ND. Note the aramaizing *dagesh forte* in the first-root consonant and the lack of doubling of the second-root consonant in the Hiphil (GKC §67g, y; JM §82h n.17, i). The root כתת, "break into small pieces," graphically depicts the smashing of the army.

בְּשֵׂעִיר עַד־חָרְמָה. PP adjuncts of the verb ויכתו. The versions regard בשעיר as "*from* Seir" (so also NASB, NIV). This could be based on a misreading of מ as ב, or, possibly as an instance of ב acting interchangeably with מן, mirroring Ugaritic usage (cf. Sarna). The alternative is to render it "*in* Seir" (ESV, NRSV). The answer partly depends on what is meant by חרמה. If it is the same Hormah as the place later named as such because of defeat of the Canaanites (Num 21:3; though cf. Judg 1:17), then the direction of pursuit *toward* the land is puzzling (Tigay 1996: 348 n. 121). Perhaps it is a different place or even a common noun, "to destruction" not a place name (cf. Num 14:45, החרמה). The people end up in Hormah, "destruction" (cf. חרם). The people experience anti-Exodus (1:40; 2:1) and "unholy war" (Moran 1963b). On this reading, "in Seir" in the sense of "in the region of Seir" is preferable.

1:45 וַתָּשֻׁבוּ וַתִּבְכּוּ לִפְנֵי יְהוָה וְלֹא־שָׁמַע יְהוָה בְּקֹלְכֶם וְלֹא הֶאֱזִין אֲלֵיכֶם׃

ND. D2. Moses recounts the end of their abortive attempt and Yhwh's response. Two *wayyiqtols* are followed by two disjunctive לא + *qatal* clauses. In the only other preceding לא + *qatal* clauses, the people "were not willing" (1:26) and "did not listen (1:43) "(שמע). Now, Yhwh "did not listen (שמע)" nor did he "give ear" to their weeping.

וַתָּשֻׁבוּ וַתִּבְכּוּ לִפְנֵי יְהוָה. *Wayyiqtol* 2mp Qal √שוב and √בכה. ND. לפני יהוה is PP spatial adjunct. The consonants of ותשבו could also come from ישב, "*you sat* and wept" (cf. LXX; Judg 21:2), but probably that reading arises from assimilation to ותשבו in v. 46 (*BHQ: Deuteronomy*, 56*). Often שוב is used with a second verb to express repetition of the second verb's action (JM §102g, §177b): they "wept again" (cf. Num 11:4). Since in Deuteronomy they have not yet wept, it is more likely that the MT further highlights the reversals. In 1:25 the spies brought back (√שוב) a good report. Now they "returned" (√שוב) in abject defeat.

וְלֹא־שָׁמַע יְהוָה בְּקֹלְכֶם. *Qatal* 3ms Qal √שמע. For the sense of שמע בקול as "hear and accept a request," see HALOT 1572. בקלכם is oblique complement of שמע.

וְלֹא הֶאֱזִין אֲלֵיכֶם. *Qatal* 3ms Hiph √אזן. The Hiphil can have a **denominative** function, speaking of the use of particular body parts, in this case the ear, אזן (WO §27.4a; cf. the English expression, "give ear to").

1:46 וַתֵּשְׁבוּ בְקָדֵשׁ יָמִים רַבִּים כַּיָּמִים אֲשֶׁר יְשַׁבְתֶּם:

ND. D2. Moses' speech began with the declaration that Israel had spent long enough "staying (√ישב)" at this mountain. The denouement of the debacle is their "staying (√ישב)" at Kadesh-Barnea for as many days as they "stayed (√ישב)."

וַתֵּשְׁבוּ בְקָדֵשׁ יָמִים רַבִּים. *Wayyiqtol* 2mp Qal √ישב. בקדש is locative adjunct PP of the verb ותשבו. ימים רבים is an adverbial time adjunct NP, expressing the duration of their stay.

כַּיָּמִים אֲשֶׁר יְשַׁבְתֶּם. *Qatal* 2mp Qal √ישב. כימים is temporal adjunct PP of the verb ותשבו. אשר ישבתם is a restrictive relative clause, with (כ)ימים as the **head**. When the **head** of a relative clause is a period of time, there is never a resumptive pronoun referring to that word of time (GKC §138c; JM §158k; contrast the resumptive pronoun in 1:22 and the resumptive adverb in 4:5). כ introduces a point of correspondence or comparison. The repetition within the comparison without further elucidation (Driver, 31: "idem per idem") is an idiomatic way of being intentionally nonspecific: "you stayed at Kadesh as many days as the days you stayed" (cf. 9:25).

2:1 וַנֵּ֜פֶן וַנִּסַּ֤ע הַמִּדְבָּ֙רָה֙ דֶּ֣רֶךְ יַם־ס֔וּף כַּאֲשֶׁ֛ר דִּבֶּ֥ר יְהוָ֖ה אֵלָ֑י וַנָּ֥סָב אֶת־הַר־שֵׂעִ֖יר יָמִ֥ים רַבִּֽים׃ ס

ND. D2. Three *wayyiqtol* clauses conclude the section begun in 1:6 (n.b., the **inclusio** with פנה and נסע [1:7; 2:1]). For the first time since the spies brought back the fruit of the land (1:25), Moses includes himself with the people ("*we* turned . . ."); he shares their destiny, but not their culpability.

וַנֵּ֜פֶן וַנִּסַּ֤ע הַמִּדְבָּ֙רָה֙ דֶּ֣רֶךְ יַם־ס֔וּף. *Wayyiqtol* 1cp Qal √פנה and √נסע. ND. המדברה is a directional adjunct (cf. on ההרה in 1:24). דרך ים סוף is adverbial adjunct construct NP specifying the route to be travelled (cf. on דרך הר־שעיר in 1:2).

כַּאֲשֶׁ֛ר דִּבֶּ֥ר יְהוָ֖ה אֵלָ֑י. *Qatal* 3ms Piel √דבר (see on 1:1 for pointing). Comparative clause with subordinating conjunction כאשר and **triggered inversion**. אלי is the oblique PP complement. They have finally done as commanded, but only after needless defeat.

וַנָּ֥סָב אֶת־הַר־שֵׂעִ֖יר יָמִ֥ים רַבִּֽים. *Wayyiqtol* 1cp Qal √סבב. את הר שעיר is the accusative construct NP complement. They "circled" (NASB) or "went round" in the sense of avoiding Seir (HALOT 739; cf. Num 21:4; "skirted" NRSV). הר שעיר is a **metonymy** for the whole territory of the Edomites (cf. v. 5; 1:7, הר האמרי). ימים רבים is an adverbial time adjunct NP, expressing the duration of their circling.

Travelling through Edom (2:2-8a)

The historical recollection from 2:2–3:29 gives the counterpart to 1:6–2:1. The opening chapter was characterized by Israel's unbelief and Yhwh's wrath and destruction. This next section, begun by "enough of your circling this mountain" (v.2; cf. 1:6) recounts Israel's success in taking the Transjordanian region through heeding Yhwh's voice. In 2:2-8a and 2:8b-15, Yhwh's instructions are followed by the people's obedient response.

²*Then Yhwh said to me,* ³*"Enough of your circling this mountain! Turn to the north.* ⁴*Command the people, 'You are about to pass through the territory of your brothers, the descendants of Esau, who live in Seir, and they*

may be afraid of you, so be very careful. ⁵Do not engage with them, for I will not give to you [any] of their land, not even so much as a footprint, for it is as a possession for Esau that I have given the hill country of Seir. ⁶Food you may buy from them with silver so you can eat, and water, too, you may purchase from them with silver so you can drink.'" ⁷For Yhwh your God has blessed you in all the work of your hand—he has known your going through this great wilderness; these forty years Yhwh your God has been with you; you have not lacked anything. ⁸ªSo we passed by, away from our brothers, the descendants of Esau who live in Seir, away from the Arabah route, from Elath and from Ezion-geber.

2:2   וַיֹּאמֶר יְהוָה אֵלַי לֵאמֹר:

ND. D2. The next event of significance for Moses' retelling is Yhwh's command to head to the land. The events of the intervening years, time sufficient for the rebellious generation to die out, are irrelevant to Moses' narration. The wandering is over.

וַיֹּאמֶר. *Wayyiqtol* 3ms Qal √אמר. ND. יהוה is the overt subject, necessary because Yhwh now is the **topic**. For לאמר as a **complementizer**, see on 1:5.

2:3   רַב־לָכֶם סֹב אֶת־הָהָר הַזֶּה פְּנוּ לָכֶם צָפֹנָה:

ED then HD. Moses recalls Yhwh's words (D3). The impetus for chapters 2–3 comes from this verse. In 1:6, Yhwh said they had stayed "long enough" (רב לכם) at "this mountain." Now they have "circled" "long enough" (רב לכם) "this mountain." Yhwh declares it is time to head to the land.

רַב־לָכֶם סֹב אֶת־הָהָר הַזֶּה. ED. **Null-copula** clause, with P–S subject order. Literally "circling this mountain [is] much for you." See on 1:6.

סֹב. Inf constr Qal √סבב. It stands here as the subject of the **null-copula** clause and should be translated as a verbal noun, or **gerund**. As a *verbal* noun, the infinitive construction takes an accusative complement, את ההר הזה.

אֶת־הָהָר הַזֶּה. Although the referent is the whole hill country (see on 2:1), the translation renders הר "mountain" to preserve the parallel with 1:6.

פְּנוּ לָכֶם צָפֹנָה. Impv mp Qal √פנה. HD. For its meaning and for the reflexive nuance of לכם, see on 1:7. צפנה is the directional adjunct. The locative ה on צפן indicates motion toward (WO §10.5a, b).

2:4 וְאֶת־הָעָם֙ צַ֣ו לֵאמֹ֔ר אַתֶּ֣ם עֹֽבְרִ֗ים בִּגְבוּל֙ אֲחֵיכֶ֣ם בְּנֵי־עֵשָׂ֔ו הַיֹּשְׁבִ֖ים בְּשֵׂעִ֑יר וְיִֽירְא֣וּ מִכֶּ֔ם וְנִשְׁמַרְתֶּ֖ם מְאֹֽד׃

After the more general instruction, Yhwh gives instructions to Moses (HD, D3) and tells him what to say to the people (D4). Their crossing may precipitate fear amongst their "brothers," the descendants of Esau, so they should be careful (PD/ED, HD).

וְאֶת־הָעָם֙ צַ֣ו לֵאמֹ֔ר. Impv ms Piel √צוה. HD. For the **apocopation** of ה in III-ה verbs in ms imperative, see JM §79j. ואת העם is accusative complement of the verb צוה. Since the **topic** is not in doubt, it must be fronted for **focus**. But that raises the question of whom Moses might command if not the people. Presumably it is Joshua (cf. 3:21). Responsibility rests with the people as a whole.

אַתֶּ֣ם עֹֽבְרִ֗ים בִּגְבוּל֙ אֲחֵיכֶ֣ם בְּנֵי־עֵשָׂ֔ו הַיֹּשְׁבִ֖ים בְּשֵׂעִ֑יר. Ptcp mp Qal √עבר. PD/ED. The personal pronoun does not carry **topic** or **focus** as it is syntactically necessary. Contrary to JM §154fd, S–P word is the unmarked order in **null-copula** participial clause (see Buth). The first of eighteen occurrences of √עבר in chapters 2–3. The participle in Hebrew can indicate a future action that is already in progress (JM §121e).

בִּגְבוּל֙ אֲחֵיכֶ֣ם. Oblique complement construct PP of verb עברים. עבר ב means "pass *through*." It is striking that the Edomites, the children of Esau, are included in the "fraternity" (אח).

בְּנֵי־עֵשָׂ֔ו. Constr NP appositional to אחיכם.

הַיֹּשְׁבִ֖ים בְּשֵׂעִ֑יר. Ptcp mp Qal √ישׁב, with the relative use of the article (see on 1:30) introducing a non-restrictive relative clause. The **head** is אחיכם. בשעיר is oblique PP complement with the verb ישׁב.

וְיִֽירְא֣וּ מִכֶּ֔ם. Yiqtol (modal) 3mp Qal √ירא. PD. It is very unusual to have a *yiqtol* after a **null-copula** participial clause. It is much more common for modal *qatal* to follow, usually indicating a (con)sequence. The only other instances are in 1 Kgs 12:9 and Neh 5:3. Probably the nuance here is modal, "they *may* be afraid of you." מכם is oblique complement.

וְנִשְׁמַרְתֶּ֖ם מְאֹֽד. *Qatal* (modal) 2mp Niph √שמר. HD. The modal *qatal* (cf. note on 1:16) is used to indicate actions contingent on previous actions, here with imperatival force. מאד is used as an adverbial adjunct, intensifying the force of the verbal idea (AC §4.2.12).

2:5 אַל־תִּתְגָּר֣וּ בָ֔ם כִּ֠י לֹֽא־אֶתֵּ֤ן לָכֶם֙ מֵֽאַרְצָ֔ם עַ֖ד מִדְרַ֣ךְ כַּף־רָ֑גֶל כִּֽי־יְרֻשָּׁ֣ה לְעֵשָׂ֔ו נָתַ֖תִּי אֶת־הַ֥ר שֵׂעִֽיר׃

HD. D4. Yhwh forbids military engagement and gives the grounds for that prohibition.

אַל־תִּתְגָּר֣וּ בָ֔ם. Jussive 2mp Hitp √גרה. HD. אל + jussive expresses a prohibition (see on 1:17). With ב, גרה Hitpael has the sense of "engage [in battle]/strive with." בם is oblique complement.

כִּ֠י לֹֽא־אֶתֵּ֤ן לָכֶם֙ מֵֽאַרְצָ֔ם עַ֖ד מִדְרַ֣ךְ כַּף־רָ֑גֶל. *Yiqtol* 1cs Qal √נתן. Explanatory clause, giving the grounds for the prohibition on engagement.

מֵֽאַרְצָ֔ם. PP. The preposition מן in מארצם is partitive, used when taking a part from the whole (cf. WHS §324). In negative clauses, it indicates "none of" the object of the preposition (cf. WO §11.2.11e). The part that is actually given is a **null** accusative complement of נתן: "Ø from their [Edom's] land."

עַ֖ד מִדְרַ֣ךְ כַּף־רָ֑גֶל. Adjunct PP. Construct chain, with רגל as the absolute. כף denotes the hollow of hand or foot, hence כף רגל is the "sole of the foot." מדרך, an OT **hapax** related to the verb דרך, is a place on which the foot treads. The construct chain phrase constitutes a "footprint" (cf. 11:24). With לא, עד indicates "not even as much as" (BDB 724).

כִּֽי־יְרֻשָּׁ֣ה לְעֵשָׂ֔ו נָתַ֖תִּי אֶת־הַ֥ר שֵׂעִֽיר. *Qatal* 1cs Qal √נתן. A further explanatory clause, explaining why Yhwh will not give any Edomite land to Israel. נתן with two accusatives can have a number of nuances, including "turn" X "into" Y or "make" X Y. Here, it is used of "giving X *as* Y."

יְרֻשָּׁ֣ה לְעֵשָׂ֔ו. Indirect accusative NP (cf. JM §126c). The preposition ל connects its object closely with ירשה, "a possession *for* Esau" (n.b., the conjunctive accent, *munakh*, יְרֻשָּׁה). The phrase stands in for the datival complement of √נתן. When the second noun is definite and the first is indefinite, the construct relationship is usually avoided and replaced by ל (JM §130b). The phrase is fronted for **focus**. Of all the possible grounds for the gift of this land and of all the possible recipients of the gift, it is "as a possession for Esau." Although possessing of land is central to the plot, others too can be beneficiaries. Israel should possess only the land Yhwh has promised (cf. 1:8, 21).

אֶת־הַר שֵׂעִיר. Accusative complement construct NP (cf. on 1:2). It denotes what is given.

2:6 אֹכֶל תִּשְׁבְּרוּ מֵאִתָּם בַּכֶּסֶף וַאֲכַלְתֶּם וְגַם־מַיִם תִּכְרוּ מֵאִתָּם בַּכֶּסֶף וּשְׁתִיתֶם׃

HD. D4. Having given instructions as to what the Israelites should *not* do, now Yhwh indicates what they *may* do on their journey.

אֹכֶל תִּשְׁבְּרוּ מֵאִתָּם בַּכֶּסֶף. *Yiqtol* (modal) 2mp Qal √שׁבר. A **homonym** of שׁבר I, "to break," the verb means "to buy," usually of grain. אֹכֶל is accusative complement, fronted as the **topic** (see below).

מֵאִתָּם. Adjunct PP comprising two prepositions, מן and את, with 3mp pronoun as their object. It expresses from whom they may buy.

בַּכֶּסֶף. Adjunct PP, expressing how they may buy the food.

וַאֲכַלְתֶּם. *Qatal* (modal) 2mp Qal √אכל. The modal *qatal* here expresses logical consecution (JM §119e).

וְגַם־מַיִם תִּכְרוּ מֵאִתָּם בַּכֶּסֶף. *Yiqtol* (modal) 2 mp Qal √כרה. A rare **homonym** of כרה I, "to dig," the verb means "to get by trade, buy" (cf. Hos 3:2). גם is an item adverb (for which, see on 1:28), given the fronting for **topic** of the accusative complement, מים. The statement is the counterpart of the previous injunction and coordinated with it. Together they build up a complementary picture, which accounts for the **topicalization** (cf. Moshavi 2010: 160–61).

וּשְׁתִיתֶם. *Qatal* (modal) 2 mp Qal √שׁתה. The modal *qatal* here expresses logical consecution (JM §119e).

2:7 כִּי יְהוָה אֱלֹהֶיךָ בֵּרַכְךָ בְּכֹל מַעֲשֵׂה יָדֶךָ יָדַע לֶכְתְּךָ אֶת־הַמִּדְבָּר הַגָּדֹל הַזֶּה | אַרְבָּעִים שָׁנָה יְהוָה אֱלֹהֶיךָ עִמָּךְ לֹא חָסַרְתָּ דָּבָר:

D2. Yhwh's speech to Moses, including the words he has told Moses to say, has ended (Yhwh is spoken of now in the 3rd person). This is the first of many occasions in the book where the call to obedience is rooted in Yhwh's prior blessing. That blessing is illustrated by three clauses that follow asyndetically.

כִּי יְהוָה אֱלֹהֶיךָ בֵּרַכְךָ בְּכֹל מַעֲשֵׂה יָדֶךָ. Explanatory clause. *Qatal* 3ms Piel √ברך with 2ms pronominal suffix. After כי, a *qatal* verb form normally follows directly, due to **triggered inversion**. Thus the S–P order here, which would be unmarked in a main clause, is due to the fronting of יהוה אלהיך. Given that the domain of others who might have blessed Israel is not in view, יהוה אלהיך must be the **topic**, with attention shifted to what *Yhwh* has done.

בְּכֹל מַעֲשֵׂה יָדֶךָ. Adjunct construct PP.

יָדַע לֶכְתְּךָ אֶת־הַמִּדְבָּר הַגָּדֹל הַזֶּה. *Qatal* 3ms Qal √ידע. ND. Yhwh's knowledge is not awareness, but providential care (cf. Ps 1:6). The first of three clauses following asyndetically from Yhwh's blessing, explaining the nature and extent of that blessing.

לֶכְתְּךָ. Inf constr Qal √הלך with 2ms pronominal suffix. הלך is the only I-ה verb that behaves like a I-ו (JM §75g). As a verbal noun, the infinitive is accusative complement of the verb ידע.

אֶת־הַמִּדְבָּר הַגָּדֹל הַזֶּה. NP complement of infinitive construct of הלך. See on 1:19 for את following הלך. WO §10.3.1c interpret slightly differently, albeit with the same effect, suggesting that the particle את can sometimes be used with adverbial accusatives, here of space, "through."

זֶה | אַרְבָּעִים שָׁנָה יְהוָה אֱלֹהֶיךָ עִמָּךְ. A **null-copula** clause joined asyndetically, explaining Yhwh's blessing. The word order is standard S–P, with subject יהוה אלהיך and predicate PP עמך. The temporal frame of the clause is set by the opening fronted temporal adverbial phrase, זה ארבעים שנה. זה often precedes numerals or words speaking of time. On these occasions it neither agrees with what follows nor takes the article, but has its original function as a demonstrative adverb, "*these* forty years" (cf. GKC §136d; WO §17.4.2b; JM §143a). The singular noun occurs with tens (GKC §134h; JM §142f). The fronting of the opening phrase could be for **focus**, giving "these forty years" as one among a number of alternative time frames in which Yhwh has been with them. However it is not obvious what the other times could be. More likely, then, it is fronted as **topic**, providing scene-setting information about the time. Although it has been a time of judgment, wandering in the wilderness, Yhwh has not been absent, but with them.

לֹא חָסַרְתָּ דָּבָר. *Qatal* 2ms Qal √חסר. A third clause joined asyndetically, further illustrating Yhwh's blessing. דבר is accusative complement. **Litotes**: "you did not lack anything" means "you had *everything*."

2:8a וַנַּעֲבֹר מֵאֵת אַחֵינוּ בְנֵי־עֵשָׂו הַיֹּשְׁבִים בְּשֵׂעִיר
מִדֶּרֶךְ הָעֲרָבָה מֵאֵילַת וּמֵעֶצְיֹן גָּבֶר ס

ND. D2. Moses recalls their subsequent travel in conformity with the instructions Yhwh gave.

וַנַּעֲבֹר. *Wayyiqtol* 1cp Qal √עבר. ND.

מֵאֵת אַחֵינוּ. Adjunct PP. For מאת, see on 2:6.

בְנֵי־עֵשָׂו הַיֹּשְׁבִים בְּשֵׂעִיר. See on 2:4 for the identical phrase.

מִדֶּרֶךְ הָעֲרָבָה מֵאֵילַת וּמֵעֶצְיֹן גָּבֶר. Three adjunct PPs. All express what the Israelites left behind.

Travelling through Moab (2:8b-15)

The MT begins a new section here in the middle of a verse (ס). This relatively rare occurrence probably indicates "a break in content" (Tov, 50), here the shift in attention from Edom to Moab. As in the previous section, Yhwh's instruction is followed by a dutiful response. There are two extra features here. First, there is a narratorial explanation about the identity of different occupants of the land. Second, Moses highlights the death of the entire wilderness generation in conformity with Yhwh's word. The choice of two destinies runs throughout the historical prologue as well as the rest of Deuteronomy (cf. 1:1-5; 30:19).

⁸ᵇ*Then we turned and went on by the way to the wilderness of Moab.* ⁹*Yhwh said to me, "Do not be hostile to Moab and do not engage in battle with them, for I shall not give to you [any] of their land as a possession, since it is to the descendants of Lot that I have given Ar as a possession."* (¹⁰*The*

Emites formerly lived in it—a people great and numerous and as tall as the Anakites. ¹¹*Like the Anakites, they too are considered Rephaites, but the Moabites call them Emites.* ¹²*And in Seir the Horites lived previously, but the children of Esau dispossessed them and destroyed them from before them and lived there instead of them, just as Israel did to the land of its possession, which Yhwh gave to them.)* ¹³ *"Now arise and cross the Wadi Zered." So we crossed Wadi Zered.* ¹⁴*Now the time that we journeyed from Kadesh-Barnea until we crossed Wadi Zered was thirty-eight years, until the finishing off of the whole generation—that is, the fighting men—from the midst of the camp, just as Yhwh swore to them.* ¹⁵*Yes, indeed the hand of Yhwh was against them, so as to throw them into confusion from the midst of the camp until they were finished off.*

2:8b   וַנֵּ֣פֶן וַֽנַּעֲבֹ֔ר דֶּ֖רֶךְ מִדְבַּ֥ר מוֹאָֽב׃

ND. D2.

וַנֵּ֣פֶן וַֽנַּעֲבֹ֔ר דֶּ֖רֶךְ מִדְבַּ֥ר מוֹאָֽב. *Wayyiqtol* 1cp Qal √פנה and עבר. For the sense of "turn and go on" for פנה, see on 1:7. דרך מדבר מואב is an adverbial adjunct construct NP specifying the route they travelled. For the syntax of the whole phrase, see on דרך הר־שעיר in 1:2.

2:9   וַיֹּ֨אמֶר יְהוָ֜ה אֵלַ֗י אַל־תָּ֨צַר֙ אֶת־מוֹאָ֔ב וְאַל־תִּתְגָּ֥ר
בָּ֖ם מִלְחָמָ֑ה כִּ֠י לֹֽא־אֶתֵּ֨ן לְךָ֤ מֵֽאַרְצוֹ֙ יְרֻשָּׁ֔ה כִּ֣י
לִבְנֵי־ל֔וֹט נָתַ֥תִּי אֶת־עָ֖ר יְרֻשָּֽׁה׃

Moses recalls (ND, D2) what Yhwh said to him (D3). Yhwh makes two prohibitions concerning their conduct toward Moab (HD), and gives an explanation for those prohibitions ("for I will not give . . .") which itself is grounded in a further explanation ("for I have given . . .").

וַיֹּ֨אמֶר יְהוָ֜ה אֵלַ֗י. *Wayyiqtol* 3ms Qal √אמר. ND.

אַל־תָּ֨צַר֙ אֶת־מוֹאָ֔ב. *Yiqtol* (modal) 2ms Qal √צור, a **by-form** of צרר II, "attack." The form with *patakh* as theme vowel is probably due to ר as the final consonant (cf. *wayyiqtol* וַיֵּ֫צַר, 1 Kgs 20:1; GKC §72t). That the root is צור is clear from 2:19. Context, meaning, other Hebrew manuscripts, and the Versions all demonstrate that אֶל should be pointed אַל (*BHQ: Deuteronomy*, 57*). A prohibition (see further on 1:17).

וְאַל־תִּתְגָּ֥ר בָּ֖ם מִלְחָמָֽה. *Yiqtol* (modal) 2ms Hitp √גרה. For the **apocopated** ה in the jussive and the *qamets* in the final syllable, see GKC §75bb. For the verb and the oblique complement, בם, see on 2:5. מלחמה is an adverbial accusative, describing "more precisely the *manner* in which an action or state takes place" (GKC §118m, q), "in battle" (also 2:24; cf. 2:5, 19).

כִּ֠י לֹֽא־אֶתֵּ֨ן לְךָ֤ מֵֽאַרְצוֹ֙ יְרֻשָּׁ֔ה. *Yiqtol* 1cs Qal √נתן. Explanatory clause, giving the grounds for the prohibition on engagement. The preposition מן in מארצו is partitive, used when taking a part from the whole (cf. WHS §324). The part that is actually given is a **null** accusative complement of נתן: "Ø from its [Moab's] land." נתן is used of "giving X *as* Y" (cf. v. 5). X is the **null** complement, Y is "possession" (ירשה), an indirect accusative (hence indefinite; cf. JM §126c).

כִּ֚י לִבְנֵי־ל֔וֹט נָתַ֥תִּי אֶת־עָ֖ר יְרֻשָּֽׁה. *Qatal* 1cs Qal √נתן. Explanatory clause, in which Yhwh gives the reason why he will not give any of the land of Moab as a possession. נתן is used of "giving X *as* Y" (cf. v. 5). Here it is a three-place predicate. The recipient of the gift is designated by the oblique complement לבני לוט, which is fronted for **focus**. Of the domain of possible recipients, including Israel, it is to the descendants of Lot that Yhwh has given the land of Ar.

2:10 הָאֵמִ֥ים לְפָנִ֖ים יָ֣שְׁבוּ בָ֑הּ עַ֣ם גָּד֥וֹל וְרַ֛ב וָרָ֖ם כָּעֲנָקִֽים׃

ND. This and the next verse follow asyndetically. The clause is disjunctive, breaking narrative flow and giving background information in the form of a parenthetical aside that explains more about the inhabitants. The narrator's voice is heard directly (D1).

הָאֵמִ֥ים לְפָנִ֖ים יָ֣שְׁבוּ בָ֑הּ. *Qatal* 3cp Qal √ישב. לפנים is a temporal adjunct PP. ישבו, taken with לפנים, is an instance of a *qatal* acting akin to a pluperfect, designating an action that took place and was completed before other actions or conditions occurred (GKC §106f). בה is locative adjunct PP.

עַ֣ם גָּד֥וֹל וְרַ֛ב וָרָ֖ם כָּעֲנָקִֽים. NP, appositional to האמים. Three adjectives modify עם. The final one, ptcp ms Qal √רום, is modified by the comparative adjunct PP כענקים (cf. JM §133g). For the ו-conjunction with *qamets* (וָרָם), see on 1:28. N.b., in contrast, the ו-conjunction (וְרַב)

with *sheva* before the tone syllable even with a minor disjunctive accent (cf. GKC §104g).

2:11 רְפָאִ֛ים יֵחָשְׁב֥וּ אַף־הֵ֖ם כָּעֲנָקִ֑ים וְהַמֹּ֣אָבִ֔ים יִקְרְא֥וּ לָהֶ֖ם אֵמִֽים׃

ED. The narratorial aside continues (D1).

רְפָאִים יֵחָשְׁבוּ אַף־הֵם כָּעֲנָקִים. *Yiqtol* 3mp Niph √חשב. The *yiqtol* is used for what is (or used to be) generally the case, "are/used to be regarded" (cf. WO §31.3e). Some verbs, such as חשב, are doubly transitive, with two accusatives/direct objects ("they thought X [as] Y"). When they are found in the passive, the second accusative, here רפאים, remains in the accusative (JM §128c). רפאים is fronted for **focus**. The occurrence of the personal pronoun subject הם after אף has no special emphasis; it serves to clarify the subject of יחשבו as the (**discourse active**) Emites. The particle means little more than "also" (cf. WO §16.3.5b).

כָּעֲנָקִים. Comparative adjunct PP.

וְהַמֹּאָבִים יִקְרְאוּ לָהֶם אֵמִים. *Yiqtol* 3mp Qal √קרא, continuing to describe what is generally the case. להם is oblique complement PP. קרא ל means "to name" (HALOT 1129). The S–P word order indicates contrastive **focus**, highlighting the difference between what the Emites are regarded as and what the Moabites call them.

2:12 וּבְשֵׂעִ֞יר יָשְׁב֣וּ הַחֹרִים֮ לְפָנִים֒ וּבְנֵ֧י עֵשָׂ֣ו יִֽירָשׁ֗וּם וַיַּשְׁמִידוּם֙ מִפְּנֵיהֶ֔ם וַיֵּשְׁב֖וּ תַּחְתָּ֑ם כַּאֲשֶׁ֧ר עָשָׂ֣ה יִשְׂרָאֵ֗ל לְאֶ֙רֶץ֙ יְרֻשָּׁת֔וֹ אֲשֶׁר־נָתַ֥ן יְהוָ֖ה לָהֶֽם׃

ND. The final verse of this narratorial aside (D1).

וּבְשֵׂעִיר יָשְׁבוּ הַחֹרִים לְפָנִים. *Qatal* 3cp Qal √ישב. בשעיר is adjunct PP, in the preverbal field to indicate that the **topic** of the rest of the clause is what happened in Seir. For לפנים, see on 2:10.

וּבְנֵי עֵשָׂו יִירָשׁוּם. *Yiqtol* 3mp Qal √ירש with a 3mp suffix. In the context of ND, the *yiqtol* here is probably an archaic past, or preterite (cf. Cook 2012: 260). The durative aspect would make little sense. The Qal can mean either "take possession of" something (e.g., 1:8) or "dispossess" someone (as here). בני עשו in the preverbal field here indicates a secondary **topic**. The clause is disjunctive. Its effect is to provide a contrast, "but . . ."

וַיַּשְׁמִידוּם מִפְּנֵיהֶֽם. *Wayyiqtol* 3mp Hiph √שמד with a 3mp suffix. ND. מפניהם is adjunct PP.

וַיֵּשְׁבוּ תַחְתָּֽם. *Wayyiqtol* 3mp Qal √ישׁב. ND. תחתם is adjunct PP. Pronoun suffixes on תחת almost always are appended to the "pseudo-plural" form תַּחְתֵּי. However, on eleven occasions, the 3mp suffix yields the form found here (JM §103n n. 49).

כַּאֲשֶׁר עָשָׂה יִשְׂרָאֵל לְאֶרֶץ יְרֻשָּׁתוֹ אֲשֶׁר־נָתַן יְהוָה לָהֶם. *Qatal* 3ms Qal √עשה. For כאשר introducing a comparative clause and with P–S word order (**triggered inversion**), see on 1:19. The temporal perspective of looking *back* to what Israel has done indicates a post-conquest frame of reference.

לְאֶרֶץ יְרֻשָּׁתוֹ. Adjunct construct PP. The pronominal suffix refers to the new **topic**, ישראל.

אֲשֶׁר־נָתַן יְהוָה לָהֶם. *Qatal* 3ms Qal √נתן. After אשר, there is usually P–S word order (**triggered inversion**).

2:13 עַתָּה קֻמוּ וְעִבְרוּ לָכֶם אֶת־נַחַל זָרֶד וַנַּעֲבֹר אֶת־נַחַל זָֽרֶד׃

In v. 13a, Yhwh's speech (HD, D3) from v. 9 resumes after the parenthetical narratorial comment in vv. 10-12, but there is a shift from singular to plural. Instructions for what *Moses* should not do give way to the command to Israel to set out again. In v. 13b, Moses recounts (ND, D2), in solidarity with the people (1cp, "we"; cf. 1:19; 2:1, 8), Israel's obedient response to the command.

עַתָּה קֻמוּ. Impv mp Qal √קום; the only time the mp imperative is written defectively. HD. עתה is an adjunct temporal adverb. In its characteristic fronted position, it functions as a scene-setting (temporal) **topic** (cf. Holmstedt 2011: 22) indicating a "shift from past to present" (Lundbom, 197).

וְעִבְרוּ לָכֶם אֶת־נַחַל זָרֶד. Impv mp Qal √עבר. HD. See on 1:7 for reflexive nuance for לכם. את־נחל זרד is accusative complement construct NP, with the absolute specifying the name of the wadi (cf. GKC §128k; comment on 1:24).

וַֽנַּעֲבֹ֖ר אֶת־נַ֥חַל זָֽרֶד. *Wayyiqtol* 1cp Qal √עבר. ND.

2:14 וְהַיָּמִ֞ים אֲשֶׁר־הָלַ֣כְנוּ ׀ מִקָּדֵ֣שׁ בַּרְנֵ֗עַ עַ֤ד אֲשֶׁר־עָבַ֙רְנוּ֙ אֶת־נַ֣חַל זֶ֔רֶד שְׁלֹשִׁ֥ים וּשְׁמֹנֶ֖ה שָׁנָ֑ה עַד־תֹּ֨ם כָּל־הַדּ֜וֹר אַנְשֵׁ֤י הַמִּלְחָמָה֙ מִקֶּ֣רֶב הַֽמַּחֲנֶ֔ה כַּאֲשֶׁ֛ר נִשְׁבַּ֥ע יְהוָ֖ה לָהֶֽם׃

ND. In a parenthetical comment, Moses indicates (D2) the length of their wandering. In three short verses, thirty-eight years of narrated time are covered.

וְהַיָּמִ֞ים . . . שְׁלֹשִׁ֥ים וּשְׁמֹנֶ֖ה שָׁנָ֑ה. Circumstantial **null-copula** clause. The substantival predicate, שלשים ושמנה שנה, complements the subject, הימים, giving the time length. When the numbered object (here שנה) has both tens and units, there are three normal patterns (1) the numbered object is repeated, in the singular with tens and in the plural with units; (2) the units precede the tens, and the numbered object is in the singular; and (3) the numbered object precedes the tens and units. It is uncommon to find, as here, tens followed by units, with the numbered object in the singular (cf. GKC §134h).

אֲשֶׁר־הָלַ֣כְנוּ ׀ מִקָּדֵ֣שׁ בַּרְנֵ֗עַ עַ֤ד אֲשֶׁר־עָבַ֙רְנוּ֙ אֶת־נַ֣חַל זֶ֔רֶד. *Qatal* 1cp Qal √הלך, followed by two spatial adjunct PPs, indicating the extent of the travel. The second PP, introduced by עד, consists of a **null-head** restrictive relative clause. The predicate is *qatal* 1cp Qal √עבר.

עַד־תֹּ֨ם כָּל־הַדּ֜וֹר אַנְשֵׁ֤י הַמִּלְחָמָה֙ מִקֶּ֣רֶב הַֽמַּחֲנֶ֔ה. Inf constr Qal √תמם. Adjunct temporal PP. The construct NP, כל־הדור functions as the subject of the infinitive construct. עד indicates extent, whether temporal or spatial. Here, it is temporal, leading up to an event, the end of the wilderness generation.

אַנְשֵׁ֤י הַמִּלְחָמָה֙. Appositional construct NP, limiting "the entire generation (כל־הדור)" to those who can fight. The phrase is an "adjectival genitive," where the absolute (genitive) gives, in this case, the nature of the construct, איש (cf. WO §9.5.3a).

מִקֶּ֣רֶב הַֽמַּחֲנֶ֔ה. Spatial adjunct PP. The addition of the construct noun קרב shows the loss is not peripheral; the description is "military" (Weinfeld, 163).

כַּאֲשֶׁר נִשְׁבַּע יְהוָה לָהֶם. *Qatal* 3ms Niph √שבע. For כאשר introducing a comparative clause and with P–S word order (**triggered inversion**), see on 1:19. This had not taken Yhwh by surprise, but was what Yhwh had sworn.

2:15 וְגַם יַד־יְהוָה הָיְתָה בָּם לְהֻמָּם מִקֶּרֶב הַמַּחֲנֶה עַד תֻּמָּם׃

ND. D2. If there was any doubt about the cause of their demise, Moses highlights Yhwh's agency. The end of that generation had not just been sworn by Yhwh, but was at Yhwh's hand.

וְגַם יַד־יְהוָה הָיְתָה בָּם. *Qatal* 3fs Qal √היה. Rather than signalling further comment, "and also," וגם serves to explain and intensify, "Yes indeed" (Lundbom, 198). The oblique complement PP, בם, forms part of the idiom (Judg 2:15; 1 Sam 12:15; cf. Ruth 1:13) with ב having an adversative sense (cf. JM §133c), "against."

לְהֻמָּם מִקֶּרֶב הַמַּחֲנֶה. Inf constr Qal √המם with preposition ל and with 3mp object suffix. The verb המם speaks of the panic of commotion in war (cf. 7:23). Adjunct PP, ל + infinitive construct here could be explanatory, akin to the Latin **gerund**, "by X-ing," showing *how* Yhwh's hand was against them, "throwing them into confusion" (cf. JM §124o), or it could express the purpose or result of Yhwh's hand being against them (so NRSV; cf. JM §124l), "so as to throw them into confusion." Comparison with Judg 2:15 suggests the latter.

עַד תֻּמָּם. Inf constr Qal √תמם with 3mp subject suffix. With pronominal suffixes, the second מ, latent in the infinitive construct (תֹּם; v. 14), reappears. Temporal adjunct PP. For עד, see on 2:14.

Yhwh's instructions about the Ammonites and Sihon (2:16-25)

The account of thirty-eight years of wilderness wandering is quickly over. Characteristic of Deuteronomy, attention returns to Yhwh's words, mediated by Moses. His hearers are left in no doubt that the rebellious generation—all fighting men—have died. Three times תמם has been used; כל has been used twice: כל־הדור and כל־אנשי מלחמה once each (v. 16). They are not to engage with Ammonites in battle. However, after a further narratorial explanation of territory (vv. 21-23), the instruction to engage finally comes, against king Sihon (vv. 24-25).

¹⁶*When all the fighting men had completely died from the midst of the people,* ¹⁷*Yhwh spoke to me, saying,* ¹⁸*"You are crossing today the territory of Moab, Ar,* ¹⁹*and you will draw near, opposite the descendants of Ammon; do not be hostile to them and do not engage with them, for I will not give [any] of the land of the descendants of Ammon to you as a possession, for it is to the descendants of Lot that I have given it as a possession."* ²⁰*(It, too, is reckoned as the land of the Rephaites. Rephaites formerly lived in it, although the Ammonites call them Zamzummites—*²¹*a people great and numerous and as tall as the Anakites—and Yhwh destroyed them [the Rephaites] from before them [the Ammonites] and they [the Ammonites] dispossessed them [the Rephaites] and settled instead of them,* ²²*just as he did for the descendants of Esau, who live in Seir, from before whom he destroyed the Horites, and they dispossessed them and have settled instead of them to this day. And as for the Avvites, who were living in settlements near Gaza—the Caphtorim, who come from Caphtor, destroyed them and settled instead of them.)* ²⁴*"Arise, set out and cross Wadi Arnon. See! I hereby give into your hand Sihon, king of Heshbon, the Amorite, and his land. Begin, take possession and engage with him in battle.* ²⁵*This day I will begin to put fear of you and dread of you upon the peoples under all the heavens, who will hear report of you and tremble and writhe because of you."*

2:16 וַיְהִי כַאֲשֶׁר־תַּמּוּ כָּל־אַנְשֵׁי הַמִּלְחָמָה לָמוּת מִקֶּרֶב הָעָם: ס

ND. D2. A temporal protasis fixes the time of the subsequent event (v. 17) against the total demise of the rebellious soldiers. Although the subject matter goes with what precedes, hence MT's *setumah*, the break is better seen as occurring at the end of v. 15, before the start of the temporal protasis, rather between the protasis and the apodosis.

וַיְהִי. *Wayyiqtol* 3ms √היה. ND. For ויהי followed by a temporal phrase or clause, see on 1:3.

כַאֲשֶׁר־תַּמּוּ כָּל־אַנְשֵׁי הַמִּלְחָמָה. *Qatal* 3cp Qal √תמם. כאשר, as well as introducing comparative clauses, can also, as here, introduce a dependent temporal clause (cf. WO §38.7a; JM §166n). See on 2:15 for construct NP אנשי המלחמה. Note the P–S word order due to **triggered inversion**.

לָמוּת מִקֶּרֶב הָעָם:ס. Inf constr Qal √מות with preposition ל. For the *qamets* with ל before the tone syllable, see JM §103c. תמם + ל + infinitive construct of X means "finish X-ing" (cf. Josh 3:7; 5:8). מקרב העם is adjunct PP; the more obviously militaristic מחנה gives way to עם, "people."

2:17 וַיְדַבֵּר יְהוָה אֵלַי לֵאמֹר:

ND. D2.

וַיְדַבֵּר יְהוָה אֵלַי. *Wayyiqtol* 3ms Piel √דבר. ND. Temporal apodosis.

לֵאמֹר:. Inf constr Qal √אמר with preposition ל. **Complementizer**. See on 1:5.

2:18 אַתָּה עֹבֵר הַיּוֹם אֶת־גְּבוּל מוֹאָב אֶת־עָר:

ED/PD. Moses recalls Yhwh's words (D3) that highlight their imminent crossing, words that will resonate when Moses speaks of the crossing of the Jordan (9:1).

אַתָּה עֹבֵר הַיּוֹם אֶת־גְּבוּל מוֹאָב. Ptcp ms Qal √עבר. **Null-copula** clause, with unmarked S–P word order, personal pronoun subject and participial predicate (cf. on 2:4). היום is adverbial time adjunct NP (see on 1:10 for "today").

אֶת־עָר. Appositional NP, specifying the particular territory of Moab.

2:19 וְקָרַבְתָּ מוּל בְּנֵי עַמּוֹן אַל־תְּצֻרֵם וְאַל־תִּתְגָּר בָּם כִּי לֹא־אֶתֵּן מֵאֶרֶץ בְּנֵי־עַמּוֹן לְךָ יְרֻשָּׁה כִּי לִבְנֵי־לוֹט נְתַתִּיהָ יְרֻשָּׁה:

D3. PD, then two HD clauses, giving prohibitions. The coordinated HD clauses follow asyndetically and explain the nature of their approach. In v. 19b, Yhwh gives grounds for the prohibitions. Yhwh is not giving the territory to Israel because he has allocated it to Lot's descendants.

וְקָרַבְתָּ מוּל בְּנֵי עַמּוֹן. *Qatal* (modal) 2ms Qal √קרב. PD. מול בני עמון is a spatial adjunct PP. For מול, see on 1:1. בני עמון is an adjectival genitive, indicating "the relationship of an individual to a class of beings" (WO §9.5.3a).

אַל־תְּצֻרֵם. Jussive 2ms Qal √צור with 3mp suffix. HD. A prohibition.

וְאַל־תִּתְגָּר בָּם. Jussive 2ms Hitp √גרה. HD. See on 2:9 for the verb and for בם. Two prohibitions, unlike two imperatives, almost always are joined syndetically. For prohibitions more generally, see on 1:17.

כִּי לֹא־אֶתֵּן מֵאֶרֶץ בְּנֵי־עַמּוֹן לְךָ יְרֻשָּׁה. *Yiqtol* 1cs Qal √נתן. This explanatory clause gives grounds for the previous prohibitions. נתן with two accusatives can have a number of nuances, including "turn" X "into" Y or "make" X Y. Here, it is used of "giving X (= [none] of the Ammonites' land) *as* Y" (cf. on 2:5, 9).

מֵאֶרֶץ בְּנֵי־עַמּוֹן. PP. For partitive מן, see on 2:5. The part that is actually given is a **null** accusative complement of נתן: "Ø from the Ammonites' land."

כִּי לִבְנֵי־לוֹט נְתַתִּיהָ יְרֻשָּׁה. *Qatal* 1cs Qal √נתן with 3fs pronominal suffix. A further explanatory clause, explaining why Yhwh will not give any Ammonite land to Israel.

לִבְנֵי־לוֹט. Oblique complement PP, fronted for **focus**.

2:20 אֶרֶץ־רְפָאִים תֵּחָשֵׁב אַף־הִוא רְפָאִים יָשְׁבוּ־בָהּ לְפָנִים וְהָעַמֹּנִים יִקְרְאוּ לָהֶם זַמְזֻמִּים׃

ND. D1. The narrator interjects again, unannounced other than by the break from *wayyiqtols*, with another explanation of the inhabitants, names and territories of earlier history. This provides an interlude for the scene to change to the location for crossing (Nelson, 41).

אֶרֶץ־רְפָאִים תֵּחָשֵׁב אַף־הִוא. *Yiqtol* 3fs Niph √חשב. See on v. 11 for the *yiqtol* being used for what is generally the case, "is regarded" and for the syntax with √חשב Niphal.

אֶרֶץ־רְפָאִים. Constr NP, the accusative complement of the verb חשב, "reckon *as*," fronted for **focus**.

אַף־הִוא. For the form of הוא, see on 1:9. The occurrence of הוא after אף has no special emphasis; it serves to clarify the subject of תחשב as the (**discourse active**) territory, which Yhwh had forbidden (v. 19). The particle means little more than "also" (cf. WO §16.3.5b), and connects this narratorial comment with the previous one that spoke of the Rephaites (vv. 10-12).

רְפָאִ֛ים יָֽשְׁבוּ־בָ֥הּ לְפָנִ֑ים. *Qatal* 3cp Qal √ישׁב. ND. Unmarked S–P word order. לפנים is a temporal adjunct PP. בה is locative adjunct PP. The clause is joined asyndetically to the previous one. It gives an explanation for the opinion articulated in that clause.

וְהָֽעַמֹּנִ֔ים יִקְרְא֥וּ לָהֶ֖ם זַמְזֻמִּֽים. *Yiqtol* 3mp Qal √קרא. The *yiqtol* speaks of what is or used to be the case, להם is oblique complement PP (for both of these, cf. on v. 11). העמנים in the preverbal field here indicates a secondary **topic**. Its effect is to provide a contrast, "but . . ."

זַמְזֻמִּֽים. Zamzummim, uniquely here (though note Gen 14:5), is onomatopoeic, "buzz-buzzers" (cf. Nelson, 41).

2:21 עַ֣ם גָּד֥וֹל וְרַ֛ב וָרָ֖ם כָּעֲנָקִ֑ים וַיַּשְׁמִידֵ֤ם יְהוָה֙ מִפְּנֵיהֶ֔ם וַיִּירָשֻׁ֖ם וַיֵּשְׁב֥וּ תַחְתָּֽם׃

D1. An appositional description of the Zamzummim (v. 21a) gives way to three *wayyiqtol* clauses (ND), explaining how it is that the Ammonites live where the Zamzummim once did. The phrasing is very similar to 2:10, 12.

עַ֣ם גָּד֥וֹל וְרַ֛ב וָרָ֖ם כָּעֲנָקִ֑ים. NP, appositional to זמזמים. The phrase is identical to that in 2:10 (s.v.).

וַיַּשְׁמִידֵ֤ם יְהוָה֙ מִפְּנֵיהֶ֔ם. *Wayyiqtol* 3ms Hiph √שמד with 3mp pronominal suffix. ND. There are two **discourse active** topics in this clause, as is evident by pronominal suffixes referring to different peoples. "Yhwh destroyed *them* (the Zamzummites) from before *them* (the Ammonites)." מפניהם is adjunct PP. Here, the subject of שמד is Yhwh, rather than the descendants of Esau (v. 12).

וַיִּירָשֻׁ֖ם. *Wayyiqtol* 3mp Qal √ירשׁ with 3mp pronominal suffix. ND. The pronouns referring to different peoples continue in this clause and the next.

וַיֵּשְׁב֥וּ תַחְתָּֽם׃. *Wayyiqtol* 3mp Qal √ישׁב. ND. See on 2:12 for תחתם.

2:22 כַּאֲשֶׁ֤ר עָשָׂה֙ לִבְנֵ֣י עֵשָׂ֔ו הַיֹּשְׁבִ֖ים בְּשֵׂעִ֑יר אֲשֶׁ֨ר הִשְׁמִ֤יד אֶת־הַחֹרִי֙ מִפְּנֵיהֶ֔ם וַיִּֽירָשֻׁם֙ וַיֵּשְׁב֣וּ תַחְתָּ֔ם עַ֖ד הַיּ֥וֹם הַזֶּֽה:

D1. ND. A comparative clause is followed by three coordinated non-restrictive relative clauses with **head** בני עשו. These three clauses give a conquest pattern (cf. 2:12; 9:3).

כַּאֲשֶׁ֤ר עָשָׂה֙ לִבְנֵ֣י עֵשָׂ֔ו הַיֹּשְׁבִ֖ים בְּשֵׂעִ֑יר. *Qatal* 3ms Qal √עשה. For כאשר introducing a comparative clause and with P–S word order (**triggered inversion**), see on 1:19. For לבני עשו and הישבים בשעיר, see on 2:4. The subject remains Yhwh.

אֲשֶׁ֨ר הִשְׁמִ֤יד אֶת־הַחֹרִי֙ מִפְּנֵיהֶ֔ם. *Qatal* 3ms Hiph √שמד. The clause could be a **null-head** restrictive relative clause, with the antecedent of אשר being a time reference, "[the day] which," i.e., "when" (Holmstedt 2002: 299–300; cf. 4:11). More likely, though, is that it is a non-restrictive relative clause with **head** בני עשו, with a resumptive pronominal suffix on מפניהם, "from before whom."

וַיִּֽירָשֻׁם֙ וַיֵּשְׁב֣וּ תַחְתָּ֔ם עַ֖ד הַיּ֥וֹם הַזֶּֽה:. For ויירשם and וישבו תחתם, see on 2:21.

עַ֖ד הַיּ֥וֹם הַזֶּֽה:. Temporal adjunct PP. The first occurrence in Deuteronomy of "this day" with the referent being not "today" in the plains of Moab but the narrator's "today." The variation in referent connects the narrator's day with the day of the narrated events.

2:23 וְהָעַוִּ֛ים הַיֹּשְׁבִ֥ים בַּחֲצֵרִ֖ים עַד־עַזָּ֑ה כַּפְתֹּרִים֙ הַיֹּצְאִ֣ים מִכַּפְתּ֔וֹר הִשְׁמִידֻ֖ם וַיֵּשְׁב֥וּ תַחְתָּֽם:

ND. The narrator extends the purview of his observations to Philistia (D1).

וְהָעַוִּ֛ים הַיֹּשְׁבִ֥ים בַּחֲצֵרִ֖ים עַד־עַזָּ֑ה. Ptcp mp Qal √ישב. For the relative use of the article in הישבים, see on 1:30 (cf. 2:4, 8). The whole phrase is **extraposed** or dislocated, occurring outside the confines of the clause to which it belongs (traditionally called *casus pendens*). It is referred to by means of a resumptive pronoun, the pronominal suffix object in השמידם (cf. JM §156a, c). Such dislocation here marks the phrase as the **topic**.

בַּחֲצֵרִ֖ים. Oblique complement PP.

עַד־עַזָּה. Adjunct PP. Locative use of עַד, indicating location near its object (WHS §310).

כַּפְתֹּרִים הַיֹּצְאִים מִכַּפְתּוֹר הִשְׁמִידֻם. *Qatal* 3cp Hiph √שמד with 3mp pronominal suffix. ND. Unmarked S–P word order.

כַּפְתֹּרִים הַיֹּצְאִים מִכַּפְתּוֹר. Ptcp mp Qal √יצא. The participle has the article, while the noun does not. Rather than seeing it as a kind of attributive usage (cf. GKC §126w), the article ה is better characterised as introducing a relative clause with the adjectival participle functioning predicatively in a **null-copula** clause (see on 1:30). The relative clause is non-restrictive, giving further information about the Caphtorim. כפתרים never takes the article (JM §137c).

וַיֵּשְׁבוּ תַחְתָּם: See on 2:21. ND.

2:24 קוּמוּ סְּעוּ וְעִבְרוּ אֶת־נַחַל אַרְנֹן רְאֵה נָתַתִּי בְיָדְךָ אֶת־סִיחֹן מֶלֶךְ־חֶשְׁבּוֹן הָאֱמֹרִי וְאֶת־אַרְצוֹ הָחֵל רָשׁ וְהִתְגָּר בּוֹ מִלְחָמָה:

A succession of imperatives mark this HD, as the narratorial parenthesis gives way to Yhwh's urgent demand (D3). After the narratorial intrusion, the singular address in vv. 18-19 changes to the plural as the people come into view. At the start, it is unclear whether the voice being heard is the narrator's (continuing from v. 23), Moses' (given the plural address), or Yhwh's (confirmed by נתתי). The voices merge with powerful rhetoric. The verse is neatly balanced, with two parallel series flanking the observation that grounds the call to action.

קומו	סעו	ועברו את־נחל ארנן
	ראה נתתי . . . ואת־ארצו	
החל	רש	והתגר בו מלחמה

In both cases the first and second imperatives are the only words in the respective clauses and are joined asyndetically. The third imperative is joined syndetically, and is followed by two words. The central observation that they are to take notice of (ראה) is what they have been waiting for. Seven times in the chapter, Yhwh has either *not* given territory to Israel or *has* given it to others (נתן, 2× in vv. 5, 9, 19; 1× in v. 12). Now at last, Israel hears the news for which they have been waiting.

קוּמוּ סְּעוּ וְעִבְרוּ אֶת־נַחַל אַרְנֹן. Impv mp Qal of three verbs, √קום, √נסע, עבר. HD. For two asyndetic imperatives, where the first is a verb of motion, see on 1:21. The *dagesh forte* in סְּעוּ is euphonic, following unaccented וּ (GKC §20g), and marks the beginning of a new syllable (cf. GKC §13c).

אֶת־נַחַל אַרְנֹן. Accusative complement construct NP. This kind of construct phrase has been termed "genitive of association" (WO §9.5.3h). See on 1:24.

רְאֵה. Impv ms Qal √ראה. HD. An interjection. See on 1:8.

נָתַתִּי בְיָדְךָ אֶת־סִיחֹן מֶלֶךְ־חֶשְׁבּוֹן הָאֱמֹרִי וְאֶת־אַרְצוֹ. *Qatal* 1cs Qal √נתן. ED. This is a "commissive" *qatal*, an "extension" of the performative *qatal*. In a performative *qatal*, the action of the verb, in this case giving, is performed *in* the saying of these words (cf. WO §30.5.1d). In a "commissive," there is a gap between the declaration and the action (Cook 2012: 213), but the purpose of a "commissive" is "to commit a speaker to a certain course of action" (Austin, 156). That this giving is not complete in the saying of the action is apparent from v. 31, where Yhwh declares, "I have *begun to* give ...." The phrase נתן ביד is a common idiom for delivering someone into the hand of another. The plural address for the imperatives in the first half of the verse gives way to the singular (ךָ-) in the second half.

מֶלֶךְ־חֶשְׁבּוֹן. Appositional construct NP, indicating Sihon's office or title (cf. JM §131k).

הָאֱמֹרִי. Gentilic adjective (see on 1:4). Unlike elsewhere in chapters 1–11, where האמרי denotes the Amorite people collectively, here it speaks of an individual. האמרי could either be substantival, in apposition, "Sihon, ..., the Amorite [man]" or attributive, modifying מלך, "Sihon, the Amorite king of Heshbon" (cf. 1 Sam 27:3). It could not modify חשבן, because place names do not take attributive adjectives, nor could it be appositional to חשבן (cf. 1 Sam 30:5), because the gentilic adjective used appositionally denotes a person/people. Given the frequent occurrence of a person's name followed by a gentilic adjective used substantivally, this is most likely here, "Sihon, ..., the Amorite."

הָחֵל רָשׁ וְהִתְגָּר בּוֹ מִלְחָמָה. Three consecutive imperatives highlight the urgency.

הָחֵל רָשׁ. Impv ms Hiph √חלל, followed by impv ms Qal √ירש. HD. The *qamets* in רָשׁ is due to the verb being in pause (GKC §69f);

note also the alternative form, רֵשׁ (1:21). When two imperatives are joined asyndetically and the first is not a verb of motion, the second effectively can be seen as subordinate to the first (GKC §110h), "begin, possess" = "begin to possess." Further, the second verb expresses the "principal idea" (GKC §120g, h).

וְהִתְגָּר בּוֹ מִלְחָמָה. Impv ms Hitp √גרה. HD. For the **apocopated** ה in the Hitpael imperative, see GKC §75cc. For the verb and its complements, see on 2:5, 9.

2:25   הַיּוֹם הַזֶּה אָחֵל֙ תֵּת֙ פַּחְדְּךָ֣ וְיִרְאָתְךָ֔ עַל־פְּנֵי֙ הָֽעַמִּ֔ים תַּ֖חַת כָּל־הַשָּׁמָ֑יִם אֲשֶׁ֤ר יִשְׁמְעוּן֙ שִׁמְעֲךָ֔ וְרָגְז֥וּ וְחָל֖וּ מִפָּנֶֽיךָ׃

PD. D3. As Israel is to "begin" (חלל) to go in to possess, so Yhwh will "begin" (חלל) to put fear and dread of them upon the peoples in the land. There is no one exempt from fear. Twice Yhwh declares others will dread "you," so any reluctance to cross is wholly unwarranted.

הַיּוֹם הַזֶּה אָחֵל תֵּת פַּחְדְּךָ וְיִרְאָתְךָ עַל־פְּנֵי הָעַמִּים תַּחַת כָּל־הַשָּׁמָיִם. Yiqtol 1cs Hiph √חלל, followed by inf constr Qal √נתן. For an explanation of the form of the infinitive construct of נתן, see on 1:8. תת, along with its complements, is infinitive phrase accusative complement after the verb חלל, "begin." חלל usually is followed by ל before the infinitive complement (JM §124c, m; GKC §114m; WO §36.2.1d).

הַיּוֹם הַזֶּה. Adverbial time adjunct NP. For "today," see on 1:10.

פַּחְדְּךָ וְיִרְאָתְךָ. Accusative complements of √נתן. Both nouns have the pronominal suffix as an "objective genitive," "fear *of* you" (JM §129e, ka).

עַל־פְּנֵי הָעַמִּים. Oblique construct phrase complement of √נתן, a three-place predicate (see further on דבר in 1:1). על־פני has a variety of meanings (HALOT 943–44); with √נתן, it need not be inherently negative, though the only other occurrence in Deuteronomy, in 11:25, mirrors this one.

תַּחַת כָּל־הַשָּׁמָיִם. Adjunct construct PP. This *could* be a PP that further specifies the location of the putting of the fear, "I will begin to put fear *upon* . . . , *under* . . . ." More likely, though, this PP serves as "nominal attribute" of the noun העמים, "peoples [who are] under . . ."

(cf. 4:19; JM §130fa, 132a). Sometimes the relative word, אשר, is present to disambiguate (e.g., Gen 7:19).

אֲשֶׁ֤ר יִשְׁמְעוּן֙ שִׁמְעֲךָ֔ וְרָגְז֥וּ וְחָל֖וּ מִפָּנֶֽיךָ. *Yiqtol* 3mp Qal √שמע with **paragogic** ן. Although some regard אשר here as introducing a final/purpose clause (GKC §112p; Driver, 41; Weinfeld, 168), there is no reason not to regard it as an **extraposed** relative clause, with **head** העמים. Indeed Holmstedt 2002: 293–307 doubts whether אשר ever introduces a purpose clause. שמעך is cognate accusative complement of √שמע. The pronominal suffix is an "objective genitive," "report *of* you" (cf. JM §129 e, ka).

וְרָגְז֥וּ וְחָל֖וּ מִפָּנֶֽיךָ. *Qatal* (modal, sometimes termed *weqatalti*) 3cp Qal √רגז and √חול/חיל. These are the "temporal or logical consequences" of the previous *yiqtol* (GKC §112p; cf. WO §32.2.1d); the collocation of hearing, trembling, and writhing, as of a woman in labor, is also found in Exod 15:14. מפניך is adjunct PP, with מן introducing the cause of their turmoil (cf. WO §11.2.11d).

The defeat of Sihon (2:26-37)

Given Yhwh's command to engage in battle (vv. 24-25), Moses' peaceful deputation (v. 26) highlights both his lack of warmongering desire and Sihon's implicit culpability in his own destruction. Nonetheless, as with Pharaoh, it is Yhwh that hardens Sihon's heart (v. 30; cf. Exod 4:21). The victory granted, although concisely narrated, is a paradigm that will live long in Israel's memory (31:4; Josh 2:10; Judg 11:19-21; Psa 135:11; 136:19; Neh 9:22). Throughout the encounter, totality (כל) is in view (5× in vv. 32-36). Everyone is involved, everyone is defeated, every city is captured, everyone is devoted to חרם, Yhwh's gift is everything.

²⁶*Then I sent messengers from the desert of Kedemoth to Sihon, king of Heshbon, with peace terms,* ²⁷*"Let me pass through your land. I will travel on the road, and only on the road. I will not turn aside to the right or to the left.* ²⁸*Sell me food for silver so I can eat, and give me water for silver, so I can drink. Only let me cross on foot,* ²⁹*just as the descendants of Esau, who live in Seir, and the Moabites, who live in Ar, did for me, until I cross the Jordan into the land which Yhwh our God is giving to us."* ³⁰*But Sihon, king of Heshbon, was unwilling to let us pass by him, for Yhwh your God had hardened his spirit and made his heart stubborn, so as to give him into your hand,*

as [is the case] this day. ³¹ Then Yhwh said to me, "See! I have begun to put Sihon and his land at your disposal. Begin to take total possession of his land." ³² So Sihon came out to confront us, he and all his people for battle at Jahaz. ³³ Yhwh our God put him at our disposal, and we struck him and his sons and all his people, ³⁴ and we captured all his cities at that time. We devoted to herem the male population of every city, and the women and children—we did not leave a survivor. ³⁵ But the livestock we did plunder for ourselves, and the booty of the cities which we had captured. ³⁶ From Aroer, which is by the bank of Wadi Arnon—and the city, which is in the wadi—as far as Gilead, there was not a city that was too high for us; Yhwh our God put everything at our disposal. But you did not approach the land of the descendants of Ammon—the whole bank of Wadi Jabbok, and the hill cities, and all that Yhwh our God forbade us.

2:26 וָאֶשְׁלַח מַלְאָכִים מִמִּדְבַּר קְדֵמוֹת אֶל־סִיחוֹן מֶלֶךְ חֶשְׁבּוֹן דִּבְרֵי שָׁלוֹם לֵאמֹר׃

ND. D2. Moses recounts his sending of the messengers with a view to peaceful terms with Sihon. For the first time since 1:43, Moses is the sole subject of a verb.

וָאֶשְׁלַח מַלְאָכִים מִמִּדְבַּר קְדֵמוֹת אֶל־סִיחוֹן מֶלֶךְ חֶשְׁבּוֹן דִּבְרֵי שָׁלוֹם. *Wayyiqtol* 1cs Qal √שלח, followed by accusative complement, מלאכים, two adjunct PPs and an adjunct accusative NP, דברי שלום. ND.

מִמִּדְבַּר קְדֵמוֹת. Spatial adjunct construct PP. The absolute specifies the name of the desert (cf. GKC §128k).

מֶלֶךְ חֶשְׁבּוֹן. Appositional construct NP. See on 2:24.

דִּבְרֵי שָׁלוֹם. Adjunct construct NP. This could be an accusative of manner, "peacefully" (cf. WO §10.2.2e), a second direct object of "means" whether "instrument" or "medium," "with terms of peace" (cf. WO §10.2.3d), or, as GKC §131k suggests, a variation on apposition, termed "permutation," whereby the second noun "*defines* the preceding substantive ... in order to prevent any possible misunderstanding." The second or third are plausible.

לֵאמֹר. Inf constr Qal √אמר with preposition ל. **Complementizer**. See on 1:5.

2:27 אֶעְבְּרָה בְאַרְצֶ֔ךָ בַּדֶּ֖רֶךְ בַּדֶּ֣רֶךְ אֵלֵ֑ךְ לֹ֥א אָס֖וּר יָמִ֥ין וּשְׂמֹֽאול׃

D3. Moses' basic request to cross (HD) is then explained by two asyndetic PD clauses. In the first, Moses states the route he will take, while in the second he rules out alternative routes. The use of the 1cs emphasizes both the personal dimension and the reasonableness of the request.

אֶעְבְּרָה בְאַרְצֶ֔ךָ. Cohortative 1cs Qal √עבר. HD. The cohortative here expresses a wish, dependent on the permission of another (GKC §108c; AC §3.3.3b; JM §114c). בארצך is oblique complement PP of verb אעברה. עבר ב means "pass *through*" (cf. 2:4).

בַּדֶּ֖רֶךְ בַּדֶּ֣רֶךְ אֵלֵ֑ךְ. *Yiqtol* 1cs Qal √הלך. PD. The repeated adjunct PP בדרך בדרך, is fronted for **focus**; the particular route is highlighted and others are implicitly identified and rejected. The repetition of the noun indicates "exclusivity or intensity" (MNK §24.3.2.vi; cf. GKC §123e), "emphasis" (WO §7.2.3c) or a particular nuance, such as "steadfastly" (JM §135e). The clausal **asyndesis** reflects the clause's function of explaining Moses' planned crossing.

לֹ֥א אָס֖וּר יָמִ֥ין וּשְׂמֹֽאול׃. *Yiqtol* 1cs Qal √סור. PD. A second asyndetic clause further delimits the crossing, almost expressing a "negative adverbial idea" modifying the previous clause (GKC §156d). ימין ושמאול is an accusative expressing motion or direction towards (cf. JM §126n). For the pointing of שמאול with vowel transposition because of the א, see GKC §23c; JM §24f, §98f.

2:28 אֹ֣כֶל בַּכֶּ֤סֶף תַּשְׁבִּרֵ֙נִי֙ וְאָכַ֔לְתִּי וּמַ֛יִם בַּכֶּ֥סֶף תִּתֶּן־לִ֖י וְשָׁתִ֑יתִי רַ֖ק אֶעְבְּרָ֥ה בְרַגְלָֽי׃

PD. In v. 27 Moses emphasises what *he* will do; in v. 28, Moses outlines what he would like from Sihon (D3). Two 2ms *yiqtols* indicate Moses' requests. They are both followed by modal *qatals*, expressing the result. The tight structuring of these clauses and the initial clausal **asyndesis** reflect these clauses' function, of expanding further on the proposed terms of crossing. The final clause, joined asyndetically, reiterates the original request (HD).

אֹ֣כֶל בַּכֶּ֤סֶף תַּשְׁבִּרֵ֙נִי֙. *Yiqtol* 2ms Hiph √שבר with 1cs pronominal suffix. A *yiqtol* in a request is close to an imperative (cf. JM §113m). For

√שבר with אכל and בכסף, see on 2:6. Here, the Hiphil + 1cs suffix, "sell me," is found instead of the Qal, "buy." The accusative complement and the adjunct PP, בכסף, are both fronted. Together this statement and the one about water build up a complementary picture, which accounts for the **topicalization** (cf. Moshavi 2010: 160–61). Before the actual request comes, Moses sets out the terms. Rather than militaristic threats he proposes a peaceful agreement.

וְאָכַ֫לְתִּי. *Qatal* (modal, sometimes termed *weqataltí*) 1cs Qal √אכל. Although the tone syllable in a modal *qatal* after ו often shifts forward to the end of the word, when in pause the accent remains in its place; sometimes, as here, this is the case with the lesser pause, *zaqef qaton* (GKC §49m). The modal *qatal* here expresses "consecution" or result (JM §119e).

וּמַ֫יִם בַּכֶּ֫סֶף תִּתֶּן־לִ֫י. *Yiqtol* 2ms Qal √נתן. For the *yiqtol* functioning as a request, and for the fronting of the accusative complement and בכסף, see above.

וְשָׁתִ֫יתִי. *Qatal* (modal, sometimes termed *weqataltí*) 1cs Qal √שתה. The modal *qatal* here expresses "consecution" or result (JM §119e).

רַ֫ק אֶעְבְּרָ֫ה בְרַגְלָ֫י. Cohortative 1cs Qal √עבר. For the nuance of permission here, see on 2:27. The clause is joined asyndetically. With the restrictive adverb, רק, Moses reiterates his basic request. Since this is effectively in addition to the previous two requests, to be able to purchase food and water, the force of the restriction must be, "[I am not really asking for anything else, but] only let me cross on my feet" (cf. WO §39.3.5c). ברגלי is adjunct PP. This probably expresses the mode of travel, "on foot," (cf. Judg 4:15, 17). The journey through may be slower, but is less threatening. Perhaps, though, in view of the context, it is an idiomatic way of expressing self-reliance, "we will take nothing for free" (Tigay 1996: 31).

2:29 כַּאֲשֶׁ֨ר עָֽשׂוּ־לִ֜י בְּנֵ֣י עֵשָׂ֗ו הַיֹּֽשְׁבִים֙ בְּשֵׂעִ֔יר
וְהַמּ֣וֹאָבִ֔ים הַיֹּשְׁבִ֖ים בְּעָ֑ר עַ֤ד אֲשֶֽׁר־אֶֽעֱבֹר֙ אֶת־
הַיַּרְדֵּ֔ן אֶל־הָאָ֕רֶץ אֲשֶׁר־יְהוָ֥ה אֱלֹהֵ֖ינוּ נֹתֵ֥ן לָֽנוּ׃

Moses offers two further grounds for Sihon to accede to his request (D3). First, in a comparative clause, he gives a precedent for a positive response. Then he indicates that his goal is not "your land" (ארצך, v. 27), but to cross the Jordan to "the land Yhwh *our* God is giving to *us*" (v. 29). The 1cp at the end of the speech is at one level stereotypical, but the shift from 1cs, along with the declaration of Yhwh's gift, perhaps gives a veiled warning.

כַּאֲשֶׁ֨ר עָֽשׂוּ־לִ֜י בְּנֵ֣י עֵשָׂ֗ו הַיֹּֽשְׁבִים֙ בְּשֵׂעִ֔יר וְהַמּ֣וֹאָבִ֔ים הַיֹּשְׁבִ֖ים בְּעָ֑ר. *Qatal* 3cp Qal √עשה. Comparative clause, introduced by כאשר. After כאשר, there is usually **triggered inversion**, with P–S word order.

בְּנֵ֣י עֵשָׂ֗ו הַיֹּֽשְׁבִים֙ בְּשֵׂעִ֔יר וְהַמּ֣וֹאָבִ֔ים הַיֹּשְׁבִ֖ים בְּעָ֑ר. Ptcp mp Qal √ישב (2×), with the relative use of the article (see on 1:30) introducing a non-restrictive relative clause. The **head** of the first is בני עשו, while המואבים is the **head** of the second. בשעיר and בער are oblique PP complements with the two occurrences of the verb ישב.

עַ֤ד אֲשֶֽׁר־אֶֽעֱבֹר֙ אֶת־הַיַּרְדֵּ֔ן אֶל־הָאָ֕רֶץ אֲשֶׁר־יְהוָ֥ה אֱלֹהֵ֖ינוּ נֹתֵ֥ן לָֽנוּ. Spatial adjunct PP, with a **null-head** restrictive relative clause as the object of the preposition עד. The predicate is *yiqtol* 1cs Qal √עבר.

אֲשֶׁר־יְהוָ֥ה אֱלֹהֵ֖ינוּ נֹתֵ֥ן לָֽנוּ. Ptcp ms Qal √נתן. Restrictive relative clause with **head** הארץ. See on 1:20.

2:30 וְלֹ֣א אָבָ֗ה סִיחֹן֙ מֶ֣לֶךְ חֶשְׁבּ֔וֹן הַעֲבִרֵ֖נוּ בּ֑וֹ
כִּֽי־הִקְשָׁה֩ יְהוָ֨ה אֱלֹהֶ֜יךָ אֶת־רוּח֗וֹ וְאִמֵּץ֙ אֶת־לְבָב֔וֹ
לְמַ֛עַן תִּתּ֥וֹ בְיָדְךָ֖ כַּיּ֥וֹם הַזֶּֽה: ס

After narrating his reasonable request to Sihon, Moses recounts Sihon's lack of willingness (ND, D2), attributing it in two parallel explanatory clauses to Yhwh's action. This explanation is itself rooted in a purpose clause. Although Sihon's unwillingness is every bit as unreasonable as Israel's was (cf. 1:26), here it is attributable also to Yhwh's hardening activity.

וְלֹ֣א אָבָ֗ה סִיחֹן֙ מֶ֣לֶךְ חֶשְׁבּ֔וֹן הַעֲבִרֵ֖נוּ בּ֑וֹ. *Qatal* 3ms Qal √אבה. The disjunctive clause (לא + *qatal*) stands in sharp contrast with the modest request. See on 2:26 for סיחן מלך חשבון.

הַעֲבִרֵ֖נוּ בּ֑וֹ. Inf constr Hiph √עבר with 1cp pronominal suffix, functioning as the infinitive complement of אבה (cf. WO §36.2.1d). בו is oblique complement, with the antecedent shifting from the land (ארצך, v. 27) to Sihon himself. The one whose land it is functions as a metonymy for the land itself (Nelson, 43).

כִּי־הִקְשָׁה֩ יְהוָ֨ה אֱלֹהֶ֜יךָ אֶת־רוּח֗וֹ. *Qatal* 3ms Hiph √קשה. Explanatory clause, introduced by כי. After כי, a *qatal* verb form normally follows directly, due to **triggered inversion**. Only here is the verb קשה associated with רוח. Elsewhere, לֵב is used (e.g., Exod 7:3); here רוח and לב are synonyms (cf. Ezek 36:26).

וְאִמֵּץ֙ אֶת־לְבָב֔וֹ. *Qatal* 3ms Piel √אמץ. When a *qatal* form follows directly from a *waw*, many grammarians identify a distinct conjugation, *weqataltí*, designated as such because the accent tends to shift forwards. This should be better seen as a modal *qatal*, with **irrealis** mood (Cook 2012: 210; cf. on 1:16). ואמץ is the only example in chapters 1–11 of a superficially similar, but semantically different, occurrence of *qatal* occurring directly after a *waw*, but with **realis** mood. The *waw* is designated as "copulative," simply joining clauses, and the form is sometimes termed *weqatálti* (because of the lack of accent shift), although the shift is by no means consistent (Revell 1985). Thus WO §32.3b comment, "The copulative construction sometimes serves in a **hendiadys**, to represent two aspects of a complex situation," giving this verse as an example. It is preferable, though, to see the *qatal* as first in the clause because of **triggered inversion** carried forward from the previous clause (cf. Gen 28:6; Ezra 6:22; Jer 10:25; 49:30; 51:9).

לְמַ֛עַן תִּתּ֥וֹ בְיָדְךָ֖ כַּיּ֥וֹם הַזֶּֽה׃ ס. Inf constr Qal √נתן with 3ms pronominal suffix. For an explanation of the form of the infinitive construct of נתן, see on 1:8. The suffix functions as the object of the infinitive. Often prepositions with infinitives construct are used in place of subordinate clauses. Here, למען, functioning as a preposition, introduces a "purpose clause" (cf. WO §36.2.1d), although syntactically it is an adjunct infinitive phrase expressing purpose.

כַּיּ֥וֹם הַזֶּֽה. Comparative temporal adjunct PP. For the significance of היום in Deuteronomy, see on 1:10 and 2:22. Here, Moses breaks the narrative frame of recounting events prior to the destruction of Sihon and speaks of the present "today" in Moab.

2:31 וַיֹּ֤אמֶר יְהוָה֙ אֵלַ֔י רְאֵ֗ה הַֽחִלֹּ֙תִי֙ תֵּ֣ת לְפָנֶ֔יךָ אֶת־סִיחֹ֖ן וְאֶת־אַרְצ֑וֹ הָחֵ֣ל רָ֔שׁ לָרֶ֖שֶׁת אֶת־אַרְצֽוֹ׃

After recounting the messengers' words and Sihon's response (vv. 26-30), Moses recapitulates Yhwh's instructions to him from v. 24 (D3).

Deuteronomy 2:31-32

וַיֹּאמֶר יְהוָה אֵלַי. *Wayyiqtol* 3ms Qal √אמר. ND. יהוה is the subject, overt as the new **discourse active** agent. אלי is adjunct PP indicating addressee. D2.

רְאֵה. Impv ms Qal √ראה. HD. An interjection. See on 1:8.

הַחִלֹּתִי תֵּת לְפָנֶיךָ אֶת־סִיחֹן וְאֶת־אַרְצוֹ. *Qatal* 1cs Hiph √חלל, followed by Inf constr Qal √נתן. ND. For the *patakh* under the initial ה due to the following ח, see GKC §67w; JM §82n. For the phrase חלל תת, see on 2:25. For the meaning of the phrase נתן לפני, see on 1:8. Yhwh grounds the call to begin (√חלל) action in the second half of the verse in what Yhwh has begun (√חלל; cf. 2:25). Sihon's refusal to grant safe passage, far from grounds for fear or an indication that possession is in jeopardy, is nothing other than the beginning of Yhwh's action to give him into their hands.

הָחֵל רָשׁ לָרֶשֶׁת אֶת־אַרְצוֹ. Impv ms Hiph √חלל, followed by impv ms Qal √ירש. See on 2:24. HD. לרשת is Inf constr Qal √ירש with preposition ל. An original I-ו verb, the ו has disappeared and a feminine ת has been added (JM §72d, §75a). The presence of both רש and לרשת after החל has led some to think there is a conflation of two readings (e.g., Nelson, 43; cf. v. 24). Alternatively it is "an idiom reinforcing the sense of the verb" (Driver, 44; *BHQ: Deuteronomy*, 59*).

2:32 וַיֵּצֵא סִיחֹן לִקְרָאתֵנוּ הוּא וְכָל־עַמּוֹ לַמִּלְחָמָה יָהְצָה:

D2. Having contextualized Sihon's actions, Moses relates the engagement. ND. Sihon came out to confront them.

וַיֵּצֵא סִיחֹן לִקְרָאתֵנוּ. *Wayyiqtol* 3ms Qal √יצא, followed by ל introducing the purpose of Sihon's foray. ND.

לִקְרָאתֵנוּ. Inf constr Qal √קרא with ל preposition and with 1cp object suffix. Adjunct PP, expressing purpose. The root קרא is a **homonym** of the more common verb, "to call" and a **by-form** of קרה (JM §78k). See further on 1:42. The verbal idea remains here: "to meet us."

הוּא וְכָל־עַמּוֹ לַמִּלְחָמָה יָהְצָה. Three adjuncts: NP, PP and locative.

הוּא וְכָל־עַמּוֹ. Adjunct NP. The personal pronoun הוּא picks up the syntactic subject, סיחן, and enables other referents to be included in the action (כל עמו) while retaining Sihon as the key agent (cf. Holmstedt 2010: 57–58). Given the hostile intent and the presence of people in cities captured later, presumably עמו is Sihon's army. Nonetheless, there is something representative about this expression.

לַמִּלְחָמָה. Adjunct PP. They have come out to meet Israel with hostile intent.

יָהְצָה. Locative adjunct. The locative ה usually indicates motion toward (WO §10.5a, b; JM §93c). The accent does not shift when locative ה is added.

2:33 וַיִּתְּנֵהוּ יְהוָה אֱלֹהֵינוּ לְפָנֵינוּ וַנַּךְ אֹתוֹ וְאֶת־בָּנָו [בניו] וְאֶת־כָּל־עַמּוֹ:

D2. In this verse and the next, four *wayyiqtols* carry the action forward with economy. "Yhwh gave ... we struck ... we captured ... we devoted to חרם." It was Yhwh's initiative and agency, with Israel as a whole ("we") following it through. Narrative time becomes much shorter than narrated time.

וַיִּתְּנֵהוּ יְהוָה אֱלֹהֵינוּ לְפָנֵינוּ. *Wayyiqtol* 3ms Qal √נתן with 3ms pronominal suffix. ND. The attention remains on Sihon (הוּ-). What Yhwh began with Sihon's hardening (vv. 30-31), he now completes. For the meaning of the phrase נתן ... לפני, see on 1:8.

וַנַּךְ אֹתוֹ וְאֶת־בָּנָו [בניו] וְאֶת־כָּל־עַמּוֹ:. *Wayyiqtol* 1cp Hiph √נכה. ND. The final ה **apocopates**; the נ that is present is not the first root letter, but is the prefix for the 1cp; the initial נ of the root assimilates, but there is no *dagesh forte* because, after the **apocopation** of the final ה, ך is the final letter. The totality of the victory is expressed in the threefold accusative complement. Once Sihon was dead, the remaining threats could only come from his sons or his people (army). But they too were struck down.

בָּנָו. The *qere* is בָּנָיו, "his sons," while the *ketiv* is (with pointing added) בְּנוֹ, "his son." All other witnesses read a plural (*BHQ: Deuteronomy*, 59*). It is reasonable to assume he had more than one son. Their appearance here, for the first time, shows that Sihon's dynasty is over.

2:34

וַנִּלְכֹּד אֶת־כָּל־עָרָיו֙ בָּעֵ֣ת הַהִ֔וא וַֽנַּחֲרֵם֙ אֶת־כָּל־
עִ֣יר מְתִ֔ם וְהַנָּשִׁ֖ים וְהַטָּ֑ף לֹ֥א הִשְׁאַ֖רְנוּ שָׂרִֽיד׃

D2. ND. With the military opposition defeated, two *wayyiqtols* recount the completion of the victory, capturing the cities and devoting the inhabitants to חרם. The asyndetic clause (v. 34b), rather than introducing a further action, unpacks the previous statement and shows the totality of the victory.

וַנִּלְכֹּד אֶת־כָּל־עָרָיו בָּעֵת הַהִוא. *Wayyiqtol* 1cp Qal √לכד. ND. The accusative complement construct NP, את כל עריו, emphasises totality. The 3ms pronominal suffix keeps Sihon central as a **discourse active topic**.

בָּעֵת הַהִוא. Temporal adjunct PP. To refer to "that time" implicitly evokes a comparison with the present day in Moab. For the form, see on 1:9.

וַֽנַּחֲרֵם אֶת־כָּל־עִיר מְתִם וְהַנָּשִׁים וְהַטָּף. *Wayyiqtol* 1cp Hiph √חרם. The final *wayyiqtol* is the first occurrence in Deuteronomy of the verb √חרם (though note חרמה in 1:44). It speaks of the irrevocable giving over to Yhwh, usually by means of destruction.

אֶת־כָּל־עִיר מְתִם. Accusative complement construct NP. The so-called definite direct object marker את, is present although the absolute is not definite because כל can have a determinative sense (GKC §117c). Masoretic accentuation treats עיר as a construct (n.b., the conjunctive accent, *munakh*), and the rare word מתם, "men," as absolute (n.b., the disjunctive accent, *zaqef qaton*).

וְהַנָּשִׁים וְהַטָּף. With the Masoretic accentuation, these are linked with the whole construct NP, not just with מתם.

לֹא הִשְׁאַרְנוּ שָׂרִיד׃. *Qatal* 1cp Hiph √שאר. Asyndetic clause, explaining further the previous action. שריד, "survivor," is accusative complement, and in Deuteronomy occurs only here and in 3:3.

2:35

רַ֣ק הַבְּהֵמָ֞ה בָּזַ֣זְנוּ לָ֑נוּ וּשְׁלַ֥ל הֶעָרִ֖ים אֲשֶׁ֥ר לָכָֽדְנוּ׃

Moses clarifies the nature of חרם in the immediately preceding clause (v. 34), using a restrictive clause (ND, D2). Along with leaving no survivor, they did, in fact, plunder cattle and booty from the captured cities.

רַק הַבְּהֵמָה בָּזַזְנוּ לָנוּ. *Qatal* 1cp Qal √בזז. With geminate (or double-'*ayin*) verbs, when there are consonantal afformatives, usually the identical second and third letters assimilate and a helping vowel is present (cf. בַּזֹּנוּ, 3:7). This is the "nondissociated" state or "contracted" form. Sometimes, though, the verb appears in the "dissociated state" or "uncontracted form," as here (JM §82k; GKC §67aa). The adverb רק introduces here a restrictive clause that gives an immediate restriction or exception on the previous clause (cf. WO §39.3.5c). הבהמה is fronted for **focus**. Cattle has been singled out and mentioned first because usually חרם involved all living things, including livestock (e.g., Deut 13:15; 1 Sam 15:3). לנו is adjunct PP, with ל indicating the beneficiary of the verbal action (cf. WO §11.2.10d).

וּשְׁלַל הֶעָרִים אֲשֶׁר לָכָדְנוּ. A second accusative complement construct NP, in addition to הבהמה. The phrase comes almost as an afterthought. Plunder from the cities was sometimes proscribed (Josh 6:18), but sometimes permitted, as here.

אֲשֶׁר לָכָדְנוּ. *Qatal* 1cp Qal √לכד. Restrictive relative clause, with **head** הערים.

2:36 מֵעֲרֹעֵר אֲשֶׁר עַל־שְׂפַת־נַחַל אַרְנֹן וְהָעִיר אֲשֶׁר בַּנַּחַל וְעַד־הַגִּלְעָד לֹא הָיְתָה קִרְיָה אֲשֶׁר שָׂגְבָה מִמֶּנּוּ אֶת־הַכֹּל נָתַן יְהוָה אֱלֹהֵינוּ לְפָנֵינוּ:

ND. D2. Moses stresses the extent of the conquest and their overwhelming superiority. Yet lest self-reliance or self-congratulation intrude, in the final asyndetic clause all is Yhwh's gift.

מֵעֲרֹעֵר אֲשֶׁר עַל־שְׂפַת־נַחַל אַרְנֹן וְהָעִיר אֲשֶׁר בַּנַּחַל וְעַד־הַגִּלְעָד. Two spatial adjunct PPs indicate the extent of their invincibility, מערער . . . ועד־הגלעד. They are fronted for **focus**.

מֵעֲרֹעֵר אֲשֶׁר עַל־שְׂפַת־נַחַל אַרְנֹן. Spatial adjunct PP, followed by non-restrictive relative clause, with **head** ערער. The relative clause itself is **null-copula**, with PP complement. The object of the preposition, על, is a construct chain.

וְהָעִיר אֲשֶׁר בַּנַּחַל. NP that consists of the **head** העיר, followed by a **null-copula** restrictive relative clause, with PP complement, בנחל. The NP serves to include the city *in* the wadi. The city remains unnamed because Aroer is more significant. But almost as an afterthought for completeness, Moses mentions the extra city.

וְעַד־הַגִּלְעָד. Spatial adjunct PP. The ו functions here as a phrasal boundary marker, rather than a conjunction (cf. 3:8 and 3:16). Although a proper name, גלעד here, as often, takes the article. See further on הירדן in 1:1.

לֹא הָיְתָה קִרְיָה אֲשֶׁר שָׂגְבָה מִמֶּנּוּ. *Qatal* 3fs Qal √היה. קריה is only here and 3:4 in chapters 1–11. Moses pointedly refutes the complaint of 1:28 (Tigay 1996: 33).

אֲשֶׁר שָׂגְבָה מִמֶּנּוּ. *Qatal* 3fs Qal √שגב. Restrictive relative clause with **head** קריה. The verb שגב is only found here in prose, and in the Qal, only here and in Job 5:11. See on 1:28 for comparative מן.

אֶת־הַכֹּל נָתַן יְהוָה אֱלֹהֵינוּ לְפָנֵינוּ. *Qatal* 3ms Qal √נתן. Asyndetic clause, explaining further the summary of the extent of the conquest, rather than giving fresh activity by Yhwh. The accusative complement, את־הכל, is fronted for **focus**. Yhwh has given "everything" (see the introduction to 2:26-37). For the meaning of the phrase נתן . . . לפני, see on 1:8.

2:37 רַק אֶל־אֶרֶץ בְּנֵי־עַמּוֹן לֹא קָרָבְתָּ כָּל־יַד נַחַל יַבֹּק וְעָרֵי הָהָר וְכֹל אֲשֶׁר־צִוָּה יְהוָה אֱלֹהֵינוּ:

ND. D2. In v. 35 Moses qualified the statement of v. 34 that they left no survivors, so Moses again qualifies, with a restrictive clause introduced by רק, the "everything" that Yhwh gave them. Verse 36 gave the geographical extent of what they had defeated. Now Moses explains what they did not approach. Lest there be any doubt, this was to conform with Yhwh's prohibition (cf. 2:19).

רַק אֶל־אֶרֶץ בְּנֵי־עַמּוֹן לֹא קָרָבְתָּ. *Qatal* 2ms Qal √קרב. The adverb רק introduces here a restrictive clause which gives an immediate restriction or exception on the previous clause (cf. WO §39.3.5c). אל־ארץ בני עמון is oblique construct PP complement of קרבת. It is fronted for **focus**.

כָּל־יַד נַחַל יַבֹּק וְעָרֵי הָהָר וְכֹל אֲשֶׁר־צִוָּה יְהוָה אֱלֹהֵינוּ:. Three NPs appositional to ארץ בני עמון.

כָּל־יַד נַחַל יַבֹּק. Construct NP. יד here has metaphorical sense, "bank" (HALOT 388).

וְכֹל אֲשֶׁר־צִוָּה יְהוָה אֱלֹהֵינוּ. *Qatal* 3ms Piel √צוה. צוה here has the sense of "forbid," because fulfilment of it involved *not* drawing near (cf. JM §160k n. 15; 4:23). כל may be the **head** of the subsequent restrictive relative clause. Alternatively, the relative clause may be **null head**, with the antecedent covert rather than overt. Not only did Israel take everything (כל) Yhwh had given, but they did not approach any place (כל) Yhwh had prohibited.

The defeat of Og (3:1-7)

Having recounted the defeat of Sihon, Moses turns to the defeat of Og, king of Bashan (cf. 1:4). There are six *wayyiqtols* in both accounts (2:31-37; 3:1b-7), each from the same verb root: the king "went out" (√יצא 2:32b; 3:1); Yhwh "said" similar words (√אמר, 2:31; 3:2); Yhwh "gave" the king (√נתן, 2:33; 3:3); the Israelites "struck" (√נכה, 2:33; 3:3), "captured" (√לכד, 2:34; 3:4), and "devoted to *herem*" (√חרם, 2:34; 3:6) the king and his people. Many other motifs recur, too, albeit with some variation in order: men, women, and children devoted to חרם; no survivor left; every city captured, regardless of how well fortified; livestock taken as plunder. Just as chapter 1 was paradigmatic of unbelief and defeat, so chapters 2–3, and the campaign against Sihon and Og, are paradigmatic of obedience and victory, taking what Yhwh has given. This conquest is a "model" not just as a paradigm, but also as a "conquest in miniature," that should serve to give confidence and courage to Israel as they prepare to enter the land, taking what Yhwh gives (e.g., 1:8). That Yhwh's encouragement comes *after* Og marches out and that Og's stature in every sense is evident (vv. 1-11) both indirectly affirm the power of Yhwh.

¹Then we turned and went up on the road to Bashan, and Og, king of Bashan, came out to confront us for battle at Edrei, he and all his people. ²Then Yhwh said to me, "Do not fear him, for into your hand I am hereby giving him and all his people and his land and you will do to him just as you did to Sihon, king of the Amorites, who reigned in Heshbon." ³So Yhwh our God gave Og, king of Bashan, too, into our hand, and all his people, and we struck him down until there was no survivor for him, ⁴and we captured all his cities at that time. There was not a city that we did not take from them, sixty cities, all the territory of Argob, the kingdom of Og in Bashan. ⁵All these were cities fortified with a high wall, doors and a bar, besides the very many cities of those living in the open country. ⁶We devoted them to herem, just as we did to Sihon, king of Heshbon, devoting to herem the male population of every city, the women and children, ⁷but all the livestock and booty of the city we plundered for ourselves.

3:1 וַנֵּ֣פֶן וַנַּ֔עַל דֶּ֖רֶךְ הַבָּשָׁ֑ן וַיֵּצֵ֣א ע֣וֹג מֶֽלֶךְ־הַבָּשָׁ֡ן לִקְרָאתֵ֜נוּ ה֧וּא וְכָל־עַמּ֛וֹ לַמִּלְחָמָ֖ה אֶדְרֶֽעִי׃

ND. D2. Moses sent a deputation to Sihon, seeking a route through. Not so with Og. Here Moses relates concisely the salient details, "we went up . . . and Og came out." The correspondence between Sihon and Og found initially in 1:4 continues in 3:1b (cf. 2:32).

וַנֵּ֣פֶן וַנַּ֔עַל דֶּ֖רֶךְ הַבָּשָׁ֑ן. *Wayyiqtol* 1cp Qal √פנה and √עלה. ND. For ונפן, see on 2:1. All through chapter 1, עלה has only and often spoken of movement toward the land Yhwh has promised and given, whether of the spies going up to enter (1:21-24), not going up when they should (1:26, 28), or of going up presumptuously (1:41-43). Here, it is part of a proto-conquest.

דֶּ֖רֶךְ הַבָּשָׁ֑ן. Adjunct adverbial accusative construct NP specifying the route to be travelled (cf. on 1:2). For the presence of the article with בשן, see on 1:4.

וַיֵּצֵ֣א ע֣וֹג מֶֽלֶךְ־הַבָּשָׁ֡ן לִקְרָאתֵ֜נוּ ה֧וּא וְכָל־עַמּ֛וֹ לַמִּלְחָמָ֖ה אֶדְרֶֽעִי׃. *Wayyiqtol* 3ms Qal √יצא. ND. The whole sentence is exactly parallel to 2:32, both in structure and content. See the comments there.

מֶֽלֶךְ־הַבָּשָׁ֡ן. Appositional construct NP.

3:2 וַיֹּ֨אמֶר יְהוָ֤ה אֵלַי֙ אַל־תִּירָ֣א אֹת֔וֹ כִּ֣י בְיָדְךָ֞ נָתַ֧תִּי אֹת֛וֹ וְאֶת־כָּל־עַמּ֖וֹ וְאֶת־אַרְצ֑וֹ וְעָשִׂ֣יתָ לּ֔וֹ כַּאֲשֶׁ֣ר עָשִׂ֗יתָ לְסִיחֹן֙ מֶ֣לֶךְ הָֽאֱמֹרִ֔י אֲשֶׁ֥ר יוֹשֵׁ֖ב בְּחֶשְׁבּֽוֹן׃

Moses recounts Yhwh's words of reassurance (D3). The injunction not to fear (HD) is rooted in Yhwh's commitment to give Og into their hands and the assurance they will do the same to Og as they did to Sihon (PD).

וַיֹּ֨אמֶר יְהוָ֤ה אֵלַי֙. *Wayyiqtol* 3ms Qal √אמר. ND. יהוה is the subject, overt as the new **discourse active** agent. אלי is adjunct PP indicating addressee. D2.

אַל־תִּירָא אֹתוֹ כִּי בְיָדְךָ נָתַתִּי אֹתוֹ וְאֶת־כָּל־עַמּוֹ וְאֶת־אַרְצוֹ. Jussive 2ms Qal √ירא. HD. D3. Prohibitions in Hebrew do not use the imperative, but rather לֹא + *yiqtol* or, as here, אַל + jussive (see on 1:17). אתו is accusative complement of תירא. The verb ירא occurs absolutely (e.g., 1:21), with מן of what is feared (e.g., 2:4), and sometimes with a direct object, as here.

כִּי בְיָדְךָ נָתַתִּי אֹתוֹ וְאֶת־כָּל־עַמּוֹ וְאֶת־אַרְצוֹ. *Qatal* 1cs Qal √נתן. Explanatory cause, introduced by כי. After כי, a finite verb form normally follows directly, due to **triggered inversion**. The oblique complement, בידך, is fronted for **focus**. This is the chief reason why Yhwh tells Moses not to be fearful. The phrase נתן ביד is a common idiom for delivering someone into the hand of another. The threefold accusative complement, אתו . . . ארצו, and the fact it is "all (כל) of his people" highlight the comprehensiveness of the gift. For the "commissive" nature of the *qatal*, נתתי, see on 2:24. This clause closely resembles the grounds for Yhwh's injunction to engage Sihon in battle (2:24).

וְעָשִׂיתָ לּוֹ כַּאֲשֶׁר עָשִׂיתָ לְסִיחֹן מֶלֶךְ הָאֱמֹרִי אֲשֶׁר יוֹשֵׁב בְּחֶשְׁבּוֹן. *Qatal* (modal, sometimes termed *weqataltí*) 2ms Qal √עשה. PD. Commentators and translations are divided on whether this continues the causal clause, giving grounds not to fear ("and you *will*", PD; NJPS, Weinfeld, 178), or resumes HD after the causal clause, giving a positive injunction or command ("so you should," HD; NRSV, ESV, Nelson, 43; Block 2012: 93; Lundbom, 212). On balance I favor the minority PD view, "and you *will*" for three reasons: (1) the closest parallel syntax (apart from the almost identical wording in Num 21:34) is in Numbers 10:31; there the modal *qatal* can only be PD; (2) elsewhere in Deuteronomy the injunction not to fear is never followed by an injunction to act, but only by reassurance; and (3) although a modal *qatal* often continues an imperative (JM §119l), it rarely continues a jussive, whether 3rd person (JM §119k), or a prohibition, as here (e.g., 1 Sam 12:20; 2 Sam 14:2).

כַּאֲשֶׁר עָשִׂיתָ לְסִיחֹן מֶלֶךְ הָאֱמֹרִי. *Qatal* 2ms Qal √עשה. Comparative clause, introduced by כאשר. לסיחון is adjunct PP. See on 1:4 for the appositional phrase, מלך האמרי.

אֲשֶׁר יוֹשֵׁב בְּחֶשְׁבּוֹן. Ptcp ms Qal √ישב. See on 1:4 for the identical phrase.

וַיִּתֵּן יְהֹוָה אֱלֹהֵינוּ בְּיָדֵנוּ גַּם אֶת־עוֹג מֶלֶךְ־הַבָּשָׁן 3:3
וְאֶת־כָּל־עַמּוֹ וַנַּכֵּהוּ עַד־בִּלְתִּי הִשְׁאִיר־לוֹ שָׂרִיד:

ND. D2. Moses narrates how Yhwh gave into their hand not just Sihon, but also Og. See further the opening comments on this section.

וַיִּתֵּן יְהֹוָה אֱלֹהֵינוּ בְּיָדֵנוּ גַּם אֶת־עוֹג מֶלֶךְ־הַבָּשָׁן וְאֶת־כָּל־עַמּוֹ. *Wayy-iqtol* 3ms Qal √נתן. ND. For נתן ביד, see on 3:2. גם את־עוג is accusative complement NP, with גם acting as an item adverb, modifying not the clause as a whole but a constituent within the clause, "Og" (see further on 1:28). For מלך־הבשן, see on 3:1.

וַנַּכֵּהוּ עַד־בִּלְתִּי הִשְׁאִיר־לוֹ שָׂרִיד:. *Wayyiqtol* 1cp Hiph √נכה with 3ms pronominal suffix. Og remains center stage, "we struck *him*," though the subsequent temporal clause makes it clear that Og is a **metonymy** for Og and all his army.

עַד־בִּלְתִּי הִשְׁאִיר־לוֹ שָׂרִיד:. Inf constr Hiph √שאר. Adjunct temporal PP, functioning as a temporal clause (GKC §164d). The form הִשְׁאִיר differs from the usual Hiphil infinitive construct, where there is a *patakh* under the prefix, הַקְטִיל (cf. הַשְׁאִיר, Ezra 9:8), and looks like a *qatal* Hiphil 3ms. Broadly speaking, there are three explanations: (1) it is *qatal* Hiphil 3ms; (2) it is an inaccurately pointed infinitive construct; and (3) it is an accurately pointed infinitive construct. Against (1), no finite verb form is found elsewhere with בלתי, which negates infinitives. With regard to (2), although on a number of occasions the infinitive construct Hiphil is found with a *hireq*, according to JM §53c, these are "suspect" (cf. GKC §53l n. 3); with regard to (3), the pointing of השאיר in the phrase עד־בלתי השאיר always has this same form on the seven occasions it occurs; this prompts a brief explanation of how the form might have arisen if it in fact were authentic (JM §53c n. 7). On balance, (3) seems correct given the consistency of the pointing elsewhere, but this should not prejudice decisions made on other verbs (e.g., 7:24, הִשְׁמִדְךָ). לו is adjunct PP, with the ל indicating the beneficiary of the verbal action (cf. WO §11.2.10d).

וַנִּלְכֹּד אֶת־כָּל־עָרָיו בָּעֵת הַהִוא לֹא הָיְתָה קִרְיָה 3:4
אֲשֶׁר לֹא־לָקַחְנוּ מֵאִתָּם שִׁשִּׁים עִיר כָּל־חֶבֶל
אַרְגֹּב מַמְלֶכֶת עוֹג בַּבָּשָׁן:

ND. D2. The opening clause expresses positively what the second, asyndetic, clause expresses negatively in what is effectively an explanatory comment. The final appositional phrases in 3:4b document the extent of the "cities" captured.

וַנִּלְכֹּד אֶת־כָּל־עָרָיו בָּעֵת הַהִוא. *Wayyiqtol* 1cp Qal √לכד. ND. Verbatim from 2:34a. See comments there.

לֹא הָיְתָה קִרְיָה אֲשֶׁר לֹא־לָקַחְנוּ מֵאִתָּם שִׁשִּׁים עִיר֙ כָּל־חֶבֶל אַרְגֹּב מַמְלֶכֶת עוֹג בַּבָּשָׁן. *Qatal* 3fs Qal √היה. See on 2:36 for לא היתה קריה.

אֲשֶׁר לֹא־לָקַחְנוּ מֵאִתָּם. *Qatal* 1cp Qal √לקח. Restrictive relative clause, with **head** קריה. מאתם is adjunct PP. There is no overt antecedent of the 3mp suffix, but the shift signifies that the Amorites more generally, rather than the king, Og, are now the **topic**.

שִׁשִּׁים עִיר֙ כָּל־חֶבֶל אַרְגֹּב מַמְלֶכֶת עוֹג בַּבָּשָׁן. Three NPs, appositional to כל־עריו, each giving a different perspective on the comprehensive conquest. For numerals above eleven, the noun which follows is often in the singular if common and countable; this is true sometimes of עיר, as here in ששים עיר (cf. JM §142e). כל־חבל ארגב is construct NP; חבל is a cord or measuring line, used figuratively to speak of a territory (Driver, 48). ממלכת עוג is construct NP, with ממלכת the construct from מַמְלָכָה. בבשן is adjunct PP, modifying the nearest constituent. For the presence of the article with בשן, see on 1:4.

3:5 כָּל־אֵלֶּה עָרִים בְּצֻרוֹת חוֹמָה גְבֹהָה דְּלָתַיִם וּבְרִיחַ לְבַד מֵעָרֵי הַפְּרָזִי הַרְבֵּה מְאֹד:

Having articulated the comprehensive victory, Moses turns to the nature of the settlements defeated. The clause is **null-copula**, joined asyndetically, indicating that the narrative has not moved on, but there is further description (ED). D2. As with 2:36, where no city was too high, again Moses emphasizes the fortifications of the cities they defeated, directly rebutting the grumbling of 1:28.

כָּל־אֵלֶּה עָרִים בְּצֻרוֹת חוֹמָה גְבֹהָה דְּלָתַיִם וּבְרִיחַ. **Null-copula** clause, with the construct NP כל־אלה the subject, and the predicate ערים בצרות. As a demonstrative pronoun, אלה can act as the genitive or absolute after a construct (JM §143b).

חוֹמָה גְבֹהָה דְּלָתַיִם וּבְרִיחַ. The relationship between the predicate, ערים בצרות, and the subsequent phrase requires some explaining.

According to GKC §128c, these are "words of nearer definition standing in apposition" (cf. 1 Kgs 4:13), yielding "fortified cities, with high walls, gates and bars." Similarly JM §131m sees these words as in "loose apposition," translating as *"fortified cities: high walls, gates and bars."* An alternative is that בצור, as a Qal passive participle, retains the verbal idea; it is in the absolute state with the determining word, which expresses how the city was fortified, in the accusative (cf. GKC §116k), "cities fortified *with*. . . ." Given what would be *very* loose apposition, the latter is preferable. The use of ו joining nouns in series is "variable" (JM §177o). The three nouns function distributively, with all of them found in each fortified city. דלתים is dual, indicating the twin doors of a fortified city. The absolute dual form of דלת always assimilates with pretonic *qamets* to the plural form (דְּלָתוֹת), giving דְּלָתַיִם rather than the expected דַּלְתַיִם (GKC §93n).

לְבַד מֵעָרֵי הַפְּרָזִי הַרְבֵּה מְאֹד: Adjunct PP. לבד is made up of the preposition ל and the substantive, בַּד. Without מן following, it functions adverbially, "apart" (JM §102d); when followed by מן, it is akin to a preposition, "apart from," "besides." The adjectival ending -ִי on הפרזי connotes "belonging to" (cf. gentilic adjectives; JM §88Mg); they are "belonging to the open country." Here it is used substantivally, as the absolute after the construct עָרֵי, indicating ownership of the settlements. The presence of the article with the adjective indicates the referent is the entire group (cf. WO §13.5.1g; cf. GKC §126m).

הַרְבֵּה. Inf abs Hiph √רבה. הרבה is a specialized adverbial use of the infinite absolute, "much" (JM §79q, §102a, e). Alongside the fortified cities, they took countless settlements in the open country.

3:6 וַנַּחֲרֵם אוֹתָם כַּאֲשֶׁר עָשִׂינוּ לְסִיחֹן מֶלֶךְ חֶשְׁבּוֹן הַחֲרֵם כָּל־עִיר מְתִם הַנָּשִׁים וְהַטָּף:

ND. D2. Moses recounts the final action, the devotion to חרם of men, women, and children. The parallel treatment of Sihon and Og commanded by Yhwh (3:2) and highlighted by the narrative (see the introduction to 3:1-7) is now explicitly articulated by Moses.

וַנַּחֲרֵם אוֹתָם כַּאֲשֶׁר עָשִׂינוּ לְסִיחֹן מֶלֶךְ חֶשְׁבּוֹן. *Wayyiqtol* 1cp Hiph √חרם. ND.

כַּאֲשֶׁר עָשִׂינוּ לְסִיחֹן מֶלֶךְ חֶשְׁבּוֹן. *Qatal* 1cp Qal √עשׂה. Comparative clause, introduced by כאשר. See further on 3:2.

הַחֲרֵם֙ כָּל־עִיר מְתִם הַנָּשִׁים וְהַטָּף׃. Inf abs Hiph √חרם. Adverbial use of infinitive absolute, "in order to add a more precise piece of information" (JM §123r n. 19).

כָּל־עִיר מְתִם הַנָּשִׁים וְהַטָּף. See on 2:34. Unlike in 2:34, ו is not found with הנשים. The use of ו joining nouns in series is "variable" (JM §177o).

3:7   וְכָל־הַבְּהֵמָה וּשְׁלַל הֶעָרִים בַּזּוֹנוּ לָנוּ׃

As with Sihon and Heshbon, there is plentiful livestock and plunder from the settlements. Moses recalls the bounty (ND, D2). The shift from *wayyiqtol* to a disjunctive clause with *qatal* and with fronted accusative complement gives a contrast with what they devoted to חרם.

וְכָל־הַבְּהֵמָה וּשְׁלַל הֶעָרִים בַּזּוֹנוּ לָנוּ׃. *Qatal* 1cp Qal √בזז. ND. For the "non-dissociated" form, with the identical second and third letters assimilating, see on 2:35. וכל־הבהמה ושלל הערים are conjoined accusative complement NPs, fronted for **focus**. See on 2:35 for לנו.

Allocation of the Amorite land of Sihon and Og (3:8-17)

This section is characterized by further geographical details, both in Moses' reports and in a number of narratorial parentheses (vv. 9, 11, 13b-14). These details reinforce the reality. There is another powerful message behind these details. In 2:24 and 3:2, Moses had recalled Yhwh's words of reassurance, "I am giving" (נתתי). In vv. 8-12a, Moses reminds them in summary of the land they had captured, with ונקח בעת ההוא את־הארץ (v. 8) and ואת־הארץ הזאת ירשׁנו בעת ההוא (v. 12a) marking the *inclusio*. In 3:12b-17, Moses is now the agent of giving/allocation (נתתי, vv. 12, 13, 15, 16). This prepares the ground for the injunction to the Transjordanian tribes in 3:18-20. Both the narratorial parentheses interwoven with Moses' speeches and the parallels between Yhwh and Moses serve to align Yhwh, Moses, and the narrator and to actualize Yhwh's and Moses' words in the narrator's "today" (cf. vv. 11, 14).

[8] *So at that time we took the land from the hand of the two kings of the Amorites who were in the Jordan region, from Wadi Arnon to Mount Hermon"* [9] *(the Sidonians call Hermon Sirion, while the Amorites call it Senir),*

¹⁰"all the cities of the plateau and all of Gilead and all of Bashan as far as Salecah and Edrei, the cities of the kingdom of Og in Bashan." ¹¹(For only Og, the king of Bashan, was left, out of the rest of the Rephaites. See! His bed is an iron bed! It is in Rabbah of the descendants of Ammon! Nine cubits is its length, and four cubits its width—according to the standard cubit). ¹²"It was this land that we took possession of at that time. From Aroer, which is by Wadi Arnon, and half the hill country of Gilead along with its cities, I gave to the Reubenites and to the Gadites. ¹³The rest of Gilead and all of Bashan, the kingdom of Og, I gave to the half tribe of the Manassites, all the territory of Argob (that whole Bashan is called the land of the Rephaites; Jair, the descendant of Manasseh, took the whole territory of Argob up to the border of the Geshurites and the Maacathites, and called it—that is, Bashan—after his name, Havvoth-Jair, [as is the case] until this day); ¹⁵to Machir I gave Gilead, ¹⁶and to the Reubenites and the Gadites I gave [the territory] from Gilead to Wadi Arnon—the middle of the wadi being the boundary—and to Wadi Jabbok, the border of the Ammonites, ¹⁷and the Arabah—the Jordan being the boundary—from Chinnereth as far as the sea of the Arabah, the salty sea, beneath the slopes of Pisgah to the east.

3:8   וַנִּקַּח בָּעֵת הַהִוא אֶת־הָאָרֶץ מִיַּד שְׁנֵי מַלְכֵי הָאֱמֹרִי אֲשֶׁר בְּעֵבֶר הַיַּרְדֵּן מִנַּחַל אַרְנֹן עַד־הַר חֶרְמוֹן׃

ND. D2. Moses summarizes the previous campaign with a *wayyiqtol*; the territory taken is identified by a restrictive relative clause. They "took" (לקח√) what Yhwh "gave" (נתן√, 3:3).

וַנִּקַּח בָּעֵת הַהִוא אֶת־הָאָרֶץ מִיַּד שְׁנֵי מַלְכֵי הָאֱמֹרִי. *Wayyiqtol* 1cp Qal לקח√. ND. The verb לקח behaves like a I-נ verb, hence the *dagesh forte* in the ק (JM §72j). Rather than being a subsequent event, this *wayyiqtol* summarizes the previous campaigns (cf. JM §118i). Temporal sequentiality is not a semantic property of the *wayyiqtol* form, though often there is a strong correlation between the two (Cook 2004). Rather, it is a pragmatic implication (i.e., a natural reading) of such bound forms occurring consecutively in narrative. But other contextual factors can override this, as here. בעת ההוא is temporal adjunct PP. For the form הַהִוא, see on 1:9.

מִיַּד֙ שְׁנֵי֙ מַלְכֵ֣י הָאֱמֹרִ֔י. Adjunct construct chain PP. The syntax of the numeral two, which agrees in gender with the noun it modifies, can have one of three forms: (1) absolute form, before the noun; (2) absolute form, after the noun; or (3) construct form, before the noun, as here (JM §142c). For האמרי, see on 1:4.

אֲשֶׁר֙ בְּעֵ֣בֶר הַיַּרְדֵּ֔ן מִנַּ֥חַל אַרְנֹ֖ן עַד־הַ֥ר חֶרְמֽוֹן׃. **Null-copula** restrictive relative clause, with **head** הארץ. The complement is construct chain PP בעבר הירדן. See on 1:1 for its referent.

מִנַּ֥חַל אַרְנֹ֖ן עַד־הַ֥ר חֶרְמֽוֹן׃. Two spatial adjunct construct PPs, indicating the extent of the territory taken. The absolutes, ארנן and חרמון, specify the names of the constructs (cf. GKC §128k).

3:9 צִידֹנִ֛ים יִקְרְא֥וּ לְחֶרְמ֖וֹן שִׂרְיֹ֑ן וְהָ֣אֱמֹרִ֔י יִקְרְאוּ־ל֖וֹ שְׂנִֽיר׃

ED. D1. The breaking of the *wayyiqtol* main clause sequence and the shift to *yiqtol* indicate that it is now expository discourse. Although formally it could be Moses still speaking, given the other narratorial intrusions in the chapter, it is likely that this explanatory comment belongs to the narrator.

צִידֹנִ֛ים יִקְרְא֥וּ לְחֶרְמ֖וֹן שִׂרְיֹ֑ן. *Yiqtol* 3mp Qal √קרא. The *yiqtol* describes what is generally the case (cf. WO §31.3e). לחרמון is oblique complement PP (cf. on 2:11). Unmarked S–P word order. Note the **asyndesis** marking a break.

וְהָ֣אֱמֹרִ֔י יִקְרְאוּ־ל֖וֹ שְׂנִֽיר׃. *Yiqtol* 3mp Qal √קרא. See comments on previous clause. For האמרי, see on 1:4. Because it has collective force, the verb is plural (Driver, 51). Unmarked S–P word order. The two disjunctive clauses overlay each other temporally.

3:10 כֹּ֣ל ׀ עָרֵ֣י הַמִּישֹׁ֗ר וְכָל־הַגִּלְעָד֙ וְכָל־הַבָּשָׁ֔ן עַד־ סַלְכָ֖ה וְאֶדְרֶ֑עִי עָרֵ֛י מַמְלֶ֥כֶת ע֖וֹג בַּבָּשָֽׁן׃

Three conjoined accusative noun phrases, resuming from v. 8, describe further by apposition the territory (הארץ, v. 8) taken. The threefold repetition of כל highlights the comprehensive victory. These noun phrases are followed by an adjunct PP, indicating the extent. After the *'atnakh*, another appositional accusative construct phrase gives yet more description.

כֹּל ׀ עָרֵי הַמִּישֹׁר וְכָל־הַגִּלְעָד וְכָל־הַבָּשָׁן עַד־סַלְכָה וְאֶדְרֶעִי. Three accusative NPs, each joined by ו, occur in apposition to the captured land in v. 8. המישר is "the plain" or "the plateau" of Argob. עד־סלכה ואדרעי is spatial adjunct PP. Although normally a preposition is repeated before each object, sometimes there is "preposition override," when the preposition is omitted before subsequent objects (WO §11.4.2a). According to Masoretic accentuation, with the disjunctive *zaqef qaton* just preceding, the PP phrase does not just refer to וכל־הבשן (as NIV takes it), but to all three NPs (so NRSV, ESV, NASV).

עָרֵי מַמְלֶכֶת עוֹג בַּבָּשָׁן. Appositional construct NP (see on 3:4 for ממלכת עוג בבשן). For the presence of the article with בשן, see on 1:4.

3:11 כִּי רַק־עוֹג מֶלֶךְ הַבָּשָׁן נִשְׁאַר מִיֶּתֶר הָרְפָאִים הִנֵּה עַרְשׂוֹ עֶרֶשׂ בַּרְזֶל הֲלֹה הִוא בְּרַבַּת בְּנֵי עַמּוֹן תֵּשַׁע אַמּוֹת אָרְכָּהּ וְאַרְבַּע אַמּוֹת רָחְבָּהּ בְּאַמַּת־אִישׁ:

D1. Explanatory exceptive clause by the narrator that gives encouragement and explanation. Og was the last of the Rephaites and the size of his bed, evident even in the narrator's day, gives proof of Yhwh's power.

כִּי רַק־עוֹג מֶלֶךְ הַבָּשָׁן נִשְׁאַר מִיֶּתֶר הָרְפָאִים. *Qatal* 3ms Niph √שאר. Explanatory clause, introduced by כי. Since normally there is triggered inversion after כי, the NP עוג מלך הבשן is fronted for **focus**. The adverb רק, rather than introducing a restrictive clause which gives an immediate restriction or exception on the previous clause (cf. WO §39.3.5c), is functioning as an item adverb (for which, see WO §39.3.2 and on 1:28), "only Og."

מִיֶּתֶר הָרְפָאִים. Adjunct PP. Partitive use of מן, "remained *of / from*" (cf. JM §133e).

הִנֵּה עַרְשׂוֹ עֶרֶשׂ בַּרְזֶל. **Null-copula** ED, with subject ערשו and predicate ערש ברזל. When there are two nouns in a **null-copula** clause, it is not always certain which is the subject. One way of determining the subject is by identifying what is already known by context. This is indicated by the presence of a pronominal suffix, which indicates the **discourse active topic**. Here there is the unmarked S–P word order. It is not straightforward to capture the force and function of הִנֵּה, still less to translate it. Traditionally it has been translated with "behold." It is a **deictic** particle that draws particular attention to what follows (Miller-Naudé and van der Merwe). The **null-copula** clause itself has occasioned debates: whether עֶרֶשׂ, "bed," actually denotes a sarcophagus or a dolmen (funerary monument); whether ברזל is "iron" or, in fact, "basalt." As war booty, though, with dimensions the same as Marduk's bed, there is no reason to posit unprecedented meanings for these two words (Lindquist): "his bed is an iron bed."

הֲלֹה הִוא בְּרַבַּת בְּנֵי עַמּוֹן. Asyndetic **null-copula** clause with construct PP ברבת בני עמון as the predicate. ED. The form הלה with final ה is a *hapax*; there are more than 250 occurrences of הֲלֹא or הֲלוֹא (cf. *BHQ: Deuteronomy*, 59*); presumably it is a scribal error (Driver, 53; Weinfeld, 182). Traditionally, הלא has been regarded as comprising ה-interrogative and לא, the negative marker, serving to introduce a rhetorical question expecting the answer "yes" (= Latin *nonne*) (e.g., GKC §100i). Certainly some instances are like that. But some instances do not fit, and are closer to "presentative" in function (WO §40.3b n. 48; JM §161c). These awkward examples are in fact one strand of evidence for a **homonym**, הלא, which is a presentative clausal adverb similar to הִנֵּה (cf. Moshavi 2007; 2011b). While often the two are pragmatically indistinguishable, on some occasions there is a significant difference: regarding it as introducing a rhetorical question carries the implication that the speaker believes the addressee does or should know (Moshavi 2007: 52). Here, since הלה (הלא) occurs in parallel with a clause beginning with הנה, it makes more sense to see it as the presentative clausal adverb. For הוּא, see on 1:9.

תֵּשַׁע אַמּוֹת אָרְכָּהּ וְאַרְבַּע אַמּוֹת רָחְבָּהּ. Two **null-copula** clauses with P–S word order. The pronominal suffix ־ָהּ marks both nouns as the subject of the two clauses. Both numbers are fronted for **focus**, in this case giving salient information. The numerals from 3 to 10 are substantives; the marked feminine form is found with masculine nouns, and vice versa (cf. JM §100d).

בְּאַמַּת־אִישׁ׃. Adjunct construct PP. The phrase is unique; the more usual expression is בָּאַמָּה with the numeral, with **ellipsis** of the actual measure (e.g., 1 Kgs 6:6; cf. JM §142m). The indefinite use of אִישׁ implies it is a common measure (cf. Isa 8:1). Presumably the fuller description is to clarify which cubit is in view (cf. 2 Chr 3:3; Tigay 1996: 35) and to ward off incredulity, given the size of the bed.

3:12 וְאֶת־הָאָ֧רֶץ הַזֹּ֛את יָרַ֖שְׁנוּ בָּעֵ֣ת הַהִ֑וא מֵעֲרֹעֵ֞ר
אֲשֶׁר־עַל־נַ֣חַל אַרְנֹ֗ן וַחֲצִ֤י הַר־הַגִּלְעָד֙ וְעָרָ֔יו נָתַ֕תִּי
לָרֽאוּבֵנִ֖י וְלַגָּדִֽי׃

ND. D2. The first half of the verse concludes the summary of what they had captured "at that time (בעת ההוא), begun at v. 8 (see opening comment). In the second half, Moses switches to recounting the allocation of land.

וְאֶת־הָאָ֧רֶץ הַזֹּ֛את יָרַ֖שְׁנוּ בָּעֵ֣ת הַהִ֑וא. *Qatal* 1cp Qal √ירש. ND. The accusative complement of ירשנו, ואת־הארץ הזאת, is fronted for **focus**: of all the possible lands, it was *this* one. A **cleft** construction in English captures the force, "It was this land that we possessed. . . ." בעת ההוא is temporal adjunct PP. For the form הַהִוא, see on 1:9.

מֵעֲרֹעֵ֞ר אֲשֶׁר־עַל־נַ֣חַל אַרְנֹ֗ן וַחֲצִ֤י הַר־הַגִּלְעָד֙ וְעָרָ֔יו נָתַ֕תִּי לָרֽאוּבֵנִ֖י וְלַגָּדִֽי. *Qatal* 1cs Qal √נתן. As a three-place predicate (see further on דבר in 1:1), the verb נתן has conjoined accusative complements and an oblique complement. The accusative complement is fronted for **focus**, giving a contrast between what was given to the Reubenites and Gadites (v. 12) and what was given to the half-tribe of Manasseh (v. 13).

מֵעֲרֹעֵ֞ר אֲשֶׁר־עַל־נַ֣חַל אַרְנֹ֗ן. The accusative complement is covert: "[the territory] from Aroer . . ."; מן is not partitive here, but spatial. Aroer is **head** of a non-restrictive **null-copula** relative clause, which gives further information about Aroer (cf. 2:36). The predicate is the construct PP, על־נחל ארנן. על is often used to speak of "by" a place, particularly water (BDB s.v.).

וַחֲצִ֤י הַר־הַגִּלְעָד֙ וְעָרָ֔יו. A second accusative complement construct phrase, followed by a loosely conjoined noun, עריו. הר is in the construct state and need not indicate a specific mountain, but can designate "hill country." Although a proper name, גלעד here, as often, takes the article. See further on הירדן in 1:1. The pronominal suffix on עריו has "the hill country of Gilead" as its referent. עריו is neither a standalone accusative complement, given the suffix, nor is it another absolute after חצי.

לָרֽאוּבֵנִ֖י וְלַגָּדִֽי. Oblique complement. ראובני and גדי are patronymic (or gentilic) adjectives, designating belonging to a group based on the (male) ancestor. Patronymic adjectives characteristically end in יִ- (JM §88Mg). Here both are used substantively. The presence of the article with the adjective indicates the referent is the entire group (WO §13.5.1g; cf. GKC §126m).

3:13 וְיֶ֨תֶר הַגִּלְעָ֜ד וְכָל־הַבָּשָׁ֗ן מַמְלֶ֣כֶת ע֔וֹג נָתַ֕תִּי לַחֲצִ֖י שֵׁ֣בֶט הַֽמְנַשֶּׁ֑ה כֹּ֣ל חֶ֤בֶל הָֽאַרְגֹּב֙ לְכָל־הַבָּשָׁ֔ן הַה֥וּא יִקָּרֵ֖א אֶ֥רֶץ רְפָאִֽים׃

Moses explains the rest of the Transjordan allocation (D2, ND); the final part of the verse, לכל־הבשן . . . רפאים, is a narratorial parenthesis (D1), indicating what used to be the case (ED).

וְיֶ֨תֶר הַגִּלְעָ֜ד וְכָל־הַבָּשָׁ֗ן מַמְלֶ֣כֶת ע֔וֹג נָתַ֕תִּי לַחֲצִ֖י שֵׁ֣בֶט הַֽמְנַשֶּׁ֑ה. *Qatal* 1cs Qal √נתן. ND. As a three-place predicate (see further on דבר in 1:1), the verb נתן has both an accusative complement and an oblique complement.

וְיֶ֨תֶר הַגִּלְעָ֜ד וְכָל־הַבָּשָׁ֗ן. Conjoined accusative construct NP complements, fronted for **focus**. For the presence of the article with בשן (and, by analogy, with גלעד), see on הירדן in 1:1.

מַמְלֶ֣כֶת ע֔וֹג. Construct NP, appositional to accusative complement. See on 3:4.

לַחֲצִ֖י שֵׁ֣בֶט הַֽמְנַשֶּׁ֑ה. Oblique complement construct NP. The presence of the article with מנשה has prompted two explanations: (1) it is not a proper name, but a patronymic or gentilic adjective, used substantively, since proper names designating a definite individual do not take the article (GKC §125d n. 1); or (2) it is a rare instance of a proper name taking an article (Driver, 54); a variant on this second is that the article really belongs with חצי (JM §137b n. 2). Although the distinctive gentilic adjective form, מְנַשִּׁי, *is* found, the former explanation is more likely: proper names do not normally take the article; the gentilic form is only found four times in the OT (including Deut 4:43), while המנשה occurs twelve times, including on one occasion as a gentilic attributive adjective (Josh 13:7); in 29:7, the same phrasing is found as here, but with the gentilic adjective (שבט המנשי), suggesting interchangeability.

כֹּ֣ל חֶ֤בֶל הָֽאַרְגֹּב֙ לְכָל־הַבָּשָׁ֔ן הַה֥וּא יִקָּרֵ֖א אֶ֥רֶץ רְפָאִֽים׃. *Yiqtol* 3ms Niph √קרא. ED. The *yiqtol* is used for what used to be generally the case, "used to be called" (cf. WO §31.3e). Translators and commentators have struggled with v. 13b (Weinfeld, 182; *BHQ: Deuteronomy*, 60*). The difficulties are twofold: (1) whether כל חבל הארגב is in apposition to what precedes (Nelson, 50 n. b, ESV, NASB) or part of the following parenthetical narratorial comment, following the MT (n.b., the *ʾatnakh*; so NIV); and (2) how to construe לכל־הבשן. It is hard to make sense of לכל־הבשן if the Masoretic accentuation is retained. However, if כל חבל הארגב is taken with what precedes, then לכל הבשן ההוא is the start of a narratorial aside, an asyndetic, parenthetical explanatory clause. Although MT has *zaqef qaton*, the major break after the *ʾatnakh*, at הבשן, the lack of a noun before ההוא would be unprecedented, so ההוא should be taken with what precedes (Driver, 54). The phrase לכל הבשן ההוא is the oblique complement of יקרא, designating the object that is named (cf. on 2:11). Since בשן has the article, indicating that it is not a true proper noun (cf. on 1:4), it is also possible for בשן to take the (quasi-)demonstrative adjective, ההוא (for the determined personal pronoun's function as a demonstrative, see WO §17.3). ארץ רפאים is not the subject of יקרא (ארץ is feminine), but accusative complement, giving the name (cf. on יחשבו in 2:11, where a second accusative remains in the accusative with a passive verb). יקרא has an impersonal subject, "there is called to . . . ," hence "is called" (cf. Gen 2:23; 2 Sam 18:18).

כָּל־חֶבֶל הָאַרְגֹּב. Appositional construct NP (see the comment above and on 3:4). Unlike in 3:4, 14, ארגב ("top"?) has the article (cf. on הירדן in 1:1). This variation is evident in textual traditions, with the Samaritan Pentateuch having the article in all three cases, while the LXX does not render it anywhere (*BHQ: Deuteronomy*, 59*).

לְכָל־הַבָּשָׁן הַהוּא. Oblique complement of verb יקרא. For the article on הבשן, see on 1:4; for ההוא and for the function of the phrase, see comment above.

3:14 יָאִיר בֶּן־מְנַשֶּׁה לָקַח אֶת־כָּל־חֶבֶל אַרְגֹּב
עַד־גְּבוּל הַגְּשׁוּרִי וְהַמַּעֲכָתִי וַיִּקְרָא אֹתָם עַל־שְׁמוֹ
אֶת־הַבָּשָׁן חַוֹּת יָאִיר עַד הַיּוֹם הַזֶּה:

D1. A further asyndetic clause continues the narratorial aside. ND. The subsequent *wayyiqtol*, ויקרא, and the time reference, עד היום הזה, serve to connect the events of Moses's day with the narrator's own day.

יָאִיר בֶּן־מְנַשֶּׁה לָקַח אֶת־כָּל־חֶבֶל אַרְגֹּב עַד־גְּבוּל הַגְּשׁוּרִי וְהַמַּעֲכָתִי.
Qatal 3ms Qal √לקח. ND. Asyndetic clause, with unmarked S–P word order. את כל חבל ארגב (see on 3:4) is the accusative complement.

יָאִיר בֶּן־מְנַשֶּׁה. The proper name, יאיר, is followed by an appositional construct NP. The absence of the article with מנשה indicates it is a proper name (cf. v. 13). בן here designates a descendant (Tigay 1996: 36).

עַד־גְּבוּל הַגְּשׁוּרִי וְהַמַּעֲכָתִי. Adjunct construct chain PP. גשורי and מעכתי are gentilic adjectives, which characteristically end in ‑י (JM §88Mg). Here they are used substantivally, as two absolutes after the construct גבול. Generally the noun in the construct state is repeated before each absolute, but if the nouns in the absolute state are closely related, it may not be (GKC §128a). The presence of the article with the adjective indicates the referent is the entire group (WO §13.5.1g; cf. GKC §126m).

וַיִּקְרָא אֹתָם עַל־שְׁמוֹ אֶת־הַבָּשָׁן חַוֹּת יָאִיר עַד הַיּוֹם הַזֶּה׃. *Wayyiqtol* 3ms Qal √קרא. ND. אתם is accusative complement; the plural suffix refers back to כל חבל ארגב in syntactically imprecise fashion. על־שמו is oblique complement. קרא + acc + על is an idiom for naming something *after* someone (cf. Gen 48:6; 2 Sam 18:18; 1 Kgs 16:24).

אֶת־הַבָּשָׁן. Appositional and parenthetical, explaining further אתם. The singular is "particularly harsh" after the plural, אתם (Driver, 55), although really it is אתם that is awkward.

עַד הַיּוֹם הַזֶּה׃. Temporal adjunct PP. See on 2:22.

3:15   וּלְמָכִיר נָתַתִּי אֶת־הַגִּלְעָד׃

ND. D2. After the narratorial aside, Moses recapitulates the allocation in reverse order (cf. Tigay 1996: 36). Machir and Jair are both from the half-tribe of Manasseh.

וּלְמָכִיר נָתַתִּי אֶת־הַגִּלְעָד׃. *Qatal* 1cs Qal √נתן. ND. ולמכיר is oblique complement, fronted for **focus**. For the article on הגלעד, see on הירדן in 1:1.

Deuteronomy 3:16-17

3:16 וְלָרֻאוּבֵנִ֨י וְלַגָּדִ֜י נָתַ֗תִּי מִן־הַגִּלְעָד֙ וְעַד־נַ֣חַל אַרְנֹ֔ן
תּ֥וֹךְ הַנַּ֖חַל וּגְבֻ֑ל וְעַד֙ יַבֹּ֣ק הַנַּ֔חַל גְּב֖וּל בְּנֵ֥י עַמּֽוֹן׃

ND. D2. Moses continues his recapitulation of the allocation, with expanded geographical details.

וְלָרֻאוּבֵנִ֨י וְלַגָּדִ֜י נָתַ֗תִּי מִן־הַגִּלְעָד֙ וְעַד־נַ֣חַל אַרְנֹ֔ן תּ֥וֹךְ הַנַּ֖חַל וּגְבֻ֑ל.
Qatal 1cs Qal √נתן. ND.

וְלָרֻאוּבֵנִ֨י וְלַגָּדִ֜י. Oblique complement PP, fronted for **focus**. For the forms, see on 3:12.

מִן־הַגִּלְעָד֙ וְעַד־נַ֣חַל אַרְנֹ֔ן. Adjunct PP. The accusative complement is covert: "[the territory] from Gilead (and) to . . ."; מן is not partitive here, but spatial. The ו functions here as a phrasal boundary marker, rather than a conjunction (cf. 2:36). For the article on גלעד, see הירדן in 1:1; for נחל ארנן as "genitive of association" (WO §9.5.3h), see on 2:24 (and 1:24).

תּ֥וֹךְ הַנַּ֖חַל וּגְבֻ֑ל. Appositional conjoined NPs, explaining the boundary of what was allotted. The ו in וגבל should be understood as "explicative," so "the middle of the wadi *and* border" is best rendered "the middle of the wadi *being* the boundary." The idiom is used when the boundary is the middle of a body of water (so Weinfeld, 186; *pace* Nelson, 50, who thinks it denotes "and its adjacent territory"). Cf. e.g., Josh 13:23; 15:12.

וְעַד֙ יַבֹּ֣ק הַנַּ֔חַל גְּב֖וּל בְּנֵ֥י עַמּֽוֹן. Spatial adjunct PP, giving a second outer boundary (עד) for the land allocation, followed by appositional construct NP, גבול בני עמון. The word order of ועד יבק הנחל is surprising, though the identical phrase is found in Josh 12:2. הנחל is in apposition to יבק, serving to identify what has just been named (cf. WO §12.3e).

3:17 וְהָעֲרָבָ֖ה וְהַיַּרְדֵּ֣ן וּגְבֻ֑ל מִכִּנֶּ֗רֶת וְעַ֨ד יָ֤ם הָעֲרָבָה֙ יָ֣ם
הַמֶּ֔לַח תַּ֛חַת אַשְׁדֹּ֥ת הַפִּסְגָּ֖ה מִזְרָֽחָה׃

Moses continues the description of what he gave to the Reubenites and Gadites (D2, ND). The verse contains no predicate, but gives a second accusative complement (after the covert one in v. 16), followed by a succession of adjunct PPs and NPs.

וְהָעֲרָבָה וְהַיַּרְדֵּן וּגְבֻל. Conjoined accusative complements of נתתי in v. 16. For the article on ירדן (and on ערבה), see on 1:1. For וגבל, see on 3:16.

מִכִּנֶּרֶת וְעַד יָם הָעֲרָבָה. Two spatial adjunct PPs indicating the extent of the allocation of the Arabah territory and modifying it (cf. v. 12; Tigay 1996: 37).

יָם הַמֶּלַח. Appositional construct NP, identifying ים הערבה. By means of an adjectival genitive (WO §9.5.3a, d), what is known now as the Dead Sea is designated the Salt Sea.

תַּחַת אַשְׁדֹּת הַפִּסְגָּה. Spatial adjunct construct PP. אשד, for a long time disputed (n.b., Driver, 58), is now recognised as "slope" (Weinfeld, 186). For the presence of the article on הפסגה, see on הירדן in 1:1.

מִזְרָחָה:. Locative adjunct. The locative ה on מזרחה indicates motion toward (WO §10.5a, b; JM §93c). The accent does not shift when locative ה is added.

Instructions to the Transjordanian tribes and to Joshua (3:18-22)

Throughout the chapter up to this point, although Moses has been the speaker, the focus has been on action, whether of Israel's defeat of Og (3:1-7) or Moses' allocation (√נתן, 3:12b-17) of what they had captured (3:8-12a). In the remainder of the chapter, Moses turns to the words he spoke to three different addressees "at that time" (בעת ההוא, vv. 18, 21, 23): the Transjordanian tribes; Joshua; and Yhwh. All three have in common the theme of crossing (√עבר; vv. 18, 21, 25-28) although those crossing are in each case different; further, the first two are Moses' commands (√צוה), rooted in indicatives and tailored to the respective addressees so as to be compelling, while the third is Moses' plea.

18At that time, I commanded you, "Yhwh your God has given you this land, to possess it. As storm troops, you must cross before your brothers, the Israelites, all the warriors, 19though your women and children and livestock—I know that you have abundant livestock—may stay in your cities which I have given you, until Yhwh gives rest to your brothers, as to you, and they too possess the land which Yhwh your God is giving to them across the Jordan; then return, each one to his possession which I have given to you." 21Joshua, too, I commanded at that time, "Your eyes are the ones which have seen all that Yhwh your God did to these two kings. This is what Yhwh will do to all the kingdoms to where you are crossing. ²²Do not be afraid of them, for it is Yhwh your God who is the one who fights for you."

3:18 וָאֲצַ֣ו אֶתְכֶ֔ם בָּעֵ֥ת הַהִ֖וא לֵאמֹ֑ר יְהוָ֣ה אֱלֹהֵיכֶ֗ם נָתַ֨ן לָכֶ֜ם אֶת־הָאָ֤רֶץ הַזֹּאת֙ לְרִשְׁתָּ֔הּ חֲלוּצִ֣ים תַּעַבְר֗וּ לִפְנֵ֛י אֲחֵיכֶ֥ם בְּנֵֽי־יִשְׂרָאֵ֖ל כָּל־בְּנֵי־חָֽיִל׃

Although the referent of "you" is not directly indicated, thus implicitly bracketing the Transjordanian tribes with the others, Moses recalls (ND, D2) the command (√צוה) to the Transjordanian tribes. The first clause of the command is in fact an indicative, what Yhwh *has* done (ND, D3). The second then gives the command to cross (HD, D3).

וָאֲצַ֣ו אֶתְכֶ֔ם בָּעֵ֥ת הַהִ֖וא לֵאמֹ֑ר. *Wayyiqtol* 1cs Piel √צוה. Often there is **apocopation** of the ה- with *wayyiqtol* of III-ה verbs, as here, but sometimes the form occurs in full, especially in 1cs (e.g., 1:16, 18; GKC §75t). It is followed by two direct objects as complements (GKC §117gg; AC §2.3.1e), indicating the recipients of Moses' command (אתכם) and what he commanded introduced by the **complementizer**, לאמר (see on 1:5).

בָּעֵ֥ת הַהִ֖וא. Temporal adjunct PP. See on 1:9.

יְהוָ֣ה אֱלֹהֵיכֶ֗ם נָתַ֨ן לָכֶ֜ם אֶת־הָאָ֤רֶץ הַזֹּאת֙ לְרִשְׁתָּ֔הּ. *Qatal* 3ms Qal √נתן. ND. Unmarked S–P word order. Until now Yhwh has set the land before them (נתן לפני, 1:8, 21). Now the declaration is a bit stronger: Yhwh "*has* given" (no לפני). √נתן is three-place predicate (cf. on דבר in 1:1); the subject (יהוה אלהיכם), accusative complement (את־הארץ הזאת) and oblique complement (לכם) are all overt.

לְרִשְׁתָּ֔הּ. Inf constr Qal √ירש with 3fs pronominal suffix (object) with ל preposition. An original I-ו verb, the ו has disappeared and a feminine ת has been added (JM §72d, 75a). With pronominal suffixes, the segholate infinitive רֶ֫שֶׁת becomes רִשְׁת (GKC §69m). Adjunct infinitive construct phrase, indicating the purpose of Yhwh's gift.

חֲלוּצִ֣ים תַּעַבְר֗וּ לִפְנֵ֛י אֲחֵיכֶ֥ם בְּנֵֽי־יִשְׂרָאֵ֖ל כָּל־בְּנֵי־חָֽיִל׃. *Yiqtol* 2mp Qal √עבר. HD. The *yiqtol* here is an injunction carrying the modal nuance, "must" (cf. JM §113m), since it forms the basic action of the command (√צוה).

חֲלוּצִים. Ptcp mp Qal pass √חלץ, functioning as adverbial accusative of state, which "specifies a feature of the verb's subject or object at the time of the verbal action or in relation to that action" and is always indefinite (WO §10.2.2d n. 18). It is fronted for **focus**, giving an implicit contrast with all other modes of crossing. In Deuteronomy the root only occurs elsewhere in 25:9-10, where it is associated with the "removing" of a sandal. This might suggest a meaning like "selected," or perhaps "vanguard," or "storm troops" (Tigay 1996: 37); an alternative lies in the verb's association with the word for loins, "girded" (Weinfeld, 188). Usage is determinative. The word is used for armed troops, strikingly often at the front (e.g., Num 32:19-32), sometimes in contrast with the rearguard (Josh 6:9, 13; cf. Isa 52:12). If anachronism be forgiven, "storm troops" fits.

לִפְנֵי אֲחֵיכֶם בְּנֵי־יִשְׂרָאֵל. Adjunct PP, followed by appositional construct, בני ישראל. Moses emphasizes familial connections.

כָּל־בְּנֵי־חָיִל: Not the syntactic subject of תעברו, but adjunct construct NP, specifying the "you" of the **null subject** of the verb. חיל is an attributive adjectival genitive; with בן, it forms an idiom expressing the quality of those so described (WO §9.5.3a).

3:19 רַק נְשֵׁיכֶם וְטַפְּכֶם וּמִקְנֵכֶם יָדַ֫עְתִּי כִּי־מִקְנֶה רַב לָכֶם יֵשְׁבוּ בְּעָרֵיכֶם אֲשֶׁר נָתַתִּי לָכֶם:

Having given the injunction, Moses articulates an exception, granting permission for some to stay (D3, HD). Rhetorical force comes not just from the exception itself but also from Moses' articulation of their (implicit) thoughts (ידעתי, ED) and their indebtedness to him (נתתי).

רַק נְשֵׁיכֶם וְטַפְּכֶם וּמִקְנֵכֶם ... יֵשְׁבוּ בְּעָרֵיכֶם אֲשֶׁר נָתַתִּי לָכֶם: *Yiqtol* 3mp Qal √ישב. The *yiqtol*, as here, can carry the "modal nuance of permission" (JM §113l; cf. WO §31.4d). Restrictive clause, clarifying what Moses has previously enjoined (cf. WO §39.3.5c). The singular nouns טף and מקנבם have a collective meaning. The latter noun may initially seem to be plural, since מִקְנֵכֶם is, according to the Masorah Parva, מקניכם written defectively. The *plene* form מקניכם is found in Gen 47:16; Josh 1:14; 2 Kgs 3:17. But the י is not the indication of a plural noun: the absolute form of the noun only occurs in the singular; the singular noun follows directly in this verse, and the form with י (מִקְנֶיךָ), is found with a singular verb in Isa 30:23 (cf. Driver, 59; GKC §93ss).

אֲשֶׁר נָתַתִּי לָכֶם׃. *Qatal* 1cs Qal √נתן. Restrictive relative clause, with עריכם as the **head**. Moses' claim that *he* has given the cities to them reinforces their obligation to obey.

יָדַעְתִּי כִּי־מִקְנֶה רַב לָכֶם. *Qatal* 1cs Qal √ידע. Asyndetic clause (ED), with the accusative complement being a **null-copula** noun clause introduced by the **complementizer** כי. The **asyndesis** indicates that Moses is breaking off from the flow, almost as an aside, here indicating that he knows what (he assumes) they are thinking.

כִּי־מִקְנֶה רַב לָכֶם. **Null**-copula noun clause, as accusative complement of ידעתי. The S–P word order is unmarked, since there is not normally **triggered inversion** after כי in a **null-copula** clause. מקנה רב is the subject, רב being an attributive adjective. לכם is the complement, indicating possession (cf. WO §11.2.10d).

3:20 עַד אֲשֶׁר־יָנִיחַ יְהוָה ׀ לַאֲחֵיכֶם כָּכֶם וְיָרְשׁוּ גַם־הֵם
אֶת־הָאָרֶץ אֲשֶׁר יְהוָה אֱלֹהֵיכֶם נֹתֵן לָהֶם בְּעֵבֶר
הַיַּרְדֵּן וְשַׁבְתֶּם אִישׁ לִירֻשָּׁתוֹ אֲשֶׁר נָתַתִּי לָכֶם׃

In the previous verses, Moses has given the command to cross (v. 18) and permission for an exception (v. 19). In v. 20a, he gives an endpoint to the injunction, using a temporal adjunct PP. Once their brothers have also possessed the land Yhwh is giving them, and only then, can the Transjordanian fighters return to their possession (v. 20b).

עַד אֲשֶׁר־יָנִיחַ יְהוָה ׀ לַאֲחֵיכֶם כָּכֶם. Temporal adjunct PP, introduced by עד, followed by a **null-head** restrictive relative clause. The predicate of the relative clause is *yiqtol* (modal) 3ms Hiph √נוח, following אשר directly due to **triggered inversion**. With an oblique complement, the Hiphil means "give rest to (ל)." Within the wider HD, this is not a prediction, but an indication of potentiality. Although not found in chapters 1–11, it should be noted that there is an alternative Hiphil form with a geminated first root letter, הֵנִיחַ (JM §80p).

לַאֲחֵיכֶם כָּכֶם. Oblique complement לאחיכם followed by comparative adjunct PP ככם. Instead of ככם, the form כְּלָכֶם might have been expected, "as *to* you," but after כ, the corresponding preposition is often missing (JM §133h). The vertical line ׀ between יהוה and לאחיכם is the first occurrence in Deuteronomy of the *paseq*. It is not an accent, but a mark used to provide a separation between two words for varied reasons.

The function is not certain (JM §15m), though proposals have been made (Wickes, 120–29; GKC §15f n. 6; Himmelfarb).

וְיָרְשׁוּ גַם־הֵם אֶת־הָאָרֶץ אֲשֶׁר יְהוָה אֱלֹהֵיכֶם נֹתֵן לָהֶם בְּעֵבֶר הַיַּרְדֵּן. Qatal (modal, sometimes termed *weqataltí*) 3cp Qal √ירשׁ. The verb continues the modality of יניח. The clause is coordinated with the previous one. Together, they specify the temporal endpoint of the Transjordanian tribal involvement.

גַם־הֵם. Syntactically, גם here is an item adverb, modifying neither the predicate nor the clause as a whole, but just the constituent, הם (see on 1:28). The pragmatic effect is to make הם the **focus**, contrasting with the Transjordanian addressees. The 3mp independent personal subject pronoun occurs in one of two forms, הֵם and הֵמָּה. The different forms have no particular significance, indeed the alternative המה is found in the parallel passage to this in Joshua 1:15 (JM §39a n. 11).

אֲשֶׁר יְהוָה אֱלֹהֵיכֶם נֹתֵן לָהֶם בְּעֵבֶר הַיַּרְדֵּן. Ptcp ms Qal √נתן. Restrictive relative clause, with **head** הארץ. For the clausal syntax, see on 1:20. בעבר הירדן is adjunct PP. For its form and significance, see on 1:1.

וְשַׁבְתֶּם אִישׁ לִירֻשָּׁתוֹ אֲשֶׁר נָתַתִּי לָכֶם: Qatal (modal, sometimes termed *weqataltí*) 2mp Qal √שׁוב. HD. Rather than continuing עד אשר יניח (so Driver, 59), this clause resumes, after the intervening exceptive and temporal clauses, the mainline begun by תעברו: "cross . . ., however . . ., until . . ., and (then) return."

אִישׁ לִירֻשָּׁתוֹ. Adjunct NP, expressing distributive meaning, "each" (cf. WO §15.6b; JM §147d).

אֲשֶׁר נָתַתִּי לָכֶם: Qatal 1cs Qal √נתן. Restrictive relative clause with **head** ירשׁתו. Moses concludes his address with a further reminder of his addressees' indebtedness.

3:21 וְאֶת־יְהוֹשׁוּעַ צִוֵּיתִי בָּעֵת הַהִוא לֵאמֹר עֵינֶיךָ הָרֹאֹת אֵת כָּל־אֲשֶׁר עָשָׂה יְהוָה אֱלֹהֵיכֶם לִשְׁנֵי הַמְּלָכִים הָאֵלֶּה כֵּן־יַעֲשֶׂה יְהוָה לְכָל־הַמַּמְלָכוֹת אֲשֶׁר אַתָּה עֹבֵר שָׁמָּה:

Moses turns now to recall his instructions to Joshua (ND, D2). The command (v. 22) is rooted in two realities—Joshua's eyes are the ones that saw what Yhwh did in the past (ED); Yhwh will act in conformity with that past (PD).

וְאֶת־יְהוֹשׁוּעַ צִוֵּיתִי בָּעֵת הַהִוא לֵאמֹר. *Qatal* 1cs Piel √צוה. ND. It is followed by two direct objects as complements (GKC §117gg; AC §2.3.1e) indicating the recipients of Moses' command (ואת־יחושוע) and what Moses commanded, introduced by the **complementizer**, לאמר (see on 1:5). ואת־יחושוע is fronted for **focus**. In contrast to the Transjordanian tribes (vv. 18-20), Moses had a different command for Joshua. בעת ההוא is temporal adjunct PP. For the form הַהִוא, see on 1:9.

עֵינֶיךָ הָרֹאֹת אֵת כָּל־אֲשֶׁר עָשָׂה יְהוָה אֱלֹהֵיכֶם לִשְׁנֵי הַמְּלָכִים הָאֵלֶּה. Ptcp fp Qal √ראה with the article. ED. The presence of the article with the participle here has generated a lot of attention (GKC §116q, 126k; JM §137l; WO §13.5.2d, 37.5a). Recent study suggests that the article ה is best characterized as introducing a **null-head** relative clause with the adjectival participle functioning predicatively in a **null-copula** clause (Barr, 322–25; Holmstedt 2002: 83–90; Cook 2008; cp. WO §19.7): "your eyes [are] [*the one*s] *which have seen.* . . ."

אֵת כָּל־אֲשֶׁר עָשָׂה יְהוָה אֱלֹהֵיכֶם לִשְׁנֵי הַמְּלָכִים הָאֵלֶּה. *Qatal* 3ms Qal √עשה. Syntactically, this is the accusative complement of the verb הראת, comprising כל followed by a restrictive relative clause. כל may be the **head**, or the relative clause may be **null-head**, with the antecedent covert, rather than overt. Typically Deuteronomic, כל shows that Joshua saw *everything*. לשני המלכים האלה is an adjunct construct chain PP, with ל introducing the one affected by the verbal action, in this case negatively (cf. WO §11.2.10d). For the syntax of the numeral 2, see on 3:8.

כֵּן־יַעֲשֶׂה יְהוָה לְכָל־הַמַּמְלָכוֹת אֲשֶׁר אַתָּה עֹבֵר שָׁמָּה׃. *Yiqtol* 3ms Qal √עשה. PD. כן is a demonstrative adverb (JM §102h), drawing an explicit comparison between the previous clause and Yhwh's future action (n.b., the repeated √עשה). It typically comes first in the clause, leading to **triggered inversion** and a כן–P–S rather than a S–P order. The **asyndesis** requires Joshua to take the two statements and connect them.

אֲשֶׁר אַתָּה עֹבֵר שָׁמָּה׃. Ptcp ms Qal √עבר. The participle in Hebrew can indicate a future action that is already in progress (JM §121e). With participial clauses, the unmarked order after אשר is S-P. Restrictive relative clause, with **head** כל־הממלכות. שמה is a locative resumptive adverb, loosely resuming the geographical reference implicit within כל־הממלכות.

3:22 לֹ֥א תִּֽירָא֑וּם כִּ֚י יְהוָ֣ה אֱלֹֽהֵיכֶ֔ם ה֖וּא הַנִּלְחָ֥ם לָכֶֽם׃ ס

HD. D3. The command to Joshua is introduced asyndetically. It is for Joshua to make the connection between the indicatives of v. 21 and the injunction not to fear, although Moses does give further grounds not to fear in the subsequent explanatory clause.

לֹ֥א תִּֽירָא֑וּם כִּ֚י יְהוָ֣ה אֱלֹֽהֵיכֶ֔ם ה֖וּא הַנִּלְחָ֥ם לָכֶֽם׃. *Yiqtol* (modal) 2mp √ירא with 3mp pronominal suffix. A prohibition (see on 1:17 for לא + *yiqtol*).

כִּ֚י יְהוָ֣ה אֱלֹֽהֵיכֶ֔ם ה֖וּא הַנִּלְחָ֥ם לָכֶֽם׃. Ptcp ms Niph √לחם, with the article. For the article with the participle, see on v. 21. The root לחם almost always occurs in the Niphal and is intransitive. לכם is adjunct PP, indicating for whom Yhwh will fight (cf. 1:30). The clause is a **tripartite** nominal/verbless explanatory clause, giving the reason Joshua should not fear. For more on these **tripartite** clauses and ways to interpret them, see on כִּ֣י הַמִּשְׁפָּ֤ט לֵֽאלֹהִים֙ ה֔וּא in 1:17. In contrast to 1:17, here the order is X+S(=PronX)–P. Rather than regarding הוא as a pronominal copula here, I favor seeing הוא as a resumptive pronoun, referring to the **extraposed** (or dislocated or *casus pendens*) NP, יהוה אלהיכם. The effect is that "the subject . . . is singled out and contrasted with other possible or actual alternatives" (WO §16.3.3c; cf. Muraoka 1985: 72–74). In other words, "the repetition of the Subject referent in the pronoun הוא becomes Focal and should receive focus intonation" (Buth, 104–5). This phrase is **extraposed** for contrast and can (often) be translated by a **cleft** sentence in English, "it is Yhwh your God [and not others] that is the one who fights for you." Where Yhwh is in view, the contrastive view makes more sense (cf. Geller 1991; and 9:3).

Moses recalls his unsuccessful plea to Yhwh to let him cross the Jordan (3:23-29)

This is the third of Moses' addresses "at that time" (בעת ההוא; cf. on 3:18-22). Moses adopts the same persuasive rhetorical strategy, here rooting his desire to cross in Yhwh's prior actions. Throughout the section, there is skillful interplay between themes of seeing (√ראה, vv. 24, 25, 27, 28) and crossing (or being angry!) (√עבר, vv. 25, 26, 27, 28).

Yhwh's refusal to grant Moses' request highlights the impending death of Moses (cf. Olson) and Joshua's pivotal role as successor.

²³At that time I implored Yhwh's favor, ²⁴"Yhwh God, you have begun to show your servant your greatness and your strong hand. What god is there in heaven and earth who can perform [anything] like your deeds and mighty acts? ²⁵Let me please cross and see the good land which is across the Jordan, this good hill country and the Lebanon." ²⁶Yhwh was very cross with me because of you, and he did not listen to me. Yhwh said to me, "Enough of you. Never again speak to me further on this matter. ²⁷Ascend the summit of Pisgah and lift up your eyes to the west, to the north, to the south, and to the east. Take a good look, for you will not cross this Jordan. ²⁸Charge Joshua and say to him, 'Be strong and courageous,' for it is he that will cross before this people and it is he that will make them inherit the land that you see." ²⁹Then we remained in the valley opposite Beth-peor.

3:23 וָאֶתְחַנַּ֖ן אֶל־יְהוָ֑ה בָּעֵ֥ת הַהִ֖וא לֵאמֹֽר׃

ND. D2. The third of Moses' recollections of his words בעת ההוא (see introduction to 3:18-22), and the most painful for him.

וָאֶתְחַנַּ֖ן אֶל־יְהוָ֑ה בָּעֵ֥ת הַהִ֖וא לֵאמֹֽר׃. *Wayyiqtol* 1cs Hitp √חנן. ND. Note the *patakh* in the final syllable (cf. GKC §54k). אל־יהוה is oblique complement. The **complementizer**, לאמר (see on 1:5), introduces what Moses pleaded.

בָּעֵ֥ת הַהִ֖וא. Temporal adjunct PP. See on 1:9.

3:24 אֲדֹנָ֣י יְהוִ֗ה אַתָּ֤ה הַֽחִלּ֙וֹתָ֙ לְהַרְא֣וֹת אֶֽת־עַבְדְּךָ֔
אֶת־גָּדְלְךָ֖ וְאֶת־יָדְךָ֣ הַחֲזָקָ֑ה אֲשֶׁ֤ר מִי־אֵל֙ בַּשָּׁמַ֣יִם
וּבָאָ֔רֶץ אֲשֶׁר־יַעֲשֶׂ֥ה כְמַעֲשֶׂ֖יךָ וְכִגְבוּרֹתֶֽךָ׃

As with his previous speeches (vv. 18-20, 21-22), again Moses looks to persuade his addressee, here Yhwh. Yhwh has [only] *begun* to show him. D3. ND.

אֲדֹנָ֣י יְהוִ֗ה אַתָּ֤ה הַֽחִלּ֙וֹתָ֙ לְהַרְא֣וֹת אֶֽת־עַבְדְּךָ֔ אֶת־גָּדְלְךָ֖ וְאֶת־יָדְךָ֣ הַחֲזָקָ֑ה. *Qatal* 2ms Hiph √חלל, followed by ל +Inf constr Hiph √ראה as an infinitive complement. ND. For the *patakh* under the initial ה in החלות due to the following ח, see GKC §67w; JM §82n.

אֲדֹנָי יְהוִה. Vocative NP, indicating addressee. The vocative in Hebrew is not the subject, but here stands in apposition to the subsequent 2nd person subject pronoun, אתה (WO §4.7d). When יהוה stands alone, it normally has, as a *qere perpetuum*, the vowels of אֲדֹנָי (though note the simple vocal *sheva* with the י, יְהוָה). However, when יהוה is preceded by אֲדֹנָי, the vocalization is יְהוִה, indicating that the *qere* is אֱלֹהִים (JM §16f). This way of speaking of Yhwh only occurs here and 9:26 in Deuteronomy, both times on the lips of Moses as he prays (Craigie, 126).

אֶת־עַבְדְּךָ אֶת־גָּדְלְךָ וְאֶת־יָדְךָ הַחֲזָקָה. The Hiphil of √ראה often has two accusative complements, "to show X, Y"; X is the person shown (את־עבדך); Y comprises two conjoined NPs. החזקה is an attributive adjective, modifying ידך. When the noun is definite by virtue of a pronominal suffix, the adjective is also definite (GKC §126u).

אֲשֶׁר מִי־אֵל בַּשָּׁמַיִם וּבָאָרֶץ. The אשר here is awkward, especially with מי following. It is not a **complementizer** (*pace* Holmstedt 2006: 10), since what is described is not the content of what Yhwh showed Moses. The ancient versions rendered אשר as causal. The alternative, preferable because אשר retains its relative function, is to see it as a relative with antecedent אתה and resumptive pronouns on כמעשיך וכגבורתך, though translating this idiomatically requires rephrasing. Lit. "you ... who what god is there in heaven and earth who can perform like your deeds and your mighty acts," yielding "you ... the like of whose deeds and mighty acts what god is there who can perform them" (cf. Weinfeld, 190; Nelson, 51). Embedded within the relative clause is an interrogative clause, begun with the interrogative pronoun מי. מי can govern another clause (WO §18.2c). Although in English the appropriate gloss is "what god," in Hebrew the personal dimension of the deity explains מי rather than מה as the interrogative (cf. WO §18.2d; JM §144a, b).

בַּשָּׁמַיִם וּבָאָרֶץ. Adjunct PPs. Together, they form a **merism**. There is no conceivable place where a comparable deity may be found.

אֲשֶׁר־יַעֲשֶׂה כְמַעֲשֶׂיךָ וְכִגְבוּרֹתֶךָ׃. *Yiqtol* 3ms Qal √עשה. Restrictive relative clause, with **head** אל (note the 3ms). כמעשיך וכגבורתך are comparative adjunct PPs (cf. JM §133g). The pronominal suffixes are resumptive, within the relative clause begun by the first אשר.

3:25 אֶעְבְּרָה־נָּא וְאֶרְאֶה אֶת־הָאָ֫רֶץ הַטּוֹבָ֫ה אֲשֶׁ֫ר בְּעֵ֫בֶר הַיַּרְדֵּ֑ן הָהָ֥ר הַטּ֛וֹב הַזֶּ֖ה וְהַלְּבָנֹֽן׃

D3. HD. Having prepared the ground (v. 24), Moses now makes his request. His intent had already been apparent in 2:29, in the deputation he sent to Sihon. Yhwh had begun to "show" (√ראה) his servant Moses his greatness. Moses moves quickly past "cross" and focuses on his desire to "see" (√ראה) the good land generously given by Yhwh (טוב, 3:25 [2×]; cf. 1:25).

אֶעְבְּרָה־נָּא. Cohortative 1cs Qal √עבר. The cohortative here expresses a wish or desire, where permission is needed; the נא furthers the petitionary dimension (JM §114b-d, §163a). There is **ellipsis** of the complement.

וְאֶרְאֶה אֶת־הָאָ֫רֶץ הַטּוֹבָ֫ה אֲשֶׁ֫ר בְּעֵ֫בֶר הַיַּרְדֵּן הָהָר הַטּוֹב הַזֶּה וְהַלְּבָנֹֽן. Cohortative 1cs Qal √ראה. HD. III-ה verbs retain the ordinary *yiqtol* form for the cohortative (GKC §75l).

אֲשֶׁ֫ר בְּעֵ֫בֶר הַיַּרְדֵּן. **Null-copula** restrictive relative clause, with **head** הארץ. The complement is construct chain PP בעבר הירדן. For its referent, see on 1:1.

הָהָר הַטּוֹב הַזֶּה וְהַלְּבָנֹֽן. NPs, appositional to the accusative complement, את־הארץ הטובה. For the order of the attributive adjective chain, see AC §2.5.2 and on 1:19. See on 1:7 for הלבנון.

3:26 וַיִּתְעַבֵּ֨ר יְהוָ֥ה בִּי֙ לְמַ֣עַנְכֶ֔ם וְלֹ֥א שָׁמַ֖ע אֵלָ֑י וַיֹּ֨אמֶר יְהוָ֤ה אֵלַי֙ רַב־לָ֔ךְ אַל־תּ֗וֹסֶף דַּבֵּ֥ר אֵלַ֛י ע֖וֹד בַּדָּבָ֥ר הַזֶּֽה׃

D2. ND. Moses recounts Yhwh's angry response to his request, reckoning his representative role for the people as the cause (cf. 1:37). Yhwh commands Moses never to bring up the matter of his crossing the Jordan again (D3, HD).

וַיִּתְעַבֵּ֨ר יְהוָ֥ה בִּי֙ לְמַ֣עַנְכֶ֔ם. *Wayyiqtol* 3ms Hitp √עבר. This rare root, related to the noun עֶבְרָה and only in the Hitpael, is regarded by both BDB and HALOT as a **homonym** of the more common verb, עבר I, "to cross" (cf. v. 25), meaning "to be angry." The only "crossing" (√עבר) was Yhwh's, in his anger (√עבר). I have retained the pun by translating it as "Yhwh was very *cross* with me." בִּי is oblique complement of the verb וַיִּתְעַבֵּר.

לְמַעַנְכֶם. Adjunct PP, giving the grounds for Yhwh's anger with Moses (WHS §366; AC §4.1.11). לְמַעַן can be a preposition, as here, or a subordinating conjunction (e.g., 4:1).

וְלֹא שָׁמַע אֵלָי. *Qatal* 3ms Qal √שׁמע. ND. אֵלַי is oblique complement, found often when שׁמע moves beyond the act of audition. Yhwh had clearly heard what Moses said. If what Yhwh did do was be angry, what Yhwh did not do is "listen," in the sense of accede to Moses' request.

וַיֹּאמֶר יְהוָה אֵלַי. *Wayyiqtol* 3ms Qal √אמר. ND.

רַב־לָךְ. ED. Incomplete clause, an exclamation. See on 1:6 for the idiom. For the pausal pointing of לָךְ, see on 1:21.

אַל־תּוֹסֶף דַּבֵּר אֵלַי עוֹד בַּדָּבָר הַזֶּה. Jussive 2ms Hiph √יסף. HD. With the accent drawn to the first syllable because of אַל, the final *tsere* becomes a *segol* (GKC §69v). The verb √יסף is "quasi-defective" (see on 1:11). A prohibition (see further on 1:17). The verb is followed by an infinitive phrase complement, with infinitive construct Piel √דבר. When followed by another verb, יסף has an adverbial force, "again" (JM §102g, §177b). עוֹד is an adverbial adjunct, here pleonastic. בדבר הזה is an adjunct PP.

3:27 עֲלֵה | רֹאשׁ הַפִּסְגָּה וְשָׂא עֵינֶיךָ יָמָּה וְצָפֹנָה וְתֵימָנָה וּמִזְרָחָה וּרְאֵה בְעֵינֶיךָ כִּי־לֹא תַעֲבֹר אֶת־הַיַּרְדֵּן הַזֶּה:

D3. After Yhwh's angry prohibition (v. 26), now a series of six imperatives to Moses follows (vv. 27-28). HD. The first three relate to Moses, giving him sight of the land (√ראה, cf. vv. 24-25), while at the same time confirming, in an explanatory clause, introduced by כי, that he will not cross (√עבר). In v. 28 the second three imperatives relate to Joshua, and Moses' commissioning of him, for *he* will cross (√עבר) and enable the people to inherit what Moses sees (√ראה). The tight structure ("you see," "you will not cross," "*he* will cross," "you see") reinforces the themes of Moses' death and the transition to Joshua.

עֲלֵה | רֹאשׁ הַפִּסְגָּה. Impv ms Qal √עלה. HD. ראש הפסגה is accusative complement construct NP. A preposition might have been expected, since elsewhere in Deuteronomy עלה is followed by a preposition (ב, e.g., 5:5; אל, e.g., 34:1) if not by locative ה (e.g., 1:24, 43). Although not necessary (cf. Exod 17:10), some ancient versions do include or suggest the presence of a preposition (*BHQ: Deuteronomy*, 60*; Weinfeld, 190; Nelson, 51).

וְשָׂא עֵינֶיךָ יָמָּה וְצָפֹנָה וְתֵימָנָה וּמִזְרָחָה. Impv ms Qal √נשא. HD. The accusative complement, עיניך, is followed by four conjoined locative adjuncts. The locative ה on each indicates motion toward (WO §10.5a, b; JM §93c). The accent does not shift when locative ה is added.

וּרְאֵה בְעֵינֶיךָ כִּי־לֹא תַעֲבֹר אֶת־הַיַּרְדֵּן הַזֶּה:. Impv ms Qal √ראה. HD. בעיניך is an adjunct PP. There is a certain redundancy about the PP, since seeing requires eyes. The nuance is similar to the English, "take a good look," meaning that is *all* you will experience (cf. 34:4; 2 Kgs 7:2, 19).

כִּי־לֹא תַעֲבֹר אֶת־הַיַּרְדֵּן הַזֶּה:. Yiqtol 2ms Qal √עבר. An explanatory clause introduced by כי, saying why Moses should take a good look. Although כי can introduce an accusative complement noun clause (e.g., 5:24) and ראה has no (other) overt accusative complement, this cannot be a noun clause, because no amount of looking would reveal that Moses will not cross. It also cannot be an exceptive clause, "look with your eyes, *but* you will not cross," since after a positive statement אֶפֶס כִּי would be expected, while כִּי אִם would follow a negative statement (JM §173a, b). For הירדן, see on 1:1. The presence of the near demonstrative, זה, shows how close Moses is.

3:28 וְצַו אֶת־יְהוֹשֻׁעַ וְחַזְּקֵהוּ וְאַמְּצֵהוּ כִּי־הוּא יַעֲבֹר לִפְנֵי הָעָם הַזֶּה וְהוּא יַנְחִיל אוֹתָם אֶת־הָאָרֶץ אֲשֶׁר תִּרְאֶה:

D3. HD. Yhwh gives Moses three further instructions, followed by two explanatory clauses. Joshua, not Moses, will cross (√עבר) and lead this people to inherit what Moses sees (√ראה). See the comments on v. 27.

וְצַו אֶת־יְהוֹשֻׁעַ וְחַזְּקֵהוּ וְאַמְּצֵהוּ. Impv ms Piel √צוה, followed by Impv ms Piel √חזק and √אמץ with 3ms pronominal suffix. For the **apocopation** of ה (וצו) in III-ה verbs in ms imperative, see JM §79j (also 2:4). √צוה has the sense of "commission" or "charge" (HALOT 1011; cf.

Num 27:19; 31:14). The two subsequent Piels are what has been termed "delocutive" (Hillers); that is, commands for Moses to *say* to Joshua, "be strong and courageous": "say to him, 'be strong'" (see on 1:38).

כִּי־הוּא יַעֲבֹר לִפְנֵי הָעָם הַזֶּה. *Yiqtol* 3ms Qal √עבר. Explanatory clause. After כי, there is normally **triggered inversion** with a *yiqtol*. הוא is syntactically unnecessary and fronted for **focus**. In contrast to Moses, *he* (Joshua) will cross. לפני העם הזה is an adjunct PP. To be "in front of the people" has been Moses' role (10:11). No longer.

וְהוּא יַנְחִיל אוֹתָם אֶת־הָאָרֶץ אֲשֶׁר תִּרְאֶה׃. *Yiqtol* 3ms Hiph √נחל. The Hiphil has two accusative complements. Instead of X inheriting (Qal) Y, we have Z causing X to inherit (Hiph) Y (WO §10.2.3e; AC §3.1.6[a]). הוא is syntactically unnecessary and fronted for **focus** (cf. AC §5.1.2[a.2]). See previous comment and on 1:38.

אֲשֶׁר תִּרְאֶה׃. *Yiqtol* 2ms Qal √ראה. Restrictive relative clause, with **head** הארץ.

3:29 וַנֵּשֶׁב בַּגַּיְא מוּל בֵּית פְּעוֹר׃ פ

ND. D2. Moses has finished recounting not just his plea, but also the wilderness history. The name Peor is redolent with disaster (cf. Num 25), but the details remain hidden (Geller 1994: 107).

וַנֵּשֶׁב בַּגַּיְא מוּל בֵּית פְּעוֹר׃. *Wayyiqtol* 1cp Qal √ישב. ND. בגיא is oblique complement, as ישב is almost always followed by a preposition indicating where or with whom. מול בית פעור is adjunct PP. For מול, see on 1:1.

Call to Obedience
Deuteronomy 4:1-40

Chapters 1–3 have set out in historical retrospect the two choices with which Moses will confront the people in the plains of Moab. Now the scene shifts (ועתה; imperative, שמע; 4:1). Up until now, all the imperatives have occurred within reported direct speech. In chapter 4, the exhortation moves from being implicit to explicit as Moses confronts his addressees directly with a call to action in the present.

Structurally within the book of Deuteronomy as a whole, there are close links with chapters 29–30: e.g., bowing down (השתחוה) and serving (עבד) gods of the nations that have been allotted (חלק) to those nations (4:19; 29:25 [ET 26]); calling heaven and earth as witnesses against them (הַעִידֹתִי בָכֶם הַיּוֹם אֶת־הַשָּׁמַיִם וְאֶת־הָאָרֶץ; 4:26; 30:19); a forward look to exile (4:25-28; 29:22-28 [ET 23-29]) and possible restoration (4:29-31 and 30:1-10) (see Nelson, 63). The central section, giving the basic command, the statutes and the ordinances, needs to be read within Deuteronomy's storyline of anticipated rebellion, exile, and possible new future (Levenson; Robson; Weinfeld, 214–21).

Within 4:1-40, there are important unifying structural markers, alongside common motifs (e.g., seeing, 4:3, 9, 12, 15, 19, 34-36), phrases and words (e.g., יוֹם [17×]):

*4:1-2 and 4:40: observing (שׁמר) Yhwh's commandments (מצות), only in 4:2, 40; "which I am teaching/commanding you" (4:1, 2, 6, 40); motivation clause for instruction (לְמַעַן), only in 4:1, 40.

*4:1-8 and 4:32-40: "great (גדול)," prominent and only in these two sections in this chapter (4:6-8, 32, 34, 36-38); rhetorical questions (4:7-8; 32-34); "explicit universalism of outlook" (Mayes 1981: 26).

*4:9-31: "Be careful (שׁמר) . . . lest (פן)" (vv. 9, 15, 23) (Nelson, 63). Each of these sections (as indeed also vv. 4-1 and vv. 5-8) has this "warning to obey the law" "reinforced through reference to history" (Mayes 1981, 25).

*4:1-8 and 4:32-40 have as their theme "no other gods" (cf. 5:7), founded in the uniqueness of Israel's historical experience of Yhwh ("I am Yhwh your God, who brought you out of Egypt") and the particularity of the law given to them. Verses 9-31 have "no idols" as their theme (cf. 5:8-10).

No other gods: Israel is unique in having a near god and a just law (4:1-8)

This opening section breaks into two parts, vv. 1-4 and vv. 5-8. Both start with a call to obey, and then give a historical reference (Mayes 1981: 25). Israel needs to listen to, not tinker with, the "statutes and judgments" that Moses is setting before them (vv. 1, 5, 8); it was a disaster in the past not listening to Yhwh (v. 3); it is the way to life and land (v. 1; cf. v. 4); they are uniquely privileged and the envy of nations around about for having them (vv. 5-8).

[1]Now, Israel, listen to the statutes and judgments which I am teaching you to do, so that you may live and enter and possess the land which Yhwh, the God of your ancestors, is giving to you—[2]do not add to the word which I am commanding you, and do not take away from it—by keeping the

commandments of Yhwh your God which I am commanding you. ³*Your eyes are the ones which have seen all that Yhwh did at Baal-Peor, that everyone who went after Baal-Peor Yhwh your God destroyed from your midst,* ⁴*but you who clung to Yhwh your God are alive, all of you, today.* ⁵*See! I am teaching you statutes and judgments, just as Yhwh my God commanded me, for you to do exactly in the midst of the land to which you are entering to possess.* ⁶*You should keep [them] and do [them], for that is your wisdom and your understanding in the eyes of the nations, who will hear all these statutes and say, "Surely this great nation is a wise and understanding people."* ⁷*For what great nation is there which has a god near to it like Yhwh our God in all our calling to him?* ⁸*And what great nation is there which has righteous statutes and judgments like all of this torah, which I am setting before you today?*

4:1 וְעַתָּה יִשְׂרָאֵל שְׁמַע אֶל־הַחֻקִּים וְאֶל־הַמִּשְׁפָּטִים אֲשֶׁר אָנֹכִי מְלַמֵּד אֶתְכֶם לַעֲשׂוֹת לְמַעַן תִּחְיוּ וּבָאתֶם וִירִשְׁתֶּם אֶת־הָאָרֶץ אֲשֶׁר יְהוָה אֱלֹהֵי אֲבֹתֵיכֶם נֹתֵן לָכֶם:

HD. D2. Moses turns to exhortation that they should listen to what he is about to say. He grounds the call with three tightly connected purpose/result clauses introduced by למען. The gift of land lies before them, but they need to enter and possess it.

וְעַתָּה יִשְׂרָאֵל שְׁמַע אֶל־הַחֻקִּים וְאֶל־הַמִּשְׁפָּטִים אֲשֶׁר אָנֹכִי מְלַמֵּד אֶתְכֶם לַעֲשׂוֹת. Impv ms Qal √שמע. HD. The ms form is common at the start of instruction (cf. 5:1; 6:4; 9:1; Prov 1:8; see Weinfeld, 199). ישראל is vocative. Oblique complements, like אל־החקים ואל־המשפטים here, are often found when שמע moves beyond the act of audition. This is a slightly different usage from the call to listen used absolutely (e.g., 6:4; Weinfeld, 199). עתה "indicates a logical conclusion: in the light of, therefore.... Sometimes the grounds for a conclusion extend over several chapters of a biblical book. For example, the grounds for the conclusion reached in Deut. 4.1 are to be found in Deut. 1-3" (MNK §44.6.1; see also on 2:13).

אֲשֶׁר אָנֹכִי מְלַמֵּד אֶתְכֶם. Ptcp ms Piel √למד. The first occurrence in the Pentateuch of √למד; it occurs five times in 4:1-14. Teaching and learning are critical. Restrictive relative clause, with **head** החקים and המשפטים. While relative clauses with *yiqtol* or *qatal* verb forms have typical P–S word order with **triggered inversion**, **null-copula** relative clauses with the participle have S–P word order, as here. This is the first occurrence in Deuteronomy of אנכי, the 1cs independent personal subject pronoun. It is noteworthy on two counts: (1) it is one of a few words where *qamets* remains in an open syllable two syllables away from the tone (JM §30e, §39a), hence often with *meteg* (JM §14b); and (2) its usage, given that an alternative form, אֲנִי, also occurs, has generated significant discussion. אנכי is found twenty-five times in chapters 4–11. The other form אֲנִי is never found. This is in marked contrast to Ezekiel, in particular (אנכי once; אני [169×]). Explanations for the profile of occurrence have included chronology, sources, and social/pragmatic function. Revell suggests that אנכי is more deferential, and when predicated of Yhwh is usually concerned with the addressee "on a personal level" (1995: 212–14).

לַעֲשׂוֹת. Inf constr Qal √עשה with preposition ל. It is an infinitive phrase complement after מלמד.

לְמַעַן תִּחְיוּ וּבָאתֶם וִירִשְׁתֶּם אֶת־הָאָרֶץ אֲשֶׁר יְהוָה אֱלֹהֵי אֲבֹתֵיכֶם נֹתֵן לָכֶם׃. *Yiqtol* 2mp Qal √חיה, followed by modal *qatal* (sometimes termed *weqataltí*) 2mp Qal √בוא and ירש, continuing the modality of תחיו (cf. GKC §112p). למען is a subordinating conjunction that can introduce purpose or result clauses (JM §168d, §169g). Since what is in view is less the "effect" of that action than the "aim," these clauses should be seen as a succession of purpose rather than result clauses, although the dividing line is not sharp. The vocalization of וִירִשְׁתֶּם, with theme vowel *hireq* rather than *patakh*, occurs in some I-ו verbs (ילד, ירשׁ), either because of assimilation to the preceding sounded vowel, whether *sheva*, or, as here, *hireq-yod*, or because of variant form יָרֵשׁ (GKC §44d, 69s; cf. JM §41b, §42d).

אֲשֶׁר יְהוָה אֱלֹהֵי אֲבֹתֵיכֶם נֹתֵן לָכֶם׃. Ptcp ms Qal √נתן. Restrictive relative clause with **head** הארץ. For יהוה אלהי אבתיכם, see on 1:11. לכם is oblique complement of נתן. Until now, the gift in this formulaic relative clause has been לנו (1:20, 25; 2:29). But Moses has been told he will not enter (3:23–29).

4:2 לֹא תֹסִפוּ עַל־הַדָּבָר אֲשֶׁר אָנֹכִי מְצַוֶּה אֶתְכֶם
וְלֹא תִגְרְעוּ מִמֶּנּוּ לִשְׁמֹר אֶת־מִצְוֺת יְהוָה אֱלֹהֵיכֶם
אֲשֶׁר אָנֹכִי מְצַוֶּה אֶתְכֶם׃

HD. D2. Verse 2 continues from v. 1 asyndetically, suggesting that v. 2a illuminates what it means to "listen" (v. 1). To add is to dilute the word's authority; to take away is to usurp it. The second half of the verse follows from v. 1b rather than 2a (see below). Keeping Yhwh's commands is the way of entering and possessing the land.

לֹא תֹסִפוּ עַל־הַדָּבָר֙ אֲשֶׁ֣ר אָנֹכִ֔י מְצַוֶּ֖ה אֶתְכֶ֑ם. *Yiqtol* 2mp Hiph √יסף. The verb יסף is "quasi-defective," and followed by עַל it means "add" or "increase" (see on 1:11). A prohibition (see on 1:17).

אֲשֶׁ֣ר אָנֹכִ֔י מְצַוֶּ֖ה אֶתְכֶ֑ם. Ptcp ms Piel √צוה. Restrictive relative clause, with **head** הדבר. For word order and אנכי, see on v. 1.

וְלֹ֥א תִגְרְע֖וּ מִמֶּ֑נּוּ. *Yiqtol* 2mp Hiph √גרע. A prohibition (see on 1:17). The verb is used elsewhere of trimming a beard (Jer 48:37). The preposition מן in ממנו is partitive, used when taking a part from the whole (cf. WHS §324). The part that they are not to take away is the **null** accusative complement of גרע: "Ø from it."

לִשְׁמֹ֗ר אֶת־מִצְוֺת֙ יְהוָ֣ה אֱלֹֽהֵיכֶ֔ם אֲשֶׁ֥ר אָנֹכִ֖י מְצַוֶּ֥ה אֶתְכֶֽם׃. Inf constr Qal √שמר with ל preposition. Adjunct infinitive construct phrase, but how it relates to what precedes is tricky. Broadly there are four ways of taking it: (1) explanatory, taken with the clauses immediately prior, "keeping" (Nelson, 57), but it is then not obvious how the not adding or taking away is *itself* "keeping"; (2) purpose, "in order to keep" (Weinfeld, 193, ESV, NASB); not adding or taking away is not in itself "keeping," but rather enables that to happen. However, when ל + infinitive construct follows a prohibition, whether the force is purpose or explanatory, syntactically it is always *within* the clause that is prohibited, rather than a comment on the prohibition itself, external to the clause (e.g., 20:19, Lev 26:1); (3) loosely appositional adjunct to דבר, explaining what this "word" is, "to keep" (cf. 11:13); and (4) explanatory, joined with the end of v. 1, with the intervening "do not add . . . do not take away" as parenthetical (n.b., the **asyndesis**). The phrase then expands and further explains how they enter and possess the land (cf. 11:8). (3) and (4) are possible. NRSV and NIV's "but keep" is impossible.

אֲשֶׁ֥ר אָנֹכִ֖י מְצַוֶּ֥ה אֶתְכֶֽם׃. Identical phrase to earlier in the verse. The **head** of the restrictive relative clause here is מצות.

4:3 עֵינֵיכֶם הָרֹאֹת אֵת אֲשֶׁר־עָשָׂה יְהוָה בְּבַעַל פְּעוֹר כִּי כָל־הָאִישׁ אֲשֶׁר הָלַךְ אַחֲרֵי בַעַל־פְּעוֹר הִשְׁמִידוֹ יְהוָה אֱלֹהֶיךָ מִקִּרְבֶּךָ׃

ED. D2. Moses reminds them, from what their eyes have seen, of twin destinies (vv. 3-4); in v. 3, Yhwh destroyed all those who went after Baal-Peor. The more vague "what Yhwh did" followed by the more specific appositional clause, כי . . . מקרבך, invites addresses to consider for themselves what Yhwh had done. The clausal **asyndesis** between verses 2 and 3 draws a comparison between adding to or taking away from Yhwh's word and the idolatry that brought death. There is a canonical consciousness, which affirms not only "textual integrity" but also that the integrity's "status" is "ranking with the person of God Himself" (Geller 1994: 118). There is a close relationship between Yhwh and his word (Robson, 111 n. 96).

עֵינֵיכֶם הָרֹאֹת אֵת אֲשֶׁר־עָשָׂה יְהוָה בְּבַעַל פְּעוֹר. Ptcp fp Qal √ראה with the article. See on 3:21 for the syntax of עיניכם הראת.

אֲשֶׁר־עָשָׂה יְהוָה בְּבַעַל פְּעוֹר. *Qatal* 3ms Qal √עשה. The **null-head** restrictive relative clause acts as the accusative complement of the participle, הראת (cf. on 3:21). בבעל פעור is an adjunct PP. It can be the name of place, not just the name of a deity, so there is no need to suggest, as NRSV and NASB do, an unusual gloss for ב (Hos 9:10; Weinfeld, 195).

כִּי כָל־הָאִישׁ אֲשֶׁר הָלַךְ אַחֲרֵי בַעַל־פְּעוֹר הִשְׁמִידוֹ יְהוָה אֱלֹהֶיךָ מִקִּרְבֶּךָ׃. *Qatal* 3ms Hiph √שמד with 3ms pronominal suffix. כי . . . מקרבך is an appositional accusative noun clause, showing what their eyes saw, introduced by the **complementizer** כי. In apposition to את אשר . . . פעור, it articulates precisely what Yhwh did. Given that there is a resumptive pronoun, the pronominal suffix object in השמידו, the phrase כל־האיש . . . בעל־פעור must be an **extraposed** NP (*casus pendens*). Such **extraposition** (or dislocation) here marks the phrase as the **topic** (see on 2:23). מקרבך is an adjunct PP (cf. 2:14).

אֲשֶׁר הָלַךְ אַחֲרֵי בַעַל־פְּעוֹר. *Qatal* 3ms Qal √הלך. אחרי בעל־פעור is the oblique complement. הלך אחרי is a common phrase for following a deity, usually one (or more) other than Yhwh (cf. 6:14; 8:19). אחרי has a spatial or locative sense (cf. WHS §358).

4:4 וְאַתֶּם֙ הַדְּבֵקִ֔ים בַּיהוָ֖ה אֱלֹהֵיכֶ֑ם חַיִּ֥ים כֻּלְּכֶ֖ם הַיּֽוֹם׃

ED. D2. Moses turns to what is now the case. There is a sharp contrast with those whom Yhwh destroyed because of idolatry (v. 3). The key is sticking fast to Yhwh (√דבק; cf. 10:20; 11:22).

וְאַתֶּם֙ הַדְּבֵקִ֔ים בַּיהוָ֖ה אֱלֹהֵיכֶ֑ם חַיִּ֥ים כֻּלְּכֶ֖ם הַיּֽוֹם׃. **Null-copula** clause, with subject אתם and predicate חיים.

הַדְּבֵקִים בַּיהוָה אֱלֹהֵיכֶם. דבקים is a verbal adjective (mp). The verb √דבק, although often showing an active (or fientive) pattern (qatal דָּבַק), reveals its stative origins in pausal forms (e.g., דָּבֵק; 2 Kgs 3:3) and in its parallel verbal adjective, דָּבֵק, rather than a participle (WO §22.3k; JM §41b, c). ביהוה אלהיכם is oblique complement of √דבק. Whether the whole phrase is an appositional NP, with the substantival use of the adjective, or the ה in הדבקים introduces a **null-copula** relative clause (cf. on 1:30), is not certain. הדבקים cannot be an attributive adjective, because these do not modify personal pronouns.

כֻּלְּכֶם. Adjunct NP. With rhetorical flourish, the adjunct draws attention to and clarifies the scope of אתם.

הַיּוֹם׃. Adverbial time adjunct NP. For "today," see on 1:10.

4:5 רְאֵ֣ה| לִמַּ֣דְתִּי אֶתְכֶ֗ם חֻקִּים֙ וּמִשְׁפָּטִ֔ים כַּאֲשֶׁ֥ר צִוַּ֖נִי יְהוָ֣ה אֱלֹהָ֑י לַעֲשׂ֣וֹת כֵּ֔ן בְּקֶ֣רֶב הָאָ֔רֶץ אֲשֶׁ֥ר אַתֶּ֛ם בָּאִ֥ים שָׁ֖מָּה לְרִשְׁתָּֽהּ׃

D2. ED. Echoes of 4:1, but here Moses establishes the chain between what Yhwh "commanded" him (comparative clause), what he is now doing ("teaching," ED, performative), and what Israel should "do" in the land to which they are heading.

|רְאֵה. Impv ms Qal √ראה. HD. An interjection. See on 1:8.

לִמַּדְתִּי אֶתְכֶם חֻקִּים וּמִשְׁפָּטִים. Qatal 1cs Piel √למד. ED. This is a performative *qatal*, whereby the action of teaching is performed in the saying of these words (cf. WO §30.5.1d). The teaching is not complete (contrast ESV and NIV's "have taught"), but in process. The **resultative** Piel takes a double accusative (AC §2.3.1e, 3.1.3a; cf. JM §125u).

כַּאֲשֶׁר צִוַּנִי יְהוָה אֱלֹהָי. *Qatal* 3ms Piel √צוה with 1cs pronominal suffix. כאשר often introduces, as here, a comparative clause. After כאשר, there is usually **triggered inversion**, with P–S word order.

לַעֲשׂוֹת כֵּן בְּקֶרֶב הָאָרֶץ אֲשֶׁר אַתֶּם בָּאִים שָׁמָּה לְרִשְׁתָּהּ׃ Inf constr Qal √עשה with ל preposition. Adjunct infinitive construct phrase. כן is a demonstrative adverb (JM §102h), drawing an explicit comparison between what Moses is teaching and what they should do. As Weinfeld (195) notes, כן is awkward. When Piel √למד has one accusative complement, the infinitive construct phrase is a second complement (e.g., 4:1; n.b., the modal *qatal* instead of the infinitive in 5:31), and what the people are being taught to do is the object of the infinitive construct phrase (4:1; 6:1). Where Piel √למד has two accusative complements, as here (also 4:14; 11:19), the infinitive construct phrase follows more loosely, as an adjunct, and has a resumptive adverb (כן) or pronoun (4:14; 11:19) referring to the second accusative complement.

אֲשֶׁר אַתֶּם בָּאִים שָׁמָּה. Ptcp mp Qal √בוא. The participle in Hebrew can indicate a future action that is already in progress (JM §121e). With **null-copula** participial clauses, the unmarked order after אשר is S–P. Restrictive relative clause, with **head** הארץ. שמה is a locative resumptive adverb.

לְרִשְׁתָּהּ׃ Inf constr Qal √ירש with 3fs pronominal suffix (object) with preposition ל. Adjunct infinitive construct phrase, indicating the purpose of crossing. For the form, see on 3:18.

4:6 וּשְׁמַרְתֶּם וַעֲשִׂיתֶם כִּי הִוא חָכְמַתְכֶם וּבִינַתְכֶם
לְעֵינֵי הָעַמִּים אֲשֶׁר יִשְׁמְעוּן אֵת כָּל־הַחֻקִּים
הָאֵלֶּה וְאָמְרוּ רַק עַם־חָכָם וְנָבוֹן הַגּוֹי הַגָּדוֹל הַזֶּה׃

HD. D2. With two modal *qatals* (HD), Moses tells Israel to keep and do what he is teaching them. Their obedience will be their wisdom and understanding (cf. 1:13). The chain established in the previous verse goes one further: the nations will take notice and draw a striking conclusion (D3). Wisdom is particularized as obedience to Torah; Torah has a universal grammar that all will recognize (Robson, 177–78).

וּשְׁמַרְתֶּם וַעֲשִׂיתֶם. *Qatal* (modal, sometimes termed *weqatalti*) 2mp Qal √שמר and √עשה. HD. According to HALOT 1381, √שמר with a second verb means "to do something *carefully*," whether the second verb is coordinated (with ו) or subordinated (with ל + infinitive construct). Although this phenomenon of the first verb functioning adverbially is found (JM §124n), in the case of שמר√ and עשׂה√, it is more likely that שמר√ functions as an independent verb (Muraoka and Malessa; JM §124n n. 24), because there are different syntactic combinations that occur without difference in meaning, some of which have שמר√ followed by an accusative complement (e.g., 19:9; 29:8; cf. 1 Kgs 6:12). Here both verbs have covert accusative complements. The modal *qatal* in Deuteronomy is often used to convey a volitional force after narrative discourse (cf. WO §32.2.3d).

כִּי הִוא חָכְמַתְכֶם וּבִינַתְכֶם לְעֵינֵי הָעַמִּים. **Null-copula** explanatory clause with conjoined substantival predicate, חכמתכם ובינתכם. For the form הוא, see on 1:9. The antecedent is an implicit noun, the act of keeping and doing in the opening two verbs (cf. Num 14:41; GKC §135p; WO §16.3.1a).

לְעֵינֵי הָעַמִּים. Adjunct PP.

אֲשֶׁר יִשְׁמְעוּן אֵת כָּל־הַחֻקִּים הָאֵלֶּה. *Yiqtol* 3mp Qal שמע√ with a **paragogic** ן (see on 1:17). Non-restrictive relative clause giving further, but not essential, information about the **head**, העמים.

וְאָמְרוּ. *Qatal* (modal, sometimes termed *weqataltí*) 3cp Qal אמר√, carrying on the modality the previous *yiqtol*. The reported speech is the complement of the verb.

רַק עַם־חָכָם וְנָבוֹן הַגּוֹי הַגָּדוֹל הַזֶּה. **Null-copula** clause, the complement of ואמרו. With two substantives in a **null-copula** clause, the subject is the more definite (cf. Dyk and Talstra, 178–82; Lowery), here הגוי הגדול הזה (for the order of the attributive adjective chain, see AC §2.5.2 and on 1:19). The substantival predicate is indefinite, עם־חכם ונבון. נבון is ptcp ms Niph בין√, functioning adjectivally, meaning here "discerning," "understanding" (cf. on 1:13). Both adjectives (חכם ונבון) pick up on the substantival predicates of the **null-copula** explanatory clause in 6a, חכמתכם ובינתכם. The P–S word order indicates that the P is fronted for **focus**. Of all the possible descriptions of "this great nation" that the other peoples could have, the one they arrive at because of Israel's obedience to what Moses is commanding them is "wise and discerning." רק, as a restrictive adverb, has an emphatic or asseverative effect when the situation qualified is not described (WO §39.3.5c; hence AC §4.2.15b, "surely"): "This great nation is [nothing] *but* a wise and discerning people" (cf. Weinfeld, 195).

4:7 כִּ֚י מִי־ג֣וֹי גָּד֔וֹל אֲשֶׁר־ל֥וֹ אֱלֹהִ֖ים קְרֹבִ֣ים אֵלָ֑יו
כַּיהוָ֣ה אֱלֹהֵ֔ינוּ בְּכָל־קָרְאֵ֖נוּ אֵלָֽיו׃

D2. ID (ED). Moses gives the reason why the nations will come to their conclusion with an explanatory clause that contains two identically structured rhetorical questions (vv. 7-8). Each has a relative clause outlining the privilege that all other great nations lack, followed by a comparative phrase and a further statement connecting with Israel's present experience. The presupposition is that Israel is already a great nation; the question is in what way is Israel great (cp. NIV).

כִּ֚י מִי־ג֣וֹי גָּד֔וֹל אֲשֶׁר־ל֥וֹ אֱלֹהִ֖ים קְרֹבִ֣ים אֵלָ֑יו. Explanatory clause. ID. The clause is **null-copula**. The predicate is, effectively, the **null-head** with the subsequent relative clause (see below). Although in English the appropriate gloss is "*what* great nation," in Hebrew the personal dimension of the people explains מי rather than מה as the interrogative (WO §18.2d; JM §144a, b).

אֲשֶׁר־ל֥וֹ אֱלֹהִ֖ים קְרֹבִ֣ים אֵלָ֑יו. **Null-head** relative clause, functioning as the predicate of the question: "What great nation is Ø, who to him (i.e., which has). . . ."; לו is PP indicating possession. When אלהים has a plural adjective or predicate, one of three possible referents is in view: (1) "gods," where the plural is numerical (e.g., 6:14); (2) "a god," where the designation is a non-Israelite deity (e.g., 1 Kgs 11:33); or (3) God, that is, Yhwh. Although normally אלהים, as a plural of majesty, takes singular adjectives and predicates when referring to a singular deity, the presence of the plural does not demand that the referent is plural here. Sometimes the referent is clearly singular, yet the participle or adjective is plural (e.g., Josh 24:19; 1 Sam 17:26). See JM §136d, §148a, §150f; Tigay 1996: 352 n. 32. Since the contrast is being made with Yhwh, here the referent must be either (1) (or 2). In favor of the singular is the comparison being drawn (Tigay 1996: 45); the plural adjective avoids association with Israel's God. אליו is adjunct PP, going closely with קרבים.

כַּיהוָ֣ה אֱלֹהֵ֔ינוּ. Comparative adjunct PP; possibly a predicate is implicit, "is near to us"; but only rarely does the preposition כ have the force of a comparative conjunction (JM §174d).

בְּכָל־קָרְאֵנוּ אֵלָיו. Inf constr Qal √קרא with 1cp pronominal suffix. Temporal adjunct construct PP. As a verbal noun (or **gerund**), the infinitive construct here is the genitive or *nomen regens* in a construct chain; the 1cp suffix functions as the subject of the verbal noun, "our calling"; it is unusual to have כל followed by an infinitive construct (cf. 1 Kgs 8:52). אליו is oblique complement of קראנו.

4:8 וּמִי גּוֹי גָּדוֹל אֲשֶׁר־לוֹ חֻקִּים וּמִשְׁפָּטִים צַדִּיקִם
כְּכֹל הַתּוֹרָה הַזֹּאת אֲשֶׁר אָנֹכִי נֹתֵן לִפְנֵיכֶם הַיּוֹם׃

See on 4:7.

וּמִי גּוֹי גָּדוֹל אֲשֶׁר־לוֹ חֻקִּים וּמִשְׁפָּטִים צַדִּיקִם. For the syntax, see on v. 7. According to GKC §128p, צדיקם is the only instance of צדיק being used of an impersonal object. Other instances are expressed by **periphrasis** with צֶדֶק or צְדָקָה.

כְּכֹל הַתּוֹרָה הַזֹּאת. Comparative adjunct PP; see on v. 7. An implicit predicate would be ". . . is righteous."

אֲשֶׁר אָנֹכִי נֹתֵן לִפְנֵיכֶם הַיּוֹם׃. Ptcp ms Qal √נתן. Restrictive relative clause, with **head** התורה הזאת. Yhwh does not just set the land before them as a gift, but also the statutes and commandments (cf. 1:8). Unmarked S–P word order (see on 1:20). For אנכי, see on 4:1. היום is adverbial time adjunct NP. For "today," see on 1:10.

Be careful of amnesia (4:9-14)

The first of three sections begun by Niph √שמר, followed by פן (vv. 9, 15, 23). Moses makes two critical points in this section. Both are rooted in his addressees' experience. First, sight is important: what "Israel 'saw' and 'experienced' was in fact the immediacy and primacy of Yhwh's revelation in word" (Robson, 123; cf. Geller 1994; Carasik 1999: 261). Second, *who* heard *what* is important: at Horeb, Yhwh told them all the decalogue (v. 13), but he commanded Moses to teach them statutes and commandments (v. 14), something Moses is in the process of doing in Deuteronomy's speeches. Together they establish *from their experience* the importance of Moses' words in the plains of Moab.

⁹*Only be on your guard and watch yourself closely lest you forget the things which your eyes saw, and lest they turn aside from your heart all the days of your life, but you should make them known to your children and to*

your children's children—*¹⁰the day when you stood before Yhwh your God at Horeb, when Yhwh said to me, "Gather for me the people that I may let them hear my words, which they should learn, so as to fear me all the days which they are alive in the land, and which they should teach their children." ¹¹You drew near and stood beneath the mountain—the mountain was burning with fire to the heart of the heavens, with darkness, cloud and thick darkness—¹²and Yhwh spoke to you from the midst of the fire—you heard the sounds of words, but you did not see a form, except for a voice—¹³and he told you his covenant which he commanded you to do, the ten words, and he wrote them on two stone tablets. ¹⁴But Yhwh commanded me at that time to teach you statutes and judgments, for you to do them in the land to where you are crossing, to possess.*

4:9 רַ֡ק הִשָּׁ֣מֶר לְךָ֩ וּשְׁמֹ֨ר נַפְשְׁךָ֜ מְאֹ֗ד פֶּן־תִּשְׁכַּ֣ח אֶת־הַדְּבָרִ֗ים אֲשֶׁר־רָא֣וּ עֵינֶיךָ֮ וּפֶן־יָס֣וּרוּ מִלְּבָבְךָ֒ כֹּ֖ל יְמֵ֣י חַיֶּ֑יךָ וְהוֹדַעְתָּ֥ם לְבָנֶ֖יךָ וְלִבְנֵ֥י בָנֶֽיךָ׃

D2. HD. Two tautologous imperatives are then followed by two negative final clauses introduced by פֶּן, outlining what they should guard against. The last clause says positively what should happen to "the words (things)" they "saw." Characteristic of the chapter, they are to pass it on to subsequent generations.

רַ֡ק הִשָּׁ֣מֶר לְךָ֩. Impv ms Niph √שמר. HD. When followed by the tone syllable (לְךָ counted as monosyllabic), the accent is shifted back. The final syllable, closed and unaccented, takes *segol* not *tsere* (GKC §51n). רק is a restrictive adverb whose sense depends on what precedes. If the previous clause(s) are negative, then the best translation is "but, except," while if the previous clause(s) are positive, then the best translation is "only." Here, it picks up all that precedes, and, according to WO §39.3.5c, is best translated, "Only [the most important thing is / the upshot is], take heed." לְךָ is a reflexive adjunct PP (cf. on 1:7). The reflexive Niphal goes with a reflexive preposition, yielding the doubly reflexive construction, "Guard yourself for yourself" (as WO §23.4c translate it). The reflexive pronoun is often found with Niphal imperative √שמר, "in order to give emphasis to the significance of the occurrence in question for a particular subject" (GKC §119s).

וּשְׁמֹר נַפְשְׁךָ מְאֹד. Impv ms Qal √שמר. HD. The reflexive opening clause is followed by an active and transitive repetition of the same root. נפשך is accusative complement; נפש, "throat," "neck," is often used as a metonymy for the whole person. מאד is used as an adverbial adjunct, intensifying the force of the verbal idea (AC §4.2.12).

פֶּן־תִּשְׁכַּח אֶת־הַדְּבָרִים אֲשֶׁר־רָאוּ עֵינֶיךָ. *Yiqtol* (modal) 2ms Qal √שכח. פן introduces a negative purpose clause and is followed by a *yiqtol*. It serves "to indicate a negative wish of a speaker or speakers . . . 'I (or: we) do not wish the following to be, become or have become a reality'" (JM §168g).

אֲשֶׁר־רָאוּ עֵינֶיךָ. *Qatal* 3cp Qal √ראה. Restrictive relative clause with **head** הדברים.

וּפֶן־יָסוּרוּ מִלְּבָבְךָ כֹּל יְמֵי חַיֶּיךָ. *Yiqtol* 3mp Qal √סור. The subject is covert, but from the context the **discourse active** topic is הדברים. מלבבך is adjunct PP. The "heart" (i.e., "mind," "will") is critical for Deuteronomy (cf. 4:29; 5:29; 6:5; 7:17; 8:2; 8:17; 9:4-5). כל ימי חייך is temporal adjunct construct NP. It is an indirect or adverbial accusative (i.e., not the object of the verb), giving a length of time (cf. GKC §118k; JM §126i; WO §10.2.2c).

וְהוֹדַעְתָּם לְבָנֶיךָ וְלִבְנֵי בָנֶיךָ: *Qatal* (modal, sometimes termed *weqatalti*) 2ms Hiph √ידע with 3mp pronominal suffix. לבניך ולבני בניך is oblique complement.

4:10 יוֹם אֲשֶׁר עָמַדְתָּ לִפְנֵי יְהוָה אֱלֹהֶיךָ בְּחֹרֵב בֶּאֱמֹר יְהוָה אֵלַי הַקְהֶל־לִי אֶת־הָעָם וְאַשְׁמִעֵם אֶת־דְּבָרָי אֲשֶׁר יִלְמְדוּן לְיִרְאָה אֹתִי כָּל־הַיָּמִים אֲשֶׁר הֵם חַיִּים עַל־הָאֲדָמָה וְאֶת־בְּנֵיהֶם יְלַמֵּדוּן:

HD (*cont*). D2. The whole verse is in apposition to את־הדברים אשר ראו עיניך in v. 9 and a "temporal modifier" for the main clauses in the following four verses (Holmstedt 2002: 300). Moses reminds them of Yhwh's words Horeb (D3) and in doing so articulates a theology redolent of synagogue and church: "assemble the people . . . that I may let them hear my words, which they should learn, so as to revere . . . and which they should teach their children." An imperative is followed by an indirect cohortative (HD), with two relative clauses continuing to outline their obligations. The gathering is to hear Yhwh's words.

יוֹם אֲשֶׁר עָמַדְתָּ לִפְנֵי יְהוָה אֱלֹהֶיךָ בְּחֹרֵב. *Qatal* 2ms Qal √עמד. יוֹם, appositional to את־הדברים (v. 9) is the **head** of the following restrictive relative clause. לפני יהוה אלהיך and בחרב are spatial adjunct PPs.

בֶּאֱמֹר יְהוָה אֵלַי. Inf constr Qal √אמר with preposition ב. Temporal adjunct PP. As a *verbal* noun, the infinitive construct takes a subject, יהוה, an oblique complement, אלי, and an accusative complement, which is the reported speech that follows.

הַקְהֶל־לִי אֶת־הָעָם. Impv ms Hiph √קהל. לי is not a spatial adjunct PP, "to/before me" (NIV, ESV, NASV), but a "dative of advantage" giving the beneficiary of the action of the verb (cf. JM §133d; GKC §119s). The place of gathering is introduced by אל not by ל (e.g., Lev 8:3).

וְאַשְׁמִעֵם אֶת־דְּבָרָי אֲשֶׁר יִלְמְדוּן לְיִרְאָה אֹתִי כָּל־הַיָּמִים אֲשֶׁר הֵם חַיִּים עַל־הָאֲדָמָה. *Yiqtol* (modal) 1cs Hiph √שמע with 3mp pronominal suffix. It is an indirect cohortative after the previous imperative, expressing purpose (cf. JM §116a, b; WO §34.6a). The clauses are syntactically coordinate, but semantically the second is subordinate. Rather than "assemble . . . *and* I *will* let them hear" (cf. NRSV) it is "assemble . . . *that* I *may* let them hear."

אֲשֶׁר יִלְמְדוּן. *Yiqtol* (modal) 3mp Qal √למד with a **paragogic** ן (see on 1:17). Many grammarians note that the relative אשר sometimes indicates purpose (GKC §165b; MNK §40.6.4) and propose that it must be purpose here (so AC §5.2.3a; WO §38.3b; JM §168f). This would make ליראה אתי the infinitive phrase complement of ילמדון (cf. 14:23; 17:19; 31:13; also LXX, ὅπως μάθωσιν). However, Holmstedt (2002: 293–307) doubts, on the grounds of economy, whether אשר ever introduces a purpose clause. Although overstated (see on 4:40 below), the basic point is well made. If there is a way of taking it as a relative or a **complementizer**, it should be taken. Here, it *is* possible to regard the clause as a relative clause with **head** דברי, if ליראה אתי is taken as an infinitive phrase adjunct, expressing purpose (cf. Holmstedt 2006: 19). An argument in favor of this construal is that this ensures that the final verb of the verse, יְלַמְּדוּן, has two accusative complements (see below). Elsewhere in Deuteronomy, √למד Piel always has two accusatives or an accusative and an infinitive phrase complement (e.g., vv. 1, 5, 14). The verb has a modal force, "should," arising from the HD discourse context.

Deuteronomy 4:10-11

לְיִרְאָה אֹתִי. Inf constr Qal √ירא with preposition לְ. The phrase is an infinitive phrase adjunct of ילמדון, expressing purpose. Some verbs, almost always stative, have an infinitive construct Qal ending in ־ה (JM §49d). As a verbal noun, the infinitive construct retains the verbal power to govern an object, אתי (GKC §114d; WO §36.3.1a).

כָּל־הַיָּמִים אֲשֶׁר הֵם חַיִּים עַל־הָאֲדָמָה. Adverbial temporal adjunct NP, כל־הימים, acting as **head** of restrictive relative **null-copula** clause. חיים is the adjectival predicate of the **null-copula** clause. This is the unmarked S–P word order in **null-copula** clauses, even after אשר (cf. on 1:20). על־האדמה is spatial adjunct PP.

וְאֶת־בְּנֵיהֶם יְלַמֵּדוּן׃. Yiqtol (modal) 3mp Piel √למד with **paragogic** ן (see on 1:17). "In pause, the preceding vowel is retained and occasionally given secondary lengthening" (as here) (JM §44e). Given the discourse context, the verb is still modal, expressing obligation. את־בניהם is accusative complement, fronted for **focus**. The other accusative complement is אשר (for דברי, the **head** of the following relative clause; see comment above).

4:11 וַתִּקְרְבוּן וַתַּעַמְדוּן תַּחַת הָהָר וְהָהָר בֹּעֵר בָּאֵשׁ עַד־לֵב הַשָּׁמַיִם חֹשֶׁךְ עָנָן וַעֲרָפֶל׃

ND. D2. Within the exhortation not to forget (v. 9; HD) and the temporal setting established in v. 10, Moses recounts the events at Horeb with two *wayyiqtols* (v. 11a). These are followed by a circumstantial clause, giving vivid additional pictorial information (v. 11b).

וַתִּקְרְבוּן וַתַּעַמְדוּן תַּחַת הָהָר. *Wayyiqtol* 3mp Qal √קרב and √עמד both with **paragogic** ן (see on 1:17). תחת ההר is spatial adjunct PP.

וְהָהָר בֹּעֵר בָּאֵשׁ עַד־לֵב הַשָּׁמַיִם חֹשֶׁךְ עָנָן וַעֲרָפֶל׃. Ptcp ms Qal √בער. **Null-copula** circumstantial clause. The disjunctive S–P **null-copula** participial clause indicates a durative action alongside the action of the main verb (cf. JM §159a, d; WS §494). The fact that it follows the *wayyiqtol* indicates it is "pure circumstance" (JM §166h). באש is adjunct PP.

עַד־לֵב הַשָּׁמַיִם. Spatial adjunct construct PP. לב is used metaphorically, for the "middle."

חֹשֶׁךְ עָנָן וַעֲרָפֶל׃. Three nouns syntactically unrelated to the clause proper. They form an accusative of manner, " used . . . in order to describe more precisely the manner in which an action or state takes place" (GKC §118 m, q). In a series of nouns, the use of ו is "variable" (JM §177o). עֲרָפֶל is "thick darkness"; the three nouns also occur in 5:22.

4:12 וַיְדַבֵּ֨ר יְהוָ֤ה אֲלֵיכֶם֙ מִתּ֣וֹךְ הָאֵ֔שׁ ק֣וֹל דְּבָרִ֖ים אַתֶּ֣ם שֹׁמְעִ֔ים וּתְמוּנָ֛ה אֵינְכֶ֥ם רֹאִ֖ים זוּלָתִ֥י קֽוֹל׃

D2. Yhwh's speaking (v. 12a, ND) is explained by two syntactically similar but semantically contrasting **null-copula** participial clauses that are introduced asyndetically (ED). The **focus**-fronting contrasts what was heard and what was seen. The final exception with rhetorical flourish insists that "you . . . were seeing a voice."

וַיְדַבֵּ֨ר יְהוָ֤ה אֲלֵיכֶם֙ מִתּ֣וֹךְ הָאֵ֔שׁ. *Wayyiqtol* 3ms Piel √דבר. ND. מתוך האש is adjunct construct PP.

ק֣וֹל דְּבָרִ֖ים אַתֶּ֣ם שֹׁמְעִ֔ים. Ptcp mp Qal √שמע. **Null-copula** participial clause. ED. The **asyndesis** suggests this clause explains further the event of Yhwh speaking (cf. JM §177a). The participles here and in the following clause give a "very dramatic" (Craigie, 134) durative force, hard to capture in English: lit. "a sound of words you were hearing. . . ." קול דברים, the accusative complement construct NP of שמעים, is fronted for **focus**.

וּתְמוּנָ֛ה אֵינְכֶ֥ם רֹאִ֖ים זוּלָתִ֥י קֽוֹל׃. Ptcp mp Qal √ראה. **Null-copula** participial clause, coordinated with the previous explanatory clause. ED. תמונה, the accusative complement, is fronted for **focus**. It is a "form," or "manifestation," which cannot itself be manufactured, but is rather what an image is shaped to resemble (Weinfeld, 289; Tigay 1996: 352 nn. 42, 55). אין is used here "to negate the veracity of a statement expressed with a nominal clause" (JM §160g). For more on this adverb of nonexistence and the pronominal suffix functioning as the subject, see on 1:32.

זוּלָתִ֥י קֽוֹל׃. זולתי introduces an exception after a negation. For the **paragogic** ־ִי, see JM §93q. Since אין serves here to negate a nominal clause, "you were seeing a form" becomes "you were not seeing a form—except a voice." This notion of "seeing a voice," missed by many commentators and English versions, does not reify "voice," but is part of a dramatic rhetorical flourish. Two observations favor rendering the phrase as an extension of the accusative complement of ראים: the notion of seeing words is already present in v. 9; there is parallel syntax in 1 Kgs 3:18, where there is a more extended nominal/verbless clause with אין followed by זולה.

Deuteronomy 4:13-14

4:13 וַיַּגֵּ֣ד לָכֶ֗ם אֶת־בְּרִיתוֹ֙ אֲשֶׁ֨ר צִוָּ֤ה אֶתְכֶם֙ לַעֲשׂ֔וֹת עֲשֶׂ֖רֶת הַדְּבָרִ֑ים וַֽיִּכְתְּבֵ֔ם עַל־שְׁנֵ֖י לֻח֥וֹת אֲבָנִֽים׃

ND. D2. Moses continues to recount the events at Horeb with two *wayyiqtols* (see the comment on v. 11). Yhwh told the people the decalogue and wrote them down on stone tablets.

וַיַּגֵּ֣ד לָכֶ֗ם אֶת־בְּרִיתוֹ֙ אֲשֶׁ֨ר צִוָּ֤ה אֶתְכֶם֙ לַעֲשׂ֔וֹת עֲשֶׂ֖רֶת הַדְּבָרִ֑ים. *Wayyiqtol* 3ms Hiph √נגד. ND. The verb √נגד Hiphil is a three-place predicate. לכם is oblique complement; את־בריתו is accusative complement. The subject is covert.

אֲשֶׁ֨ר צִוָּ֤ה אֶתְכֶם֙ לַעֲשׂ֔וֹת. *Qatal* 3ms Piel √צוה. Restrictive relative clause, with **head** בריתו. לעשות is an infinitive phrase complement (inf constr Qal √עשה with preposition ל). As a three-place predicate, √צוה is followed by two complements, here an accusative complement, indicating the recipients of Moses' command (אתכם) and an infinitive phrase complement (לעשות).

עֲשֶׂ֖רֶת הַדְּבָרִ֑ים. NP, appositional to the accusative complement, בריתו. For the feminine form of the collective substantive with the masculine noun, see JM §100d. For the syntax, see on 3:8.

וַֽיִּכְתְּבֵ֔ם עַל־שְׁנֵ֖י לֻח֥וֹת אֲבָנִֽים׃. *Wayyiqtol* 3ms Qal √כתב with 3mp pronominal suffix. ND. על־שני לחות אבנים is adjunct construct PP. This construct chain is a type of adjectival genitive, where the absolute indicates the material of which the construct is made (cf. WO §9.5.3d). When the compound idea in a construct chain is plural, sometimes the absolute is singular (e.g., בני־חיל, 3:18), sometimes the construct is singular (e.g., בית־אבות, Exod 6:14) and sometimes, as here, both nouns are plural (לחות, אבנים; cf. GKC §124q; JM §136o). For the syntax with the numeral two, see on 3:8.

4:14 וְאֹתִ֞י צִוָּ֤ה יְהוָה֙ בָּעֵ֣ת הַהִ֔וא לְלַמֵּ֣ד אֶתְכֶ֔ם חֻקִּ֖ים וּמִשְׁפָּטִ֑ים לַעֲשֹׂתְכֶ֣ם אֹתָ֔ם בָּאָ֕רֶץ אֲשֶׁ֥ר אַתֶּ֛ם עֹבְרִ֥ים שָׁ֖מָּה לְרִשְׁתָּֽהּ׃

ND. D2. Moses continues to recount the events at Horeb with a *qatal* in a disjunctive clause (see the comment on v. 11). In contrast to the declaring of the ten words to everyone (v. 13), Yhwh commanded Moses to teach the statutes and commandments, something that Moses is in the process of doing in the speeches in Deuteronomy.

וְאֹתִ֞י צִוָּ֤ה יְהוָה֙ בָּעֵ֣ת הַהִ֔וא. *Qatal* 3ms Piel √צוה. ND. אתי is accusative complement, fronted for **focus**, giving a contrast between Yhwh telling Israel (v. 13) and Yhwh commanding Moses.

בָּעֵת הַהִוא. Temporal adjunct PP. See on 1:9.

לְלַמֵּ֣ד אֶתְכֶ֔ם חֻקִּ֖ים וּמִשְׁפָּטִ֑ים. Inf constr Piel √למד with preposition ל. Infinitive phrase complement. The **resultative** Piel takes a double accusative (AC §2.3.1e, 3.1.3a; cf. JM §125u).

לַעֲשֹׂתְכֶ֣ם אֹתָ֔ם בָּאָ֕רֶץ אֲשֶׁ֥ר אַתֶּ֛ם עֹבְרִ֥ים שָׁ֖מָּה לְרִשְׁתָּֽהּ. Inf constr Qal √עשה with preposition ל and with 2mp pronominal suffix. The suffix is the subject of the infinitive construct. Adjunct infinitive construct phrase (see on 4:5). אתם is the accusative complement. בארץ is adjunct PP, **head** of the following restrictive relative clause.

אֲשֶׁ֥ר אַתֶּ֛ם עֹבְרִ֥ים שָׁ֖מָּה. Ptcp mp Qal √עבר. Restrictive relative clause. Apart from עברים instead of באים, the same wording as 4:5. See comments there.

לְרִשְׁתָּֽהּ. See on 3:18.

Be careful of idols (4:15-22)

In 4:9-14, Moses urged the Israelites not to forget what they had seen, but to teach their children: they had seen the immediacy of Yhwh's word and the primacy of that word for subsequent generations. Now, because the Israelites did not see a form, only a voice (v. 12), Moses warns them against making visual representations. If it is appropriate for the nations, it is not for those whom Yhwh rescued from Egypt and made his people. The warning is all the more urgent since they will be crossing without Moses.

[15]*So watch yourselves very closely, since you did not see any form on the day Yhwh spoke to you at Horeb from the midst of the fire,* [16]*lest you act corruptly and make for yourselves an idol, a form of any figure, a representation of a male or female,* [17]*a representation of any animal that is on the earth, a representation of any winged bird that flies in the heavens,* [18]*a representation of anything that creeps on the ground, a representation of any fish that is in the waters beneath the earth,* [19]*and lest you lift your eyes to the heavens and see the sun and the moon and the stars—all the host of heaven—and let*

yourself be led astray and bow down to them and serve them, which Yhwh your God allotted to all the peoples under all the heavens. [20]But Yhwh took you and brought you out from the iron furnace, from Egypt, to become for him a people of his own inheritance, as [is the case] this day. [21]But Yhwh was angry with me because of your words, and he swore that I would not cross the Jordan and would not come into the good land which Yhwh your God is giving to you as an inheritance; [22] for I am about to die in this land—I am not crossing the Jordan—but you are crossing and you will possess that good land.

4:15 וְנִשְׁמַרְתֶּם מְאֹד לְנַפְשֹׁתֵיכֶם כִּי לֹא רְאִיתֶם
כָּל־תְּמוּנָה בְּיוֹם דִּבֶּר יְהוָה אֲלֵיכֶם בְּחֹרֵב מִתּוֹךְ
הָאֵשׁ׃

The main clause (HD, v. 15a) is rooted in the previous narrative and in the subsequent explanatory clause that further grounds the call for care (v. 15b). D2.

וְנִשְׁמַרְתֶּם מְאֹד לְנַפְשֹׁתֵיכֶם. *Qatal* (modal, sometimes termed *weqataltí*) 2mp Niph √שמר. HD. The modal *qatal* in Deuteronomy is often used to convey a volitional force after narrative discourse (cf. WO §32.2.3d). This opening clause comprises a blend of the first two clauses of v. 9. Along with the 9aβ, שמר is followed by מאד and נפש. But, along with 9aα, it is Niphal here, hence followed by an adjunct PP, לנפשתיכם, corresponding to the reflexive לך in v. 9; see further on v. 9. The subsequent negative final clauses start in vv. 16 and 19.

כִּי לֹא רְאִיתֶם כָּל־תְּמוּנָה. *Qatal* 2mp Qal √ראה. Explanatory clause. כל־תמונה is the accusative complement. When כל is found with לא, there is potential ambiguity (JM §160k): "not any" (e.g., Gen 9:11) or "not every" (e.g., Gen 3:1). Here, clearly it is "not . . . any."

בְּיוֹם דִּבֶּר יְהוָה אֲלֵיכֶם בְּחֹרֵב מִתּוֹךְ הָאֵשׁ׃. *Qatal* 3ms Piel √דבר. Not an anomalously pointed infinitive construct (so Qimḥi), but Piel *qatal* (GKC §52o). For the form with *segol*, see on 1:1. For the construct governing an otherwise independent sentence, and for ביום in particular, see GKC §130d. The noun clause has a genitival function, as absolute or *nomen regens*. בחרב and מתוך האש are adjunct PPs.

4:16 פֶּן־תַּשְׁחִתוּן וַעֲשִׂיתֶם לָכֶם פֶּסֶל תְּמוּנַת כָּל־סָמֶל
תַּבְנִית זָכָר אוֹ נְקֵבָה׃

HD. D2. The negative final clause introduced by פן + modal *yiqtol* is then followed by a modal *qatal*. The initial adverbial Hiphil speaks of "acting corruptly." The subsequent clause proclaims the corrupt action. The accusative complement, פסל, is then followed by two appositional construct NPs. The many words for forms and images are indicative of the strong stance against visual representations, a stance rooted in their experience at Horeb.

פֶּן־תַּשְׁחִתוּן. *Yiqtol* (modal) 2mp Hiph √שחת with **paragogic** ן (see on 1:17). פן is a subordinating conjunction following from the warning of v. 15. It introduces a negative final clause, articulating the unwanted action (cf. on 4:9). The Hiphil can be, as here, intransitive and give the "mode of action," an "adverbial hiphil" (JM §54d).

וַעֲשִׂיתֶם לָכֶם פֶּסֶל תְּמוּנַת כָּל־סָמֶל תַּבְנִית זָכָר אוֹ נְקֵבָה׃. *Qatal* (modal, sometimes termed *weqatalti*) 2mp Qal √עשה. The continuation of the negative final clause, introduced by פן, with a modal *qatal* (for which, see GKC §112p; JM §168h) suggests that this constitutes the acting corruptly (√שחת). The repetition of פן in v. 19 reinforces this, indicating that there are two main actions that they should avoid. This demonstrates that *weqatalti* is not essentially consecutive or sequential, whether temporally or logically.

לָכֶם. Adjunct PP. ל introduces here what is sometimes called "the dative of advantage" giving the beneficiaries of the action of the verb (GKC §119q-s; JM §133d; WO §11.2.10d; WHS §271a).

פֶּסֶל תְּמוּנַת כָּל־סָמֶל. There are four words פסל, תמונה, סמל, and תבנית that together are used to condemn the construction of visible images in the worship of Yhwh. According to MT accentuation, the construct NP תמונת כל־סמל is in apposition to פסל (n.b., the disjunctive accent, *tiphah*, פֶּסֶל). פסל is an "idol"; this is then modified: "a form of any figure" (cf. vv. 23, 25; 5:8). While תמונה cannot strictly be manufactured (see on v. 12), the apposition here serves to connect the object made and the "form" on which it was modelled, with a certain "inexactness of language" (Driver, 84).

תַּבְנִית זָכָר אוֹ נְקֵבָה׃. A further appositional construct NP. תבנית is "copy" or "reproduction."

4:17 תַּבְנִית כָּל־בְּהֵמָה אֲשֶׁר בָּאָרֶץ תַּבְנִית כָּל־צִפּוֹר
כָּנָף אֲשֶׁר תָּעוּף בַּשָּׁמָיִם:

H2 (*cont.*). D2. There is no main verb here; the verse consists of two further construct phrases in apposition to פסל.

תַּבְנִית כָּל־בְּהֵמָה אֲשֶׁר בָּאָרֶץ. Appositional construct phrase (to פסל), with **null-copula** restrictive relative clause, **head** בהמה. בארץ is PP complement.

תַּבְנִית כָּל־צִפּוֹר כָּנָף אֲשֶׁר תָּעוּף בַּשָּׁמָיִם:. Appositional construct phrase (to פסל), with restrictive relative clause, **head** צפור. כל־צפור כנף is an attributive adjectival genitive, where the absolute indicates by what the construct is characterized (cf. WO §9.5.3a, k). Although tautologous, the phrase does occur elsewhere (Ps 148:10; cf. Ezek 17:23). תעוף is *yiqtol* 3fs Qal √עוף. The *yiqtol* is used for what is generally the case, "fly" (cf. WO §31.3e).

4:18 תַּבְנִית כָּל־רֹמֵשׂ בָּאֲדָמָה תַּבְנִית כָּל־דָּגָה
אֲשֶׁר־בַּמַּיִם מִתַּחַת לָאָרֶץ:

H2 (*cont.*). D2. There is no main verb here; the verse consists of two further construct phrases in apposition to פסל. The order reverses that of Genesis (Fishbane, 321–22). Idolatry and decreation belong together.

תַּבְנִית כָּל־רֹמֵשׂ בָּאֲדָמָה. Appositional construct phrase (to פסל). The absolute, רמשׂ, is ptcp ms Qal √רמשׂ, used substantively. באדמה is adjunct PP, going closely with רמש.

תַּבְנִית כָּל־דָּגָה אֲשֶׁר־בַּמַּיִם מִתַּחַת לָאָרֶץ:. Appositional construct phrase (to פסל), with **null-copula** restrictive relative clause, **head** דגה. במים is PP complement. The form מתחת can be either a compound preposition, "from under" (e.g., 7:24; Prov 22:27) or an adverb, with the preposition מן joined to the substantive, תחת, "below" (e.g., 4:39). With the addition of ל, the phrase becomes a (compound) preposition, "beneath"; sometimes ל is omitted (GKC §119c).

וּפֶן־תִּשָּׂא עֵינֶיךָ הַשָּׁמַיְמָה וְֽרָאִיתָ אֶת־הַשֶּׁמֶשׁ 4:19
וְֽאֶת־הַיָּרֵחַ וְאֶת־הַכּֽוֹכָבִים כֹּל צְבָא הַשָּׁמַיִם וְנִדַּחְתָּ
וְהִשְׁתַּחֲוִיתָ לָהֶם וַעֲבַדְתָּם אֲשֶׁר חָלַק יְהוָה אֱלֹהֶיךָ
אֹתָם לְכֹל הָעַמִּים תַּחַת כָּל־הַשָּׁמָיִם׃

HD (*cont.*). D2. A second negative final clause introduced by פֶּן + *yiqtol* is then followed by four modal *qatals*, giving the anticipated chain of degeneration. The warning is grounded in the final relative clause. These heavenly bodies were allotted to all other peoples, not to Israel. What starts innocently enough ends with idolatry like the other nations.

וּפֶן־תִּשָּׂא עֵינֶיךָ הַשָּׁמַיְמָה. *Yiqtol* (modal) 2ms Qal √נשׂא. פֶּן is a subordinating conjunction following from the warning of v. 15. It introduces a (second) negative final clause, articulating the unwanted action (cf. on 4:9). JM §168h observes, "Where פֶּן extends its force to a second juxtaposed verb, the first clause can be logically subordinate (temporal or conditional) . . . '*lest, lifting your eyes to the sky and seeing the sun* etc. . . ., *you are tempted.* . . .'" The problem is not the act of lifting eyes to the sky *per se*, nor indeed what they see, but what they do when they have seen.

הַשָּׁמַיְמָה. Directional adjunct. The locative ה indicates motion toward (WO §10.5a, b; JM §93c).

וְֽרָאִיתָ אֶת־הַשֶּׁמֶשׁ וְֽאֶת־הַיָּרֵחַ וְאֶת־הַכּֽוֹכָבִים כֹּל צְבָא הַשָּׁמַיִם. *Qatal* (modal, sometimes termed *weqataltí*) 2ms Qal √ראה.

אֶת־הַשֶּׁמֶשׁ וְֽאֶת־הַיָּרֵחַ וְאֶת־הַכּֽוֹכָבִים. Conjoined accusative complement NPs of וראית. In a series of nouns or NPs, ו-conjunction may join each item apart from the first, as here (JM §177o).

כֹּל צְבָא הַשָּׁמַיִם. Construct chain NP, appositional to the accusative complement. צבא, only here in chapters 1–11, is often used with השמים in the sense of "heavenly bodies."

וְנִדַּחְתָּ. *Qatal* (modal) 2ms Niph √נדח. This is an instance of the "tolerative" Niphal, which combines "the reflexive notion with the notion of permission" (WO §24.3f). Being "led astray" is something that they have allowed, rather than something inflicted on them (cf. 30:17 and the synonymous phrase in 11:16).

וְהִשְׁתַּחֲוִיתָ לָהֶם. *Qatal* (modal) 2ms Hishtaphel √חוי/חוה. Traditionally this verb was thought to be the Hitpalel from √שחה (e.g.,

GKC §75kk; BDB s.v.). More recently, based on a proposed Ugaritic cognate, most scholars think it is the Hishtaphel from √חוה/ חוי (e.g., Kreuzer; WO §21.2.3d; JM §59g; HALOT s.v.), but not all (e.g., CDCH 455). The verb only occurs in this *binyan*, and it is the only verb in this *binyan*. Both *binyanim* are unusual alternatives to the Hitpael. The meaning is not in dispute, "bow down." להם is adjunct PP.

וַעֲבַדְתָּם. *Qatal* (modal) 2ms Qal √עבד with 3mp pronominal suffix.

אֲשֶׁר חָלַק יְהוָה אֱלֹהֶיךָ אֹתָם לְכֹל הָעַמִּים תַּחַת כָּל־הַשָּׁמָיִם: *Qatal* 3ms Qal √חלק. The verb is a three-place predicate here, "W allotted X to Y." Non-restrictive relative clause. Because the relative clause is separated from the true **head**, את־השמש ... ואת־הכוכבים (as opposed to the pronominal suffix on עבדתם), אתם, the direct object marker with the resumptive pronoun, is added (Weinfeld, 196). לכל העמים is oblique complement of √חלק. תחת כל־השמים is adjunct PP, modifying העמים.

4:20 וְאֶתְכֶם לָקַח יְהוָה וַיּוֹצִא אֶתְכֶם מִכּוּר הַבַּרְזֶל מִמִּצְרָיִם לִהְיוֹת לוֹ לְעַם נַחֲלָה כַּיּוֹם הַזֶּה:

ND. D2. There is "a certain asymmetry" between v. 20 and v. 19. Here, Yhwh has made Israel his own in and through the act of rescue from Egypt. In v. 19, one might have expected Yhwh to have given the nations to the heavenly host. But the reverse is found; the heavenly host is assigned to the peoples (Tigay 1996: 50). Yhwh is not just sovereign, as the agent of √חלק (v. 19) and √לקח (v. 20), but also supreme over the astral bodies that have nothing assigned to them, but are themselves allotted.

וְאֶתְכֶם לָקַח יְהוָה. *Qatal* 3ms Qal √לקח. ND. ואתכם is accusative complement, fronted for **focus**. The contrast is between "you" and "all the [other] peoples."

וַיּוֹצִא אֶתְכֶם מִכּוּר הַבַּרְזֶל מִמִּצְרָיִם. *Wayyiqtol* 3ms Hiph √יצא. ND. Only four out of fifteen instances of ויוצא in the OT have an anomalous *hireq* in the final syllable (GKC §74l; JM §78i). More generally, where an anomalous *hireq* occurs, it almost always is in a III-א verb (JM §54c). מכור הברזל is oblique complement of the three-place predicate √יצא Hiphil. כור, a "furnace," is used elsewhere of a fierce affliction (Isa 48:10) and, with הברזל, of Egypt (1 Kgs 8:51; Jer 11:4). הברזל, the absolute, does not indicate the material from which the furnace is made, but the purpose for which it exists, an objective genitive (cf. JM §129d).

מִמִּצְרָיִם. Appositional PP. The fierce purging spoken of in the oblique complement now has further definition.

לִהְיוֹת לוֹ לְעַם נַחֲלָה כַּיּוֹם הַזֶּה:. Inf constr Qal √היה with preposition ל. √היה often is followed by ל . . . ל. One introduces the beneficiary of the action, the so-called "dative of advantage" (GKC §119s; JM §133d; WO §11.2.10d), here לוֹ. This is a PP adjunct. The other indicates the new role that the subject will take on (cf. MNK §39.11.I.1c; WO §11.2.10d; WHS §278), and is an adverbial PP complement of √היה, here the construct PP לעם נחלה. Usually it is the land that is Israel's נחלה (e.g., 4:21, 38). But here Israel is Yhwh's (cf. 9:26, 29; 32:8-9). The construct NP is an attributive adjectival genitive (cf. 7:6; WO §9.5.3a).

כַּיּוֹם הַזֶּה:. Temporal adjunct PP. See on 2:30.

4:21 וַיהוָה הִתְאַנַּף־בִּי עַל־דִּבְרֵיכֶם וַיִּשָּׁבַע לְבִלְתִּי עָבְרִי
אֶת־הַיַּרְדֵּן וּלְבִלְתִּי־בֹא אֶל־הָאָרֶץ הַטּוֹבָה אֲשֶׁר
יְהוָה אֱלֹהֶיךָ נֹתֵן לְךָ נַחֲלָה:

Having begun the historical retrospect by drawing a contrast between "the peoples" (v. 19) and "you" (v. 20), Moses continues by returning to his own exclusion from the land. A disjunctive clause with *qatal* introduces the contrast; the ND continues with a *wayyiqtol*, followed by two infinitive phrase complements giving the content of what Yhwh swore.

וַיהוָה הִתְאַנַּף־בִּי עַל־דִּבְרֵיכֶם. *Qatal* 3ms Hitp √אנף. Although Codex Leningradensis (M^L) reads הִתְאַנַּף here, this is probably an error and should read, with two other Tiberian Masoretic mss (M^L17 and M^S5), הִתְאַנָּף (*BHQ: Deuteronomy*, 15; cf. 1:37 and comments; 9:20). Disjunctive clause. יהוה is a fronted **topic**. Given that Yhwh was already the **discourse active** topic, an overt subject is indication here that there is a break and a contrast. This event is not sequential to, but happened alongside, the events of v. 20. בי is oblique complement of the verb הִתְאַנַּף. על־דבריכם is adjunct PP, giving the grounds for Yhwh's anger with Moses (cf. 1:37; 3:26).

וַיִּשָּׁבַע. *Wayyiqtol* 3ms Niph √שבע. The consequence of Yhwh's anger.

לְבִלְתִּ֣י עָבְרִ֔י אֶת־הַיַּרְדֵּ֑ן. Inf constr Qal √עבר with 1cs pronominal suffix acting as the subject of the infinitive (WHS §109). לבלתי is the usual way of negating an infinitive construct (JM §124e, §160l). For the **paragogic** (word-extending) -ִי, see JM §93q. The whole is an infinitive phrase complement, indicating what Yhwh swore.

וּלְבִלְתִּי־בֹא֙ אֶל־הָאָ֣רֶץ הַטּוֹבָ֔ה אֲשֶׁר֙ יְהוָ֣ה אֱלֹהֶ֔יךָ נֹתֵ֥ן לְךָ֖ נַחֲלָֽה׃. Inf constr Qal √בוא. The subject of the infinitive is carried forward from the previous clause. See above for comments on לבלתי. אל־הארץ הטובה is oblique complement of בוא, and **head** of the following restrictive relative clause.

אֲשֶׁר֙ יְהוָ֣ה אֱלֹהֶ֔יךָ נֹתֵ֥ן לְךָ֖ נַחֲלָֽה׃. Ptcp ms Qal √נתן. Restrictive relative clause. For the formulaic phrase, see on 1:20. Note that the gift is "to you" (לך), with Moses not entering (cf. on 4:1). נחלה is an indirect accusative (hence indefinite; cf. JM §126c). נתן with two accusatives can have a number of nuances, including "turn" X "into" Y or "make" X Y. Here, it is used of "giving X *as* Y" (cf. 2:5, 9).

4:22 כִּ֣י אָנֹכִ֥י מֵת֙ בָּאָ֣רֶץ הַזֹּ֔את אֵינֶ֥נִּי עֹבֵ֖ר אֶת־הַיַּרְדֵּ֑ן
וְאַתֶּם֙ עֹֽבְרִ֔ים וִֽירִשְׁתֶּ֕ם אֶת־הָאָ֥רֶץ הַטּוֹבָ֖ה הַזֹּֽאת׃

Moses unpacks the previous verse, explaining why he will not cross and why Yhwh is giving the good land to them. PD. D2. The opening כי introduces a **null-copula** participial explanatory clause, giving the imminent future, "I am about to die." An asyndetic **null-copula** participial clause follows, spelling out the implications of Moses' death in an almost parenthetical fashion. The third clause, again **null-copula** participial, continues the explanation of the first clause, while contrasting with it (כי אנכי . . . ואתם . . .). The final clause, with a modal *qatal*, confidently states what will happen when "you cross."

כִּ֣י אָנֹכִ֥י מֵת֙ בָּאָ֣רֶץ הַזֹּ֔את. Ptcp ms Qal √מות. The participle here indicates imminent future action (GKC §116d; cf. 2:4); the "progressive sense" characteristic of the participle remains, but the "prospective sense" is evident from "logical" clues (Cook 2012: 232–33). This is the unmarked S–P word order for a **null-copula** clause, even after a subordinating conjunction. For אנכי, see on 4:1. בארץ הזאת is spatial adjunct PP.

אֵינֶנִּי עֹבֵר אֶת־הַיַּרְדֵּן. Ptcp ms Qal √עבר. אין is an adverb of nonexistence (JM §154k, §160g); see further on 1:32 for its form and function. This clause follows the previous one asyndetically, indicating that it explains and draws out the critical implication of Moses' death.

וְאַתֶּם עֹבְרִים. Ptcp mp Qal √עבר. In contrast with אנכי, Moses declares what אתם will do. **Null-copula** participial clause.

וִירִשְׁתֶּם אֶת־הָאָרֶץ הַטּוֹבָה הַזֹּאת׃. *Qatal* (modal) 2mp Qal √ירש. For the pointing, see on 4:1. The demonstrative for the land they will inherit, זאת, matches the demonstrative pointing to the land where Moses will die. While English says, "this . . . that . . .," Hebrew says "this (זאת) . . . this (זאת)" (cf. JM §143c).

Be careful: The consequences of amnesia and idolatry are devastating, but not final (4:23-31)

What begins as a warning (v. 23; cf. vv. 9, 15) becomes an unfolding narrative of the future (PD). The line between what will and what might be the case is not sharply defined. Perhaps the PD is an **indirect speech act**, formally declaring the future, but pragmatically seeking a response (HD). There are three striking contrasts: (1) between the active, engaged, powerful Yhwh and the gods Israel make and serve; (2) between faithful Yhwh and unfaithful Israel (שכח√, ברית, שחת√); and (3) between judgment and mercy (e.g., v. 23, אל קנא, אש אכלה and v. 31, אל רחום; מצא√ (vv. 29-30); v. 28, שם, and v. 29, משם). Although a return from exile is not explicitly stated, hope rests in Yhwh's mercy and covenant (v. 31), with the demand on Israel for wholehearted searching, repentance and obedience (vv. 29-30).

[23]Watch yourselves lest you forget the covenant of Yhwh your God which he made with you, and make for yourself an idol, the form of anything that Yhwh your God forbade, [24]since Yhwh your God is a consuming fire, a jealous god. [25]When you father children and children's children and grow old in the land, and act corruptly, and make an idol, a form of anything, and do what is evil in the sight of Yhwh your God, so as to vex him, [26]I call heaven and earth as witnesses against you that you will certainly perish quickly from the land which you are crossing the Jordan to there to possess; you will not prolong days upon it, but you will certainly be destroyed, [27]and Yhwh will scatter you among the peoples and you will be left few in number among the nations to where Yhwh will drive you, [28]and there you will serve gods, the work of human hands, wood and stone, which do not see or hear or eat

or smell; ^{29}and you will seek Yhwh your God from there, and you will find [him] if you search for him with all your heart and with your whole being. ^{30}When disaster strikes you and all these things find you in later days, then you will return to Yhwh your God and listen to his voice, ^{31}for Yhwh your God is a compassionate god: he will not abandon you, nor will he destroy you, nor will he forget the covenant with your ancestors that he swore to them.

4:23 הִשָּׁמְר֣וּ לָכֶ֔ם פֶּֽן־תִּשְׁכְּח֗וּ אֶת־בְּרִ֤ית יְהוָה֙ אֱלֹ֣הֵיכֶ֔ם אֲשֶׁ֥ר כָּרַ֖ת עִמָּכֶ֑ם וַעֲשִׂיתֶ֨ם לָכֶ֥ם פֶּ֛סֶל תְּמ֥וּנַת כֹּ֖ל אֲשֶׁ֥ר צִוְּךָ֖ יְהוָ֥ה אֱלֹהֶֽיךָ׃

HD. The **asyndesis** marks the start of a new section. For the third time (cf. vv. 9, 15), Moses urges watchfulness (√שמר Niphal). He returns to the theme of forgetfulness (cf. 4:9), while integrating the danger of idolatry (vv. 15-22).

הִשָּׁמְר֣וּ לָכֶ֔ם. Impv mp Niph √שמר. HD. For Niphal imperative √שמר with reflexive adjunct PP (לכם), see on 4:9.

פֶּֽן־תִּשְׁכְּח֗וּ אֶת־בְּרִ֤ית יְהוָה֙ אֱלֹ֣הֵיכֶ֔ם אֲשֶׁ֥ר כָּרַ֖ת עִמָּכֶ֑ם. *Yiqtol* (modal) 2mp Qal √שכח. For פן introducing a negative purpose clause, see on 4:9.

אֲשֶׁ֥ר כָּרַ֖ת עִמָּכֶ֑ם. *Qatal* 3ms Qal √כרת. Restrictive relative clause, with **head** עמכם. ברית יהוה אלהיכם is oblique complement.

וַעֲשִׂיתֶ֨ם לָכֶ֥ם פֶּ֛סֶל תְּמ֥וּנַת כֹּ֖ל אֲשֶׁ֥ר צִוְּךָ֖ יְהוָ֥ה אֱלֹהֶֽיךָ׃. *Qatal* (modal) 2mp Qal √עשה. For the continuation of a negative final clause introduced by פן with a modal *qatal*, see on 4:16. Forgetting Yhwh's covenant is intimately linked with, even demonstrated by, making idols. פסל is accusative complement, as in v. 16. The disjunctive *pashtah* indicates that it is not a construct, bound to what follows. תמונת כל, "a form of anything," is a construct phrase in apposition (similar to v. 16, but no סמל here; see comments on v. 16). כל is the **head** of the subsequent restrictive relative clause.

אֲשֶׁ֥ר צִוְּךָ֖ יְהוָ֥ה אֱלֹהֶֽיךָ׃. *Qatal* 3ms Piel √צוה with 2ms pronominal suffix. צוה here has the sense of forbid, because fulfilment of it involved not making idols (JM §160k n.15; cf. 2:37). It is followed by two direct objects as complements (GKC §117gg; AC §2.3.1e), indicating the recipients of Moses' command (-ךָ) and what Moses commanded (the **head** of the restrictive relative clause).

4:24 כִּ֚י יְהוָ֣ה אֱלֹהֶ֔יךָ אֵ֥שׁ אֹכְלָ֖ה ה֑וּא אֵ֖ל קַנָּֽא׃ פ

Moses grounds the caution of v. 23 in an explanatory clause that spells out Yhwh's dangerous nature.

כִּ֚י יְהוָ֣ה אֱלֹהֶ֔יךָ אֵ֥שׁ אֹכְלָ֖ה ה֑וּא. This is a **tripartite** nominal clause. As discussed on 1:17, there are two ways of understanding such clauses. Here, the **extraposed** NP יהוה אלהיך is established as the **topic**. The resumptive pronoun הוא is the subject of the **null-copula** clause. אש אכלה is the predicate, with the Qal fs participle, אכלה (√אכל), functioning as an attributive adjective (WO §4.6.1a, 37.4.b; WS §215; MNK §20.3.3; WHS §215a). This reading fits with the P–S word order and the pragmatic sense (also Holmstedt and Jones, 77). The word order highlights יהוה אלהיך as the **topic** and אש אכלה as the **focus**. When it comes to "Yhwh your God," of all that might possibly be predicated of Yhwh, the salient one is that Yhwh is "a consuming fire" (cf. 3:22, where there is S–P order).

אֵ֖ל קַנָּֽא׃. NP, appositional to אש אכלה. קנא is an attributive adjective. The adjective is only predicated of Yhwh (cf. 5:9; 6:15).

4:25 כִּֽי־תוֹלִ֤יד בָּנִים֙ וּבְנֵ֣י בָנִ֔ים וְנוֹשַׁנְתֶּ֖ם בָּאָ֑רֶץ
וְהִשְׁחַתֶּ֗ם וַעֲשִׂ֤יתֶם פֶּ֙סֶל֙ תְּמ֣וּנַת כֹּ֔ל וַעֲשִׂיתֶ֥ם הָרַ֛ע
בְּעֵינֵ֥י יְהוָֽה־אֱלֹהֶ֖יךָ לְהַכְעִיסֽוֹ׃

D2. The verse opens with a temporal protasis looking at future events (כי + initial *yiqtol*). The *yiqtol* is followed by a sequence of four modal *qatals*. The main interpretative question is whether this sequence suggests an inevitable succession of events (NASV; Nelson, 58) or there is an implicit, unmarked conditional present, with והשחתם being the protasis (NIV, ESV, NRSV; Weinfeld, 194). On balance it makes sense to see an unbroken chain into a pessimistic future (see below).

כִּֽי־תוֹלִ֤יד בָּנִים֙ וּבְנֵ֣י בָנִ֔ים. *Yiqtol* 2ms Hiph √ילד. The subordinating conjunction כי + *yiqtol* introduces a temporal clause in future time (GKC §164d; JM §166o; WO §38.7a; WHS §445, §497). Although כי can also begin a conditional protasis and sometimes it is hard to determine which is right (e.g., 30:1; AC §4.3.4f), here having children and growing old in the land are not in doubt, so כי should be understood as temporal.

וְנוֹשַׁנְתֶּ֖ם בָּאָֽרֶץ. *Qatal* (modal) 2mp Niph √ישׁן, continuing the temporal protasis. While BDB regards this verb as the Niphal of יָשֵׁן, "to sleep," HALOT and CDCH regard it as a **homonym**, ישׁן II, "to grow old" (cf. Isa 22:11; Ugaritic *ytn*). בארץ is adjunct PP.

וְהִשְׁחַתֶּ֗ם. *Qatal* (modal) 2mp Hiph √שחת. Note the contraction of the ת of the root and the ת of the afformative (GKC §44o). Moses looks ahead to when the danger warned of in 4:16 becomes a reality. Although Hebrew does sometimes begin a conditional protasis with a modal *qatal* rather than a subordinating conjunction (cf. Gen 44:22; GKC §112kk, 159g; JM §167b), there is usually some indication of a break, either no directly preceding modal *qatal* (e.g., Ruth 2:9) or a shift in person (e.g., 25:9). This should be seen as continuing the temporal protasis.

וַעֲשִׂיתֶ֥ם פֶּ֙סֶל֙ תְּמ֣וּנַת כֹּ֔ל. *Qatal* (modal) 2mp Qal √עשה. For ועשיתם following √שחת, see on 4:16. For פסל תמונת כל, see on 4:16.

וַעֲשִׂיתֶ֥ם הָרַ֛ע בְּעֵינֵ֥י יְהוָֽה־אֱלֹהֶ֖יךָ לְהַכְעִיסֽוֹ׃. *Qatal* (modal) 2mp Qal √עשה. This is not a different action, but a further commentary on the previous action. הרע is accusative complement. בעיני יהוה־אלהיך is adjunct construct PP. Sight is an important motif in the chapter (see opening comments).

לְהַכְעִיסֽוֹ׃. Inf constr Hiph √כעס with ל preposition and with 3ms pronominal suffix. Adjunct infinitive construct phrase. ל introduces "consecution," or "result" (JM §124l, §169g; WO §36.2.3d; MNK §20.1.3[vi]). WS §198 suggests the translation, "thus provoking him to anger," an instance of a more general principle that ל + infinitive construct be translated "thus . . . -ing."

4:26 הַעִידֹ֨תִי בָכֶ֜ם הַיּ֗וֹם אֶת־הַשָּׁמַ֙יִם֙ וְאֶת־הָאָ֔רֶץ
כִּֽי־אָבֹ֣ד תֹּאבֵדוּן֮ מַהֵר֒ מֵעַ֣ל הָאָ֔רֶץ אֲשֶׁ֨ר אַתֶּ֜ם
עֹבְרִ֧ים אֶת־הַיַּרְדֵּ֛ן שָׁ֖מָּה לְרִשְׁתָּ֑הּ לֹֽא־תַאֲרִיכֻ֤ן
יָמִים֙ עָלֶ֔יהָ כִּ֥י הִשָּׁמֵ֖ד תִּשָּׁמֵדֽוּן׃

A performative *qatal* prefaces the temporal apodosis, which begins with the accusative complement noun clause of העידתי. The initial assertion of swift destruction is then restated in v. 26b (n.b., the **asyndesis**). Two **paronomastic** infinitive constructions (see below) in the verse emphasize the certain and total destruction.

עוּד√ Qatal 1cs Hiph. הַעִידֹ֨תִי בָכֶ֤ם הַיּוֹם֙ אֶת־הַשָּׁמַ֣יִם וְאֶת־הָאָ֔רֶץ
A performative *qatal*, whereby the action of calling as witnesses is performed in the saying of these words (cf. WO §30.5.1d). The *patakh* with the prefixed ה, הַעִידֹתִי instead of הַעִידֹתִי, is rare (JM §80m). The **asyndesis** shows that the temporal protasis has ended. בכם is oblique complement, "against you." היום is adverbial time adjunct NP.

כִּֽי־אָבֹ֣ד תֹּאבֵדוּן֮ מַהֵר֒ מֵעַ֣ל הָאָ֔רֶץ אֲשֶׁ֨ר אַתֶּ֜ם עֹבְרִ֧ים אֶת־הַיַּרְדֵּ֛ן שָׁ֖מָּה לְרִשְׁתָּ֑הּ. *Yiqtol* 2mp Qal √אבד with a **paragogic** ן (for which see on 1:17), preceded by infinitive absolute Qal √אבד. This is the so-called **paronomastic** infinitive construction, the "concatenation of an infinitive absolute and a verb of the same root" (Callaham, 4–5). This construction accents the modality of its cognate verb in modal contexts, such as this one, where the truth of the proposition is being asserted. כי is a **complementizer**, introducing a noun clause expressing what is being testified. The noun clause functions as the temporal apodosis. PD.

מַהֵר. Inf abs Piel √מהר, functioning adverbially (JM §102e, §123r).

מֵעַ֣ל הָאָ֔רֶץ. Spatial adjunct PP. Compound preposition comprising מן and על, "from upon." Until now, the prepositions with הארץ have been "to" or "into" the land (אל or ל) or "in" it (ב). Now there is a danger of perishing "from upon" the land. The notion of "perishing . . . from upon" the land is a striking one. Death is associated with losing the land, life with gaining the land (Weinfeld, 60).

אֲשֶׁ֨ר אַתֶּ֜ם עֹבְרִ֧ים אֶת־הַיַּרְדֵּ֛ן שָׁ֖מָּה לְרִשְׁתָּ֑הּ. Ptcp mp Qal √עבר. Restrictive relative clause, with **head** הארץ. Almost identical phrasing as 4:5, 14; see comments there. See on 3:18 for לרשתה.

לֹֽא־תַאֲרִיכֻ֤ן יָמִים֙ עָלֶ֔יהָ. *Yiqtol* 3mp Hiph √ארך with **paragogic** ן. PD. Clausal **asyndesis**, serving to explain or expand upon what Moses has just said. ימים is accusative complement. עליה is adjunct PP; the object is a pronoun referring to the (**discourse active**) ארץ.

כִּ֥י הִשָּׁמֵ֖ד תִּשָּׁמֵדֽוּן׃. *Yiqtol* 2mp Niph √שמד with a **paragogic** ן (for which see on 1:17), preceded by infinitive absolute Niphal √שמד. The Niphal infinitive absolute in the regular verb most commonly has the form as here, הִשָּׁמֵד, rather than הִקָּטֹל; the difference is probably due to assonance (JM §51b; cf. GKC §51k). The alternative form נִקְטֹל is found with *qatal* (e.g., 1 Sam 20:6). See the comments above for the **paronomastic** infinitive construction. When the conjunction כִּי follows a clause with לֹא, it often indicates an adversative clause (cf. GKC §163a; JM §172c; AC §5.2.10).

4:27 וְהֵפִ֨יץ יְהוָ֤ה אֶתְכֶם֙ בָּעַמִּ֔ים וְנִשְׁאַרְתֶּם֙ מְתֵ֣י מִסְפָּ֔ר בַּגּוֹיִ֕ם אֲשֶׁ֨ר יְנַהֵ֧ג יְהוָ֛ה אֶתְכֶ֖ם שָֽׁמָּה׃

The temporal apodosis, which began with the accusative complement NP of Moses' invoking of witnesses, continues with two modal *qatals*, the second of which is a consequence of the former. PD. D2. The language of death and destruction in v. 26 is associated with exile from the land. The judgment reverses the Abrahamic promises (1:8–11).

וְהֵפִ֨יץ יְהוָ֤ה אֶתְכֶם֙ בָּעַמִּ֔ים. *Qatal* (modal) 3ms Hiph √פוץ. PD. Temporal apodosis (*cont.*). בָּעַמִּים is spatial adjunct PP. For the extended spatial sense of בְּ, "among" (a group), see AC §4.1.5a.

וְנִשְׁאַרְתֶּם֙ מְתֵ֣י מִסְפָּ֔ר בַּגּוֹיִ֕ם אֲשֶׁ֨ר יְנַהֵ֧ג יְהוָ֛ה אֶתְכֶ֖ם שָֽׁמָּה׃. *Qatal* (modal) 2mp Niph √שאר. The modal *qatal* here expresses the result or consequence of the previous verb (AC §3.5.2b). PD. In 28:62 מתי מספר is the construct NP object of the preposition בְּ. The absolute, מספר, is a type of explanatory or appositional genitive, giving further definition to the construct (cf. GKC §128n). The absence of בְּ means that the construct phrase is a loose accusative, further refining the verb. JM §133c term it a "predicative accusative" (an indeterminate, complementary phrase relating to the subject or object, subordinated to the verbal predicate; JM §126a) while GKC §163q call it an adverbial accusative, "specifying a number more accurately."

אֲשֶׁ֨ר יְנַהֵ֧ג יְהוָ֛ה אֶתְכֶ֖ם שָֽׁמָּה׃. *Yiqtol* 3ms Piel √נהג. The Piel of a fientive verb which occurs transitively in the Qal can be seen as **resultative**, "bringing about of a state corresponding to the verbal meaning of the *Qal*" (WO §24.3b), although challenges in understanding the function of Piel remain (JM §52d). Restrictive relative clause. שמה is resumptive locative adverb.

4:28 וַעֲבַדְתֶּם־שָׁם אֱלֹהִים מַעֲשֵׂה יְדֵי אָדָם עֵץ וָאֶבֶן אֲשֶׁר לֹא־יִרְאוּן וְלֹא יִשְׁמְעוּן וְלֹא יֹאכְלוּן וְלֹא יְרִיחֻן׃

The temporal apodosis continues with another modal *qatal*. PD. D2. The object, אלהים, is modified by two appositional phrases and four restrictive relative clauses with *yiqtols* indicating what is habitually (not) the case.

וַעֲבַדְתֶּם־שָׁם אֱלֹהִים מַעֲשֵׂה יְדֵי אָדָם עֵץ וָאֶבֶן. *Qatal* (modal) 2mp Qal √עבד. PD. שׁם, a locative adverb, reinforces the displacement. אלהים, the indeterminate accusative complement, is then modified by two appositional NPs. The first, a construct chain מעשה ידי אדם, contrasts these gods with Yhwh the "agent" (עשה; 1:30; 4:34). The second, עץ ואבן, gives the material from which they are made. The ו-conjunction is often pointed with *qamets* before the tone syllable, especially when the words are closely paired (GKC §104g; JM §104d).

אֲשֶׁר לֹא־יִרְאוּן וְלֹא יִשְׁמְעוּן וְלֹא יֹאכְלוּן וְלֹא יְרִיחֻן׃. *Yiqtol* 3mp Qal √ראה, √שמע, √אכל, Hiph √רוח, all with **paragogic** ן (see on 1:17). There is some discussion whether there are homonyms I and II רוח (HALOT s.v.), with the latter sometimes classified as √ריח Qal (e.g., *CDCH* 415, 421), since if it were regarded as II רוח, it would only occur in the Hiphil. The clause is a restrictive relative clause, with **head** אלהים.

4:29 וּבִקַּשְׁתֶּם מִשָּׁם אֶת־יְהוָה אֱלֹהֶיךָ וּמָצָאתָ כִּי תִדְרְשֶׁנּוּ בְּכָל־לְבָבְךָ וּבְכָל־נַפְשֶׁךָ׃

PD. A further modal *qatal* continues the temporal apodosis begun in v. 26. This is followed by a conditional apodosis (ומצאת; see below) and protasis (v. 29b). If seeking Yhwh can be assumed, it is only a wholehearted searching that will result in finding. There is, after all, future hope, rhetorically contingent on Israel's action, but dependent ultimately on Yhwh's compassion and covenant (v. 31).

וּבִקַּשְׁתֶּם מִשָּׁם אֶת־יְהוָה אֱלֹהֶיךָ. *Qatal* (modal) 2mp Piel √בקש. PD. משם is spatial adjunct PP.

וּמָצָאתָ. *Qatal* (modal) 2ms Qal √מצא. Beginning here, the rest of the verbs until 4:40 are 2nd sg., as are the suffixes (except for לכם and

אלהיכם in v. 34). For textual issues here, see *BHQ: Deuteronomy*, 63*. One explanation is that the shift to 2ms וּמְצָאתָ signals a break from the PD; this is a conditional apodosis, preceding the protasis in the final clause in the verse (cf. NRSV, NASV, McConville 110).

כִּ֤י תִדְרְשֶׁ֙נּוּ֙ בְּכָל־לְבָבְךָ֖ וּבְכָל־נַפְשֶֽׁךָ׃. *Yiqtol* 2ms Qal √דרש with 3ms pronominal suffix. כי here introduces a conditional protasis, although the dividing line between conditional and temporal protases after כי is not always clear (cf. on 4:25). בכל־לבבך ובכל־נפשך are adjunct PPs. They are typically Deuteronomic terms (cf. on 4:9; note also 6:5).

4:30 בַּצַּ֣ר לְךָ֔ וּמְצָא֕וּךָ כֹּ֖ל הַדְּבָרִ֣ים הָאֵ֑לֶּה בְּאַחֲרִית֙ הַיָּמִ֔ים וְשַׁבְתָּ֙ עַד־יְהוָ֣ה אֱלֹהֶ֔יךָ וְשָׁמַעְתָּ֖ בְּקֹלֽוֹ׃

An adverbial temporal phrase is followed by ו and a modal *qatal*. Together, they form a temporal protasis. The temporal apodosis consists of two modal *qatals* outlining Israel's repentance and what it entails. Because they heard a voice (4:12), they need to listen to it (שמע, קול√). The clausal **asyndesis** suggests that this expands on the preceding verse.

בַּצַּ֣ר לְךָ֔. Adjunct PP. Broadly there are two interpretative questions. One is whether this phrase goes with what precedes or what follows. The second is how בצר should be parsed. Regarding the first, JM §166n takes this phrase with what precedes, "*if you seek Him with all your heart and soul when you are in distress*" (so too Smr, LXX), but this represents an attempt to simplify the syntax (*BHQ: Deuteronomy*, 63*) and leaves ומצאוך hanging, not consequent on the preceding actions. בצר, as pointed, is the noun, צַר, with the article (**syncopated**) and the preposition ב. Driver, however, regards it to be originally intended as infinitive construct of √צרר with preposition ב, בְּצֵר, or בְּצֹר, with a *waw* + suffix conjugation following (74; cf. GKC §112v). According to Weinfeld, צר is a noun, part of an "idiomatic expression meaning 'when disaster strikes'" (197). The subsequent modal *qatal* is then "subordinated to adverbial expressions of time" (WO §32.2.6b), as is found elsewhere (e.g., Isa 16:4). Weinfeld's view is probably to be preferred. The phrase is more common than Driver's assertion suggests, and it is always pointed as a noun (e.g., Hos 5:15). Further, LXX regards it as a noun. The phrase as a whole begins a temporal protasis.

וּמְצָא֗וּךָ כֹּ֤ל הַדְּבָרִים֙ הָאֵ֔לֶּה בְּאַחֲרִית֙ הַיָּמִ֔ים. *Qatal* (modal) 3cp Qal √מצא with 2ms pronominal suffix. The verb continues the temporal protasis (see above for relationship with בצר לך).

בְּאַחֲרִית הַיָּמִים. Temporal adjunct construct PP. Masoretic pointing links this with the following clause, rather than with what precedes (n.b., the ʾ*atnakh*; so Driver, 74; Nelson, 60 n. u). On the other hand, in 31:29 the phrase אחרית הימים is associated with the affliction, suggesting that it should be taken with the preceding clause (Weinfeld, 197–98). At first it looks as though the second half of the verse matches the first half, with a temporal phrase followed by a modal *qatal*. But in v. 30a the modal *qatal* has a coordinate relationship with the temporal phrase, "when you are in distress and all these things find you"; while in v. 30b, if באחרית הימים were taken with what follows, the modal *qatal* would have a *subordinate* relationship, "in later days, [then] you will return." It is unlikely, given the coordination in v. 30a, that באחרית הימים begins a temporal protasis, so it should be taken with the preceding clause.

וְשַׁבְתָּ֙ עַד־יְהוָ֣ה אֱלֹהֶ֔יךָ. *Qatal* (modal) 2ms Qal √שוב. Temporal apodosis. PD. עד־יהוה אלהיך is the oblique complement. Although usually שוב is followed by אל, it can also be followed by עד (e.g., 30:2; Amos 4:6-11).

וְשָׁמַעְתָּ֖ בְּקֹלֽוֹ׃ *Qatal* (modal) 2ms Qal √שמע. Temporal apodosis (*cont.*). PD. בקולו is oblique complement. שמע בקול denotes "listening to" or "obeying" (e.g., 8:20; 9:23; cf. 1:45).

4:31 כִּ֣י אֵ֤ל רַחוּם֙ יְהוָ֣ה אֱלֹהֶ֔יךָ לֹ֥א יַרְפְּךָ֖ וְלֹ֣א יַשְׁחִיתֶ֑ךָ
וְלֹ֤א יִשְׁכַּח֙ אֶת־בְּרִ֣ית אֲבֹתֶ֔יךָ אֲשֶׁ֥ר נִשְׁבַּ֖ע לָהֶֽם׃

The promise that a wholeheartedly penitent people will "find" (v. 29) is rooted in the character of Yhwh, unpacked in the explanatory clause at the start of v. 31, which is in turn developed by three negated *yiqtols*. They are coordinated with each other, but the **asyndesis** before the first shows that Yhwh's compassion is evidenced by all three, taken together: there are three things Yhwh will *not* do. A second ground for hope is the covenant that Yhwh swore to their ancestors.

כִּ֣י אֵ֤ל רַחוּם֙ יְהוָ֣ה אֱלֹהֶ֔יךָ. Subordinating conjunction כי introducing an explanatory **null-copula** clause. Although after כי verbal clauses have **triggered inversion**, **null-copula** clauses do not. The P–S word order in a **null-copula** clause marks the P, רחום אל as the **focus**. Of all that Yhwh might be, he is a compassionate god (cf. v. 24).

לֹא יַרְפְּךָ. *Yiqtol* 3ms Hiph √רפה with 2ms pronominal suffix. Following asyndetically from the opening clause, this develops what is meant by Yhwh being "a compassionate god."

וְלֹא יַשְׁחִיתֶךָ. *Yiqtol* 3ms Hiph √שחת with 2ms pronominal suffix. With accusative complement, √שחת Hiphil is "destroy"; but Moses' hearers will likely have in their minds vv. 16 and 25, where Israel is the subject and √שחת is followed by a verb, carrying the sense "act corruptly" with the following verb showing how.

וְלֹא יִשְׁכַּח אֶת־בְּרִית אֲבֹתֶיךָ אֲשֶׁר נִשְׁבַּע לָהֶם. *Yiqtol* 3ms Qal √שכח. ברית אבתיך is the accusative complement construct NP. It is an example of an objective genitive, "in which the first noun indicates an action performed to, for, or against a person indicated by the second noun . . . 'the pact with your fathers'" (JM §129e). Yhwh is very different from Israel (cf. v. 23, √שכח, ברית).

אֲשֶׁר נִשְׁבַּע לָהֶם. *Qatal* 3ms Niph √שבע. Restrictive relative clause, with **head** ברית. √שבע takes ב for what is sworn "by," and ל of the recipient of the oath.

No other gods: Israel is unique in having a speaking and redeeming god (4:32-40)

As the chapter has continued, time references have gone further back, here right back to creation (Mayes 1981: 27). The final words of the section hold out the land as a permanent gift into the indefinite future. Against the time frame going as far back as possible, two rhetorical questions assert that no other people has experienced revelation as they have with Yhwh; no other deity has acted as Yhwh has in redeeming. They saw in order to know Yhwh's uniqueness (v. 35). Verse 36 provides the bridge between seeing and hearing. The causal clause in vv. 37-38 grounds three modal *qatals* (vv. 39-40), which give the only instructions in vv. 32-40 (beyond the call to "ask" in 4:32): to "know" (וידעת) and "bring to mind" (והשבת אל-לבבך) Yhwh's uniqueness, and to "keep" (ושמרת) Yhwh's commands that Moses is commanding "today."

[32]For ask about former days which were before you, from the day God created humanity on the earth, and from one end of heaven to the other, has the like of this great thing happened, or has the like of it been heard? [33]Has

a people heard a god's voice speaking from the midst of fire, as you have, and lived, ³⁴or has a god tried to come to take for himself a nation from the midst of a nation with trials, with signs and with wonders and with war, and with a strong hand and with an outstretched arm and with great terrors, like all that Yhwh your God did for you in Egypt before your eyes. ³⁵You were shown so as to know that it is Yhwh that is God; there is none besides him. ³⁶From heaven he caused you to hear his voice, to discipline you, while on earth he showed you his great fire, and his words you heard from the midst of the fire. ³⁷Precisely because he loved your ancestors and chose their seed after them and brought you out from Egypt by his presence, by his great strength, ³⁸to dispossess nations greater and stronger than you, from before you, to bring you [in], to give you their land as an inheritance" (as it is today), ³⁹"so know today and bring back to your mind that it is Yhwh that is God in the heavens above and on the earth beneath—there is no other—⁴⁰and keep his statutes and his commands which I am commanding you today, so that it may go well with you and your children after you, and so that you may prolong [your] time on the land which Yhwh your God is giving to you for all time."

4:32 כִּי שְׁאַל־נָא לְיָמִים רִאשֹׁנִים אֲשֶׁר־הָיוּ לְפָנֶיךָ לְמִן־הַיּוֹם אֲשֶׁר בָּרָא אֱלֹהִים ׀ אָדָם עַל־הָאָרֶץ וּלְמִקְצֵה הַשָּׁמַיִם וְעַד־קְצֵה הַשָּׁמָיִם הֲנִהְיָה כַּדָּבָר הַגָּדוֹל הַזֶּה אוֹ הֲנִשְׁמַע כָּמֹהוּ׃

D2. An opening explanatory clause grounds the previous assertions. Moses with rhetorical force stretches out time (from היום of creation to היום of Moab) and space, and urges Israel to ask two rhetorical questions (ID): Has a similar event happened? Has anyone heard of it? They are uniquely privileged.

כִּי שְׁאַל־נָא לְיָמִים רִאשֹׁנִים. Impv ms Qal √שאל. Explanatory clause, introduced by כי. Although Lundbom (252) regards the כי here as "asseverative," it makes more sense to see what follows as giving grounds for the assertions of v. 31 (Driver, 75). נא with the imperative carries the force of entreaty, and often of energy (JM §105c, §114m). The accusative complement of the verb is the question itself, cited as direct speech (. . . הנהיה). The preposition ל after √שאל can introduce the addressee of the question (e.g., 2 Kgs 8:6), or the subject about which the question is asked (e.g., Gen 26:7). Given the way the PP לימים ראשנים is unpacked in the following appositional phrase, it should be regarded as an adjunct PP indicating the subject of the question. Were it introducing addressees, a personal object of the preposition would have been expected (cf. Job 8:8; n.b., also 32:7; Jer 6:16). For the form of the adjective ראשון, see on 9:18.

אֲשֶׁר־הָיוּ לְפָנֶיךָ. *Qatal* 3cp Qal √היה. Restrictive relative clause, with **head** ימים ראשנים. לפניך functions as PP adverbial predicate.

לְמִן־הַיּוֹם אֲשֶׁר בָּרָא אֱלֹהִים ׀ אָדָם עַל־הָאָרֶץ. *Qatal* 3ms Qal √ברא, the predicate of the restrictive relative clause after the **head**, היום. למן is "pleonastic" synonym of מן (Weinfeld, 198), with ל giving "the starting point, as an exact *terminus a quo*" ("end from which") of place (e.g., Exod 11:7) or, as here and 9:7, of time (GKC §119c n. 2; cf. Driver, 75). The adjunct PP is in apposition to לימים ראשנים, going back to the moment of creation (only occurrence of √ברא in Deuteronomy). The vertical line between אלהים and אדם is a *paseq* (cf. on 3:20).

וּלְמִקְצֵה הַשָּׁמַיִם וְעַד־קְצֵה הַשָּׁמָיִם. Spatial adjunct PPs. See above for למן.

הֲנִהְיָה כַּדָּבָר הַגָּדוֹל הַזֶּה. *Qatal* 3ms Niph √היה with ה-interrogative. The Niph √היה here is "happen" (cf. 1 Kgs 12:24). ID (ND). כ here functions here as a "quasi-nominal phrasal **head**," similar to the English "Has *the like*... happened?" In other words, "Has there been *anything like* this great event? Has *anything like* it been heard of?" (WO §11.2.9d). WS §256 describes it as a "comparative" use of the preposition כ. This question and the ones that follow are rhetorical, making a point strongly (JM §161k; Moshavi 2011a).

אוֹ הֲנִשְׁמַע כָּמֹהוּ. *Qatal* 3ms Niph √שמע with ה-interrogative. ID (ND). או is the coordinating conjunction similar to English "or" (JM §175a). As in the previous clause, כ functions as a "quasi-nominal phrasal head." Note that the inseparable preposition כ has the longer form, כמו, with some pronominal suffixes (GKC §h, k; JM §103g).

4:33 הֲשָׁמַע עָם קוֹל אֱלֹהִים מְדַבֵּר מִתּוֹךְ־הָאֵשׁ
כַּאֲשֶׁר־שָׁמַעְתָּ אַתָּה וַיֶּחִי׃

A second pair of rhetorical questions joined by או follows v. 32 asyndetically (vv. 33-34). The initial **asyndesis** indicates that these two questions explain the unprecedented happening in 4:32b, an event of which no one had ever heard. Formally ID, rhetorically ND. The opening question is generic. A comparative clause (כאשר) is followed by the outcome of hearing.

הֲשָׁמַע עָם֩ קוֹל אֱלֹהִ֨ים מְדַבֵּ֧ר מִתּוֹךְ־הָאֵ֛שׁ. *Qatal* 3ms Qal √שמע with ה-interrogative. ID (ND). Both subject עם and accusative complement קול אלהים are indefinite. A number of English versions (e.g., NASV, NKJV, NIV; also Weinfeld, 198) regard אלהים as "God," Israel's deity, here (NKJV and Wright [60] do in v. 34, too). Possible reasons include in 4:32, אלהים refers to Israel's deity; LXX and Smr read the attributive adjective חיים here (cf. 5:26). To respond: (1) in v. 34, אלהים refers to "a god," since the contrast is between "any god" and Yhwh, so the shift from אלהים as Israel's deity (v. 32) does happen in these verses; (2) there is no definite direct object marker, את (cf. 4:10, 36; 5:23, 25; n.b., though, v. 36c; 5:26); and (3) the parallel with v. 34 indicates that the contrast is between any other nation's experience of *any* deity and Israel's experience of Yhwh (cf. Driver, 75).

מְדַבֵּ֧ר מִתּוֹךְ־הָאֵ֛שׁ. Ptcp ms Piel √דבר. The participle is an "attributive accusative of state" (cf. JM §127a), modifying a noun (hence termed "attributive") rather than the predicate (adverbial or indirect accusative). מתוך־האש is spatial adjunct construct PP.

כַּאֲשֶׁר־שָׁמַ֥עְתָּ אַתָּ֖ה. *Qatal* 2ms Qal √שמע. After כאשר, there is usually **triggered inversion**, with P–S word order. אתה is unnecessary syntactically. It is very unusual for a subject pronoun to follow the finite predicate in a clause introduced by אשר (1 Sam 20:23; Qoh 5:17; Jer 44:17; Ezek 16:48). The word order has not marked it out as the **focus**. Instead, it seems almost to act as an adjunct (cf. 1 Sam 20:23; Ezek 16:48), "you have heard, [yes] you."

וַיֶּֽחִי׃. *Wayyiqtol* 3ms Qal √חיה. The form is analogous to that of ויהי in 1:3 (s.v.). The *segol* is due to it being in pause (n.b., the *silluq*). The *wayyiqtol* here has a "consequential sense," following the previous *qatal* (Cook 2012: 264, 299), expressing "indefinite perfective" value (WO §33.3.1a).

4:34 א֣וֹ ׀ הֲנִסָּ֣ה אֱלֹהִ֗ים לָ֠בוֹא לָקַ֨חַת ל֣וֹ גוֹי֮ מִקֶּ֣רֶב גּוֹי֒
בְּמַסֹּת֩ בְּאֹתֹ֨ת וּבְמוֹפְתִ֜ים וּבְמִלְחָמָ֗ה וּבְיָ֤ד חֲזָקָה֙
וּבִזְר֣וֹעַ נְטוּיָ֔ה וּבְמוֹרָאִ֖ים גְּדֹלִ֑ים כְּ֠כֹל אֲשֶׁר־עָשָׂ֨ה
לָכֶ֜ם יְהוָ֧ה אֱלֹהֵיכֶ֛ם בְּמִצְרַ֖יִם לְעֵינֶֽיךָ׃

The second rhetorical question of the second pair that explains the unprecedented happening of v. 32 (see comments on vv. 32, 33). The seven adjunct PPs are an example of Deuteronomy's enthusiasm for seven (cf. 7:1).

אֽוֹ ׀ הֲנִסָּ֨ה אֱלֹהִ֜ים לָ֠בוֹא לָקַ֨חַת ל֣וֹ גוֹי֮ מִקֶּ֣רֶב גּוֹי֒. *Qatal* 3ms Piel √נסה with הֵ-interrogative. ID (ND).

לָבוֹא. Inf constr Qal √בוא, with preposition לְ. Infinitive complement of verb נסה. Before the tone syllable of an infinitive construct, the preposition לְ often has *qamets* (GKC §102f; JM §103c).

לָקַ֨חַת ל֣וֹ גוֹי֮ מִקֶּ֣רֶב גּוֹי֒. Inf constr Qal √לקח, with preposition לְ. לקח is the only I-ל verb that functions like a I-נ (JM §72j). There is **aphaeresis** of the initial נ, and feminine ת is added (JM §72c, d). The a-class vowels are due to the ח. Adjunct infinitive phrase to verb לבוא, expressing purpose. See above for לְ. לוֹ is an adjunct PP, with the ל introducing what is sometimes called "the dative of advantage" giving the beneficiary of the action of the verb (GKC §119s; JM §133d; WO §11.2.10d; WHS §271a). מקרב גוי is adjunct construct PP.

בְּמַסֹּת֩ בְּאֹתֹ֨ת וּבְמוֹפְתִ֜ים וּבְמִלְחָמָ֗ה וּבְיָ֤ד חֲזָקָה֙ וּבִזְר֣וֹעַ נְטוּיָ֔ה וּבְמוֹרָאִ֖ים גְּדֹלִ֑ים. A succession of seven adjunct PPs, indicating how Yhwh acted. The final six are joined syndetically and fall into two groups of three. Each of the final three has an attributive adjective modifying the noun. נטויה is Ptcp fs Qal pass √נטה, used as an attributive adjective (WO §37.4.c). It is possible that the six are appositional to במסת, but in 7:19 מסה is just one of the list. מוראים, "terrors," is related to √ירא, not √ראה (cf. LXX and Smr, which seem to register במראים).

כְּ֠כֹל אֲשֶׁר־עָשָׂ֨ה לָכֶ֜ם יְהוָ֧ה אֱלֹהֵיכֶ֛ם בְּמִצְרַ֖יִם לְעֵינֶֽיךָ׃. *Qatal* 3ms Qal √עשה. For ככל אשר־עשה, see on 1:30. לכם is an adjunct PP, with the ל introducing "the dative of advantage" (see above). For במצרים לעיניך, see on 1:30.

4:35 אַתָּה֙ הָרְאֵ֣תָ לָדַ֔עַת כִּ֥י יְהוָ֖ה ה֣וּא הָאֱלֹהִ֑ים אֵ֥ין ע֖וֹד מִלְבַדּֽוֹ׃

ND. D2. Moses indicates the purpose of Israel being shown the signs and wonders. Yhwh's uniqueness is evident not from assertion but from what they have seen (cf. vv. 3, 6, 9, 12, 15, 34, 36).

אַתָּה הָרְאֵתָ לָדַעַת. *Qatal* 2ms Hoph √ראה. The **asyndesis** marks a shift from the rhetorical questions, while there is continuity found in the motif of "seeing" (cf. לְעֵינֶיךָ at the end of v. 34).

לָדַעַת. Inf constr Qal √ידע with preposition ל. An original I-ו verb, the ו has disappeared (**aphaeresis**; see JM §17d) and a feminine ת has been added (JM §72d). It now has the form of a segholate noun, with the a-class vowels because of the guttural ע (JM §75g). Adjunct infinitive phrase to verb הראת, expressing purpose. Before the tone syllable of an infinitive construct, the ל often has *qamets* (GKC §102f; JM §103c).

כִּי יְהוָה הוּא הָאֱלֹהִים. A **tripartite** nominal/verbless explanatory clause, with X+S(PronX)–P word order (see on 1:17; 3:22). Although the function of הוא is "ambiguous," since it *could* be a pronominal predicate or a resumptive pronoun (Holmstedt and Jones, 85–86), the fact that the issue of choice and uniqueness is explicitly raised in the final clause of the verse suggests that יהוה is **extraposed** as the **topic**, and the resumptive pronoun הוא is the **focus** (see on 3:22).

אֵין עוֹד מִלְּבַדּוֹ. Asyndetic **null-copula** clause with prepositional predicate. אין is an adverb of nonexistence (JM §154k, §160g). עוד is a scalar adverb, indicating the repeatability (here unrepeatability, with אין) of a situation (cf. WO §39.3.1i). These two can occur on their own, "there is none besides" (e.g., 4:39). מלבדו is adjunct PP, comprising מן, ל, בד, and the 3ms pronominal suffix. The noun בד, "part," often is joined to ל, "in separation"; when it functions as a preposition, rather than adverbially, it is followed by מן (e.g., Exod 12:37). Sometimes the מן precedes לבד, מלבד, as here, not because of transposition of מן but because מן often loses its spatial sense when forming adverbial phrases and the preposition מן is omitted afterwards (GKC §119c n. 2).

4:36 מִן־הַשָּׁמַיִם הִשְׁמִיעֲךָ אֶת־קֹלוֹ לְיַסְּרֶךָּ וְעַל־הָאָרֶץ הֶרְאֲךָ אֶת־אִשּׁוֹ הַגְּדוֹלָה וּדְבָרָיו שָׁמַעְתָּ מִתּוֹךְ הָאֵשׁ:

The contrast between heaven and earth, both fronted for **focus**, on the one hand, and seeing and hearing, on the other, continues. The opening *qatal* is followed by an adjunct infinitive phrase expressing the purpose of Yhwh causing them to hear. A second *qatal* clause gives the contrast, suggesting a sharp *hearing Yhwh/heaven* and *seeing fire/earth* distinction. The final *qatal* clause blurs that distinction (cf. MacDonald 2006: 215).

מִן־הַשָּׁמַיִם הִשְׁמִיעֲךָ אֶת־קֹלוֹ לְיַסְּרֶךָּ. *Qatal* 3ms Hiph √שמע with 2ms pronominal suffix. מן־השמים is an adjunct PP, fronted for **focus**.

לְיַסְּרֶךָּ. Inf constr Piel √יסר with 2ms pronominal suffix (object) and with preposition ל. Only three infinitives (4:36; 23:5; Job 33:22) have the 2nd ms suffix with "נ *energicum*" (*dagesh forte* / נ present in pronominal suffix). All are in pause (cf. GKC §61d; WO §36.1.1e; JM §61f n. 3, §65d). Adjunct infinitive phrase to verb השמיעך, expressing purpose.

וְעַל־הָאָרֶץ הֶרְאֲךָ אֶת־אִשּׁוֹ הַגְּדוֹלָה. *Qatal* 3ms Hiph √ראה with 2ms pronominal suffix. על־הארץ is an adjunct PP, fronted for **focus**, contrasting with "from heaven."

וּדְבָרָיו שָׁמַעְתָּ מִתּוֹךְ הָאֵשׁ׃. *Qatal* 2ms Qal √שמע. דבריו, the accusative complement, is fronted for **focus**. The contrast is not with different locations, but with different auditory experiences.

4:37 וְתַחַת כִּי אָהַב אֶת־אֲבֹתֶיךָ וַיִּבְחַר בְּזַרְעוֹ אַחֲרָיו
וַיּוֹצִאֲךָ בְּפָנָיו בְּכֹחוֹ הַגָּדֹל מִמִּצְרָיִם׃

ND. D2. Causal clause, introduced by תחת כי, followed by two *wayyiqtols* that spell out what Yhwh did as a result of his "love" (cf. 7:7-8).

וְתַחַת כִּי אָהַב אֶת־אֲבֹתֶיךָ. *Qatal* 3ms Qal √אהב. GKC §158b regards תחת כי together as a causal conjunction, "*for the reason that.*" WHS §353 observes that תחת can have as its object a causal clause, introduced by כי or אשר. This draws attention to the nature of the preposition itself, and its strong reciprocal connotation (cf. WO §11.2.15b n. 18, 38.4a).

וַיִּבְחַר בְּזַרְעוֹ אַחֲרָיו. *Wayyiqtol* 3ms Qal √בחר. There are three choices for when the main clause begins after the causal clause: (1) most see the main clause, or apodosis, as beginning with ויבחר; (2) some see the causal clause as continuing with ויבחר, and the main clause beginning with ויצאך (McConville, 99; Lundbom 247; NIV); and (3) some regard the whole verse as three causal clauses, with the main clause beginning with וידעת (v. 39; so Driver, 76; ESV; cf. Nelson, 70). Syntactically, (2) is unlikely since there is no syntactic trigger for the switch at ויצאך. When כי introduces a causal clause that is in "first position," often the apodosis begins with what Joüon-Muraoka term a "Waw of apodosis" (JM §170o; cf. JM §176e). In other words, a *wayyiqtol* can follow as the predicate in the main clause (so option (1); cf. GKC §111q); so too can a modal *qatal* (so option (3); cf. GKC §112nn). This might suggest either (1) or (3) is possible. However, as Driver (76) notes, the way the causal clause is introduced, with תחת כי, "in return for the fact that" (cf. 21:14; 22:29; 28:47), shows that (3) is best. Israel should act "in return for the fact that" Yhwh has loved, chosen, and delivered them from Egypt to bring them into the land he has promised to them. בזרעו is oblique complement. The transitive English verb "choose" has, as its Hebrew counterpart, an intransitive verb: בחר ב (WO §10.2.1c). The singular pronominal suffixes in MT are curious given the plural antecedent, אבתיך. All versions have the plural. *BHQ: Deuteronomy*, 64* notes two choices: either MT suffixes are "distributive sg. ('the descendants of each one of them')," in which case the plurals of the versions do not reflect a different *Vorlage*, or the singular suffixes refer to one particular ancestor, Jacob, to avoid other nations being included in the promises. The translation above treats them as distributive. אחריו is adjunct PP.

וַיּוֹצִאֲךָ בְּפָנָיו בְּכֹחוֹ הַגָּדֹל מִמִּצְרָיִם: *Wayyiqtol* 3ms Hiph √יצא with 2ms pronominal suffix. בפניו is adjunct PP. The object of the preposition, פנים, is a metonymy for Yhwh (cf. Exod 33:14; Lundbom 255). בכחו הגדל is PP, appositional to בפניו. ממצרים is adjunct PP.

4:38 לְהוֹרִישׁ גּוֹיִם גְּדֹלִים וַעֲצֻמִים מִמְּךָ מִפָּנֶיךָ לַהֲבִיאֲךָ לָתֶת־לְךָ אֶת־אַרְצָם נַחֲלָה כַּיּוֹם הַזֶּה:

D2. This verse comprises three asyndetic adjunct infinitive phrases expressing purpose. Yhwh remains the subject of all three verbs. Yhwh's actions in the past and purposes for the future serve as grounds for knowledge in the present (v. 39). The narrator breaks the narrative frame at the end of the verse (D1) to merge the horizons of Moses' and his addressees.

לְהוֹרִישׁ גּוֹיִם גְּדֹלִים וַעֲצֻמִים מִמְּךָ מִפָּנֶיךָ. Inf constr Hiph √ירש with preposition ל. Adjunct infinitive phrase, expressing purpose. Although some English versions (NRSV, ESV, NASV) treat the infinitive as a **gerund**, "driving out," this is not a past action, but an intended future one. The phrasing here is always used of nations west of the Jordan (7:1; 9:1, 14; 11:23), not of those defeated as part of the exodus. Two attributive adjectives גדלים ועצמים modify the indefinite accusative complement גוים. Although Israel is a גוי גדול (4:6-8), others are greater and stronger (cf. 7:1; 9:1, 14; 11:23). Lacking particular forms for the comparative, Hebrew uses the preposition מן attached to the noun (here the pronominal suffix on ממך) that is excelled when both nouns are present (JM §141g; AC §4.1.13h). מפניך is spatial adjunct PP.

לַהֲבִיאֲךָ. Inf constr Hiph √בוא with 2ms pronominal suffix and with preposition ל. Adjunct infinitive phrase, expressing purpose.

לָתֶת־לְךָ אֶת־אַרְצָם נַחֲלָה כַּיּוֹם הַזֶּה׃. Inf constr Qal √נתן with preposition ל. Adjunct infinitive phrase, expressing purpose. When followed directly by the tone syllable (לְךָ counted as monosyllabic), the accent is shifted back (GKC §29e), so instead of לָתֵת there is לָתֶת. The final syllable, closed and unaccented, takes *segol* not *tsere*. נחלה is an indirect accusative (hence indefinite; cf. JM §126c). נתן with two accusatives can have a number of nuances, including "turn" X "into" Y or "make" X Y. Here, it is used of "giving X *as* Y" (cf. 2:5, 9).

כַּיּוֹם הַזֶּה׃. Comparative temporal adjunct PP. For the significance of "today," see on 1:10. Since Israel does not possess the land in Moses' day, the "today" is the narrator's "today" (cf. 2:22). "The text temporarily breaks the dramatic frame of Moses' speech" (Nelson, 70). This could be an oversight (von Rad, 51), or, more likely, an intentional merging of horizons. A proposed alternative is that Moses is speaking of the possession of the Transjordan (Lundbom 255). It is true that כיום הזה in 2:30 and 4:20 speaks of Moses' "today" in Moab and that language of possession (√ירש) *can* speak of Transjordan (e.g., 3:12) and not just the land west of Jordan (e.g., 1:8). However, language of entering (√בוא; e.g., 4:1, 5, 34) and "nations" that are "greater and mightier" (גדלם ועצמים; 9:1; 11:23; cf. 7:1; 9:14) are always predicated of the land west of the Jordan, so that alternative should be rejected.

4:39 וְיָדַעְתָּ הַיּוֹם וַהֲשֵׁבֹתָ אֶל־לְבָבֶךָ כִּי יְהוָה הוּא הָאֱלֹהִים בַּשָּׁמַיִם מִמַּעַל וְעַל־הָאָרֶץ מִתָּחַת אֵין עוֹד׃

HD. D2. Moses draws out the implications for Israel of Yhwh's actions in the past and purposes for the future on their behalf, rooting them again in Yhwh's "transcendent uniqueness" (cf. Bauckham, 210–12).

וְיָדַעְתָּ֣ הַיּ֗וֹם. *Qatal* (modal) 2ms Qal √ידע. The modal *qatal* in Deuteronomy is often used to convey a volitional force after narrative discourse (cf. WO §32.2.3d). This is the main clause in the sentence that began with the causal clause at the start of v. 37. היום is adverbial time adjunct NP (see on 1:10). The accusative complement is the noun clause beginning כי.

וַהֲשֵׁבֹתָ֮ אֶל־לְבָבֶ֒ךָ֒. *Qatal* (modal) 2ms Hiph √שוב. The *qatal* 2ms Hiphil characteristically has a helping vowel i before the afformative and a *khatef-patakh* for the initial syllable (GKC §72i, w). Note the propretonic *tsere* instead of *hireq-yod* (JM §80m). The accusative complement is the noun clause beginning כי.

כִּ֤י יְהוָה֙ ה֣וּא הָֽאֱלֹהִ֔ים בַּשָּׁמַ֣יִם מִמַּ֔עַל וְעַל־הָאָ֖רֶץ מִתָּ֑חַת. כי is a **complementizer**, introducing the accusative complement noun clause. The clause itself is a **tripartite** verbless/nominal clause (see on 3:22 for its construal, and on 1:17 for such clauses more generally). יהוה is the **extraposed topic**, while הוא is the **focus**.

בַּשָּׁמַ֣יִם מִמַּ֔עַל וְעַל־הָאָ֖רֶץ מִתָּ֑חַת. Spatial adjunct PPs. Together they form a **merism**. ממעל and מתחת are locative adverbs, formed originally from a substantive and the preposition מן (GKC §119c, 119c n. 2).

אֵ֥ין עֽוֹד׃. See on 4:35.

וְשָׁמַרְתָּ֞ אֶת־חֻקָּ֣יו וְאֶת־מִצְוֹתָ֗יו אֲשֶׁ֨ר אָנֹכִ֤י מְצַוְּךָ֙ הַיּ֔וֹם אֲשֶׁר֩ יִיטַ֨ב לְךָ֜ וּלְבָנֶ֣יךָ אַחֲרֶ֗יךָ וּלְמַ֨עַן תַּאֲרִ֤יךְ יָמִים֙ עַל־הָ֣אֲדָמָ֔ה אֲשֶׁ֨ר יְהוָ֧ה אֱלֹהֶ֛יךָ נֹתֵ֥ן לְךָ֖ כָּל־הַיָּמִֽים׃ פ   4:40

HD. A third modal *qatal* (with וידעת and והשבת [v. 39]) brings to an end the exhortation (4:1-40) built upon the recounting of history (1:6–3:29). Moses reinforces the call to obedience to what he is commanding "today" in Moab by highlighting two motivations in two purpose clauses: that it may go well with them and that they may prolong their days in the land. The final phrase, כל־הימים, holds out the reality of the gift in perpetuity. It is a permanent gift, even if an individual generation's prospering and length of days in the land depends on their obedience. There are many echoes of 4:1-2.

וְשָׁמַרְתָּ֞ אֶת־חֻקָּ֣יו וְאֶת־מִצְוֺתָ֗יו אֲשֶׁ֨ר אָנֹכִ֤י מְצַוְּךָ֙ הַיּ֔וֹם. *Qatal* (modal) 2ms Qal √שמר.

אֲשֶׁ֨ר אָנֹכִ֤י מְצַוְּךָ֙ הַיּ֔וֹם. Ptcp ms Piel √צוה with 2ms pronominal suffix. Restrictive relative clause, with **head** the conjoined NPs, את־חקיו ואת־מצוותיו (cf. on 4:2). היום is adverbial time adjunct NP (see on 1:10).

אֲשֶׁ֨ר יִיטַ֥ב לְךָ֖ וּלְבָנֶ֣יךָ אַחֲרֶ֑יךָ. *Yiqtol* 3ms Qal √יטב. The verb is one of seven genuine I-י verbs (JM §76d). It is defective, meaning that parts of the conjugation come from different roots (*qatal*: √טוב, cf. 5:33; *yiqtol*: √יטב; see JM §85a). As an impersonal verb, the one experiencing or undergoing the verbal action is the object of the subsequent preposition, ל (WO §22.7b). אשר introduces a final or purpose clause here (GKC §165b; JM §168f; WHS §175, §466, §523). This is evident from the parallel between אשר ייטב לך (4:40; 6:3) and למען ייטב לך (e.g., 5:18; 6:18) and from the lack of both a possible **head** and a place in the clause where the **head** might fit. That its role introducing a purpose clause is part of a diachronic development in אשר is doubtful, given its rarity (Holmstedt 2006). More likely it is intelligible but "ungrammatical" (Holmstedt 2006: 21–22), perhaps as an abbreviation of למען אשר.

וּלְמַ֨עַן תַּאֲרִ֤יךְ יָמִים֙ עַל־הָ֣אֲדָמָ֔ה אֲשֶׁ֨ר יְהוָ֧ה אֱלֹהֶ֛יךָ נֹתֵ֥ן לְךָ֖ כָּל־הַיָּמִֽים׃ פ. *Yiqtol* 2ms Hiph √ארך. Purpose clause introduced by the subordinating conjunction למען (cf. on 4:1). ימים is accusative complement. Although Codex Leningradensis (M^L) reads הָאֲדָמָה here, this is an error and should read, with two other Tiberian Masoretic mss (M^L17 and M^S5), הָאֲדָמָה (*BHQ: Deuteronomy*, 17).

אֲשֶׁ֨ר יְהוָ֧ה אֱלֹהֶ֛יךָ נֹתֵ֥ן לְךָ֖ כָּל־הַיָּמִֽים׃ פ. Ptcp ms Qal √נתן. Restrictive relative clause, with **head** האדמה. For the formulaic phrase, see on 1:20. כל־הימים is adverbial time adjunct construct NP.

Moses' Assignment of Transjordanian Cities of Refuge
Deuteronomy 4:41-43

The narrator breaks off from recounting Moses' speeches to describe Moses' allocation of cities of refuge east of the Jordan.

[41]Then Moses set apart three cities in the Transjordanian region on the east side [42]for a homicide to flee there; the one who unintentionally kills his neighbor—and he had not previously been his enemy—shall flee to one of these cities and live: [43]Bezer in the wilderness, in the plateau-land, for the Reubenites, Ramoth in Gilead, for the Gadites, and Golan in Bashan for the Manassites.

4:41 אָ֣ז יַבְדִּ֤יל מֹשֶׁה֙ שָׁלֹ֣שׁ עָרִ֔ים בְּעֵ֖בֶר הַיַּרְדֵּ֑ן מִזְרְחָ֖ה שָֽׁמֶשׁ׃

ND. D1. The narrator describes with loose temporal connection the designation of three cities of refuge east of the Jordan.

אָ֣ז יַבְדִּ֤יל מֹשֶׁה֙ שָׁלֹ֣שׁ עָרִ֔ים בְּעֵ֖בֶר הַיַּרְדֵּ֑ן. *Yiqtol* 3ms Hiph √בדל. After אז, *yiqtol* occurs frequently, always directly (cf. Holmstedt 2002: 184). It probably is an "archaic past" form, though the lack of shortening (יַבְדִּיל not יַבְדֵּל) is puzzling (WHS §177c; Cook 2012: 260–63; cf. JM §113i; GKC §107c). אז does not necessarily indicate that the allocation of cities was subsequent to Moses' opening speech, rather that it was about at that time. The narrator has chosen not to interrupt (Tigay 1996: 58).

בְּעֵ֖בֶר הַיַּרְדֵּ֑ן. Spatial adjunct PP. See on 1:1 for its referent.

מִזְרְחָ֖ה שָֽׁמֶשׁ. Directional adjunct construct NP. The locative ה on מזרחה indicates motion toward (cf. WO §10.5a, b; JM §93c), "toward the rising of the sun," hence "to the east" (cf. on 3:17). Although the locative ה is normally unaccented, in three places מזרחה has the accent on the final syllable, including here. This may be because of the subsequent pause (JM §93c) or, more likely, because it is in the construct state (BDB s.v; HALOT s.v.; cf. Josh 12:1; Judg 21:19; GKC §90i).

4:42 לָנֻ֣ס שָׁ֗מָּה רוֹצֵ֙חַ֙ אֲשֶׁ֨ר יִרְצַ֤ח אֶת־רֵעֵ֙הוּ֙ בִּבְלִי־דַ֔עַת וְה֛וּא לֹא־שֹׂנֵ֥א ל֖וֹ מִתְּמֹ֣ל שִׁלְשֹׁ֑ם וְנָ֗ס אֶל־אַחַ֛ת מִן־הֶעָרִ֥ים הָאֵ֖ל וָחָֽי׃

D1. The opening three words continue v. 41. The rest of the verse clarifies the general provision—the one who kills his neighbor accidentally and with no history of hostility (v. 42a) may flee to one of the cities and live. ED.

לָנֻ֣ס שָׁ֗מָּה רוֹצֵ֙חַ֙. Inf constr Qal √נוס with preposition ל. Adjunct infinitive phrase expressing purpose. Weinfeld (230–31) has the best construal of the syntax. This phrase completes the previous verse (cf. 19:3b). שמה is a locative adverb, functioning as the oblique complement. רוצח is Ptcp ms Qal √רצח, used substantivally, as the subject of the infinitive construct נס.

Deuteronomy 4:42

אֲשֶׁר יִרְצַח אֶת־רֵעֵהוּ בִּבְלִי־דַעַת. *Yiqtol* 3ms Qal √רצח. Characteristic of legal texts, the preceding general statement of provision is now specified. אשר does not have as its **head** רוצח, but it is **null-head**, "[the one] who" (cf. 15:2; 19:4b). This begins the second sentence and gives further details (Weinfeld, 231).

בִּבְלִי־דַעַת. Adjunct construct PP. בלי is a rare negative, usually found in poetry (JM §160m). Here it occurs with preposition ב and is "privative," indicating "a lack of," or "un-," negating the noun that follows (WHS §420; cf. MNK §41.5.5).

וְהוּא לֹא־שֹׂנֵא לוֹ מִתְּמוֹל שִׁלְשׁוֹם. Ptcp ms Qal √שנא. The root √שנא sometimes shows both fientive and stative characteristics at the same time. The use of the participle suggests a "progressive and thus fientive sense" but the verb itself is stative (WO §22.2.3b). Although normally a **null-copula** clause, including one with a participle, is negated with אין not with לא, when the pronoun הוא is necessary, as it is here because of the circumstantial nature of the clause, לא is used (JM §160b; cf. JM §160b; GKC §152d). לו is oblique complement of שנא.

מִתְּמוֹל שִׁלְשׁוֹם. Adverbial temporal phrase. מתמול is an adverb, constructed from תמול, "yesterday" (e.g., Job 8:9; and also an adverb) and מן (cf. GKC §119c). שלשום is an adverb, "three days ago." For the ending ם- as due to it being an Akkadian loan word, rather than adverbial, see JM §102b. Together, they form a phrase, "formerly."

וְנָס אֶל־אַחַת מִן־הֶעָרִים הָאֵל. *Qatal* (modal) 3ms Qal √נוס. The ו marks the clause boundary, and the modal *qatal* indicates permission. The corresponding injunction in 19:5 has הוּא יָנוּס. A prepositional phrase, . . . אחת מן, can be used to express the partitive (JM §142ma). הָאֵל is a rare variant of the demonstrative הָאֵלֶּה (JM §36b).

וָחָי. *Qatal* (modal) 3ms Qal √חיה. The root developed from √חיי, but the 3ms *qatal* Qal retains the characteristics of the original, hence חַי (e.g., Gen 5:5; cf. GKC §76i; JM §79s). In pause, it is חָי, with the ו-conjunction pointed as וָ before the tone syllable (GKC §102g). The modality continues from the previous clause (cf. GKC §112m).

4:43 אֶת־בֶּ֧צֶר בַּמִּדְבָּ֛ר בְּאֶ֥רֶץ הַמִּישֹׁ֖ר לָרֽאוּבֵנִ֑י
וְאֶת־רָאמֹ֤ת בַּגִּלְעָד֙ לַגָּדִ֔י וְאֶת־גּוֹלָ֥ן בַּבָּשָׁ֖ן לַֽמְנַשִּֽׁי׃

Three accusative NPs, appositional to שלש ערים in v. 41, give the names of the cities and their tribal beneficiaries.

אֶת־בֶּ֧צֶר בַּמִּדְבָּ֛ר בְּאֶ֥רֶץ הַמִּישֹׁ֖ר לָרֽאוּבֵנִ֑י. בארץ המישר is appositional construct PP. לראובני is adjunct PP. The ל could indicate possession or, more likely, the beneficiaries (cf. on לשבטים in 1:16, לנו in 1:22). See on 3:12 for לראובני.

וְאֶת־רָאמֹ֤ת בַּגִּלְעָד֙ לַגָּדִ֔י. See on 3:12 for לגדי.

וְאֶת־גּוֹלָ֥ן בַּבָּשָׁ֖ן לַֽמְנַשִּֽׁי׃. Rare use of the patronymic (or gentilic) adjective, מנשי (see on 3:13 for מנשי and on האמרי in 1:4 for gentilic adjectives).

Looking Backward and Forward in Preparation for Moses' Second Address
Deuteronomy 4:44-49

Scholars have debated how this section relates to what precedes (esp. 1:1-5) and what follows, and, in particular, whether there are two introductions here (4:44, 45). This relates to compositional questions about the book as a whole. As the section stands, it looks both ways, functioning in some senses as a subscription to the first four chapters (Lundbom 260–64), but also preparing the way for what follows (e.g., Driver, 79–80; Weinfeld, 233–34). Although it may have the appearance of a double introduction, תורה (4:44) echoes 1:5, and references to Sihon, Og, striking down (√נכה Hiphil; 1:4; 4:46), and בעבר הירדן in 4:45-49 recapitulate 1:1-4. The effort to construct these connections may go some way to explaining von Rad's observation that the syntax here is "something of a monstrosity" (55; see Lundbom 261).

⁴⁴*This is the torah that Moses put before the Israelites.* ⁴⁵*These are the precepts, the statutes and the judgments which Moses spoke to the Israelites when they came out from Egypt,* ⁴⁶*across the Jordan in the valley opposite Beth-peor in the land of Sihon, king of the Amorites, who reigned in Heshbon, whom Moses and the Israelites struck down when they came out from Egypt,* ⁴⁷*and so they possessed his land and the land of Og, king of Bashan, the two Amorite*

kings, who were across the Jordan to the east: ⁴⁸[the territory] from Aroer, which is by the bank of Wadi Arnon, up to Mount Śion (that is, Hermon) ⁴⁹and all the Arabah across the Jordan to the east, up to the Sea of the Arabah beneath the slopes of Pisgah.

4:44   וְזֹאת הַתּוֹרָה אֲשֶׁר־שָׂם מֹשֶׁה לִפְנֵי בְּנֵי יִשְׂרָאֵל׃

D1. ED. With the brief historical retrospect over, the narrator turns to introduce the תורה that follows. It recapitulates the introduction of 1:5.

וְזֹאת הַתּוֹרָה. **Null-copula** clause, with unmarked S–P word order and substantival predicate (cf. on 1:1).

אֲשֶׁר־שָׂם מֹשֶׁה לִפְנֵי בְּנֵי יִשְׂרָאֵל׃. *Qatal* 3ms Qal √שׂים. Restrictive relative clause, with **head** התורה. לפני בני ישראל is oblique complement construct PP.

4:45   אֵלֶּה הָעֵדֹת וְהַחֻקִּים וְהַמִּשְׁפָּטִים אֲשֶׁר דִּבֶּר מֹשֶׁה
אֶל־בְּנֵי יִשְׂרָאֵל בְּצֵאתָם מִמִּצְרָיִם׃

D1. ED. Having resumed the introduction of 1:5, the narrator expands upon the תורה, reiterating what he has just said.

אֵלֶּה הָעֵדֹת וְהַחֻקִּים וְהַמִּשְׁפָּטִים. **Null-copula** clause, with unmarked S–P word order and substantival predicate (cf. on 1:1). עֵדֹת is plural of עֵדוּת, a "precept." When written *plene*, it is sometimes pointed עֵדְוֹת, but there is no difference between the words (Driver, 80; Weinfeld, 235). The clausal **asyndesis** could mark a new section (the view of most scholars), but it could also reflect the explanatory nature of the clause, as it expands upon v. 44 (cf. DeRouchie 2007: 278).

אֲשֶׁר דִּבֶּר מֹשֶׁה אֶל־בְּנֵי יִשְׂרָאֵל. *Qatal* 3ms Piel √דבר. For the form of דבר and the word order, see on 1:1.

בְּצֵאתָם מִמִּצְרָיִם׃. Inf constr Qal √יצא with 3mp pronominal suffix and preposition ב. For the form of the infinitive construct of the I-ו and III-א verb יצא, see GKC §69m; JM §75g. Adjunct temporal PP. The suffix ־ָם is the subject of the infinitive construct. ממצרים is oblique locative complement.

בְּעֵ֥בֶר הַיַּרְדֵּן֙ בַּגַּ֔יְא מ֖וּל בֵּ֣ית פְּע֑וֹר בְּאֶ֗רֶץ סִיחֹן֙ 4:46
מֶ֣לֶךְ הָֽאֱמֹרִ֔י אֲשֶׁ֥ר יוֹשֵׁ֖ב בְּחֶשְׁבּ֑וֹן אֲשֶׁ֨ר הִכָּ֤ה
מֹשֶׁה֙ וּבְנֵ֣י יִשְׂרָאֵ֔ל בְּצֵאתָ֖ם מִמִּצְרָֽיִם׃

בְּעֵ֥בֶר הַיַּרְדֵּן֙ בַּגַּ֔יְא מ֖וּל בֵּ֣ית פְּע֑וֹר בְּאֶ֗רֶץ סִיחֹן֙ מֶ֣לֶךְ הָֽאֱמֹרִ֔י. A succession of spatial adjunct PPs, giving the location of Moses' speaking (v. 45). They pick up phrases that have occurred before: בעבר הירדן (1:1); בגיא (3:29); מול בית פעור [בארץ] (1:4). סיחן מלך האמרי

אֲשֶׁ֥ר יוֹשֵׁ֖ב בְּחֶשְׁבּ֑וֹן. Ptcp ms Qal √ישׁב. Restrictive relative clause, with **head** סיחן. See on 1:4 for identical wording.

אֲשֶׁ֨ר הִכָּ֤ה מֹשֶׁה֙ וּבְנֵ֣י יִשְׂרָאֵ֔ל. *Qatal* 3ms Hiph √נכה. Non-restrictive relative clause, giving additional information. Note the **triggered inversion** after אשר. This is an example of a clause where there is not full agreement between the subject and the predicate; the verb agrees with the first constituent, משה. This has taxed grammarians (see, e.g., GKC §145o). Recently Holmstedt has proposed a different syntactical explanation, rooted in Hebrew being a *pro*-drop language. Because the finite verb carries person, number and gender within it, subject pronouns are often not overt, and are allowed to "drop." What is found instead is the **null subject pro** (in the verb). The **pro** identifies the key figure in the narrative (Holmstedt 2009: 121–27). Here it is Moses (as in 1:4).

בְּצֵאתָ֖ם מִמִּצְרָֽיִם. See on 4:45 for the same phrase.

וַיִּֽירְשׁ֣וּ אֶת־אַרְצ֗וֹ וְאֶת־אֶ֙רֶץ֙ ׀ ע֚וֹג מֶ֣לֶךְ־הַבָּשָׁ֔ן שְׁנֵי֙ 4:47
מַלְכֵ֣י הָֽאֱמֹרִ֔י אֲשֶׁ֥ר בְּעֵ֖בֶר הַיַּרְדֵּ֑ן מִזְרַ֖ח שָֽׁמֶשׁ׃

ND. D2. This and the following two verses have a "loose connection" to what precedes (Driver, 81). In giving the location of Moses' speaking, the narrator has not been able to resist recapitulating the defeat and dispossession of Sihon and Og.

וַיִּֽירְשׁ֣וּ אֶת־אַרְצ֗וֹ וְאֶת־אֶ֙רֶץ֙ ׀ ע֚וֹג מֶ֣לֶךְ־הַבָּשָׁ֔ן שְׁנֵי֙ מַלְכֵ֣י הָֽאֱמֹרִ֔י. *Wayyiqtol* 3mp Qal √ירשׁ. ND. The adjunct phrase in 4:46, משה ובני ישראל, has allowed the shift in **pro** from 3ms to 3mp. Syntactically, this continues the events within the relative clause of v. 46. See on 1:4 for עוג מלך־הבשן. See on 3:8 for שני מלכי האמרי, construct NP appositional to Sihon (as referred to in 3ms pronominal suffix in ארצו) and Og.

אֲשֶׁ֨ר בְּעֵ֧בֶר הַיַּרְדֵּ֛ן מִזְרַ֥ח שָֽׁמֶשׁ׃. **Null-copula** restrictive relative clause, with **head** שני מלכי האמרי, with PP adverbial predicate, בעבר הירדן (for which see on 1:1). מזרח שמש is locative adjunct NP (cf. 4:41).

4:48 מֵעֲרֹעֵ֞ר אֲשֶׁ֣ר עַל־שְׂפַת־נַ֤חַל אַרְנֹן֙ וְעַד־הַ֣ר שִׂיאֹ֔ן ה֖וּא חֶרְמֽוֹן׃

ND. D2. A covert appositional accusative is followed by adjunct PPs giving the extent of the territory possessed, continuing the clause from v. 47. They are similar to, although slightly shorter than, 2:36 (3:12) and 3:8b-9. This describes the highlands (Tigay 1996: 59).

מֵעֲרֹעֵ֞ר אֲשֶׁ֣ר עַל־שְׂפַת־נַ֤חַל אַרְנֹן֙. See on 2:36 for the same phrase. Note, though, that as with 3:12, the appositional accusative is covert: "[the territory] from Aroer . . ."; the phrase is appositional to את ארצו ואת־ארץ עוג (v. 46), as is evident from the continuation in v. 49.

וְעַד־הַ֣ר שִׂיאֹ֔ן. Adjunct construct PP (cf. 3:8b). שיאן is another variant name for Hermon, perhaps arising through confusion of letters (cf. 3:9; Craigie, 147; Tigay 1996: 59).

ה֖וּא חֶרְמֽוֹן׃. Asyndetic **null-copula** clause, with unmarked S–P word order, explaining the previous (unusual) name, שיאן.

4:49 וְכָל־הָ֨עֲרָבָ֜ה עֵ֤בֶר הַיַּרְדֵּן֙ מִזְרָ֔חָה וְעַ֖ד יָ֣ם הָעֲרָבָ֑ה תַּ֖חַת אַשְׁדֹּ֥ת הַפִּסְגָּֽה׃ פ

ND. D2. This describes the other part of what the Israelites possessed, the Jordan valley (cf. Tigay 1996: 59). The wording is very similar to 3:17.

וְכָל־הָ֨עֲרָבָ֜ה עֵ֤בֶר הַיַּרְדֵּן֙ מִזְרָ֔חָה. וכל־הערבה is a second NP coordinated with the covert appositional accusative, "[Ø] from Aroer." עבר הירדן, an appositional construct NP, only here in chapters 1–11 lacks the preposition ב; along with the locative adverb מזרחה (cf. on 3:17; 4:41), it specifies the location of the Arabah.

וְעַ֖ד יָ֣ם הָעֲרָבָ֑ה תַּ֖חַת אַשְׁדֹּ֥ת הַפִּסְגָּֽה׃ פ. See on 3:17 for the identical phrase.

MOSES' SECOND ADDRESS
DEUTERONOMY 5:1–11:32(26:19)

The Events at Horeb Mean Israel Should Listen in Moab: Deuteronomy 5:1-33

Moses reminds them of the events at Horeb, because it was there that they heard Yhwh's voice giving the decalogue, pleaded with Moses to mediate with Yhwh and committed to hearing and doing what Moses might tell them. For such a desire and commitment, they received a rare commendation (5:28). In the chapter there are no fewer than four domains of speech, from the narrator (5:1a) through to the narrator citing Moses citing Yhwh telling Moses what he should say (5:30b). The logic is as below:

* Hear, learn and observe by doing (v. 1);
* Yhwh gave the decalogue and nothing else; you heard Yhwh's voice, pleaded with me to mediate and said you would obey; Yhwh agreed and said he would tell me what to say to you (vv. 2-31);
* so observe by doing, just as Yhwh commanded (vv. 32-33).

The purpose of reciting the events at Horeb is twofold: (1) to tie Moses' addressees in Moab to Horeb (cf. v. 3); and (2) to reinforce Moses' exhortation to them to observe the statutes and commandments given in Moab: they had requested Moses as mediator and Yhwh had endorsed that request.

The introduction to the decalogue (5:1-5)

Moses' initial command to his addressees in Moab to hear, learn and observe the statutes and commandments (v. 1) is buttressed by recounting events at Horeb and affirming their close connection with those events.

¹Then Moses summoned all Israel and said to them, "Hear, Israel, the statutes and judgments which I am speaking in your hearing today; learn them and observe [them] by doing them. ²Yhwh our God made a covenant with us at Horeb. ³It was not with our ancestors that Yhwh made this covenant, but with us, yes us, these ones here today, all of us [who are] alive. ⁴Face to face, Yhwh spoke with you on the mountain from the midst of the fire ⁵(I was mediating between Yhwh and you at that time, to tell you the word of Yhwh because you were afraid of the fire and did not go up on the mountain), saying:

5:1 וַיִּקְרָ֤א מֹשֶׁה֙ אֶל־כָּל־יִשְׂרָאֵ֔ל וַיֹּ֣אמֶר אֲלֵהֶ֔ם שְׁמַ֤ע יִשְׂרָאֵל֙ אֶת־הַחֻקִּ֣ים וְאֶת־הַמִּשְׁפָּטִ֔ים אֲשֶׁ֧ר אָנֹכִ֛י דֹּבֵ֥ר בְּאָזְנֵיכֶ֖ם הַיּ֑וֹם וּלְמַדְתֶּ֣ם אֹתָ֔ם וּשְׁמַרְתֶּ֖ם לַעֲשֹׂתָֽם׃

The narrator introduces Moses' speech with two *wayyiqtols* (D1, ND). Moses begins (D2) with a call to Israel to hear (HD), followed by two modal *qatals* (HD): hear, learn, be mindful [of them] by doing them.

וַיִּקְרָ֤א מֹשֶׁה֙ אֶל־כָּל־יִשְׂרָאֵ֔ל. *Wayyiqtol* 3ms Qal √קרא. ND. אל־כל־ישראל is oblique complement.

וַיֹּ֣אמֶר אֲלֵהֶ֔ם. *Wayyiqtol* 3ms Qal √אמר. אלהם is oblique complement, written defectively (see on 1:3). The accusative complement is the direct speech that follows until 26:19.

שְׁמַ֤ע יִשְׂרָאֵל֙ אֶת־הַחֻקִּ֣ים וְאֶת־הַמִּשְׁפָּטִ֔ים אֲשֶׁ֧ר אָנֹכִ֛י דֹּבֵ֥ר בְּאָזְנֵיכֶ֖ם הַיּ֑וֹם. Impv ms Qal √שמע. HD. See on 4:1. ישראל is vocative.

אֲשֶׁ֧ר אָנֹכִ֛י דֹּבֵ֥ר בְּאָזְנֵיכֶ֖ם הַיּ֑וֹם. Ptcp ms Qal √דבר. The finite forms of √דבר are always Piel. However, on forty-one occasions the Qal is found, thirty-nine of which are active participles (exceptions are Ps 51:6; Prov 25:11). Possibly some other Qal forms have become assimilated to the Piel (Weinfeld, 236). The clause is a **null-copula** restrictive relative clause, with **head** את־החקים ואת־המשפטים. The participle indicates the ongoing process of proclamation. The S–P word order is unmarked (see on 1:20). For אנכי, see on 4:1. באזניכם is adjunct PP (cf. Jer 28:7). היום is a locative adverb (see on 1:10).

וּלְמַדְתֶּ֥ם אֹתָֽם. *Qatal* (modal) 2mp Qal √למד. HD. The modal *qatal* continues an imperative when "the second action does not belong to the present moment, but to a more or less distant time" (JM §119l).

וּשְׁמַרְתֶּ֖ם לַעֲשֹׂתָֽם׃. *Qatal* (modal) 2mp Qal √שמר, followed by Inf constr Qal √עשה with 3mp pronominal suffix and preposition ל. HD. Rather than this being an instance of שמר having an adverbial force (see on 4:6), the infinitive construct לעשׂתם is **gerundial**, "by doing them" (cf. WO §36.2.3e, although they confusingly or erroneously describe this kind as "**gerundive**"); the accusative complement of √שמר is covert.

5:2 יְהוָ֣ה אֱלֹהֵ֗ינוּ כָּרַ֥ת עִמָּ֛נוּ בְּרִ֖ית בְּחֹרֵֽב׃

D2. ND. Moses insists that the covenant at Horeb was with his addressees, though that generation had died out (1:35; 2:14). The **asyndesis** serves to demarcate a long section (vv. 2-31), which provides the grounds for the commands of v. 1 (DeRouchie 2007: 125).

יְהוָ֣ה אֱלֹהֵ֗ינוּ כָּרַ֥ת עִמָּ֛נוּ בְּרִ֖ית בְּחֹרֵֽב׃. *Qatal* 3ms Qal √כרת. ND. Unmarked S–P word order. עמנו is adjunct PP; often, but not always (e.g., Gen 21:32), a preposition introduces the one with whom a covenant (ברית) is made (√כרת). Usually in Deuteronomy it is עם or את (e.g., here, v. 3; 9:9; 31:16). In Deuteronomy it is ל only when making a covenant with the inhabitants of the land (7:2; cf. Exod 34:12, 15; Josh 9:15; Judg 2:2), though that usage is not exclusively negative (cf. Psa 89:4 [ET 89:3]; 1 Chr 11:3; 2 Chr 29:10; Ezra 10:3). בחרב is spatial adjunct PP.

5:3 לֹ֣א אֶת־אֲבֹתֵ֔ינוּ כָּרַ֥ת יְהוָ֖ה אֶת־הַבְּרִ֣ית הַזֹּ֑את כִּ֣י אִתָּ֣נוּ אֲנַ֗חְנוּ אֵ֣לֶּה פֹ֥ה הַיּ֛וֹם כֻּלָּ֖נוּ חַיִּֽים׃

ND. D2. The clausal **asyndesis**, the dramatic contrast between לא את־אבתינו and כי אתנו and the pleonastic rhetorical hammer-blows of 5:3b all serve to stress the immediacy of the Horeb covenant for the people in Moab. Given the covenant in Moab's validity for all future generations (29:13-14), this immediacy is also for the *book*'s hearers.

לֹ֣א אֶת־אֲבֹתֵ֔ינוּ כָּרַ֥ת יְהוָ֖ה אֶת־הַבְּרִ֣ית הַזֹּ֑את. *Qatal* 3ms Qal √כרת. ND. לא is an item adverb, modifying the adjunct PP rather than the main clause (cf. WO §39.3.2). את־אבתינו is adjunct PP, fronted for focus. The implied contrast is then spelled out fully in the second half of the verse. The clausal **asyndesis** suggests that v. 3a expands upon or explains v. 2.

כִּ֣י אִתָּ֔נוּ אֲנַ֣חְנוּ אֵ֥לֶּה פֹ֛ה הַיּ֖וֹם כֻּלָּ֥נוּ חַיִּֽים. When the conjunction כי follows a clause or phrase with לא, it often indicates an adversative clause or phrase (cf. GKC §163a; JM §172c; AC §5.2.10). The "awkward" syntax reinforces the "direct relationship" (Craigie, 148). After the PP אתנו, contrasting with את־אבתינו, two appositional words describe the people (אנחנו אלה); two adverbial phrases then follow, giving place (פה) and time (היום; cf. on 1:10) in Moab; finally there is a further appositional NP and an adjective. The use of the independent personal subject pronoun, אנחנו, after אתנו gives strong emphasis (GKC §135g; WO §16.3.4.a; JM §146d; WHS §107a). The whole phrase is **elliptical**. Effectively it provides the correct answer that can be substituted for the incorrect one found in the **focus**-fronted phrase in 5:3a (Moshavi 2010: 139).

5:4 פָּנִ֣ים ׀ בְּפָנִ֗ים דִּבֶּ֨ר יְהוָ֧ה עִמָּכֶ֛ם בָּהָ֖ר מִתּ֥וֹךְ הָאֵֽשׁ׃

ND. D2. Moses declares to the people the directness of the encounter the people had, further reactualizing Horeb for the Moab generation (cf. 4:9-10).

פָּנִ֣ים ׀ בְּפָנִ֗ים דִּבֶּ֨ר יְהוָ֧ה עִמָּכֶ֛ם בָּהָ֖ר מִתּ֥וֹךְ הָאֵֽשׁ׃. *Qatal* 3ms Piel √דבר. For the form, see on 1:1. This asyndetic clause explains further v. 2, rather than v. 3, which itself was joined asyndetically to v. 2. There is no direct relationship warranting a ו between v. 3 and v. 4 (cf. DeRouchie 2007: 125).

פָּנִ֣ים ׀ בְּפָנִ֗ים. פנים בפנים is an indirect accusative. JM §126f characterizes it as a "predicative accusative of state" because it is subordinated to the predicate, and complements the action of the predicate. It is fronted for **focus**: out of the possible ways that Yhwh could speak, it was "face to face." Since Deuteronomy is clear that no form was seen (4:12), perhaps the preposition ב indicates a reticence (cf. Weinfeld, 239–40). Only here is the preposition ב used, rather than אל (e.g., 34:10; 5× in total). The vertical line | after פנים is not the *paseq* (see on 3:20), but a disjunctive accent, *legarmeh*.

עִמָּכֶ֛ם בָּהָ֖ר מִתּ֥וֹךְ הָאֵֽשׁ׃. Three adjunct PPs, indicating with whom, where, and from where Yhwh spoke.

5:5 אָנֹכִי עֹמֵד בֵּין־יְהוָה וּבֵינֵיכֶם בָּעֵת הַהִוא לְהַגִּיד לָכֶם אֶת־דְּבַר יְהוָה כִּי יְרֵאתֶם מִפְּנֵי הָאֵשׁ וְלֹא־עֲלִיתֶם בָּהָר לֵאמֹר׃ס

ND. D2. This circumstantial clause gives further information, clarifying the picture expressed in the previous verse.

אָנֹכִי עֹמֵד בֵּין־יְהוָה וּבֵינֵיכֶם בָּעֵת הַהִוא. Ptcp ms Qal √עמד. **Null-copula** clause, with unmarked S–P word order. The S–P word order with a participle indicates that it is a circumstantial clause, giving background, sometimes parenthetical, ongoing activity. It is not advancing the storyline. Usually such a clause begins with ו (GKC §141e; JM §159d), but sometimes it is asyndetic (JM §159b). For אנכי see on 4:1. The use of prepositions בין . . . בין . . . either "distinguishes different parties . . . that are each actively involved in a process" or "indicates localization in a space: between two or more points" (MNK §39.7). The former is clearly the case here. For בעת ההוא, see on 1:9.

לְהַגִּיד לָכֶם אֶת־דְּבַר יְהוָה. Inf constr Hiph √נגד with preposition ל. Adjunct infinitive phrase to verb עמד, indicating purpose. As a three-place predicate, it has both an accusative complement, the construct NP את־דבר יהוה, and an oblique complement, לכם.

כִּי יְרֵאתֶם מִפְּנֵי הָאֵשׁ. Qatal 2mp Qal √ירא. מפני האש is oblique complement. √ירא sometimes takes an oblique complement (with מן, מפני; e.g., 1:29) and sometimes an accusative complement (e.g., 3:2). A stative verb, it is sometimes absolute (e.g., 1:21). The cause is an explanatory clause, introduced by the subordinating conjunction, כי, explaining why Moses had to mediate.

וְלֹא־עֲלִיתֶם בָּהָר. Qatal 2mp Qal √עלה. בהר is spatial adjunct PP.

לֵאמֹר׃. Inf constr Qal √אמר with preposition ל. A **complementizer** (see on 1:5), it resumes the clause begun in v. 4, after the circumstantial clause in the rest of v. 5, and introduces the cited discourse.

The decalogue (5:6-21)

Moses' reciting of the decalogue, with Deuteronomic characteristics, needs to be understood within the rhetoric of the chapter as a whole (see introductory comments).

Although there are ten words (4:13), there have been different ways of numbering, which place weight on features of the decalogue that either connect commandments or separate them. Broadly speaking, the following factors need to be considered:

1. The distinctively Yhwh-focused characteristics of commandments between vv. 6 and 16. Each is grounded in motive clauses related to the action or words of "Yhwh your God" (vv. 6, 9, 11, 12, 14, 15, 16) (Tigay 1996: 62).
2. The role of historical references. The commandments from vv. 6-16 are bound together by the narrative of Yhwh bringing the people out of Egypt (v. 6) and entering the land (v. 16) (Weinfeld, 313). Their allegiance to Yhwh and obedience to Yhwh's commands are rooted in Yhwh's redemptive action in history.
3. The significance of pronouns (or their absence):
   a. whether the pronouns are in the same commandment as their antecedents: על־פני (v. 7) relates to Yhwh (v. 6); להם (v. 9) relates to אלהים אחרים (v. 7);
   b. whether the absence of pronouns indicates separate commandments: ברעך occurs in both clauses in v. 21 (also v. 20). Only within v. 21b do pronouns occur, referring to רעך.
4. Because there are more than ten injunctions, the significance of syndesis and **asyndesis** (cf. DeRouchie 2007: 115–16, 128–32).
   a. whether **asyndesis** marks explanation of a commandment (so, e.g., v. 9) or the introduction of a new commandment (e.g., vv. 16, 17).
   b. whether the syndesis in v. 21b is consistent with the start of a new commandment, beginning ולא תתאוה (cf. the syndesis found in vv. 18-21, unlike in Exodus)?
5. The significance of the variations from the Exodus commandments (esp. Exod 20:17 and 5:21).
6. The traditions of interpretation, including those found in the MT and represented in different traditions of accentuation (cf. Weinfeld, 243–45).

Commentators discuss the numbering at length. I favor taking vv. 6-10 as the first commandment, and regarding v. 21 as containing

⁶"I am Yhwh your God, who brought you out from the land of Egypt, from the house of slaves—⁷You shall have no other gods in my sight. ⁸You shall not make for yourself an idol, any form that is in the heavens above or on the earth beneath or in the waters under the earth. ⁹You shall not bow down to them and you shall not serve them, for I am Yhwh your God, a jealous god, visiting fathers' iniquity on children and on the third and fourth [generation] of those that hate me, ¹⁰while acting with faithful love to thousands [of generations] of those who love me and keep my commandments. ¹¹You shall not take up the name of Yhwh your God in vain, for Yhwh will not leave unpunished the one who takes up his name in vain. ¹²Keep the sabbath day by sanctifying it, just as Yhwh your God commanded you— ¹³six days you shall labor and do all your work, ¹⁴while the seventh day is a sabbath to Yhwh your God. Do not do any work, you, your son or daughter, your servant or maidservant, your ox, donkey or any of your livestock, or your resident alien who is in your communities, so that your servant and maidservant may rest, as you do. ¹⁵You should remember that you were a slave in the land of Egypt, and Yhwh your God brought you out from there with a strong hand and outstretched arm. Therefore, Yhwh your God commands you to observe the sabbath day. ¹⁶Honor your father and your mother, just as Yhwh your God commanded you, so that your days may be long and so that it may go well with you on the land which Yhwh your God is giving to you. ¹⁷Do not murder ¹⁸and do not commit adultery ¹⁹and do not steal ²⁰and do not testify for or against your neighbor as a false witness ²¹and do not covet your neighbor's wife and do not crave your neighbor's household: his field, his servant or maidservant, his ox, his donkey, or anything that belongs to your neighbor."

5:6 אָנֹכִי יְהוָה אֱלֹהֶיךָ אֲשֶׁר הוֹצֵאתִיךָ מֵאֶרֶץ מִצְרָיִם מִבֵּית עֲבָדִים׃

ED. D3. This verse functions both as an introduction to the first commandment (cf. Ps 81:10-11) and to the commandments in general (Tigay 1996: 63).

אָנֹכִי יְהוָה אֱלֹהֶיךָ. **Null-copula** clause, with S–P word-order. ED. For אנכי, see on 4:1. The main interpretative question is whether יהוה is an apposition to אנכי, with אלהיך the substantival complement, "I, Yhwh, am your God," or אלהיך in apposition to יהוה, with יהוה the substantive complement, "I am Yhwh, your God." The former takes Yhwh's name for granted, and insists Yhwh, and not any other deity, is their god and focuses on the action of deliverance (cf. Mayes 1979: 166; Nelson, 75 n. d). The latter emphasises Yhwh's self-identification as Yhwh (cf. Zimmerli). The latter is to be preferred on four grounds: (1) MT accentuation, with אנכי having a disjunctive *pashtah* and יהוה having a conjunctive *munah*; (2) elsewhere in Deuteronomy, אלהים is always appositional to יהוה (e.g., 5:9); (3) in other contexts, אלהיך may be omitted, and the phrase "I am Yhwh" is found (see esp. Gen 15:7; Lev 19:36-37); and (4) self-presentations are common in ANE royal inscriptions (Lundbom 276–77).

אֲשֶׁר הוֹצֵאתִ֛יךָ מֵאֶ֥רֶץ מִצְרַ֖יִם מִבֵּ֥ית עֲבָדִֽים׃. *Qatal* 1cs Hiph √יצא with 2ms pronominal suffix. Non-restrictive relative clause, giving further information about Yhwh. The 1cs is because Hebrew tends to use the same person in the relative clause, if 1st or 2nd person, as the antecedent (GKC §138d; JM §158n). The verb connotes "releasing," not merely physical movement (Tigay 1996: 64; cf. 2 Sam 22:49). מארץ מצרים is oblique complement construct phrase with √יצא Hiphil, "bring out *from*." מבית עבדים is appositional PP; the lack of the article with עבדים may be due to its effective function as a place name (JM §137s). In BHS, there is a double accentuation pattern due to differing traditions of verse division. The Masoretes retained both traditions by giving some words two accents on the stressed syllable (n.b., the ʾ*atnakh* and *silluq* in the last syllable of עֲבָדִֽים). See Tigay 1996: 63, 342.

5:7 לֹ֣א יִהְיֶֽה־לְךָ֛ אֱלֹהִ֥ים אֲחֵרִ֖ים עַל־פָּנָֽי׃

HD. D3. The **asyndesis** here connects this verse with v. 6, rather than beginning something new. This is confirmed by the pronominal suffix on על־פני, the antecedent of which is in v. 6. This is the basic injunction of the first commandment.

לֹ֣א יִהְיֶֽה־לְךָ֛ אֱלֹהִ֥ים אֲחֵרִ֖ים. *Yiqtol* (modal) 3ms Qal √היה. The longer form יהיה with לא can indicate both PD, what "will not" be the case (e.g., 7:14), and HD, what "should not" be the case (e.g., 15:4; 25:13-14). Context is determinative, and the apodictic commands that follow indicate HD; the *yiqtol* has the nuance of "must/should (not)" (cf. GKC §107o; JM §113m). The other way of expressing negative HD, the **apocopated** jussive form יְהִי negated with אַל, would indicate a negative wish (e.g., Job 16:18). לֹא + *yiqtol* is characteristic of apodictic or universal laws. The verb is singular, while the subject following, אלהים אחרים is plural. This is quite common when the subject follows the predicate and the subject is not personal; it is also often the case, as here, with the verb היה as the copula (GKC §145q; WHS §228; JM §150j). לְךָ is the adverbial PP complement, indicating possession (cf. WO §11.2.10d).

עַל־פָּנָֽי. Adjunct PP. For the double accentuation, see on v. 6. The meaning of the phrase has been much discussed. JM §103p notes that Hebrew "makes extensive use of pseudo-prepositions," a preposition attached to a substantive. Sometimes the substantive is used as such (e.g., for עַל־פְּנֵי, Ezek 1:28, "I fell *on my face*"), but usually a figurative sense of the noun is meant, and the whole effectively seems a preposition. Interpretative questions for עַל־פְּנֵי revolve around: (1) the significance of the object of the preposition (whether inanimate, personal, or Yhwh); (2) the importance of a prior preposition, such as מִן (e.g., 2 Kgs 17:23); (3) the appropriate corpus that should be considered; (4) the construction of Israelite religious history for what is plausible (cf. Lundbom, 279); and (5) the weight given to the ancient versions (e.g., LXX: 5:7—πρὸ προσώπου μου, "in my presence"; Exod 20:3—πλὴν ἐμοῦ, "except for me"). A spatial sense is by far the most common; it is also the most plausible, but even here there are three possible connotations: (1) "above," in the sense of "preference" (cf. 21:16); (2) "before," in the sense of literal presence (cf. 16:21; Exod 33:19); or (3) "before," in the sense of "in my sight." The second and the third are not far apart and should be preferred: when Yhwh is the object of the preposition, this sense is always in view, whether more literally (Ps 9:20) or more figuratively (compounded with מִן, e.g., 2 Kgs 13:23; 17:23; 23:27; 24:3; Jer 7:15; 23:39). However עַל־פְּנֵי is understood, the point is clear: they should have no deities but Yhwh.

5:8 לֹֽא־תַעֲשֶׂה־לְךָ֣ פֶ֣סֶל ׀ כָּל־תְּמוּנָ֗ה אֲשֶׁ֤ר בַּשָּׁמַ֙יִם֙ ׀ מִמַּ֔עַל וַאֲשֶׁ֥ר בָּאָ֖רֶץ מִתָּ֑חַת וַאֲשֶׁ֥ר בַּמַּ֖יִם ׀ מִתַּ֥חַת לָאָֽרֶץ׃

HD. D3. The **asyndesis** here serves to explain "other gods" in terms of the construction of idols. It remains part of the opening command (see the introduction to the decalogue and the comment on להם in v. 9). The scope is comprehensive.

לֹא־תַעֲשֶׂה־לְךָ֣ פֶ֣סֶל׀ כָּל־תְּמוּנָ֡ה. *Yiqtol* (modal) 2ms Qal √עשה. Prohibitions in Hebrew do not use the imperative, but either אל + jussive or, as here, לא + *yiqtol*. The difference between them has been disputed (WO §34.2.2 n. 6; JM §113m). לא + *yiqtol* may be "more solemn" (JM §113m) or "more emphatic" (GKC §107o). For the notion of √עשה + פסל + לכם/לך, see on 4:16. The vertical line | after פסל is not the *paseq* (see on 3:20), but a disjunctive accent, *legarmeh*; the other accentuation tradition also has a disjunctive accent, a *pashtah*. כל־תמונה is, then, in apposition to פסל, and is an inversion of תמונת־כל (4:23-25): "any form." While the notion of making a "form" might seem problematic (see on 4:12), it is not necessarily so (see on 4:16).

אֲשֶׁ֣ר בַּשָּׁמַ֣יִם׀ מִמַּ֡עַל וַאֲשֶׁ֣ר בָּאָ֣רֶץ מִתַּ֑חַת וַאֲשֶׁ֥ר בַּמַּ֖יִם׀ מִתַּ֥חַת לָאָֽרֶץ׃. Three **null-copula** restrictive relative clauses, with **head** תמונה (cf. 4:23, where כל is the **head**) and PP complements. For בשמים ממעל and for בארץ מתחת see on 4:39 (n.b., על־הארץ there, not בארץ); for במים מתחת לארץ, see on 4:18.

5:9 לֹֽא־תִשְׁתַּחֲוֶ֥ה לָהֶ֖ם וְלֹ֣א תָעָבְדֵ֑ם כִּ֣י אָנֹכִ֞י יְהוָ֤ה אֱלֹהֶ֙יךָ֙ אֵ֣ל קַנָּ֔א פֹּ֠קֵד עֲוֺ֨ן אָב֧וֹת עַל־בָּנִ֛ים וְעַל־שִׁלֵּשִׁ֥ים וְעַל־רִבֵּעִ֖ים לְשֹׂנְאָֽי׃

HD. D3. Two prohibitions are followed by the grounds for them (כי): Yhwh is a jealous god, who will punish iniquity. Although mercy endures longer than grace (v. 10), it is Yhwh's jealousy that comes first and is prominent here, unlike in, e.g., Exod 34:6-7 (Weinfeld, 294–95). The antecedent of להם (אלהים אחרים) in v. 7 indicates that this verse is still part of the first commandment. The **asyndesis** reinforces the connection, indicating that these two prohibitions continue to expand on what it means not to have other gods: not making idols and not bowing down to them. The repeated self-identification, אנכי יהוה אלהיך connects this verse with v. 6.

לֹֽא־תִשְׁתַּחֲוֶ֥ה לָהֶ֖ם. *Yiqtol* (modal) 2ms Hishtaphel √חוי/חוה (see on 4:19). HD. A prohibition (see on v. 8). להם is adjunct PP. The antecedent could be פסל, with the plural arising from an implied multitude of idols. It is more likely, though, that the antecedent is אלהים אחרים (v. 7);

everywhere else in chapters 1–11, √חוי/חוה Hishtaphel (always with √עבד) is associated with bowing down to other deities, not to images (4:19; 8:19; 11:16).

וְלֹא תָעָבְדֵם. *Yiqtol* (modal) 2ms Qal √עבד with 3mp pronominal suffix. HD. A prohibition (see on v. 8). The form initially appears to be a Hophal (so HALOT s.v.; 2ms = תָּעֳבַד); further, the MT pointing is confirmed by the *plene* reading (with a *mater lectionis*, ו) of four different sources at Qumran (4QDeut^n, 1QPhyl, 4QPhyl^b, 4QPhyl^j). Weinfeld (277) suggests that Masoretic vocalization as a Hophal is "tendentious," with the meaning "you shall not allow yourself to be brought to worship them" (a possibility raised in GKC §60b). It expresses "contempt": "servitude" not "service" (Cassuto, 242, on Exod 20:5). However, based on "the unanimous interpretation of the textual tradition" and the Masorah Parva note to 13:3 (וְנַעַבְדֵם), *BHQ: Deuteronomy*, 66* argues that the forms are, in fact, "unusual or anomalous *qal* forms" (so too JM §63b).

כִּי אָנֹכִי יְהוָה אֱלֹהֶיךָ אֵל קַנָּא. **Null-copula** explanatory clause, introduced by כי, giving (further) grounds for not making idols. There are two NPs, יהוה אלהיך and אל קנא. In the former, אלהיך is in apposition to יהוה (cf. v. 6); in the latter, קנא is an attributive adjective, modifying אל (see on 4:24). The main question is where the copula should come or, from another perspective, which NP occurs in apposition: "I, Yhwh . . . *am* a jealous god" (Nelson, 73; NIV, ESV, NRSV, NASV) or "I *am* Yhwh . . ." (LXX; Weinfeld, 275; Lundbom, 280). In 6:15 אל קנא is the NP predicate, favoring the former. On the other hand, almost every instance in the Hebrew Bible (55 in all) of a 1cs pronoun preceding "Yhwh your God" may or must be read "I *am* Yhwh your God. . . ." The exception, where "Yhwh your God" is definitely in apposition, has the predicate (קדוש) first, fronted for **focus** (Lev 19:2). On balance the latter should be preferred, given either that an alternative order for the former was available and not chosen or the weight of evidence from other occurrences, including v. 6.

פֹּקֵד עֲוֹן אָבוֹת עַל־בָּנִים וְעַל־שִׁלֵּשִׁים וְעַל־רִבֵּעִים לְשֹׂנְאָי. Ptcp ms Qal √פקד. The whole is an adjunct NP. The participle is an attributive accusative of state, used as the attribute of a noun (יהוה אלהיך). The lack of an article shows it is neither in apposition nor a relative clause (cf. JM §127a). As a verbal adjective, the participle can take an accusative, as here (עון), showing it is primarily functioning verbally (cf. JM §121l). עון אבות is indefinite accusative complement construct

NP. עָוֹן can denote either the misdeed itself, or the guilt incurred for the misdeed, or the punishment meted out (HALOT s.v.). √פקד can speak of punishment without עָוֹן (Isa 27:1; Amos 3:14). Together, פקד עָוֹן then speaks of "visiting (by punishing) the sin of . . ."; the construct NP is then a subjective genitive, "sins fathers have committed" (cf. WO §9.5.1b); other senses of עָוֹן yield objective genitives: "guilt of fathers" (i.e., incurred by) or "punishment of fathers" (i.e., punishment due to fathers). Three coordinated oblique complements follow, indicating on whom the "iniquity" is visited. שִׁלֵּשִׁים are grandchildren (third generation); רִבֵּעִים are great-grandchildren (fourth generation).

לְשֹׂנְאָי. Ptcp mp Qal √שׂנא with 1cs pronominal suffix and with preposition לְ. The participle is used substantivally, but retains the verbal idea by taking a pronominal suffix (cf. JM §121k). Because שִׁלֵּשִׁים and רִבֵּעִים are indefinite, like the other nouns in the verse, while שֹׂנְאַי is definite (given the pronominal suffix), the construct-absolute relationship is avoided, and the "genitive" is instead the object of לְ (cf. JM §130b).

5:10 וְעֹ֥שֶׂה חֶ֖סֶד לַאֲלָפִ֑ים לְאֹהֲבַ֖י וּלְשֹׁמְרֵ֥י מִצְוֺתָֽו [מצותי]: ס

D3. This verse continues the grounds for the two prohibitions (HD) of v. 9. In contrast to the dire warning for those who make (√עשׂה) idols, Yhwh does (√עשׂה) חסד for those who are loyal and obedient. The end of the first commandment is marked by the *setumah* (ס) and by the end of Yhwh speaking in the first person.

וְעֹ֥שֶׂה חֶ֖סֶד לַאֲלָפִ֑ים. Ptcp ms Qal √עשׂה. While the accusative complement of פקד was an action of the people, here, the accusative complement of עשׂה is Yhwh's own action. חסד is "covenantal love" (cf. 7:9). לַאֲלָפִים is adjunct PP, indicating the recipients of Yhwh's חסד. It speaks of thousands *of generations*, given the contrast with v. 9 and לְאֶלֶף דּוֹר in 7:9.

לְאֹהֲבַ֖י וּלְשֹׁמְרֵ֥י מִצְוֺתָֽו [מצותי]: ס. Ptcp mp Qal √אהב with 1cs pronominal suffix and with preposition לְ; followed by Ptcp mp Qal √שׁמר, the construct before the absolute/genitive, מצותו (*ketiv*; see below). This is an objective genitive, where the construct "does" the genitive (cf. WO §9.5.2b). These substantival participles occur, as in v. 9, as the objects of the preposition לְ, in place of a "genitive" after an indefinite noun (לַאֲלָפִים; cf. JM §130b). This is the first instance of Israel's obligations to "love" (√אהב) Yhwh. The language is covenantal and resonant of vassal treaties (Moran 1963a), but such love is not reducible to affectionless loyalty (Lapsley; Arnold); the filial relationship is significant (McKay; cf. 8:5) and perhaps prior (Arnold, 556). The *qere* is מִצְוֺתָי, "my commandments," while the *ketiv* is (with pointing added) מִצְוֺתוֹ, "his commandment," a scribal error (*BHQ: Deuteronomy*, 67*).

5:11 לֹא תִשָּׂא אֶת־שֵׁם־יְהוָה אֱלֹהֶיךָ לַשָּׁוְא כִּי לֹא יְנַקֶּה יְהוָה אֵת אֲשֶׁר־יִשָּׂא אֶת־שְׁמוֹ לַשָּׁוְא׃ ס

HD. D3. The **asyndesis** here marks the start of a new commandment, confirmed by the shift to Yhwh now spoken of in the 3rd person. The second commandment.

לֹא תִשָּׂא אֶת־שֵׁם־יְהוָה אֱלֹהֶיךָ לַשָּׁוְא. *Yiqtol* (modal) 2ms Qal √נשׂא. HD. A prohibition (see on v. 8). The accusative complement is אֶת־שֵׁם־יהוה, with אלהיך in apposition to יהוה. לשׁוא is adjunct PP, "empty," futile," "worthless," though it can have the connotation of "falsehood" when associated with words (cf. v. 20; Prov 30:8; Exod 20:16). What is prohibited here has been much discussed. There is no exact parallel elsewhere (beyond the corresponding verse in Exod 20:7). Probably what is in view is the swearing of false or empty oaths (cf. Jer 7:9; Hos 4:2) or blaspheming (cf. Lev 24:10-17, 23). As Tigay (1996: 357 n. 79) suggests, the phrase is **elliptical** for taking it on the lips or uttering it (cf. Pss 16:4; 24:4; 50:16).

כִּי לֹא יְנַקֶּה יְהוָה אֵת אֲשֶׁר־יִשָּׂא אֶת־שְׁמוֹ לַשָּׁוְא׃ ס. *Yiqtol* 3ms Piel √נקה, "leave unpunished." Explanatory clause introduced by the subordinating conjunction כי.

אֵת אֲשֶׁר־יִשָּׂא אֶת־שְׁמוֹ לַשָּׁוְא׃ ס. *Yiqtol* 3ms Qal √נשׂא. The **null-head** restrictive relative clause acts as the accusative complement of the verb ינקה.

5:12 שָׁמוֹר אֶת־יוֹם הַשַּׁבָּת לְקַדְּשׁוֹ כַּאֲשֶׁר צִוְּךָ ׀ יְהוָה אֱלֹהֶיךָ׃

HD. D3. While the first two commandments have been prohibitions, this is framed positively, although it will be circumscribed further (v. 14).

Deuteronomy 5:12-13

This injunction is grounded in a comparative clause that recalls the command in Exodus.

שָׁמ֛וֹר אֶת־י֥וֹם הַשַׁבָּ֖ת לְקַדְּשׁ֑וֹ. Inf abs Qal √שמר. The infinitive absolute functions here as a command (see on שָׁמֵעַ in 1:16). For שמר + ל + infinitive construct, see on 5:1. The presence of accusative complements for both verbs (שמר and קדש) shows that שמר is not functioning adverbially, but that ל + infinitive construct here is explanatory.

אֶת־י֥וֹם הַשַׁבָּ֖ת. את־יום השבת is accusative complement construct phrase (cf. GKC §113f). The absolute, or genitive, specifies which type of day it is, a type of genitive of species, where the construct gives the class, and the absolute narrows it down (WO §9.5.3g).

לְקַדְּשׁ֑וֹ. Inf constr Piel √קדש with 3ms pronominal object suffix and with preposition ל. **Gerundial** explanatory use of ל + infinitive construct, "by sanctifying it." See above and WO §36.2.3e.

כַּאֲשֶׁ֥ר צִוְּךָ֖ ׀ יְהוָ֥ה אֱלֹהֶֽיךָ. *Qatal* 3ms Piel √צוה with 2ms pronominal suffix. A comparative clause. After כאשר, there is usually **triggered inversion**, with P–S word order.

5:13 שֵׁ֣שֶׁת יָמִים֮ תַּֽעֲבֹד֒ וְעָשִׂ֖יתָ כָּל־מְלַאכְתֶּֽךָ׃

HD. D3. The **asyndesis** indicates that this explains further *how* the Israelites are to "sanctify" the sabbath day. It specifies the number of days they are to work, and what they are to accomplish in those days.

שֵׁ֣שֶׁת יָמִים֮ תַּֽעֲבֹד֒. *Yiqtol* (modal) 2ms Qal √עבד. The *yiqtol* has the nuance of obligation (cf. JM §113m). ששת ימים is an indirect or adverbial accusative (i.e., not the object of the verb), giving the length of time they are to work (GKC §118k; JM §126i; WO §10.2.2c). It is fronted for **focus**, to give a contrast with the "seventh day" (5:14). The numerals from 3–10 are substantives; the marked feminine form is found with masculine nouns, and vice versa (cf. JM §100d). The syntax can have one of three forms: (1) absolute, before the noun; (2) absolute, after the noun; and (3) construct, before the noun, as here (JM §142d).

וְעָשִׂ֖יתָ כָּל־מְלַאכְתֶּֽךָ׃. *Qatal* (modal) 2ms Qal √עשה. The modal *qatal* continues the force of the previous *yiqtol* (WO §32.2.1d#18).

וְיוֹם֙ הַשְּׁבִיעִ֜י שַׁבָּ֣ת ׀ לַיהוָ֣ה אֱלֹהֶ֗יךָ לֹ֣א תַעֲשֶׂ֣ה 5:14
כָל־מְלָאכָ֡ה אַתָּ֣ה וּבִנְךָֽ־וּ֠בִתֶּךָ וְעַבְדְּךָֽ־וַ֨אֲמָתֶ֜ךָ
וְשׁוֹרְךָ֣ וַחֲמֹֽרְךָ֘ וְכָל־בְּהֶמְתֶּ֒ךָ וְגֵרְךָ֙ אֲשֶׁ֣ר בִּשְׁעָרֶ֔יךָ
לְמַ֗עַן יָנ֛וּחַ עַבְדְּךָ֥ וַאֲמָתְךָ֖ כָּמֽוֹךָ׃

D3. Verse 14a makes a statement that contrasts with the six days of v. 13 (ED). It is then followed asyndetically by a prohibition (HD) that explains the implication of a seventh-day sabbath (v. 14b). Adjunct NPs give the broad scope of the command. The final clause is a purpose clause, giving the reason for the prohibition.

וְיוֹם֙ הַשְּׁבִיעִ֜י שַׁבָּ֣ת ׀ לַיהוָ֣ה אֱלֹהֶ֗יךָ. **Null-copula** clause with substantival predicate (שבת). ED. After the indefinite noun, יום, ordinals always take the article "as a subsequent limitation," despite being attributive adjectives (GKC §126w; cf. WO §14.3.1d), a so-called "appositional genitive" (WS §98; WHS §98a; cf. 2 Kgs 17:6). ליהוה אלהיך is adjunct PP. After an indefinite noun, ל is used with a definite object of the preposition instead of the absolute/genitive after the construct. The nuance here is probably that of ownership, but other types of relationship are possible (cf. JM §133d).

לֹ֣א תַעֲשֶׂ֣ה כָל־מְלָאכָ֡ה. *Yiqtol* (modal) 2ms Qal √עשה. A prohibition (see on v. 8). לא . . . כל introduces an "*absolute* negation," "none whatever" (GKC §156b). The **asyndesis** suggests that it is explaining and affirming, negatively, what has been commanded positively.

אַתָּ֣ה וּבִנְךָֽ־וּבִתֶּךָ וְעַבְדְּךָֽ־וַאֲמָתֶ֜ךָ וְשׁוֹרְךָ֣ וַחֲמֹֽרְךָ֘ וְכָל־בְּהֶמְתֶּ֒ךָ וְגֵרְךָ֙ אֲשֶׁ֣ר בִּשְׁעָרֶ֔יךָ. The ms pronoun does not exclude the wife (a suggestion counter to 12:12, 18; Weinfeld, 307–8), but rather is indicative of the "priority of the masculine gender" (WO §6.5.3a). Because the finite verb carries person, number, and gender within it, subject pronouns are often not overt, and are allowed to "drop." What is found instead is the **null subject pro** (in the verb) (Holmstedt 2009: 121–27). אתה is not the subject of the verb. Rather, this whole phrase is a series of coordinated adjunct NPs, indicating the comprehensive nature of the command. The 2ms pronominal suffix on all the nouns highlights the relational dimension and the responsibility for ensuring it happens.

אֲשֶׁ֣ר בִּשְׁעָרֶ֔יךָ. **Null-copula** restrictive relative clause, with **head** גרך and PP complement. The referent of the phrase, by metonymy, is "your towns," or perhaps even "your covenant communities" (so Frese; see on 6:9).

לְמַ֨עַן יָנ֜וּחַ עַבְדְּךָ֤ וַאֲמָֽתְךָ֙ כָּמֽוֹךָ. *Yiqtol* 3ms Qal √נוח. למען is a subordinating conjunction that can introduce purpose or result clauses (JM §168d, §169g). Here it is a purpose clause, since what is in view is less the "effect" of that action than the "aim." For the singular verb agreeing with the nearest subject, see on 4:46 above.

כָּמֽוֹךָ:. Comparative adjunct PP. For the different forms of כ with pronominal suffixes, see JM §103g. English translations regard this as a kind of comparative clause, "as you [rest]"; that is the most probable rendering (cf. 5:26). However, as GKC §118s observes, כ has the "power of representing a great many pregnant relations," and perhaps it is possible that the similarity is in identity, not in the action of resting: "[who is] like you" (cf. 18:15; Schüle on Lev 19:18). If so, the point is that the servant and maidservant are no different from the addressee (cf. 15:12, although there it is a Hebrew bondservant in view, while here it could be bondservant or slave).

5:15 וְזָכַרְתָּ֞ כִּי־עֶ֣בֶד הָיִ֣יתָ ׀ בְּאֶ֣רֶץ מִצְרַ֗יִם וַיֹּצִ֨אֲךָ֜ יְהֹוָ֤ה אֱלֹהֶ֙יךָ֙ מִשָּׁ֔ם בְּיָ֥ד חֲזָקָ֖ה וּבִזְרֹ֣עַ נְטוּיָ֑ה עַל־כֵּ֗ן צִוְּךָ֙ יְהֹוָ֣ה אֱלֹהֶ֔יךָ לַעֲשׂ֖וֹת אֶת־י֥וֹם הַשַּׁבָּֽת: ס

HD. D3. They should only work (√עבד; v. 13) six days and should keep the sabbath, including making sure the slave (עבד) rested, because they too once were slaves (עבד) in Egypt, and Yhwh brought them out. They should always remember this.

וְזָכַרְתָּ֞ כִּי־עֶ֣בֶד הָיִ֣יתָ ׀ בְּאֶ֣רֶץ מִצְרַ֗יִם. *Qatal* (modal) 2ms Qal √זכר. The modal *qatal* continues the HD. It builds on the reference to עבד in v. 14, but it also serves to ground in their history the call to observe יום השבת (v. 15bβ; cf. v. 12).

כִּי־עֶ֣בֶד הָיִ֣יתָ ׀ בְּאֶ֣רֶץ מִצְרַ֗יִם. *Qatal* 2ms Qal √היה. The clause is an accusative complement noun clause, with **complementizer** כי. After כי there is normally **triggered inversion** with a fientive verb and with the copula היה; here עבד is fronted for **focus**. Of all the statuses they could have had in Egypt, they were slaves. The singular, עבד, matches the 2ms address throughout the decalogue. בארץ מצרים is spatial adjunct construct PP.

וַיּוֹצִאֲךָ֩ יְהוָ֨ה אֱלֹהֶ֤יךָ מִשָּׁם֙ בְּיָ֣ד חֲזָקָ֔ה וּבִזְרֹ֖עַ נְטוּיָ֑ה. *Wayyiqtol* 3ms Hiph √יצא with 2ms pronominal suffix. With pronominal suffixes, the shortened form (cf. on ויוצא in 4:20) reverts to the longer, with a *hireq-yod*, here written defectively. The clause continues the accusative complement noun clause, with a *wayyiqtol* following the *qatal*. משם is spatial adjunct PP. For the adjunct PPs ביד חזקה ובזרע נטויה, see on 4:34.

עַל־כֵּ֗ן צִוְּךָ֙ יְהוָ֣ה אֱלֹהֶ֔יךָ לַעֲשׂ֖וֹת אֶת־י֥וֹם הַשַּׁבָּֽת׃ ס. *Qatal* 3ms Qal √צוה with 2ms pronominal suffix. The three-place predicate, √צוה, takes an accusative complement (ךָ-) and an infinitive phrase complement (לעשות . . . השבת). על־כן is adjunct PP. The adverb כן has acquired substantival value, and so may be the object of a preposition, על, "therefore" (GKC §119ii); here it refers back to the previous clauses, and, as the object of על, gives the cause for the action of this clause (cf. JM §170h).

לַעֲשׂ֖וֹת אֶת־י֥וֹם הַשַּׁבָּֽת׃ ס. Inf constr Qal √עשה with preposition ל. The phrase forms an infinitive phrase complement, after √צוה. As a *verbal* noun, the infinitive construct can take objects. את־יום השבת is accusative complement of √עשה (for the phrase, see on 5:12). The sabbath command is framed by the *inclusio* with this phrase.

5:16 כַּבֵּ֤ד אֶת־אָבִ֙יךָ֙ וְאֶת־אִמֶּ֔ךָ כַּאֲשֶׁ֥ר צִוְּךָ֖ יְהוָ֣ה אֱלֹהֶ֑יךָ לְמַ֣עַן ׀ יַאֲרִיכֻ֣ן יָמֶ֗יךָ וּלְמַ֙עַן֙ יִ֣יטַב לָ֔ךְ עַ֚ל הָֽאֲדָמָ֔ה אֲשֶׁר־יְהוָ֥ה אֱלֹהֶ֖יךָ נֹתֵ֥ן לָֽךְ׃ ס

D3. The fourth commandment. An opening command (HD) is followed by a comparative clause (with כאשר) then two purpose clauses introduced by the subordinating conjunction למען. The close links between 4:40 and 5:16 suggest that the honouring of parents is the counterpart of the parental responsibility to teach their children the commandments. It is covenant loyalty and continuity rather than family stability that is in view (Craigie, 158).

כַּבֵּ֤ד אֶת־אָבִ֙יךָ֙ וְאֶת־אִמֶּ֔ךָ. Inf abs Piel √כבד. The alternative, that it is Piel imperative, is unlikely given שמור (5:12; cf. WO §35.5.1a n. 52; JM §123v n. 31). It is followed by coordinated accusative complements.

כַּאֲשֶׁ֥ר צִוְּךָ֖ יְהוָ֣ה אֱלֹהֶ֑יךָ. See on 5:12.

לְמַ֣עַן ׀ יַאֲרִיכֻ֣ן יָמֶ֗יךָ. *Yiqtol* 3mp Hiph √ארך with a **paragogic** ן (for which see on 1:17). For למען introducing a purpose clause, see on 4:1.

The phrase is similar to 4:40, except that יָמֶיךָ is the subject here, not the object (also 6:2; cf. HALOT s.v.).

וּלְמַעַן יֵיטַב לָךְ עַל הָאֲדָמָה אֲשֶׁר־יְהוָה אֱלֹהֶיךָ נֹתֵן לָךְ׃. Impv ms Qal √יטב. For a purpose clause with the impersonal use of the verb יטב, see on 4:40. For the pausal pointing of לָךְ, see on 1:21. הָאֲדָמָה is the **head** of the subsequent restrictive relative clause.

אֲשֶׁר־יְהוָה אֱלֹהֶיךָ נֹתֵן לָךְ׃. Ptcp ms Qal √נתן. For the phrase, see on 1:20; 4:21.

5:17 לֹא תִּרְצָח׃ ס

HD. D3. The fifth commandment. The following six commandments, unlike in Exodus, are joined by ו, making them one sentence and reinforcing the organic interconnection between them. After two positive commandments, the final six return to לֹא + *yiqtol*, indicating prohibitions (cf. on 1:17).

לֹא תִּרְצָח׃. *Yiqtol* (modal) 2ms Qal √רצח. The semantic domain of the verb includes both premeditated killing, or murder (e.g., Hos 6:9), and unintentional killing (e.g., 19:3-6). On one occasion it is used of sanctioned judicial execution (Num 35:30). It is never used of warfare, which is elsewhere accepted or mandated. Translation into English is difficult: "'murder' is too narrow, but 'kill' is too broad" (Nelson, 75 n. o). All unsanctioned ending of a person's life is in view.

5:18 וְלֹא תִּנְאָף׃ ס

HD. D3. The sixth commandment. The singling out of this particular sexual offence is because of the context of a "relationship of commitment" (Craigie, 160). The order of this and the preceding commandment varies in different manuscript traditions (see *BHQ: Deuteronomy*, 68*).

וְלֹא תִּנְאָף׃. *Yiqtol* 2ms Qal √נאף. A prohibition (see on 1:17). This verb occurs thirty-one times in twenty-six verses. It is narrower in scope than זנה and focuses on sexual intercourse that breaks a marriage or engagement bond (cf. Lev 20:10).

5:19 וְלֹא תִּגְנֹב׃ ס

HD. D3. The seventh commandment.

וְלֹא תִּגְנֹב׃. *Yiqtol* (modal) 2ms Qal √גנב. A prohibition (see on 1:17). This focuses on stealing more generally (Weinfeld, 314–15). The lack of an overt accusative complement ensures comprehensive scope.

5:20 וְלֹא־תַעֲנֶה בְרֵעֲךָ עֵד שָׁוְא׃ ס

HD. D3. The eighth commandment. Yhwh, as one who speaks and has a concern for justice, places a premium on truthful testimony.

וְלֹא־תַעֲנֶה בְרֵעֲךָ. *Yiqtol* (modal) 2ms Qal √ענה. A prohibition (see on 1:17). The verb ענה has a specialized meaning in legal contexts, "testify." The preposition ב often introduces the one about whom a person is testifying, usually denoting "against" (e.g., Num 35:30), but on one occasion "for" (Gen 30:33). ברעך is adjunct PP.

עֵד שָׁוְא׃. Adjunct construct NP. The NP is an attributive adjectival genitive, where the absolute indicates what the construct is characterized by (cf. WO §9.5.3a, k). The absolute, שוא, when used of words, has the connotation of "false" (cf. on 5:11; also Exod 20:16, שֶׁקֶר). עד does not denote the verbal report that is made; rather it is a person (cf. 19:16, 18; Weinfeld, 283). Thus the NP is not the accusative complement of √ענה, but is an accusative of manner, describing the way in which the verb, in this case "testify," is to be performed (cf. WO §10.2.2e): "as a false witness."

5:21 וְלֹא תַחְמֹד אֵשֶׁת רֵעֶךָ ס וְלֹא תִתְאַוֶּה בֵּית רֵעֶךָ שָׂדֵהוּ וְעַבְדּוֹ וַאֲמָתוֹ שׁוֹרוֹ וַחֲמֹרוֹ וְכֹל אֲשֶׁר לְרֵעֶךָ׃ ס

The final verse comprises two HD prohibitions that are the final two commandments (see comments on the introduction to the decalogue and below). They both move beyond actions to desires, and to a sphere untouchable by a judicial framework with sanctions.

וְלֹא תַחְמֹד אֵשֶׁת רֵעֶךָ ס. *Yiqtol* (modal) 2ms Qal √חמד. Note the silent *sheva* in תַחְמֹד instead of the compound vocal *sheva* (cf. JM §63c).

A prohibition (see on 1:17). אֵשֶׁת רֵעֶךָ is accusative complement construct NP. אֵשֶׁת is fs construct of אִשָּׁה (cf. GKC §96; JM §89h, §99c).

וְלֹא תִתְאַוֶּה בֵּית רֵעֶךָ שָׂדֵהוּ וְעַבְדּוֹ וַאֲמָתוֹ שׁוֹרוֹ וַחֲמֹרוֹ וְכֹל אֲשֶׁר לְרֵעֶךָ׃ ס. *Yiqtol* (modal) 2ms Hitp √אוה. A prohibition (see on 1:17). בֵּית רֵעֶךָ is accusative complement construct NP. Two pairs of three nouns follow appositionally, explaining what is meant by בֵּית רֵעֶךָ. Three features point to it being a separate commandment: (1) the continued syndesis, ולא, which has served to demarcate the commandments since v. 18; (2) the profile of absence and presence of pronominal reference to רֵעֶךָ. The noun itself is present in vv. 20, 21a, and 21b, but is referred to by a pronoun *within* the same commandment in v. 21b after the initial occurrence; and (3) the presence of two (different—only in Deuteronomy) verbs.

אֲשֶׁר לְרֵעֶךָ׃ ס. **Null-copula** restrictive relative clause, with **head** כל and PP complement, with ל indicating possession (cf. WO §11.2.10d).

Moses appointed as mediator (5:22-33)

After the decalogue, there is a clear break. This section explains the appointment of Moses as mediator, in preparation for the giving of the statutes and judgments in Moab. In vv. 22-28, √שמע occurs eight times and קול occurs seven. Seeing also is important: √ראה occurs twice in v. 24. Two key points: (1) They have seen certain things: Yhwh has revealed (√ראה) his glory and greatness and they have seen (√ראה) it has (on this one occasion) proved possible for people to hear Yhwh speaking and live; (2) the overwhelming experience they have had is hearing (√שמע) Yhwh's voice (קול). Both of these points echo 4:9-14. Fear lest they die next time led to a request for a mediator. Confirmation came because Yhwh in turn heard (√שמע) their voice (קול) (v. 28) and approved of their words (v. 29). The result was that Moses was deputed by the people and mandated by Yhwh to mediate, and now in the plains of Moab he is proclaiming the statutes and judgments, the fruit of that mediation. This ties Moab to Horeb, and gives twin grounds for the people to listen: their request for him to mediate and Yhwh's commission.

²²It was these words that Yhwh spoke to your whole assembly on the mountain from the midst of the fire, the cloud and the deep darkness, in a loud voice, and he added nothing. He wrote them on two stone tablets and he gave them to me. ²³As soon as you heard the voice from the midst of the darkness—the mountain was burning with fire—you approached me, all the leaders of your tribes and your elders, ²⁴and you said, "Look! Yhwh our God has shown us his glory and his greatness, and his voice we have heard from the midst of the fire; this very day we have seen that God may speak with people and they may live. ²⁵Now, why should we die, for this great fire will consume us? If we hear any further the voice of Yhwh our God, we will die. ²⁶For whatever mortal is there who has heard the voice of the living God speaking from the midst of fire, as we have, and lived? ²⁷You draw near and hear all that Yhwh our God may say, and you speak to us all that Yhwh our God may speak to you and we will listen and do it." ²⁸Yhwh heard your words when you spoke to me. Then Yhwh said to me, "I have heard this people's words that they have spoken to you. They have done well in all they have spoken. ²⁹Would that they have this as their heart: to fear me and to keep all my commandments always, so that it may go well for them and for their children for ever! ³⁰Go, say to them, 'Return to your tents!' ³¹But as for you, stand here with me that I may tell you the whole commandment and the statutes and the judgments that you should teach them and they should do in the land which I am giving to them to possess." ³²So observe [them] by doing [them], just as Yhwh your God commanded you—do not turn aside to the right or to the left; ³³exactly in the way Yhwh your God has commanded you, you should walk—so that you may live and it may go well for you and you may prolong [your] days in the land you will possess.

5:22 אֶת־הַדְּבָרִ֣ים הָאֵ֡לֶּה דִּבֶּר֩ יְהוָ֨ה אֶל־כָּל־קְהַלְכֶ֜ם בָּהָ֗ר מִתּ֤וֹךְ הָאֵשׁ֙ הֶֽעָנָ֣ן וְהָֽעֲרָפֶ֔ל ק֥וֹל גָּד֖וֹל וְלֹ֣א יָסָ֑ף וַֽיִּכְתְּבֵ֗ם עַל־שְׁנֵי֙ לֻחֹ֣ת אֲבָנִ֔ים וַֽיִּתְּנֵ֖ם אֵלָֽי׃

ND. D2. Having finished recounting Yhwh's words in the decalogue, Moses highlights their uniqueness in two ways. They alone were spoken by Yhwh at that point; they alone were written by Yhwh and given to Moses.

אֶת־הַדְּבָרִים הָאֵלֶּה דִּבֶּר יְהוָה אֶל־כָּל־קְהַלְכֶם בָּהָר מִתּוֹךְ הָאֵשׁ הֶעָנָן וְהָעֲרָפֶל קוֹל גָּדוֹל. *Qatal* 3ms Piel √דבר. ND. For the pointing and for √דבר as a three-place predicate, see on 1:1.

אֶת־הַדְּבָרִים הָאֵלֶּה. Accusative complement NP, fronted for **focus**. Of all the words that Yhwh might have spoken or have been said to have spoken, it was these [and no others].

אֶל־כָּל־קְהַלְכֶם. Oblique complement of verb √דבר. The noun קהל becomes a semi-technical term in the phrase, "the day of the assembly" (9:10; 10:4). All the people were involved in receiving the decalogue.

בָּהָר מִתּוֹךְ הָאֵשׁ הֶעָנָן וְהָעֲרָפֶל. Two spatial adjunct PPs. The latter consists of a construct followed by three absolutes. Although generally the noun in the construct state is repeated before each absolute (e.g., Jer 8:1), if the three nouns are closely related, it may not be (GKC §128a).

קוֹל גָּדוֹל. Adjunct NP. It is not the direct object of the verb, but an internal accusative, characterized as such by being indefinite, having a qualifier (גדול), and being closely related to the verb's action: "with a loud voice" (JM §125s; GKC §117t; WO §10.2.1g).

וְלֹא יָסָף. *Qatal* 3ms Qal √יסף. ND. When coordinated with a following verb, √יסף often functions adverbially, defining the manner of the action, "again"; but when it is found with a negative and coordinated with a verb, it emphasizes that the action was not repeated (GKC §120d n. 4).

וַיִּכְתְּבֵם עַל־שְׁנֵי לֻחֹת אֲבָנִים. *Wayyiqtol* 3ms Qal √כתב with 3mp pronominal suffix. ND. For the whole phrase, see on 4:13.

וַיִּתְּנֵם אֵלָי: *Wayyiqtol* 3ms Qal √נתן with 3mp pronominal suffix.

5:23 וַיְהִי כְּשָׁמְעֲכֶם אֶת־הַקּוֹל מִתּוֹךְ הַחֹשֶׁךְ וְהָהָר
בֹּעֵר בָּאֵשׁ וַתִּקְרְבוּן אֵלַי כָּל־רָאשֵׁי שִׁבְטֵיכֶם
וְזִקְנֵיכֶם:

ND. D2. Moses reminds them of their response to Yhwh speaking. Although a deputation of leaders came and, in reality, this was their parents' generation (cf. 1:35; 2:14), Moses attributes the action to the "you" of those in the plains of Moab (cf. on 1:30; 5:3).

וַיְהִי. *Wayyiqtol* 3ms Qal √היה. For the form ויהי and for it being followed by a temporal phrase or clause, see on 1:3. Since the infinitive construct does not in itself indicate time, the opening verb ויהי anchors the action in the past (ND).

כְּשָׁמְעֲכֶם אֶת־הַקּוֹל מִתּוֹךְ הַחֹשֶׁךְ. Inf constr Qal √שמע with 2mp pronominal suffix and with preposition כ. For the retention of the *o* in the infinitive construct with suffixes, see JM §70d; GKC §61a, 65a. The suffix functions as the subject of the infinitive. כ + infinitive construct typically introduces a temporal clause, "when . . .," and has the connotation "as soon as" (AC §3.4.1b2; JM §166m). מִתּוֹךְ הַחֹשֶׁךְ is spatial adjunct construct NP.

וְהָהָר בֹּעֵר בָּאֵשׁ. Ptcp ms Qal √בער. **Null-copula** circumstantial clause. For the phrase, see on 4:11.

וַתִּקְרְבוּן אֵלַי כָּל־רָאשֵׁי שִׁבְטֵיכֶם וְזִקְנֵיכֶם. *Wayyiqtol* 2mp Qal √קרב with a **paragogic** ן (for which see on 1:17). Some have seen here an example of a *t*-prefix 3mp prefix verb in Hebrew, as is found in Ugaritic (cf. WO §31.1.1a n. 2). More likely, the subject of the verb is **pro**, and כל־ראשי שבטיכם וזקניכם are coordinate adjunct NPs, giving a more precise description of the **pro** ("you") in the verb. Since the key figure in the narrative is the one identified by the **pro** (Holmstedt 2009: 121–27), this keeps as the key figure not the deputation of leaders, but "you," the people as a whole.

5:24 וַתֹּאמְרוּ הֵן הֶרְאָנוּ יְהוָה אֱלֹהֵינוּ אֶת־כְּבֹדוֹ
וְאֶת־גָּדְלוֹ וְאֶת־קֹלוֹ שָׁמַעְנוּ מִתּוֹךְ הָאֵשׁ הַיּוֹם הַזֶּה
רָאִינוּ כִּי־יְדַבֵּר אֱלֹהִים אֶת־הָאָדָם וָחָי:

After the introductory recollection, "you said" (ND, D2), Moses relates the words of the leaders when they came to him (D3, ND). The opening presentative adverb, הן, highlighted to Moses what they had seen; when retold by Moses, it draws his addressees' attention to what they had seen. The motifs of seeing and hearing recur (cf. 4:9-14), this time with the notion of living. Again, what was seen is (the primacy of) Yhwh speaking (cp. Exod 33:20).

וַתֹּאמְרוּ. *Wayyiqtol* 2mp Qal √אמר. ND. The accusative complement is the direct speech that follows.

הֵן הֶרְאָנוּ יְהוָה אֱלֹהֵינוּ אֶת־כְּבֹדוֹ וְאֶת־גָּדְלוֹ. *Qatal* 3ms Hiph √ראה with 1cp pronominal suffix. In the Hiphil, III-ה verbs often begin הֶ (JM §54c). With pronominal suffixes, a final ה in III-ה verbs **syncopates** (JM §79k). This is a case of a perfective *qatal* relating to the recent past, hence the translation, "we *have* seen" (WO §30.5.1b). The Hiphil often takes, as here, a double accusative complement, with the person who would have been the subject of the Qal becoming the first accusative complement of the Hiphil, here -נו pronominal suffix (WO §10.2.3e; JM §125u).

הֵן. Like הִנֵּה, הן highlights what follows for particular attention (JM §105d). Originally "here," it became an interjection (GKC §105b), more specifically a "presentational adverb" (JM §105d), "Behold!" It usually is clause-initial.

וְאֶת־קֹלוֹ שָׁמַעְנוּ מִתּוֹךְ הָאֵשׁ. *Qatal* 1cp Qal √שמע. ND. ואת־קלו is accusative complement, fronted for **focus**. Of all that they could have heard, it was Yhwh's voice. מתוך האש is spatial adjunct construct NP.

הַיּוֹם הַזֶּה רָאִינוּ כִּי־יְדַבֵּר אֱלֹהִים אֶת־הָאָדָם וָחָי. *Qatal* 1cp Qal √ראה. ND. היום הזה is adverbial time adjunct NP, probably fronted as the **topic**, providing scene-setting information about the time. The alternative, that it is fronted as the **focus**, sets "this very day" in contrast to all other days. This is the "today" of Horeb (cf. on 1:10). The accusative complement is a noun clause, introduced by the **complementizer** כי.

כִּי־יְדַבֵּר אֱלֹהִים אֶת־הָאָדָם. *Yiqtol* (modal) 3ms Piel √דבר. The modal *yiqtol* can indicate what is generally the case (cf. WO §31.3e). However, here what they saw is not able to be generalized, but an event that proved possible on one occasion after all (cf. McConville, 118). The *yiqtol* shows the contingency of what has happened. The referent of אלהים is Israel's deity, "God," rather than "a god." In 4:33-34 the contrast is between their deity and those of other nations; here, it is the surprise that *their* God should act one way rather than another. את־האדם is an adjunct PP. The article with the collective singular of a noun is often used to denote a class (JM §126m).

וָחָי. *Qatal* (modal) 3ms Qal √חיה. See on 4:42.

5:25 וְעַתָּה֙ לָ֣מָּה נָמ֔וּת כִּ֣י תֹאכְלֵ֔נוּ הָאֵ֥שׁ הַגְּדֹלָ֖ה הַזֹּ֑את אִם־יֹסְפִ֣ים ׀ אֲנַ֗חְנוּ לִ֠שְׁמֹעַ אֶת־ק֨וֹל יְהוָ֧ה אֱלֹהֵ֛ינוּ ע֖וֹד וָמָֽתְנוּ׃

D3. Moses continues to recall the leaders' words to him. A deliberative question is grounded in their fear of the fire consuming them (ID). This then is reframed (n.b., the **asyndesis**) in terms of hearing Yhwh's voice again, using a conditional protasis and apodosis (v. 25b). The chiastic structure (A: die / B: fire consume / B´: hear Yhwh's voice / A´: die) shows the intimate relationship in their thinking between B and B´, fire consuming them and their hearing Yhwh's voice again.

וְעַתָּה֙ לָ֣מָּה נָמ֔וּת. *Yiqtol* 1cp Qal √מות. ID. עתה introduces a conclusion based on what has preceded (cf. on 2:13; 4:1). למה begins ID, though here it is a deliberative question. These typically have a *yiqtol* predicate (JM §107t, §150c n. 4).

כִּ֣י תֹאכְלֵ֔נוּ הָאֵ֥שׁ הַגְּדֹלָ֖ה הַזֹּ֑את. *Yiqtol* 3fs Qal √אכל with 1cp pronominal suffix. The clause is explanatory, introduced by כי. The P–S word order is due to **triggered inversion** after כי. When a noun is modified by an attributive adjective and a demonstrative, all three characteristically have the article, with the demonstrative placed last (GKC §126v).

אִם־יֹסְפִ֣ים ׀ אֲנַ֗חְנוּ לִ֠שְׁמֹעַ אֶת־ק֨וֹל יְהוָ֧ה אֱלֹהֵ֛ינוּ ע֖וֹד. Ptcp mp Qal √יסף. When followed by another verb (here לשמע), יסף has an adverbial force, "again" (JM §102g, §177b). **Null-copula** conditional protasis, introduced by אם (GKC §159v). The participial predicate in such a conditional invokes a sense of imminent action (WO §37.6f) and precedes an independent pronoun. This conditional follows asyndetically, reframing the first half of the verse.

לִ֠שְׁמֹעַ אֶת־ק֨וֹל יְהוָ֧ה אֱלֹהֵ֛ינוּ ע֖וֹד. Inf constr Qal √שמע with adverb ל. עוד is an adverbial adjunct, here pleonastic after √יסף.

וָמָֽתְנוּ׃. *Qatal* (modal) 1cp Qal √מות. ו + modal *qatal* often introduces a conditional (or temporal) apodosis (GKC §112ff; JM §176d).

5:26 כִּ֣י מִ֣י כָל־בָּשָׂ֡ר אֲשֶׁ֣ר שָׁמַ֣ע קוֹל֩ אֱלֹהִ֨ים חַיִּ֜ים
מְדַבֵּ֧ר מִתּוֹךְ־הָאֵ֛שׁ כָּמֹ֖נוּ וַיֶּֽחִי׃

D3. Explanatory clause, followed by a rhetorical question that highlights the unprecedented experience they have had. In so doing, they look to justify their desire to hear no further words from Yhwh.

כִּ֣י מִ֣י כָל־בָּשָׂ֡ר. Explanatory clause introducing a rhetorical question. כל־בשר is a construct NP that emphasizes mortality and fragility, and contrasts with "living god" (cf. Jer 17:5; Craigie, 165). With an indeterminate absolute, the substantive כל has varied meanings, here (with בשר) something like "*whoever is the man?*" (JM §139h). Although in English the appropriate gloss is "*whatever* mortal," in Hebrew the personal connotation of כל־בשר explains מי rather than מה as the interrogative (cf. WO §18.2d; JM §144a, b). מי can govern another clause, in this case a relative clause (WO §18.2c; cf. 3:24).

אֲשֶׁר שָׁמַע קוֹל אֱלֹהִים חַיִּים מְדַבֵּר מִתּוֹךְ־הָאֵשׁ כָּמֹנוּ. *Qatal* 3ms Qal √שמע. **Null-head** relative clause, functioning as the predicate of the question: "whatever mortal is Ø, who. . . ."

קוֹל אֱלֹהִים חַיִּים. Accusative complement construct NP. The presence of חיים strongly suggests that the referent here is to "the voice of *the living* God" (cp. 4:33). 4QDtⁿ reads the singular, חי, rather than חיים, and 4QPhyl^h reads קול יהוה אלהים.

מְדַבֵּר מִתּוֹךְ־הָאֵשׁ. Ptcp ms Piel √דבר. The participle is an "attributive accusative of state" (cf. JM §127a), modifying a noun (hence termed "attributive") rather than the predicate (adverbial or indirect accusative). מתוך־האש is adjunct construct PP.

כָּמֹנוּ. Comparative adjunct PP, "as we have" (cf. on כמוך in 5:14).

וַיֶּחִי. *Wayyiqtol* 3ms Qal √חיה. See on 4:33.

5:27 קְרַב אַתָּה וּשֲׁמָע אֵת כָּל־אֲשֶׁר יֹאמַר יְהוָה אֱלֹהֵינוּ וְאַתְּ ׀ תְּדַבֵּר אֵלֵינוּ אֵת כָּל־אֲשֶׁר יְדַבֵּר יְהוָה אֱלֹהֵינוּ אֵלֶיךָ וְשָׁמַעְנוּ וְעָשִׂינוּ׃

HD. D3. Moses reminds all those in Moab of the people's request and enthusiastic commitment. The sequence highlights the roles: Moses is to approach, hear, speak; the people will hear and do. The repetition of "all Yhwh says" and the unqualified declaration demonstrate the commitment.

קְרַב אַתָּה. Impv ms Qal √קרב. אתה is adjunct personal pronoun, syntactically unnecessary, therefore present for emphasis (GKC §135a), in this case to highlight what *Moses* should do.

וּשֲׁמָע אֵת כָּל־אֲשֶׁר יֹאמַר יְהוָה אֱלֹהֵינוּ. Impv ms Qal √שמע. On some occasions, with a degree of unpredictability, compound vocal *shevas* are found with non-gutturals (JM §9b). One pattern is when a sibilant follows ו (JM §9c). The accusative complement is the following noun clause.

אֵת כָּל־אֲשֶׁר יֹאמַר יְהוָה אֱלֹהֵינוּ. *Yiqtol* 3ms Qal √אמר. The *yiqtol* is used for the modal nuance of "may" (cf. JM §119l). כל may be the **head** of the subsequent restrictive relative clause. Alternatively, the relative clause may be **null-head**, with the antecedent covert rather than overt. The whole phrase is the accusative complement of √שמע.

וְאַתְּ ׀ תְּדַבֵּר אֵלֵינוּ אֵת כָּל־אֲשֶׁר יְדַבֵּר יְהוָה אֱלֹהֵינוּ אֵלֶיךָ. *Yiqtol* (modal) 2ms Piel √דבר. A modal *yiqtol* follows two imperatives; when associated with a request or command, this *yiqtol* is tantamount to an imperative (JM §113m).

וְאַתְּ ׀. Independent personal subject pronoun. The form looks fs, but it is clearly intended to be ms. On five occasions, the 2ms is אַתָּ, while on three, the 2ms form is as found here (GKC §32g; JM §39a nn. 5, 6; Blau, 162). It is fronted for **focus**; the people want Moses (and not Yhwh) to speak to them.

כָּל־אֲשֶׁר יְדַבֵּר יְהוָה אֱלֹהֵינוּ אֵלֶיךָ. *Yiqtol* 3ms Piel √דבר. The *yiqtol* is used for the modal nuance of "may" (cf. JM §119l). The verb דבר is a three-place predicate here (cf. on 1:1). כל may be the **head** of the subsequent restrictive relative clause. Alternatively, the relative clause may be **null-head**, with the antecedent covert rather than overt.

וְשָׁמַעְנוּ וְעָשִׂינוּ׃. *Qatal* (modal) 1cp Qal √שמע and √עשה. The modal *qatals* constitute the clauses for which they are the predicates. Nothing qualifies or attenuates their enthusiastic response to Moses speaking Yhwh's words. Had they been modal *yiqtols*, that would have indicated purpose or result; modal *qatals* signify temporal consequence.

5:28 וַיִּשְׁמַע יְהוָה אֶת־קוֹל דִּבְרֵיכֶם בְּדַבֶּרְכֶם אֵלָי
וַיֹּאמֶר יְהוָה אֵלַי שָׁמַעְתִּי אֶת־קוֹל דִּבְרֵי הָעָם הַזֶּה
אֲשֶׁר דִּבְּרוּ אֵלֶיךָ הֵיטִיבוּ כָּל־אֲשֶׁר דִּבֵּרוּ׃

ND. D2. Moses recounts Yhwh's response to the elders' words. Yhwh has "heard" (√שמע) the "voice" (קוֹל) of their words (cf. introductory comments to this section). Unusually for Israel, Yhwh approves of all they said (D3; cp. 1:34).

וַיִּשְׁמַע יְהוָה אֶת־קוֹל דִּבְרֵיכֶם בְּדַבֶּרְכֶם אֵלָי. *Wayyiqtol* 3ms Qal √שמע. ND. את . . . אֵלָי is accusative complement construct NP.

בְּדַבֶּרְכֶם אֵלָי. Inf constr Piel √דבר with 2mp pronominal suffix and with preposition ב. Adjunct temporal PP. The suffix -כֶם is the subject of the infinitive construct. אֵלָי is oblique complement.

וַיֹּאמֶר יְהוָה אֵלַי. *Wayyiqtol* 3ms Qal √אמר. The repetition of יהוה as an overt subject suggests either a minor break between the first two clauses, or, perhaps more likely, it helps with narrative cohesion, since ויאמר

alone could be the *narrator*'s voice describing what *Moses*, the antecedent of the most recent ms pronominal suffix, then said.

שָׁמַ֗עְתִּי אֶת־ק֤וֹל דִּבְרֵי֙ הָעָ֣ם הַזֶּ֔ה אֲשֶׁ֥ר דִּבְּר֖וּ אֵלֶ֑יךָ. *Qatal* 1cs Qal √שמע. את־קול דברי העם is accusative complement construct NP. קול is not strictly necessary as the accusative complement of √דבר (cf. 4:10). But it serves to connect Israel's experience of Yhwh (cf. 4:12; 5:24, 26) with Yhwh's of Israel.

אֲשֶׁ֥ר דִּבְּר֖וּ אֵלֶ֑יךָ. *Qatal* 3cp Piel √דבר. Restrictive relative clause. The **head** is דברי. It is not קול, since קול can hardly be the object of √דבר, nor is it העם, since there is no need to identify the people (they are already designated as "*this* people") or to supply this further information about them.

הֵיטִ֖יבוּ כָּל־אֲשֶׁ֥ר דִּבֵּֽרוּ׃. *Qatal* 3cp Hiph √יטב. Often an impersonal verb (see on 4:40), here the subject is 3mp **null subject pro** ("they"), and the connotation is "do [X] well" (HALOT s.v.). The accusative complement is כל followed by the restrictive relative clause.

כָּל־אֲשֶׁ֥ר דִּבֵּֽרוּ׃. *Qatal* 3cp Piel √דבר. In pause, with the *silluq*, the *sheva* is raised to a *tsere* (cf. GKC §29m). Restrictive relative clause. As in the previous verse, כל may be the **head** of the subsequent restrictive relative clause. Alternatively, the relative clause may be **null-head**, with the antecedent (possibly הדברים) covert rather than overt.

5:29 מִֽי־יִתֵּ֡ן וְהָיָה֩ לְבָבָ֨ם זֶ֜ה לָהֶ֗ם לְיִרְאָ֥ה אֹתִ֛י וְלִשְׁמֹ֥ר
אֶת־כָּל־מִצְוֺתַ֖י כָּל־הַיָּמִ֑ים לְמַ֨עַן יִיטַ֥ב לָהֶ֛ם
וְלִבְנֵיהֶ֖ם לְעֹלָֽם׃

D3. Yhwh's praise for Israel is short-lived, as he expresses unfulfilled longing for Israel's heart to be obedient to him so they can prosper. There is a sceptical realism about the people's vow of commitment (5:27bβ), one that proved accurate in subsequent experience (cf. Exod 24:7; 32:8).

מִֽי־יִתֵּ֡ן וְהָיָה֩ לְבָבָ֨ם זֶ֜ה לָהֶ֗ם. *Yiqtol* 3ms Qal √נתן. מי יתן introduces something that is possible, but unfulfilled. Sometimes it simply introduces a wish (= Latin *utinam*; sense 1); at other times, the sense of √נתן remains (GKC §151b; JM §163d; sense 2). Within the book of Deuteronomy as a whole, the call to Israel to act gives way to a recognition that only Yhwh can do so (cf. 10:16; 30:6). In light of this, perhaps the longing (sense 1) blends into the need for the gift (sense 2; cf. 29:3). Only here is מי יתן followed by ו + modal *qatal* as the accusative complement noun clause (GKC §151c; JM §177h).

וְהָיָה לְבָבָם זֶה לָהֶם. *Qatal* (modal) 3ms Qal √היה. There are two possible ways of taking the syntax of this accusative complement noun clause: (1) זה could be a demonstrative pronoun functioning as the subject of the clause, "*this* will be . . ."; or (2) זה could be a demonstrative pronoun used in attributive apposition, as happens when the substantive is made definite with a pronominal suffix (WHS §74b; cf. GKC §126y; WO §17.4.1a), "they have this as their heart. . . ." The latter is more likely given: (1) the demonstrative follows the noun (cf. Gen 40:12); (2) the attributive appositional usage is recognisable syntax (e.g., 11:18; Judg 6:14); (3) להם makes more sense, functioning as the adverbial PP predicate indicating possession (cf. WO §11.2.10d). For the significance of לבב in Deuteronomy, see on 4:9.

לְיִרְאָה אֹתִי. Inf constr Qal √ירא with preposition ל. For the form and phrase, see on 4:10. This infinitive construct and the coordinated one, ולשמר, are adjunct infinitive construct phrases, identifying what kind of heart is in view.

וְלִשְׁמֹר אֶת־כָּל־מִצְוֹתַי כָּל־הַיָּמִים. Inf constr Qal √שמר with preposition ל. כל־הימים is adverbial time adjunct construct NP.

לְמַעַן יִיטַב לָהֶם וְלִבְנֵיהֶם לְעֹלָם׃ *Yiqtol* 3ms Qal √יטב. For a purpose clause introduced by למען with the impersonal use of the verb יטב, see on 4:40. Continued observance (כל־הימים) leads to continued prospering (לעלם).

5:30 לֵךְ אֱמֹר לָהֶם שׁוּבוּ לָכֶם לְאָהֳלֵיכֶם׃

Yhwh commands Moses with two imperatives (HD, D3) to relay words dismissing the people (HD, D4).

לֵךְ אֱמֹר לָהֶם. Impv ms Qal √הלך and √אמר. Two imperatives frequently occur asyndetically, especially where the first involves movement (JM §177e). This coordination is an alternative mode of expression to subordination, and the second verb expresses the main idea (cf. GKC §120d, g). It is a mark of elevated or rhetorical style (cf. GKC §120h).

שׁוּבוּ לָכֶם לְאָהֳלֵיכֶם׃. Impv mp Qal √שׁוב. See on 1:7 for reflexive לכם. לאהליכם is adjunct PP. The ל is "terminative," indicating to where they should return (WO §11.2.10d n. 78).

5:31 וְאַתָּ֞ה פֹּה֙ עֲמֹ֣ד עִמָּדִ֔י וַאֲדַבְּרָ֣ה אֵלֶ֗יךָ אֵ֧ת כָּל־הַמִּצְוָ֛ה וְהַחֻקִּ֥ים וְהַמִּשְׁפָּטִ֖ים אֲשֶׁ֣ר תְּלַמְּדֵ֑ם וְעָשׂ֣וּ בָאָ֔רֶץ אֲשֶׁ֧ר אָנֹכִ֛י נֹתֵ֥ן לָהֶ֖ם לְרִשְׁתָּֽהּ׃

HD. D3. The opening imperative gives Moses clear instruction to remain; it is followed by an **indirect volitive**, indicating the purpose of that remaining: to give him words to teach the Israelites so that they do them.

וְאַתָּ֞ה פֹּה֙ עֲמֹ֣ד עִמָּדִ֔י. Impv ms Qal √עמד. אתה is not the subject, but is an adjunct personal pronoun, present for emphasis (GKC §135a) to highlight what Moses should do (cf. WHS §106). It is fronted as the **topic** (cf. v. 27). פה is adverbial spatial adjunct. It is fronted for **focus**. עמדי is adjunct PP; it is a variant form of עמי (JM §103i).

וַאֲדַבְּרָ֣ה אֵלֶ֗יךָ אֵ֧ת כָּל־הַמִּצְוָ֛ה וְהַחֻקִּ֥ים וְהַמִּשְׁפָּטִ֖ים. Cohortative 1cs Piel √דבר. The sequence of verbs of which it is a part indicates it is an **indirect volitive** (cf. JM §116b). The clause is syntactically coordinated with the previous clause, "stand ... *and* I *will* speak," but semantically subordinate, providing the purpose of the choosing, "stand ... *that* I *may* speak. ..." The accusative complement comprises three conjoined NPs, which are the **head** of the following relative clause. This is the first time that מצוה is found in the singular in chapters 1–11. It sometimes refers to the whole law given in Moab (cf. 11:8; 19:9; 27:1; n.b., כל, "all of," "the whole") while at other times it has a narrower focus, the basic command for allegiance and loyalty as found particularly in chapters 5–11 (cf. Weinfeld, 326). The statutes and judgments, then, should not be seen as something fundamentally different but rather the expression of מצוה (cf. DeRouchie 2007: 122). The apparently neat division of chapters 5–11 into המצוה and chapters 12–26 into החקים והמשפטים (cf. 12:1) is too neat and thus misguided. This double sense explains why here and in 7:11, ו precedes החקים, while in 6:1 החקים והמשפטים stand in apposition to המצוה.

אֲשֶׁר תְּלַמְּדֵם. *Yiqtol* (modal) 2ms Piel √למד with 3mp pronominal suffix. The *yiqtol* has the modal nuance of obligation (cf. JM §113m). Restrictive relative clause.

וְעָשׂוּ בָאָרֶץ אֲשֶׁר אָנֹכִי נֹתֵן לָהֶם לְרִשְׁתָּהּ. *Qatal* (modal) 3cp Qal √עשׂה. Following on from the modal *yiqtol*, the *qatal* here has the modal nuance of obligation (cf. JM §119h, w). בארץ is spatial adjunct PP, the **head** of the following restrictive relative clause.

אֲשֶׁר אָנֹכִי נֹתֵן לָהֶם לְרִשְׁתָּהּ. A variation on a characteristic Deuteronomic expression. For the **null-copula** participial clause expressing Yhwh's gift of the land, see on 1:18. See on 4:1 for אנכי and on 3:18 for לרשתה.

5:32 וּשְׁמַרְתֶּם לַעֲשׂוֹת כַּאֲשֶׁר צִוָּה יְהוָה אֱלֹהֵיכֶם אֶתְכֶם לֹא תָסֻרוּ יָמִין וּשְׂמֹאל׃

HD. D2. The shift in person from 3cp (v. 31) to 2mp (v. 32) indicates that the lengthy section from 5:2-31 is over (see comments on 5:1-33). This verse opens with the same injunction as that found at the end of 5:1, as Moses confronts Israel in the plains of Moab and recapitulates those commands.

וּשְׁמַרְתֶּם לַעֲשׂוֹת. *Qatal* (modal) 2mp Qal √שמר. For the relationship with לעשׂות (inf constr Qal √עשׂה with preposition ל), see on 5:1.

כַּאֲשֶׁר צִוָּה יְהוָה אֱלֹהֵיכֶם אֶתְכֶם. *Qatal* 3ms Piel √צוה. Comparative clause introduced by כאשר (cf. on 1:18).

לֹא תָסֻרוּ יָמִין וּשְׂמֹאל׃. *Yiqtol* (modal) 2mp Qal √סור. לא + *yiqtol* introduces a prohibition (cf. on 1:17). For the idiom with ימין ושׂמאל, see on 2:27. There it was literal, here it is metaphorical. The **asyndesis** suggests that diligent observance entails undeviating focus.

5:33 בְּכָל־הַדֶּרֶךְ אֲשֶׁר צִוָּה יְהוָה אֱלֹהֵיכֶם אֶתְכֶם תֵּלֵכוּ לְמַעַן תִּחְיוּן וְטוֹב לָכֶם וְהַאֲרַכְתֶּם יָמִים בָּאָרֶץ אֲשֶׁר תִּירָשׁוּן׃

HD. D2. The opening **asyndesis** shows that this further modifies the call to diligent observance. If v. 32b expressed the modification negatively, "don't deviate from . . .," this expresses it positively, "walk wholly in"—every part should be followed, nothing should be ignored. This injunction is then followed by three syndetic purpose clauses, introduced by an initial למען.

בְּכָל־הַדֶּ֗רֶךְ אֲשֶׁ֨ר צִוָּ֜ה יְהוָ֧ה אֱלֹהֵיכֶ֛ם אֶתְכֶ֖ם תֵּלֵ֑כוּ. *Yiqtol* (modal) 3mp Qal √הלך. When associated with a request or command, *yiqtol* is tantamount to an imperative (JM §113m). בכל־הדרך . . . אתכם is adjunct PP, fronted for **focus**. Of all possible ways of "walking" (= living), they should walk only in the way Yhwh has commanded. The substantive כל in the construct PP בכל־הדרך almost has an adverbial meaning, "completely," or "exactly" (JM §139e n. 2). The **asyndesis** indicates that this is a further explanation of the command for diligent observance.

אֲשֶׁ֨ר צִוָּ֜ה יְהוָ֧ה אֱלֹהֵיכֶ֛ם אֶתְכֶ֖ם. *Qatal* 3ms Piel √צוה. For the double accusative following the verb of commanding, see on 1:18. Restrictive relative clause, with **head** הדרך.

לְמַ֣עַן תִּֽחְי֑וּן. *Yiqtol* (modal) 2mp Qal √חיה with a **paragogic** ן (for which see on 1:17). למען is a subordinating conjunction that can introduce purpose or result clauses (JM §168d, §169g). Since what is in view is less the "effect" of the action than the "aim," this and the following two clauses should be seen as a succession of purpose rather than result clauses.

וְט֖וֹב לָכֶ֑ם. *Qatal* (modal) 3ms Qal √טוב. The modal *qatal* continues the modality of the previous *yiqtol*. As noted on 4:40, the verb is defective (*qatal*: √טוב; *yiqtol*: √יטב; cf. JM §85a). As an impersonal verb, the one experiencing or undergoing the verbal action is the object of the subsequent preposition, ל (WO §22.7b).

וְהַאֲרַכְתֶּ֣ם יָמִ֔ים בָּאָ֖רֶץ אֲשֶׁ֥ר תִּֽירָשֽׁוּן׃. *Qatal* (modal) 2mp Qal √ארך. The modal *qatal* continues the modality of the previous *yiqtol*. ימים is the accusative complement (cf. 4:26, 40; cp. 5:16). בארץ . . . תירשון is adjunct PP.

אֲשֶׁ֥ר תִּֽירָשֽׁוּן׃. *Yiqtol* 2mp Qal √ירש with a **paragogic** ן (for which see on 1:17). Restrictive relative clause, with **head** בארץ.

The Appeal for Undivided Love of Yhwh
Deuteronomy 6:1-25

Hear and fear Yhwh (6:1-3)

As with 4:44, this looks both backward and forward. It connects backward with the call to "hear" (שמע√; 5:1; 6:3) and with verbal links to 5:27-33: שמע√, עשׂה√, ירא√, שמר√, למד√ Piel (Lundbom, 304–5). It also connects forward, particularly with 6:24-25 (n.b., esp. the next occurrence of המצוה in 6:25) and anticipating 12:1.

> ¹*And this is the commandment—the statutes and the judgments—that Yhwh your God commanded [me] to teach you to do in the land to where you are crossing, to possess it,* ²*so that you may fear Yhwh your God, by keeping all his statutes and commandments which I am commanding you—you, your son, and your son's son—all the days of your life, and so that your days may be long.* ³*So hear, Israel, and observe [them] by doing [them], so that it may go well for you and so that you may multiply greatly, just as Yhwh the God of your ancestors promised you, [in] the land oozing with milk and honey.*

6:1 וְזֹאת הַמִּצְוָה הַחֻקִּים וְהַמִּשְׁפָּטִים אֲשֶׁר צִוָּה יְהוָה אֱלֹהֵיכֶם לְלַמֵּד אֶתְכֶם לַעֲשׂוֹת בָּאָרֶץ אֲשֶׁר אַתֶּם עֹבְרִים שָׁמָּה לְרִשְׁתָּהּ:

ED. D2. This opening echoes what precedes and anticipates what follows (cf. 4:44).

וְזֹאת הַמִּצְוָה הַחֻקִּים וְהַמִּשְׁפָּטִים. **Null-copula** clause, with unmarked S-P word order and substantival predicate (cf. on 1:1). The backward connection is marked by the clausal syndesis. החקים והמשפטים are in apposition to המצוה (see on 5:31).

אֲשֶׁר צִוָּה יְהוָה אֱלֹהֵיכֶם. *Qatal* 3ms Piel צוה√. Restrictive relative clause, with **head** המצוה.

לְלַמֵּד אֶתְכֶם. Inf constr Piel למד√ with preposition ל. Infinitive phrase complement of צוה√. The subject of למד√ is covert, "me" (cf. 4:14; Craigie, 167). The **resultative** Piel takes here an accusative complement אתכם and an infinitive phrase complement.

לַעֲשׂוֹת בָּאָרֶץ אֲשֶׁר אַתֶּם עֹבְרִים שָׁמָּה לְרִשְׁתָּהּ. Inf constr Qal עשׂה√ with preposition ל. It is an infinitive phrase complement after

ללמד (cf. 4:1; see on 4:5). The accusative complement of √עשׂה is אשר in the phrase אשר צוה יהוה אלהיכם (**head** = המצוה). בארץ is spatial adjunct PP, the **head** of the following restrictive relative clause.

אֲשֶׁ֨ר אַתֶּ֥ם עֹבְרִ֛ים שָׁ֖מָּה לְרִשְׁתָּֽהּ׃. See on 4:14 for identical phrase.

6:2 לְמַ֨עַן תִּירָ֜א אֶת־יְהוָ֣ה אֱלֹהֶ֗יךָ לִ֠שְׁמֹר אֶת־כָּל־חֻקֹּתָ֣יו וּמִצְוֺתָיו֮ אֲשֶׁ֣ר אָנֹכִי֮ מְצַוֶּךָ֒ אַתָּה֙ וּבִנְךָ֣ וּבֶן־בִּנְךָ֔ כֹּ֖ל יְמֵ֣י חַיֶּ֑יךָ וּלְמַ֖עַן יַאֲרִכֻ֥ן יָמֶֽיךָ׃

D2. Two subordinate purpose clauses indicate that the learning, even the observing, is not an end in itself, but the purpose is that people learn to fear Yhwh and that their days may be long.

לְמַ֨עַן תִּירָ֜א אֶת־יְהוָ֣ה אֱלֹהֶ֗יךָ. *Yiqtol* (modal) 2ms Qal √ירא. There is a wrong (1:21, 29; 3:2, 22) and a right (1:19; 4:10; 5:29) object of fear. The subordinating conjunction למען here introduces a purpose clause (cf. on 4:1).

לִ֠שְׁמֹר אֶת־כָּל־חֻקֹּתָ֣יו וּמִצְוֺתָיו֮ אֲשֶׁ֣ר אָנֹכִי֮ מְצַוֶּךָ֒. Inf constr Qal √שמר with preposition ל. The phrase is an adjunct infinitive construct phrase. The infinitive construct is **gerundial** or explanatory, "by keeping" (cf. WO §36.2.3e). The conjoined accusative complement NPs, את כל־חקתיו ומצותיו, are the **head** of the following restrictive relative clause. The lack of repetition of את־כל means that ומצותיו is a second absolute. Although generally the noun in the construct state is repeated before each absolute (e.g., Jer 8:1), if the nouns are closely related, it may not be (GKC §128a).

אֲשֶׁ֣ר אָנֹכִי֮ מְצַוֶּךָ֒. Ptcp ms Piel √צוה with 2ms pronominal suffix. See on 4:40 for the identical phrase.

אַתָּה֙ וּבִנְךָ֣ וּבֶן־בִּנְךָ֔. Adjunct conjoined NPs that serve to extend the "you" of the plains of Moab (2ms **null subject pro** in תירא) to children and grandchildren.

כֹּ֖ל יְמֵ֣י חַיֶּ֑יךָ. Adverbial temporal construct NP.

וּלְמַ֖עַן יַאֲרִכֻ֥ן יָמֶֽיךָ׃. *Yiqtol* (modal) 3mp Hiph √ארך with a **paragogic** ן (for which see on 1:17). למען here introduces a second purpose clause in the verse (cf. on 4:1). See on 5:16 for the identical phrase, though here יארכן is doubly defective in the way it is written.

Deuteronomy 6:3

וְשָׁמַעְתָּ֣ יִשְׂרָאֵ֗ל וְשָׁמַרְתָּ֙ לַעֲשׂ֔וֹת אֲשֶׁר֙ יִיטַ֣ב 6:3
לְךָ֔ וַאֲשֶׁ֥ר תִּרְבּ֖וּן מְאֹ֑ד כַּאֲשֶׁר֩ דִּבֶּ֨ר יְהוָ֜ה אֱלֹהֵ֤י
אֲבֹתֶ֙יךָ֙ לָ֔ךְ אֶ֛רֶץ זָבַ֥ת חָלָ֖ב וּדְבָֽשׁ׃ פ

HD. D2. Given what Moses has set out (ED, v. 1), the injunction to Israel follows, with two modal *qatals* followed by two purpose clauses. The final section of the verse provides further motivation—this is nothing other than Yhwh has promised; further, the land involved is bountiful.

וְשָׁמַעְתָּ֣ יִשְׂרָאֵ֗ל. *Qatal* (modal) 2ms Qal √שמע. HD. The modal *qatal* in Deuteronomy is often used to convey a volitional force after narrative discourse (cf. WO §32.2.3d); it can also convey the same force after **null-copula** clauses (ED; WO §32.2.4a). Here it follows the opening declaration of 6:1 (ED). ישראל is vocative (cf. 5:1).

וְשָׁמַרְתָּ֙ לַעֲשׂ֔וֹת. *Qatal* (modal) 2ms Qal √שמר. See previous comment for modal *qatal*. Both accusative complements are covert (cf. on 5:1).

לַעֲשׂ֔וֹת. Inf constr Qal √עשה with preposition ל. Adjunct infinitive construct phrase. The infinitive construct is **gerundial** or explanatory, "by doing" (cf. WO §36.2.3e).

אֲשֶׁר֙ יִיטַ֣ב לְךָ֔. See on 4:40 for the identical phrase, including a discussion of אשר introducing a purpose clause.

וַאֲשֶׁ֥ר תִּרְבּ֖וּן מְאֹ֑ד . . . אֶ֛רֶץ זָבַ֥ת חָלָ֖ב וּדְבָֽשׁ׃ פ. *Yiqtol* (modal) 2mp Qal √רבה with a **paragogic** ן (for which see on 1:17). See on 4:40 for אשר introducing a purpose clause. מאד is used as an adverbial adjunct, intensifying the force of the verbal idea (AC §4.2.12).

אֶ֛רֶץ זָבַ֥ת חָלָ֖ב וּדְבָֽשׁ׃. Ptcp fs construct Qal √זוב. The participle is not strictly functioning as an attributive adjective (n.b., in 31:20, האדמה is definite, while זבת is not), but as an "attributive accusative of state" (cf. JM §127a), modifying a noun (hence termed "attributive") rather than the predicate (adverbial or indirect accusative). The following absolutes, חלב ודבש, are a type of "objective genitive" where the absolute "receives the action implied by the construct term" (WHS §38); they are also known as a type of "adverbial genitive" (WO §9.5.2d). The relationship of this phrase to what precedes is awkward, with no preposition before ארץ. LXX attempts to ameliorate this by adding δοῦναι before לך, probably assimilating to use elsewhere (e.g., 4:38; see

BHQ: *Deuteronomy*, 71*). On a number of occasions the accusative of place can follow a verb, without a preposition (1:2, 19; cf. GKC §118g although they follow LXX here), "multiply [*in*] a land flowing. . . ." The alternative, based on the fact that the phrase is usually appositional to a phrase designating the gift of land, is that the phrase is somehow appositional to the land in v. 1 (Tigay 1996: 358 n. 7). On balance, regarding it as an accusative of place without a preposition is preferable, because the modal *qatals* in v. 2 provide too significant a break to allow apposition to bridge them (though n.b. 4:43).

כַּאֲשֶׁר דִּבֶּר יְהוָה אֱלֹהֵי אֲבֹתֶיךָ לָךְ. See on 1:21 for the identical phrase, כאשר . . . לך.

Love Yhwh exclusively (6:4-9)

The foundational declaration in 6:4 that Yhwh, and only Yhwh, is to be their deity, gives rise to a succession of corollaries: wholehearted love (v. 5), internalization and appropriation of Yhwh's words (vv. 6-8), and public propagation of those same words (v. 9). Yhwh has *spoken*, so the right response is to heed those words. Although private ("on your hearts"), Yhwh's words are not to be privatized, but are to be "within your towns/communities" (6:9).

⁴*Hear, Israel! Yhwh our God, Yhwh is one,* ⁵*so you should love Yhwh your God with all your heart and with all your being and with all your resources.* ⁶*These words that I am commanding you today should be on your heart.* ⁷*You should recite them to your children, and talk about them when you stay in your house and when you are travelling on the road, when you lie down and when you get up.* ⁸*You should bind them as a sign upon your hand, and they should be as a headband on your forehead.* ⁹*You should write them on the doorposts of your house and in your communities.*

6:4   שְׁמַע יִשְׂרָאֵל יְהוָה אֱלֹהֵינוּ יְהוָה ׀ אֶחָד׃

The Shemaʿ. A call to Israel to listen (HD, D2), followed by a statement about Yhwh (ED, D2).

שְׁמַע יִשְׂרָאֵל. Impv ms Qal √שמע. For the phrase, see on 4:1. Used without an accusative, as here, it is closer to a call to attention (cf. 9:1; Weinfeld, 199).

יְהוָ֣ה אֱלֹהֵ֔ינוּ יְהוָ֖ה ׀ אֶחָֽד׃. The Hebrew mss have large letters (*literae maiusculae*), שמע ... אחד, to draw attention to the verse (MNK §9.8.3[i]; cf. Driver, 90). That it is these two letters is probably because עד is "testimony" (cf. Weinfeld, 338); the first ש and the last ד yield שד, "a demon"! These four words have spawned a bewildering variety of translations, both ancient and modern. Commentaries and articles discuss them at great length (e.g., Block 2004; Bruno; Janzen; Kraut; MacDonald 2003; McBride; Miller 1999; Moberly 1990, 1999). Broadly speaking, interpretation depends on two interlocking aspects: first, *semantic and syntactical questions* surrounding the text; second, *relative weighting of factors* affecting which answer is preferred. On the first, there is a large measure of agreement: (a) what is/are the subject(s) and predicate(s)?; (b) are there one or two clauses?; (c) how does אחד fit?; and (d) what does אחד mean? On the second, the weighting affects, even determines, interpretation. Factors include (1) the unique syntax (WO §8.4.2g; though see Kraut, 595–99, who cites Hos 12:6; Exod 15:3); (2) the literary context in Deuteronomy (e.g., how it connects with v. 5; whether אלהינו could be a substantival predicate); (3) the theological context (e.g., wider questions about monotheism in Deuteronomy); (4) the wider Hebrew Bible context (e.g., use of אחד elsewhere); (5) the history of interpretation (e.g., how LXX and the New Testament take it).

I favor the translation, "Yhwh our God, Yhwh is one." A few explanatory comments on how this should be understood and why this has been adopted follow: First, the opening two words are **extraposed** or dislocated, occurring outside the confines of the clause (traditionally called *casus pendens*). They function as the **topic**. Although a resumptive pronoun might have been expected in what is a **tripartite** verbless/nominal clause (cf. 1:17), the restatement of the name, יהוה, is for **focus**, Yhwh and no other deity. Recognizing the recurrence is not superfluous, but for **focus**, removes what Kraut (592) calls the "one devastating problem" for this interpretation. Second, the **null-copula** clause that follows has יהוה as the subject and אחד as the adjectival predicate. To say that יהוה *is* אחד is not to make a statement about Yhwh's nature or essence; nor is it in and of itself to make a monotheistic claim. Rather, it is a statement of allegiance and loyalty (hence some prefer the rendering "alone"): Yhwh is the only one for them (cf. Cant 6:8-9; Zech 14:9). Third, this fits with how v. 5 continues, using a modal *qatal* coordinated with ו, "*so* you shall love . . ." (cf. NAB); it also fits the wider context of Deuteronomy. Fourth, elsewhere in Deuteronomy, יהוה אלהינו are always together in apposition, never as subject and predicate. Fifth, אחד cannot be functioning as an attributive adjective, "one Yhwh," since it would be qualifying a proper name. Sixth, it makes little sense to have the copula after אלהינו, "Yhwh our God *is* Yhwh. . . ." For a concise discussion of the issues, see Nelson, 91–89.

וְאָהַבְתָּ אֵת יְהוָה אֱלֹהֶיךָ בְּכָל־לְבָבְךָ וּבְכָל־נַפְשְׁךָ 6:5
וּבְכָל־מְאֹדֶךָ׃

HD. The modal *qatal* follows from the declaration of v. 4. Complete devotion is commanded, pointing to the covenantal context.

וְאָהַבְתָּ אֵת יְהוָה אֱלֹהֶיךָ. *Qatal* (modal) 2ms Qal √אהב. HD. Here, the modal *qatal* does not follow the imperative, שמע (see comment above). Rather, as in 6:3, it is used to convey a volitional force after a **null-copula** clause (cf. WO §32.2.4a; Ruth 3:9). The grounds for the injunction lie in the statement (ED) יהוה אלהינו אחד. For the notion of loving Yhwh, see on 5:9.

בְּכָל־לְבָבְךָ וּבְכָל־נַפְשְׁךָ וּבְכָל־מְאֹדֶךָ׃. Three adjunct construct PPs describe the extent of this love. Rather than referring to three different aspects of the human person, the nouns have expanding extent. לבב is a person's mind or will (cf. on 4:9); נפש is a metonymy for the whole person (cf. on 4:9); together they speak of "full devotion"; מאד is used as a substantive rather than an adverb (WO §39.3.1). This happens only here and in 2 Kgs 23:25 (the only other place where these three nouns appear together), and speaks of a person's wealth or resources as well as their "might" (Weinfeld, 332, 338–40).

וְהָיוּ הַדְּבָרִים הָאֵלֶּה אֲשֶׁר אָנֹכִי מְצַוְּךָ הַיּוֹם 6:6
עַל־לְבָבֶךָ׃

HD. D2. There is an intimate connection between loving Yhwh with complete devotion (v. 5) and having the word of Yhwh internalized (v. 6).

וְהָיוּ הַדְּבָרִים הָאֵלֶּה . . . עַל־לְבָבֶךָ׃. *Qatal* (modal) 3cp Qal √היה. Although the subject shifts to 3cp, "these words," the same modality continues. This is not a prediction, but a command. The referent of the subject, הדברים האלה, could be the most recent words, 6:4-5 (Driver, 92), or, more likely, the whole teaching of Moses (cf. 1:1; 4:40; 11:18; McConville, 142). עַל־לְבָבֶךָ functions as an adverbial complement with the copula. The phrase can be used literally, of the high priest bearing the names of the songs of Israel on his breastplate (Exod 28:29-30). Here it is used metaphorically, of internalized words.

אֲשֶׁר אָנֹכִי מְצַוְּךָ הַיּוֹם. See on 4:40 for the identical phrase.

> וְשִׁנַּנְתָּם לְבָנֶיךָ וְדִבַּרְתָּ בָּם בְּשִׁבְתְּךָ בְּבֵיתֶךָ   6:7
> וּבְלֶכְתְּךָ בַדֶּרֶךְ וּבְשָׁכְבְּךָ וּבְקוּמֶךָ:

HD. Two modal *qatals* continue Moses' exhortation, focusing on the internalization of Yhwh's words. Twin **merisms** emphasise the ubiquitous and constant repetition.

וְשִׁנַּנְתָּם לְבָנֶיךָ. *Qatal* (modal) 2ms Piel √שׁנן with 3mp pronominal suffix. The Piel of √שׁנן is not found elsewhere. Some regard this form as a **by-form** of the verb √שׁנה II, "repeat," "recite" (HALOT s.v; Tigay 1996: 78). Others associate it with the verb √שׁנן I, "sharpen" (cf. 32:41), "drill them into" (Lundbom, 313). On balance, the former should be preferred: (a) √שׁנן is never used elsewhere in the sense of teaching or impressing upon; (b) the parallel in 11:19 uses √למד Piel, "teach"; (c) Cognate languages point toward the existence of the **by-form**. See Tigay 1996: 358–59 n. 25.

וְדִבַּרְתָּ בָּם. *Qatal* (modal) 2ms Piel √דבר. The significance of the preposition ב is debated. It could be either oblique complement, "recite *them*" (Weinfeld, 333; cf. קרא ב in 17:19) or PP adjunct: "speak *about them*" (GKC §119l; Tigay 1996: 78; the translation in WO §11.2.5f). The latter is preferable given how √דבר Piel followed by ב is best understood elsewhere (3:26; 1 Sam 19:3-4), and that reciting or repeating has already been enjoined.

בְּשִׁבְתְּךָ בְּבֵיתֶךָ וּבְלֶכְתְּךָ בַדֶּרֶךְ וּבְשָׁכְבְּךָ וּבְקוּמֶךָ. Inf constr Qal √ישׁב, √הלך, √שׁכב, and √קום, all with 2ms pronominal suffix (subject) and with preposition ב. √ישׁב was an original I-ו verb; in the infinitive construct, the ו has disappeared and a feminine ת has been added; the *segols* characteristic of the form without pronominal suffixes disappear when suffixes are present (JM §72d, §75a). √הלך is the only I-ה verb that behaves like a I-ו (JM §75g). The preposition ב attached to infinitives construct characteristically has a temporal sense, "when" *sensu* "while" (JM §166l; MNK §39.6.2; AC §4.1.5b; cf. WO §36.2.2a, b), and is a common alternative way of expressing a temporal clause. The four temporal adjunct PPs split into two pairs, both of which form **merisms** indicating "always." The first pair has spatial adjunct PPs, בביתך and בדרך.

6:8 וּקְשַׁרְתָּ֥ם לְא֖וֹת עַל־יָדֶ֑ךָ וְהָי֥וּ לְטֹטָפֹ֖ת בֵּ֥ין עֵינֶֽיךָ׃

HD. D2.

וּקְשַׁרְתָּ֥ם לְא֖וֹת עַל־יָדֶ֑ךָ. Qatal (modal) 2ms Qal √קשר with 3mp pronominal suffix. לאות is an adjunct PP. This is "quasi datival" use of ל, making something *into* something (cf. AC §4.1.10e.2); it often speaks of the purpose or goal of the action (WO §11.2.10d).

וְהָי֥וּ לְטֹטָפֹ֖ת בֵּ֥ין עֵינֶֽיךָ׃. Qatal (modal) 3cp Qal √היה. The meaning of טטפת is debated. Probably it is a "headband" (Tigay 1982; 1996: 79). For the ל, see the comment above. בין עיניך is an adjunct PP. Literally "between your eyes," it denotes the forehead (cf. 14:1).

6:9 וּכְתַבְתָּ֛ם עַל־מְזוּז֥וֹת בֵּיתֶ֖ךָ וּבִשְׁעָרֶֽיךָ׃ ס

HD. The final injunction speaks of public display.

וּכְתַבְתָּ֛ם עַל־מְזוּז֥וֹת בֵּיתֶ֖ךָ וּבִשְׁעָרֶֽיךָ׃ ס. Qatal (modal) 2ms Qal √כתב with 3mp pronominal suffix. על מזוזת ביתך is adjunct construct PP; מזוזת are "doorposts" (cf. Exod 12:7). בשעריך is adjunct PP. In Deuteronomy, the noun שער occurs frequently in the plural with 2ms pronominal suffix, as the object of the preposition ב. In such cases, שעריך (lit. "your gates") is a metonymy for "your (i.e., Israelite) towns" (cf. LXX, which changes translation from πύλαι, "gates," to πόλεις, "towns," in 12:15) or, perhaps, covenantal communities (Frese). Thus what is in view is more than just writing these words "on your gates" (so, e.g., Driver, 93; Nelson, 86), even if gates are understood as the gates of the town, but public display throughout the Israelite town or community (n.b., the shift in preposition from על to ב).

Entry to the land, plenty, and diligent loyalty (6:10-19)

With the imminent possession of the land and the fulfilment of the promises made to their ancestors, Moses looks to the future and the danger of forgetting amidst the prosperity. The temporal protasis (vv. 10-11) is followed by an imperatival apodosis, השמר (v. 12) and a negative purpose clause, "lest you forget" (פן תשכח) that governs all that follows. Four main injunctions/prohibitions (*yiqtol* clauses) follow asyndetically, explaining what forgetting and not forgetting look like:

- 13: injunctions (תשבע, תעבד, תירא; all coordinated, suggesting a unity);
- 14: prohibition (לא תלכון אחרי);
- 16: prohibition (לא תנסו);
- 17-18: injunction (שמור תשמרון; coordinated with ועשית).

Forgetting consists in following other gods (v. 14) and testing Yhwh (v. 16); remembering entails exclusive loyalty to Yhwh (v. 13) and obedience to Yhwh's commands (vv. 17-18).

[10] When Yhwh your God brings you into the land which he swore to your ancestors, to Abraham, to Isaac and to Jacob, to give to you—great and good cities that you did not build, [11] houses full of every good thing, which you did not fill, hewn wells that you did not hew, vineyards and olive groves that you did not plant—and you eat and are satisfied, [12] be on your guard lest you forget Yhwh, who brought you out from the land of Egypt, from the house of slaves; [13] it is Yhwh your God that you should fear; it is he that you should serve; it is in his name that you should swear. [14] Do not follow other gods, any of the gods of the peoples who are around you, [15] for Yhwh your God is a jealous god in your midst, lest the anger of Yhwh your God is kindled against you so that he destroys you from upon the face of the ground. [16] Do not test Yhwh your God, as you tested [him] at Massah. [17] Make sure you observe the commandments of Yhwh your God, and his decrees and his statutes that he commanded you, [18] and do what is right and good in the eyes of Yhwh, so that it may go well for you and you may enter and possess the good land which Yhwh swore to your ancestors, [19] by driving out all your enemies from before you, just as Yhwh promised.

6:10 וְהָיָ֞ה כִּ֥י יְבִיאֲךָ֣ ׀ יְהוָ֣ה אֱלֹהֶ֗יךָ אֶל־הָאָ֜רֶץ אֲשֶׁ֨ר נִשְׁבַּ֧ע לַאֲבֹתֶ֛יךָ לְאַבְרָהָ֛ם לְיִצְחָ֥ק וּֽלְיַעֲקֹ֖ב לָ֣תֶת לָ֑ךְ עָרִ֛ים גְּדֹלֹ֥ת וְטֹבֹ֖ת אֲשֶׁ֥ר לֹא־בָנִֽיתָ׃

D2. The start of a new section, the initial temporal protasis is dependent syntactically on the warning in v. 12, which is HD. Moses begins to cast a vision of the future, with the assumption that the people will enter.

וְהָיָ֞ה. *Qatal* (modal) 3ms Qal √היה. והיה can function as a copula in future time. When there is no subject or complement, as here, it serves to anchor discourse time in the future (Cook 2012: 309–10). It is typically followed by a temporal phrase, a preposition with the infinitive construct, or, as here, a subordinating conjunction. Typically, it begins a new section (MNK §44.4).

כִּ֥י יְבִיאֲךָ֣ ׀ יְהוָ֣ה אֱלֹהֶ֗יךָ אֶל־הָאָ֜רֶץ. *Yiqtol* 3ms Hiph √בוא with 2ms pronominal suffix. As well as introducing causal or explanatory clauses and being a **complementizer** for noun clauses, כי can also, as here, introduce temporal clauses (GKC §164d; WHS §445, §497). Since כי can also introduce conditional clauses (JM §167c, i; WHS §446, §515), the line between temporal, "when," and conditional, "if," in future time is not always obvious (AC §4.3.4e-f). Here there is no doubt whether Yhwh will bring them in or not, hence "when"; but in 15:16 the context requires a conditional, "if" (cf. 6:25).

אֲשֶׁ֨ר נִשְׁבַּ֧ע לַאֲבֹתֶ֛יךָ לְאַבְרָהָ֛ם לְיִצְחָ֥ק וּֽלְיַעֲקֹ֖ב לָ֥תֶת לָ֑ךְ. *Qatal* 3ms Niph √שבע. The verb here is a three-place predicate, with subject יהוה, the action of giving the land as what is sworn, and the oblique complement, לאבתיכם, indicating the recipients of the oath. לאברהם ליצחק וליעקב are three PPs in apposition to לאבתיכם. The clause is a restrictive relative clause, with **head** הארץ.

לָ֥תֶת לָ֑ךְ. Inf constr Qal √נתן with ל preposition (see on 1:8 for the form; also on 4:38 for לָ֥תֶת not לָ֣תֶת). Infinitive phrase complement, describing what was sworn. The accusative complement is הארץ, represented in the clause by אשר. לך is oblique complement; the pointing is due to it being in pause (see on 1:21).

עָרִ֛ים גְּדֹלֹ֥ת וְטֹבֹ֖ת אֲשֶׁ֥ר לֹא־בָנִֽיתָ׃. The NP ערים גדלת וטבת is in apposition to הארץ, the accusative complement of what was given (represented in the clause by אשר). It is the **head** of the following restrictive relative clause. There is a rhythmic, poetic quality to this and the subsequent conjoined NPs (Craigie, 172–73).

אֲשֶׁ֥ר לֹא־בָנִֽיתָ׃. *Qatal* 2ms Qal √בנה. Before consonantal afformatives, III-ה verbs revert to an original י (JM §75f-g). Restrictive relative clause.

6:11 וּבָתִּים מְלֵאִים כָּל־טוּב֮ אֲשֶׁ֣ר לֹא־מִלֵּ֒אתָ֒ וּבֹרֹ֤ת חֲצוּבִים֙ אֲשֶׁ֣ר לֹא־חָצַ֔בְתָּ כְּרָמִ֥ים וְזֵיתִ֖ים אֲשֶׁ֣ר לֹא־נָטָ֑עְתָּ וְאָכַלְתָּ֖ וְשָׂבָֽעְתָּ׃

Three further rhythmic and poetic NPs describe the land sworn as a gift, continuing the apposition from the previous verse. All stress the land's bounty and Yhwh's generosity, as they will have done nothing. After the *'atnakh*, two modal *qatals* continue and complete the temporal protasis. Little prepares for the warning that follows abruptly.

וּבָתִּים מְלֵאִים כָּל־טוּב֮ אֲשֶׁ֣ר לֹא־מִלֵּ֒אתָ֒. A second NP appositional to הארץ, but conjoined with the previous NP. As a stative verb, √מלא does not strictly have a participle, but a verbal adjective, מָלֵא (GKC §116b; JM §41c). Since stative verbs may be transitive (JM §111h), as a *verbal* adjective, מָלֵא can take an accusative complement, the NP כל־טוב (DHS §98a; WO §10.2.1h; JM §125d; though Joüon-Muraoka note that some grammarians regard this accusative as adverbial and Davidson regards the form as a participle). The noun בַּיִת has an irregular plural, בָּתִּים, but here it occurs without the *meteg* (GKC §96). It is the **head** of the following restrictive relative clause.

אֲשֶׁ֣ר לֹא־מִלֵּ֒אתָ֒. *Qatal* 2ms Piel √מלא. As a stative verb, the Qal does not denote an action; hence the Piel is used for "fill" (JM §78j). Restrictive relative clause.

וּבֹרֹ֤ת חֲצוּבִים֙ אֲשֶׁ֣ר לֹא־חָצַ֔בְתָּ. A third NP appositional to הארץ, but conjoined with the previous NP. Ptcp mp Qal pass √חצב. The noun בּוֹר is masculine, although the plural ends in ־וֹת, hence the ending ־ים on the participle. It is the **head** of the following restrictive relative clause.

אֲשֶׁ֣ר לֹא־חָצַ֔בְתָּ. *Qatal* 2ms Qal √חצב.

כְּרָמִ֥ים וְזֵיתִ֖ים אֲשֶׁ֣ר לֹא־נָטָ֑עְתָּ. A fourth NP appositional to הארץ. In a list of items, although the use of ו is "variable" (JM §177o), it is unusual for ו to be omitted only before the final item. The plural of זַיִת is regular (cp. בַּיִת above). The conjoined NP כרמים וזיתים is the **head** of the following restrictive relative clause.

אֲשֶׁ֣ר לֹא־נָטָ֑עְתָּ. *Qatal* 2ms Qal √נטע. Restrictive relative clause.

וְאָכַלְתָּ֖ וְשָׂבָֽעְתָּ. *Qatal* (modal) 2ms Qal √אכל and √שבע. GKC §49m cites ושבעת to illustrate that the "waw-consecutive of the perfect" (= modal *qatal*) retains the tone in the penultimate syllable when in pause. In another context, these modal *qatals* could form the temporal apodosis, since ו + modal *qatal* often introduces a conditional or temporal apodosis (GKC §112ff; JM §176d). But here the abrupt **asyndesis** and imperative in v. 12 indicate that the apodosis begins there. These modal *qatals* both continue the temporal protasis.

6:12 הִשָּׁ֣מֶר לְךָ֔ פֶּן־תִּשְׁכַּ֖ח אֶת־יְהוָ֑ה אֲשֶׁ֧ר הוֹצִיאֲךָ֛ מֵאֶ֥רֶץ מִצְרַ֖יִם מִבֵּ֥ית עֲבָדִֽים׃

HD. D2. The temporal apodosis begins with an (asyndetic) imperative, followed by a negative purpose clause. Echoes of 5:6 suggest that the first commandment is in view. This is confirmed by what follows.

הִשָּׁ֣מֶר לְךָ֔. Impv ms Niph √שמר. See on 4:9 for the identical phrase.

פֶּן־תִּשְׁכַּ֖ח אֶת־יְהוָ֑ה. *Yiqtol* (modal) 2ms Qal √שכח. See on 4:9 for פן־תשכח.

אֲשֶׁ֧ר הוֹצִיאֲךָ֛ מֵאֶ֥רֶץ מִצְרַ֖יִם מִבֵּ֥ית עֲבָדִֽים׃. *Qatal* 3ms Hiph √יצא with 2ms pronominal suffix. Non-restrictive relative clause, giving further, but not essential, information about the **head** יהוה. After a proper name, a relative clause is non-restrictive since further identification is not necessary. The whole clause echoes Yhwh's self-introduction in 5:6 (see comments there).

6:13 אֶת־יְהוָ֧ה אֱלֹהֶ֛יךָ תִּירָ֖א וְאֹת֣וֹ תַעֲבֹ֑ד וּבִשְׁמ֖וֹ תִּשָּׁבֵֽעַ׃

HD. D2. Three coordinated modal *yiqtols* follow asyndetically from v. 12. Given the **asyndesis** and the shift from imperative to *yiqtols*, this verse is explanatory, unpacking what it means to be on their guard against forgetting. The three complements are all fronted for **focus**: "it is Yhwh [and no other deity] that you should. . . ." The pronominal reference to יהוה in the second and third clauses and the coordinating ו-conjunction confirm the essential unity as well as the complementarity of these three injunctions.

אֶת־יְהוָ֧ה אֱלֹהֶ֛יךָ תִּירָ֖א. *Yiqtol* (modal) 2ms Qal √ירא. The accusative complement construct NP, את־יהוה אלהיך, is fronted for **focus**.

וְאֹתוֹ תַעֲבֹד. *Yiqtol* (modal) 2ms Qal √עבד. The accusative complement, אתו, is fronted for **focus**. Yhwh set them free from the house of slaves (עבד) so they would serve (√עבד) him [and no one else].

וּבִשְׁמוֹ תִּשָּׁבֵעַ׃ *Yiqtol* 2ms Niph √שבע. The oblique complement, בשמו, is fronted for **focus**: "in Yhwh's [and no other] name you should swear."

6:14 לֹא תֵלְכוּן אַחֲרֵי אֱלֹהִים אֲחֵרִים מֵאֱלֹהֵי הָעַמִּים אֲשֶׁר סְבִיבוֹתֵיכֶם׃

HD. D2. The prohibition follows asyndetically, a counterpart to, rather than an explanation of, the positively framed triad of commands in 6:13. It continues to unpack what it means to be on their guard against forgetting (v. 12).

לֹא תֵלְכוּן אַחֲרֵי אֱלֹהִים אֲחֵרִים. *Yiqtol* (modal) 2mp Qal √הלך with a **paragogic** ן (for which see on 1:17). A prohibition (see on 1:17). אחרי אלהים אחרים is the oblique complement. הלך אחרי is a common phrase for following a deity, usually one (or more) other than Yhwh (cf. 4:9; 8:19).

מֵאֱלֹהֵי הָעַמִּים אֲשֶׁר סְבִיבוֹתֵיכֶם׃. Adjunct construct PP followed by restrictive relative clause with **head** העמים. The preposition מן here could be partitive, "any of the gods" (NRSV) or explicative, giving further definition to the preceding substantive (McConville, 137; NIV; cf. WHS §326). Both are possible (cf. JM §133e). On balance the former is preferable, partly on grounds of frequency and partly because examples of explicative מן do not have the same noun in the explanation as the noun being explained. The **null-copula** restrictive relative clause has a PP predicate, סביבותכם. סביב is a noun, sometimes functioning as a preposition. The plural, סביבות (rarely סביבים) can also act as a substantive, and sometimes, as here, as a preposition, "around" (JM §103n).

6:15 כִּי אֵל קַנָּא יְהוָה אֱלֹהֶיךָ בְּקִרְבֶּךָ פֶּן־יֶחֱרֶה אַף־יְהוָה אֱלֹהֶיךָ בָּךְ וְהִשְׁמִידְךָ מֵעַל פְּנֵי הָאֲדָמָה׃ ס

Three dependent clauses, an explanatory clause (ED) followed by two negative purpose clauses, are subordinate to the prohibition of v. 14. The explanatory clause gives grounds for thinking the negative purpose clauses will happen. The ultimate danger if they "follow other gods" (v. 14) is in the second negative purpose clause.

כִּי אֵל קַנָּא יְהוָה אֱלֹהֶיךָ בְּקִרְבֶּךָ. **Null-copula** explanatory clause, introduced by the subordinating conjunction כי, with substantival predicate. In **null-copula** clauses, even after כי, the unmarked word order is S–P. The P–S word order here indicates that אל קנא is fronted for **focus**. בקרבך is adjunct PP.

פֶּן־יֶחֱרֶה אַף־יְהוָה אֱלֹהֶיךָ בָּךְ. *Yiqtol* (modal) 3ms Qal √חרה. The verb חרה, "to be hot," often has אף "nose," "anger," as the subject, as an idiom for a person's wrath being kindled. In that idiom, an adjunct PP with preposition ב denotes the person against whom the wrath is kindled (HALOT s.v.). The pointing of בך as בָּךְ is due to it being in pause (see on לָךְ in 1:21). פן introduces a negative purpose clause and is followed by a *yiqtol* (JM §168g; cf. on 4:9). Where, as here, a second verb (השמידך) also depends on פן, the first verb can be subordinate. The real danger lies in the final verb (cf. JM §168h).

וְהִשְׁמִידְךָ מֵעַל פְּנֵי הָאֲדָמָה: ס. *Qatal* (modal) 3ms Hiph √שמד with 2ms pronominal suffix. The modal *qatal* continues the force of the previous *yiqtol* after פן (see previous comment). מעל פני האדמה is spatial adjunct construct PP.

6:16 לֹא תְנַסּוּ אֶת־יְהוָה אֱלֹהֵיכֶם כַּאֲשֶׁר נִסִּיתֶם בַּמַּסָּה:

HD. D2. The prohibition follows asyndetically, a counterpart to the prohibition in v. 14. It continues to unpack what it means to be on their guard against forgetting (v. 12).

לֹא תְנַסּוּ אֶת־יְהוָה אֱלֹהֵיכֶם. *Yiqtol* (modal) 2mp Piel √נסה. A prohibition (see on 1:17).

כַּאֲשֶׁר נִסִּיתֶם בַּמַּסָּה:. *Qatal* 2mp Piel √נסה. Comparative clause, with subordinating conjunction כאשר. After כאשר, there is usually **triggered inversion**, with P–S word order. The accusative complement is covert, but obvious. במסה is spatial adjunct PP. The presence of the (**syncopated**) article shows that Massah was not originally a proper name (see on הירדן in 1:1).

Deuteronomy 6:17-18

6:17 שָׁמ֣וֹר תִּשְׁמְר֔וּן אֶת־מִצְוֺ֖ת יְהוָ֣ה אֱלֹהֵיכֶ֑ם וְעֵדֹתָ֥יו וְחֻקָּ֖יו אֲשֶׁ֥ר צִוָּֽךְ׃

HD. D2. This injunction, like the ones in v. 13, follows asyndetically and explains v. 12.

שָׁמ֣וֹר תִּשְׁמְר֔וּן אֶת־מִצְוֺ֖ת יְהוָ֣ה אֱלֹהֵיכֶ֑ם וְעֵדֹתָ֥יו וְחֻקָּ֖יו. *Yiqtol* 2mp Qal √שמר with a **paragogic** ן (for which see on 1:17), preceded by Inf abs Qal √שמר. This **paronomastic** infinitive construction, of infinitive absolute with finite verb of the same root, accents the modality of its cognate verb in modal contexts, such as this one (see on 4:26). The *yiqtol* here, as an injunction, has the virtual nuance of must (cf. JM §113m).

אֶת־מִצְוֺ֖ת יְהוָ֣ה אֱלֹהֵיכֶ֑ם וְעֵדֹתָ֥יו וְחֻקָּ֖יו. Conjoined accusative complement NPs of תשמרון. The particle את usually precedes every member of a list, but sometimes the initial את serves for every accusative complement (WO §10.3.1a). The first is a construct chain; the following two accusative complements have pronominal suffixes referring back to the absolute.

אֲשֶׁ֥ר צִוָּֽךְ׃. *Qatal* 3ms Piel √צוה with 2ms pronominal suffix. Restrictive relative clause.

6:18 וְעָשִׂ֛יתָ הַיָּשָׁ֥ר וְהַטּ֖וֹב בְּעֵינֵ֣י יְהוָ֑ה לְמַ֙עַן֙ יִ֣יטַב לָ֔ךְ וּבָ֗אתָ וְיָֽרַשְׁתָּ֙ אֶת־הָאָ֣רֶץ הַטֹּבָ֔ה אֲשֶׁר־נִשְׁבַּ֥ע יְהוָ֖ה לַאֲבֹתֶֽיךָ׃

HD. D2. A modal *qatal* continues the injunctive force from תשמרון (v. 17). This is then followed by three purpose clauses. The threefold repetition of טוב/יטב gives implicit motivation to heed the command. Doing what is "good" (טוב) enables them to "do well" (יטב) and possess the "good" (טוב) land.

וְעָשִׂ֛יתָ הַיָּשָׁ֥ר וְהַטּ֖וֹב בְּעֵינֵ֣י יְהוָ֑ה. *Qatal* (modal) 2ms Qal √עשה. The modal *qatal* continues the force of the previous *yiqtol* (cf. WO §32.2.1d), though note the shift from 2mp to 2ms. הישר והטוב are conjoined accusative complement NPs. Both are adjectives, used substantivally. בעיני יהוה is adjunct construct PP.

לְמַ֫עַן יִ֥יטַב לָ֑ךְ. *Yiqtol* 3ms Qal √יטב. For a purpose clause introduced by למען with the impersonal use of the verb יטב, see on 4:40. For the vocalization of לך due to being in pause, see on 1:21.

וּבָאתָ֗ וְיָרַשְׁתָּ֙ אֶת־הָאָ֣רֶץ הַטֹּבָ֔ה. *Qatal* (modal) 2ms Qal √בוא and √ירש. Note the accent shift to the final syllable in the modal *qatal*, וירשת (cf. JM §119a). The modal *qatals* take on the purpose or telic usage after a *yiqtol* (DHS §53c; cf. WO §32.2.1d).

אֲשֶׁר־נִשְׁבַּ֥ע יְהוָ֖ה לַאֲבֹתֶֽיךָ׃. *Qatal* 3ms Niph √שבע. Restrictive relative clause with **head** הארץ הטבה. For the phrase, see on 1:8; 6:10.

6:19 לַהֲדֹ֥ף אֶת־כָּל־אֹיְבֶ֖יךָ מִפָּנֶ֑יךָ כַּאֲשֶׁ֖ר דִּבֶּ֥ר יְהוָֽה׃ ס

D2. The verse depends on the HD of v. 18, explaining how the final clauses will happen.

לַהֲדֹ֥ף אֶת־כָּל־אֹיְבֶ֖יךָ מִפָּנֶ֑יךָ. Inf constr Qal √הדף with preposition ל. Adjunct PP. This is the **gerundial** or epexegetical use of the infinitive construct, explaining how the previous action (√ירש, v. 18) should be carried out (cf. WO §36.2.3e; JM §124o). את־כל־איביך is accusative complement construct NP. מפניך is spatial adjunct PP.

כַּאֲשֶׁ֖ר דִּבֶּ֥ר יְהוָֽה׃ ס. *Qatal* 3ms Piel √דבר. Comparative clause. For the identical phrase (although with an expanded subject NP), see on 1:21.

Answering children's questions (6:20-25)

Moses' future perspective continues, as he imagines a child asking a question about the meaning of the commandments and instructs on the response. A retold history explains present observance. After setting the scene with their plight, "we were slaves," three *wayyiqtol* clauses, each with Yhwh overt as subject, outline the foundational actions: Yhwh *brought us out* (ויציאנו, v. 21) . . . Yhwh *gave* great signs (ויתן, v. 22) . . . Yhwh *commanded us* to do (ויצונו, v. 24). . . ." Moses fosters motivation by outlining the purposes or results of obedience (vv. 24b-25a), which also characterize the journey and not merely the endpoint.

[20]*When your son asks you in the future, "What do the decrees, the statutes and the judgments mean that Yhwh our God commanded you?"* [21]*then you shall say to your son, "We were nothing but slaves to Pharaoh in Egypt, and*

Yhwh brought us out of Egypt with a strong hand; Yhwh performed great and grievous signs and wonders against Egypt, against Pharaoh and against all his house, before our eyes. And it was we that he brought out from there, to bring us in so as to give us the land which he swore to our ancestors. And Yhwh commanded us to do all these statutes, to fear Yhwh our God, so that it may go well for us always and so as to keep us alive, as [is the case] today. ²⁵*We will have righteousness, if we observe this entire commandment by doing it before Yhwh our God, just as he commanded us."*

6:20 כִּי־יִשְׁאָלְךָ בִנְךָ מָחָר לֵאמֹר מָה הָעֵדֹת וְהַחֻקִּים וְהַמִּשְׁפָּטִים אֲשֶׁר צִוָּה יְהוָה אֱלֹהֵינוּ אֶתְכֶם׃

A temporal protasis (D2) looks forward to life in the land and to a son's question about the meaning of Yhwh's instructions (ID [ED]; D3). Moses' expectation is that the people will (or, at least, should!) be obeying in such a way that a son is curious.

כִּי־יִשְׁאָלְךָ בִנְךָ מָחָר לֵאמֹר. *Yiqtol* 3ms Qal √שאל with 2ms pronominal suffix. מחר is an adverbial time adjunct (cf. GKC §100c), "tomorrow" hence "in the future." See on 1:5 for the **complementizer** לאמר. The conjunction כי can introduce temporal or conditional clauses (cf. on 6:10). Given the temporal frame established by v. 10 and the imminent expectation of entering the land, a temporal clause here is more probable. Further, a temporal clause fits better rhetorically, establishing the expectation that a son will ask, rather than merely catering for that eventuality.

מָה הָעֵדֹת וְהַחֻקִּים וְהַמִּשְׁפָּטִים. ID. Null-copula clause with three coordinated substantival complements. מה is an interrogative pronoun with a wide variety of senses (WO §18.3b). The response to the question indicates that the desire is to understand the significance (cf. Exod 12:26; 13:14; Josh 4:6, 21).

אֲשֶׁר צִוָּה יְהוָה אֱלֹהֵינוּ אֶתְכֶם. *Qatal* 3ms Piel √צוה. It is followed by two direct objects as complements (GKC §117gg; AC §2.3.1e). Restrictive relative clause with **head** העדת והחקים והמשפטים.

6:21 וְאָמַרְתָּ לְבִנְךָ עֲבָדִים הָיִינוּ לְפַרְעֹה בְּמִצְרָיִם וַיּוֹצִיאֵנוּ יְהוָה מִמִּצְרַיִם בְּיָד חֲזָקָה׃

Temporal apodosis (D2, HD) is then followed by the parent's reply (D3, ND). Meaning is found in history. There is continuity between the "we" of Egypt and the exodus and the "we" of future generations in the land.

וְאָמַרְתָּ֖ לְבִנְךָ֑. *Qatal* (modal) 2ms Qal √אמר. HD. The modal *qatal* with ו is common after temporal and conditional clauses (JM §176d, f; they term it *"waw* of apodosis" and regard the protasis here as conditional, not temporal, though).

עֲבָדִ֛ים הָיִ֥ינוּ לְפַרְעֹ֖ה בְּמִצְרָ֑יִם. *Qatal* 1cp Qal √היה. ED. In past and future time, the copula (√היה) is usually overt. The subject is **pro**. The predicative complement, עבדים, is fronted for **focus**. לפרעה is PP adjunct, expressing possession (cf. WHS §270). במצרים is adjunct PP.

וַיּוֹצִיאֵ֧נוּ יְהוָ֛ה מִמִּצְרַ֖יִם בְּיָ֥ד חֲזָקָֽה׃. *Wayyiqtol* 3ms Hiph √יצא with 1cp pronominal suffix. ND. In direct speech, narrative discourse never begins with a *wayyiqtol*, but narrative begun with a *qatal* often continues with *wayyiqtols*. ממצרים is oblique complement, indicating from where Yhwh had brought them out. ביד חזקה is adjunct PP.

6:22 וַיִּתֵּ֣ן יְהוָ֡ה אוֹתֹ֣ת וּ֠מֹפְתִים גְּדֹלִ֨ים וְרָעִ֧ים ׀ בְּמִצְרַ֛יִם בְּפַרְעֹ֥ה וּבְכָל־בֵּית֖וֹ לְעֵינֵֽינוּ׃

D3. ND. Moses continues to instruct on the parent's reply, again stressing the continuity between past and present (לעינינו).

וַיִּתֵּ֣ן יְהוָ֡ה אוֹתֹ֣ת וּ֠מֹפְתִים גְּדֹלִ֨ים וְרָעִ֧ים ׀. *Wayyiqtol* 3ms Qal √נתן. ND. The verb is sometimes used of "performing" a sign or wonder (e.g., 13:2; cf. Exod 7:9, with מופת). The *wayyiqtol* indicates a narratival continuity with what preceded, but the repetition of the subject, יהוה, despite already being **discourse active** (cp. v. 23), marks a break. Along with v. 24, it suggests a threefold declaration of Yhwh's action. The accusative complement consists of paired nouns followed by paired adjectives. Despite the ending ־ת, the noun אות is usually masculine (n.b., though, Josh 24:17). רע speaks not of the moral quality of the actions, but of the effect they had (cf. 7:15); there is a stark contrast with the prospering desired for the people (טוב, v. 24).

בְּמִצְרַ֛יִם בְּפַרְעֹ֥ה וּבְכָל־בֵּית֖וֹ לְעֵינֵֽינוּ׃. Four adjunct PPs to the verb נתן, specifying against whom Yhwh acted and who saw it. The first three, with ב, indicate "against" whom Yhwh performed the signs, a common adversative use of ב (cf. WO §11.2.5d; WHS §242). The final one,

לְעֵינֵינוּ, is adjunct PP, expressing who saw it. Sight is important (cf. on 1:30; 4:6, 34).

6:23 וְאוֹתָ֛נוּ הוֹצִ֥יא מִשָּׁ֖ם לְמַ֙עַן֙ הָבִ֣יא אֹתָ֔נוּ לָ֤תֶת לָ֙נוּ֙ אֶת־הָאָ֔רֶץ אֲשֶׁ֥ר נִשְׁבַּ֖ע לַאֲבֹתֵֽינוּ׃

ND. D3. Rather than advancing the storyline (note the *qatal* not *wayyiqtol*), Moses recapitulates the event to explain Yhwh's intention (cp. 1:27).

וְאוֹתָ֛נוּ הוֹצִ֥יא מִשָּׁ֖ם. *Qatal* 3ms Hiph √יצא. ND. The accusative complement, אותנו, is fronted for **focus**: "it was we . . . (and no one else, and can you believe it?)." משם is spatial adjunct PP. The only times it has occurred before in Deuteronomy are to speak of the exodus (5:15) and of seeking Yhwh from exile (4:29). The break from the *wayyiqtol* sequence indicates that the storyline is not advancing; this is a comment on the preceding *wayyiqtols* (n.b., too, the repetition of √יצא).

לְמַ֙עַן֙ הָבִ֣יא אֹתָ֔נוּ. Inf constr Hiph √בוא. Adjunct PP. As well as a subordinating conjunction, למען can act as a preposition with the infinitive construct, expressing purpose, as here, or result (cf. JM §168d).

לָ֤תֶת לָ֙נוּ֙ אֶת־הָאָ֔רֶץ אֲשֶׁ֥ר נִשְׁבַּ֖ע לַאֲבֹתֵֽינוּ׃. Inf constr Qal √נתן with preposition ל (see on 1:8 for the form; also on 4:38 for לָתֵת not לָתֵת). Since only very rarely does an infinitive construct after למען have the preposition ל, this infinitive phrase is adjunct to הביא, "to bring in *in order to give*." The ל indicates purpose (cf. GKC §114g; WHS §197, §277).

אֲשֶׁ֥ר נִשְׁבַּ֖ע לַאֲבֹתֵֽינוּ׃. *Qatal* 3ms Niph √שבע. Restrictive relative clause with **head** הארץ.

6:24 וַיְצַוֵּ֣נוּ יְהוָ֗ה לַעֲשׂוֹת֙ אֶת־כָּל־הַחֻקִּ֣ים הָאֵ֔לֶּה לְיִרְאָ֖ה אֶת־יְהוָ֣ה אֱלֹהֵ֑ינוּ לְט֥וֹב לָ֙נוּ֙ כָּל־הַיָּמִ֔ים לְחַיֹּתֵ֖נוּ כְּהַיּ֥וֹם הַזֶּֽה׃

ND. D3. A third *wayyiqtol* gets to the heart of the son's question. It is followed by an infinitive phrase complement then an appositional infinitive phrase. Both express the essence of the command. The final two infinitive phrases express the purpose of those commands: prospering and life.

וַיְצַוֵּ֣נוּ יְהוָ֔ה. *Wayyiqtol* 3ms Piel √צוה with 1cp pronominal suffix. As a three-place predicate, √צוה has a subject and is followed by two complements, an accusative complement indicating the recipients of Moses' command (נו- pronominal suffix) and an infinitive phrase complement (לעשׂות . . .). For the repetition of יהוה as an overt subject, despite being **discourse active**, see on v. 22.

לַעֲשׂוֹת֙ אֶת־כָּל־הַחֻקִּ֣ים הָאֵ֔לֶּה. Inf constr Qal √עשׂה with preposition ל. Infinitive phrase complement.

לְיִרְאָ֖ה אֶת־יְהוָ֣ה אֱלֹהֵ֑ינוּ. Inf constr Qal √ירא with preposition ל. Appositional infinitive phrase. For the form and syntax of the phrase, see on 4:10. The **asyndesis** suggests this is the equivalent of observing the commands (Tigay 1996: 83).

לְט֥וֹב לָ֖נוּ כָּל־הַיָּמִ֑ים. Inf constr Qal √טוב with preposition ל. As noted on 4:40, יטב/טוב is a defective verb. Different parts of the conjugation come from one or other of these roots. The infinitive construct comes from טוב. The ל indicates purpose (cf. GKC §114g; WHS §197, §277). Since טוב is an impersonal verb, the one experiencing or undergoing the verbal action is the object of the subsequent preposition, לנו (cf. WO §22.7b).

לְחַיֹּתֵ֖נוּ כְּהַיּ֥וֹם הַזֶּֽה׃. Inf constr Piel √חיה with 1cp pronominal suffix and with preposition ל. The ל indicates purpose (cf. GKC §114g; WHS §197, §277). The pronominal suffix of לחיתנו is the accusative complement, since the verb is Piel. Presumably Yhwh is the subject, "to maintain us" (Lohfink) or "to keep us alive" (cf. 20:16).

כְּהַיּ֥וֹם הַזֶּֽה׃. Temporal adjunct PP. See on 2:30. Normally there is **syncopation** of the article consonant, ה, with the prepositions ב, כ, ל. Sometimes, as here, there is no **syncopation**. There is no difference in meaning between כהיום הזה and כיום הזה (JM §35e).

6:25 וּצְדָקָ֖ה תִּֽהְיֶה־לָּ֑נוּ כִּֽי־נִשְׁמֹ֨ר לַעֲשׂ֜וֹת אֶת־כָּל־הַמִּצְוָ֣ה הַזֹּ֗את לִפְנֵ֛י יְהוָ֥ה אֱלֹהֵ֖ינוּ כַּאֲשֶׁ֥ר צִוָּֽנוּ׃ ס

PD. D3. A conditional apodosis precedes the protasis. It is likely, given the chiastic structuring in vv. 24-25, that Moses is still completing instructions on the parental response. They will be rightly related to Yhwh.

וּצְדָקָ֖ה תִּֽהְיֶה־לָּ֣נוּ. *Yiqtol* 3fs Qal √היה. In past and future time, the copula (√היה) is usually overt. לנו is the prepositional predicate, indicating possession (cf. WO §11.2.10d). It is pointed with a euphonic *dagesh forte* because the accent is on the first syllable and it follows an accented ־ָה (GKC §20c). The clause is a conditional apodosis, preceding the protasis. Although some commentators see צדקה as "merit" here (Weinfeld, 349; Tigay 1996: 83; Lundbom, 325), the chiastic structuring between v. 24 and v. 25 (n.b., √צוה, √עשה) suggests that צדקה, "righteousness," is no more meritorious than the "life" or "prospering" of v. 24b (cf. Ps 24:4-5; Block 2005: 17–19; Robson, 138–41).

כִּֽי־נִשְׁמֹ֨ר לַעֲשׂ֜וֹת אֶת־כָּל־הַמִּצְוָ֣ה הַזֹּ֗את לִפְנֵ֛י יְהוָ֥ה אֱלֹהֵ֖ינוּ. *Yiqtol* 1cp Qal √שמר followed by infinitive construct Qal √עשה with preposition ל. For the meaning of this syntax with these roots, see on 5:1. את־כל־המצוה is the accusative complement construct NP; the repetition of המצוה forms an ***inclusio*** with 6:1. לפני אלהינו is adjunct PP. Although כי can introduce both conditional and temporal clauses (see on 6:10), here it introduces a conditional protasis because the protasis is hardly assumed.

כַּאֲשֶׁ֥ר צִוָּֽנוּ׃ ס. *Qatal* 3ms Piel √צוה with 1cp pronominal suffix. Comparative clause introduced by כאשר.

Conquest, Canaanites, and Constancy
Deuteronomy 7:1-26

The chapter as a whole mandates severe treatment for the Canaanites and their religious symbols. The impetus comes from Israel's identity, rooted in their history with Yhwh. There are some ways in which this chapter fits part of a larger whole from chapters 6–8, splitting it into two with a break after 7:11: the reference to "doing" (√עשה infinitive construct with preposition ל) משפטים, and חקים, מצוה (6:1; 7:11); the only occurrences of עקב . . . תשמעון (7:12; 8:20).

However, alongside this, there is an internal coherence and a discernible chiastic structure to the chapter (cf. Lundbom, 328):

- A 1-6a—Yhwh dislodging (נשל) and putting at their disposal (נתן√ לפני) bigger nations (רבים גוים)
    - B 7b-11—Yhwh's love (√אהב) in election and keeping (√שמר) covenant loyalty (הברית והחסד).

B′ 12-16—Yhwh will love (√אהב) and keep (√שמר) covenant loyalty (הברית והחסד)

A′ 17-26—Yhwh dislodging (נשל) and putting at their disposal (נתן\√ לפני) bigger nations (רבים גוים).

But there is also development. The opening call to חרם and to religious iconoclasm is rooted in Israel's consecration to Yhwh (vv. 1-6a); an excursus from vv. 6b-24 grounds the call to covenant commitment (obedience) and to covenant action (fearlessness and uncompromising response) in Yhwh's action on their behalf in history. The final two verses return to the opening call to uncompromising religious iconoclasm (cf. 7:25 with 7:5) and have the sober warning that *they* could become *herem* (v. 26) if they fail to carry out *herem* (v. 2).

Uncompromising treatment of the Canaanites and their gods (7:1-6a)

Moses looks forward to entering the land and insists on an uncompromising approach to the inhabitants and their religious symbols. The structure (see below) establishes the temporal apodosis in v. 2 as the key command, החרם תחרים. Three coordinated prohibitions follow **asyndetically** by way of explanation; the last of these, "do not intermarry," is itself expanded upon with two further prohibitions that are grounded in a breathless sequence that connects intermarriage with destruction by Yhwh.

In contrast to these five prohibitions, there are five injunctions, with the first anticipating the following four. Destruction of Canaanite religious symbols and artefacts is the positive application of חרם. The final clause (v. 6) roots this in Yhwh's special relationship with Israel.

When Yhwh brings you in . . . and dislodges . . . and delivers them to you . . . and you defeat them . . .

[Then] . . . devote them to *herem*:

A   Do not make a covenant . . . and do not show favor . . . and do not intermarry . . .
     —do not give your daughter . . . or take his daughter . . .
        For he would turn your son away . . . and they will serve . . . and Yhwh's
    anger shall be kindled . . . and he will destroy you . . .;

A   But do this to them:
     Pull down... and smash... and cut down... and burn,
     For you are a *holy* people... (v. 6)

¹*When Yhwh your God brings you into the land to where you are entering to possess and he dislodges many nations from before you—Hittites, Girgashites, Amorites, Canaanites, Perizzites, Hivites, Jebusites, seven nations more numerous and mightier than you—²and Yhwh your God puts them at your disposal and you strike them, be sure to devote them utterly to herem: do not make a covenant with them, do not show them favor, ³and do not intermarry with them—your daughter you should not give to his son, while his daughter you should not take for your son, ⁴for he will turn your son from following me, they will serve other gods, Yhwh's anger will burn against you and he will destroy you swiftly—⁵but this is what you should do to them: their altars you should pull down, their memorial stones you should smash, their sacred poles you should cut down, and their idols you should burn with fire, ⁶for you are a holy people to Yhwh your God.*

7:1 כִּי יְבִיאֲךָ֣ יְהוָ֣ה אֱלֹהֶ֗יךָ אֶל־הָאָ֙רֶץ֙ אֲשֶׁר־אַתָּ֣ה
בָא־שָׁ֣מָּה לְרִשְׁתָּ֔הּ וְנָשַׁ֣ל גּוֹיִם־רַבִּ֣ים ׀ מִפָּנֶ֗יךָ הַחִתִּ֡י
וְהַגִּרְגָּשִׁ֡י וְהָאֱמֹרִי֩ וְהַכְּנַעֲנִ֨י וְהַפְּרִזִּ֜י וְהַחִוִּ֣י וְהַיְבוּסִ֗י
שִׁבְעָ֣ה גוֹיִ֔ם רַבִּ֥ים וַעֲצוּמִ֖ים מִמֶּֽךָּ׃

D2. Temporal protasis, with time anchored in the future (cf. 6:10, 20). The two appositional NPs describing the nations emphasize their significance ("seven") and might. But by being appositional, they are an aside in a confident future narrative.

כִּי יְבִיאֲךָ יְהוָה אֱלֹהֶיךָ אֶל־הָאָרֶץ. *Yiqtol* 3ms Hiph √בוא with 2ms pronominal suffix. כִּי introduces a temporal protasis (cf. on 6:10), since "whether" is not in doubt; it is a matter of "when."

אֲשֶׁר־אַתָּה בָא־שָׁמָּה לְרִשְׁתָּהּ. Ptcp ms Qal √בוא. Restrictive relative clause, with **head** הארץ. See on 4:5 for the near-identical phrase (plural, not singular).

וְנָשַׁל גּוֹיִם־רַבִּים ׀ מִפָּנֶיךָ. *Qatal* (modal) 3ms Qal √נשל. A rare verb. The Qal is used transitively of "dislodging" nations (7:1, 22). Elsewhere it is used of loosening and taking off a sandal (Exod 3:5; Josh 5:15). In Deuteronomy it is also used intransitively (19:5; 28:40). The modal *qatal* continues the temporal protasis. The accusative complement, גוים רבים, is further explained by two appositional NPs. מפניך is spatial adjunct PP.

הַחִתִּי וְהַגִּרְגָּשִׁי וְהָאֱמֹרִי וְהַכְּנַעֲנִי וְהַפְּרִזִּי וְהַחִוִּי וְהַיְבוּסִי. Seven coordinated gentilic adjectives, used substantivally, follow in apposition to גוים רבים. Gentilic adjectives characteristically end in -ִי (JM §88Mg). The presence of the article with the adjective indicates the referent is the entire group (WO §13.5.1g; cf. GKC §126m). In a series of nouns or NPs, ו-conjunction may join each item apart from the first, as here (JM §177o).

שִׁבְעָה גוֹיִם רַבִּים וַעֲצוּמִים מִמֶּךָּ. Appositional NP. The numerals from 3–10 are substantives; the marked feminine form is found with masculine nouns, and vice versa (cf. JM §100d). Lacking particular forms for the comparative adjective, Hebrew uses the preposition מן attached to the noun (here the pronominal suffix on ממך) that is excelled when both nouns are present (JM §141g; AC §4.1.13h).

7:2 וּנְתָנָם יְהוָה אֱלֹהֶיךָ לְפָנֶיךָ וְהִכִּיתָם הַחֲרֵם תַּחֲרִים אֹתָם לֹא־תִכְרֹת לָהֶם בְּרִית וְלֹא תְחָנֵּם:

D2. HD. In v. 2a, the temporal protasis continues. The subtle shift from 3ms (Yhwh) to 2ms indicates victory is a foregone conclusion (v. 2a). It is the manner and aftermath that is the greater concern (v. 2b).

וּנְתָנָם יְהוָה אֱלֹהֶיךָ לְפָנֶיךָ. *Qatal* (modal) 3ms Qal √נתן with 3mp pronominal suffix. To נתן something לפני someone is to lay something out before someone with a view to them acting appropriately, almost to "put X at Y's disposal," where Y is the object of the preposition לפני (cf. on 1:8). A continuation of the temporal protasis.

וְהִכִּיתָם. *Qatal* (modal) 2ms Hiph √נכה with 3mp pronominal suffix. A continuation of the temporal protasis, despite the change of person.

הַחֲרֵם תַּחֲרִים אֹתָם. *Yiqtol* (modal) 2ms Hiph √חרם preceded by Inf abs Hiph √חרם. This **paronomastic** infinitive construction, of infinitive absolute with finite verb of the same root, accents the modality of its cognate verb in modal contexts, such as this one (see on 4:26 above). The *yiqtol* here, as an injunction, has the virtual nuance of must (cf. JM §113m). √חרם speaks of the irrevocable giving over to Yhwh, usually by means of destruction (cf. 2:34). The **asyndesis** here marks this clause as the start of the temporal apodosis (cf. 6:12).

לֹא־תִכְרֹת לָהֶם בְּרִית. *Yiqtol* (modal) 2ms Qal √כרת. A prohibition (see on 1:17). להם is adjunct PP. Often, but not always (e.g., Gen 21:32), a preposition introducing the one with whom a covenant is made is present. Often it is ל, as here (but cf. 5:2). This clause and the two following, to which it is coordinated, follow asyndetically from the previous injunction. Together, they serve to interpret the injunction negatively, in terms of what they should not do.

וְלֹא תְחָנֵּם. *Yiqtol* (modal) 2ms Qal √חנן with 3mp pronominal suffix. A prohibition (see on 1:17).

7:3 וְלֹא תִתְחַתֵּן בָּם בִּתְּךָ לֹא־תִתֵּן לִבְנוֹ וּבִתּוֹ
לֹא־תִקַּח לִבְנֶךָ:

HD. D2. This verse comprises three prohibitions. The first (v. 3a), coordinated with two at the end of 7:2, continues the explanation of the basic injunction, החרם תחרים (see on v. 2). In v. 3b, the two prohibitions are coordinated. Together, they follow the first asyndetically, expanding on what it means not to "intermarry." The "giving" and "taking" of daughters demonstrates the patrilocal nature of marriage.

וְלֹא תִתְחַתֵּן בָּם. *Yiqtol* 2ms Hitp √חתן (cf. חָתָן, "son-in-law"; חֹתֵן, "father-in-law," חֹתֶנֶת, "mother-in-law"). A prohibition (see on 1:17). בם is the oblique complement.

בִּתְּךָ לֹא־תִתֵּן לִבְנוֹ. *Yiqtol* (modal) 2ms Qal √נתן. A prohibition (see on 1:17). בתך is fronted as the **topic** (see below). The **asyndesis** indicates that this clause (and the one following, joined to this with ו) explains the intermarrying that is forbidden. The shift from 3mp to 3ms narrows the focus to an individual father with whom an agreement might be struck.

וּבִתּוֹ לֹא־תִקַּח לִבְנֶךָ. *Yiqtol* (modal) 2ms Qal √לקח. The verb לקח behaves like a I-נ verb, hence the *dagesh forte* in the ק (JM §72j). A prohibition (see on 1:17). בתו is fronted as the **topic**. The statement is the counterpart of the previous prohibition, coordinated with it. Together they build up a complementary picture, which accounts for the **topicalization** (Moshavi 2010: 160–61).

7:4 כִּי־יָסִיר אֶת־בִּנְךָ֙ מֵאַחֲרַ֔י וְעָבְד֖וּ אֱלֹהִ֣ים אֲחֵרִ֑ים
וְחָרָ֤ה אַף־יְהוָה֙ בָּכֶ֔ם וְהִשְׁמִידְךָ֖ מַהֵֽר׃

D2. An explanatory clause tells a story in future time. It is dependent syntactically on the prohibition on intermarriage (HD), and gives the grounds for it. An unbroken sequence, from a father causing a son's turning aside to destruction of the people as a whole, reinforces the original prohibition. The shift in pronouns graphically highlights the spreading effect.

כִּי־יָסִיר אֶת־בִּנְךָ֙ מֵאַחֲרַ֔י. *Yiqtol* 3ms Hiph √סור. Three subjects have been proposed: the "foreigner in general" (so Weinfeld, 365); impersonal, referring in a subjunctive manner to the verbal idea of the previous clause (McConville, 149); the foreign daughter's father (so ESV; Nelson, 99; Lundbom, 335). The third option is preferable: evidence in favor is the unseen presence of the father in the giving to "his son" (v. 3) and the unbroken chain from individual father's agreement to destruction of "you" as a nation. כי introduces an explanatory clause, giving grounds for the stark injunction (cf. JM §170a). מאחרי is adjunct PP. The 1cs pronominal suffix indicates that Moses' voice has merged with Yhwh's (cf. 11:14-15).

וְעָבְד֖וּ אֱלֹהִ֣ים אֲחֵרִ֑ים. *Qatal* (modal) 3cp Qal √עבד. The modal *qatal* with ו continues the future sequence, outlining the consequences of the previous *yiqtol* (cf. WO §32.2.1d). The shift to 3cp indicates that husband and wife together will serve other deities.

וְחָרָ֤ה אַף־יְהוָה֙ בָּכֶ֔ם. *Qatal* (modal) 3ms Qal √חרה. The verb חרה, "to be hot," often has אף "nose," "anger," as the subject, as an idiom for a person's wrath being kindled. In that idiom, an adjunct PP with preposition ב denotes the person against whom the wrath is kindled (HALOT s.v.). The 2mp pronominal object of the pronoun means everyone experiences Yhwh's wrath, presumably for failing to do anything about the situation.

וְהִשְׁמִידְךָ֖ מַהֵֽר׃. *Qatal* (modal) 3ms Hiph √שמד with 2ms pronominal suffix. This modal *qatal* ends the unbroken chain. A final pronominal shift, to 2ms, perhaps returns to the father. More likely, though, is that it speaks of the people as a whole (cf. vv. 1-2a; 6:15).

מַהֵֽר׃. Inf abs Piel √מהר, functioning adverbially (JM §102e, §123r).

Deuteronomy 7:5-6a

7:5 כִּֽי־אִם־כֹּ֣ה תַעֲשׂוּ֮ לָהֶם֒ מִזְבְּחֹתֵיהֶ֣ם תִּתֹּ֔צוּ
וּמַצֵּבֹתָ֖ם תְּשַׁבֵּ֑רוּ וַאֲשֵֽׁירֵהֶם֙ תְּגַדֵּע֔וּן וּפְסִילֵיהֶ֖ם
תִּשְׂרְפ֥וּן בָּאֵֽשׁ׃

D2. Adversative clause. HD. After the basic injunction החרם תחרים (v. 2), there were five prohibitions. These are balanced by five injunctions (v. 5). The initial command is followed asyndetically by four coordinated *yiqtols* which together define what they *should* do. In discussions of חרם, it is important to notice that *all* of the positive commands are associated with religious iconoclasm.

כִּֽי־אִם־כֹּ֣ה תַעֲשׂוּ֮ לָהֶם֒. *Yiqtol* (modal) 2mp Qal √עשׂה. כי־אם introduces an adversative clause after a negative (WHS §555; JM §172c): "[Do not do X . . .] *but* [do Y]." כה is a demonstrative adverbial adjunct (cf. JM §102h), and typically comes first in the clause, leading to **triggered inversion** and a X–P–S rather than a S–P order. It is cataphoric, referring to what follows rather than to what precedes.

מִזְבְּחֹתֵיהֶ֣ם תִּתֹּ֔צוּ וּמַצֵּבֹתָ֖ם תְּשַׁבֵּ֑רוּ וַאֲשֵֽׁירֵהֶם֙ תְּגַדֵּע֔וּן וּפְסִילֵיהֶ֖ם תִּשְׂרְפ֥וּן בָּאֵֽשׁ׃. A succession of four 2mp *yiqtols* with modal nuance, expressing obligation (cf. JM §113m): Qal √נתץ, Piel √שׁבר, Piel √גדע and Qal √שׂרף, the final two with **paragogic** ן (for which see on 1:17). In each case, the accusative complement NP is fronted as the **topic** (Moshavi 2010: 160). Together they build up a complementary picture, rather than a sequential narrative (n.b., they are all disjunctive clauses). Although each of the four is coordinated with ו, the **asyndesis** at the start indicates that these together explain precisely what they *are* to do (כי־אם־כה תעשׂו להם). באשׁ is adjunct PP.

מִזְבְּחֹתֵיהֶ֣ם וּמַצֵּבֹתָ֖ם. For ם- on plural nouns, instead of ־יהֶם, see JM §94g. While מצבתם is the characteristic form with 3mp pronominal suffix, מזבחתיהם is also found, for euphonic reasons, as מזבחתם (12:3).

תְּגַדֵּע֔וּן. Note that *tsere* is kept even before the relatively minor pause of *zaqef qaton* (GKC §52n).

7:6a כִּ֣י עַ֤ם קָדוֹשׁ֙ אַתָּ֔ה לַיהוָ֖ה אֱלֹהֶ֑יךָ

An explanatory clause (v. 6a) grounds the previous injunctions and prohibitions. Israel's unique relationship with Yhwh is the foundation for everything.

כִּי עַם קָדוֹשׁ אַתָּה לַיהוָה אֱלֹהֶיךָ. Subordinating conjunction כִּי introducing an explanatory **null-copula** clause. Although after כִּי verbal clauses have **triggered inversion**, **null-copula** clauses do not. The P–S word order in a **null-copula** clause marks P, the substantival complement עַם קָדוֹשׁ as the **focus**. Of all that the people might be, they are a people holy to Yhwh. לַיהוָה אֱלֹהֶיךָ is adjunct PP. Holiness in Deuteronomy is always "to Yhwh" and speaks of a status of "consecration to" more than "separation from" (cf. Costecalde et al.).

Israel's unique status as grounds for obedience (7:6b-11)

An opening asyndetic clause marks the start of a long *excursus* from 7:6b-24; the modal *yiqtol* in 7:25a picks up from 7:5b (Weinfeld, 376; DeRouchie 2007: 242–43). This initial section expands on Yhwh's choice and uses his action in history to ground exhortations to "know" (v. 9) and "keep" (v. 11). Yhwh's choice of Israel, and no other nation, brings special status and special responsibilities. The macrostructure illuminates some of the key points being made:

> 6bIt was you that Yhwh chose . . .
> 7Not because of your being more numerous than
> all the peoples   A
> did Yhwh desire you   X
> and so choose you
> for you [were] the least of all the peoples)
> 8But rather, because of Yhwh's loving you   B
> and because of his keeping the oath he swore to your fathers
> did Yhwh bring you out by a strong hand   Y
> and redeem you from the house of slaves...
> 9so know that Yhwh your God is God, the faithful God. . . .
> 11and keep . . .

A 'not A but X'-type contrast is set up in v. 7, and then repeated with variation in v. 8: "it was not because of A that X happened, but because of B that Y happened." This entire statement then forms the ground for the commands to "know" (v. 9) and "keep" (v. 11). This structure conveys three things:

1. Israel's identity as Yhwh's people arises from their history (X, Yhwh's desire and choice, and Y, Yhwh's bringing out and redeeming, correspond; cf. 4:20);

2. Israel's knowledge of Yhwh is rooted in their history; and
3. Israel's obligation to obey is rooted in their identity and their knowledge of Yhwh, both of which are established through their history.

⁶ᵇ—*it was you that Yhwh your God chose to be a treasured possession for himself, out of all the peoples who are on the face of the earth.* ⁷*It was not because you were numerous than all peoples that Yhwh desired you and chose you, for you were the fewest of all peoples,* ⁸*but it was because Yhwh loves you and because he kept his oath which he swore to your ancestors that Yhwh brought you out with a strong hand and redeemed you from the house of slaves, from the hand of Pharaoh, king of Egypt.* ⁹*So know that Yhwh your God, he is God, the faithful god, keeping his covenant loyalty with those who love him and keep his commandments, to a thousand generations,* ¹⁰*but repaying those who hate him to their face, by destroying them—he will not delay with the one who hates him; to their face he will repay them*—¹¹*and keep the commandment, the statutes and the judgments that I am commanding you today, by doing them.*

7:6b בְּךָ֞ בָּחַ֣ר ׀ יְהוָ֣ה אֱלֹהֶ֗יךָ לִהְי֥וֹת לוֹ֙ לְעַ֣ם סְגֻלָּ֔ה מִכֹּל֙ הָֽעַמִּ֔ים אֲשֶׁ֖ר עַל־פְּנֵ֥י הָאֲדָמָֽה: ס

D2. An asyndetic *qatal* clause (ND) marks the start of an excursus. Israel's consecration to Yhwh (v. 6a) is founded on Yhwh's choice.

בְּךָ֞ בָּחַ֣ר ׀ יְהוָ֣ה אֱלֹהֶ֗יךָ. *Qatal* 3ms Qal √בחר. בך is the oblique complement, fronted for **focus**: "you [and no one else]." This clause follows on asyndetically from the explanatory clause (v. 6a). It, and the subsequent clauses that follow asyndetically, serve to explain what it means for "you" to be "a holy people."

לִהְי֥וֹת לוֹ֙ לְעַ֣ם סְגֻלָּ֔ה. Inf constr Qal √היה with preposition ל. This adjunct infinitive phrase is the result of the choice (AC §3.4.1[d]). For √היה followed by ל . . . ל, see on 4:20. לעם סגלה is construct PP. As an attributive adjectival genitive, סגלה characterizes עם (cf. WO §9.5.3a-b). סגלה is a king's treasure (cf. 1 Chr 29:3; Qoh 2:8); the noun is one of thirty-six with this vocalization (WO §5.5b).

מִכֹּל֙ הָעַמִּ֔ים אֲשֶׁ֖ר עַל־פְּנֵ֥י הָאֲדָמָֽה: ס. Adjunct construct PP, with absolute העמים as **head** of the following restrictive relative clause. מן is partitive, "out of all . . ." (cf. JM §133e; WHS §324). The relative clause is **null-copula**, with construct PP predicate.

7:7 לֹא מֵרֻבְּכֶ֞ם מִכָּל־הָעַמִּ֗ים חָשַׁ֧ק יְהוָ֛ה בָּכֶ֖ם וַיִּבְחַ֣ר בָּכֶ֑ם כִּֽי־אַתֶּ֥ם הַמְעַ֖ט מִכָּל־הָעַמִּֽים׃

ND. D2. A *qatal* then a *wayyiqtol* tell the story of Yhwh's love and choice. Erroneous grounds are fronted for **focus** and assertively dismissed. The explanatory clause (v. 7b) gives the reason for that dismissal.

לֹא מֵרֻבְּכֶ֞ם מִכָּל־הָעַמִּ֗ים חָשַׁ֧ק יְהוָ֛ה בָּכֶ֖ם. *Qatal* 3ms Qal √חשק. ND. Again there is clausal **asyndesis**. It signals the start of the explanation of the choice Yhwh made. Because of the fronting for **focus**, the word order is PP–P–S. בכם is oblique complement of √חשק.

לֹא מֵרֻבְּכֶ֞ם מִכָּל־הָעַמִּ֗ים. Inf constr Qal √רבב with 2mp pronominal suffix (subject) and with preposition מן. Adjunct infinitive phrase with מן expressing causation (WHS §319, §535; MNK §39.14.5; cf. WO §36.2.2b). The phrase is fronted for **focus**: of all possible reasons for Yhwh's affection, being more numerous is not one. לא is an item adverb, modifying the adjunct phrase rather than the main clause (cf. WO §39.3.2). The whole does *not* mean, "Because you were more numerous, Yhwh did *not* love you . . .," but "It is *not* because you were more numerous . . . that Yhwh loved you." מכל־העמים is adjunct construct PP. Where the verb has an adjectival idea, comparison is expressed by the preposition מן, denoting difference and connoting comparison (JM §141h).

וַיִּבְחַ֣ר בָּכֶ֑ם. *Wayyiqtol* 3ms Qal √בחר. The *wayyiqtol* continues the ND after the *qatal*. בכם is oblique complement, marking the direct object (MNK §32.2.2[i], §39.1.3[ii]a).

כִּֽי־אַתֶּ֥ם הַמְעַ֖ט מִכָּל־הָעַמִּֽים׃. Subordinating conjunction כי introducing an explanatory **null-copula** clause. Note the unmarked S–P word order. Lacking a superlative form, Hebrew uses the article, here with predicate nominative, to indicate the superlative (WHS §33b, §77b, §93; MNK §24.4.3[iii]). מכל־העמים is adjunct PP, with partitive מן (cf. JM §133e; WHS §324).

7:8 כִּ֣י מֵֽאַהֲבַ֣ת יְהוָה֩ אֶתְכֶ֨ם וּמִשָּׁמְר֤וֹ אֶת־הַשְּׁבֻעָה֙
אֲשֶׁ֤ר נִשְׁבַּע֙ לַאֲבֹ֣תֵיכֶ֔ם הוֹצִ֧יא יְהוָ֛ה אֶתְכֶ֖ם בְּיָ֣ד
חֲזָקָ֑ה וַֽיִּפְדְּךָ֙ מִבֵּ֣ית עֲבָדִ֔ים מִיַּ֖ד פַּרְעֹ֥ה מֶֽלֶךְ־
מִצְרָֽיִם׃

ND. D2. A mirrored structure with v. 7. See comments on vv. 6b–11.

כִּ֣י מֵֽאַהֲבַ֣ת יְהוָה֩ אֶתְכֶ֨ם. Inf constr Qal √אהב. The verb √אהב has the feminine ending ־ה for the infinitive construct, as do some other stative verbs, notably √ירא (JM §49d). Here, it is bound as construct with יהוה, hence the ־ת ending. The genitive (or absolute), יהוה, is subjective; Yhwh is the subject of the verbal action expressed in the construct (WHS §37). As a *verbal* noun, the infinitive construct takes an accusative complement, אתכם. The phrase is an adjunct infinitive phrase with מן expressing causation (WO §36.2.2b; cf. WHS §319, §535); the phrase is fronted for **focus**, inviting a contrast with other possible reasons. כי is adversative after a negative, לא (v. 7; cf. JM §172c).

וּמִשָּׁמְר֤וֹ אֶת־הַשְּׁבֻעָה֙ אֲשֶׁ֤ר נִשְׁבַּע֙ לַאֲבֹ֣תֵיכֶ֔ם. Inf constr Qal √שמר with 3ms pronominal suffix. The comments on the previous clause apply here on: (1) subjective genitive (this time the pronominal suffix); (2) *verbal* noun taking an accusative complement, את־השבעה; (3) מן expressing causation; and (4) fronting for **focus**.

אֲשֶׁ֤ר נִשְׁבַּע֙ לַאֲבֹ֣תֵיכֶ֔ם. *Qatal* 3ms Niph √שבע. Restrictive relative clause, with **head** השבעה.

הוֹצִ֧יא יְהוָ֛ה אֶתְכֶ֖ם בְּיָ֣ד חֲזָקָ֑ה. *Qatal* 3ms Hiph √יצא. ביד חזקה is adjunct PP (cf. 4:34). Because of the fronted PPs, the word order is PPs–P–S.

וַֽיִּפְדְּךָ֙ מִבֵּ֣ית עֲבָדִ֔ים מִיַּ֖ד פַּרְעֹ֥ה מֶֽלֶךְ־מִצְרָֽיִם׃. *Wayyiqtol* 3ms Qal √פדה with 2ms pronominal suffix. מבית עבדים is adjunct PP (see on 5:6). מיד פרעה is adjunct construct PP, appositional to מבית עבדים, giving further information. Only here in Deuteronomy is יד פרעה found. The contrast with Yhwh's יד חזקה is sharp. מלך־מצרים is appositional construct NP, giving more information about Pharaoh.

7:9 וְיָדַעְתָּ֗ כִּֽי־יְהוָ֤ה אֱלֹהֶ֙יךָ֙ ה֣וּא הָֽאֱלֹהִ֔ים הָאֵל֙ הַֽנֶּאֱמָ֔ן שֹׁמֵ֧ר הַבְּרִ֣ית וְהַחֶ֗סֶד לְאֹהֲבָ֛יו וּלְשֹׁמְרֵ֥י מִצְוֹתָ֖ו [מצוותיו] לְאֶ֥לֶף דּֽוֹר׃

HD. D2. The modal *qatal* gives an exhortation rooted in the history just recounted. They know who Yhwh is and what Yhwh is like because of their history. Yhwh's faithfulness (√אמן) is manifest both in keeping his covenant (v. 9b) and in repaying those who hate him (v. 10). There are strong echoes of the first commandment (cf. 5:9-10). Yhwh's keeping (√שמר) of his oath and covenant (vv. 8-9) gives grounds for Israel's keeping (√שמר) of Yhwh's commands (vv. 9, 11).

. . . וְיָדַעְתָּ֗ כִּֽי. *Qatal* (modal) 2ms Qal √ידע. This exhortation is grounded in the events in history in vv. 6-8 (cf. WO §32.2.3d and on 4:39). כי is a **complementizer**, introducing the accusative complement noun clause, what they should "know." The essential knowledge is expressed succinctly in the following nominal clause, but the full extent continues to the end of v. 10.

כִּֽי־יְהוָ֤ה אֱלֹהֶ֙יךָ֙ ה֣וּא הָֽאֱלֹהִ֔ים הָאֵל֙ הַֽנֶּאֱמָ֔ן. A **tripartite** verbless/nominal clause (see on 3:22 for its construal, and on 1:17 for such clauses more generally). יהוה אלהיך is **extraposed** as the **topic**, הוא is the **focus**.

הָאֵל֙ הַֽנֶּאֱמָ֔ן. Ptcp ms Niph √אמן. For the article with the participle as introducing a **null-copula** relative clause, see on 1:30. Appositional NP.

שֹׁמֵ֧ר הַבְּרִ֣ית וְהַחֶ֗סֶד לְאֹהֲבָ֛יו וּלְשֹׁמְרֵ֥י מִצְוֹתָ֖ו [מצוותיו] לְאֶ֥לֶף דּֽוֹר׃. Ptcp ms Qal √שמר. The participle is an attributive accusative of state, used as the attribute of a noun (האל הנאמן), "keeping." The lack of an article shows it is neither in apposition nor a relative clause (cf. JM §127a).

הַבְּרִ֣ית וְהַחֶ֗סֶד. Accusative complement NP, functioning as a **hendiadys**, expressing one concept through two words: "covenant loyalty" (Nelson, 95–96; cf. WHS §72; AC §4.3.3(g.1); MNK §40.8.1[v]) or "gracious covenant" (Weinfeld, 370); cf. also v. 12.

לְאֹהֲבָ֛יו וּלְשֹׁמְרֵ֥י מִצְוֹתָ֖ו [מצוותיו]. Ptcp mp Qal √אהב with 3ms pronominal suffix (object) and with preposition ל, followed by Ptcp mp constr Qal √שמר with absolute מצותו (*ketiv*), an objective genitive (cf. 5:10; WO §9.5.2b). Adjunct PPs. These substantival participles occur as the objects of the preposition לְ, with the לְ introducing what is sometimes called "the dative of advantage" giving the beneficiaries of the action of the verb (GKC §119q-s; JM §133d; WO §11.2.10d; WHS §271a). The *qere* is מִצְוֹתָיו, "his commandments," while the *ketiv* is (with pointing added) מִצְוָתוֹ, "his commandment." The MT, Smr, and ancient versions all read the plural here. It is possible that the singular, "his commandment" was intended. There is variation in the pattern of usage of מצוה with √שמר in chapters 1–11. Factors include whether מצוה has a pronominal suffix or not (e.g., 6:1-2); whether כל precedes or not (e.g., 6:25; 7:11); whether and how מצוה is coordinated with other terms or not (e.g., 4:2, 40). Probably the plural is preferable, given the profile with suffixes (*BHQ: Deuteronomy*, 72*).

לְאֶלֶף דּוֹר. Adjunct PP. The so-called "terminative" לְ, "up to" (WO §11.2.10c; WHS §266). For the singular noun דור with אלף, see GKC §134g.

7:10 וּמְשַׁלֵּם לְשֹׂנְאָיו אֶל־פָּנָיו לְהַאֲבִידוֹ לֹא יְאַחֵר
לְשֹׂנְאוֹ אֶל־פָּנָיו יְשַׁלֶּם־לוֹ׃

D2. Yhwh's faithfulness is also evident in his repaying those who hate him (v. 10a). Two asyndetic PD clauses unfold and reassert what Yhwh's repayment looks like (v. 10b).

וּמְשַׁלֵּם לְשֹׂנְאָיו אֶל־פָּנָיו לְהַאֲבִידוֹ. Ptcp ms Piel √שלם. The participle is a second attributive accusative of state, used as the attribute of a noun (האל הנאמן), a counterpart of שמר (v. 9).

לְשֹׂנְאָיו. Ptcp mp Qal √שנא with 3ms pronominal suffix (object) and with preposition לְ. Oblique complement of √שלם. The participle is used substantivally, but retains the verbal idea by taking a pronominal suffix as the object (cf. JM §121k).

אֶל־פָּנָיו. Adjunct PP. This shift from the plural, "*those* who hate him" to "to *his* face" is "distinctive: every one of them" (Weinfeld, 360). GKC §145l notes the "*distributive* singular" when the "class of individuals," represented by the participle, gives way to a singular predicate and regards pronominal suffixes as "analogous" (GKC §145m). The rest of the verse speaks of an individual, using the singular.

לְהַאֲבִידוֹ. Inf constr Hiph √אבד with 3ms pronominal suffix (object) and with preposition לְ. לְ + infinitive construct here is explanatory, a **gerundial** use of the infinitive, "by X-ing," showing *how* Yhwh would be repaying them (cf. WO §36.2.3e; JM §124o).

לֹ֤א יְאַחֵר֙ לְשֹׂ֣נְא֔וֹ. *Yiqtol* 3ms Piel √אחר. לשנאו (ptcp ms Qal √שנא; see above) could be an adjunct PP, the dative of disadvantage, the analogue of the dative of advantage (see on 7:9). Alternatively, there is **ellipsis** of the expected ל + infinitive construct, לְשַׁלֵּם, in which case the NP is the oblique complement of √שלם, "he will not delay [in repaying] the one who hates him." The clausal **asyndesis** indicates that this spells out the previous clause, reaffirming the immediacy of Yhwh's repayment.

אֶל־פָּנָ֖יו יְשַׁלֶּם־לֽוֹ׃. *Yiqtol* 3ms Piel √שלם. אל־פני is adjunct PP, fronted for **focus**, inviting a contrast with other times or places of repaying. לו is oblique complement of √שלם. The clause follows asyndetically, explaining the previous clause about lack of delay.

וְשָׁמַרְתָּ֨ אֶת־הַמִּצְוָ֜ה וְאֶת־הַֽחֻקִּ֣ים וְאֶת־הַמִּשְׁפָּטִ֗ים 7:11
אֲשֶׁ֨ר אָנֹכִ֧י מְצַוְּךָ֛ הַיּ֖וֹם לַעֲשׂוֹתָֽם׃ פ

HD. D2. The move from Yhwh's action in history to the exhortation to "know (√ידע; v. 9)" then to "keep (√שמר)" occurs elsewhere (4:39-40; 8:5-6; 11:2, 8). It echoes back to 5:31 and 6:1, and warrants a break after it (note the *petuhah*, פ).

וְשָׁמַרְתָּ֨ אֶת־הַמִּצְוָ֜ה וְאֶת־הַֽחֻקִּ֣ים וְאֶת־הַמִּשְׁפָּטִ֗ים . . . לַעֲשׂוֹתָֽם׃ פ. *Qatal* (modal) 2ms Qal √שמר. See on 5:31 for the accusative complement, את־המצוה . . . המשפטים. For √שמר followed by infinitive construct Qal √עשה (here with 3mp pronominal suffix), see on 5:1. The presence of accusative complements for √שמר and √עשה provides evidence for the view taken there, that √שמר is not functioning adverbially, "carefully," but that ל + infinitive construct is explanatory.

אֲשֶׁ֨ר אָנֹכִ֧י מְצַוְּךָ֛ הַיּ֖וֹם. Ptcp ms Piel √צוה with 2ms pronominal suffix. See on 4:40 for the identical phrase.

*Obedience will bring blessing, but compromise
remains dangerous (7:12-16)*

This section explores what happens on the assumption that the exhortations of vv. 1-11 are acted upon. A string of seven modal *qatals* declare what Yhwh will do for them, followed by an eighth, ואכלת, which the people will do in response to Yhwh's "giving" (√נתן, v. 16a). Only in v. 16b are there uncompromising injunctions. The big danger is idolatry.

¹²And precisely because you hear these judgements and keep [them] and do them, Yhwh your God will keep for you the covenant loyalty which he swore to your ancestors, ¹³and will love you and bless you and multiply you and bless your fruit of the womb and your fruit of the ground: your grain and wine and oil, the offspring of your cattle and the young of your flock, upon the ground which he swore to your ancestors to give to you —¹⁴you will be blessed more than all peoples: there will not be among you a barren man or woman, nor among your livestock—¹⁵and Yhwh will remove from you every sickness, and as for all the dreadful diseases of Egypt that you knew, he will not set them on you, but will put them among all your enemies. You will devour all the peoples that Yhwh your God is giving to you—never let your eye have pity on them and do not serve their gods, for that would be nothing but a snare for you.

7:12 וְהָיָה ׀ עֵקֶב תִּשְׁמְעוּן אֵת הַמִּשְׁפָּטִים הָאֵלֶּה
וּשְׁמַרְתֶּם וַעֲשִׂיתֶם אֹתָם וְשָׁמַר יְהוָה אֱלֹהֶיךָ לְךָ
אֶת־הַבְּרִית וְאֶת־הַחֶסֶד אֲשֶׁר נִשְׁבַּע לַאֲבֹתֶיךָ׃

PD. D2. Moses looks forward to the future. There is a direct correspondence and correlation between Israelite obedience to Yhwh's judgments (√שמע, √שמר, √עשה; v. 12a; causal clauses) and Yhwh's response, expressed in a modal *qatal* (√שמר) in v. 12b and in subsequent modal *qatals* in the following verses.

וְהָיָה ׀. *Qatal* (modal) 3ms Qal √היה. This serves to anchor what follows in future time. See on 6:10.

עֵקֶב תִּשְׁמְעוּן אֵת הַמִּשְׁפָּטִים הָאֵלֶּה. *Yiqtol* 2mp Qal √שמע with a **paragogic** ן (for which see on 1:17). The *yiqtol* here expresses the "past future," *"as a reward for the fact that you will have . . ."* (JM §113b). √שמע with an accusative complement usually denotes the act of hearing (e.g., 4:6), while with a preposition (ב or אל) it denotes "listening to" (e.g., 9:23; 11:13). Since the verb is linked with the two clauses that follow (see below), "hear" is a better translation (cf. 6:3, where the three verbs occur and שמע is "hear"). The subordinating conjunction עקב is relatively uncommon, only occurring elsewhere in Deuteronomy in 8:20. JM §170g comments (on this, and similar instances) that it has "the special nuance of *in recompense for the fact that*" in positive cases (cf. Gen 22:18; 26:5; GKC §158b; AC §5.2.5[b]").

וּשְׁמַרְתֶּ֤ם וַעֲשִׂיתֶם֙ אֹתָ֔ם. *Qatal* (modal) 2mp Qal √שמר and √עשה. The modal *qatals* continue the force of the previous *yiqtol*. See on 5:1 for √שמר followed by √עשה. אתם, the accusative complement of √עשה, refers back to המשפטים, tying these three clauses together into one compound action.

וְשָׁמַר֩ יְהוָ֨ה אֱלֹהֶ֤יךָ לְךָ֙ אֶֽת־הַבְּרִית֙ וְאֶת־הַחֶ֔סֶד. *Qatal* (modal) 3ms Qal √שמר. The modal *qatal* with ו often introduces the main clause when a causal clause comes first (cf. JM §170o, §176e; they term it "Waw of apodosis"). לך is dative of "advantage" (see on 7:9). The accusative complement, את־הברית ואת־החסד is a **hendiadys** (see on 7:9).

אֲשֶׁ֥ר נִשְׁבַּ֖ע לַאֲבֹתֶֽיךָ׃. For the identical phrase, see on 6:10. Restrictive relative clause, with את־הברית ואת־החסד as the **head**. Yhwh can be said to swear (√שבע, Niphal) his חסד (Ps 89:50; Micah 7:20) and his ברית (4:31).

7:13 וַאֲהֵ֣בְךָ֔ וּבֵרַכְךָ֖ וְהִרְבֶּ֑ךָ וּבֵרַ֣ךְ פְּרִֽי־בִטְנְךָ֣ וּפְרִֽי־אַדְמָתֶ֗ךָ דְּגָנְךָ֤ וְתִֽירֹשְׁךָ֙ וְיִצְהָרֶ֔ךָ שְׁגַר־אֲלָפֶ֖יךָ וְעַשְׁתְּרֹ֣ת צֹאנֶ֑ךָ עַ֚ל הָֽאֲדָמָ֔ה אֲשֶׁר־נִשְׁבַּ֥ע לַאֲבֹתֶ֖יךָ לָ֥תֶת לָֽךְ׃

D2. PD. Four modal *qatals* continue the future blessing contingent on obedience.

וַאֲהֵ֣בְךָ֔ וּבֵרַכְךָ֖ וְהִרְבֶּ֑ךָ. *Qatal* (modal) 3ms Qal √אהב, Piel √ברך, Hiph √רבה each with 2ms pronominal suffix. The modal *qatals* continue from ושמר (v. 12).

וּבֵרַ֣ךְ פְּרִֽי־בִטְנְךָ֣ וּפְרִֽי־אַדְמָתֶ֗ךָ דְּגָנְךָ֤ וְתִֽירֹשְׁךָ֙ וְיִצְהָרֶ֔ךָ שְׁגַר־אֲלָפֶ֖יךָ וְעַשְׁתְּרֹ֣ת צֹאנֶ֑ךָ. *Qatal* (modal) 3ms Piel √ברך, with a succession of grouped NPs. **Asyndesis** indicates that the second (דגנך ותירשך ויצהרך) and third (שגר־אלפיך ועשתרת צאנך) group explain the first (פרי־בטנך ופרי־אדמתך).

פְּרִֽי־בִטְנְךָ֣ וּפְרִֽי־אַדְמָתֶ֗ךָ. Conjoined accusative complement NPs. "When the logical union between the two nouns which make up a genitive group is very close, the suffix logically affects the block and not the second noun"; thus, here, "*your offspring* (lit. *your fruit-of-womb*, Germ.

Leibesfrucht; not *the fruit of your womb*, for this could not be said about a man)" (JM §140b).

דְּגָנְךָ וְתִירֹשְׁךָ וְיִצְהָרֶךָ. Appositional conjoined NPs. When these three nouns occur together and joined by ו, the order is always the same; it is also common (e.g., 11:14; 12:17).

שְׁגַר־אֲלָפֶיךָ וְעַשְׁתְּרֹת צֹאנֶךָ עַל הָאֲדָמָה. Two appositional conjoined construct NPs, followed by adjunct PP. שגר derives from "what is dropped, thrown," hence "offspring" (HALOT s.v.). עשתרת is construct plural of עַשְׁתֶּרֶת, "offspring (of smaller animals)." Both words are rare, only occurring here and in 28:4, 18 (שגר is found once elsewhere as a segholate, שֶׁגֶר (Exod 7:13). The repetition of האדמה probably indicates that the two appositional NPs describing crops and livestock are "your fruit from the ground" (פרי־אדמתך) that Yhwh has blessed. It is conceivable, though, that all three groups of NPs are separate (cf. the separation of fruit of womb, soil, and cattle in 28:4, 11, 18).

אֲשֶׁר־נִשְׁבַּע לַאֲבֹתֶיךָ לָתֶת לָךְ: Restrictive relative clause. For the identical phrase (but with patriarchal names included after לאבתיך), see on 6:10.

7:14 בָּרוּךְ תִּהְיֶה מִכָּל־הָעַמִּים לֹא־יִהְיֶה בְךָ עָקָר וַעֲקָרָה וּבִבְהֶמְתֶּךָ:

PD. D2. Two asyndetic *yiqtol* clauses unpack further the nature and extent of the blessing.

בָּרוּךְ תִּהְיֶה מִכָּל־הָעַמִּים. *Yiqtol* 2ms Qal √היה. ברוך is Qal passive participle √ברך. ברוך occupies first position in a clause when a blessing is uttered and there is no copula (√היה). Here, however, there is a copula and it is PD. ברוך is the participial predicate, fronted for **focus**: of all that Israel could be they will be *blessed*." מכל־העמים is adjunct construct NP. Lacking particular forms for the comparative, Hebrew uses the preposition מן attached to the noun that is excelled (JM §141g; AC §4.1.13h). Clausal **asyndesis** indicates that this expands upon the blessing articulated in v. 13b.

לֹא־יִהְיֶה בְךָ עָקָר וַעֲקָרָה וּבִבְהֶמְתֶּךָ: *Yiqtol* 3ms Qal √היה. PD. בך is spatial adjunct PP, עקר, "barren," is only here predicated of men. בבהמתך is spatial adjunct PP, slightly awkwardly placed, but such placement is not uncommon (cf. 1:36; Driver, 103). Clausal **asyndesis**, explaining further the nature of the blessing.

7:15 וְהֵסִ֧יר יְהוָ֛ה מִמְּךָ֖ כָּל־חֹ֑לִי וְכָל־מַדְוֵי֩ מִצְרַ֨יִם הָרָעִ֜ים אֲשֶׁ֣ר יָדַ֗עְתָּ לֹ֤א יְשִׂימָם֙ בָּ֔ךְ וּנְתָנָ֖ם בְּכָל־שֹׂנְאֶֽיךָ׃

PD. D2. A further modal *qatal* continues Yhwh's contingent action (v. 15a). In v. 15b, a *yiqtol* followed by a modal *qatal* spell out what will happen to the (syntactically **extraposed**) grievous Egyptian diseases.

וְהֵסִ֧יר יְהוָ֛ה מִמְּךָ֖ כָּל־חֹ֑לִי. *Qatal* (modal) 3ms Hiph √סור. ממך is adjunct PP. כל־חלי is accusative complement construct NP. כל in construct relationship with an indeterminate noun has the connotation "every" (JM §139h).

וְכָל־מַדְוֵי֩ מִצְרַ֨יִם הָרָעִ֜ים אֲשֶׁ֣ר יָדַ֗עְתָּ. **Extraposed** or hanging construct NP, followed by restrictive relative clause, with predicate *qatal* 2ms Qal √ידע (cf. 1:31, אשר ראית). The construct chain וכל־מדוי מצרים הרעים includes the rare word מַדְוֶה, "sickness," found only here and in 28:60. In a construct chain, the adjective (הרעים) follows the absolute and usually qualifies the construct (GKC §132a; JM §139a); here, it takes the article because the chain is definite, owing to the absolute being definite (a proper name, מצרים; cf. GKC §127a).

לֹ֤א יְשִׂימָם֙ בָּ֔ךְ. *Yiqtol* 3ms Qal √שים with 3mp pronominal suffix. Normally pronominal suffixes attached to the *yiqtol* have an i-class vowel (3mp, םֵ֖-; e.g., 9:3, יַשְׁמִידֵם), but here it is a-class (GKC §60d). The pronominal suffix is resumptive, picking up the **extraposed** NP. בך is spatial adjunct PP, "among" (cf. WO §11.2.5b).

וּנְתָנָ֖ם בְּכָל־שֹׂנְאֶֽיךָ׃. *Qatal* (modal) 3ms Qal √נתן with 3mp pronominal suffix. בכל־שנאיך is spatial adjunct construct PP. שנאיך is ptcp mp Qal √שנא with 2ms pronominal suffix, used substantivally.

7:16 וְאָכַלְתָּ֣ אֶת־כָּל־הָֽעַמִּ֗ים אֲשֶׁ֨ר יְהוָ֤ה אֱלֹהֶ֙יךָ֙ נֹתֵ֣ן לָ֔ךְ לֹא־תָחֹ֥ס עֵֽינְךָ֖ עֲלֵיהֶ֑ם וְלֹ֤א תַעֲבֹד֙ אֶת־אֱלֹ֣הֵיהֶ֔ם כִּֽי־מוֹקֵ֥שׁ ה֖וּא לָֽךְ׃ ס

D2. A final modal *qatal* contingent on Israel's action (v. 12, PD) gives way to the only injunctions (modal *yiqtols*) of this section, introduced **asyndetically**. Moses justifies the charge not to let their eye pity or to serve other gods, for to do so would be a "snare."

וְאָכַלְתָּ֙ אֶת־כָּל־הָ֣עַמִּ֔ים אֲשֶׁ֨ר יְהוָ֤ה אֱלֹהֶ֙יךָ֙ נֹתֵ֣ן לָ֔ךְ. *Qatal* (modal) 2ms Qal √אכל. PD. Although Yhwh is said to be a "consuming (√אכל) fire", this is the only figurative occurrence of אכל predicated of people in chapters 1–11; elsewhere it is literal, "eat."

אֲשֶׁ֨ר יְהוָ֤ה אֱלֹהֶ֙יךָ֙ נֹתֵ֣ן לָ֔ךְ. Ptcp ms Qal √נתן. For the phrase, see on 1:20; 4:21. Strikingly the **head** of the characteristic relative clause is elsewhere always territory or land. But here the **head** is כל־העמים.

לֹא־תָח֥וֹס עֵֽינְךָ֖ עֲלֵיהֶ֑ם. *Yiqtol* (modal) 3fs Qal √חוס. The morphology and syntax here is awkward. Given the coordination with the following prohibition, לא תעבד, the verb here must be volitional. A negative volitional form is either אל with the jussive (JM §114i; cf. Ezek 9:5 *qere*) or לא + *yiqtol*. Here, the shortened form תָחֹס (rather than תָחוּס) might seem to be jussive, but the negative is לא (cf. לא תחוס in 13:9; 19:13, 21; 25:12). These forms could either be לא + jussive, with instances like 13:9 irregular *plene* jussives, or they may have originally intended to be לֹא תָחוּס, with the occurrence here written defectively (for these, see GKC §72r, 109d). However, only twice is the *yiqtol* 2nd or 3rd person found with ו, both with indicative force (Isa 13:8; Jer 21:7); normally the vowel is וּ, whether the force is a prohibition or indicative (13:9; Ezek 5:11; see JM §80k). Only here is a prohibition found just with a *holem*. Perhaps it should be read as לא + *yiqtol*, written defectively.

וְלֹ֥א תַעֲבֹ֖ד אֶת־אֱלֹהֵיהֶֽם. *Yiqtol* (modal) 2ms Qal √עבד. A prohibition (see on 1:17).

כִּֽי־מוֹקֵ֥שׁ ה֖וּא לָֽךְ׃ ס. Subordinating conjunction כי introducing an explanatory **null-copula** clause. The antecedent of הוא is an "implicit" noun, the act of keeping and doing in the opening two verbs (cf. 4:6; GKC §135p; WO §16.3.1a). Although verbal clauses have **triggered inversion** after כי, **null-copula** clauses do not. The P–S word order in a **null-copula** clause marks P, the substantival complement מוקש, as the **focus**. Of all that the action might be to them, it is a "snare." לך is adjunct PP. For the pausal form, see on 1:21.

> *Do not fear the inhabitants, because Yhwh will do*
> *what he has done and is in your midst (7:17-24)*

The second part of the excursus deals with the opposite thought pattern from that envisaged in the first part, but both have their roots in "militarism" (Olson, 52) or "self-importance" (Robson, 128): vv. 7-8 refute "arrogance," insisting that their election was not on the grounds of being impressive; these verses refute "despair" (Olson, 54). The conditional protasis (v. 17) outlines the errant thinking. Two injunctions not to fear (vv. 18, 21) are the key clauses in the apodosis (cf. 1:29, where they occur together). Both are introduced asyndetically. Both are then expanded upon in order to ground them.

> [18a]Do not fear them
> [18b]Make sure you remember . . .
> [19b]Yhwh will do all this and more . . .
> [21a]Do not be afraid of them
> [21b]For Yhwh is in your midst
> [22]and Yhwh will bring victory . . .

[17]If you say to yourself, "These nations are more numerous than we are. How can I dispossess them?" [18]do not fear them. Be very sure to remember what Yhwh your God did to Pharaoh and to all Egypt—[19]the great trials that your eyes saw, and the signs and the wonders and the strong hand and the outstretched arm [by] which Yhwh your God brought you out—Yhwh your God will do this to all the peoples of whom you are afraid. [20]What is more, Yhwh your God will send the hornet against them, until those who are left and those who have hidden themselves have perished from before you. [21]Do not be afraid of them, for Yhwh your God is in your midst, a great and fearful god—[22]and Yhwh your God will dislodge these nations from before you little by little—you will not be able to make a swift end to them, lest the wild animals of the countryside multiply against you—[23]and Yhwh your God will put them at your disposal and will throw them into great confusion until they are destroyed, [24]and he will give their kings into your hand and you will destroy their name from under heaven—No one will stand against you until you have destroyed them.

7:17 כִּי תֹאמַר֮ בִּלְבָבְךָ֒ רַבִּ֗ים הַגּוֹיִ֤ם הָאֵ֙לֶּה֙ מִמֶּ֔נִּי אֵיכָ֥ה אוּכַ֖ל לְהוֹרִישָֽׁם׃

A conditional protasis (D2) is followed by the verbalized thoughts (D3). These thoughts comprise two clauses, ED then ID. The **asyndesis** shows they are connected.

כִּי תֹאמַר֮ בִּלְבָבְךָ֒. *Yiqtol* 2ms Qal √אמר. Although כי can introduce both conditional and temporal clauses (see on 6:10), here it introduces a conditional protasis because its occurrence is hardly assumed. A reflexive action, "say to yourself," "think," is here expressed by a circumlocution (בלבבך, adjunct PP) rather than the Niphal (WO §23.4c).

רַבִּים הַגּוֹיִם הָאֵלֶּה מִמֶּנִּי. **Null-copula** clause, with P–S word order. The adjectival predicate is fronted for **focus**. ממנו is adjunct PP, with comparative מן (see on 7:14). Because of the P–S word order in this bipartite nominal clause, the preposition מן is separated from the predicate (JM §154q).

אֵיכָה אוּכַל לְהוֹרִישָׁם: *Yiqtol* 1cs Hoph √יכל. For the form, see on 1:9. The interrogative particle, איכה, "how," occurs more rarely than its synonym, אֵיךְ. Clausal **asyndesis**. The question follows quickly from the feelings of inferiority.

לְהוֹרִישָׁם: Inf constr Hiph √ירש with 3mp pronominal suffix (object) and with preposition ל. Infinitive phrase complement of √יכל.

7:18 לֹא תִירָא מֵהֶם זָכֹר תִּזְכֹּר אֵת אֲשֶׁר־עָשָׂה יְהוָה אֱלֹהֶיךָ לְפַרְעֹה וּלְכָל־מִצְרָיִם:

HD. D2. The apodosis begins **asyndetically** with a prohibition. An emphatic injunction follows this prohibition, again **asyndetically**. The way of not fearing is to remember what Yhwh did. Again Moses refers to collective memory.

לֹא תִירָא מֵהֶם. *Yiqtol* (modal) 2ms Qal √ירא. The apodosis is introduced **asyndetically** (cf. 6:12; 7:2). A prohibition (see on 1:17). מהם is oblique complement.

זָכֹר תִּזְכֹּר אֵת אֲשֶׁר־עָשָׂה יְהוָה אֱלֹהֶיךָ לְפַרְעֹה וּלְכָל־מִצְרָיִם: *Yiqtol* (modal) 2ms Qal √זכר preceded by infinitive absolute Qal √זכר. This **paronomastic** infinitive construction, of infinitive absolute with finite verb of the same root, accents the modality of its cognate verb in modal contexts, such as this one (see on 4:26). The *yiqtol* here, as an injunction, has the nuance of "must" (JM §123h n. 11). GKC §113bb sees the infinitive absolute here as indicating an "emphatic imperative." The **null-head** restrictive relative clause acts as the accusative complement of תזכר. The injunction follows the opening prohibition **asyndetically**, pointing to the importance of memory if they are not to be afraid.

אֲשֶׁר־עָשָׂה יְהוָה אֱלֹהֶיךָ לְפַרְעֹה וּלְכָל־מִצְרָיִם: *Qatal* 3ms Qal √עשה. **Null-head** restrictive relative clause, with P–S word order due to

triggered inversion. Two adjunct PPs follow, with ל introducing the one affected by the verbal action, in this case negatively (cf. WO §11.2.10d).

7:19 הַמַּסֹּת֙ הַגְּדֹלֹ֗ת אֲשֶׁר־רָא֣וּ עֵינֶ֘יךָ֙ וְהָאֹתֹ֤ת וְהַמֹּֽפְתִים֙ וְהַיָּ֤ד הַחֲזָקָה֙ וְהַזְּרֹ֣עַ הַנְּטוּיָ֔ה אֲשֶׁ֥ר הוֹצִֽאֲךָ֖ יְהוָ֣ה אֱלֹהֶ֑יךָ כֵּֽן־יַעֲשֶׂ֜ה יְהוָ֤ה אֱלֹהֶ֙יךָ֙ לְכָל־הָ֣עַמִּ֔ים אֲשֶׁר־אַתָּ֥ה יָרֵ֖א מִפְּנֵיהֶֽם׃

D2. The first half of the verse is a series of conjoined appositional NPs, outlining what Israel should remember (HD). The second half, with a *yiqtol*, declares what Yhwh will do (PD). A chiastic structure for vv. 18-19 reinforces the rhetoric:

- A Do not fear (√ירא)
  - B Remember what Yhwh did (√עשׂה)
  - B′ Yhwh will do (√עשׂה) the same
- A′ To all the nations you fear (√ירא).

הַמַּסֹּת֙ הַגְּדֹלֹ֗ת אֲשֶׁר־רָא֣וּ עֵינֶ֘יךָ֙. המסת הגדלת is appositional NP, describing what Yhwh did (cf. v. 18); the **head** of the following restrictive relative clause.

אֲשֶׁר־רָא֣וּ עֵינֶ֘יךָ֙. *Qatal* 3cp Qal √ראה. Restrictive relative clause, with P–S word order due to **triggered inversion**. For the rhetorical significance of sight, see on 1:30 (לעיניך) and comments on 4:9-14.

וְהָאֹתֹ֤ת וְהַמֹּֽפְתִים֙ וְהַיָּ֤ד הַחֲזָקָה֙ וְהַזְּרֹ֣עַ הַנְּטוּיָ֔ה אֲשֶׁ֥ר הוֹצִֽאֲךָ֖ יְהוָ֣ה אֱלֹהֶ֑יךָ. A succession of conjoined NPs, continuing the apposition. Each NP appears also in 4:34 (see comments there).

אֲשֶׁ֥ר הוֹצִֽאֲךָ֖ יְהוָ֣ה אֱלֹהֶ֑יךָ. *Qatal* 3ms Hiph √יצא with 2ms pronominal suffix. For the "extreme" omission of the preposition and resumptive pronoun here (*by which* he brought you out), see JM §158i (cf. Weinfeld, 361).

כֵּֽן־יַעֲשֶׂ֜ה יְהוָ֤ה אֱלֹהֶ֙יךָ֙ לְכָל־הָ֣עַמִּ֔ים אֲשֶׁר־אַתָּ֥ה יָרֵ֖א מִפְּנֵיהֶֽם׃. *Yiqtol* 3ms Qal √עשׂה. PD. כן is a demonstrative adverbial adjunct (cf. JM §102h), and typically comes first in the clause, leading to **triggered inversion** and a X–P–S rather than a S–P order. לכל־העמים is adjunct construct PP, with ל introducing the one affected by the verbal action, in this case negatively (cf. WO §11.2.10d).

אֲשֶׁר־אַתָּה יָרֵא מִפְּנֵיהֶם׃. **Null-copula** restrictive relative clause. Although WO §37.3b#6 call יָרֵא a "quasi-fientive stative participle," as a stative verb, √ירא does not strictly have a participle, but a verbal adjective, יָרֵא (GKC §116b; JM §41c). As a *verbal* adjective, it can take an oblique complement, מפניהם; the resumptive pronoun ־הֶם refers back to the **head**, כל־העמים. Unmarked S–P word order.

7:20 וְגַם֙ אֶת־הַצִּרְעָ֔ה יְשַׁלַּ֞ח יְהוָ֧ה אֱלֹהֶ֛יךָ בָּ֖ם עַד־אֲבֹ֑ד
הַנִּשְׁאָרִ֥ים וְהַנִּסְתָּרִ֖ים מִפָּנֶֽיךָ׃

D2. PD. Yhwh's action in the future will surpass that in the past.

וְגַם֙ אֶת־הַצִּרְעָ֔ה יְשַׁלַּ֞ח יְהוָ֧ה אֱלֹהֶ֛יךָ בָּ֖ם. *Yiqtol* 3ms Piel √שלח. גם serves to alert Moses' addressees that something is to be added to what Yhwh will do (cf. MNK §41.4.5.2[i]). It is probable that the scope of גם is the clause as a whole rather than just a constituent within the clause, את־הצרעה, since there are different predicates in this and the previous clause. בם is adjunct PP, with either an adversative sense (cf. JM §133c), "against them" (NRSV, NASV) or a spatial sense (cf. WO §11.2.5b), "among them" (NIV, ESV).

אֶת־הַצִּרְעָֽה. Accusative complement NP, fronted for **focus**. The referent of the word has been disputed. The ancient versions took it as the "hornet" (cf. HALOT s.v.). Presumably these will flush out any Canaanites that hide (cf. Driver, 104). Other interpretations of צרעה include a disease (cf. צרעת, Lev 13:2; NRSV), but that would be an unlikely agent of "driving out" (Exod 23:28); a metaphor for an army (e.g., Weinfeld, 375), but the reference in Joshua 24:12 precludes military interpretations and the comparison with the simile in 1:44 is tenuous; metonymy for "fear" (e.g., McConville, 149, 161), but the presence of "panic" (7:23) or "fear" (אימה, in parallel; Exod 23:27-28), rather than supporting this understanding, undermines it because צרעה is separable from it.

עַד־אֲבֹ֑ד הַנִּשְׁאָרִ֥ים וְהַנִּסְתָּרִ֖ים מִפָּנֶֽיךָ׃. Inf constr Qal √אבד. Although normally I-א verbs have *khatef-segol* in the infinitive construct (cf. בֶּאֱמֹר in 4:10), sometimes, as here, they have *khatef-patakh* (GKC §63i). Temporal adjunct infinitive construct phrase. There are two absolutes, both substantival Niphal mp participles (√שאר, √סתר) with the article (see on 1:30 for their syntax).

מִפָּנֶֽיךָ. Adjunct PP. There are two possible ways of taking it: first, closely with וְהַנִּשְׁאָרִים, "hidden from you" (cf. Gen 4:14; Job 13:20; so LXX, ESV, NIV); second with the second half of the verse as a whole, "perishing ... from before you," (cf. 8:20; Ps 9:4; so Weinfeld, 358; Lundbom, 327). On balance, the latter is to be preferred: (a) the disjunctive *tiphah* on והנסתרים shows that the Masoretes favored the latter; (b) in 7:22 (also 7:1), מפניך is associated with the dislodging of the nations "from before you"; (c) the close parallel in 8:20 with √אבד.

7:21 לֹ֥א תַעֲרֹ֖ץ מִפְּנֵיהֶ֑ם כִּֽי־יְהוָ֤ה אֱלֹהֶ֙יךָ֙ בְּקִרְבֶּ֔ךָ אֵ֥ל גָּד֖וֹל וְנוֹרָֽא׃

D2. HD. The second prohibition against fear is again rooted (cf. v. 18), this time with an explanatory clause asserting Yhwh's presence in their midst.

לֹ֥א תַעֲרֹ֖ץ מִפְּנֵיהֶ֑ם. *Yiqtol* (modal) 2ms Qal √ערץ. A prohibition (see on 1:17). מפניהם is oblique complement.

כִּֽי־יְהוָ֤ה אֱלֹהֶ֙יךָ֙ בְּקִרְבֶּ֔ךָ אֵ֥ל גָּד֖וֹל וְנוֹרָֽא. Subordinating conjunction כי introducing an explanatory **null-copula** clause. Although after כי, verbal clauses have **triggered inversion**, **null-copula** clauses do not. Some aspects of the syntax are straightforward: יהוה אלהיך is the characteristic appositional NP; אל גדול ונורא is a NP, with the substantive אל modified by an attributive adjective, גדול, and a Niphal ms participle √ירא, נורא, functioning adjectivally, having what WO §23.3d term the "**gerundive**" use of the Niphal, indicating what is proper or possible, here "dread*ful*" or "fear*ful*." But the location of the copula is contested. There are two possible ways to understand the syntax: (1) The substantival complement is אל גדול ונורא, with בקרבך as a PP either modifying יהוה אלהיך or the PP complement of an unmarked relative clause "for Yhwh your God [who is] in your midst, is a great and awesome God" (so NRSV, NIV; cf. 6:15); or (2) בקרבך is the predicate, with the final phrase אל גדול ונורא in apposition (so Weinfeld, 358; Tigay 1996: 90; McConville, 148; Nelson, 95, ESV, NASB), "for Yhwh your God is in your midst, a great and fearful god." The latter is preferable. The *zaqef-qaton* on בקרבך shows that the Masoretes favored it. Further, the key point is Yhwh's presence in their midst, not that the one in their midst is great and awesome.

Deuteronomy 7:22-23

7:22 וְנָשַׁל֩ יְהוָ֨ה אֱלֹהֶ֜יךָ אֶת־הַגּוֹיִ֥ם הָאֵ֛ל מִפָּנֶ֖יךָ מְעַ֣ט מְעָ֑ט לֹ֤א תוּכַל֙ כַּלֹּתָ֣ם מַהֵ֔ר פֶּן־תִּרְבֶּ֥ה עָלֶ֖יךָ חַיַּ֥ת הַשָּׂדֶֽה׃

HD. PD. Yhwh's presence will result in action, in dislodging the nations (v. 22a; cf. 7:1). This is then qualified by an asyndetic *yiqtol* clause, which is itself explained by a negative purpose clause. Any delay in conquest will not be determined by the power of the enemy but by the consideration of Yhwh.

וְנָשַׁל֩ יְהוָ֨ה אֱלֹהֶ֜יךָ אֶת־הַגּוֹיִ֥ם הָאֵ֛ל מִפָּנֶ֖יךָ מְעַ֣ט מְעָ֑ט. *Qatal* (modal) 3ms Qal √נשל. See on 7:1 for √נשל. הָאֵל is a rare variant of the demonstrative הָאֵלֶּה (cf. 4:42; JM §36b). מפניך is spatial adjunct PP. For the repetition of מעט in the "stock phrase" "little by little" (and other noun repetitions), see WO §7.2.3c. Yhwh's presence in their midst (ED) flows into what Yhwh will do (modal *qatal*) (cf. Exod 6:6).

לֹא תוּכַל כַּלֹּתָם מַהֵר. *Yiqtol* 2ms Hoph √יכל. PD. For יוכל as Hophal, see on 1:9 (cf. 7:17). Asyndetic explanatory comment, explaining the nature of Yhwh's dislodging.

כַּלֹּתָם. Inf constr Piel √כלה with 3mp pronominal suffix (object). Infinitive phrase complement of √יכל.

מַהֵר. Inf abs Piel √מהר, functioning adverbially (JM §102e, §123r), modifying כלתם.

פֶּן־תִּרְבֶּה עָלֶיךָ חַיַּת הַשָּׂדֶה. *Yiqtol* (modal) 3fs Qal √רבה. פן introduces a negative purpose clause and is followed by a *yiqtol*. It serves "to indicate a negative wish of a speaker or speakers ... 'I (or: we) do not wish the following to be, become or have become a reality'" (JM §168g). עליך is adjunct PP. The spatial sense of "on" extends to "against" or "above" in an oppressive sense, effectively creating a dative of disadvantage "to indicate a victim" (JM §133f). חית השדה is construct NP, the subject of תרבה. חיה is almost always a collective noun (but see Gen 37:20); השדה is "countryside," since the animals are wild.

7:23 וּנְתָנָ֞ם יְהוָ֤ה אֱלֹהֶ֙יךָ֙ לְפָנֶ֔יךָ וְהָמָם֙ מְהוּמָ֣ה גְדֹלָ֔ה עַ֖ד הִשָּׁמְדָֽם׃

D2. PD. After the brief qualification (v. 22b), two further modal *qatals* continue (from וּנְשַׁל) what Yhwh's presence in the midst will achieve.

וּנְתָנָם יְהוָה אֱלֹהֶיךָ לְפָנֶיךָ. *Qatal* (modal) 3ms Qal √נתן with 3mp pronominal suffix. See on 7:2 for the identical phrase.

וְהָמָם מְהוּמָה גְדֹלָה עַד הִשָּׁמְדָם׃. *Qatal* (modal) 3ms Qal √הום with 3mp pronominal suffix. The verb is הום, possibly a **by-form** of המם (cf. Exod 23:27, where the root is המם; see Tigay 1996: 90–91), and is followed by an internal accusative, מהומה גדלה, "an abstract noun of action, identical with, or analogous to the action expressed by the verb" (JM §125q), sometimes known as a cognate accusative, "He will confuse them [with] a great confusion. . . ."

עַד הִשָּׁמְדָם׃. Inf constr Niph √שמד with 3mp pronominal suffix acting as the subject. For Niphal infinitives construct with pronominal suffixes, see GKC §61e. Temporal adjunct PP to the verb המם. The action of the main clause continues *until* the time of the event specified by the infinitive construct (cf. MNK §20.1.5[iii]).

7:24 וְנָתַן מַלְכֵיהֶם בְּיָדֶךָ וְהַאֲבַדְתָּ אֶת־שְׁמָם מִתַּחַת הַשָּׁמָיִם לֹא־יִתְיַצֵּב אִישׁ בְּפָנֶיךָ עַד הִשְׁמִדְךָ אֹתָם׃

ND. PD. A further modal *qatal* continues to outline Yhwh's future action (v. 24aα). The subject then shifts to 2ms, but the modal *qatal*, האבדת, remains PD, serving to reassure against fear. An **asyndetic** *yiqtol* clause gives further grounds for confidence (v. 24b).

וְנָתַן מַלְכֵיהֶם בְּיָדֶךָ. *Qatal* (modal) 3ms Qal √נתן. בידך is oblique complement.

וְהַאֲבַדְתָּ אֶת־שְׁמָם מִתַּחַת הַשָּׁמָיִם. *Qatal* (modal) 2ms Hiph √אבד. מתחת השמים is spatial adjunct PP; מתחת is a compound preposition (see on 4:18).

לֹא־יִתְיַצֵּב אִישׁ בְּפָנֶיךָ עַד הִשְׁמִדְךָ אֹתָם׃. *Yiqtol* 3ms Hitp √יצב. This verb only occurs in the Hitpael. All other *binyanim* use √נצב, the "true root" (JM §77b). With בפני, as opposed to לפני, it has the connotation of hostility, "stand against," "resist" (Driver, 105; HALOT s.v; Weinfeld, 361). Clausal **asyndesis** shows this explains the previous clause.

עַד הִשָּׁמְדְךָ אֹתָם. Inf constr Hiph √שמד with 2ms pronominal suffix acting as the subject. In general it is unusual for the Hiphil infinitive construct to have *hireq* rather than *patakh* in the first syllable (GKC §53l; Driver, 105; JM §54c), although this verb does so elsewhere (28:48; Josh 11:14; 1 Kgs 15:29; 2 Kgs 10:17), albeit not consistently (e.g., Josh 23:15). See on הִשְׁאִיר in 3:3. Temporal adjunct PP to the verb עַד־הִשָּׁמְדָם in v. 23) (cf. on הַמֵּם).

Avoid idols, which are an abomination, lest you too become herem (7:25-26)

The final two verses of the chapter resume the theme begun in 7:1-6, exhorting uncompromising iconoclasm. A thinly veiled threat ends the chapter (v. 26a), as *herem* is not intrinsically nationalistic.

²⁵*The idols of their gods you should burn with fire. Do not desire the silver or gold on them and so take [it] for yourself, in case you are ensnared by it, for it is nothing but an abomination to Yhwh your God,* ²⁶*and do not bring an abomination into your home and so become devoted to herem like it. Utterly loathe it and regard it as an abomination, for it is devoted to herem.*

7:25 פְּסִילֵי אֱלֹהֵיהֶם תִּשְׂרְפוּן בָּאֵשׁ לֹא־תַחְמֹד כֶּסֶף וְזָהָב עֲלֵיהֶם וְלָקַחְתָּ לָךְ פֶּן תִּוָּקֵשׁ בּוֹ כִּי תוֹעֲבַת יהוה אֱלֹהֶיךָ הוּא:

D2. HD. The opening clause resumes from 7:5. This destructive command is then explained by an asyndetic prohibition (לא־תחמד), followed by a modal *qatal* (ולקחת), with the ultimate fear introduced in a negative purpose clause (פן). The move from (wrong) desire to action to being ensnared is given conclusive disapproval in the explanatory clause ending the verse.

פְּסִילֵי אֱלֹהֵיהֶם תִּשְׂרְפוּן בָּאֵשׁ. *Yiqtol* (modal) 2mp Qal √שרף with a **paragogic** ן (for which see on 1:17). The *yiqtol* has a modal nuance, expressing obligation (cf. JM §113m). The accusative complement construct NP, פסילי אלהיהם is fronted as the **topic**. The clausal **asyndesis** here marks a break from what has preceded. It resumes the HD from 7:5.

לֹא־תַחְמֹד כֶּסֶף וְזָהָב עֲלֵיהֶם. *Yiqtol* (modal) 2ms Qal √חמד. A prohibition (see on 1:17). עליהם is adjunct PP, going closely with the accusative complement, כסף וזהב. The antecedent is the "gods" rather than the inhabitants of the land.

וְלָקַחְתָּ֣ לָ֔ךְ. *Qatal* (modal) 2ms Qal √לקח. According to GKC §152z, the negative, לֹא, extends to this clause from the previous one thus continuing the prohibition. Given that the same syntax occurs in v. 26, the force should be regarded slightly differently: the ו and modal *qatal* emphasises the sequence, "do not desire . . . *and so* take." The accusative complement is covert, but easily recoverable from the context. לך is adjunct PP, with ל introducing the "dative of advantage" giving the beneficiaries of the action of the verb (WO §11.2.10d; cf. GKC §119s; JM §133d; WHS §271a).

פֶּ֥ן תִּוָּקֵ֖שׁ בּ֑וֹ. *Yiqtol* 2ms Niph √יקש. פן introduces a negative purpose clause and is followed by a *yiqtol* (JM §168g; cf. on v. 22). בו is adjunct PP, referring back to כסף וזהב.

כִּ֧י תוֹעֲבַ֛ת יְהוָ֥ה אֱלֹהֶ֖יךָ הֽוּא׃. Subordinating conjunction כי introducing an explanatory **null-copula** clause. Although after כי, verbal clauses have **triggered inversion**, **null-copula** clauses do not. The P–S word order in a **null-copula** clause marks P, the construct NP complement תועבת יהוה אלהיך as the **focus**. Although their silver and gold might seem desirable, they are "[nothing but] an abomination. . . ." Note that the noun in the construct state is regarded as indefinite, despite the absolute being definite (a proper name), "*an* abomination to Yhwh your God" (GKC §127e; JM §139c).

7:26 וְלֹא־תָבִ֤יא תֽוֹעֵבָה֙ אֶל־בֵּיתֶ֔ךָ וְהָיִ֥יתָ חֵ֖רֶם כָּמֹ֑הוּ שַׁקֵּ֧ץ ׀ תְּשַׁקְּצֶ֛נּוּ וְתַעֵ֥ב ׀ תְּתַעֲבֶ֖נּוּ כִּי־חֵ֥רֶם הֽוּא׃ פ

D2. HD. The opening prohibition continues with a modal *qatal* outlining the severe consequence of ignoring the prohibition. The final two HD clauses in the verse follow **asyndetically**. Both are emotive. They are essentially to have the same attitude as Yhwh toward idols (cf. תעבה).

וְלֹא־תָבִ֤יא תֽוֹעֵבָה֙ אֶל־בֵּיתֶ֔ךָ. *Yiqtol* (modal) 2ms Hiph √בוא. A prohibition (see on 1:17). אל־ביתך is oblique complement, with אל here as "spatially terminative," with its object "an ending location" (WHS §298).

וְהָיִיתָ חֵרֶם כָּמֹהוּ. *Qatal* (modal) 2ms Qal √היה. This is the first instance of the substantive, חרם, rather than the verb. כמהו is comparative adjunct PP. For the different forms of כ with pronominal suffixes, see JM §103g.

שַׁקֵּץ ׀ תְּשַׁקְּצֶנּוּ וְתַעֵב ׀ תְּתַעֲבֶנּוּ. *Yiqtol* 2ms Piel √שקץ with 3ms pronominal suffix, preceded by Inf abs Piel √שקץ, then *yiqtol* 2ms Piel √תעב with 3ms pronominal suffix, preceded by infinitive absolute Piel √תעב. The **paronomastic** infinitive construction, of infinitive absolute with finite verb of the same root, accents the modality of its cognate verb in modal contexts, such as this one (see on 4:26 above). The *yiqtol* has a modal nuance, expressing obligation, "must" (cf. JM §113m). √שקץ Piel is elsewhere associated with loathing something as unclean (Lev 11:11-13). WO §24.4g regard the type of Piel in תעב תתעבנו as "estimative": "lit. *regard* it as an abomination" (emphasis added).

כִּי־חֵרֶם הוּא: פ. Subordinating conjunction כי introducing an explanatory **null-copula** clause, with P-S word order and the substantival complement, חרם, fronted for **focus** (cf. on 7:25).

Warning Against Forgetting Yhwh
Deuteronomy 8:1-20

Chapter 7 focused on the need for uncompromising treatment of inhabitants and their idols and presented the danger of self-importance or militarism. Chapter 8 looks at the land from a different angle, that of prosperity and flourishing. They need to remember and not forget. The danger is "materialism" (Olson, 52) or "self-satisfaction" (Robson, 128) (cf. 8:17). The lessons of dependence in the hardship of the wilderness are to shape them as they enter the prosperity of the land.

Scholars give significant attention to the matter of structure here, discerning, in particular, palistrophic organization (in addition to the commentaries, n.b., van Leeuwen 1984; 1985; O'Connell). There *are* striking parallels, such as the repeated call to "remember" (modal *qatal*, וזכרת, in vv. 2, 18), and the central exhortation to be careful not to "forget" (v. 11). But palistrophic structures can mask temporal advance and rhetorical development. The story moves on. Life on the edge of the land merges with life in the land. Memory remains important throughout. As with the beginning and ending of chapter 7, obedience brings life and possession of the land (v. 1). Disobedience brings destruction, the same destiny as the nations they are dispossessing (v. 20).

Remember, for the events of the past are to shape the present and the future (8:1-10)

The opening injunction is programmatic, with the call to keep (√שמר), by doing, the whole commandment (v. 1). The subunit of vv. 2-6 is shaped by three modal *qatals*, "remember" (v. 2), "know" (v. 5), "keep" (√שמר, v. 6), with v. 6 arriving at the place v. 1 set out (√שמר, מצוה). Their experience of the past is to inform their present and future. This is evident from the rhetoric of remembering (v. 2), the link between past and present with Yhwh's discipline (v. 3), the question of whether Israel would obey or not (√שמר, v. 2; cf. vv. 1, 6), the modal *qatal* "know" building on the recounting of history (v. 5), and from repetition of the motif of walking in/on the way: in v. 2, of Yhwh leading them (√הלך) on the wilderness route (דרך); in v. 6, of their need to walk (√הלך) in Yhwh's ways (דרך) (cp. v. 19, "walking (√הלך) after other gods"). While chapter 7 focused on Yhwh's power to defeat enemies in the past (and future), chapter 8 focuses on Yhwh's provision and Israel's dependence on Yhwh for food and word. Life comes through obedience to Yhwh's word, not just from bread (vv. 1, 3; √חיה).

Verses 7-10 build upon this, looking forward to life in the land. As with vv. 2-6, there are three modal *qatals* (v. 10). They should "eat" and "be satisfied" and "bless" Yhwh (v. 10). The lessons of the wilderness (vv. 2-6) are to inform their times of plenty (vv. 7-10).

[1] The entire commandment that I am commanding you today you are to keep, by doing [it], so that you may live and multiply and enter and possess the land that Yhwh swore to your ancestors; [2] so remember the whole route that Yhwh your God caused you to go these forty years in the wilderness, so as to afflict you, to test you, to know what is in your heart, whether you would keep his commandments or not. [3] He afflicted you and caused you to hunger and fed you manna, which you did not know, nor did your ancestors know, so as to make you know that it is not on bread alone that people live, but it is on everything that proceeds from the mouth of Yhwh that people live—[4] your clothing did not wear out from upon you, nor did your foot swell these forty years—[5] so know in your heart that, just as a man disciplines his son, so Yhwh your God disciplines you, [6] and keep the commandments of Yhwh your God, by walking in his ways and by fearing him. [7] For Yhwh your God is bringing you into a good land, a land of streams of water, of springs and of watery deeps, coming forth in valley and hill, [8] a land of wheat and barley and vine and fig and pomegranate, a land of olives bearing oil and of honey, [9] a land

in which you will eat bread without poverty—you will lack nothing in it—a land whose stones are iron and from whose peaks you can dig copper. ¹⁰*So eat and be satisfied and bless Yhwh your God upon the good land that he will have given you.*

8:1 כׇּל־הַמִּצְוָ֗ה אֲשֶׁ֨ר אָנֹכִ֧י מְצַוְּךָ֛ הַיּ֖וֹם תִּשְׁמְר֣וּן לַעֲשׂ֑וֹת לְמַ֨עַן תִּֽחְי֜וּן וּרְבִיתֶ֗ם וּבָאתֶם֙ וִֽירִשְׁתֶּ֣ם אֶת־הָאָ֔רֶץ אֲשֶׁר־נִשְׁבַּ֥ע יְהֹוָ֖ה לַאֲבֹתֵיכֶֽם׃

D2. HD. The programmatic call to obedience to "the entire commandment" is followed by four purpose clauses: a modal *yiqtol* followed by three modal *qatals*. Commands characteristically are rooted in persuasion.

כׇּל־הַמִּצְוָה אֲשֶׁר אָנֹכִי מְצַוְּךָ הַיּוֹם תִּשְׁמְרוּן לַעֲשׂוֹת. *Yiqtol* (modal) 2mp Qal √שמר with a **paragogic** ן (for which see on 1:17) followed by infinitive construct Qal √עשה with preposition ל. Rather than this being an instance of שמר having an adverbial force, the infinitive construct לעשות is **gerundial**, "by doing" (see on 5:1); the accusative complement of √שמר is covert. The accusative complement of לעשות, the construct NP כל־המצוה followed by a restrictive relative clause, is fronted for **focus**: it is "the whole commandment . . ." they are to "observe by doing." Cf. on 4:6.

אֲשֶׁר אָנֹכִי מְצַוְּךָ הַיּוֹם. See on 4:40 for the identical phrase. The **head** of the restrictive relative clause is כל־המצוה. The different **heads** of this same phrase (4:40; 6:6; 7:11) show that כל־המצוה denotes here all of Moses's teaching in Moab (cf. on 5:31).

לְמַעַן תִּחְיוּן. *Yiqtol* (modal) 2mp Qal √חיה with a **paragogic** ן (for which see on 1:17). למען is a subordinating conjunction that can introduce purpose or result clauses (JM §168d, §169g). Since what is in view is less the "effect" of the action than the "aim," this and the following modal *qatal* clauses should be seen as a succession of purpose rather than result clauses.

וּרְבִיתֶם וּבָאתֶם וִירִשְׁתֶּם אֶת־הָאָרֶץ אֲשֶׁר־נִשְׁבַּע יְהוָה לַאֲבֹתֵיכֶם. *Qatal* (modal) 2mp Qal √רבה and √בוא and √ירש. The modal *qatals* continue the force of the previous *yiqtol*, a series of purpose clauses (cf. on 4:1; also for the pointing of וירשתם).

אֲשֶׁר־נִשְׁבַּע יְהוָה לַאֲבֹתֵיכֶם. See on 1:8 for the identical phrase.

8:2 וְזָכַרְתָּ֣ אֶת־כָּל־הַדֶּ֗רֶךְ אֲשֶׁ֨ר הֹלִֽיכֲךָ֜ יְהוָ֧ה אֱלֹהֶ֛יךָ
זֶ֥ה אַרְבָּעִ֛ים שָׁנָ֖ה בַּמִּדְבָּ֑ר לְמַ֨עַן עַנֹּֽתְךָ֜ לְנַסֹּֽתְךָ֗
לָדַ֜עַת אֶת־אֲשֶׁ֧ר בִּֽלְבָבְךָ֛ הֲתִשְׁמֹ֥ר מִצְוֺתָ֖ו
[מצותיו] אִם־לֹֽא׃

D2. HD. If v. 1b gave the motivation for keeping the commandment (v. 1a), vv. 2–5 give the method (cf. DeRouchie 2007: 248). The modal *qatal* calls Israel first to remember Yhwh's action (v. 2a) and Yhwh's motivation (v. 2b), expressed in three adjunct infinitive phrases expressing purpose.

וְזָכַרְתָּ֣ אֶת־כָּל־הַדֶּ֗רֶךְ. *Qatal* (modal) 2ms Qal √זכר. The accusative complement construct NP, את־כל־הדרך, speaks of "the entire path." Previous occurrences of this phrase refer to the exodus (1:31) and the "way" of the commandments (5:33). These senses coalesce in these verses, as the wilderness lessons on the "way" (דרך) are to provide a foundation for obedience to Yhwh's "ways" in the land (cf. דרכיו in v. 6).

אֲשֶׁ֨ר הֹלִֽיכֲךָ֜ יְהוָ֧ה אֱלֹהֶ֛יךָ זֶ֥ה אַרְבָּעִ֛ים שָׁנָ֖ה בַּמִּדְבָּ֑ר. *Qatal* 3ms Hiph √הלך with 2ms pronominal suffix. After the relative, אשר, there is **triggered inversion** with finite verbs, hence the P–S word order.

זֶ֥ה אַרְבָּעִ֛ים שָׁנָ֖ה. Adverbial temporal adjunct NP. See on 2:7 for this phrase.

לְמַ֨עַן עַנֹּֽתְךָ֜. Inf constr Piel √ענה with 2ms pronominal suffix, the object of the verb. Adjunct infinitive phrase indicating purpose. As well as a subordinating conjunction, למען can act as a preposition with the infinitive construct, expressing purpose, as here, or result (cf. JM §168d; WO §36.2.1d).

לְנַסֹּֽתְךָ֗. Inf constr Piel √נסה with 2ms pronominal suffix, the object of the verb, and with preposition ל. Adjunct infinitive phrase indicating purpose. It is a little strange to follow למען by ל + infinitive construct (cf. the repeated למען in v. 16b). Although syntactically it could be explanatory, "by testing," this and the previous verb are then in the wrong order: "To test *by afflicting*" would make more sense than "to afflict *by testing*." The **asyndesis** here indicates that the previous phrase, "to afflict" is explained by this one. Yhwh had a purpose for their affliction.

לָדַ֫עַת אֶת־אֲשֶׁ֣ר בִּלְבָבְךָ֗. Inf constr Qal √ידע with preposition ל. For the form, see on 4:35. Adjunct infinitive phrase indicating purpose. The **null-head** restrictive relative clause acts as the accusative complement.

אֶת־אֲשֶׁ֣ר בִּלְבָבְךָ֗. **Null-copula** restrictive relative clause with PP predicate.

הֲתִשְׁמֹ֛ר מִצְוֺתָ֖יו [מצותו] אִם־לֹֽא׃. *Yiqtol* 2ms Qal √שמר, preceded by ה-interrogative, which introduces here an indirect question (JM §161f). The *ketiv-qere* here mirrors that in 7:9. See comments there. אם־לא introduces the alternative in the indirect question (cf. GKC §150i; JM §161d, f).

וַיְעַנְּךָ֗ וַיַּרְעִבֶ֔ךָ וַיַּֽאֲכִֽלְךָ֤ אֶת־הַמָּן֙ אֲשֶׁ֣ר לֹא־יָדַ֔עְתָּ וְלֹ֥א יָדְע֖וּן אֲבֹתֶ֑יךָ לְמַ֣עַן הוֹדִֽיעֲךָ֗ כִּ֠י לֹ֣א עַל־הַלֶּ֤חֶם לְבַדּוֹ֙ יִחְיֶ֣ה הָֽאָדָ֔ם כִּ֛י עַל־כָּל־מוֹצָ֥א פִֽי־יְהוָ֖ה יִחְיֶ֥ה הָאָדָֽם׃   8:3

ND. D2. Three *wayyiqtol* clauses describe Yhwh's action (v. 3a); in v. 3b, the purpose (לְמַעַן) is given, "to make Israel *know*. . . ." The testing of Israel in the wilderness wanderings was a journey of discovery (√ידע) for Yhwh (v. 2) and Israel (v. 3). Israel was to understand how people can live (√חיה, cf. v. 1).

וַיְעַנְּךָ֗ וַיַּרְעִבֶ֔ךָ וַיַּֽאֲכִֽלְךָ֤ אֶת־הַמָּן֙ אֲשֶׁ֣ר לֹא־יָדַ֔עְתָּ וְלֹ֥א יָדְע֖וּן אֲבֹתֶ֑יךָ. *Wayyiqtol* 3ms Piel √ענה, Hiph √רעב, Hiph √אכל, all with 2ms pronominal suffix. The causative nature of the Hiphil (ויאכלך) gives rise to two accusative complements, "he fed *you manna*" (JM §125u; WO §10.2.3e). These three *wayyiqtols* continue the accusative complement NP of v. 2a.

אֶת־הַמָּן֙. Accusative complement of √אכל. Intriguingly, M^L has אֶת הַמָּן֙, clearly an error, while M^{L17} + M^{S5} have the reading above with *maqqef* (*BHQ: Deuteronomy*, 27*). While *BHQ* omits the *maqqef*, both *BHL* and *BHS* print with it, despite being presentations of the same Ms (M^L=B19^A). BHL says that "the editor undertakes to present the scribe's intention" (*BHL*, xv) and part of this includes restoring inadvertent omission of *maqqef* (as here). Where the editor of BHL does this, it should appear in the list of variants. 8:3, however, is missing from list of variants (p. 1231) when it should be present.

Deuteronomy 8:3-4

אֲשֶׁר לֹא־יָדַעְתָּ וְלֹא יָדְעוּן אֲבֹתֶיךָ. *Qatal* 2ms Qal √ידע, followed by *qatal* 3cp Qal √ידע with a **paragogic** ן (for which see on 1:17). JM §42f notes the "suspect or faulty" **paragogic** ן, which only occurs in three places with *qatal* 3cp: 8:3, 16; Isa 26:16 (cf. WO §31.7.1a n. 49). GKC §44l suggests that the instances here and in 8:16 are "no doubt, if the text is correct, to avoid a hiatus," because they precede א. Nonrestrictive relative clauses, providing additional information about the **head** המן.

לְמַעַן הוֹדִעֲךָ כִּי . . . הָאָדָם׃. Inf constr Hiph √ידע with 2ms pronominal suffix as the object. Adjunct infinitive phrase expressing purpose. למען acts as a preposition with the infinitive construct, expressing purpose (cf. JM §168d; WO §36.2.1d; see on 8:2). The Hiphil has two accusative complements, the pronominal suffix ־ךָ and the noun clause introduced by the **complementizer** כי.

כִּי לֹא עַל־הַלֶּחֶם לְבַדּוֹ יִחְיֶה הָאָדָם. *Yiqtol* 3ms Qal √חיה. The adjunct PP על־הלחם לבדו is fronted for **focus**, establishing a contrast that the second half of the noun clause addresses. לא is an item adverb, modifying the adjunct phrase rather than the main clause (cf. WO §39.3.2). לבדו comprises the noun בַּד and the preposition לְ, together with the 3ms pronominal suffix, "it alone." Often in Hebrew a preposition and noun together function adverbially, as with לְבַד here (JM §102d).

כִּי עַל־כָּל־מוֹצָא פִי־יְהוָה יִחְיֶה הָאָדָם׃. *Yiqtol* 3ms Qal √חיה. The adjunct construct PP על־כל מוצא פי יהוה is fronted for **focus**. כל in construct relationship with an indeterminate noun has the connotation "every" (JM §139h). כי introduces a contrastive or adversative clause after לא (cf. 7:7-8; 5:3; JM §172c).

8:4 שִׂמְלָתְךָ לֹא בָלְתָה מֵעָלֶיךָ וְרַגְלְךָ לֹא בָצֵקָה זֶה אַרְבָּעִים שָׁנָה׃

D2. ND. A parenthetical comment, marked by initial clausal **asyndesis**, describes Yhwh's leading (v. 2). Yhwh's provision was miraculous and total.

שִׂמְלָתְךָ לֹא בָלְתָה מֵעָלֶיךָ. *Qatal* 3fs Qal √בלה, only here and 29:4 in Deuteronomy, "wear out." There are two very similar words for garment in the Hebrew Bible, שַׂלְמָה and שִׂמְלָה (e.g., 29:4, שלמה, and 8:4; 10:18, שמלה). This gave plenty of scope for scribal variation, hence a large Masorah Magna note (*BHQ: Deuteronomy*, 74*). מַעֲלִיד is adjunct PP. This and the following clause to which this one is coordinated with ו follow asyndetically. They are not part of what Yhwh was trying to teach, but describe further the way Yhwh led them (v. 2). Note the unmarked S–P word order.

וְרַגְלְךָ לֹא בָצֵקָה זֶה אַרְבָּעִים שָׁנָה׃. *Qatal* 3fs Qal √בצק, "swell." A rare verb, only here and Neh 9:21; it is related to בָּצֵק, "dough," which similarly swells. Note the unmarked S–P word order.

זֶה אַרְבָּעִים שָׁנָה׃. Adverbial temporal adjunct NP (see on 2:7; cf. 8:2).

8:5 וְיָדַעְתָּ עִם־לְבָבֶךָ כִּי כַּאֲשֶׁר יְיַסֵּר אִישׁ אֶת־בְּנוֹ יְהוָה אֱלֹהֶיךָ מְיַסְּרֶךָּ׃

D2. HD. The modal *qatal* calls Israel to draw the right conclusions from the past: hardships experienced were part of Yhwh's fatherly education (cf. 1:31). The call to "know" is the second part of the method of keeping Yhwh's commandment (cf. on 8:1-10 and on v. 2).

וְיָדַעְתָּ עִם־לְבָבֶךָ כִּי ... מְיַסְּרֶךָּ. *Qatal* (modal) 2ms Qal √ידע. This exhortation is grounded in Israel's experience (cf. 4:39; 7:9; WO §32.2.3d). עם־לבבך is spatial adjunct PP, giving "the locus of psychological interest" (WO §11.2.14b; cf. MNK §39.20.3[ii]). What they are to know is an accusative complement noun clause, introduced by the **complementizer** כי.

כַּאֲשֶׁר יְיַסֵּר אִישׁ אֶת־בְּנוֹ. *Yiqtol* 3ms Piel √יסר. For כאשר introducing a comparative clause with P–S word order (**triggered inversion**), see on 1:19. The *yiqtol* is used because it speaks of a repeated general or habitual situation (cf. WO §31.3e; JM §113c n. 7).

יְהוָה אֱלֹהֶיךָ מְיַסְּרֶךָּ. Ptcp ms Piel √יסר with 2ms pronominal suffix. The "pausal form ךָּ" with "energic נ," normally found with *yiqtol* and *wayyiqtol*, can also be found with other verb conjugations including the participle, as here (JM §61f n. 3; GKC §61h; cf. JM §66b). **Null-copula** clause with participial predicate and unmarked S–P word order. The participle indicates that Yhwh continues to "chastise"; the lesson of the past continues to the present (and to the future). After a comparative clause, often כן completes the comparison (so 4QDeut^j; LXX; cf. JM §174b).

Deuteronomy 8:6-7

8:6 וְשָׁמַרְתָּ֙ אֶת־מִצְוֺ֣ת יְהוָ֣ה אֱלֹהֶ֔יךָ לָלֶ֥כֶת בִּדְרָכָ֖יו
וּלְיִרְאָ֥ה אֹתֽוֹ׃

D2. HD. Having remembered (v. 2) and known (v. 5), the call to "keep" (שמר√) Yhwh's commandments returns once more (v. 1; cf. v. 3).

וְשָׁמַרְתָּ֙ אֶת־מִצְוֺ֣ת יְהוָ֣ה אֱלֹהֶ֔יךָ. *Qatal* (modal) 2ms Qal שמר√.

לָלֶ֥כֶת בִּדְרָכָ֖יו. Inf constr Qal הלך√ with preposition ל. הלך is the only I-ה verb that behaves like a I-ו (JM §75g). Before the tone syllable of an infinitive construct, the ל often has *qamets* (GKC §102f; JM §103c). The phrase is an adjunct infinitive construct phrase. The infinitive construct is **gerundial** or explanatory, "by walking" (cf. WO §36.2.3e). בדרכיו is spatial adjunct PP (cf. comments on v. 2).

וּלְיִרְאָ֥ה אֹתֽוֹ׃. Inf constr Qal ירא√ with preposition ל. For the form ליראה, see on 4:10. Explanatory phrase (see previous comment).

8:7 כִּ֚י יְהוָ֣ה אֱלֹהֶ֔יךָ מְבִֽיאֲךָ֖ אֶל־אֶ֣רֶץ טוֹבָ֑ה אֶ֚רֶץ נַ֣חֲלֵי
מָ֔יִם עֲיָנֹת֙ וּתְהֹמֹ֔ת יֹצְאִ֥ים בַּבִּקְעָ֖ה וּבָהָֽר׃

D2. An explanatory clause (see below), introduced by כי, explains why their previous history and the commands of vv. 1-6 matter. The section from vv. 7-9 is thus subordinate to the HD clauses before and after with modal *qatals* (vv. 2, 5, 6, 10). The land to which Yhwh is bringing them is bountiful in every way.

כִּ֚י יְהוָ֣ה אֱלֹהֶ֔יךָ מְבִֽיאֲךָ֖ אֶל־אֶ֣רֶץ טוֹבָ֑ה. Ptcp ms Hiph בוא√ with 2ms pronominal suffix. Unmarked S–P word order in a **null-copula** clause, even after כי. There is significant disagreement whether the opening כי introduces a temporal protasis, "when," anticipating what follows, or an explanatory clause, "for," grounding what has preceded.

Arguments in favor of a temporal clause, including those put forward by exponents (Mayes 1979: 191; Weinfeld, 391; McConville, 165; Nelson, 105–6, 112–13) are:

* close parallels between 8:7-11 and 6:10-12, "when Yhwh brings you in . . . be careful not to forget";
* gives greater rhetorical force to v. 11 as a climax, beginning the apodosis;

- v. 6 marks the end of a section (see the arguments above); further, elsewhere (4:39-40; 7:9-11), "know" (√ידע modal *qatal*) is followed by "keep" (√שמר modal *qatal*) as the climax;
- it is not obvious why the quality of the land is the *reason* to keep the commands;
- it is "the first part of an extended argument" (Nelson, 113);
- although rare, there *are* instances of כי + participle introducing a temporal clause (e.g., 18:9).

Arguments in favor of an explanatory clause, including those put forward by exponents (Driver, 108; Craigie, 183; WO §37.5e; Tigay 1996: 94; DeRouchie 2007: 244–48; Lundbom, 345) are:

- the parallel with 6:10-12 is not exact; there it was כי + *yiqtol* √בוא Hiphil (so too 7:1; 11:29);
- temporal clauses introduced by כי need a verb (WHS §445);
- since the participle is a verbal adjective (Cook 2008), it should be possible in a **null-copula** clause to supply the copula "is" or "will be" and still make sense, but that is not possible here (DeRouchie 2007: 247);
- if it were a temporal clause, "when Yhwh brings," הארץ rather than ארץ would be expected (DeRouchie 2007: 246);
- LXX reads "for" (γάρ);
- the modal *qatals* in v. 10 make better sense as continuing to say what *should* be the case (HD), rather than what *will* be the case (PD). It is syntactically unlikely that the final verb in v. 10, וברכת, introduces the temporal apodosis. It is also implausible, in terms of meaning, that it is the final verb of the temporal protasis, before the apodosis begins in v. 11 (see on v. 10).

In my view, the syntax favors taking כי as explanatory, "for." The main arguments against it—of sense and structural awkwardness—dissolve if the explanatory clause is not tied too closely to v. 6, but rather picks up vv. 1-6 as a whole. Moses' addressees should apply the lessons of the wilderness as they prepare to enter a bountiful land.

אֶל־אֶרֶץ טוֹבָה. Oblique complement of verb מביאך. It is then qualified by a succession of appositional NPs, each beginning with the indefinite ארץ. The whole has a poetic quality.

אֶרֶץ נַחֲלֵי מַיִם עֲיָנֹת וּתְהֹמֹת יֹצְאִים בַּבִּקְעָה וּבָהָר׃. Appositional construct NP. The construct, ארץ, is followed by three NPs, נחלי מים, עינת, תהמת. Although generally the noun in the construct state is repeated before each absolute (e.g., Jer 8:1), if the nouns are closely related, it may not be (GKC §128a). Each describes a different type of water: "wadis of water" (נחלי מים), "springs" (עינת), "deeps" (תהמת). ארץ נחלי מים is an attributive adjectival genitive (cf. WO §9.5.3; JM §129f); the construct, נחלי is modified by the absolute, מים, to show that the wadis are not dry but full of water. These NPs are followed by Ptcp mp Qal √יצא, an "attributive accusative of state" (cf. JM §127a), modifying a noun (hence termed "attributive") rather than the predicate (adverbial or indirect accusative). בבקעה ובהר are two adjunct PPs, expressing where the waters flow. Together they form a **merism** (cf. Ps 104:8). The emphasis is on subterranean water (Weinfeld, 391).

8:8 אֶרֶץ חִטָּה וּשְׂעֹרָה וְגֶפֶן וּתְאֵנָה וְרִמּוֹן אֶרֶץ־זֵית שֶׁמֶן וּדְבָשׁ׃

D2. Two further appositional construct NPs graphically depict the land (ארץ).

אֶרֶץ חִטָּה וּשְׂעֹרָה וְגֶפֶן וּתְאֵנָה וְרִמּוֹן. Appositional construct NP. Five absolutes (genitives) follow the construct, ארץ. Although generally the noun in the construct state is repeated before each absolute (e.g., Jer 8:1), if the nouns are closely related, it may not be (GKC §128a). חטה, "wheat," sometimes is found as a plural, חטים. The singular, חטה, denotes "wheat as a species," while the plural, חטים, denotes "wheat as a collection of grains and stalks" ("plural of composition") (JM §136b).

אֶרֶץ־זֵית שֶׁמֶן וּדְבָשׁ׃. Appositional construct NP. Two NPs follow the construct ארץ. The first, זית שמן, could be an adverbial genitive, where the construct "roughly . . . causes" the absolute (cf. WO §9.5.2c), or, more likely, an attributive adjectival genitive, in which the construct is "characterized by" the absolute (cf. WO §9.5.3a). Nouns of the form זַיִת have זֵית as the construct (JM §96Am). The olives in view are ones that bear oil (Weinfeld, 386; Lundbom, 352). דבש is date honey (Weinfeld, 392).

8:9 אֶרֶץ אֲשֶׁר לֹא בְמִסְכֵּנֻת תֹּאכַל־בָּהּ לֶחֶם
לֹא־תֶחְסַר כֹּל בָּהּ אֶרֶץ אֲשֶׁר אֲבָנֶיהָ בַרְזֶל
וּמֵהֲרָרֶיהָ תַּחְצֹב נְחֹשֶׁת׃

D2. Two further appositional NPs continue the portrait of the bountiful land (ארץ). Both comprise ארץ as the **head** of restrictive relative clauses. Both move from the essential qualities of the land to what the Israelites will be able to do in the land. The first restrictive relative clause is expanded by an asyndetic *yiqtol* clause (PD). The second appositional NP has two coordinated restrictive relative clauses; the second of these introduces what the Israelites will be able to do, to "dig."

אֶרֶץ אֲשֶׁר לֹא בְמִסְכֵּנֻת תֹּאכַל־בָּהּ לֶחֶם. Appositional NP, with ארץ **head** of the following restrictive relative clause. *Yiqtol* 2ms Qal √אכל. בה is spatial adjunct PP, with the resumptive pronominal suffix -הָ referring back to ארץ.

בְמִסְכֵּנֻת לֹא. Adjunct PP, fronted for **focus**. לא is an item adverb, modifying the adjunct phrase rather than the main clause (cf. WO §39.3.2). The abstract noun, מסכנת, is a *hapax*. It derives from the adjective מִסְכֵּן, "poor," only found four times in the Hebrew Bible, all in Qohelet (cf. Weinfeld, 387). The effect of the focus-fronting and the item adverb לא is to create a **litotes**: "*not in poverty*" = "in abundance."

לֹא־תֶחְסַר כֹּל בָּהּ. *Yiqtol* 2ms Qal √חסר. כל is accusative complement. See above for בה. Asyndetic clause, reinforcing what preceded. PD.

אֶרֶץ אֲשֶׁר אֲבָנֶיהָ בַרְזֶל. Appositional NP, with ארץ **head** of the following **null-copula** restrictive relative clause. When there are two nouns in a **null-copula** clause, it is not always certain which is the subject. One way of determining the subject is by identifying what is already known by context. This is indicated by the presence of a (resumptive) pronominal suffix that indicates the **discourse active topic**. Here there is the unmarked S–P word order.

וּמֵהֲרָרֶיהָ תַּחְצֹב נְחֹשֶׁת. *Yiqtol* 2ms Qal √חצב. A second relative clause introduced by אשר with **head** ארץ. ומהרריה is spatial adjunct PP, fronted for **focus**. The pronominal suffix is resumptive, referring back to ארץ. Note the unusual "poetic" (GKC §93aa) three-lettered root (הרר) lying behind the plural (+ suffix), rather than the usual two-lettered root (הר).

8:10 וְאָכַלְתָּ וְשָׂבָעְתָּ וּבֵרַכְתָּ אֶת־יְהוָה אֱלֹהֶיךָ
עַל־הָאָרֶץ הַטֹּבָה אֲשֶׁר נָתַן־לָךְ׃

D2. Three modal *qatal* main clauses resume the HD after the lengthy subordinate clause (vv. 7-9). The climax is that they should "bless" or "give thanks" to Yhwh (√ברך), since Yhwh has "blessed" them with the plenty of vv. 7-9 (cf. √ברך; 7:13, 14).

וְאָכַלְתָּ וְשָׂבָעְתָּ וּבֵרַכְתָּ אֶת־יְהוָה אֱלֹהֶיךָ עַל־הָאָרֶץ הַטֹּבָה אֲשֶׁר נָתַן־לָךְ׃. *Qatal* (modal) 2ms Qal √אכל, √שבע, and Piel √ברך. Note that only ושבעת has the accent on the penultimate syllable, due to being in pause (cf. on 6:11). The three 2ms modal *qatals* continue the HD from ושמרת (v. 6), after the explanatory clause introduced by כי (v. 7). Where a sequence of modal *qatals* occurs, it can indicate a "contingent succession of future actions" (GKC §164b; cf. JM §166b), effectively yielding a temporal clause, "when . . ., then" (cf. NIV, NASV, "when . . .," v. 10). Whether it is translated as such or not, it is less a command to "eat and be full" than, a command, having done so, to "bless" Yhwh (cf. vv. 12-14; Tigay 1996: 94–95; Block 2012: 232). But the fact that they are modal *qatals* indicates that "eating" and "being full" are something good and to be affirmed.

If כי (v. 7) is taken as the start of a temporal protasis, then that raises the question of where the apodosis begins. The most natural sequence is to see all three modal *qatals* in v. 10 continuing the protasis, and the apodosis beginning asyndetically with the imperative השמר in v. 11 (cf. 6:10-12; so Nelson, 105; McConville, 165–66). If so, Moses makes the extraordinary assumption that a person can "bless Yhwh" and *still* forget him! That is unlikely, and this awkwardness provides further evidence for taking כי as explanatory in v. 7 (see comments there).

עַל־הָאָרֶץ הַטֹּבָה. Spatial adjunct PP. There is disagreement whether to take על as "in" or "upon," the location of the blessing (cf. 23:21; so, e.g., Lundbom, 345), or as "for," the grounds for blessing Yhwh (cf. 2 Sam 8:10; so, e.g., Weinfeld, 385; Nelson, 105; McConville, 165). Given that על very rarely follows √ברך to express the grounds for blessing and that על־הארץ occurs frequently in Deuteronomy to speak of the location, the former is preferable. Reference to "good land" serves as an ***inclusio*** with v. 7.

אֲשֶׁר נָתַן־לָךְ׃. *Qatal* 3ms Qal √נתן. The *qatal* here probably speaks of future time, but anterior relative to the action of the main verb (JM §112i; WO §30.3b). Although sometimes the gift of the land is future (e.g., 6:23) or ongoing (participle; e.g., 1:25), sometimes it is either handed over in the act of speaking (e.g., 1:8) or *has been* given (e.g., 1:21; 9:23).

Remember, and do not forget, in your plenty that Yhwh who sustained you in the wilderness is the one who empowers you in the land (8:11-20)

An opening warning not to "forget" is then expanded upon in vv. 12-17. The triple danger is expressed in three modal *qatals* (vv. 14, 17): have a haughty heart, forget, think they have done it all themselves. The plenty of the future can give rise to "self-satisfaction." They should remember Yhwh is the one who has given them even the ability to prosper, for forgetting Yhwh leads to the same destruction as the nations they are to dispossess.

¹¹Be on your guard lest you forget Yhwh your God, by not keeping his commandments and judgments and statutes which I am commanding you today, ¹²lest [when] you eat and are satisfied, [when] you build good houses and live [in them], ¹³[when] your cattle and flocks multiply, [when] your silver and gold multiplies for you, [when] all that you have multiplies, ¹⁴your heart is haughty and you forget Yhwh your God, who brought you from the land of Egypt, from the house of slaves, ¹⁵who led you in the great and dreadful wilderness, with fiery serpents and scorpions, and with thirsty ground where there is no water, who brought out water for you from the flinty rock, ¹⁶who in the wilderness fed you manna, which your ancestors did not know, [all] so as to humble you and to test you so that it may go well for you in the end, ¹⁷ and you say to yourself, "My strength and the might of my hand have made this wealth for me." So remember that Yhwh your God is the one who gives you the strength to make wealth, so as to confirm his covenant that he swore to your ancestors—as [is the case] this day. And if you should forget Yhwh your God and go after other gods and serve them and bow down to them, I testify against you today that you will certainly perish. Like the nations that Yhwh is destroying from before you, so you will perish, precisely because you have not obeyed the voice of Yhwh your God.

8:11 הִשָּׁ֣מֶר לְךָ֔ פֶּן־תִּשְׁכַּ֖ח אֶת־יְהוָ֣ה אֱלֹהֶ֑יךָ לְבִלְתִּ֨י שְׁמֹ֤ר מִצְוֺתָיו֙ וּמִשְׁפָּטָ֣יו וְחֻקֹּתָ֔יו אֲשֶׁ֛ר אָנֹכִ֥י מְצַוְּךָ֖ הַיּֽוֹם׃

D2. HD. An imperative is followed by a negative final clause introduced by פֶּן, outlining what they should guard against. This is clarified by an explanatory adjunct infinitive phrase. Forgetting is demonstrated by failure to observe Yhwh's commands given through Moses in Moab.

הִשָּׁמֶר לְךָ פֶּן־תִּשְׁכַּח אֶת־יְהוָה אֱלֹהֶיךָ. For תשכח השמר לך פן, see on 4:9 (cf. 6:12). Negative purpose clause introduced by פֶּן.

לְבִלְתִּי שְׁמֹר מִצְוֹתָיו וּמִשְׁפָּטָיו וְחֻקֹּתָיו אֲשֶׁר אָנֹכִי מְצַוְּךָ הַיּוֹם:
Inf constr Qal √שמר. לבלתי is the usual way of negating an infinitive construct (JM §124e, 160l). For the **paragogic** (word-extending) ־ִי, see JM §93q. The whole is an infinitive phrase adjunct, indicating how the forgetting is manifest. The infinitive construct is **gerundial**, or explanatory, "by [not] observing" (AC §5.3.5(c); cf. 5:1; WO §36.2.3e).

מִצְוֹתָיו וּמִשְׁפָּטָיו וְחֻקֹּתָיו. Conjoined accusative complement NPs, each of them a characteristic noun denoting Yhwh's commands. Masorah Parva note the varied ordering of these three words, using the abbreviations צ׳ מצותיו "his commandments"), פ׳ משפטיו "his ordinances"), ק׳ חקתיו "his statutes"). The verses are 8:11 (צפק); 11:1 (קפצ); 26:17 (קצפ); 30:16 (צקפ); 1 Kgs 2:3 (קצפ); 1 Kgs 8:58 (צקפ).

אֲשֶׁר אָנֹכִי מְצַוְּךָ הַיּוֹם:. See on 4:40 for the identical phrase.

8:12 פֶּן־תֹּאכַל וְשָׂבָעְתָּ וּבָתִּים טוֹבִים תִּבְנֶה וְיָשָׁבְתָּ:

D2. The subordinating conjunction, פֶּן, is repeated from v. 11, but is then omitted, although it governs modal *qatals* and modal *yiqtols* until ואמרת (v. 17). The lack of the ו-conjunction before פֶּן (cp. 4:9, וּפֶן) indicates that this whole sequence further explains v. 11. The verbs here are not what they should guard against (eating and being full have been encouraged, v. 10), but are effectively part of a temporal protasis, with the apodosis beginning in v. 14. Here, a *yiqtol* is twice followed by a modal *qatal*. Both have an internal sequence, while the clauses with *yiqtols* are temporally overlaid, one with another.

פֶּן־תֹּאכַל. *Yiqtol* (modal) 2ms Qal √אכל. Negative purpose clause. The sequence of negative purpose clauses running down to ושכחת is effectively a long temporal protasis, "... lest *when* you ..., (then) your heart is lofty and you forget (v. 14) ... and you say to yourself (v. 17)" (cf. on v. 10). JM §168h observes, "where פֶּן extends its force to a second juxtaposed verb, the first clause can be logically subordinate (temporal or conditional) ... Dt 8.12-14 lest, having eaten your fill etc...., your heart is lifted up ..." (cf. 4:19; also Driver, 110).

וְשָׂבָ֑עְתָּ. *Qatal* (modal) 2ms Qal √שׂבע. Negative purpose clause. For the accent location, see on 6:11.

וּבָתִּ֥ים טוֹבִ֛ים תִּבְנֶ֖ה. *Yiqtol* 2ms Qal √בנה. Negative purpose clause. The accusative complement, בתים טובים, is fronted. This could be for **focus**, inviting comparison with other types of houses and highlighting טוב (cf. vv. 7, 10); more likely it is fronted as the **topic**, giving a complementary picture with v. 12a (cf. Moshavi 2010: 160–61). The shift in word order suggests temporal overlay rather than sequentiality between this action and the ones preceding (JM §119f).

וְיָשָֽׁבְתָּ׃. *Qatal* (modal) 2ms Qal √ישׁב. Negative purpose clause. For the accent location, see on 6:11. This action follows logically and temporally on the previous one. Although ישׁב can occur absolutely, there is an expectation here of an oblique complement, indicating where they lived. Originally **null** and easily supplied, other versions supplied one, בם, to make it explicit (*BHQ: Deuteronomy*, 28).

8:13 וּבְקָרְךָ֤ וְצֹֽאנְךָ֙ יִרְבְּיֻ֔ן וְכֶ֥סֶף וְזָהָ֖ב יִרְבֶּה־לָּ֑ךְ וְכֹ֥ל אֲשֶׁר־לְךָ֖ יִרְבֶּֽה׃

D2. Three further modal *yiqtols* continue the negative final clause from v. 12, while effectively being still part of a temporal protasis (see comment on v. 12). The threefold repetition of √רבה picks up this key motif (cf. 7:13; 8:1). The S–P word order in all three clauses may simply be a case of unmarked word order; alternatively, each subject is topicalized, giving a complementary picture (cf. Moshavi 2010: 160–61), not a sequential one.

וּבְקָרְךָ֤ וְצֹֽאנְךָ֙ יִרְבְּיֻ֔ן. *Yiqtol* 3mp Qal √רבה with a **paragogic** ן (for which see on 1:17). Although normally III-ה verbs with vocalic afformatives lose the ה, sometimes, as here, the original י is found, particularly when in pause or when there is a **paragogic** ן (GKC §75u).

וְכֶ֥סֶף וְזָהָ֖ב יִרְבֶּה־לָּ֑ךְ. *Yiqtol* 3ms Qal √רבה. Normally the "postpositive [verb occurring after the subject] verb" is plural, but "the verb sometimes remains in the singular when the two nouns, forming a single idea, are taken as a single concept" (JM §150p). לך is pointed with a euphonic *dagesh forte* because the accent is on the first syllable and it follows an originally accented ־הָ (GKC §20c); for the pausal form, see on 1:21.

וְכֹל אֲשֶׁר־לְךָ יִרְבֶּה׃. *Yiqtol* 3ms Qal √רבה.

אֲשֶׁר־לְךָ. **Null-copula** restrictive relative clause with **head** כֹל and PP complement. לְךָ indicates possession (cf. WO §11.2.10d).

8:14 וְרָם לְבָבֶךָ וְשָׁכַחְתָּ אֶת־יְהוָה אֱלֹהֶיךָ הַמּוֹצִיאֲךָ מֵאֶרֶץ מִצְרַיִם מִבֵּית עֲבָדִים׃

D2. Two modal *qatals* continue the negative final clause, now introducing the temporal apodosis. This is where Moses was heading with his concern, "be careful lest . . ." (v. 11, HD). Having arrived again at the point of "forgetting" Yhwh (√שכח; cf. v. 11), Moses now demonstrates the culpability and stupidity of such an action by a succession of four Hiphil participles that spell out all Yhwh has done for them (vv. 14b-16).

וְרָם לְבָבֶךָ. *Qatal* (modal) 3ms Qal √רום. A "heart" being "high" connotes arrogance (cf. 17:20; Ezek 31:10). The heart (לבב) is critical (cf. on 4:9). This verb effectively starts the temporal apodosis (see on v. 12).

וְשָׁכַחְתָּ אֶת־יְהוָה אֱלֹהֶיךָ. *Qatal* (modal) 2ms Qal √שכח.

הַמּוֹצִיאֲךָ מֵאֶרֶץ מִצְרַיִם מִבֵּית עֲבָדִים׃. Ptcp ms Hiph √יצא with 2ms pronominal suffix. The article ה introduces a relative clause with the adjectival participle functioning predicatively in a **null-copula** clause (see on 1:30); this analysis accounts for the fact that the participle here is prefixed with ה while having a pronominal suffix, something that would not normally be found with a noun or adjective (cf. WHS §82d). For the PPs מארץ מצרים מבית עבדים, see on 5:6.

8:15 הַמּוֹלִיכֲךָ בַּמִּדְבָּר הַגָּדֹל וְהַנּוֹרָא נָחָשׁ שָׂרָף וְעַקְרָב וְצִמָּאוֹן אֲשֶׁר אֵין־מָיִם הַמּוֹצִיא לְךָ מַיִם מִצּוּר הַחַלָּמִישׁ׃

D2. Two further Hiphil participles serve to expound what Yhwh has done (see on v. 14).

הַמּוֹלִיכֲךָ בַּמִּדְבָּר הַגָּדֹל וְהַנּוֹרָא נָחָשׁ שָׂרָף וְעַקְרָב וְצִמָּאוֹן אֲשֶׁר אֵין־מָיִם. Ptcp ms Hiph √הלך with 2ms pronominal suffix, with article ה introducing a **null-copula** relative clause (see on v. 14). The *compound* vocal *sheva* with כ is noteworthy. On some occasions, with a degree of unpredictability, compound vocal *shevas* are found with non-gutturals (JM §9b). Pertinent patterns are "under a consonant which is then repeated" and "with כ, ר, in certain forms, after an etymologically long vowel and before the stress" (JM §9c). The lack of coordinating ו gives a certain poetic quality to the expression of Yhwh's actions.

בַּמִּדְבָּר ׀ הַגָּדֹל וְהַנּוֹרָא. Spatial adjunct PP. See 1:19 for המדבר הגדל והנורא.

נָחָשׁ ׀ שָׂרָף וְעַקְרָב וְצִמָּאוֹן. נחש שרף are two nouns in apposition, with the second, שרף, defining the first (cf. Num 21:8, where it is a substantive), "fiery serpent[s]"; עקרב are "scorpions"; צמאון is "thirsty ground" (cf. √צמא). For the form, see JM §88Mb. There are two possible ways of taking these nouns: either "words of nearer definition standing in apposition" (cf. GKC §128c) or, less likely, as the absolutes "in a genitive relationship to an implied repetition of the noun *midbar* 'wilderness'" (a possibility suggested by Weinfeld, 387).

אֲשֶׁר אֵין־מָיִם. **Null-copula** restrictive relative clause. אין is an adverb of nonexistence (JM §154k, §160g) that introduces a **null-copula** clause (GKC §152m). Although there is no resumptive adverb or preposition with resumptive pronoun in the relative clause, there is a gap where one would fit (cf. שָׁמָּה, 4:5; בָּהּ, 8:9). The omission is similar to that in 1:31 (n.b., also 7:19).

הַמּוֹצִיא לְךָ מַיִם מִצּוּר הַחַלָּמִישׁ. Ptcp ms Hiph √יצא with article ה introducing a **null-copula** relative clause (see on v. 14). לך is adjunct PP, the "dative of advantage," giving the beneficiary of the action of the verb (cf. JM §133d; GKC §119s). מצור החלמיש is construct PP complement, indicating from where Yhwh brought water out. The absolute, חלמיש, indicates from what the rock is made, "flint," an attributive adjectival genitive (cf. WO §9.5.3d). The source of water is rather unlikely (cf. 32:13).

8:16 הַמַּאֲכִלְךָ מָן בַּמִּדְבָּר אֲשֶׁר לֹא־יָדְעוּן אֲבֹתֶיךָ לְמַעַן עַנֹּתְךָ וּלְמַעַן נַסֹּתֶךָ לְהֵיטִבְךָ בְּאַחֲרִיתֶךָ:

D2. A further Hiphil participle continues to spell out what Yhwh has done (v. 16a; see on v. 14). Tigay (1996: 95, 361 n. 15) notes the "sonorous" repetition of מ in vv. 14-16 and the fourfold occurrence of ע in five words in this verse. In v. 16b, two adjunct infinitive PPs show Yhwh's purposes in the actions spelled out (vv. 14-16); the final adjunct infinitive PP shows the ultimate purpose—Yhwh has their best interests at heart.

הַמַּאֲכִלְךָ מָן בַּמִּדְבָּר אֲשֶׁר לֹא־יָדְעוּן אֲבֹתֶיךָ. Ptcp ms Hiph √אכל with 2ms pronominal suffix with article ה introducing a **null-copula** relative clause (see on v. 14). The second accusative complement, מָן, is **head** of the following non-restrictive relative clause, but separated or **extraposed** from אשר by the spatial adjunct PP, במדבר (cf. Holmstedt 2002: 301).

אֲשֶׁר לֹא־יָדְעוּן אֲבֹתֶיךָ. *Qatal* 3cp Qal √ידע with a **paragogic** ן, for which see on 8:3. The P–S word order is due to **triggered inversion** after אשר.

לְמַעַן עַנֹּתְךָ. See on 8:2 for the identical phrase. This and the following phrase should not be restricted just to the feeding with manna (as in the translation of Nelson, 106), but to the whole wilderness experience (cf. vv. 2-3).

וּלְמַעַן נַסֹּתֶךָ. Inf constr Piel √נסה with 2ms pronominal suffix, the object of the verb. In contrast to 8:2, where the preposition ל was prefixed to the verb and the PP followed asyndetically from למען ענתך, here the infinitive is the object of the preposition למען and the two phrases are coordinated with ו. In both places, the afflicting/humbling and the testing are complementary explanations of the same events.

לְהֵיטִבְךָ בְּאַחֲרִיתֶךָ. Inf constr Hiph √יטב with 2ms pronominal suffix (object) and with preposition ל. באחריתך is temporal adjunct PP. A positive outcome (אחרית, "end") after present testing is common in the wisdom tradition (e.g., Job 8:7; see Weinfeld, 395).

8:17 וְאָמַרְתָּ בִּלְבָבֶךָ כֹּחִי וְעֹצֶם יָדִי עָשָׂה לִי אֶת־הַחַיִל הַזֶּה׃

After the lengthy exposition of Yhwh's actions, a third modal *qatal* (after ורם and ושכחת, v. 14) introduces the erroneous thoughts which Moses wants them to watch out for (v. 11; cf. 7:17; 9:4). Verse 17a is a further negative final clause (D2). Verse 17b spells out the content of these thoughts (D3, ND). The unpacking of the condensed negative purpose clause (v. 11) by the negative purpose clauses in vv. 12-17 comes to an end.

וְאָמַרְתָּ֖ בִּלְבָבֶ֑ךָ. *Qatal* (modal) 2ms Qal √אמר. See on 7:17 for √אמר בלבבך.

כֹּחִי֙ וְעֹ֣צֶם יָדִ֔י עָ֥שָׂה לִ֖י אֶת־הַחַ֥יִל הַזֶּֽה׃. *Qatal* 3ms Qal √עשׂה. ND. עצם ידי is construct NP; עצם is "strength," "might." Normally the "postpositive [verb occurring after the subject] verb" is plural when the subject is plural, but "the verb sometimes remains in the singular when the two nouns, forming a single idea, are taken as a single concept" (JM §150p). לי is adjunct PP, the "dative of advantage" giving the beneficiary of the action of the verb (cf. JM §133d; GKC §119s). The interpretation of events (ND) is way off the mark.

8:18 וְזָֽכַרְתָּ֙ אֶת־יְהוָ֣ה אֱלֹהֶ֔יךָ כִּ֣י ה֗וּא הַנֹּתֵ֥ן לְךָ֛ כֹּ֖חַ לַעֲשׂ֣וֹת חָ֑יִל לְמַ֨עַן הָקִ֧ים אֶת־בְּרִית֛וֹ אֲשֶׁר־נִשְׁבַּ֥ע לַאֲבֹתֶ֖יךָ כַּיּ֥וֹם הַזֶּֽה׃פ

D2. HD. The opening modal *qatal* has a double function: it continues from the warning of v. 11 to "be careful" (השמר), framing it positively; it also gives Moses' response to the erroneous thought of v. 17. Rather than forgetting, they are to "remember" Yhwh as the giver. It is not that producing or having plenty is inherently negative (cf. v. 10). This is no asceticism. But the danger is "self-satisfaction," forgetting Yhwh as the giver.

... וְזָֽכַרְתָּ֙ אֶת־יְהוָ֣ה אֱלֹהֶ֔יךָ כִּ֣י. *Qatal* (modal) 2ms Qal √זכר. Verbs of perceiving sometimes have a double accusative, with the first the thing/person perceived, and the second a noun clause, giving what is perceived (cf. Gen 6:2; JM §157d). Here, the one to be remembered is יהוה אלהיך, and what is to be remembered is the accusative complement noun clause following the **complementizer** כי (see below). Translations should combine the two: "remember that Yhwh your God is the one who...."

כִּ֣י ה֗וּא הַנֹּתֵ֥ן לְךָ֛ כֹּ֖חַ לַעֲשׂ֣וֹת חָ֑יִל. Ptcp ms Qal √נתן. **Null-copula** accusative complement noun clause, with **complementizer** כי. Note the unmarked S–P word order. הנתן is the predicate (or complement). Where, as here, the "nominal predicate" is definite, the article is needed with the participle (GKC §127k; JM §137l). The article ה in הנתן is best characterized as introducing a **null-head** relative clause with the adjectival participle functioning predicatively in a **null-copula** clause (see on

3:21): "he is [the one] who gives. . . ." לְךָ is oblique complement. כֹחַ is accusative complement.

לַעֲשׂוֹת חָיִל. Inf constr Qal √עשׂה with preposition ל. ל + infinitive construct functions here "as an *adverbial* after a noun," "the strength to produce wealth" (WO §36.2.3b).

לְמַעַן הָקִים אֶת־בְּרִיתוֹ אֲשֶׁר־נִשְׁבַּע לַאֲבֹתֶיךָ כַּיּוֹם הַזֶּה: פ. Inf constr Hiph √קום. Often prepositions with infinitives construct are used in place of subordinate clauses. Here, למען, acting as a preposition rather than as a subordinating conjunction (as in 4:1), introduces a purpose "clause" (cf. WO §36.2.1d), although syntactically it is an adjunct infinitive phrase indicating purpose. √קום Hiphil is used metaphorically with accusative complements denoting words or speech with the sense of "confirm," or "keep" (HALOT s.v.).

אֲשֶׁר־נִשְׁבַּע לַאֲבֹתֶיךָ. *Qatal* 3ms Niph √שבע. See on 6:10 for the identical phrase (cf. 1:8). The **head** of the restrictive relative clause is בריתו (cf. 4:31; 7:8, 12).

כַּיּוֹם הַזֶּה: פ. Comparative temporal adjunct PP. See further on 2:30.

8:19 וְהָיָה אִם־שָׁכֹחַ תִּשְׁכַּח אֶת־יְהוָה אֱלֹהֶיךָ וְהָלַכְתָּ אַחֲרֵי אֱלֹהִים אֲחֵרִים וַעֲבַדְתָּם וְהִשְׁתַּחֲוִיתָ לָהֶם הַעִדֹתִי בָכֶם הַיּוֹם כִּי אָבֹד תֹּאבֵדוּן:

D2. After warning against forgetting (vv. 11-18), Moses spells out the profile and consequences of forgetting using a conditional clause. A conditional protasis rooted in future time comprises a *yiqtol* followed by three coordinated modal *qatals*. A performative *qatal* prefaces the apodosis, which begins with the accusative complement noun clause of העידתי.

וְהָיָה. *Qatal* (modal) 3ms Qal √היה. When there is no subject or complement, as here, it serves to anchor discourse time in the future (Cook 2012: 309–10), and marks a break from what precedes. See on 6:10.

אִם־שָׁכֹחַ תִּשְׁכַּח אֶת־יְהוָה אֱלֹהֶיךָ. *Yiqtol* 2ms Qal √שכח preceded by Inf abs Qal √שכח. This **paronomastic** infinitive construction, of infinitive absolute with finite verb of the same root, accents the modality of its cognate verb in modal contexts, such as this one (see on 4:26). Conditional protasis, introduced by subordinating conjunction אם.

וְהָלַכְתָּ֗ אַחֲרֵי֙ אֱלֹהִ֣ים אֲחֵרִ֔ים. *Qatal* (modal) 2ms Qal √הלך. אחרי אלהים אחרים is adjunct PP. הלך אחרי is a common phrase for following a deity, usually one (or more) other than Yhwh (cf. 4:23; 6:14). The modal *qatal* continues the conditional protasis.

וַעֲבַדְתָּ֖ם וְהִשְׁתַּחֲוִ֣יתָ לָהֶ֑ם. *Qatal* (modal) 2ms Qal √עבד with 3mp pronominal suffix, followed by *qatal* (modal) 2ms Hishtaphel √חוה/חוי (see on 4:19). להם is adjunct PP. The modal *qatal*s continue the conditional protasis. The **anaphoric** pronouns, -הֶם/-ם, tie these clauses with the preceding clause. They are not three sequential activities, but one compound defection (n.b., the different order of √חוה and √עבד in 4:19).

הַעִדֹ֤תִי בָכֶם֙ הַיּ֔וֹם. *Qatal* 1cs Hiph √עוד. A performative *qatal*, whereby the action of calling as witnesses is performed in the saying of these words. See on 4:26 for the identical phrase.

כִּ֥י אָבֹ֖ד תֹּאבֵדֽוּן׃. *Yiqtol* 2mp Qal √אבד with a **paragogic** ן (for which see on 1:17), preceded by Inf abs Qal √אבד. See on 4:26 for the identical phrase. The phrase functions as the apodosis of the conditional, as well as the accusative complement of העדתי.

8:20 כַּגּוֹיִ֗ם אֲשֶׁ֤ר יְהוָה֙ מַאֲבִ֣יד מִפְּנֵיכֶ֔ם כֵּ֖ן תֹּאבֵד֑וּן
עֵ֚קֶב לֹ֣א תִשְׁמְע֔וּן בְּק֖וֹל יְהוָ֥ה אֱלֹהֵיכֶֽם׃ פ

ND. Comparative clause, with comparison drawn between the nations Yhwh is destroying and the destruction Yhwh will mete out on Israel because of their disobedience. A "chilling" end (Wright, 128).

כַּגּוֹיִ֗ם אֲשֶׁ֤ר יְהוָה֙ מַאֲבִ֣יד מִפְּנֵיכֶ֔ם. Comparative adjunct PP (cf. JM §133g), with גוים the **head** of the following restrictive relative clause. . . . כ . . . כן is a characteristic way of expressing a comparative clause, with כ + substantive followed by כן introducing the apodosis (JM §174c; AC §5.2.6[b]).

אֲשֶׁ֤ר יְהוָה֙ מַאֲבִ֣יד מִפְּנֵיכֶ֔ם. Ptcp ms Hiph √אבד. **Null-copula** restrictive relative clause, with participial predicate. Unmarked S–P word order. מפניכם is adjunct PP (cf. 7:20).

כֵּ֖ן תֹּאבֵד֑וּן. *Yiqtol* 2mp Qal √אבד with a **paragogic** ן (for which see on 1:17). PD. כן is a demonstrative adverb (JM §102h), introducing the apodosis in a comparative clause, drawing an explicit comparison between the previous clause and Yhwh's future action (see on כְגוֹיִם above).

שמע√ Qal 2mp *Yiqtol*. עֵ֕קֶב לֹ֣א תִשְׁמְע֔וּן בְּק֖וֹל יְהוָ֣ה אֱלֹהֵיכֶֽם׃ פ with a **paragogic** ן (for which see on 1:17). See on 7:12 for עקב ... תשמעון. This is the direct counterpart of 7:12; there it was positive, here it is negative. Further, √שמע here has an oblique complement, בקול יהוה אלהיכם rather than the accusative complement of 7:12. שמע בקול denotes "listening to" or "obeying" (e.g., 4:30; 9:23; cf. 1:45).

Moses Warns Against Self-righteousness in the Land Given Israel's History on the Way to It
Deuteronomy 9:1–10:11

This larger unit, begun by the call to listen and declaration that they are crossing the Jordan "today" (v. 1), tackles the third of three erroneous thoughts: that they are possessing the land because of their righteousness (9:4-5; cf. 7:17; 8:17). Moses insists the opposite, for they are "nothing but stiff-necked" (v. 6). Such an opinion requires a delicate balancing act—demonstrating it to be true, but not cultivating despair. Moses first recounts their history to demonstrate his point (vv. 7-24). But given that history, it might seem that all is lost. So Moses records his own intercession (vv. 25-29) and the renewal of the covenant by Yhwh's reissuing of the tablets (10:1-10). With Yhwh's declaration that he will not "destroy" them (10:10) comes Yhwh's renewed call to enter and possess the land, a call rooted in his patriarchal promise (10:11).

Right knowledge of Yhwh and themselves is vital as they prepare to cross the Jordan (9:1-6)

The opening exhortation to listen marks the beginning of a new section. There are two pairs of three verses, both climaxing with "so know" (וידעת, vv. 3, 6). In vv. 1-3, given the apparent invincibility of the inhabitants and the certainty of imminent crossing (היום, √עבר, v. 1), they are to get reassurance "today" (היום) in Yhwh as the one who crosses (√עבר) before them. In vv. 4-6, there is a further warning against erroneous thoughts (9:4; cf. 7:17; 8:18; √אמר בלבבך). The danger here is "moralism" (Olson, 52) or "self-righteousness" (Robson, 128–29). The conclusion, as with v. 3, is "so know" (וידעת, v. 6). Right knowledge is important.

¹*Hear, Israel! You are crossing the Jordan today to enter to dispossess nations greater and stronger than you—cities great and fortified to the heavens, ²a people great and tall, the Anakites, whom you yourselves know and of whom you yourselves have heard, "Who can stand before the Anakites?"—³So know today that it is Yhwh your God who is the one crossing before you, a consuming fire. He will demolish them and he will subdue them before you so you can dispossess them and destroy them quickly, just as Yhwh promised you. ⁴Do not think to yourself when Yhwh your God drives them out from before you, "It is because of my righteousness that Yhwh has brought me in to possess this land," seeing as it is because of the wickedness of these nations that Yhwh is driving them out from before you. ⁵It is not because of your righteousness and the uprightness of your heart that you are entering to possess their land, but it is because of the wickedness of these nations that Yhwh your God is driving them out from before you, and to confirm the word that Yhwh swore to your ancestors, to Abraham, to Isaac and to Jacob. ⁶So know that it is not because of your righteousness that Yhwh your God is giving to you this good land, to possess it, for you are nothing but a stiff-necked people.*

9:1 שְׁמַע יִשְׂרָאֵל אַתָּה עֹבֵר הַיּוֹם אֶת־הַיַּרְדֵּן לָבֹא לָרֶשֶׁת גּוֹיִם גְּדֹלִים וַעֲצֻמִים מִמֶּךָ עָרִים גְּדֹלֹת וּבְצֻרֹת בַּשָּׁמָיִם׃

D2. The opening call to listen (HD) is then followed by a statement declaring imminent crossing "today" (cf. on 1:10). This statement (ED) is expanded by two adjunct infinitive phrases expressing purpose. Moses begins to refresh their memories on the nature of their enemy.

שְׁמַע יִשְׂרָאֵל. Impv ms Qal √שמע. HD. The ms form is common at the start of instruction; here it is used absolutely as a call to listen. See on 4:1; 6:4.

אַתָּה עֹבֵר הַיּוֹם אֶת־הַיַּרְדֵּן. Ptcp ms Qal √עבר. ED. The personal pronoun does not carry **topic** or **focus** as it is syntactically necessary. Contrary to JM §154fd, S–P word is the unmarked order in **null-copula** participial clause (see Buth). היום is adverbial time adjunct NP (see on 1:10 for "today"). See on 1:1 for the article in הירדן.

לָבֹא לָרֶשֶׁת גּוֹיִם גְּדֹלִים וַעֲצֻמִים מִמֶּךָ עָרִים גְּדֹלֹת וּבְצֻרֹת בַּשָּׁמָיִם. Inf constr Qal √בוא and √ירש, both with preposition ל. Before the tone syllable of an infinitive construct, the ל often has *qamets* (GKC §102f;

JM §103c). As an original I-ו verb, the ו in לרשת has disappeared and a feminine ת has been added (JM §72d, §75a). Both are adjunct infinitive phrases, expressing purpose. Until now, √ירש Qal has only been used by Moses to "possess" land; where it has spoken of "dispossessing" people, it has been the voice of the narrator (2:12, 21, 22); from now, Moses also uses the Qal for dispossessing (e.g., 11:23; 12:2, 29). גוים גדלים ועצמים ממך is accusative complement NP of verb לרשת, with comparative מן. See on 4:38 for the identical phrase. ערים גדלת ובצרת בשמים is appositional NP; together with the appositional NPs in 9:2, it spells out precisely what the גוים are. See on 1:28 for the identical phrase.

9:2 עַם־גָּד֥וֹל וָרָ֖ם בְּנֵ֣י עֲנָקִ֑ים אֲשֶׁ֨ר אַתָּ֤ה יָדַ֙עְתָּ֙ וְאַתָּ֣ה שָׁמַ֔עְתָּ מִ֣י יִתְיַצֵּ֔ב לִפְנֵ֖י בְּנֵ֥י עֲנָֽק׃

D2. Two appositional NPs, with the second expanded by two relative clauses, the second of which includes a proverbial quotation (ID, D3). Moses shows the people he is not underestimating the enemy that they know only too well.

עַם־גָּד֥וֹל וָרָ֖ם. Ptcp ms Qal √רום. Appositional NP. See on 1:28 for the identical phrase.

בְּנֵ֣י עֲנָקִ֑ים אֲשֶׁ֨ר אַתָּ֤ה יָדַ֙עְתָּ֙ וְאַתָּ֣ה שָׁמַ֔עְתָּ. Appositional construct NP, בני ענקים, the **head** of the following non-restrictive relative clause. The plural of both the construct and the absolute (cp. v. 2b, בני ענק) is due to "grammatical attraction," where the plural of the construct is "mechanically passed" to the absolute (JM §136o).

אֲשֶׁ֨ר אַתָּ֤ה יָדַ֙עְתָּ֙ וְאַתָּ֣ה שָׁמַ֔עְתָּ. *Qatal* 2ms Qal √ידע and √שמע. Non-restrictive relative clauses. The independent personal subject pronoun אתה is unnecessary in both these clauses, and only appears very rarely elsewhere with similar syntax (e.g., Jer 29:25). Since normally there is **triggered inversion** after אשר with finite verbs and there is no reason to think it is fronted as the **topic**, it must be fronted for **focus**: "you" (and not "others"). They have had direct experience of the Anakites (cf. 1:28). The enemy is known to them, not unknown.

מִ֣י יִתְיַצֵּ֔ב לִפְנֵ֖י בְּנֵ֥י עֲנָֽק׃. *Yiqtol* 3ms Hitp √יצב. ID. The *yiqtol* expresses the notion of possibility (cf. JM §111g, §113l). See on 7:24 for the verb and adjunct PPs לפני and בפני. Since with לפני there is no necessary connotation of hostility, the Anakites are so terrifying that even the lesser "standing *before*" is impossible, let alone "standing *against*."

9:3 וְיָדַעְתָּ הַיּוֹם כִּי יְהוָה אֱלֹהֶיךָ הוּא־הָעֹבֵר לְפָנֶיךָ
אֵשׁ אֹכְלָה הוּא יַשְׁמִידֵם וְהוּא יַכְנִיעֵם לְפָנֶיךָ
וְהוֹרַשְׁתָּם וְהַאֲבַדְתָּם מַהֵר כַּאֲשֶׁר דִּבֶּר יְהוָה לָךְ:

D2. HD. Given their imminent crossing (v. 1) and the enemy, Moses urges the Israelites to be aware of Yhwh's nature and initiative at the vanguard (v. 3a): they know their enemy (√ידע, v. 2b); they should know Yhwh's involvement (√ידע, v. 3a). Their activity is contingent and derivative on Yhwh's action (modal *qatals*, following the two *yiqtols*, v. 3b).

... וְיָדַעְתָּ הַיּוֹם כִּי. *Qatal* (modal) 2ms Qal √ידע. HD. The modal *qatal* in Deuteronomy is often used to convey a volitional force after narrative discourse (cf. WO §32.2.3d); it can also convey the same force after **null-copula** clauses (ED; WO §32.2.4a). Here it builds on the affirmation "you are crossing" (v. 1). היום is adverbial time adjunct NP (see on 1:10 for "today"). כי is a **complementizer**, introducing the accusative complement noun clause, what they should "know."

כִּי יְהוָה אֱלֹהֶיךָ הוּא־הָעֹבֵר לְפָנֶיךָ אֵשׁ אֹכְלָה. Ptcp ms Qal √עבר. Where, as here, the "nominal predicate" is definite, the article is needed with the participle (GKC §127k; JM §137l). The article ה in העבר is best characterised as introducing a **null-head** relative clause with the adjectival participle functioning predicatively in a **null-copula** clause (see on 3:21). The clause is a **tripartite** verbless/nominal clause, with יהוה אלהיך **extraposed** as the **topic**, and הוא a resumptive pronoun, rather than a copula, as is evident from the repeated הוא in the following clauses (Muraoka 1999: 199; JM §154j n. 48). See on 3:22 for the construal of these clauses, and on 1:17 for such clauses more generally.

אֵשׁ אֹכְלָה. Ptcp fs Qal √אכל. The participle functions as an attributive adjective (WO §37.4b n. 33; cf. on 4:24). The phrase could be an "implicit" or adverbial accusative (so Driver, 111; Nelson, 115; cf. GKC §118q), "as a consuming fire," or it could be appositional to יהוה אלהיך (Weinfeld, 400; Lundbom, 362). The latter is preferable, since this clause focuses on who Yhwh *is*. What follows asyndetically in two *yiqtol* clauses is what Yhwh will *do*.

הוּא יַשְׁמִידֵם וְהוּא יַכְנִיעֵם לְפָנֶיךָ. *Yiqtol* 3ms Hiph √שמד and √כנע, both with 3mp pronominal suffix. PD. Two coordinated *yiqtol* clauses follow asyndetically from v. 3aα. They expand on what it means for Yhwh to be the one crossing ahead of them. √כנע is reminiscent of כנעני (1:7; 7:1; 11:30).

וְהוֹרַשְׁתָּם וְהַאֲבַדְתָּם מַהֵר. *Qatal* (modal) 2ms Hiph √ירש and √אבד, both with 3mp pronominal suffixes. PD. Two modal *qatal* clauses continue the PD. They are temporally and logically contingent on Yhwh's prior action.

מַהֵר. Inf abs Piel √מהר, functioning adverbially (JM §102e, §123r). Sudden victory in war does not contradict lack of swift eradication (מהר, 7:22). See Lundbom, 362.

כַּאֲשֶׁר דִּבֶּר יְהוָה לָךְ. *Qatal* 3ms Piel √דבר. See on 1:21 for the almost identical phrase.

9:4 אַל־תֹּאמַר בִּלְבָבְךָ בַּהֲדֹף יְהוָה אֱלֹהֶיךָ אֹתָם ׀ מִלְּפָנֶיךָ לֵאמֹר בְּצִדְקָתִי הֱבִיאַנִי יְהוָה לָרֶשֶׁת אֶת־הָאָרֶץ הַזֹּאת וּבְרִשְׁעַת הַגּוֹיִם הָאֵלֶּה יְהוָה מוֹרִישָׁם מִפָּנֶיךָ:

D2. HD. A prohibition against erroneous thoughts, which are then spelled out (ND, D3). Verse 4b is a circumstantial clause that paints the real picture (D2, ED).

אַל־תֹּאמַר בִּלְבָבְךָ . . . לֵאמֹר. Jussive 2ms Qal √אמר. HD. A prohibition (cf. on 1:17). A reflexive action, "say to yourself," "think," is here expressed by a circumlocution (בלבבך, adjunct PP) rather than the Niphal (WO §23.4c; cf. 7:17; 8:17). לאמר is a **complementizer** introducing a direct speech complement, and should not be translated (cf. on 1:5, including for the form). The **asyndesis** shows that this builds on what has preceded (v. 3). Yhwh's nature and action rule out self-righteousness.

בַּהֲדֹף יְהוָה אֱלֹהֶיךָ אֹתָם ׀ מִלְּפָנֶיךָ. Inf constr Qal √הדף with preposition ב. The infinitive construct as a *verbal* noun still retains the ability to govern an accusative complement (אתם) and to require a subject (יהוה אלהיך). Temporal adjunct PP, functioning as an infinitival temporal clause (cf. WO §36.2.2b). The preposition ב attached to the infinitive construct often introduces temporal expressions (see on 6:7). מלפניך is spatial adjunct PP.

בְּצִדְקָתִי הֱבִיאַנִי יְהוָה לָרֶשֶׁת אֶת־הָאָרֶץ הַזֹּאת. *Qatal* 3ms Hiph √בוא with 1cs pronominal suffix. D3. ND. בצדקתי is adjunct PP, fronted for **focus**: of all the possible reasons Yhwh might have brought me in, it is "because of my righteousness." For the causal use of ב, an extension of the instrumental, "with," see WO §11.2.5e; JM §170j; WHS §247.

לָרֶשֶׁת אֶת־הָאָרֶץ הַזֹּאת. Inf constr Qal √ירש with preposition ל. For the form, see on 9:1. Adjunct infinitive construct phrase, indicating the purpose of Yhwh bringing "me" in.

וּבְרִשְׁעַת הַגּוֹיִם הָאֵלֶּה יְהוָה מוֹרִישָׁם מִפָּנֶיךָ. Ptcp ms Hiph √ירש with 3mp pronominal suffix. Note the PP–S–P word order. וברשעת הגוים האלה is adjunct construct PP, fronted for **focus**, giving a contrast with the Israelites' erroneous thoughts. מפניך is spatial adjunct PP. The clause is a **null-copula** circumstantial clause with a participial predicate (Nelson, 117 n. c; cf. WHS §219, §494). It sets the scene for the main clause, in this case pointing out that something contrary to that asserted in the main clause is in fact the case.

9:5 לֹא בְצִדְקָתְךָ וּבְיֹשֶׁר לְבָבְךָ אַתָּה בָא לָרֶשֶׁת אֶת־אַרְצָם כִּי בְּרִשְׁעַת׀ הַגּוֹיִם הָאֵלֶּה יְהוָה אֱלֹהֶיךָ מוֹרִישָׁם מִפָּנֶיךָ וּלְמַעַן הָקִים אֶת־הַדָּבָר אֲשֶׁר נִשְׁבַּע יְהוָה לַאֲבֹתֶיךָ לְאַבְרָהָם לְיִצְחָק וּלְיַעֲקֹב:

D2. ED. Moses refutes directly the erroneous self-righteous thoughts with an adversative clause (לא . . . כי), and gives two reasons for Yhwh's action: the inhabitants' wickedness and Yhwh's faithfulness to his patriarchal promise.

לֹא בְצִדְקָתְךָ וּבְיֹשֶׁר לְבָבְךָ אַתָּה בָא לָרֶשֶׁת אֶת־אַרְצָם. Ptcp ms Qal √בוא. **Null-copula** verbless clause with participial predicate. Note the PP–S–P word order. לא בצדקתך ובישר לבבך comprises two adjunct PPs, the second of which is construct PP. The item adverb, לא, modifies the adjunct phrases rather than the main clause (cf. WO §39.3.2). This explains why, though a **null-copula** clause, לא rather than אין is used as the negative (cf. GKC §152d; JM §160b). The whole phrase is fronted for **focus** (cf. on 9:4). The clausal **asyndesis** here marks this verse out as explanatory, spelling out the preceding statement. Although much is repetition, there are expansions.

לָרֶ֫שֶׁת אֶת־אַרְצָם. Inf constr Qal √ירש with preposition ל. For the form, see on 9:1. Adjunct infinitive construct phrase, indicating the purpose of entering.

כִּ֤י בְרִשְׁעַת֙ | הַגּוֹיִ֣ם הָאֵ֔לֶּה יְהוָ֥ה אֱלֹהֶ֖יךָ מוֹרִישָׁ֣ם מִפָּנֶ֑יךָ. See on 9:4 for almost identical phrase. The construction of לא followed by כי indicates an adversative clause (cf. GKC §163a; JM §172c; AC §5.2.10).

וּלְמַ֜עַן הָקִ֣ים אֶת־הַדָּבָ֗ר. Inf constr Hiph √קום with preposition ל. Adjunct infinitive phrase expressing purpose. See on 8:18 for למען הקים + object of what is confirmed.

אֲשֶׁ֨ר נִשְׁבַּ֤ע יְהוָה֙ לַאֲבֹתֶ֔יךָ לְאַבְרָהָ֥ם לְיִצְחָ֖ק וּֽלְיַעֲקֹֽב׃. Qatal 3ms Niph √שבע. Restrictive relative clause with **head** הדבר. For the almost identical phrase, see on 1:8.

9:6 וְיָדַעְתָּ֗ כִּ֠י לֹ֤א בְצִדְקָֽתְךָ֙ יְהוָ֣ה אֱלֹהֶ֗יךָ נֹתֵ֨ן לְךָ֜ אֶת־הָאָ֧רֶץ הַטּוֹבָ֛ה הַזֹּ֖את לְרִשְׁתָּ֑הּ כִּ֥י עַם־קְשֵׁה־עֹ֖רֶף אָֽתָּה׃

D2. HD. It is one thing for Moses to state the situation. It is another for the people to acknowledge it, so Moses exhorts them to "know" it (cf. v. 3). The final explanatory clause gives an unpalatable but realistic assessment. Just how realistic it is Moses goes on to demonstrate (vv. 7-24).

וְיָדַעְתָּ֗ כִּ֠י . . . Qatal (modal) 2ms Qal √ידע. The modal *qatal* conveys volitional force (see on 9:3). כי is a **complementizer**, introducing the accusative complement noun clause, what they should "know."

כִּ֠י לֹ֤א בְצִדְקָֽתְךָ֙ יְהוָ֣ה אֱלֹהֶ֗יךָ נֹתֵ֨ן לְךָ֜ אֶת־הָאָ֧רֶץ הַטּוֹבָ֛ה הַזֹּ֖את לְרִשְׁתָּ֑הּ. Ptcp ms Qal √נתן. **Null-copula** clause with participial predicate. As a three-place predicate, √נתן has an overt subject, יהוה אלהיך, an oblique complement, לך, and an accusative complement NP, את־הארץ הטובה הזאת. Note the PP–S–P word order. לא בצדקתך is adjunct PP, fronted for **focus**, with לא functioning as an item adverb (see on 9:5).

לְרִשְׁתָּ֑הּ. Inf constr Qal √ירש with 3fs pronominal suffix (object) with preposition ל (for the form, see on 3:18). Adjunct infinitive construct phrase, indicating the purpose of Yhwh's gift.

כִּי עַם־קְשֵׁה־עֹרֶף אַתָּה. Subordinating conjunction כִּי introducing an explanatory **null-copula** clause. Although after כִּי verbal clauses have **triggered inversion**, **null-copula** clauses do not. The P–S word order in a **null-copula** clause marks the predicate (P), the construct NP עַם־קְשֵׁה־עֹרֶף, as the **focus**. The construct-absolute phrase is an attributive adjectival genitive. WO §9.5.3c term it an "epexegetical genitive, wherein G[enitive] is characterized by C[onstruct]."

Israel should remember that they have been rebellious (9:7-24)

Having made the startling assertion about the people being stiff-necked, Moses follows with an extended exposition of this theme, introduced (asyndetically) by the call to remember and not forget their past. Although the wilderness was the scene of consistent rebellion, it was at Horeb—of all places—that the people showed their true mettle, while it was also evident elsewhere (vv. 22-23). The call to remember, not forget, continues until 10:11, but this subsection is marked by an *inclusio*, ממרים הייתם עם־יהוה (vv. 7, 24) and by references to place names introduced by בְּ (vv. 8, 22-23). Self-righteousness is unwarranted in view of their history.

> [7]Remember, do not forget, that you angered Yhwh your God in the wilderness—from the time you came out from the land of Egypt until your coming to this place, you have been constantly rebelling in dealing with Yhwh—[8]at Horeb you angered Yhwh and Yhwh was furious with you so as to destroy you. [9]When I went up on the mountain to receive the stone tablets, the tablets of the covenant that Yhwh made with you, I stayed on the mountain for forty days and forty nights—I did not eat bread, nor did I drink water—[10]Yhwh gave to me the two stone tablets, written with the finger of God, and upon them were just like all the words that Yhwh spoke with you on the mountain from the midst of the fire on the day of the assembly. [11]And at the end of forty days and forty nights, Yhwh gave to me the two stone tablets, the tablets of the covenant. [12]Then Yhwh said to me, "Get up, go down quickly from here, for your people, whom you brought out from Egypt, have acted corruptly: they have turned aside quickly from the way I commanded them; they have made for themselves a molten image." [13]Then Yhwh said to me, "I have seen this people—look—they are nothing but a stiff-necked people. [14]Let go of me that I may destroy them and wipe their name from under heaven and make you into a nation that is mightier and more numerous than it." [15]So I turned and

went down the mountain—the mountain was burning with fire and the two tablets of the covenant were in my two hands—¹⁶And I looked—and there it was—you had sinned against Yhwh your God—you had made for yourselves a molten calf; you had turned aside quickly from the way Yhwh commanded you. ¹⁷I grasped the two tablets, I hurled them down from my two hands, and I smashed them before your eyes. ¹⁸Then I prostrated myself before Yhwh as formerly for forty days and forty nights—I did not eat bread, nor did I drink water—because of your sin that you had committed by doing what is evil in the sight of Yhwh, so as to vex him; for I was afraid of the ire and the anger that Yhwh raged against you, enough to destroy you. And at that time, too, Yhwh listened to me. ²⁰With Aaron in particular Yhwh was so angry as to destroy him, so I prayed on behalf of him too at that time. ²¹And your sinful thing that you had made, the calf, I took and I burned it with fire, and I smashed it, crushing it up thoroughly, until it was fine as dust. Then I hurled its dust into the wadi that goes down from the mountain. ²²And at Taberah, at Massah, and at Kibroth-Hattaavah, you kept angering Yhwh. ²³And when Yhwh sent you from Kadesh Barnea, saying, "Go up and take possession of the land that I have given you!" you defied the word of Yhwh your God, and you did not trust him or obey him. ²⁴You have been constantly rebelling in dealing with Yhwh from the day that I knew you.

9:7 זְכֹר אַל־תִּשְׁכַּח אֵת אֲשֶׁר־הִקְצַפְתָּ אֶת־יְהוָה אֱלֹהֶיךָ בַּמִּדְבָּר לְמִן־הַיּוֹם אֲשֶׁר־יָצָאתָ ׀ מֵאֶרֶץ מִצְרַיִם עַד־בֹּאֲכֶם עַד־הַמָּקוֹם הַזֶּה מַמְרִים הֱיִיתֶם עִם־יְהוָה׃

HD. D2. An asyndetic imperative, to "remember," is followed by a prohibition, "do not forget," reinforcing it. In the rest of the verse, two accusative complement noun clauses spell out what they are to remember. The first has a *qatal* predicate, seeing their angering of Yhwh as a past event, *in toto* (ND). The second is past progressive—a constant history of rebelliousness.

זְכֹר אַל־תִּשְׁכַּח. Impv ms Qal √זכר followed asyndetically by jussive 2ms Qal √שׁכח (a prohibition with אל; see on 1:17; WHS §186). HD. The double command expresses the same call (hence the **asyndesis**) positively and negatively for emphasis. In an exhortation, *"remember"* as opposed to a legal injunction, "*you shall/must remember*," the imperative is used rather than the infinitive absolute (cp. 5:12; JM §123v n. 30).

אֵת אֲשֶׁר־הִקְצַפְתָּ אֶת־יְהוָה אֱלֹהֶיךָ בַּמִּדְבָּר. *Qatal* 2ms Hiph √קצף. In 1:34 Yhwh was angry (√קצף Qal); here, they are to recall how they "angered" Yhwh (√קצף Hiphil). The **null-head** restrictive relative clause acts as the accusative complement of the imperative, זכר. אשר here acts as a **complementizer**, "that" (WHS §464; cf. WO §10.3.1a#14), since there is no resumed position within the clause (cf. Holmstedt 2006: 10–11). במדבר is spatial adjunct PP.

לְמִן־הַיּוֹם אֲשֶׁר־יָצָאתָ ׀ מֵאֶרֶץ מִצְרַיִם. Temporal adjunct PP, with היום as **head** of the following restrictive relative clause with predicate *qatal* 2ms Qal √יצא. למן is pleonastic synonym of מן (see on 4:32). מארץ מצרים is spatial adjunct PP. This and the following temporal adjunct PPs begin a new clause that follows asyndetically. It expands upon the fact they had angered Yhwh in the wilderness.

עַד־בֹּאֲכֶם עַד־הַמָּקוֹם הַזֶּה. Inf constr Qal √בוא with 2mp subject suffix. Temporal adjunct PP. See on 1:31 for the identical phrase. When the **head** of a relative clause is a period of time, there is never a resumptive pronoun referring to that word of time (GKC §138c; JM §158k; cf. on 1:46).

מַמְרִים הֱיִיתֶם עִם־יְהוָה׃ *Qatal* 2mp Qal √היה, with ptcp mp Hiph √מרה. When the copula (√היה) is combined with a participle, there are various possible ways of understanding it. Sometimes a **periphrastic** verb is created (e.g., Job 1:14; JM §121f, §154m). GKC §116r thinks that the presence of the overt copula is for emphasis. WO §37.7.1b make a distinction between participles that appear after the copula, which have a "progressive" sense, and those that appear before, which are "adjectival" or "substantival." They regard the instance here as substantival (WO §37.7.1b n. 51). JM §121f n. 6 agrees in thinking this instance is not **periphrastic**, but regards ממרים here as having a quasi-adjectival meaning, "rebellious." However, rather than seeing the participle as a substantive ("rebels") or quasi-adjectival ("rebellious"), it makes better sense to see it as an instance of a past progressive (so Cook 2012: 229), with the participle fronted for **focus**, "you have been [doing nothing but] rebelling. . . ." The participle speaks of events, unlike normal adjectives. The presence of the copula with the participle is not distinctive from **null-copula** clauses with a participial predicate. Rather, with participial predicates, Hebrew uses the copula in past time and sometimes in the future, but has a **null-copula** for the present (Cook 2012: 229). עִם־יְהוָה is adjunct PP to the participial predicate, "in dealing with" (Driver, 113); it expresses negatively what אֵת expresses positively (1:30; 10:21).

9:8 וּבְחֹרֵב הִקְצַפְתֶּם אֶת־יְהוָה וַיִּתְאַנַּף יְהוָה בָּכֶם לְהַשְׁמִיד אֶתְכֶם:

D2. Moses continues by recounting the past events (ND) they should remember. A *qatal* (due to the fronting of בחרב as the **topic**, "at Horeb") is followed by a *wayyiqtol*. Yhwh's anger looms large.

וּבְחֹרֵב הִקְצַפְתֶּם אֶת־יְהוָה. *Qatal* 2mp Hiph √קצף. It is attractive to regard the spatial adjunct PP בחרב as fronted for **focus**: "at Horeb [as opposed to anywhere else / of all places]...." More likely, though, in view of the parallel with v. 22, it is fronted as the **topic**, providing scene-setting information about the place where the provocation occurred.

וַיִּתְאַנַּף יְהוָה בָּכֶם. *Wayyiqtol* 3ms Hitp √אנף. For the *patakh*, ויתאנף, see GKC §54k; WO §26.1.1c. בכם is oblique complement of the verb ויתאנף.

לְהַשְׁמִיד אֶתְכֶם: Inf constr Hiph √שמד with preposition ל. The ל with the infinitive construct here indicates "degree," "angry *enough to*" (cf. WHS §199, §275).

9:9 בַּעֲלֹתִי הָהָרָה לָקַחַת לוּחֹת הָאֲבָנִים לוּחֹת הַבְּרִית אֲשֶׁר־כָּרַת יְהוָה עִמָּכֶם וָאֵשֵׁב בָּהָר אַרְבָּעִים יוֹם וְאַרְבָּעִים לַיְלָה לֶחֶם לֹא אָכַלְתִּי וּמַיִם לֹא שָׁתִיתִי:

D2. Moses continues by recounting the past events (ND) they should remember. A temporal protasis (v. 9a) is followed by a *wayyiqtol* temporal apodosis (v. 9bα). Two coordinated circumstantial *qatal* clauses follow asyndetically (v. 9bβ). Yhwh's anger (vv. 7-8) is followed narratively by Moses' action (v. 9), but the opening **asyndesis** indicates that the action of this verse is developing the previous verse.

בַּעֲלֹתִי הָהָרָה. Inf constr Qal √עלה with 1cs pronominal suffix (subject) and with preposition ב. Temporal adjunct PP, functioning as an infinitival temporal clause (cf. WO §36.2.2b). The preposition ב attached to the infinitive construct often introduces temporal expressions (see on 6:7). ההרה is the directional adjunct. The locative ה on ההר indicates motion toward (WO §10.5a, b; JM §93c). The accent does not shift when ה is added. The clausal **asyndesis** at the start of v. 9 shows that this does not follow the preceding events, but explains them.

לָקַ֣חַת לוּחֹ֣ת הָאֲבָנִ֗ים לוּחֹ֣ת הַבְּרִ֔ית. Inf constr Qal √לקח with preposition ל. לקח is the only I-ל verb which functions like a I-נ (JM §72j). Adjunct infinitive phrase to verb בעלתי, expressing purpose. Before the tone syllable of an infinitive construct, the ל often has *qamets* (GKC §102f; JM §103c). לוחת האבנים is accusative complement construct NP. For the phrase, see on 4:13. לוחת הברית is appositional construct NP, making the point that the ten tablets contain the Horeb covenant's terms.

אֲשֶׁר־כָּרַ֧ת יְהוָ֛ה עִמָּכֶ֖ם. *Qatal* 3ms Qal √כרת. Restrictive relative clause with **head** הברית. For the idea that the covenant was made with Moses' addressees in Moab, see 5:2-3.

וָאֵשֵׁ֣ב בָּהָ֗ר אַרְבָּעִ֥ים יוֹם֙ וְאַרְבָּעִ֣ים לַ֔יְלָה. *Wayyiqtol* 1cs Qal √ישב. A *wayyiqtol* often follows a temporal adjunct PP and introduces the temporal apodosis (GKC §111b; WO §33.3.5c; MNK §39.6.2). בהר is spatial adjunct PP. ארבעים יום וארבעים לילה is an indirect or adverbial accusative (i.e., not the object of the verb), giving the length of time Moses was on the mountain (cf. GKC §118k; JM §126i; WO §10.2.2c). The singular noun occurs with tens (GKC §134h; JM §142f).

לֶ֚חֶם לֹ֣א אָכַ֔לְתִּי וּמַ֖יִם לֹ֥א שָׁתִֽיתִי׃ *Qatal* 1cs Qal √אכל and √שתה. These coordinated clauses follow asyndetically, further describing Moses' stay on the mountain. The accusative complements, לחם and מים, are fronted as **topics.** The clauses are coordinated and are counterparts of each other. Together they build up a complementary picture, which accounts for the topicalization (cf. Moshavi 2010: 160–61). The clauses are circumstantial (Driver, 113).

9:10 וַיִּתֵּ֨ן יְהוָ֜ה אֵלַ֗י אֶת־שְׁנֵי֙ לוּחֹ֣ת הָאֲבָנִ֔ים כְּתֻבִ֖ים בְּאֶצְבַּ֣ע אֱלֹהִ֑ים וַעֲלֵיהֶ֗ם כְּכָל־הַדְּבָרִ֡ים אֲשֶׁ֣ר דִּבֶּר֩ יְהוָ֨ה עִמָּכֶ֥ם בָּהָ֛ר מִתּ֥וֹךְ הָאֵ֖שׁ בְּי֥וֹם הַקָּהָֽל׃

ND. D2. Moses continues recounting the past events (ND) they should remember. Here it is the subnarrative begun in v. 9 that continues with a *wayyiqtol* (v. 10a) and a circumstantial clause (v. 10b).

וַיִּתֵּ֨ן יְהוָ֜ה אֵלַ֗י אֶת־שְׁנֵי֙ לוּחֹ֣ת הָֽאֲבָנִ֔ים כְּתֻבִ֖ים בְּאֶצְבַּ֣ע אֱלֹהִ֑ים. *Wayyiqtol* 3ms Qal √נתן. √נתן is a three-place predicate, here with an overt subject (יהוה), an overt oblique complement (אלי) and an overt accusative complement (את־שני לוחת האבנים; see on 4:13 for the identical phrase).

כְּתֻבִ֖ים בְּאֶצְבַּ֣ע אֱלֹהִ֑ים. Ptcp mp Qal pass √כתב. The participle is not strictly functioning as an attributive adjective, since the participle does not have the article, but as an "attributive accusative of state" (cf. JM §127a), modifying a noun (hence termed "attributive") rather than the predicate (adverbial or indirect accusative). באצבע אלהים is adjunct construct PP.

וַעֲלֵיהֶ֕ם כְּכָל־הַדְּבָרִ֗ים. **Null-copula** circumstantial clause, with PP subject and predicate. The subject, (ו)עליהם, is identifiable as such because the pronominal suffix marks it as more definite. The predicate construct PP, ככל־הדברים, has the comparative preposition כ, that "expresses a relation of either perfect (equality), or imperfect (resemblance) similitude" (JM §133g), here exact given כל. The preposition does not make the predication "nonsensical," as DeRouchie (2007: 318 n. 12) claims. Rather, the written words match the spoken words.

אֲשֶׁ֨ר דִּבֶּ֧ר יְהוָ֛ה עִמָּכֶ֥ם בָּהָ֖ר מִתּ֣וֹךְ הָאֵ֑שׁ בְּי֖וֹם הַקָּהָֽל׃. *Qatal* 3ms Piel √דבר (for the pointing, see on 1:1). Restrictive relative clause with **head** הדברים. Four adjunct PPs follow, indicating with whom (עמכם), where (בהר), from where (מתוך האש) and when (ביום הקהל) Yhwh spoke.

9:11 וַיְהִ֗י מִקֵּ֛ץ אַרְבָּעִ֥ים י֖וֹם וְאַרְבָּעִ֣ים לָ֑יְלָה נָתַ֨ן יְהוָ֜ה אֵלַ֗י אֶת־שְׁנֵ֧י לֻחֹ֛ת הָאֲבָנִ֖ים לֻח֥וֹת הַבְּרִֽית׃

ND. D2. Moses continues the subnarrative begun in v. 9. Verse 11a sets the temporal context for Yhwh's gift of the stone tablets (v. 11b).

וַיְהִ֗י מִקֵּ֛ץ אַרְבָּעִ֥ים י֖וֹם וְאַרְבָּעִ֣ים לָ֑יְלָה. *Wayyiqtol* 3ms Qal √היה. ויהי followed by a temporal phrase expresses the time in which subsequent events happen; it usually begins a new section. See further on 1:3 for form and syntax. מקץ ארבעים יום וארבעים לילה is adjunct temporal construct

PP. The object of מִן can be the time of an event (WO §11.2.11c; WHS §323b).

נָתַ֨ן יְהוָ֜ה אֵלַ֗י אֶת־שְׁנֵ֛י לֻחֹ֥ת הָאֲבָנִ֖ים לֻח֥וֹת הַבְּרִֽית׃. *Qatal* 3ms Qal √נתן. For √נתן with the identical subject and complements as a three-place predicate, see on v. 10. See on v. 9 for the appositional construct NP, לחות הברית.

9:12 וַיֹּ֧אמֶר יְהוָ֣ה אֵלַ֗י ק֣וּם רֵ֤ד מַהֵר֙ מִזֶּ֔ה כִּ֚י שִׁחֵ֣ת עַמְּךָ֔ אֲשֶׁ֥ר הוֹצֵ֖אתָ מִמִּצְרָ֑יִם סָ֣רוּ מַהֵ֗ר מִן־הַדֶּ֙רֶךְ֙ אֲשֶׁ֣ר צִוִּיתִ֔ם עָשׂ֥וּ לָהֶ֖ם מַסֵּכָֽה׃

Moses continues the subnarrative begun in v. 9 (ND, D2). He recounts Yhwh's words to him (D3). Two asyndetic imperatives (HD) are followed by an explanatory clause introduced by כי. That explanatory clause is in turn expounded by two asyndetic *qatal* clauses. Haste (מהר) is important for Moses, because of the Israelites' hasty departure (מהר) from the right path.

וַיֹּ֧אמֶר יְהוָ֣ה אֵלַ֗י. *Wayyiqtol* 3ms Qal √אמר. The inclusion of an **overt** subject, יהוה, when already **discourse active**, marks a sense break.

ק֣וּם רֵ֤ד מַהֵר֙ מִזֶּ֔ה. Impv ms Qal √קום and √ירד. For the form רֵד, customary for I-נ verbs, see GKC §69b. Two imperatives frequently occur asyndetically, especially where the first involves movement (JM §177e). This coordination is an alternative mode of expression to subordination, and the second verb expresses the main idea (cf. GKC §120d, g). It is a mark of elevated or rhetorical style (cf. GKC §120h).

מַהֵר֙. Inf abs Piel √מהר, functioning adverbially (JM §102e, §123r; WO §35.4a).

מִזֶּ֔ה. Spatial adjunct PP. זה originally was a demonstrative adverb (JM §143a).

כִּ֚י שִׁחֵ֣ת עַמְּךָ֔ אֲשֶׁ֥ר הוֹצֵ֖אתָ מִמִּצְרָ֑יִם. *Qatal* 3ms Piel √שחת. The middle guttural is "virtually strengthened" so there is no compensatory lengthening in the first syllable (cf. GKC §64d). Explanatory clause, introduced by the subordinating conjunction כי; note the **triggered inversion**. Yhwh calls Israel "your" people to Moses.

אֲשֶׁ֥ר הוֹצֵ֖אתָ מִמִּצְרָ֑יִם. *Qatal* 2ms Hiph √יצא. Non-restrictive relative clause with **head** עמך. Yhwh declares that Moses brought the

Deuteronomy 9:12-13

people out from Egypt. Everywhere else in chapters 1–11, Yhwh has been the agent of deliverance, including the programmatic 5:6 (cf. v. 24 below).

סָ֣רוּ מַהֵ֔ר מִן־הַדֶּ֖רֶךְ אֲשֶׁ֣ר צִוִּיתִ֑ם. *Qatal* 3cp Qal √סור. See above for מהר. מן־הדרך is spatial adjunct PP. דרך has been an important motif, whether literal or figurative (cf. 5:33; 8:2, 6). The clausal **asyndesis** with this and the following clause marks these clauses as explaining or illustrating the way they have acted corruptly. In that sense, they are similar to an adverbial accusative of manner, "by . . . -ing" (cf. WHS §491; v. 16).

אֲשֶׁ֣ר צִוִּיתִ֑ם. *Qatal* 1cs Piel √צוה with 3mp pronominal suffix. Restrictive relative clause with **head** הדרך.

עָשׂ֥וּ לָהֶ֖ם מַסֵּכָֽה׃. *Qatal* 3cp Qal √עשה. ל introduces here what is sometimes called "the dative of advantage" giving the beneficiaries of the action of the verb (cf. GKC §119q-s; JM §133d; WO §11.2.10d; WHS §271a).

9:13 וַיֹּ֥אמֶר יְהוָ֖ה אֵלַ֣י לֵאמֹ֑ר רָאִ֙יתִי֙ אֶת־הָעָ֣ם הַזֶּ֔ה וְהִנֵּ֥ה עַם־קְשֵׁה־עֹ֖רֶף הֽוּא׃

Moses continues the subnarrative begun in v. 9 (ND, D2). He recounts Yhwh's words to him (D3). A *qatal* clause (ND) is then followed by Yhwh's conclusion (ED). Yhwh's verdict reinforces Moses': Israel are nothing but a stiff-necked people (cf. v. 6).

וַיֹּ֥אמֶר יְהוָ֖ה אֵלַ֣י לֵאמֹ֑ר. *Wayyiqtol* 3ms Qal √אמר. The inclusion of an overt subject, יהוה, when already **discourse active**, marks a sense break. The repeated root, "Yhwh said (√אמר) . . . saying (√אמר)" illustrates לאמר as a **complementizer** which can hardly be translated (see on 1:5).

רָאִ֙יתִי֙ אֶת־הָעָ֣ם הַזֶּ֔ה. *Qatal* 1cs Qal √ראה.

וְהִנֵּ֥ה עַם־קְשֵׁה־עֹ֖רֶף הֽוּא׃. **Null-copula** clause. The P–S word order in a **null-copula** clause marks P, the construct NP complement עַם־קְשֵׁה־עֹרֶף as the **focus** (see on 1:14; for the construct NP, see on 9:6). It is not straightforward to capture the force and function of הנה, still less to translate it. Traditionally it has been translated with "behold." It is a **deictic** particle, that draws particular attention to what follows (Miller-Naudé and van der Merwe). The ו connects this clause to the preceding proposition.

9:14 הֶ֤רֶף מִמֶּ֙נִּי֙ וְאַשְׁמִידֵ֔ם וְאֶמְחֶ֣ה אֶת־שְׁמָ֔ם מִתַּ֖חַת הַשָּׁמָ֑יִם וְאֶֽעֱשֶׂה֙ אֽוֹתְךָ֔ לְגוֹי־עָצ֥וּם וָרָ֖ב מִמֶּֽנּוּ׃

Yhwh's speech continues from v. 13 (D3). A strikingly anthropomorphic imperative (Weinfeld, 402) is followed by three indirect cohortatives, expressing purpose (HD). While Israel would suffer the same fate as the inhabitants of the land, Yhwh is keen to begin again with Moses and make a nation similar in might and number to the inhabitants of the land. The subnarrative returns to Yhwh's anger and intention to destroy (√שמד) Israel (cf. v. 8).

הֶ֤רֶף מִמֶּ֙נִּי֙. Impv ms Hiph √רפה. HD. The Hiphil imperative of √רפה, like other III-ה verbs, sometimes **apocopates** (though note Judg 11:37; 2 Kgs 4:23). The (notional) form הַרְפְּ acquires helping *segols*, like a segholate noun, giving the form הֶ֤רֶף (n.b., the accent on the first syllable). See GKC §75gg. The accusative complement is covert, "[your hand/ your grip]" (cf. Driver, 114). ממני is PP adjunct.

וְאַשְׁמִידֵ֔ם. Cohortative 1cs Hiph √שמד with 3mp pronominal suffix. The cohortative is 1st person volitive, expressing the will of the one(s) speaking. Although not morphologically marked here, its position at the start of the clause and the sequence of verbs of which it is a part indicate it is an **indirect volitive** (cf. JM §116b). The clause is syntactically coordinated with the previous clause, "let go of me... and I will destroy," but semantically subordinate, providing the purpose of the letting go, "let go of me... *that* I *may* destroy them."

וְאֶמְחֶ֣ה אֶת־שְׁמָ֔ם מִתַּ֖חַת הַשָּׁמָ֑יִם. Cohortative 1cs Qal √מחה. III-ה verbs retain the ordinary *yiqtol* form for the cohortative (GKC §75l). **Indirect volitive** (see above). מתחת השמים is spatial adjunct PP; מתחת is a compound preposition (see on 4:18). At the outset, the Israelites nearly suffered the same fate as they were to mete on the inhabitants of the land (cf. 7:24).

וְאֶֽעֱשֶׂה֙ אֽוֹתְךָ֔ לְגוֹי־עָצ֥וּם וָרָ֖ב מִמֶּֽנּוּ׃. Cohortative 1cs Qal √עשה. III-ה verbs retain the ordinary *yiqtol* form for the cohortative (GKC §75l). **Indirect volitive** (see above).

לְגוֹי־עָצ֥וּם וָרָ֖ב מִמֶּֽנּוּ׃. Adjunct PP. The ל of "product," where the object of the preposition is the outcome of an action (WHS §278). Lacking particular forms for the comparative, Hebrew uses the preposition מן attached to the noun (here the pronominal suffix in ממנו)

that is excelled when both nouns are present (JM §141g; AC §4.1.13h). The antecedent of the suffix is גוי. The phrase echoes 7:1.

9:15 וָאֵ֗פֶן וָֽאֵרֵד֙ מִן־הָהָ֔ר וְהָהָ֖ר בֹּעֵ֣ר בָּאֵ֑שׁ וּשְׁנֵי֙ לֻחֹ֣ת הַבְּרִ֔ית עַ֖ל שְׁתֵּ֥י יָדָֽי׃

D2. ND. Two *wayyiqtols* signal the end of Yhwh's embedded direct speech. The two actions are then followed by two circumstantial clauses. The scene is dramatic and foreboding. Fire is reminiscent of Yhwh (cf. 9:3); the tablets containing the commandments to which they had given eager assent prohibit what Israel has been doing. Yhwh has declared his anger and his intentions (vv. 12-14; cf. v. 8). Now Moses' reaction is center stage.

וָאֵ֗פֶן וָֽאֵרֵד֙ מִן־הָהָ֔ר. *Wayyiqtol* 1cs Qal √פנה and √ירד. As a III-ה verb, the ה **apocopates** in the *wayyiqtol*. For the vocalization of that form, see JM §79i. מן־ההר is spatial adjunct PP.

וְהָהָ֖ר בֹּעֵ֣ר בָּאֵ֑שׁ. Ptcp ms Qal √בער. **Null-copula** circumstantial clause. For the phrase, see on 4:11.

וּשְׁנֵי֙ לֻחֹ֣ת הַבְּרִ֔ית עַ֖ל שְׁתֵּ֥י יָדָֽי׃. **Null-copula** circumstantial clause, with construct NP subject, שני לחת הברית, and PP predicate, על שתי ידי. The syntax of the numeral two, which agrees in gender with the noun it modifies, can have one of three forms: (1) absolute form, before the noun; (2) absolute form, after the noun; or (3) construct form, before the noun, as in both cases here (JM §142c).

9:16 וָאֵ֗רֶא וְהִנֵּ֤ה חֲטָאתֶם֙ לַיהוָ֣ה אֱלֹֽהֵיכֶ֔ם עֲשִׂיתֶ֣ם לָכֶ֔ם עֵ֖גֶל מַסֵּכָ֑ה סַרְתֶּ֣ם מַהֵ֔ר מִן־הַדֶּ֕רֶךְ אֲשֶׁר־צִוָּ֥ה יְהוָ֖ה אֶתְכֶֽם׃

ND. D2. A *wayyiqtol* is followed by a *qatal* after והנה. What Yhwh reported to Moses, Moses now sees with his own eyes (והנה . . . √ראה, cf. v. 13). Two asyndetic *qatal* clauses then make the sin plain (√עשה, √סור; cf. v. 12). The congruence of Yhwh's words (vv. 12-13) and Moses' (v. 16) corroborate Moses' authority and his verdict.

וָאֵ֗רֶא. *Wayyiqtol* 1cs Qal √ראה. As a III-ה verb, the ה **apocopates** in the *wayyiqtol*. For the vocalization of that form, see JM §79i.

וְהִנֵּה חֲטָאתֶם לַיהוָה אֱלֹהֵיכֶם. *Qatal* 2mp Qal √חטא. For the **deictic** particle הנה, see on v. 13. Here it does not connote surprise but corroborates what Yhwh had told Moses; nonetheless, it does convey the "stance of the observer" (Miller-Naudé and van der Merwe, 73). ליהוה אלהיכם is adjunct PP, specifying against whom the sin has been committed.

עֲשִׂיתֶם לָכֶם עֵגֶל מַסֵּכָה. *Qatal* 2mp Qal √עשׂה. ל introduces here what is sometimes called "the dative of advantage" giving the beneficiaries of the action of the verb (cf. GKC §119q-s; JM §133d; WO §11.2.10d; WHS §271a). The accusative complement is the construct NP, עגל מסכה. It is a type of adjectival genitive, where the absolute/genitive, מסכה, gives the material of which the construct is made (cf. WO §9.5.3d). The clausal **asyndesis** for this and the following clause marks these clauses as explaining or illustrating the way they have sinned (cf. on v. 12).

סַרְתֶּם מַהֵר מִן־הַדֶּרֶךְ אֲשֶׁר־צִוָּה יְהוָה אֶתְכֶם: *Qatal* 2mp Qal √סור. See on v. 12 for מהר and for מן־הדרך. WHS §491 regards this as a clause equivalent to an adverbial accusative of manner, "by . . . -ing." See the previous comment and on v. 12.

אֲשֶׁר־צִוָּה יְהוָה אֶתְכֶם: *Qatal* 3ms Piel √צוה. Restrictive relative clause with **head** הדרך.

9:17 וָאֶתְפֹּשׂ בִּשְׁנֵי הַלֻּחֹת וָאַשְׁלִכֵם מֵעַל שְׁתֵּי יָדָי וָאֲשַׁבְּרֵם לְעֵינֵיכֶם:

ND. Three *wayyiqtols* and the tablets are broken; the covenant is symbolically annulled (Tigay 1996: 100), and those in Moab saw it with their own eyes (cf. on 1:30).

וָאֶתְפֹּשׂ בִּשְׁנֵי הַלֻּחֹת. *Wayyiqtol* 1cs Qal √תפשׂ. בשני הלחת is oblique complement construct NP.

וָאַשְׁלִכֵם מֵעַל שְׁתֵּי יָדָי. *Wayyiqtol* 1cs Hiph √שלך with 3mp pronominal suffix. מעל שתי ידי is adjunct PP. מעל is a compound preposition, "downwards from" (HALOT s.v.).

וָאֲשַׁבְּרֵם לְעֵינֵיכֶם: *Wayyiqtol* 1cs Piel √שבר with 3mp pronominal suffix. The verb √שבר was traditionally cited as an example of the difference between the Qal ("break") and the "derived" Piel ("smash") with the Piel being a so-called "intensive" stem. However, for a more cogent and comprehensive analysis of the *binyanim*, sees √שבר Piel as

resultative, bringing about a result or state of which the transitive Qal speaks (AC §3.1.3[a]; cf. WO §24.1, 24.3). לעיניכם is adjunct PP. The Moab generation is treated as though at Horeb. See on 1:30.

9:18 וָאֶתְנַפַּל֩ לִפְנֵ֨י יְהוָ֜ה כָּרִאשֹׁנָ֗ה אַרְבָּעִ֥ים יוֹם֙ וְאַרְבָּעִ֣ים לַ֔יְלָה לֶ֚חֶם לֹ֣א אָכַ֔לְתִּי וּמַ֖יִם לֹ֣א שָׁתִ֑יתִי עַ֤ל כָּל־חַטַּאתְכֶם֙ אֲשֶׁ֣ר חֲטָאתֶ֔ם לַעֲשׂ֥וֹת הָרַ֛ע בְּעֵינֵ֥י יְהוָ֖ה לְהַכְעִיסֽוֹ׃

ND. D2. Moses moves beyond Israel's sin and Yhwh's anger and intention to destroy, to recount his prostration before Yhwh, a prostration marked by fasting (n.b., coordinated circumstantial *qatal* clauses follow asyndetically). Innocent of Israel's sin, as mediator Moses intercedes on their behalf.

וָאֶתְנַפַּל לִפְנֵי יְהוָה כָּרִאשֹׁנָה אַרְבָּעִים יוֹם וְאַרְבָּעִים לַיְלָה. *Wayyiqtol* 1cs Hitp √נפל. For the *patakh*, ואתנפל, see GKC §54k; Blau, 233 (cf. 1:37; 4:21). The Hitpael √נפל only occurs four times. The parallel in Ezra 10:1 suggests self-abasement, "prostrated myself." לפני יהוה is spatial adjunct PP. כראשנה is temporal adjunct PP. Often after כ the expected preposition is omitted (JM §133h): sometimes כבראשנה is found (e.g., Judg 20:32), but here ב is dropped. The ordinal adjective רִאשׁוֹן, "first" (JM §101a) is derived from ראש (JM §88Me). The *hireq* is attributable to "dissimilation," the reluctance to have two identical vowels in a row (JM §29h). The feminine singular form functions much more often as an adverb (JM §102c). See on v. 9 for ארבעים יום וארבעים לילה.

לֶחֶם לֹא אָכַלְתִּי וּמַיִם לֹא שָׁתִיתִי. See on 9:9 for the identical phrase.

עַל כָּל־חַטַּאתְכֶם אֲשֶׁר חֲטָאתֶם. על כל־חטאתכם is adjunct PP. The object of על indicates the cause (WHS §291). The noun חטאת has this pointing because of the quiescent א (cf. GKC §23a); the notional form חַטָּאת becomes חַטָּאת (JM §97Ff).

אֲשֶׁר חֲטָאתֶם. *Qatal* 2mp Qal √חטא. Restrictive relative clause.

לַעֲשׂוֹת הָרַע בְּעֵינֵי יְהוָה לְהַכְעִיסוֹ׃. Inf constr Qal √עשׂה with preposition ל. The infinitive construct is **gerundial** or explanatory, "by keeping" (cf. WO §36.2.3e). See on 4:25 for the identical phrase after √עשׂה.

9:19 כִּ֣י יָגֹ֗רְתִּי מִפְּנֵ֤י הָאַף֙ וְהַ֣חֵמָ֔ה אֲשֶׁ֨ר קָצַ֧ף יְהוָ֛ה עֲלֵיכֶ֖ם לְהַשְׁמִ֣יד אֶתְכֶ֑ם וַיִּשְׁמַ֤ע יְהוָה֙ אֵלַ֔י גַּ֖ם בַּפַּ֥עַם הַהִֽוא׃

D2. In the explanatory clause in v. 19a, Moses reveals the fears lying behind his action of v. 18. In v. 19b Moses recounts the positive reception Yhwh gave his prayer (ND).

כִּ֣י יָגֹ֗רְתִּי מִפְּנֵ֤י הָאַף֙ וְהַ֣חֵמָ֔ה אֲשֶׁ֨ר קָצַ֧ף יְהוָ֛ה עֲלֵיכֶ֖ם לְהַשְׁמִ֣יד אֶתְכֶ֑ם. *Qatal* 1cs Qal √יגר. The verb is stative, speaking of a temporary psychological state (WO §22.4e). It is also "defective," meaning that parts of the conjugation come from different roots (*qatal*: √יגר; *yiqtol*, imperative: √גור; cf. 1:17) (JM §75i, §85a). מפני האף והחמה is oblique complement. Explanatory clause introduced by subordinating conjunction, כי.

אֲשֶׁ֨ר קָצַ֧ף יְהוָ֛ה עֲלֵיכֶ֖ם. *Qatal* 3ms Qal √קצף. עליכם is oblique complement. Restrictive relative clause, with **head** האף והחמה. The **head** of the relative אשר functions as an internal accusative, "an abstract noun of action, identical with, or analogous to the action expressed by the verb"; it can be a cognate word (i.e., of the same root, קָצַ֖ף . . . קֶ֑צֶף, Zech 1:2), or synonymous with the verb (JM §125q), as here.

לְהַשְׁמִ֣יד אֶתְכֶ֑ם. Inf constr Hiph √שמד with preposition ל. The ל with the infinitive construct here indicates "degree," "angry *enough to*" (cf. WHS §199, §275; also vv. 8, 20).

וַיִּשְׁמַ֤ע יְהוָה֙ אֵלַ֔י גַּ֖ם בַּפַּ֥עַם הַהִֽוא׃. *Wayyiqtol* 3ms Qal √שמע. אלי is oblique complement. With the preposition אל, √שמע denotes "listening to" (see on 7:12).

גַּ֖ם בַּפַּ֥עַם הַהִֽוא׃. Temporal adjunct PP. The *ketiv* of the feminine singular pronoun is almost always הוא in the Pentateuch (see on 1:9). גם is here an item adverb, modifying the adjunct PP (see on 1:28).

9:20 וּֽבְאַהֲרֹ֗ן הִתְאַנַּ֧ף יְהוָ֛ה מְאֹ֖ד לְהַשְׁמִיד֑וֹ וָֽאֶתְפַּלֵּ֛ל גַּם־בְּעַ֥ד אַהֲרֹ֖ן בָּעֵ֥ת הַהִֽוא׃

ND. D2. Alongside anger with the people, Yhwh was angry with Aaron (v. 20a). Moses interceded for Aaron too (v. 20b).

וּֽבְאַהֲרֹ֗ן הִתְאַנַּ֧ף יְהוָ֛ה מְאֹ֖ד לְהַשְׁמִיד֑וֹ. *Qatal* 3ms Hitp √אנף. For the *patakh*, התאנף, see GKC §54k; WO §26.1.1c; Blau, 233. באהרן is oblique complement of the verb התאנף, fronted for **focus**: Yhwh was particularly angry with Aaron. מאד is used as an adverbial adjunct, intensifying the force of the verbal idea (AC §4.2.12).

לְהַשְׁמִידוֹ. Inf constr Hiph √שמד with 3ms pronominal suffix and with preposition ל. The ל with the infinitive construct here indicates "degree," "angry *enough to*" (cf. WHS §199, §275; as in vv. 8, 19).

גם בעד אהרן בעת ההוא: וָאֶתְפַּלֵּל גַּם־בְּעַד אַהֲרֹן בָּעֵת הַהִוא. *Wayyiqtol* 1cs Hitp √פלל. אהרן is adjunct PP, with item adverb גם (see on 1:28). The preposition בְּעַד, originally a noun, has different forms depending on whether it precedes a pronoun (בַּעֲדוֹ), another preposition (בְּעַד ל), or a noun (בְּעַד, as here), when it behaves like the segholate noun חֶדֶר, "room" (JM §103g n. 17; Blau, 283). בעת ההוא is temporal adjunct PP (see on 1:9).

9:21 וְאֶת־חַטַּאתְכֶ֞ם אֲשֶׁר־עֲשִׂיתֶ֣ם אֶת־הָעֵ֗גֶל לָקַ֒חְתִּי֒ וָאֶשְׂרֹ֨ף אֹת֤וֹ ׀ בָּאֵשׁ֙ וָאֶכֹּ֤ת אֹתוֹ֙ טָח֣וֹן הֵיטֵ֔ב עַ֥ד אֲשֶׁר־דַּ֖ק לְעָפָ֑ר וָאַשְׁלִךְ֙ אֶת־עֲפָר֔וֹ אֶל־הַנַּ֖חַל הַיֹּרֵ֥ד מִן־הָהָֽר׃

ND. Alongside intercession with Yhwh, Moses recalls his decisive action with the calf, described initially as "your sin." A *qatal* (due to the accusative complement fronted for **focus**) is followed by three *wayyiqtols* that together express the thorough destruction of the calf.

וְאֶת־חַטַּאתְכֶם אֲשֶׁר־עֲשִׂיתֶם אֶת־הָעֵגֶל לָקַחְתִּי. *Qatal* 1cs Qal √לקח. את־חטאתכם is accusative complement NP, fronted for **focus**. חטאתכם is biting metonymy (n.b., change of verb from √חטא to √עשה), since the Israelites would not have immediately associated "sin" with the calf. את־העגל is appositional NP, identifying—if it were needed after √עשה—חטאתכם.

אֲשֶׁר־עֲשִׂיתֶם. *Qatal* 2mp Qal √עשה. Restrictive relative clause with **head** חטאתכם.

וָאֶשְׂרֹף אֹתוֹ | בָּאֵשׁ. *Wayyiqtol* 1cs Qal √שרף. באש is adjunct PP.

וָאֶכֹּת אֹתוֹ טָחוֹן הֵיטֵב עַד אֲשֶׁר־דַּק לְעָפָר. *Wayyiqtol* 1cs Qal √כתת. Geminate verbs sometimes have aramaising *dagesh forte*, where the first root letter has a *dagesh forte*, not the second (GKC §67g; cf. 1:44).

טָחוֹן הֵיטֵב. Inf abs Qal √טחן and Hiph √יטב. Both are adverbial uses of the infinitive absolute, although they differ slightly (JM §123r n. 20;

cf. WO §35.4a; Blau, 215). The first, טחון, continues the action of the finite verb, "crushing" (cf. החרם, 3:6); the second, היטב, gives the manner, "well," or "thoroughly," almost having the characteristic of an independent adverb (GKC §113k).

עַד אֲשֶׁר־דַּק לְעָפָר. Adjunct PP, with a **null-head** relative clause as the object of עד. The predicate is *qatal* 3ms Qal √דקק. The 3ms *qatal* Qal of geminate verbs often has two letters (דַּק not דָּקַק) if it is intransitive and expressing a state (GKC §67bb). לעפר is adjunct PP, with ל introducing comparison, "*as* dust" (WO §11.2.10d#23; WHS §274b).

וָאַשְׁלִךְ אֶת־עֲפָרוֹ אֶל־הַנַּחַל הַיֹּרֵד מִן־הָהָר. *Wayyiqtol* 1cs Hiph √שלך. The *hireq* in the final syllable of *wayyiqtol* Hiphil is common for 1cs (unlike for 2ms, 3fs, 3ms), though often verbs in 1cs are spelled defectively (JM §54c). הירד is ptcp ms Qal √ירד, functioning as an attributive adjective. מן־ההר is spatial adjunct PP.

9:22 וּבְתַבְעֵרָה וּבְמַסָּה וּבְקִבְרֹת הַתַּאֲוָה מַקְצִפִים הֱיִיתֶם אֶת־יְהוָה:

ND. D2. Moses turns his attention to other scenes of Israel's behavior that triggered Yhwh's anger. The past progressive, *qatal* of the copula (√היה) with the participle, indicates the *consistently* provocative behavior.

וּבְתַבְעֵרָה וּבְמַסָּה וּבְקִבְרֹת הַתַּאֲוָה. Three spatial adjunct PPs, fronted as the **topic**, providing scene-setting information about the places where the provocation occurred (cf. v. 8).

מַקְצִפִים הֱיִיתֶם אֶת־יְהוָה. *Qatal* 2mp Qal √היה, with ptcp mp Hiph √קצף. See on v. 7.

9:23 וּבִשְׁלֹחַ יְהוָה אֶתְכֶם מִקָּדֵשׁ בַּרְנֵעַ לֵאמֹר עֲלוּ וּרְשׁוּ אֶת־הָאָרֶץ אֲשֶׁר נָתַתִּי לָכֶם וַתַּמְרוּ אֶת־פִּי יְהוָה אֱלֹהֵיכֶם וְלֹא הֶאֱמַנְתֶּם לוֹ וְלֹא שְׁמַעְתֶּם בְּקֹלוֹ:

A temporal protasis (v. 23a) is followed by a *wayyiqtol* temporal apodosis (v. 23b). This is the third instance of rebellious behavior identified by Moses. In the protasis, Moses repeats Yhwh's words (D3, HD), because the call to "possess the land" remains relevant to the Moab generation.

The apodosis is marked by a *wayyiqtol* followed by two negated *qatals*. All three combine to spell out Israel's lack of trust and obedience.

וּבִשְׁלֹחַ יְהוָה אֶתְכֶם מִקָּדֵשׁ בַּרְנֵעַ לֵאמֹר. Inf constr Qal √שלח with preposition בְּ. Temporal adjunct PP, functioning as an infinitival temporal clause (cf. WO §36.2.2b). The preposition בְּ attached to the infinitive construct often introduces temporal expressions (see on 6:7). מִקָּדֵשׁ בַּרְנֵעַ is spatial adjunct PP. See on 1:5 for the **complementizer** לֵאמֹר. The ו-conjunction at the start of the clause indicates that this continues the illustration of Israel's sinfulness from the previous verse.

עֲלוּ וּרְשׁוּ אֶת־הָאָרֶץ אֲשֶׁר נָתַתִּי לָכֶם. HD. Impv mp Qal √עלה and √ירשׁ. אֶת־הָאָרֶץ functions as the accusative complement of both verbs. הָאָרֶץ is the **head** of the following relative clause.

אֲשֶׁר נָתַתִּי לָכֶם. *Qatal* 1cs Qal √נתן. Restrictive relative clause.

וַתַּמְרוּ אֶת־פִּי יְהוָה אֱלֹהֵיכֶם. *Wayyiqtol* 2mp Hiph √מרה. A *wayyiqtol* often follows a temporal adjunct PP and introduces the temporal apodosis (GKC §111b; WO §33.3.5c; MNK §39.6.2). See on 1:26 for the identical phrase.

וְלֹא הֶאֱמַנְתֶּם לוֹ. *Qatal* 2mp Hiph √אמן. Normally √אמן Hiphil takes an oblique complement with preposition בְּ (see on 1:32). Here (and in Isa 43:10) it is with לְ, "trust," "believe."

וְלֹא שְׁמַעְתֶּם בְּקֹלוֹ. *Qatal* 2mp Qal √שמע. For √שמע with לֹא and בְּקוֹל, "not listen to," "disobey," see on 8:20.

9:24 מַמְרִים הֱיִיתֶם עִם־יְהוָה מִיּוֹם דַּעְתִּי אֶתְכֶם:

ND. D2. Moses returns to v. 7, having made his case. The past progressive shows the consistent pattern of rebelling.

מַמְרִים הֱיִיתֶם עִם־יְהוָה. *Qatal* 2mp Qal √היה, with ptcp mp Hiph √מרה. See on 9:7 for the identical phrase.

מִיּוֹם דַּעְתִּי אֶתְכֶם:. Inf constr Qal √ידע with 1cs pronominal (subject) suffix. An infinitive phrase as the object of preposition מִן, which denotes the starting time (MNK §39.14.2; WHS §316). The construct relationship is a type of subjective genitive which WO §9.5.1f term a "temporal genitive": "a verbal action G[enitive] associated with a time C[onstruct]." Some commentators favor reading דַּעְתּוֹ (so Smr), "he [i.e., Yhwh] knew" (e.g., Merrill, 196 n. 160; McConville, 177;

BHQ: Deuteronomy, 78*), but note 31:27, which shows the MT reading is plausible, since it is Moses' experience of the Israelites that is in view there.

Israel should remember Moses' intercession on their behalf (9:25-29)

Structurally, this continues from the preceding argument. This is still part of what Israel (in Moab) should remember and not forget (v. 7). In view of their inveterate rebelliousness, the only grounds for hope lay in the mediatorial intercession of Moses. Moses highlights Yhwh's promises and his reputation (vv. 27-28), with the prayer framed by Israel's identity as עמך ונחלתך rooted in Yhwh's action in bringing them out (הוצאת) with great power (vv. 26, 29).

> ²⁵*So I lay prostrate before Yhwh the forty days and forty nights that I was prostrate, for Yhwh had said that he was going to destroy you.* ²⁶*And I prayed to Yhwh and said, "Yhwh God, do not destroy your people who are your inheritance, whom you redeemed with your greatness, whom you brought out from Egypt by a strong hand.* ²⁷*Give a thought to your servants, to Abraham, Isaac, and Jacob. Do not pay attention to the stubbornness of this people or to their wickedness or to their sin,* ²⁸*lest the land from where you brought us out say, 'It is because Yhwh was unable to bring them into the land that he promised them and because he hates them that he brought them out to put them to death in the wilderness.'* ²⁹*They are your people, your inheritance, whom you brought out with your great strength and with your outstretched arm."*

9:25 וָאֶתְנַפַּל לִפְנֵי יְהוָה אֵת אַרְבָּעִים הַיּוֹם וְאֶת־אַרְבָּעִים הַלַּיְלָה אֲשֶׁר הִתְנַפָּלְתִּי כִּי־אָמַר יְהוָה לְהַשְׁמִיד אֶתְכֶם:

ND. D2. Moses recounts his prostration before Yhwh (v. 25a) and his motivation rooted in Yhwh's intention to destroy the rebellious people (v. 25b).

וָאֶתְנַפַּל לִפְנֵי יְהוָה אֵת אַרְבָּעִים הַיּוֹם וְאֶת־אַרְבָּעִים הַלַּיְלָה אֲשֶׁר הִתְנַפָּלְתִּי. *Wayyiqtol* 1cs Hitp √נפל. See on 9:18 for ואתנפל לפני יהוה.

אֵת אַרְבָּעִים הַיּוֹם וְאֶת־אַרְבָּעִים הַלַּיְלָה. Compound NP, expressing the length of time (JM §126i). It is very unusual to have the marker of the direct object, את, with indirect accusatives, including that of time

(JM §125e; WO §10.3.1c). This relates to the fact that only here is it the definite היום (rather than יום) after ארבעים (cf. GCK §118k). It is not simply a duration of forty days, but "*the* forty days . . ." (Driver, 116). The phrase is the **head** of the following relative clause.

אֲשֶׁ֣ר הִתְנַפַּ֗לְתִּי. *Qatal* 1cs Hitp √נפל (cf. on 9:18). Restrictive relative clause.

כִּֽי־אָמַ֤ר יְהוָה֙ לְהַשְׁמִ֣יד אֶתְכֶֽם׃. *Qatal* 3ms Qal √אמר. Explanatory clause introduced by subordinating conjunction כי. Note the P–S word order due to **triggered inversion**.

לְהַשְׁמִ֣יד אֶתְכֶֽם׃. Inf constr Hiph √שמד with preposition ל. This infinitive phrase is the complement of the verb אמר. ל + infinitive construct sometimes functions as the direct object of a verb (GKC §114m; WO §36.2.1d; JM §124c, m; WHS §193, §276).

9:26 וָאֶתְפַּלֵּ֣ל אֶל־יְהוָה֮ וָאֹמַר֒ אֲדֹנָ֣י יְהוִ֗ה אַל־תַּשְׁחֵ֤ת עַמְּךָ֙ וְנַחֲלָ֣תְךָ֔ אֲשֶׁ֥ר פָּדִ֖יתָ בְּגָדְלֶ֑ךָ אֲשֶׁר־הוֹצֵ֥אתָ מִמִּצְרַ֖יִם בְּיָ֥ד חֲזָקָֽה׃

Moses recalls his prayer (ND, D2). Syntactically, the prayer is a prohibition, but given the status gap between speaker and addressee, it is a request (D3, HD). His request not to "destroy" (√שחת) tacitly acknowledges the rightness of that verdict by recalling Yhwh's word for Israel's corrupt action (√שחת, v. 12; cf. 4:16, 25, 31).

וָאֶתְפַּלֵּ֣ל אֶל־יְהוָה֮ וָאֹמַר֒. *Wayyiqtol* 1cs Hitp √פלל and Qal √אמר. The *yiqtol* and *wayyiqtol* 1cs Qal of I-א verbs have one א. The direct speech that follows is the complement of √אמר.

אֲדֹנָ֣י יְהוִ֗ה אַל־תַּשְׁחֵ֤ת עַמְּךָ֙ וְנַחֲלָ֣תְךָ֔. Jussive 2ms Hiph √שחת. A prohibition (with אל); see on 1:17. Here it is a prayer, addressed to Yhwh (GKC §109c; JM §114i), and functions as an optative, expressing Moses' wish (JM §163a). אדני יהוה is vocative, indicating the addressee (for the vocalization, see on 3:24). The vocative in Hebrew is not the subject, but stands in apposition, here with the **pro** subject in תשחת. עמך ונחלתך is accusative complement of √שחת, functioning as a **hendiadys**, speaking of one referent with two words (cf. 7:9, 12).

אֲשֶׁ֥ר פָּדִ֖יתָ בְּגָדְלֶ֑ךָ. *Qatal* 2ms Qal √פדה. Restrictive relative clause, with **head** עמך ונחלתך. בגדלך is adjunct PP (cf. 3:24), with instrumental use of ב (cf. WHS §243).

אֲשֶׁר־הוֹצֵאתָ מִמִּצְרַיִם בְּיָד חֲזָקָה׃. *Qatal* 2ms Hiph √יצא. מצרים is spatial adjunct PP. ביד חזקה is adjunct PP, with instrumental use of ב (cf. WHS §243). Both גדל and יד חזקה occur in Moses' plea in 3:24. Moses "quotes" Yhwh, rejecting Yhwh's attribution of the exodus to Moses (cf. v. 12). Moses insists Yhwh brought Israel out from Egypt. This second restrictive relative clause with **head** עמך ונחלתך follows asyndetically from the previous one; together they form a complementary picture of Yhwh's action for his people, not a sequential one.

9:27 זְכֹר לַעֲבָדֶיךָ לְאַבְרָהָם לְיִצְחָק וּלְיַעֲקֹב אַל־תֵּפֶן אֶל־קְשִׁי הָעָם הַזֶּה וְאֶל־רִשְׁעוֹ וְאֶל־חַטָּאתוֹ׃

D3. HD. Moses continues his prayer. In his appeal, Moses calls on Yhwh to remember the patriarchs (imperative, v. 27a) and to turn a blind eye to the stubbornness and wickedness of the people (prohibition, אל + jussive, v. 27b).

זְכֹר לַעֲבָדֶיךָ לְאַבְרָהָם לְיִצְחָק וּלְיַעֲקֹב. *Impv* ms Qal √זכר. HD. לעבדיך is oblique complement; ל serves to introduce the direct object of the verb (JM §125k; cf. WHS §273b). לאברהם ליצחק וליעקב are three PPs in apposition to לעבדיך.

אַל־תֵּפֶן אֶל־קְשִׁי הָעָם הַזֶּה וְאֶל־רִשְׁעוֹ וְאֶל־חַטָּאתוֹ׃. *Jussive* 2ms Qal √פנה. A prohibition (with אַל); see on 1:17. As a III-ה verb, the ה **apocopates** in the jussive. For the vocalization of that form, see JM §79i. Three adjunct PPs follow the verb. √פנה followed by אל is "turn toward," whether literally (Exod 16:10) or metaphorically (31:18); here the metaphor is extended further, "[don't] pay attention to"; an idiomatic English phrase is "turn a blind eye to. . . ." The construct noun קְשִׁי is an OT *hapax* (cf. קשה, 9:6, 13). רשעו is the segholate noun רֶשַׁע with 3ms pronominal suffix. When pronominal suffixes attach to segholates, the original primitive form usually appears (JM §96c, e, g).

9:28 פֶּן־יֹאמְרוּ הָאָרֶץ אֲשֶׁר הוֹצֵאתָנוּ מִשָּׁם מִבְּלִי יְכֹלֶת יְהוָה לַהֲבִיאָם אֶל־הָאָרֶץ אֲשֶׁר־דִּבֶּר לָהֶם וּמִשִּׂנְאָתוֹ אוֹתָם הוֹצִיאָם לַהֲמִתָם בַּמִּדְבָּר׃

Moses continues recounting his prayer (D3). In a negative purpose clause, Moses gives the reason why Yhwh should turn a blind eye to

Israel's wickedness: Egypt will think Yhwh is powerless or heartless (v. 28aβ-b; D4). Yhwh's own reputation is at stake.

פֶּן־יֹאמְרוּ הָאָ֫רֶץ אֲשֶׁ֨ר הוֹצֵאתָ֫נוּ מִשָּׁ֫ם פֶּ֫ן. *Yiqtol* 3mp Qal √אמר introduces a negative purpose clause and is followed by a *yiqtol*. It serves "to indicate a negative wish of a speaker or speakers . . . 'I (or: we) do not wish the following to be, become or have become a reality'" (JM §168g). The accusative complement is the direct speech that follows. The subject, הארץ, is feminine singular, while the verb is masculine plural. הארץ is idiomatic, a metonymy for the inhabitants of the land (cf. Gen 41:57; GKC §145e).

אֲשֶׁ֨ר הוֹצֵאתָ֫נוּ מִשָּׁ֫ם. *Qatal* 2ms Hiph √יצא with 1cp pronominal suffix. Restrictive relative clause with **head** הארץ. משם is spatial adjunct PP, with שם a resumptive adverb in the relative clause: Hebrew "which . . . from there" = English "from where. . . ."

מִבְּלִ֞י יְכֹ֣לֶת יְהוָ֗ה לַהֲבִיאָ֛ם אֶל־הָאָ֖רֶץ אֲשֶׁר־דִּבֶּ֥ר לָהֶֽם. Inf constr Qal √יכל. The pointing of this infinitive construct is not unprecedented (יְבֹ֫שֶׁת, Gen 8:7), but "of a very rare type" (JM §75i; cf. GKC §45e). It is possible that the form is due to the verb being the governing or construct noun ("*nomen regens*") followed by an absolute (JM §124h). If so, יהוה is a subjective genitive, the agent of the action found in the construct (cf.; WO §9.5.1b, בשנאת יהוה in 1:27, and משנאתו here). Alternatively, יהוה is simply the subject of the infinitive. The normal way of negating an infinitive construct is לְבִלְתִּי; sometimes מִבִּלְתִּי is found (cf. parallel passage in Num 14:16). מבלי comprises the rare poetic negative בלי (see on 4:42) and the preposition מן, which expresses the grounds or cause (JM §170i; cf. 7:8). Only here does it negate an infinitive construct (JM §160l n. 17). The extended PP is fronted for **focus**, inviting a contrast with other possible reasons for why Yhwh has brought Israel out.

לַהֲבִיאָ֛ם אֶל־הָאָ֫רֶץ. Inf constr Hiph √בוא with 3mp pronominal suffix with preposition ל. Together with its direct object, the suffix ם-, and the adjunct PP אל־הארץ, the phrase forms an infinitive phrase complement, after √יכל.

אֲשֶׁר־דִּבֶּ֥ר לָהֶֽם. *Qatal* 3ms Piel √דבר. Restrictive relative clause with **head** הארץ. For the form of דבר, see on 1:1. Moses declares that Egypt is well aware of Yhwh's promise (thus corroborating it for the Israelites), but what is at stake is Yhwh's ability (or willingness) to keep it.

וּמִשִּׂנְאָתוֹ אוֹתָם. Inf constr Qal √שׂנא with 3ms pronominal suffix and with preposition מִן. The pronominal suffix functions as the subject of the verb. For the form of the infinitive construct and the syntax, see on 1:27 (where the subject is the genitive יהוה). The preposition מִן expresses the grounds or cause (see above). The extended PP is coordinated with the previous one, and is also fronted for **focus**.

הוֹצִיאָם לַהֲמִתָם בַּמִּדְבָּר. *Qatal* 3ms Hiph √יצא with 3mp pronominal suffix. ND. D4.

לַהֲמִתָם בַּמִּדְבָּר. Inf constr Hiph √מות with 3mp pronominal suffix (object), and with preposition לְ. Infinitive phrase adjunct of הוציאם, expressing purpose. במדבר is spatial adjunct PP.

9:29 וְהֵם עַמְּךָ וְנַחֲלָתֶךָ אֲשֶׁר הוֹצֵאתָ בְּכֹחֲךָ הַגָּדֹל
וּבִזְרֹעֲךָ הַנְּטוּיָה: פ

D3. ED. Moses completes his appeal by reminding Yhwh again of his special relationship with his people and his prior action (cf. v. 26).

וְהֵם עַמְּךָ וְנַחֲלָתֶךָ. ED. **Null-copula** circumstantial clause, with substantival predicate, the **hendiadys** עמך ונחלתך (see on v. 26). Unmarked S–P word order.

אֲשֶׁר הוֹצֵאתָ בְּכֹחֲךָ הַגָּדֹל וּבִזְרֹעֲךָ הַנְּטוּיָה: פ. *Qatal* 2ms Hiph √יצא. Non-restrictive relative clause, with **head** עמך ונחלתך.

בְּכֹחֲךָ הַגָּדֹל וּבִזְרֹעֲךָ הַנְּטוּיָה:. Two adjunct PPs. Both have occurred before (the first in 4:37; the second in 4:34), but the 2ms pronominal suffix is only here (and, outside Deuteronomy, in Jer 32:17, of Yhwh's creating act). Moses is reminding Yhwh of his own actions.

Israel should remember the second chance Yhwh gave (10:1-11)

Structurally, this continues what Israel (in Moab) should remember and not forget (9:7). Self-righteousness is unwarranted (9:7-24); Moses' intercession provides the only way out (9:25-29). In vv. 1-11, Moses spells out Yhwh's gracious response, a second chance for the people at Horeb expressed through the new set of stone tablets. The section concludes with Moses recalling that Yhwh heard his prayer and told him to set out so the people could take possession of the land. Those in Moab can be confident, but not in themselves.

¹At that time Yhwh said to me, "Hew for yourself two stone tablets like the first ones, and come up to me on the mountain, and make for yourself an ark of wood, ²that I may write on the tablets the words that were on the first tablets that you broke, and put them in the ark." ³So I made an ark of acacia wood and I hewed out two stone tablets like the first ones, and I went up on the mountain, with the two tablets in my hand. ⁴Then he wrote on the tablets, with the same writing as before, the ten words that Yhwh spoke to you on the mountain from the midst of the fire on the day of the assembly, and Yhwh gave them to me. ⁵Then I turned and went down from the mountain, and I put the tablets in the ark that I had made, and so they were there, just as Yhwh commanded me. [⁶The Israelites journeyed from Beeroth-benejaakan to Moserah. It was there that Aaron died, and he was buried there, and Eleazar his son acted as a priest in his place. ⁷From there they journeyed to Gudgod, and from Gudgod to Jotbah, a land of wadis with water.] ⁸At that time Yhwh set apart the tribe of Levites to carry the ark of the covenant of Yhwh, to stand before Yhwh, to serve him and to bless in his name—until this day. ⁹Therefore Levi has not had a share or inheritance with his brothers—Yhwh is his inheritance, just as Yhwh your God promised him. ¹⁰So I had stood on the mountain, as the first time, for forty days and forty nights, and Yhwh listened to me at that time, too—Yhwh was not willing to destroy you. ¹¹Then Yhwh said to me, "Get up, go to journey in front of the people that they may enter and possess the land that I swore to their ancestors, to give to them."

10:1 בָּעֵ֨ת הַהִ֜וא אָמַ֧ר יְהוָ֣ה אֵלַ֗י פְּסָל־לְךָ֞ שְׁנֵֽי־לוּחֹ֤ת אֲבָנִים֙ כָּרִ֣אשֹׁנִ֔ים וַעֲלֵ֥ה אֵלַ֖י הָהָ֑רָה וְעָשִׂ֥יתָ לְּךָ֖ אֲר֥וֹן עֵֽץ׃

With a general temporal introduction, Moses recalls Yhwh's words to him (D2, ND). Yhwh gives three instructions (HD, D3), two imperatives followed by a modal *qatal*. Moses' narrative connects his intercession with Yhwh's reissuing of the decalogue.

בָּעֵ֨ת הַהִ֜וא אָמַ֧ר יְהוָ֣ה אֵלַ֗י. *Qatal* 3ms Qal √אמר. בעת ההוא is temporal adjunct PP giving more general indication of the time of speaking (see on 1:9 for the form ההוא). It is fronted as a scene-setting (temporal) **topic**.

פְּסָל־לְךָ֞ שְׁנֵֽי־לוּחֹ֤ת אֲבָנִים֙ כָּרִ֣אשֹׁנִ֔ים. Impv ms Qal √פסל. The verb פסל, "hew," is related to פֶּסֶל, "idol" (cf. 4:16; 5:8). לך is adjunct PP.

The ל could be reflexive. When the preposition ל, attached to a pronoun that has the same referent as the subject of the verb as with לְךָ here, indicates reflexive nuance, it isolates and focuses attention on the subject (JM §133d; GKC §119s; WHS §272). Perhaps more likely given לְךָ with √עשׂה later in the verse is that ל here introduces the "dative of advantage," giving the beneficiary of the action of the verb (cf. GKC §119q-s; JM §133d; WO §11.2.10d; WHS §271a). For the accusative complement שְׁנֵי־לוּחֹת אֲבָנִים, here indefinite, see on 9:10. כָּרִאשֹׁנִים is comparative adjunct PP; the comparison is with לוּחֹת, hence the adjective is masculine plural. For the form, see on 9:18, though there it is an adverb.

וַעֲלֵה אֵלַי הָהָרָה. Impv ms Qal √עלה. הָהָרָה is the directional adjunct. The locative ה on הָהָר indicates motion toward (WO §10.5a, b; JM §93c).

וְעָשִׂיתָ לְּךָ אֲרוֹן עֵץ׃. Qatal (modal) 2ms Qal √עשׂה. A modal qatal often follows an imperative (e.g., 4:9). Here there are two imperatives followed by a modal qatal. Although the making of the ark is missing in the Exodus account, the syntax here is found elsewhere so is not evidence of an addition here (cf. Exod 9:13; 2 Kgs 8:8). The modal qatal is typically associated with, while not entailing, succession (JM §119i). Here, however, succession cannot be in view, for the making of the ark can hardly be meant to be up the mountain, and Moses does not take it that way (n.b., order in v. 3). לְךָ is adjunct PP, with ל introducing the dative of advantage (see above; cf. 4:16; 5:8; 9:16, all with √עשׂה, notwithstanding the fact that what is constructed in those three places is counter to Yhwh's commands). The euphonic *dagesh forte* in לְּךָ is due to rhythm after unaccented [ה]- (cf. GKC §20f). אֲרוֹן עֵץ is accusative complement construct NP. עֵץ is an attributive adjectival genitive, sometimes termed "material," where the absolute gives the material of which the construct is made (WHS §40a; AC §2.2.10; cf. WO §9.5.3d).

10:2 וְאֶכְתֹּב עַל־הַלֻּחֹת אֶת־הַדְּבָרִים אֲשֶׁר הָיוּ עַל־הַלֻּחֹת הָרִאשֹׁנִים אֲשֶׁר שִׁבַּרְתָּ וְשַׂמְתָּם בָּאָרוֹן׃

D3. HD. An **indirect volitive** gives the purpose of Moses' hewing and ascent (v. 2a); a modal *qatal* then continues Yhwh's instructions to Moses (v. 2b; cf. v. 1).

וָאֶכְתֹּב עַל־הַלֻּחֹת אֶת־הַדְּבָרִים. *Yiqtol* (modal) 1cs Qal √כתב. HD. Although not morphologically marked, its position at the start of the clause and the sequence of verbs (imperatives and modal *qatals*) of which it is a part indicate it is an **indirect volitive** (cf. JM §116b). The clause is syntactically coordinated with the previous clause, "hew and come up . . . and I will write," but semantically subordinate, providing the purpose of Moses' hewing and ascent, "hew and come up . . . *that* I *may* write." על־הלחת is adjunct PP. את־הדברים is accusative complement. The word order avoids the **extraposition** of the **head** of the restrictive relative clause, את־הדברים, and the displacement of על־הלחת after the relative clause.

אֲשֶׁר הָיוּ עַל־הַלֻּחֹת הָרִאשֹׁנִים אֲשֶׁר שִׁבַּרְתָּ. *Qatal* 3cp Qal √היה. Restrictive relative clause, with *qatal* copula and PP complement. For the form of הראשנים, see on 9:18.

אֲשֶׁר שִׁבַּרְתָּ. *Qatal* 2ms Qal √שבר. Restrictive relative clause with **head** הלחת הראשנים.

וְשַׂמְתָּם בָּאָרוֹן. *Qatal* (modal) 2ms Qal √שים with 3mp pronominal suffix. HD. בארון is oblique complement.

10:3 וָאַעַשׂ אֲרוֹן עֲצֵי שִׁטִּים וָאֶפְסֹל שְׁנֵי־לֻחֹת אֲבָנִים כָּרִאשֹׁנִים וָאַעַל הָהָרָה וּשְׁנֵי הַלֻּחֹת בְּיָדִי:

ND. Three *wayyiqtols* highlight Moses' obedient response. The final clause is circumstantial, preparing the way for Yhwh's action (v. 4).

וָאַעַשׂ אֲרוֹן עֲצֵי שִׁטִּים. *Wayyiqtol* 1cs Qal √עשה. There is often **apocopation** of the ה- with *wayyiqtol* of III-ה verbs. שִׁטָּה is an acacia tree. ארון עצי שטים is accusative complement construct NP, "an ark of acacia wood" (cf. on 10:1).

וָאֶפְסֹל שְׁנֵי־לֻחֹת אֲבָנִים כָּרִאשֹׁנִים. *Wayyiqtol* 1cs Qal √פסל. See on 10:1 for the rest of the clause.

וָאַעַל הָהָרָה. *Wayyiqtol* 1cs Qal √עלה. See on ויעש above for the **apocopation** of the ה. ההרה is the directional adjunct (for the locative ה, see on v. 1).

וּשְׁנֵי הַלֻּחֹת בְּיָדִי: **Null-copula** circumstantial clause with unmarked S–P word order. It gives background information rather than advancing the storyline. The predicate (or complement) is the PP, בְּיָדִי. See on 3:8 for the syntax of שְׁנַיִם, "two."

10:4 וַיִּכְתֹּב עַל־הַלֻּחֹת כַּמִּכְתָּב הָרִאשׁוֹן אֵת עֲשֶׂרֶת הַדְּבָרִים אֲשֶׁר דִּבֶּר יְהוָה אֲלֵיכֶם בָּהָר מִתּוֹךְ הָאֵשׁ בְּיוֹם הַקָּהָל וַיִּתְּנֵם יְהוָה אֵלָי׃

ND. D2. Two *wayyiqtols* continue Moses' recounting of the events on the mountain. In the previous verse, it was Moses' obedient action. Here, it is Yhwh as agent: writing and giving.

וַיִּכְתֹּב עַל־הַלֻּחֹת כַּמִּכְתָּב הָרִאשׁוֹן אֵת עֲשֶׂרֶת הַדְּבָרִים. *Wayyiqtol* 3ms Qal √כתב. עַל־הַלֻּחֹת is spatial adjunct PP. כַּמִּכְתָּב הָרִאשׁוֹן is comparative adjunct PP. The comparative preposition כ "expresses a relation of either perfect (equality), or imperfect (resemblance) similitude" (JM §133g). Presumably the fact Yhwh is inscribing them indicates the comparison is exact. מִכְתָּב is "writing," hence "inscription." Hebrew often prefixes a root with מ to form a noun (WO §5.6b). See on 9:18 for הָרִאשׁוֹן. See on 4:13 for the accusative complement, (אֵת) עֲשֶׂרֶת הַדְּבָרִים.

אֲשֶׁר דִּבֶּר יְהוָה אֲלֵיכֶם בָּהָר מִתּוֹךְ הָאֵשׁ בְּיוֹם הַקָּהָל. *Qatal* 3ms Piel √דבר. For the form with *segol*, see on 1:1. Restrictive relative clause with **head** עֲשֶׂרֶת הַדְּבָרִים. Three adjunct PPs follow (בהר . . . הקהל). See on 9:10 for all three.

וַיִּתְּנֵם יְהוָה אֵלָי. *Wayyiqtol* 3ms Qal √נתן with 3mp pronominal suffix.

10:5 וָאֵפֶן וָאֵרֵד מִן־הָהָר וָאָשִׂם אֶת־הַלֻּחֹת בָּאָרוֹן אֲשֶׁר עָשִׂיתִי וַיִּהְיוּ שָׁם כַּאֲשֶׁר צִוַּנִי יְהוָה׃

ND. D2. Three *wayyiqtols* outline Moses' further actions. A concluding phrase, "and so they were there" marks the end of Moses' narrative about the renewed gift of the tablets; Moses has been obedient throughout.

וָאֵפֶן וָאֵרֵד מִן־הָהָר. *Wayyiqtol* 1cs Qal √פנה and √ירד. מִן־הָהָר is spatial adjunct PP. See on 9:15 for the identical phrase.

וָאָשִׂם אֶת־הַלֻּחֹת בָּאָרוֹן אֲשֶׁר עָשִׂיתִי. *Wayyiqtol* 1cs Qal √שׂים. בארון is oblique complement, with ארון the **head** of the following restrictive relative clause.

אֲשֶׁר עָשִׂיתִי. *Qatal* 1cs Qal √עשׂה. Restrictive relative clause.

וַיִּהְיוּ שָׁם. *Wayyiqtol* 3mp Qal √היה. Sometimes the tone shifts back, or "recedes" (e.g., וְאֻפָן above and many *wayyiqtols*, הַשֹּׁמֵר in 4:9); the reasons can be articulated (see GKC §29d-f). Here, the shift in accent from וַיִּהְיוּ to וְיִהְיוּ is "abnormal" (GKC §29g). שָׁם is a locative adverb, functioning as the oblique complement (cf. Holmstedt 2010: 61). The *wayyiqtol* suggests past time, "were there" (cp. ETs); a temporal adjunct עַד־הַיּוֹם הַזֶּה, "until this day" would be necessary to give the perfect, "have been *and still are* there" (cf. Ruth 1:2 [no temporal adjunct]; Josh 4:9; 1 Kgs 8:8). The point is that Moses deposited the tablets in the ark as commanded; it is Moses' past obedience not the tablets' present location that is in view.

כַּאֲשֶׁר צִוַּנִי יְהוָה:. *Qatal* 3ms Piel √צוה with 1cs pronominal suffix. Comparative clause. See on 4:5 for the identical phrase.

וּבְנֵי יִשְׂרָאֵל נָסְעוּ מִבְּאֵרֹת בְּנֵי־יַעֲקָן מוֹסֵרָה שָׁם 10:6
מֵת אַהֲרֹן וַיִּקָּבֵר שָׁם וַיְכַהֵן אֶלְעָזָר בְּנוֹ תַּחְתָּיו:

ND. D1. The shift from conjunctive clauses with *wayyiqtol* to a disjunctive clause with *qatal* and the change to speaking of the Israelites in the 3rd person indicate that this is a parenthetical comment of the narrator. The opening *qatal* clause is followed asyndetically by a *qatal* clause and two *wayyiqtols*. Together they give an account of events at Moserah.

וּבְנֵי יִשְׂרָאֵל נָסְעוּ מִבְּאֵרֹת בְּנֵי־יַעֲקָן מוֹסֵרָה. *Qatal* 3cp Qal √נסע. מבארת בני־יעקן is spatial adjunct PP. מוסרה is a directional adjunct; the final ה is not locative ה because the accent is on the final syllable and locative ה does not attract the accent (cf. JM §93c). The place is Moserah, not Moser (cp. הגדגדה and יטבתה below).

שָׁם מֵת אַהֲרֹן. *Qatal* 3ms Qal √מות. שׁם is locative adverb, fronted as a scene-setting (spatial) **topic**. The clause follows asyndetically, indicating that the journeying narrative is not advancing; rather, an event at Moserah is being described.

וַיִּקָּבֵר שָׁם. *Wayyiqtol* 3ms Niph √קבר. The *wayyiqtol* continues the description begun in the previous clause.

וַיְכַהֵן אֶלְעָזָר בְּנוֹ תַּחְתָּיו:. *Wayyiqtol* 3ms Piel √כהן. The verb only occurs in the Piel, and means "to act as a priest." בנו is appositional NP to אֶלְעָזָר. תַּחְתָּיו is adjunct PP. The preposition תחת takes prepositions associated with plural nouns (cf. GKC §103n-o). The *wayyiqtol* continues the description begun in the previous clause.

10:7 מִשָּׁ֥ם נָסְע֖וּ הַגֻּדְגֹּ֑דָה וּמִן־הַגֻּדְגֹּ֙דָה֙ יָטְבָ֔תָה אֶ֖רֶץ נַ֥חֲלֵי מָֽיִם׃

ND. D1. The journey continues.

מִשָּׁ֥ם נָסְע֖וּ הַגֻּדְגֹּ֑דָה. *Qatal* 3cp Qal √נסע. משם is PP spatial adjunct, fronted as a scene-setting (spatial) **topic**. הגדגדה is a directional adjunct. The locative ה on הגדגדה indicates motion toward (WO §10.5a, b; JM §93c). The **asyndesis** marks a break from the preceding clauses.

וּמִן־הַגֻּדְגֹּ֙דָה֙ יָטְבָ֔תָה אֶ֖רֶץ נַ֥חֲלֵי מָֽיִם. ומן־הגדגדה is spatial adjunct PP. Sometimes no sense of motion toward is implied by locative ־ָה (n.b., it occurs after the preposition מן; see JM §93f). יטבתה is a directional adjunct with locative ה. ארץ נחלי מים is appositional construct NP. M^L lacks an accent in נַ֥חֲלֵי. This could be because a *maqqef* is missing (cf. Mic 6:7) or because an accent has been omitted (*BHQ: Deuteronomy*, 79*).

10:8 בָּעֵ֣ת הַהִ֗וא הִבְדִּ֤יל יְהוָה֙ אֶת־שֵׁ֣בֶט הַלֵּוִ֔י לָשֵׂ֖את אֶת־אֲר֣וֹן בְּרִית־יְהוָ֑ה לַעֲמֹד֩ לִפְנֵ֨י יְהוָ֤ה לְשָֽׁרְתוֹ֙ וּלְבָרֵ֣ךְ בִּשְׁמ֔וֹ עַ֖ד הַיּ֥וֹם הַזֶּֽה׃

ND. D2. The narrator's aside has ended (n.b., 2ms pronominal suffix, אלהיך, in v. 9 and the repeated בעת ההוא; cf. v. 1; see DeRouchie 2007: 257; Lundbom, 384–85). A *qatal* is followed by four adjunct infinitive phrases expressing purpose. The final temporal adjunct phrase connects the day of the events with Moses' own day.

בָּעֵ֣ת הַהִ֗וא הִבְדִּ֤יל יְהוָה֙ אֶת־שֵׁ֣בֶט הַלֵּוִ֔י. *Qatal* 3ms Hiph √בדל. ND. For the temporal adjunct PP בעת ההוא, see on 1:9. It is fronted as a scene-setting (temporal) **topic** (cf. v. 1), hence the subsequent word order is P–S. הלוי, the absolute in the accusative complement construct NP, has the article, indicating that it is not the proper name, but a gentilic adjective (GKC §125d n. 1; cf. on המנשה in 3:13).

לָשֵׂ֖את אֶת־אֲר֣וֹן בְּרִית־יְהוָ֑ה. Inf constr Qal √נשא with preposition ל. Without the preposition, the form is שֵׂאת (e.g., 1:9). But with ל, it is always as here (GKC §76b). Adjunct infinitive phrase to verb הַבְדִּיל, expressing purpose. אֶת־אֲרוֹן בְּרִית־יְהוָה is accusative complement construct NP.

לִפְנֵי יְהוָה. לַעֲמֹד לִפְנֵי יְהוָה. Inf constr Qal √עמד with preposition ל. לִפְנֵי יהוה is spatial adjunct PP. √עמד followed by preposition לִפְנֵי has the connotation of "stand respectfully before," whether of Joshua before Moses (1:38), of the people before Yhwh (4:10), or, as here, of the Levites before the ark (cf. HALOT s.v.).

לְשָׁרְתוֹ. Inf constr Piel √שרת with 3ms pronominal (object) suffix and with preposition ל.

וּלְבָרֵךְ בִּשְׁמוֹ עַד הַיּוֹם הַזֶּה. Inf constr Piel √ברך with preposition ל. בשמו is adjunct PP. עד היום הזה is temporal adjunct PP. For the phrase, see on 2:22 (cf. 3:14; 11:4).

עַל־כֵּן לֹא־הָיָה לְלֵוִי חֵלֶק וְנַחֲלָה עִם־אֶחָיו יְהוָה 10:9
הוּא נַחֲלָתוֹ כַּאֲשֶׁר דִּבֶּר יְהוָה אֱלֹהֶיךָ לוֹ:

ND. D2. Moses grounds the lack of inheritance for the Levites in Yhwh's separation for service (v. 9a; cf. v. 8). An asyndetic **null-copula** clause expands on that—Yhwh is their inheritance (v. 9b).

עַל־כֵּן לֹא־הָיָה לְלֵוִי חֵלֶק וְנַחֲלָה עִם־אֶחָיו. *Qatal* 3ms Qal √היה. The verb is singular, while the coordinated subject following, חלק ונחלה, is plural. This is quite common when the subject follows the predicate and the subject is not personal; it is also often the case, as here, with the verb היה as the copula (GKC §145q; WHS §228; JM §150j). The *qatal* indicates that Moses is less concerned with what is now the case, and more with the events at the time (cf. on שם ויהיו in v. 5). על־כן is adjunct PP. The adverb כן has acquired substantival value, and so may be the object of a preposition, על, "therefore" (GKC §119ii); here it refers back to the previous clauses, and together with על gives the cause for the action of this clause (cf. JM §170h). לְלֵוִי is the adverbial PP complement of the overt copula, היה, with the ל indicating possession (cf. WO §11.2.10d). The lack of article here (לְלֵוִי not לַלֵּוִי; cf. v. 8, הַלֵּוִי) shows that it is the proper name, Levi, used eponymously for the tribe of which he is the ancestor. For that reason, I have chosen to retain 3ms in translation. עִם־אחיו is adjunct PP, to be taken closely with the subject חלק ונחלה.

יְהוָה הוּא נַחֲלָתוֹ. This is a **tripartite** nominal clause. As discussed on 1:17, there are two ways of understanding such clauses: הוא is either a resumptive pronoun referring to the **extraposed** (or dislocated or *casus pendens*) noun (יהוה) or a pronominal copula. The decision is finely balanced. Given that the previous clause declares what is *not* their inheritance, it is plausible this clause provides a contrast, saying what *is*: יהוה is **extraposed**, inviting a contrast with other possible subjects (as in 3:22, where there is the same word order; so JM §154j). But reading הוא as a copula (so Holmstedt and Jones, 83) also makes good sense, because the clause follows asyndetically from the previous one. Rather than a strong affirmation, it is an almost parenthetical expansion, so I (marginally) favor הוא as pronominal copula.

כַּאֲשֶׁר דִּבֶּר יְהוָה אֱלֹהֶיךָ לוֹ׃. *Qatal* 3ms Piel √דבר. For the form of דבר, see on 1:1. Comparative clause, introduced by כאשר, emphasizing Yhwh's faithfulness. After כאשר, there is usually **triggered inversion**, with P–S word order. לו has as its object the pronoun referring back to לוי.

10:10 וְאָנֹכִי עָמַדְתִּי בָהָר כַּיָּמִים הָרִאשֹׁנִים אַרְבָּעִים יוֹם
וְאַרְבָּעִים לָיְלָה וַיִּשְׁמַע יְהוָה אֵלַי גַּם בַּפַּעַם הַהִוא
לֹא־אָבָה יְהוָה הַשְׁחִיתֶךָ׃

ND. D2. The anterior construction (Zevit) or pluperfect, with ו + X + *qatal*, enables a flashback to prior events (9:18-19; see Lundbom, 386). The *wayyiqtol* (v. 10b) affirms that Yhwh had heard Moses' prayer.

וְאָנֹכִי עָמַדְתִּי בָהָר כַּיָּמִים הָרִאשֹׁנִים אַרְבָּעִים יוֹם וְאַרְבָּעִים לָיְלָה. *Qatal* 1cs Qal √עמד. The inclusion of the overt pronominal subject, אנכי, has two functions. First, it marks Moses out again as the **discourse active topic** after the break in vv. 8-9. Second, it enables a break from the *wayyiqtol* sequence that would naturally suggest a subsequent event and enables a pluperfect, "had" (Weinfeld, 405; cf. GKC §106f and, esp. Zevit). For the form אנכי, see on 4:1. בהר is spatial adjunct PP. כימים הראשנים is comparative adjunct PP. ארבעים יום וארבעים לילה is an indirect or adverbial accusative, giving the length of time Moses was on the mountain. See on 9:9.

וַיִּשְׁמַע יְהוָה אֵלַי גַּם בַּפַּעַם הַהִוא. *Wayyiqtol* 3ms Qal √שמע. See on 9:19 for the identical phrase.

לֹא־אָבָה יְהוָה הַשְׁחִיתֶֽךָ׃. *Qatal* 3ms Qal √אבה. Asyndetic clause explaining what it meant for Yhwh to "listen" to Moses.

הַשְׁחִיתֶֽךָ׃. Inf constr Hiph √שחת with 2ms pronominal suffix (object), functioning as the infinitive complement of אבה (cf. WO §36.2.1d; WHS §193). Yhwh had been minded to destroy Israel (√שחת, 9:16); Moses had pleaded with Yhwh not to do so (√שחת, 9:26). Now closure comes—Yhwh is no longer willing to destroy them (√שחת).

10:11 וַיֹּאמֶר יְהוָה אֵלַי קוּם לֵךְ לְמַסַּע לִפְנֵי הָעָם וְיָבֹאוּ וְיִֽירְשׁוּ אֶת־הָאָרֶץ אֲשֶׁר־נִשְׁבַּעְתִּי לַאֲבֹתָם לָתֵת לָהֶֽם׃ פ

Moses recounts Yhwh's words (ND, D2). In them, Yhwh exhorts Moses (HD, D3) to get going. The two imperatives are followed by two jussives which are semantically subordinate. The people's entry and possession depended on Moses' movement.

וַיֹּאמֶר יְהוָה אֵלַי. *Wayyiqtol* 3ms Qal √אמר. ND. The accusative complement is the direct speech that follows.

קוּם לֵךְ לְמַסַּע לִפְנֵי הָעָם. Impv ms Qal √קום and Qal √הלך. HD. Two imperatives frequently occur asyndetically, especially where the first involves movement (JM §177e). This coordination is an alternative mode of expression to subordination, and the second verb expresses the main idea (cf. GKC §120d, g). It is a mark of elevated or rhetorical style (cf. GKC §120h). לפני העם is spatial adjunct PP, to be taken closely with למסע.

לְמַסַּע. Inf constr Qal √נסע with preposition ל. Rather than a substantive (so BDB s.v.), it is a rare type of infinitive construct with Aramaic מ-prefix (GKC §45e; JM §49e). Adjunct infinitive phrase, expressing purpose.

וְיָבֹאוּ וְיִֽירְשׁוּ אֶת־הָאָרֶץ. Jussive 3mp Qal √בוא and √ירש. The previous imperatives indicate the discourse as hortatory. The sequence of verbs and the *yiqtol* forms coming first in the clause indicate that these are **indirect volitives** (cf. JM §116b). The clauses are syntactically coordinated with the previous clause, "get up, go . . . and they will enter and possess," but semantically subordinate, providing the purpose, "get up, go . . . *that* they *may* enter and possess. . . ."

אֲשֶׁר־נִשְׁבַּעְתִּי לַאֲבֹתָם לָתֵת לָהֶם: פ. *Qatal* 1cs Niph √שבע. Restrictive relative clause with **head** הָאָרֶץ. For the syntax of the phrase, see on 1:9. לאבתם is oblique complement. The 3mp pronominal suffix on the plural noun אֲבוֹת is often not ־יהֶם but ־ָם (JM §94g).

לָתֵת לָהֶם. Inf constr Qal √נתן with preposition ל. For the form, see on 1:9.

The Renewed Call to Love Yhwh
Deuteronomy 10:12–11:32

As the general exhortation draws to a close, Moses resumes from his recounting of history (9:7–10:11; n.b., וְעַתָּה, 10:12; cf. 4:1) to present the summary charge to Israel in Moab: love expressed in obedience (10:12; 11:1) echoing 6:4-5. Moses draws on every avenue possible to motivate Israel: who Yhwh is and what Yhwh has done (10:12–11:1); their unique experience (11:2-9); the bounty of the land and the danger of losing it (11:10-17). In 11:18-21, he reiterates 6:6-9: making Yhwh's words pervasive is critical. The final verses turn to the significance of obedience for entering and keeping the land and set out the stark choice that faces hearer and reader (11:22-32).

Moses summarizes what Israel should do, rooting it in who Yhwh is and what Yhwh has done (10:12–11:1)

Having established that there is no warrant for self-righteousness (cf. 9:4-5) by demonstrating, through historical retrospect, Israel's stubbornness, the value of intercession and the renewed covenant, Moses highlights the qualities that the people *should* show. There is an interweaving of command and motivation, and many of the commands and motifs echo those found previously. This section summarizes the main obligations.

> 10:12-13—Now (עתה): Yhwh's requirement to fear (√ירא) by walking, to love (√אהב) and serve by keeping (√שמר) (2ms);
>
> 10:14-16—What Yhwh is and what Yhwh has done, so Israel should . . . (modal *qatal*, ומלתם);
>
> 10:17-19—What Yhwh is and what Yhwh does, so Israel should . . . (modal *qatal*, ואהבתם);

10:20–11:1—Fear Yhwh (ירא√)—What Yhwh is and what Yhwh has done now (עתה), so Israel should . . . (modal *qatals*) love (אהב√) and keep (שמר√) (2ms).

¹²*And now, Israel, what does Yhwh your God ask of you, except to fear Yhwh your God by walking in all his ways and by loving him and to serve Yhwh your God with all your heart and with all your being, ¹³by keeping Yhwh's commandments and his statutes that I am commanding you today, so that it may go well for you. ¹⁴Look! To Yhwh your God belong the heavens and the highest heavens, the earth and all that is in it. ¹⁵It was only your ancestors that Yhwh desired, so as to love them, and he chose their offspring after them—you—out of all the peoples, as [is the case] today. ¹⁶So circumcise the foreskin of your heart, while your neck you should no longer stiffen. ¹⁷Because Yhwh your God is God of gods and Lord of lords, the great, mighty and awesome God, who does not show partiality or accept a bribe, ¹⁸doing justice for orphan[s] and widow[s] and loving resident alien[s] by giving them bread and clothing, ¹⁹so you should love the resident alien, for you were resident aliens in the land of Egypt. ²⁰It is Yhwh your God that you should fear; it is he that you should serve; it is to him that you should cling; it is in his name that you should swear. ²¹He is your praise and he is your God, who did for you these great and fearful things which your eyes saw. ²²It was as seventy people that your ancestors went down to Egypt, but now Yhwh your God has made you like the stars of heaven in abundance. ¹¹:¹So love Yhwh your God and keep his charge and his statutes and his judgments and his commandments always.*

10:12 וְעַתָּה֙ יִשְׂרָאֵ֔ל מָ֚ה יְהוָ֣ה אֱלֹהֶ֔יךָ שֹׁאֵ֖ל מֵעִמָּ֑ךְ כִּ֣י
אִם־לְ֠יִרְאָה אֶת־יְהוָ֨ה אֱלֹהֶ֜יךָ לָלֶ֣כֶת בְּכָל־דְּרָכָ֗יו
וּלְאַהֲבָ֣ה אֹת֔וֹ וְלַֽעֲבֹד֙ אֶת־יְהוָ֣ה אֱלֹהֶ֔יךָ בְּכָל־לְבָבְךָ֖
וּבְכָל־נַפְשֶֽׁךָ׃

D2. ID. Moses shifts the time frame to the present (ועתה), concluding chapters 6–10. An opening (rhetorical) question (v. 12a) is followed by the adversative כי אם that introduces a series of infinitive construct phrases that run into v. 13. Although many commentators regard these as commands, it is ED, not HD.

וְעַתָּה יִשְׂרָאֵל. עתה is an adjunct temporal adverb. In its characteristic fronted position, it functions as a scene-setting (temporal) **topic** (cf. Holmstedt 2011: 22), signalling the drawing of lessons based on history (cf. on 4:1). ישראל is vocative.

מָה יְהוָה אֱלֹהֶיךָ שֹׁאֵל מֵעִמָּךְ. Ptcp ms Qal √שאל. **Null-copula** clause with participial predicate. ID. מה is interrogative pronoun, "what . . .?" It functions as the accusative complement of √שאל. מעמך is adjunct compound PP, specifying "of whom" a request is made (cf. 18:16; elsewhere usually מֵאֵת).

כִּי אִם־לְיִרְאָה אֶת־יְהוָה אֱלֹהֶיךָ. Inf constr Qal √ירא with preposition ל (see on 4:10 for the form and syntax). כי אם introduces an adversative clause after a negative (WHS §555; JM §172c; cf. 7:5). As a question followed by כי אם, מה introduces a rhetorical question, with the implicit answer, "nothing, *but* . . .," hence "except." The infinitive phrase effectively functions as the complement of √שאל, "Yhwh asks of you [nothing] except [he does ask you] to fear. . . ."

לָלֶכֶת בְּכָל־דְּרָכָיו. Inf constr Qal √הלך with preposition ל. For the form ללכת and for "walking" (√הלך) in "his ways" (דרכיו), see on 8:6. This infinitive phrase is introduced asyndetically. Rather than the phrase being an infinitive complement after √שאל, it is an adjunct of the previous infinitive phrase. The pattern here does not conform even to the varied patterns of coordination (cf. JM §177o). There are two ways of taking it that are almost synonymous: it could be appositional, "to fear . . ., *that is*, to walk. . . ." More likely the infinitive construct is **gerundial** or explanatory, "by walking" (cf. 6:2, where √ירא is followed by explanatory לשמר; 8:6; WO §36.2.3e). Fearing Yhwh is demonstrated by walking in Yhwh's ways.

וּלְאַהֲבָה אֹתוֹ. Inf constr Qal √אהב with preposition ל. The verb √אהב has the feminine ending ־ָה for the infinitive construct, like √ירא (JM §49d). As a *verbal* noun in can govern a direct object (GKC §115d; cf. JM §124f). With an infinitive ending in ־ָה, the pronominal suffix object of the infinitive is attached to the particle את (JM §125e; cf. 7:8; cp. 9:28, with the suffix as the subject). The infinitive phrase could be functioning as the complement of √שאל, parallel with ליראה. However, the use of the pronoun "him" rather than "Yhwh your God" suggests it is coordinated with ללכת and it, too, is explanatory.

וְלַעֲבֹד אֶת־יְהוָה אֱלֹהֶיךָ. Inf constr Qal √עבד with preposition ל. The repeated "Yhwh your God indicates that it is a second infinitive phrase complement, coordinated with ליראה.

בְּכָל־לְבָבְךָ וּבְכָל־נַפְשֶֽׁךָ. Adjunct PPs. See on 4:29 for the identical phrase. cf. 6:5.

10:13 לִשְׁמֹר אֶת־מִצְוֺת יְהוָה וְאֶת־חֻקֹּתָיו אֲשֶׁר אָנֹכִי מְצַוְּךָ הַיּוֹם לְטוֹב לָֽךְ:

D2. A final infinitive phrase expresses what Yhwh *does* require (v. 13a). The opening summary statement (vv. 12-13) ends with a motivational infinitive phrase (v. 13b). This is not burdensome legalism, but for their good.

לִשְׁמֹר אֶת־מִצְוֺת יְהוָה וְאֶת־חֻקֹּתָיו. Inf constr Qal √שמר with preposition ל. This infinitive phrase is introduced asyndetically, hence is explanatory (see on ללכת in v. 12). Serving Yhwh is evidenced by keeping את־מצות יהוה ואת־חקתיו (conjoined accusative complement NPs).

אֲשֶׁר אָנֹכִי מְצַוְּךָ הַיּוֹם. Ptcp ms Piel √צוה with 2ms pronominal suffix. Restrictive relative clause with **head** את־מצות יהוה ואת־חקתיו, See on 4:40 for the identical phrase.

לְטוֹב לָֽךְ:. Inf constr Qal √טוב with preposition ל. Adjunct infinitive phrase expressing purpose. See on 6:24. For the pausal form of לך, see on 1:21.

10:14 הֵן לַיהוָה אֱלֹהֶיךָ הַשָּׁמַיִם וּשְׁמֵי הַשָּׁמָיִם הָאָרֶץ וְכָל־אֲשֶׁר־בָּֽהּ:

ED. D2. The combination of "heaven" and "earth" forms a **merism**. Everything belongs to Yhwh. Having given the summary of Yhwh's commands, Moses roots the following exhortation (v. 16) in Yhwh's special relationship with Israel (vv. 14-15). This verse should be taken with what follows, not as the grounds for what precedes; vv. 12-13 are not in themselves commands.

הֵן לַיהוָה אֱלֹהֶיךָ הַשָּׁמַיִם וּשְׁמֵי הַשָּׁמָיִם. **Null-copula** clause. הן, like הִנֵּה, highlights what follows for particular attention (JM §105d). See on 5:24. ליהוה אלהיך is PP predicate, fronted for **focus** with ל indicating possession (cf. WO §11.2.10d). Typically a PP indicating possession is the complement (or predicate) and clearly so in relative clauses with no overt subject (e.g., 5:21; 8:13). Here it is less definite than the NP השמים ושמי השמים (cf. Dyk and Talstra, 149–56; Lowery).

וּשְׁמֵי הַשָּׁמָיִם. Construct NP. There are two kinds of superlative: relative and absolute. The "relative" or "comparative" superlative (sometimes simply termed "superlative") entails comparison with other corresponding entities and declares this one to excel ("-st" in English). The absolute superlative (= "elative") simply declares the entity to excel without inviting comparison ("very"). These are expressed in different ways in Hebrew (GKC §133g-l; WO §14.5; MNK §30.5.2; JM §141j-m; WHS §77–81). The definite construct NP with cognate nouns (the "superlative genitive"; WO §9.5.3j; WHS §47) here expresses a relative superlative, "the highest heaven" (cf. WO §14.5d; JM §141l; GKC §133i). The ו could be "emphatic" (an alternative suggested by Nelson, 131 n. b), "indeed," "especially," or explanatory, "namely" (cf. GKC §154a n. 1; WHS §434). But given the parallel with the הארץ וכל־אשר בה, the normal conjunctive meaning makes most sense.

הָאָרֶץ וְכָל־אֲשֶׁר־בָּהּ. NP, following asyndetically. The **asyndesis** does not indicate explanatory apposition; rather, it is the subject of a **null-copula** clause, with **ellipsis** of the PP predicate, ליהוה, supplied from the previous clause.

וְכָל־אֲשֶׁר־בָּהּ. **Null-copula** restrictive relative clause, with **head** כל and PP predicate, בה. The pronominal suffix refers back to הארץ.

10:15 רַק בַּאֲבֹתֶיךָ חָשַׁק יְהוָה לְאַהֲבָה אוֹתָם וַיִּבְחַר בְּזַרְעָם אַחֲרֵיהֶם בָּכֶם מִכָּל־הָעַמִּים כַּיּוֹם הַזֶּה:

ND. D2. Moses gives a restriction to the universal statement of v. 14; there is something particular about Israel, rooted in history (hence *qatal* then *wayyiqtol* clauses). The choice of the past continues to the present.

רַק בַּאֲבֹתֶיךָ חָשַׁק יְהוָה לְאַהֲבָה אוֹתָם. *Qatal* 3ms Qal √חשק. Like √בחר below, √חשק takes an oblique complement, with ב, for the one desired. The clausal **asyndesis** marks this clause out as modifying or explaining v. 14.

רַק בַּאֲבֹתֶיךָ. The force of רק depends on what has preceded. After a "positive" clause, it serves as a restrictive adverb, "only" (WO §39.3.5c). Here, it is an item adverb (see on 1:28; WO §39.3.1), going closely with the oblique complement, באבתיך, which is fronted for **focus**.

לְאַהֲבָה אוֹתָם. Inf constr Qal √אהב with preposition לְ. See on v. 12 for form and syntax. This adjunct infinitive phrase is the result of Yhwh's desire (cf. WO §36.2.3d; MNK §20.1.3[vi]; AC §3.4.1[d]; JM §124l, §169g).

וַיִּבְחַר בְּזַרְעָם אַחֲרֵיהֶם בָּכֶם מִכָּל־הָעַמִּים כַּיּוֹם הַזֶּה׃. *Wayyiqtol* 3ms Qal √בחר. בזרעם is oblique complement. The transitive English verb "choose" has, as its Hebrew counterpart, an intransitive verb: בחר ב (WO §10.2.1c; cf. 4:37; 7:6-7). אחריהם is adjunct PP. בכם is PP, appositional to בזרעם, identifying who "their seed" is. מכל־העמים is adjunct PP, with partitive מן (cf. JM §133e; WHS §324). For the comparative temporal adjunct PP, כיום הזה, see on 2:30.

10:16 וּמַלְתֶּם אֵת עָרְלַת לְבַבְכֶם וְעָרְפְּכֶם לֹא תַקְשׁוּ עוֹד׃

HD. D2. A command and a prohibition flow immediately from Israel's special relationship with Yhwh. The broader context is of 9:1–10:11 and Israel's inveterate stubbornness.

וּמַלְתֶּם אֵת עָרְלַת לְבַבְכֶם. *Qatal* (modal) 2mp Qal √מול. HD. The modal *qatal* in Deuteronomy is often used to convey a volitional force after narrative discourse (cf. WO §32.2.3d). את ערלת לבבכם is accusative complement construct NP. A bold metaphor, perhaps suggested by reference to the patriarchs (cf. Tigay 1996: 107–8). The heart (לבב) is critical (cf. on 4:9).

וְעָרְפְּכֶם לֹא תַקְשׁוּ עוֹד׃. *Yiqtol* 2mp Hiphil √קשה. HD. A prohibition, with לא (see on 1:17). וערפכם is accusative complement, fronted as the **topic**. The statement is the counterpart of the previous prohibition, coordinated with it. Together they build up a complementary picture, rather than a sequential or contingent one. This accounts for the **topicalization** (cf. Moshavi 2010: 160–61). עוד is an adverbial adjunct, showing "the *continual* or *persistent* nature of the verbal clause (AC §4.2.13). It highlights that their future should break with their past (cf. 9:6, 13, 27).

10:17 כִּי יְהוָה אֱלֹהֵיכֶם הוּא אֱלֹהֵי הָאֱלֹהִים וַאֲדֹנֵי הָאֲדֹנִים הָאֵל הַגָּדֹל הַגִּבֹּר וְהַנּוֹרָא אֲשֶׁר לֹא־יִשָּׂא פָנִים וְלֹא יִקַּח שֹׁחַד׃

D2. Explanatory clause, serving as the grounds of the injunction in v. 19, rather than of what has preceded (see comments on 10:12–11:1).

כִּי יְהוָה אֱלֹהֵיכֶם הוּא אֱלֹהֵי הָאֱלֹהִים וַאֲדֹנֵי הָאֲדֹנִים. Subordinating conjunction כי introducing an explanatory **tripartite null-copula** clause with substantival predicate. As discussed on 1:17, there are two ways of understanding such clauses: הוא is either a resumptive pronoun referring to the **extraposed** (or dislocated or *casus pendens*) NP (יהוה אלהיכם) or a pronominal copula. The former is on balance preferable here (see on 3:22; *pace* Holmstedt and Jones, 83).

אֱלֹהֵי הָאֱלֹהִים וַאֲדֹנֵי הָאֲדֹנִים. Two conjoined construct NP predicates. Both are relative superlatives, expressed by the superlative genitive (see on 10:14), although these do not mean a polytheistic framework in the book as a whole (see Tigay 1996: 39, 108; Lundbom, 392). Both use honorific plurals, because they are speaking of Israel's God (GKC §124g, i; WO §7.4.3b).

הָאֵל הַגָּדֹל הַגִּבֹּר וְהַנּוֹרָא. Appositional NP, with three attributive adjectives. In such a chain, all three characteristically have the article (GKC §126v; JM §138a). The final one, הנורא, is Niphal ms participle √ירא, having what WO §23.3d term the "**gerundive**" use of the Niphal, "awe*ful*," hence "awesome."

אֲשֶׁר לֹא־יִשָּׂא פָנִים וְלֹא יִקַּח שֹׁחַד׃. Two coordinated restrictive relative clauses, with **head** הָאֵל. *Yiqtol* 3ms Qal √נשא and Qal √לקח. The *yiqtol* is used for what is generally the case (cf. WO §31.3e). √נשא פנים is an idiom that can be positive, "show consideration" (e.g., 28:50), but in a legal context is negative, "show partiality" (BDB s.v.; cf. √נכר Hiphil + פנים in 1:17; 16:19). שחד is a "bribe" (cf. 16:19).

10:18 עֹשֶׂה מִשְׁפַּט יָתוֹם וְאַלְמָנָה וְאֹהֵב גֵּר לָתֶת לוֹ לֶחֶם וְשִׂמְלָה׃

D2. A continuation of the explanatory clause in v. 17. Two attributive accusative participles expand on the description of Yhwh's actions.

עֹשֶׂה מִשְׁפַּט יָתוֹם וְאַלְמָנָה. Ptcp ms Qal √עשה. The participle is an attributive accusative of state, used as the attribute of a noun (האל). The lack of an article shows it is neither in apposition nor a relative clause (cf. JM §127a). As a *verbal* adjective, the participle can take an accusative complement (here the construct NP משפט יתום ואלמנה), showing it is primarily functioning verbally (cf. JM §121l).

מִשְׁפַּט יָתוֹם וְאַלְמָנָה. Accusative complement construct NP. The absolute (or genitive) comprises a genitive phrase, "orphan and widow" (WHS §29b); it is a type of objective or adverbial genitive where the absolute is the beneficiary of the action implied in the construct (cf. WO §9.5.2e). אלמנה, "widow," is comparatively unusual in having four root letters (JM §88Ka). In Hebrew, "the definite noun directs attention to the referent's identity, while the indefinite noun focuses on the class to which the referent belongs, its quality and character" (WO §13.2b). Here, the class is in view, hence the nouns are indefinite (also 27:19; cf. 24:21).

וְאֹהֵב גֵּר לָתֶת לוֹ לֶחֶם וְשִׂמְלָה׃. Ptcp ms Qal √אהב. The root √אהב sometimes shows both fientive and stative characteristics at the same time. The use of the participle suggests a "progressive and thus fientive sense" but the verb itself is stative (WO §22.2.3b). For the lack of article with גר, see above.

לָתֶת לוֹ לֶחֶם וְשִׂמְלָה׃. Inf constr Qal √נתן with preposition ל (see on 1:8 for the form; also on 4:38 for לָתֵת not לָתֶת). ל with the infinitive construct could introduce the result of Yhwh's love (see on לאהבה in v. 15). The alternative is the **gerundial** or epexegetical use of the infinitive construct, explaining how the previous action (√אהב) is evidenced (cf. WO §36.2.3e; JM §124o). Both entail Yhwh's gift rooted in his love. √נתן takes an oblique complement, לו and an accusative complement, לחם ושמלה. For שמלה, cf. on 8:4.

10:19 וַאֲהַבְתֶּם אֶת־הַגֵּר כִּי־גֵרִים הֱיִיתֶם בְּאֶרֶץ מִצְרָיִם׃

HD. D2. Modal *qatal* rooted in the previous explanatory clause (v. 17a), with a further motivation provided in v. 19b. Because Yhwh loves the resident alien, and because the Israelites were resident aliens (cf. 5:15), they are themselves to love the resident alien. The twin grounds—the nature of the deity with whom they are in covenant and their history—coalesce to ground ethical exhortation.

וַאֲהַבְתֶּם אֶת־הַגֵּר. *Qatal* (modal) 2mp Qal √אהב. HD. The modal *qatal* follows an explanatory clause with ED, drawing a logical consequence with injunctive force (GKC §112aa; WO §32.2.5a; AC §3.5.2[c]; JM §119e). The article in the accusative complement, את־הגר, is anaphoric, based on the mention of גר in the previous verse (cf. WO §13.5.1d, 13.5.2d; JM §137f; WHS §83).

כִּי־גֵרִים הֱיִיתֶם בְּאֶרֶץ מִצְרָיִם:. *Qatal* 2mp Qal √היה. The clause is an explanatory clause with subordinating conjunction כי. After כי there is normally **triggered inversion** with a fientive verb and also with the copula היה; here גרים is fronted for **focus**. Of all the statuses they could have had in Egypt, they were resident aliens. בארץ מצרים is adjunct construct PP.

10:20 אֶת־יְהוָה אֱלֹהֶיךָ תִּירָא אֹתוֹ תַעֲבֹד וּבוֹ תִדְבָּק וּבִשְׁמוֹ תִּשָּׁבֵעַ:

HD. D2. A modal *yiqtol* follows asyndetically from v. 19. This is then followed asyndetically by three coordinated modal *yiqtols* that illuminate the opening injunction. Three of the four clauses are identical to those in 6:13, although, importantly, coordination differs. The four accusative/oblique complements are all fronted for **focus**: "it is Yhwh [and no other deity] that you should. . . ."; the coordinating ו-conjunction and the pronominal reference to יהוה after the first demonstrate the injunctions' unity and complementarity. The call to "fear" echoes the original requirement (v. 12).

אֶת־יְהוָה אֱלֹהֶיךָ תִּירָא. *Yiqtol* (modal) 2ms Qal √ירא. The accusative complement construct NP, את־יהוה אלהיך, is fronted for **focus**.

אֹתוֹ תַעֲבֹד. *Yiqtol* (modal) 2ms Qal √עבד. The accusative complement, אתו, is fronted for **focus**. This *yiqtol* follows asyndetically, indicating that it and the following two (joined syndetically) unpack what it means to fear Yhwh.

וּבוֹ תִדְבָּק. *Yiqtol* (modal) 2ms Qal √דבק. For the verb, see on 4:4. The *a*-class theme vowel is because the verb is stative. The oblique complement, בו, is fronted for **focus**: "to him [and to no one else] you should cling." This is the only phrase not directly quoted from 6:13.

וּבִשְׁמוֹ תִּשָּׁבֵֽעַ׃. *Yiqtol* (modal) 2ms Niph √שבע. The oblique complement, בשמו, is fronted for **focus**: "in his [and no other] name you should swear."

10:21 הוּא תְהִלָּתְךָ וְהוּא אֱלֹהֶיךָ אֲשֶׁר־עָשָׂה אִתְּךָ אֶת־הַגְּדֹלֹת וְאֶת־הַנּוֹרָאֹת הָאֵלֶּה אֲשֶׁר רָאוּ עֵינֶֽיךָ׃

D2. ED. Two descriptions of Yhwh follow asyndetically from the previous HD. Again, present knowledge of Yhwh is rooted in their experience of Yhwh in history.

הוּא תְהִלָּתְךָ. **Null-copula** clause with substantival predicate. ED. Unmarked S–P word order. To say Yhwh is Israel's "praise" could mean either that Yhwh is the grounds or the object of Israel's praise (cf. Nelson, 131 n. f; Lundbom, 396–97).

וְהוּא אֱלֹהֶיךָ. **Null-copula** clause with substantival predicate. ED. Unmarked S–P word order.

אֲשֶׁר־עָשָׂה אִתְּךָ אֶת־הַגְּדֹלֹת וְאֶת־הַנּוֹרָאֹת הָאֵלֶּה אֲשֶׁר רָאוּ עֵינֶֽיךָ. *Qatal* 3ms Qal √עשה. אתך is adjunct PP, indicating for whose advantage Yhwh acted (WHS §341; cf. on 1:30). Non-restrictive relative clause with head אלהים.

אֶת־הַגְּדֹלֹת וְאֶת־הַנּוֹרָאֹת הָאֵלֶּה. Accusative complement NP. Substantival use of the adjectives. For נוראת (ptcp fp Niph √ירא), see on 1:19; cf. 10:17. The demonstrative, as a **deictic** word, points to something "near" within the mental map of the speaker. Here, the use is "emphatic" (JM §143f), making immediate what would otherwise be distant (so too the following restrictive relative clause).

אֲשֶׁר רָאוּ עֵינֶֽיךָ׃. *Qatal* 3cp Qal √ראה. Restrictive relative clause (cf. 4:9; 7:19). For the rhetorical significance of sight, see on 1:30 (לעיניך) and comments on 4:9-14.

10:22 בְּשִׁבְעִים נֶפֶשׁ יָרְדוּ אֲבֹתֶיךָ מִצְרָיְמָה וְעַתָּה שָׂמְךָ יְהוָה אֱלֹהֶיךָ כְּכוֹכְבֵי הַשָּׁמַיִם לָרֹֽב׃

D2. ND. The comparison between past (v. 22a) and present (v. 22b, n.b., עתה) echoes v. 12, demonstrates Yhwh's faithfulness to the patriarchal promises (cf. 1:10-11) and prepares the way for the final exhortation.

בְּשִׁבְעִים נֶפֶשׁ יָרְדוּ אֲבֹתֶיךָ מִצְרָיְמָה. *Qatal* 3cp Qal √ירד. It is "down" (√ירד) to Egypt (or from the land, 1:25) and "up" from Egypt and into the land (√עלה; e.g., 1:21). בשבעים נפש is adjunct PP, fronted for **focus**, contrasting with what they are now. The singular noun (here נפש) occurs with tens (GKC §134h; JM §142f; cf. on 1:2). בְּ is the so-called *beth essentiae* (GKC §119i; JM §133c), by which "the object of the preposition בְּ can act as a predicate nominative . . ., meaning that the subject is equated with it" (WHS §249), "(as) seventy people." מצרימה is the directional adjunct. The locative ה indicates motion toward (WO §10.5a, b; JM §93c). The accent does not shift when ה is added.

וְעַתָּה שָׂמְךָ יְהוָה אֱלֹהֶיךָ כְּכוֹכְבֵי הַשָּׁמַיִם לָרֹב. *Qatal* 3ms Qal √שׂים with 2ms pronominal suffix. ועתה has an adverbial function, giving a contrast between "then" and "now" (MNK §41.2.6[i]; cf. on 2:13) and an *inclusio* with v. 12 (Lundbom, 389).

כְּכוֹכְבֵי הַשָּׁמַיִם לָרֹב. See on 1:10 for the identical phrase. Here, though, ככוכבי השמים is not the adverbial predicate but comparative adjunct PP.

> 11:1 וְאָהַבְתָּ אֵת יְהוָה אֱלֹהֶיךָ וְשָׁמַרְתָּ מִשְׁמַרְתּוֹ
> וְחֻקֹּתָיו וּמִשְׁפָּטָיו וּמִצְוֺתָיו כָּל־הַיָּמִים:

D2. HD. Two modal *qatals* tie the section up, echoing the opening requirement in vv. 12-13 (love, √אהב; keep √שׁמר), while also rooted in the threefold pattern of what Yhwh is and what Yhwh has done/is doing (see comments on 10:22–11:1).

וְאָהַבְתָּ אֵת יְהוָה אֱלֹהֶיךָ. *Qatal* (modal) 2ms Qal √אהב; cf. 6:5; 10:12.

וְשָׁמַרְתָּ מִשְׁמַרְתּוֹ וְחֻקֹּתָיו וּמִשְׁפָּטָיו וּמִצְוֺתָיו כָּל־הַיָּמִים: *Qatal* (modal) 2ms Qal √שמר. משמרתו, from the noun מִשְׁמֶרֶת, "charge," "obligation," occurs only here in Deuteronomy. כל־הימים is adverbial time adjunct construct NP.

Moses calls the Moab generation to know and obey, based on their unique experience (11:2-9)

The section is structured by two modal *qatals*: to "know" (v. 2) and to "keep" (v. 8). This is a pattern that has occurred before (4:39-40; 7:9-11; 8:5-6). Both are 2mp, similar to those in 10:16, 19. In the light of their unique privileged "lesson," which not even their children experienced

(vv. 2-6) but only their eyes saw (v. 7), they have greater responsibility and obligation to obey (vv. 8-9). Alongside the blurring of generations (cf. 5:2-3), Moses also recognises a distinction between them. In the long sentence of vv. 2-6, mention of Yhwh's "actions" (מעשיו) prompts a lengthy expansion of them with two parallel sections. The first deals with Yhwh's treatment of the Egyptian enemy; the second focuses on Israel. Each has a similar pair of coordinated relative clauses with **head** מעשיו (v. 3) and beginning אשר עשה; each pair is then followed by אשר acting as a **complementizer** introducing a clause with a *qatal* then a *wayyiqtol* clause expressing Yhwh's action: destroying the Egyptians (11:4b); causing the ground to swallow Dathan and Abiram (11:6aβ-b).

> ²So know today that it is not with your children, who neither knew nor saw the lesson of Yhwh your God, his greatness, his strong hand and his outstretched arm, ³and his signs and his actions which he did in the midst of Egypt to Pharaoh, king of Egypt, and to all his land, ⁴and which he did to Egypt's army, to its horses and to its chariots, how he made the water of the Sea of Reeds flow over them when they pursued after you, and so Yhwh destroyed them right up to today, ⁵and which he did to you in the wilderness until you came to this place, ⁶and which he did to Dathan and to Abiram, the sons of Eliab, the son of Reuben, how the earth opened its mouth and swallowed them and their households and their tents and every living substance that followed them, right in the midst of all Israel—⁷but your eyes are the ones that saw all Yhwh's great action that he did. ⁸So keep the whole commandment that I am commanding you today, so that you may be strong and enter and possess the land to which you are crossing to possess, ⁹and so that you may lengthen [your] days on the ground that Yhwh swore to your ancestors to give to them and to their seed, a land flowing with milk and honey.

11:2 וִידַעְתֶּם֮ הַיּוֹם֒ כִּ֣י ׀ לֹ֣א אֶת־בְּנֵיכֶ֗ם אֲשֶׁ֤ר לֹֽא־יָדְעוּ֙ וַאֲשֶׁ֣ר לֹא־רָא֔וּ אֶת־מוּסַ֖ר יְהוָ֣ה אֱלֹהֵיכֶ֑ם אֶת־גָּדְל֕וֹ אֶת־יָדוֹ֙ הַחֲזָקָ֔ה וּזְרֹע֖וֹ הַנְּטוּיָֽה׃

D2. HD. The opening modal *qatal* is followed by the **complementizer** כי introducing a lengthy accusative complement noun clause that continues until the end of v. 7 (see below). There is a contrast between what their children and what they saw (v. 7). The children neither knew nor saw Yhwh's lesson—a lesson that continues until the end of v. 6.

וִידַעְתֶּם֩ הַיּ֨וֹם כִּ֜י|. *Qatal* (modal) 2mp Qal √ידע. הַיּוֹם is adverbial time adjunct NP (see on 1:10). The opening modal *qatal* in Deuteronomy is often used to convey a volitional force building on what has preceded, "so know . . ." (cf. on 6:3). The 2mp marks a break from the preceding modal *qatals* (2ms). But what is Israel to "know today"? On any reading, the syntax is awkward. English versions smooth it out, but the awkwardness is evident from the variety of renderings.

Broadly speaking, the following questions need to be considered:

1. How should כי (v. 2) be understood? A subordinating conjunction introducing an explanatory clause (e.g., ESV), asseverative or contrastive, marking a parenthetical statement (e.g., Lundbom, 398), or a **complementizer**, "that," introducing an accusative complement noun clause (e.g., Weinfeld, 429)?
2. How should את in את־בניכם (v. 2) be understood? As a preposition, "with"? As the marker of the accusative complement? As emphatic, marking the subject (Tigay 1996: 363; Nelson, 131; Lundbom, 398; cf. Ezek 44:3; HALOT 101, 4c)? This goes closely with . . .
3. How should the lack of verb associated with את־בניכם be explained? Textual emendation or reordering? **Ellipsis**, supplying "I am speaking with" (Driver, 28–127; cf. GKC §117l)? Or, extending that further still, omission of the verb because of a breaking of the train of thought (*aposiopesis*; GKC §117l)?
4. If כי (v. 2) introduces a subordinate clause, what is the accusative complement of √ידע? Is it מוסר יהוה (Block 2012: 282; Lundbom, 398; possibly MT, given *zaqef qaton* on ראו; cf. 8:5) or גדלו (DeRouchie 2007: 262, NRSV)?
5. How should כי (v. 7) be understood? Adversative, "but" (e.g., NASB, NIV), or explanatory, "for" (e.g., Nelson, 129)?

I favor seeing כי (v. 2) as a **complementizer**, "that," followed by an accusative complement noun clause as the content of what they are to know; את (v. 2) as "with"; the lack of verb as due to the breaking of the train of thought (*aposiopesis*); the כי in v. 7 as adversative, contrasting the parents (v. 7) with the children (v. 2). There are three main reasons for this:

1. Modal *qatal* of √ידע is always elsewhere in chapters 1–11 followed by כי as a **complementizer**;
2. The close parallel with 5:3 suggests a mirrored structure, "not with ... but ... (לא את ... כי ...)";
3. The lengthy description of what the children did not experience explains how the train of thought has broken off. There is no need to supply an extra verb.

In short, what they are to know is "not with your children ... but your eyes are the ones that saw ... (v. 7)."

לֹא אֶת־בְּנֵיכֶם. את־אבתינו is adjunct PP, fronted for **focus** (cf. 5:3). לֹא is an item adverb, modifying the adjunct phrase rather than the main clause (cf. WO §39.3.2). The implied contrast is then spelled out fully only in v. 7.

אֲשֶׁר לֹא־יָדְעוּ וַאֲשֶׁר לֹא־רָאוּ אֶת־מוּסַר יְהוָה אֱלֹהֵיכֶם. *Qatal* 3cp Qal √ידע and Qal √ראה. Non-restrictive relative clauses, with **head** את־מוסר יהוה אלהיכם בניכם is accusative complement construct NP of the verbs ידע and ראה. It is a subjective attributive genitive, the "lesson" (Tigay 1996: 110) Yhwh has given (cf. WO §9.5.1b; 8:5).

אֶת־גָּדְלוֹ אֶת־יָדוֹ הַחֲזָקָה וּזְרֹעוֹ הַנְּטוּיָה׃. The profile of coordination suggests that את־גדלו is appositional to את־מוסר יהוה אלהיכם; the conjoined NPs from החזקה את־ידו to ואת־מעשיו (v. 3a) are appositional to both of these NPs. These, along with את־גדלו, expand Yhwh's "lesson." For את־גדלו, cf. 3:24; 5:24; 9:26. For את־ידו החזקה וזרעו הנטויה, see on 4:34 (cf. 7:19).

11:3 וְאֶת־אֹתֹתָיו וְאֶת־מַעֲשָׂיו אֲשֶׁר עָשָׂה בְּתוֹךְ מִצְרָיִם לְפַרְעֹה מֶלֶךְ־מִצְרַיִם וּלְכָל־אַרְצוֹ׃

D2. Moses continues to recount the lesson that their children missed. Mention of Yhwh's actions (מעשיו) prompts a crafted exposition of them (see the introduction to 11:2-9).

וְאֶת־אֹתֹתָיו וְאֶת־מַעֲשָׂיו. Two further NPs, coordinated with those in 11:2b (see comment there). Mention of מעשיו precipitates a series of relative clauses until the end of v. 6 that expand on Yhwh's "deeds."

אֲשֶׁר עָשָׂה בְּתוֹךְ מִצְרַיִם לְפַרְעֹה מֶלֶךְ־מִצְרַיִם וּלְכָל־אַרְצוֹ׃. *Qatal* 3ms Qal √עשה. Restrictive relative clause with **head** מעשיו (n.b., *inclusio* with v. 7). בתוך מצרים is spatial adjunct PP. לפרעה is adjunct PP, with ל introducing the one affected by the verbal action, in this case negatively (cf. WO §11.2.10d); so too with adjunct construct PP ולכל־ארצו. מלך־מצרים is appositional construct NP.

11:4 וַאֲשֶׁ֣ר עָשָׂה֩ לְחֵ֨יל מִצְרַ֜יִם לְסוּסָ֣יו וּלְרִכְבּ֗וֹ אֲשֶׁ֨ר הֵצִ֜יף אֶת־מֵ֤י יַם־סוּף֙ עַל־פְּנֵיהֶ֔ם בְּרָדְפָ֖ם אַחֲרֵיכֶ֑ם וַיְאַבְּדֵ֣ם יְהוָ֔ה עַ֖ד הַיּ֥וֹם הַזֶּֽה׃

D2. Moses continues to recount Yhwh's actions (מעשׂיו), with a restrictive relative clause (v. 4aα) followed by two noun clauses introduced by the **complementizer** אשׁר expanding on what the action was: destroying the pursuing Egyptians.

וַאֲשֶׁ֣ר עָשָׂה֩ לְחֵ֨יל מִצְרַ֜יִם לְסוּסָ֣יו וּלְרִכְבּ֗וֹ. *Qatal* 3ms Qal √עשׂה. Restrictive relative clause with **head** מעשׂיו. Three adjunct PPs follow, with ל introducing the one affected by the verbal action, in each case negatively (cf. WO §11.2.10d). The final noun, רֶ֫כֶב, is often used as a collective noun, "chariots" (JM §135b). The pronominal suffixes probably refer to the nearest antecedent, מצרים, rather than to פרעה.

אֲשֶׁ֨ר הֵצִ֜יף אֶת־מֵ֤י יַם־סוּף֙ עַל־פְּנֵיהֶ֔ם. *Qatal* 3ms Hiph √צוף. אשׁר functions here as a **complementizer**, "*how* he (Yhwh) . . ." (cf. Holmstedt 2006: 10; JM §157c), appositional to the previous relative clause, explaining what it was in fact that Yhwh "did." It cannot be a relative marker, unlike in the previous two clauses. In those clauses, it occupies the position of accusative complement, but in this clause the accusative complement of הציף is overt (the construct NP את־מי ים־סוף). And it cannot occupy the position of the subject, since the **null subject pro** (in the verb) is Yhwh, already **discourse active**, and there is no conceivable **head**. על־פניהם is adjunct PP, "over them."

בְּרָדְפָ֖ם אַחֲרֵיכֶ֑ם. Inf constr Qal √רדף with 3mp pronominal suffix (subject) and with preposition ב. Adjunct PP, functioning as an infinitival temporal clause (WO §36.2.2b). אחריכם is adjunct PP.

וַיְאַבְּדֵ֣ם יְהוָ֔ה עַ֖ד הַיּ֥וֹם הַזֶּֽה׃ *Wayyiqtol* 3ms Piel √אבד with 3mp pronominal suffix. This is an example of a verb that is intransitive in the Qal (e.g., 4:26; 8:19) becoming a factitive Piel, with the subject producing a state (AC §3.1.3[a]). The subject, Yhwh, is overt for the avoidance of doubt. The clause continues the previous one introduced by the **complementizer** אשר.

עַד הַיּוֹם הַזֶּה. Temporal adjunct PP. Moses appeals to what is still the case, rhetorically powerful for his hearers (hence "once for all," Tigay 1996: 110).

11:5 וַאֲשֶׁר עָשָׂה לָכֶם בַּמִּדְבָּר עַד־בֹּאֲכֶם עַד־הַמָּקוֹם הַזֶּה:

D2. Moses continues to recount Yhwh's actions (מעשיו) with another restrictive relative clause. The focus has turned to Israel.

וַאֲשֶׁר עָשָׂה לָכֶם בַּמִּדְבָּר. *Qatal* 3ms Qal √עשה. Restrictive relative clause with **head** מעשיו (v. 3). In another context, an adjunct PP with preposition ל after √עשה can be positive, suggesting לכם is "for you" (see on 4:34; so Weinfeld, 429, NIV here). But here "*to* you" is preferable (so Tigay 1996: 111, ESV, NRSV, NASB): (1) every other instance of √עשה followed by ל is negative in this context; (2) the sequence of Yhwh's actions continues with his judgment on Dathan and Abiram; and (3) further, reference here to what takes place "in the wilderness" (במדבר) echoes the discipline of 8:1-6 (n.b., במדבר, 8:2; √יסר, 8:5). The ultimate goal was "*for* you" but only through what Yhwh did "*to* you."

עַד־בֹּאֲכֶם עַד־הַמָּקוֹם הַזֶּה. Inf constr Qal √בוא with 2mp subject suffix. See on 1:31 for the identical phrase.

11:6 וַאֲשֶׁר עָשָׂה לְדָתָן וְלַאֲבִירָם בְּנֵי אֱלִיאָב בֶּן־רְאוּבֵן אֲשֶׁר פָּצְתָה הָאָרֶץ אֶת־פִּיהָ וַתִּבְלָעֵם וְאֶת־בָּתֵּיהֶם וְאֶת־אָהֳלֵיהֶם וְאֵת כָּל־הַיְקוּם אֲשֶׁר בְּרַגְלֵיהֶם בְּקֶרֶב כָּל־יִשְׂרָאֵל:

D2. Moses continues to recount Yhwh's actions with Israel (cf. v. 5), with another restrictive relative clause followed by two noun clauses, introduced by the **complementizer** אשר, expanding on what the action was.

וַאֲשֶׁר עָשָׂה לְדָתָן וְלַאֲבִירָם בְּנֵי אֱלִיאָב בֶּן־רְאוּבֵן. *Qatal* 3ms Qal √עשה. Restrictive relative clause with **head** מעשיו (v. 3). לדתן ולאבירם are two adjunct PPs, with ל introducing the one negatively affected by the verbal action (cf. WO §11.2.10d). בני אליאב is construct NP, appositional to לדתן ולאבירם בן־ראובן is construct NP, appositional to אליאב.

אֲשֶׁר פָּצְתָה הָאָרֶץ אֶת־פִּיהָ. *Qatal* 3fs Qal √פצה. אשר functions here as a **complementizer**, "*how* the ground . . ." (cf. Holmstedt 2006: 10; JM §157c), appositional to the previous relative clause, explaining what it was in fact that Yhwh "did" (see on אשר הציץ in v. 4 above). פצה פה is to "open the mouth," and is elsewhere predicated of birds (Isa 10:14) as well as of the ground (e.g., Gen 4:11).

וַתִּבְלָעֵם וְאֶת־בָּתֵּיהֶם וְאֶת־אָהֳלֵיהֶם וְאֵת כָּל־הַיְקוּם. *Wayyiqtol* 3fs Qal √בלע with 3mp pronominal suffix. Usually the pronominal accusative complement is rendered by את + pronominal suffix if a second accusative complement with ו follows, but there is an exception here (GKC §117e; Driver, 128). The noun בַּיִת has an irregular plural, בָּתִּים, which sometimes occurs without the *meteg* (GKC §96). יקום is a rare word, "living substance" (cf. Gen 7:4, 23). For the lack of *dagesh forte* in יְ, see on ויהי in 1:3. The clause continues the previous one introduced by the **complementizer** אשר.

אֲשֶׁר בְּרַגְלֵיהֶם. **Null-copula** restrictive relative clause with **head** כל־היקום. The adverbial PP predicate, lit. "at their feet," is an idiom for "in their train" (Tigay 1996: 111) or "that followed them" (Weinfeld, 444). Cf. Exod 11:8; Judg 8:5; 2 Kgs 3:9.

בְּקֶרֶב כָּל־יִשְׂרָאֵל:. Adjunct construct PP. This happened in full view of everyone.

11:7 כִּי עֵינֵיכֶם הָרֹאֹת אֶת־כָּל־מַעֲשֵׂה יְהוָה הַגָּדֹל אֲשֶׁר עָשָׂה:

D2. With an adversative clause (see on v. 2), Moses tells the Israelites the second half of what they should know. Note the parallel with v. 3 (מעשה . . . אשר עשה).

כִּי עֵינֵיכֶם הָרֹאֹת אֶת־כָּל־מַעֲשֵׂה יְהוָה הַגָּדֹל. Ptcp fp Qal √ראה with the article. See on 3:21 for the syntax of הראת עיניכם. כי is adversative; see on v. 2.

אֶת־כָּל־מַעֲשֵׂה יְהוָה הַגָּדֹל. Accusative complement construct NP. In a construct chain, the adjective (here הגדל) follows the absolute and usually qualifies the construct (GKC §132a; JM §139a); here, it takes the article because the chain is definite, owing to the absolute being definite (a proper name, יהוה). See GKC §126u, §127a; JM §138a.

אֲשֶׁר עָשָׂה׃. *Qatal* 3ms Qal √עשה. Restrictive relative clause with **head** מעשה.

> 11:8 וּשְׁמַרְתֶּם אֶת־כָּל־הַמִּצְוָה אֲשֶׁר אָנֹכִי מְצַוְּךָ הַיּוֹם לְמַעַן תֶּחֶזְקוּ וּבָאתֶם וִירִשְׁתֶּם אֶת־הָאָרֶץ אֲשֶׁר אַתֶּם עֹבְרִים שָׁמָּה לְרִשְׁתָּהּ׃

D2. HD. In the light of their privileged position, they above all should keep the whole commandment (11:8a). Three purpose clauses follow in v. 8b, with *yiqtol* followed by two modal *qatals*: so that they can have the strength to enter and possess the land.

וּשְׁמַרְתֶּם אֶת־כָּל־הַמִּצְוָה אֲשֶׁר אָנֹכִי מְצַוְּךָ הַיּוֹם. *Qatal* (modal) 2mp Qal √שמר. HD. In the light of what they should "know" (v. 2), they should now "keep" the commandment (cf. 4:39-40; 7:9-11; 8:5-6). The accusative complement construct NP, את־כל־המצוה, denotes here the whole law given in Moab (cf. on 5:31).

אֲשֶׁר אָנֹכִי מְצַוְּךָ הַיּוֹם. Ptcp ms Piel √צוה with 2ms pronominal suffix. Restrictive relative clause, with **head** המצוה. See on 4:40 for identical phrase. Note the 2ms suffix embedded in a context of 2mp forms.

לְמַעַן תֶּחֶזְקוּ וּבָאתֶם וִירִשְׁתֶּם אֶת־הָאָרֶץ אֲשֶׁר אַתֶּם עֹבְרִים שָׁמָּה לְרִשְׁתָּהּ׃. *Yiqtol* (modal) 2mp Qal √חזק followed by *qatal* (modal) 2mp Qal √בוא and Qal √ירש, continuing the modality of תחזקו (cf. GKC §112p). למען is a subordinating conjunction, here introducing a purpose clause. See on 4:1 for the almost identical phrase (תחיו there rather than תחזקו). The three verbs should be taken together as one basic idea, associated with *entering* the land.

אֲשֶׁר אַתֶּם עֹבְרִים שָׁמָּה לְרִשְׁתָּהּ׃. Restrictive relative clause with **head** הארץ. See on 4:14 for the identical phrase.

11:9 וּלְמַ֨עַן תַּאֲרִ֤יכוּ יָמִים֙ עַל־הָ֣אֲדָמָ֔ה אֲשֶׁר֩ נִשְׁבַּ֨ע
יְהוָ֤ה לַאֲבֹֽתֵיכֶם֙ לָתֵ֣ת לָהֶ֔ם וּלְזַרְעָ֑ם אֶ֛רֶץ זָבַ֥ת
חָלָ֖ב וּדְבָֽשׁ: ס

D2. A second למען introduces the counterpart of the three coordinated clauses in v. 8 that focus on entering. They should keep the whole commandment *so that* they may prolong their days *in* the land.

וּלְמַעַן תַּאֲרִיכוּ יָמִים עַל־הָאֲדָמָה. Purpose clause. See on 4:40 for the almost identical phrase (תאריך rather than תאריכו).

אֲשֶׁר נִשְׁבַּע יְהוָה לַאֲבֹתֵיכֶם לָתֵת לָהֶם וּלְזַרְעָם. Restrictive relative clause with **head** האדמה. See on 1:8 for the almost identical phrase (patriarchal names present in 1:8).

אֶרֶץ זָבַת חָלָב וּדְבָשׁ: ס. NP, appositional to האדמה. See on 6:3 for the identical phrase.

Moses reminds them of the difference between the land they left and the land they are entering (11:10-12)

Mention of a land flowing with milk and honey to which they are going (cp. Dathan and Abiram's reference to Egypt in those terms in Num 16:13) prompts an almost poetic excursus extolling the bounty of the land (cf. 6:10-11; 8:7-9). Five times ארץ occurs (once of Egypt); five times it is referred to by a pronoun; twice the adverbial directional adjunct שמה occurs. As well as linking back to what preceded (n.b., כי in v. 10), it also anticipates vv. 13-17 (n.b., the rain, מטר, associated with heaven, השמים, in vv. 11, 14, 17).

¹⁰For the land that you are entering to possess—it is not like that land of Egypt from where you came out, which you used to sow with your seed and water with your "feet" like a vegetable garden. ¹¹But the land to where you are crossing to possess is a land of hills and valleys that drinks water according to the rain of heaven, ¹²a land that Yhwh your God cares for—the eyes of Yhwh your God are continually on it, from the beginning of the year to year-end.

11:10 כִּ֣י הָאָ֗רֶץ אֲשֶׁ֨ר אַתָּ֤ה בָא־שָׁ֨מָּה֙ לְרִשְׁתָּ֔הּ לֹ֣א
כְאֶ֤רֶץ מִצְרַ֨יִם֙ הִ֔וא אֲשֶׁ֥ר יְצָאתֶ֖ם מִשָּׁ֑ם אֲשֶׁ֤ר
תִּזְרַע֙ אֶֽת־זַרְעֲךָ֔ וְהִשְׁקִ֥יתָ בְרַגְלְךָ֖ כְּגַ֥ן הַיָּרָֽק:

Deuteronomy 11:10   335

D2. In this **null-copula** explanatory clause, Moses makes a comparison and draws a contrast between the land they are entering and the land they left.

כִּי הָאָרֶץ . . . לֹא כְאֶרֶץ מִצְרַיִם֙ הִוא אֲשֶׁר יְצָאתֶם מִשָּׁם. This explanatory clause, with subordinating conjunction כי, is a **tripartite** nominal clause. As discussed on 1:17, there are two ways of understanding such clauses. Here (also 4:24) there is the same structure, X–P–S(pronX). The resumptive pronoun הוא is the subject of the **null-copula** clause. לא כארץ מצרים is the comparative adverbial (PP) predicate. This reading fits with the P–S word order and the pragmatic sense (also Holmstedt and Jones, 77). The word order establishes the **extraposed** NP הארץ . . . לרשתה as the **topic** and highlights כארץ מצרים as the **focus**. When it comes to "the land (that you are entering . . .)," of all that might possibly be predicated of it, the salient one is that it is *"not like the land of Egypt."* Although normally a **null-copula** clause, including one with a participle, is negated with אין not with לא, when the pronoun הוא is necessary, as it is here because of the **extraposed topic**, לא is used (cf. 4:42; GKC §152d; JM §160b). For the form הִוא, see on 1:9.

אֲשֶׁר אַתֶּה בָא־שָׁמָּה לְרִשְׁתָּהּ. Restrictive relative clause with **head** הארץ. See on 7:1 for the identical phrase.

אֲשֶׁר יְצָאתֶם מִשָּׁם. *Qatal* 2mp Qal √יצא. Non-restrictive relative clause with **head** ארץ מצרים. משם is spatial adjunct PP, with שם a resumptive adverb in the relative clause: Hebrew "which . . . from there" = English "from where. . . ." The relative clause is **extraposed**, with resumptive personal subject pronoun הוא intervening (cf. Holmstedt 2002: 301–2). This is due to the **focus**-fronting of לא כארץ מצרים.

אֲשֶׁר תִּזְרַע אֶת־זַרְעֲךָ. *Yiqtol* 2ms Qal √זרע. The *yiqtol* speaks of a repeated general or habitual situation of what they "used" to do (cf. WO §31.3e). Restrictive relative clause with **head** ארץ מצרים. This is an example of "stacking," whereby consecutive relative clauses have the same **head** (Holmstedt 2002: 69–70). There are two ways of making sense of את־זרעך: First, the combination √זרע and its cognate accusative, זרע, is an example of an "affected" object, whereby the object existed beforehand and is acted on by the verb [rather than (the more usual) "effected" object, whereby the object is either the result or the effect of the transitive verb's action] (WO §10.2.1f; AC §2.3.1[b] n. 25; JM §125p; cf. Gen 1:29). If את־זרעך is the only object, then this is an instance where there is no resumptive adverb or preposition with resumptive pronoun in the relative clause. There is a gap where one would fit (cf. שָׁמָּה, מִשָּׁם earlier in the verse; בָּהּ, 8:9). The omission would be similar to that in 1:31 (so Driver, 129; n.b., also 7:19; 8:15). Second, an alternative way of reading it is to see אשר (antecedent ארץ מצרים) as the accusative complement of the verb √זרע, and את־זרעך as the means of sowing, "*which* you sow *with seed*." √זרע often takes a double accusative, with "the direct object … the area planted and the means … the crop" (WO §10.2.3d#28; cf. Isa 30:23; Jer 31:27). Although elsewhere the "means" does not have את, the latter is still preferable, because in the following clause אשר (ארץ מצרים) functions as the accusative complement of √שקה Hiphil.

וְהִשְׁקִ֤יתָ בְרַגְלְךָ֙ כְּגַ֖ן הַיָּרָֽק. *Qatal* (modal) 2ms Hiph √שקה. √שקה, "water," is a defective verb; it occurs only in the Hiphil; but it and another verb, √שתה Qal ("drink"; e.g., 9:18; 11:11) "mutually complete one another," supplying the forms the other lacks (GKC §78b). The verb is transitive in more than 95 percent of its occurrences, with the accusative complement denoting what is "watered." It is very likely, then, that the accusative complement is אשר (antecedent ארץ מצרים; see previous comment). The modal *qatal* continues the force of the previous *yiqtol* (cf. GKC §112e; WO §32.2.1d).

בְרַגְלְךָ. Adjunct PP, with instrumental use of ב (cf. WHS §243). Commentators discuss at length what is meant. Probably it is a euphemism for "genitals"; they water it with urine (cf. 2 Kgs 18:27, where *ketiv* is שיניהם ["their urine"], but *qere* is מימי רגליהם, "waters *of their feet*"; Eslinger; Nicol). The reference may be pungent and satirical (Eslinger) or, perhaps more likely given that urine is a fertilizer, derogatory to the size of a garden that can be watered by a person's urine (Nicol).

כְּגַ֖ן הַיָּרָֽק. Comparative adjunct construct PP. ירק are "greens," "vegetables" (cf. 1 Kgs 21:2). The article is frequent when a class is being spoken of in a comparison (JM §137i). The construct NP is adjectival, with the construct being characterized by the absolute, "like a vegetable garden" (cf. WO §9.5.3a).

11:11 וְהָאָ֗רֶץ אֲשֶׁ֨ר אַתֶּ֜ם עֹבְרִ֥ים שָׁ֨מָּה֙ לְרִשְׁתָּ֔הּ אֶ֥רֶץ הָרִ֖ים וּבְקָעֹ֑ת לִמְטַ֥ר הַשָּׁמַ֖יִם תִּשְׁתֶּה־מָּֽיִם׃

D2. Having spelled out in more detail the land they left, Moses now turns to the land to which they are going. As with v. 10, it is a **null-copula** clause. The restrictive relative clause, as in the previous verses, maintains the contrast between past and future, Egypt and the promised land.

וְהָאָ֗רֶץ ... אֶ֤רֶץ הָרִים֙ וּבְקָעֹ֔ת. **Null-copula** clause with substantival predicate and unmarked S–P word order. The predicate is indefinite construct NP; usually a nominal predicate is indefinite (JM §137l). Although generally the noun in the construct state is repeated before each absolute (e.g., Jer 8:1), if the nouns are closely related, it may not be (cf. GKC §128a; WHS §29b).

אֲשֶׁ֨ר אַתֶּ֤ם עֹבְרִים֙ שָׁ֣מָּה לְרִשְׁתָּ֔הּ. See on 4:14 for the identical phrase.

לִמְטַ֥ר הַשָּׁמַ֖יִם תִּשְׁתֶּה־מָּֽיִם׃. *Yiqtol* 3fs Qal √שׁתה. למטר השמים is adjunct construct PP, fronted for **focus**. This is "rather an extreme case" (Driver, 130) of ל in the sense of "according to" a particular norm or standard (cf. WHS §274a; WO §11.2.10d; AC §4.1.10[j]).

11:12 אֶ֕רֶץ אֲשֶׁר־יְהוָ֥ה אֱלֹהֶ֖יךָ דֹּרֵ֣שׁ אֹתָ֑הּ תָּמִ֗יד עֵינֵ֨י יְהוָ֤ה אֱלֹהֶ֙יךָ֙ בָּ֔הּ מֵֽרֵשִׁית֙ הַשָּׁנָ֔ה וְעַ֖ד אַחֲרִ֥ית שָׁנָֽה׃ ס

D2. An appositional NP (v. 12a) is followed by an asyndetic **null-copula** clause (v. 12b). The second half of the verse is an example of synonymous parallelism with gapping.

אֶ֕רֶץ אֲשֶׁר־יְהוָ֥ה אֱלֹהֶ֖יךָ דֹּרֵ֣שׁ אֹתָ֑הּ. Ptcp ms Qal √דרשׁ. √דרשׁ can have the connotation "caring for," an extension of the more common meaning of "seek" (cf. Job 3:4). Restrictive relative clause with **head** ארץ. ארץ is appositional to the construct NP at the end of v. 11. אתה is the particle את with resumptive pronoun. Unmarked S–P word order in **null-copula** participial clause.

תָּמִ֗יד עֵינֵ֨י יְהוָ֤ה אֱלֹהֶ֙יךָ֙ בָּ֔הּ. **Null-copula** verbless clause with adverbial PP predicate, בה. Elsewhere Yhwh's protecting eyes normally have preposition אל (Ps 33:18; 34:16). תמיד is adverbial temporal adjunct, fronted for **focus**, to be taken with what follows according to Masoretic accentuation. Tigay (1996: 113; cf. Block 2012: 285; Lundbom, 402) argues that it should be taken with what precedes, because it is redundant in this clause given the closing temporal adjunct PPs, and taking it with what precedes preserves "quasi-poetic" synonymous parallelism. But pleonastic temporal expressions with תמיד occur elsewhere (e.g., Jer

52:33), the lines would become uneven were it taken with what precedes, and parallelism is still evident if MT accentuation is followed, with gapping (**ellipsis**) making space for the extended temporal adjunct PPs. The clause follows asyndetically, explaining what Yhwh's continued care looks like.

מֵרֵשִׁית הַשָּׁנָה וְעַד אַחֲרִית שָׁנָה: ס. Two temporal adjunct construct PPs. מרשׁית comprises מִן and רֵאשִׁית (cf. 26:2, מראשׁית). Sometimes quiescent א disappears completely (GKC §23f). The ו functions here as a phrasal boundary marker, rather than a conjunction (cf. 2:36). The lack of article with שנה in אחרית שנה may be due to the poetic style (cf. WO §13.7); more likely, it is because the noun has been previously quoted (cf. JM §137t) or because this instance is a variation on "the case of coordinate multiple terms" where "the article may be found only with the first of them" (cf. JM §137ta).

Obedience brings plenty in the land, but plenty brings dangers (11:13-17)

The promise of rains from heaven (vv. 11-12) is contingent upon obedience. Verses 13-15 promise plenty if there is obedience. But enjoying the land's plenty brings potential danger. So vv. 16-17 warn of the chain from idolatry to withheld bounty to perishing from the land. While there are thematic links to vv. 10-12, the opening והיה (v. 13) marks a break, reflected by a *setumah* in M^L and Smr.

13If you really do listen to my commandments which I am commanding you today—to love Yhwh your God and serve him with all your heart and with your whole being—14I will give rain for your land in its season, early rain and late rain, and you will gather your grain and your wine and your oil, 15I will give grass in your field[s] for your cattle, and you will eat and be satisfied. 16Be careful lest your heart is seduced and you turn aside and serve other gods and bow down to them, 17and Yhwh's anger burns against you and he shuts up the heavens so there is no rain and the ground does not produce its yield and you swiftly perish from upon the good land that Yhwh is giving to you.

11:13 וְהָיָה אִם־שָׁמֹעַ תִּשְׁמְעוּ אֶל־מִצְוֹתַי אֲשֶׁר אָנֹכִי
מְצַוֶּה אֶתְכֶם הַיּוֹם לְאַהֲבָה אֶת־יְהוָה אֱלֹהֵיכֶם
וּלְעָבְדוֹ בְּכָל־לְבַבְכֶם וּבְכָל־נַפְשְׁכֶם:

D2. PD. An opening conditional protasis grounds future plenty in Israel's obedience (v. 13a), an obedience that is spelled out in two adjunct infinitive phrases that speak of total commitment to Yhwh (v. 13b; cf. 10:12)

וְהָיָה. *Qatal* (modal) 3ms Qal √היה. When there is no subject or complement, as here, it serves to anchor discourse time in the future (Cook 2012: 309–10), and marks a break from what precedes. See on 6:10.

אִם־שָׁמֹעַ תִּשְׁמְעוּ אֶל־מִצְוֹתַי. *Yiqtol* 2mp Qal √שמע preceded by Inf abs Qal √שמע. This **paronomastic** infinitive construction, of infinitive absolute with finite verb of the same root, accents the modality of its cognate verb in modal contexts, such as this one (see on 4:26). Conditional protasis, introduced by subordinating conjunction אם. √שמע followed by adjunct PP with preposition אל denotes "listening to" in the sense of "obey" (cf. on 7:12). Moses speaks with Yhwh's voice (מצותי, "my commandments"; see on v. 14).

אֲשֶׁר אָנֹכִי מְצַוֶּה אֶתְכֶם הַיּוֹם. See on 4:2 for the identical phrase, apart from the temporal adjunct, היום, for which see on 1:10. It is likely that Moses is speaking given the occurrence of the phrase elsewhere; see on ונתתי below.

לְאַהֲבָה אֶת־יְהוָה אֱלֹהֵיכֶם וּלְעָבְדוֹ. Inf constr Qal √אהב with preposition ל (see on 10:12 for form and syntax) followed by inf constr Qal √עבד with 3ms pronominal suffix and with preposition ל. The pronominal suffix î- indicates that this adjunct infinitive phrase should be taken closely with what precedes, as does the Masoretic *zaqef qaton*. Both are loosely appositional adjunct infinitive phrases to מצותי, explaining what these commandments are (cf. 4:2).

בְּכָל־לְבַבְכֶם וּבְכָל־נַפְשְׁכֶם׃. Coordinated adjunct PPs. See on 4:29 (with √דרש); cf. 6:5 and 10:12 (both with √אהב). The disjunctive *zaqef qaton* with לעבדו indicates that these prepositional phrases go with *both* infinitives construct (Yeivin, 223).

11:14 וְנָתַתִּי מְטַר־אַרְצְכֶם בְּעִתּוֹ יוֹרֶה וּמַלְקוֹשׁ וְאָסַפְתָּ דְגָנֶךָ וְתִירֹשְׁךָ וְיִצְהָרֶךָ׃

D2 (Moses speaks with Yhwh's voice; see below). The conditional apodosis spells out future blessing (PD).

וְנָתַתִּ֧י מְטַֽר־אַרְצְכֶ֛ם בְּעִתּ֖וֹ. *Qatal* (modal) 1cs Qal √נתן. ו + modal *qatal* often introduces a conditional (or temporal) apodosis (GKC §112ff; JM §176d). This is another instance in MT, not evident in LXX or Smr, of Moses' voice merging with that of Yhwh (cf. 7:4; Lundbom, 405; see also Weinfeld, 446–47; *BHQ: Deuteronomy*, 82*–83*). מטר־ארצכם is accusative complement construct NP. It is a type of objective or adverbial genitive where the absolute is the beneficiary of the action implied in the construct (cf. WO §9.5.2e). בעתו is temporal adjunct PP. The antecedent of the 3ms pronominal suffix ֹו- is מטר, not ארץ, which is feminine.

יוֹרֶ֣ה וּמַלְק֑וֹשׁ. Appositional coordinated NPs. יורה is "early rain"; מלקוש is "late rain."

וְאָסַפְתָּ֣ דְגָנֶ֔ךָ וְתִֽירֹשְׁךָ֖ וְיִצְהָרֶֽךָ׃. *Qatal* (modal) 2ms Qal √אסף. The verb can speak of gathering into sheaves (Ruth 2:7), from the field (Exod 23:16) or from threshing floor and wine press (16:13). Here it is likely to designate bringing in, given what is actually gathered (cf. Weinfeld, 447; Tigay 1996: 114). A further conditional apodosis. For the nouns of the threefold accusative complement, see on 7:13.

11:15 וְנָתַתִּ֛י עֵ֥שֶׂב בְּשָׂדְךָ֖ לִבְהֶמְתֶּ֑ךָ וְאָכַלְתָּ֖ וְשָׂבָֽעְתָּ׃

D2 (Moses speaks with Yhwh's voice; see above). Conditional apodosis spells out future blessing (PD). Yhwh will give (v. 15a); they will "eat and be full" (cf. 6:11; 8:10). Obedience brings plenty.

וְנָתַתִּ֛י עֵ֥שֶׂב בְּשָׂדְךָ֖ לִבְהֶמְתֶּ֑ךָ. *Qatal* (modal) 1cs Qal √נתן (see on v. 14). בשדך is spatial adjunct PP. לבהמתך is oblique complement of √נתן.

וְאָכַלְתָּ֖ וְשָׂבָֽעְתָּ׃. *Qatal* (modal) 2ms Qal √אכל and Qal √שבע. A further conditional apodosis. See on 6:11 (cf. 8:10).

11:16 הִשָּֽׁמְר֣וּ לָכֶ֔ם פֶּ֥ן יִפְתֶּ֖ה לְבַבְכֶ֑ם וְסַרְתֶּ֗ם וַעֲבַדְתֶּם֙ אֱלֹהִ֣ים אֲחֵרִ֔ים וְהִשְׁתַּחֲוִיתֶ֖ם לָהֶֽם׃

D2. HD. The danger of affluence, evident in 8:10-17, recurs here. An opening imperative is followed by four negative purpose clauses introduced by פן. Each speaks of Israel's action.

הִשָּׁמְר֣וּ לָכֶ֔ם. Impv mp Niph √שׁמר. HD. For Niphal imperative √שׁמר with reflexive adjunct PP (לכם), see on 4:9.

פֶּ֥ן יִפְתֶּ֖ה לְבַבְכֶ֑ם. *Yiqtol* 3ms Qal √פתה. The verb is usually regarded as פתה I (HALOT s.v.), "to be simple/gullible/enticed" (cf. Hos 7:11; Job 31:9, 27). Meek (235–36) argues that it comes from פתה II (HALOT s.v.), "to be wide," "to be open" (cf. Gen 9:27; Prov 20:19). This fits both with LXX (πλατυνθῇ, "be wide") and, Meek claims, with the message of the prophets, where tolerance of other deities was the problem. However, the syntactical and conceptual parallels in Job are closer than anything found in the prophets, so "enticed" is to be preferred. For פן introducing a negative purpose clause with **triggered inversion**, see on 4:9.

וְסַרְתֶּ֗ם וַעֲבַדְתֶּם֙ אֱלֹהִ֣ים אֲחֵרִ֔ים וְהִשְׁתַּחֲוִיתֶ֖ם לָהֶֽם׃. *Qatal* (modal) 2mp Qal √סור, Qal √עבד and Hishtaphel √חוה. The negative purpose clause, introduced by פן, continues with three modal *qatals* (cf. GKC §112p; JM §168h). For √סור, "turn aside," cf. 5:32; 7:4; 9:12, 16; 11:28. For √עבד with √חוה, see on 4:19 (cf. 5:9; 8:19).

11:17 וְחָרָ֨ה אַף־יְהוָ֜ה בָּכֶ֗ם וְעָצַ֤ר אֶת־הַשָּׁמַ֙יִם֙ וְלֹֽא־יִהְיֶ֣ה מָטָ֔ר וְהָ֣אֲדָמָ֔ה לֹ֥א תִתֵּ֖ן אֶת־יְבוּלָ֑הּ וַאֲבַדְתֶּ֣ם מְהֵרָ֗ה מֵעַל֙ הָאָ֣רֶץ הַטֹּבָ֔ה אֲשֶׁ֥ר יְהוָ֖ה נֹתֵ֥ן לָכֶֽם׃

D2. Two further modal *qatals* continue the sequence of negative purpose clauses, this time focusing on Yhwh's actions. Two לא + *yiqtols* follow, indicating negative results on the land. A final modal *qatal* returns to the people and gives the endpoint of what they are to guard against (v. 16): perishing swiftly from the land.

וְחָרָ֨ה אַף־יְהוָ֜ה בָּכֶ֗ם. *Qatal* (modal) 3ms Qal √חרה. The negative purpose clauses, introduced by פן, continue with further modal *qatals* (cf. GKC §112p; JM §168h). These now follow a temporal/logical sequence. See on 7:4 for the identical phrase (cf. 6:15).

וְעָצַ֤ר אֶת־הַשָּׁמַ֙יִם֙. *Qatal* (modal) 3ms Qal √עצר. √עצר is used figuratively, "lock up" (HALOT s.v.).

וְלֹֽא־יִהְיֶ֣ה מָטָ֔ר. *Yiqtol* 3ms Qal √היה. The sequence of modal *qatals* is broken by a negative result clause, expressed by לא + *yiqtol*, "so that . . . not . . ." (cf. JM §169b).

וְהָאֲדָמָ֔ה לֹ֥א תִתֵּ֖ן אֶת־יְבוּלָ֑הּ. *Yiqtol* 3fs Qal √נתן. A further negative result clause (see above). האדמה is fronted as the **topic**. This result clause is coordinated with the previous one. Together they build up a complementary picture, which accounts for the topicalization.

וַאֲבַדְתֶּ֣ם מְהֵרָ֗ה מֵעַל֙ הָאָ֣רֶץ הַטֹּבָ֔ה. *Qatal* (modal) 2mp Qal √אבד. מהרה is an adverbial adjunct, "quickly"; everywhere else in Deuteronomy it is מהר, an adverbial use of the infinitive absolute of √מהר (see e.g., 4:26). מעל הארץ הטבה is spatial adjunct PP. See on 4:26 for "perishing (√אבה) *from upon* (מעל). . . ." See on 6:18 and 8:10 for הארץ הטבה. This is the final outcome of the heart's seduction.

אֲשֶׁ֥ר יְהוָ֖ה נֹתֵ֥ן לָכֶֽם׃. Ptcp ms Qal √נתן. Restrictive relative clause with **head** הארץ. A slight variation on the repeated refrain (see, e.g., 4:1).

Moses reiterates the call to immerse themselves in Yhwh's words (11:18-21)

These verses echo 6:6-9 closely, and serve to form an *inclusio* around the intervening chapters (Weinfeld, 446; Lundbom, 407). At the same time, the opening ו + modal *qatal* connects with vv. 13-17. The logic is, "and it will be the case, if you obey, that you will have plenty (vv. 13-15); be careful not to be seduced and so end up perishing from the land (vv. 16-17); *so take these words to heart* (vv. 18-21)."

> ¹⁸*So you should put these words of mine upon your heart and upon your very being; you should bind them as a sign upon your hand; they should be as a headband on your forehead;* ¹⁹*you should teach them to your children by talking about them when you stay in your house and when you are travelling on the road, when you lie down and when you get up;* ²⁰*you should write them on the doorposts of your house and in your communities,* ²¹*so that your days and the days of your children may be many upon the ground that Yhwh swore to your ancestors to give to them, as long as the heavens are above the earth.*

11:18 וְשַׂמְתֶּם֙ אֶת־דְּבָרַ֣י אֵ֔לֶּה עַל־לְבַבְכֶ֖ם וְעַֽל־נַפְשְׁכֶ֑ם וּקְשַׁרְתֶּ֨ם אֹתָ֤ם לְאוֹת֙ עַל־יֶדְכֶ֔ם וְהָי֥וּ לְטוֹטָפֹ֖ת בֵּ֥ין עֵינֵיכֶֽם׃

D2. HD. Moses charges the people to make Yhwh's word pervasive, internally (v. 18a; modal *qatal*) and on their person (v. 18b; two modal *qatals*).

וְשַׂמְתֶּם֙ אֶת־דְּבָרַ֣י אֵ֔לֶּה עַל־לְבַבְכֶ֖ם וְעַל־נַפְשְׁכֶ֑ם. *Qatal* (modal) 2mp Qal √שׂים. HD. עַל־לבבכם וְעל־נפשכם are coordinated oblique complements. See on 6:6 for Yhwh's words being עַל־לבב. Only here in chapters 1–11 is נפש the object of עַל. It extends the thought frame of 6:5-6. The modal *qatal* builds on what precedes.

אֶת־דְּבָרַ֣י אֵ֔לֶּה. Accusative complement NP. When the substantive is made definite with a pronominal suffix, the demonstrative pronoun is often used in attributive apposition with no article (WHS §74b; cf. GKC §126y; WO §17.4.1a). See on 5:29; cp. 6:6, הדברים האלה.

וּקְשַׁרְתֶּ֥ם אֹתָ֛ם לְא֖וֹת עַל־יֶדְכֶ֑ם. *Qatal* (modal) 2mp Qal √קשׁר. See on 6:8.

וְהָי֥וּ לְטוֹטָפֹ֖ת בֵּ֥ין עֵינֵיכֶֽם׃. *Qatal* (modal) 3cp Qal √היה. See on 6:8.

11:19 וְלִמַּדְתֶּ֥ם אֹתָ֛ם אֶת־בְּנֵיכֶ֖ם לְדַבֵּ֣ר בָּ֑ם בְּשִׁבְתְּךָ֣ בְּבֵיתֶ֗ךָ וּבְלֶכְתְּךָ֤ בַדֶּ֙רֶךְ֙ וּֽבְשָׁכְבְּךָ֖ וּבְקוּמֶֽךָ׃

D2. HD. Moses commands them to teach these same commands to their children by speaking about them everywhere (modal *qatal*).

וְלִמַּדְתֶּ֥ם אֹתָ֛ם אֶת־בְּנֵיכֶ֖ם לְדַבֵּ֣ר בָּ֑ם. *Qatal* (modal) 2mp Qal √למד. The **resultative** Piel takes a double accusative (AC §2.3.1e, 3.1.3a; cf. JM §125u). For teaching (√למד Piel) children, see 4:10 (cf. 6:20-25).

לְדַבֵּ֣ר בָּ֑ם. Inf constr Piel √דבר with preposition ל. For √דבר Piel followed by ב, see on 6:7. Adjunct infinitive construct phrase. The infinitive construct is **gerundial** or explanatory, "by speaking" (cf. WO §36.2.3e).

בְּשִׁבְתְּךָ֣ בְּבֵיתֶ֗ךָ וּבְלֶכְתְּךָ֤ בַדֶּ֙רֶךְ֙ וּֽבְשָׁכְבְּךָ֖ וּבְקוּמֶֽךָ׃. See on 6:7 for the identical phrasing.

11:20 וּכְתַבְתָּ֛ם עַל־מְזוּז֥וֹת בֵּיתֶ֖ךָ וּבִשְׁעָרֶֽיךָ׃

D2. HD. Moses insists that Yhwh's commands are not something "privatized" within the home; they should be displayed publicly.

וּכְתַבְתָּ֛ם עַל־מְזוּז֥וֹת בֵּיתֶ֖ךָ וּבִשְׁעָרֶֽיךָ׃. See on 6:9 for the identical phrasing.

11:21 לְמַ֨עַן יִרְבּ֤וּ יְמֵיכֶם֙ וִימֵ֣י בְנֵיכֶ֔ם עַ֚ל הָֽאֲדָמָ֔ה אֲשֶׁ֨ר נִשְׁבַּ֧ע יְהוָ֛ה לַאֲבֹתֵיכֶ֖ם לָתֵ֣ת לָהֶ֑ם כִּימֵ֥י הַשָּׁמַ֖יִם עַל־הָאָֽרֶץ׃ ס

D2. As throughout Deuteronomy, charges to obey are accompanied by motivations for doing so. Here, it is length of days in the land. Reference to their children's days takes these words into Israel's future.

לְמַ֨עַן יִרְבּ֤וּ יְמֵיכֶם֙ וִימֵ֣י בְנֵיכֶ֔ם עַ֚ל הָֽאֲדָמָ֔ה. *Yiqtol* 3mp Qal √רבה. Elsewhere in chapters 1–11, √רבה is associated with multiplication of people or livestock (1:10; 6:3; 7:13; 8:1, 13), while √ארך is associated with "days." למען is a subordinating conjunction introducing a purpose clause (cf. JM §168d). על האדמה is adjunct PP; האדמה is **head** of the following restrictive relative clause.

אֲשֶׁ֨ר נִשְׁבַּ֧ע יְהוָ֛ה לַאֲבֹתֵיכֶ֖ם לָתֵ֣ת לָהֶ֑ם. See on 1:8 (cf. on 11:9, where the identical phrase occurs).

כִּימֵ֥י הַשָּׁמַ֖יִם עַל־הָאָֽרֶץ׃ ס. Comparative temporal adjunct construct PP followed by adjunct PP. כימי השמים, "according to/like the days of heaven" is an expression of longevity (cf. Ps 89:30). על־הארץ, "above the earth" goes closely with the preceding PP, "as long as the heavens are above the earth." The whole phrase expands on what it means for their days to be "many" (v. 11a).

Obedience brings victory in the land (11:22-25)

An opening conditional protasis about obeying Yhwh's command(s), an expansion of מצוה including loving Yhwh, and the topic of the land all echo 11:13-17. There, however, focus was on bounty in the land, while here the apodosis promises sustained military success and territorial possession. And there is no warning here about loss of the land (cf. v. 17).

²²For if you really do keep all this commandment that I am commanding you, by doing it—to love Yhwh your God, to walk in all his ways and to cling to him—²³then Yhwh will drive out all these nations from before you and you will dispossess nations that are greater and stronger than you. ²⁴All the places on which the sole of your foot treads shall be yours; from the desert and the Lebanon, from the river, the river Euphrates, to the western sea shall be your territory. ²⁵No one will stand against you; Yhwh your God will put [nothing but] fear and terror of you upon the whole land on which you tread, just as he promised you.

11:22 כִּ֩י אִם־שָׁמֹ֨ר תִּשְׁמְר֜וּן אֶת־כָּל־הַמִּצְוָ֣ה הַזֹּ֗את אֲשֶׁ֨ר אָנֹכִ֧י מְצַוֶּ֛ה אֶתְכֶ֖ם לַעֲשֹׂתָ֑הּ לְאַהֲבָ֞ה אֶת־יְהוָ֤ה אֱלֹֽהֵיכֶם֙ לָלֶ֣כֶת בְּכָל־דְּרָכָ֔יו וּלְדָבְקָה־בֽוֹ׃

D2. Moses roots the commands to appropriate Yhwh's words in a conditional apodosis (v. 23) dependent on the conditional protasis (v. 22a). Keeping Yhwh's commandment is expressed by three adjunct infinitive phrases, "love," "walk (in his ways)," "cleave" (v. 22b).

כִּי אִם־שָׁמֹר תִּשְׁמְרוּן אֶת־כָּל־הַמִּצְוָה הַזֹּאת אֲשֶׁר אָנֹכִי מְצַוֶּה אֶתְכֶם לַעֲשֹׂתָהּ. *Yiqtol* 2mp Qal √שמר with a **paragogic** ן (for which see on 1:17), preceded by Inf abs Qal √שמר (cf. 6:17; 11:13). This **paronomastic** infinitive construction, of infinitive absolute with finite verb of the same root, accents the modality of its cognate verb in modal contexts, such as this one (see on 4:26). Conditional protasis, introduced by subordinating conjunction אם. The opening כי should neither be taken with אם (as in 7:5; 10:12), since the situation is not adversative, nor as asseverative, "indeed" (Lundbom, 410), for the asseverative use is rare. Rather, it is a subordinating conjunction, introducing an explanatory clause (Weinfeld, 430; DeRouchie 2007: 340). The conditional protasis and apodosis are embedded within this explanatory clause which grounds the injunctions of vv. 18–21.

אֶת־כָּל־הַמִּצְוָה הַזֹּאת. Accusative complement NP. It is here a summary term for the whole of Moses' words in Moab (cf. 5:31); the identical phrase is in 6:25.

אֲשֶׁר אָנֹכִי מְצַוֶּה אֶתְכֶם. See on 4:2 for the identical phrase.

לַעֲשֹׂתָהּ. Inf constr Qal √עשה with 3fs pronominal suffix and with preposition ל. Rather than this being an instance of שמר having an adverbial force, the infinitive construct לעשתה is explanatory, "by doing it" (see on 5:1; cf. WO §36.2.3e).

לְאַהֲבָה אֶת־יְהוָה אֱלֹהֵיכֶם. Inf constr Qal √אהב with preposition ל (see on 10:12 for form and syntax). Adjunct infinitive phrase. This and the following infinitive phrases could either be loosely appositional adjuncts to המצוה, explaining what this "commandment" is, "to love . . .," or explanatory, "by loving . . ." (so Block 2012: 289). Given the parallel with 11:13, I favor the former.

לָלֶ֫כֶת בְּכָל־דְּרָכָ֗יו. Inf constr Qal √הלך with preposition ל. See on 10:12 for the identical phrase. Although this could be explanatory (cf. on 10:12), this infinitive phrase occurs in a sequence that conforms to a characteristic pattern of Hebrew coordination, with ו found only before the final item (cf. JM §177o).

וּלְדָבְקָה־בֽוֹ׃. Inf constr Qal √דבק with preposition ל. The stative verb √דבק has the feminine ending ־ָה for the infinitive construct, like √ירא and √אהב (GKC §45d; cf. JM §49d). בו is oblique complement. For cleaving (√דבק) to Yhwh, cf. 4:4; 10:20. A third adjunct infinitive phrase (see above).

11:23 וְהוֹרִ֨ישׁ יְהוָ֜ה אֶת־כָּל־הַגּוֹיִ֤ם הָאֵ֨לֶּה֙ מִלִּפְנֵיכֶ֔ם
וִֽירִשְׁתֶּ֣ם גּוֹיִ֔ם גְּדֹלִ֥ים וַעֲצֻמִ֖ים מִכֶּֽם׃

D2. PD. Two modal *qatals* spell out the conditional apodosis. Contingent on their obedience (v. 22), Yhwh will dispossess (√ירש Hiphil; v. 23a) so they will too (√ירש Qal; v. 23b).

וְהוֹרִ֨ישׁ יְהוָ֜ה אֶת־כָּל־הַגּוֹיִ֤ם הָאֵ֨לֶּה֙ מִלִּפְנֵיכֶ֔ם. *Qatal* (modal) 3ms Hiph √ירש (cf. 4:38; 9:4-5). מלפניכם is spatial adjunct PP. ו + modal *qatal* often introduces a conditional apodosis (GKC §112ff; JM §176d).

וִֽירִשְׁתֶּ֣ם גּוֹיִ֔ם גְּדֹלִ֥ים וַעֲצֻמִ֖ים מִכֶּֽם׃. *Qatal* (modal) 2mp Qal √ירש. See on 4:1 for the form of the verb. See on 9:1 for √ירש Qal as "dispossess." See on 4:38 for the accusative complement NP with comparative מן, גוים גדלים ועצמים מכם.

11:24 כָּל־הַמָּק֗וֹם אֲשֶׁ֨ר תִּדְרֹ֧ךְ כַּֽף־רַגְלְכֶ֛ם בּ֖וֹ לָכֶ֣ם יִהְיֶ֑ה
מִן־הַמִּדְבָּ֨ר וְהַלְּבָנ֜וֹן מִן־הַנָּהָ֣ר נְהַר־פְּרָ֗ת וְעַד֙ הַיָּ֣ם
הָאַֽחֲר֔וֹן יִהְיֶ֖ה גְּבֻלְכֶֽם׃

D2. PD. With two *yiqtol* clauses, Moses declares what will be theirs if they obey. Both clauses follow asyndetically, unpacking what it means to dispossess these nations (v. 23).

כָּל־הַמָּק֞וֹם אֲשֶׁ֨ר תִּדְרֹ֧ךְ כַּֽף־רַגְלְכֶ֛ם בּ֖וֹ לָכֶ֣ם יִהְיֶ֑ה. *Yiqtol* 3ms Qal √היה. In past and future time, the copula (√היה) is usually overt. כל־המקום is the construct NP subject. When כל is bound in construct relationship with a determinate noun of "species or category," the absolute or genitive can occur in the singular, but with a plural connotation (JM §139g), hence "all the places" (cf. 12:13, where מקום is indeterminate). לכם is the complement, indicating possession (cf. WO §11.2.10d). It is fronted for **focus**, "yours [and not anyone else's]." The clause follows the conditional apodosis (v. 23) asyndetically, hence it serves to expand upon the nature of their possession.

אֲשֶׁ֨ר תִּדְרֹ֧ךְ כַּֽף־רַגְלְכֶ֛ם בּ֖וֹ. *Yiqtol* 3fs Qal √דרך. Restrictive relative clause with **head** כל־המקום. כף־רגלכם is construct NP; although not marked as feminine, body parts tend to be feminine (WO §6.4.1b), hence the 3fs verb, of which כף is the subject. בו is spatial adjunct PP with resumptive pronoun. For a similar notion, see 2:5.

מִן־הַמִּדְבָּ֨ר וְהַלְּבָנ֜וֹן מִן־הַנָּהָ֣ר נְהַר־פְּרָ֗ת וְעַד֙ הַיָּ֣ם הָאַֽחֲר֔וֹן יִהְיֶ֖ה גְּבֻלְכֶֽם׃ *Yiqtol* 3ms Qal √היה. In past and future time, the copula (√היה) is usually overt. The clause follows asyndetically, giving further definition to the territory possessed.

מִן־הַמִּדְבָּ֨ר וְהַלְּבָנ֜וֹן. Spatial PP, functioning as the subject of the copula clause (note the S–P word order and the parallel with the second half of the verse). Although normally a preposition is repeated before each object, sometimes there is "preposition override," when the preposition is omitted before subsequent objects (WO §11.4.2a). For the article with לבנון, see on הירדן in 1:1 (cf. 1:7).

מִן־הַנָּהָ֣ר נְהַר־פְּרָ֗ת וְעַד֙ הַיָּ֣ם הָאַֽחֲר֔וֹן. Coordinated spatial PPs, functioning as the subject of the copula clause (see above). נהר־פרת is appositional construct NP. See on 1:7. הים האחרון is "the western sea"; looking east, it is the sea "behind" (cf. אָחֵר); אחרון is an adjective, used attributively; for its form, see JM §88Me; cf. ראשון.

11:25 לֹא־יִתְיַצֵּ֥ב אִ֖ישׁ בִּפְנֵיכֶ֑ם פַּחְדְּכֶ֨ם וּמֽוֹרַאֲכֶ֜ם יִתֵּ֣ן ׀ יְהוָ֣ה אֱלֹֽהֵיכֶ֗ם עַל־פְּנֵ֤י כָל־הָאָ֙רֶץ֙ אֲשֶׁ֣ר תִּדְרְכוּ־בָ֔הּ כַּאֲשֶׁ֖ר דִּבֶּ֥ר לָכֶֽם׃ ס

D2. PD. With two further asyndetic *yiqtol* clauses, Moses declares what response they will have from the nations, if they obey. As with v. 24, these *yiqtols* unpack v. 23b. These four clauses in vv. 24-25 are framed by the motif of "treading" (√דרך), something assured for them if they walk in Yhwh's "ways" (דרך, v. 22).

לֹא־יִתְיַצֵּב אִישׁ בִּפְנֵיכֶם. *Yiqtol* 3ms Hitp √יצב. See on 7:24 for the almost identical phrase. The Israelites will be as the Anakites were reputed to be (9:2).

פַּחְדְּכֶם וּמוֹרַאֲכֶם יִתֵּן ׀ יְהוָה אֱלֹהֵיכֶם עַל־פְּנֵי כָל־הָאָרֶץ. *Yiqtol* 3ms Qal √נתן.

פַּחְדְּכֶם וּמוֹרַאֲכֶם. Accusative complements of √נתן, fronted for **focus**: of all the possible responses Yhwh will put, it will be [nothing but] fear and dread. Both nouns have the pronominal suffix as an "'objective genitive,'" "fear *of* you" (JM §129e, ka). For מורא, "terror," cf. on 4:34. Note also 2:25.

עַל־פְּנֵי כָל־הָאָרֶץ. Oblique construct phrase complement of √נתן. See on 2:25.

אֲשֶׁר תִּדְרְכוּ־בָהּ. *Yiqtol* 2mp Qal √דרך. Restrictive relative clause. בה is oblique complement of the verb דרך. The 3fs resumptive pronoun ־הָ picks up the **head** of the relative clause, הארץ.

כַּאֲשֶׁר דִּבֶּר לָכֶם: ס. *Qatal* 3ms Piel √דבר. See on 1:11 for the identical phrase. Behind every action lies Yhwh's promise.

Israel should enshrine the choice they face in a ceremony in the land (11:26-32)

This final section before "the statutes and judgments" (12:1) is framed by an *inclusio*, "that I am setting before you today" (vv. 26, 32). Attention is on enshrining the choice of blessing and curse, blessing rooted in obedience and curse in disobedience, in a ceremony in the land. The description of the two choices, of blessing and curse, and of two mountains, Ebal and Gerizim, is a climax of this opening section. But it is also a frame for chapters 12–26 (cf. chapters 27–28); and 11:31-32 are tightly bound to what follows (cf. McConville, 212–13; Nelson, 42–141):

    A   Gift of land (ארץ, נתן, ירש, "Yhwh your God") (11:31)
        B   Be careful to keep (שמר, עשה) the laws and statutes (חקים ומשפטים) (11:32)
        B′   Be careful to keep (שמר, עשה) the laws and statutes (חקים ומשפטים) (12:1)
    A′   Gift of land (ארץ, נתן, ירש, "Yhwh your God") (12:1)

This makes a strong bond between the motivational preaching of chapters 5–11 and the so-called "Deuteronomic Code" of chapters 12–26.

> ²⁶*See! I am putting before you today blessing and curse,* ²⁷*the blessing if you obey the commandments of Yhwh your God that I am commanding you today,* ²⁸*and the curse if you do not obey the commandments of Yhwh your God and turn aside from the way that I am commanding you today, walking after other gods that you have not known.* ²⁹*When Yhwh your God brings you into the land that you are entering to possess, you shall give the blessing on Mount Gerizim and the curse on Mount Ebal—*³⁰*See, they are the ones across the Jordan to the west of the western road in the land of the Canaanites who live in the Arabah opposite Gilgal beside the oaks of Moreh.* ³¹*Because you are crossing the Jordan to enter to possess the land that Yhwh your God is giving to you and you will possess it and live in it,* ³²*so you should keep, by doing, all the statutes and the judgements that I am setting before you today.*

11:26 רְאֵה אָנֹכִי נֹתֵן לִפְנֵיכֶם הַיּוֹם בְּרָכָה וּקְלָלָה:

D2. Moses follows an opening interjection (HD) with a summary statement of the options he is presenting, blessing and curse. ED.

רְאֵה. Impv ms Qal √ראה. An interjection. See on 1:8.

אָנֹכִי נֹתֵן לִפְנֵיכֶם הַיּוֹם בְּרָכָה וּקְלָלָה. Ptcp ms Qal √נתן. **Null-copula** clause with participial predicate. Unmarked S–P word order. To נתן something לפני someone is to lay something out before someone with a view to them acting appropriately (cf. on 1:8; 4:8). For אנכי, see on 4:1. היום is adverbial time adjunct NP. For "today," see on 1:10.

11:27 אֶת־הַבְּרָכָה אֲשֶׁר תִּשְׁמְעוּ אֶל־מִצְוֹת יְהוָה אֱלֹהֵיכֶם אֲשֶׁר אָנֹכִי מְצַוֶּה אֶתְכֶם הַיּוֹם:

D2. Moses expands upon the blessing. A conditional protasis insists that it depends on obedience to Moses' commands in Moab.

אֶת־הַבְּרָכָה. Appositional NP. Indeterminate ברכה (v. 26) becomes determinate, הברכה, because it has been previously mentioned (cf. JM §137f). This and the following verse expand ברכה וקללה (v. 26).

אֲשֶׁר תִּשְׁמְעוּ אֶל־מִצְוֹת יְהוָה אֱלֹהֵיכֶם. Yiqtol 2mp Qal √שמע. This is one of the very few instances of the relative particle אשר introducing a conditional protasis (GKC §159cc; WO §38.2d; MNK §40.6.7; AC §5.2.2(a); JM §167j; WHS §469, §515). The parallel with אִם־לֹא (v. 28) and the impossibility of taking it as a relative marker or **complementizer** leaves the grammarian little choice. But rather than seeing this as an example of a wider trend or an illustration of development in usage of אשר, it is better to see it as anomalous (Holmstedt 2006: 21–22). A plausible pragmatic reason for the choice of אשר and the switch to אם־לא is Moses' preference that they choose the blessing (cf. Weinfeld, 434). For שמע אל in the sense of "listen to," "obey," see on 7:12; 11:13.

אֲשֶׁר אָנֹכִי מְצַוֶּה אֶתְכֶם הַיּוֹם. See on 11:13 for the identical phrase. Restrictive relative clause with **head** מצות.

11:28 וְהַקְּלָלָה אִם־לֹא תִשְׁמְעוּ אֶל־מִצְוֺת יְהוָה אֱלֹהֵיכֶם
וְסַרְתֶּם מִן־הַדֶּרֶךְ אֲשֶׁר אָנֹכִי מְצַוֶּה אֶתְכֶם הַיּוֹם
לָלֶכֶת אַחֲרֵי אֱלֹהִים אֲחֵרִים אֲשֶׁר לֹא־יְדַעְתֶּם: ס

D2. Moses expands upon the curse, in parallel fashion to v. 27. But here the dynamic of disobedience has more detail: a conditional protasis with a *yiqtol* is then followed by a modal *qatal* and an adjunct explanatory infinitive phrase. Failure to obey, turning from the path Moses has been outlining in Moab by chasing other deities, will result in the curse. In the stark exposition of how to experience the curse, Moses looks to persuade (or indict): these are deities they have not experienced.

וְהַקְּלָלָה. Appositional NP, coordinated with אר־הברכה (v. 27). Normally in a series of definite objects, if the first has the particle את, subsequent objects do too, but sometimes את governs all (WO §11.3.1a).

אִם־לֹא תִשְׁמְעוּ אֶל־מִצְוֺת יְהוָה אֱלֹהֵיכֶם. *Yiqtol* 2mp Qal √שמע. Conditional protasis introduced by subordinating conjunction אם־לא. For שמע אל in the sense of "listen to," "obey," see on 7:12 (cf. 11:13, 27).

וְסַרְתֶּם מִן־הַדֶּרֶךְ. *Qatal* (modal) 2mp Qal √סור. The modal *qatal* continues the conditional protasis. מן־הדרך is spatial adjunct PP. דרך has been an important motif, whether literal or figurative (cf. 5:33; 8:2, 6; 9:12, 16); so too has √סור (see on 11:16).

אֲשֶׁר אָנֹכִי מְצַוֶּה אֶתְכֶם הַיּוֹם. See on 11:13 for the identical phrase (cf. v. 27). Restrictive relative clause with **head** הדרך. Yhwh has commanded a "way" (so 5:33; 9:12, 16), that Moses is relaying.

לָלֶ֫כֶת אַחֲרֵי אֱלֹהִים אֲחֵרִים. Inf constr Qal √הלך with preposition ל. For the form ללכת, see on 8:6. The phrase is an adjunct infinitive construct phrase. The infinitive construct is **gerundial** or explanatory, "by walking" (cf. WO §36.2.3e); it explains what it means to "turn aside" from the way. Following (√הלך) other deities is in sharp contrast with walking in Yhwh's ways (√הלך, דרך; 8:6; 10:12; 11:22).

אֲשֶׁ֥ר לֹֽא־יְדַעְתֶּֽם׃ ס. *Qatal* 2mp Qal √ידע. Non-restrictive relative clause with **head** אלהים אחרים. √ידע is used here in the sense of not having "experienced" (cf. 29:25; 32:17). This provides supplementary information, not strictly necessary for identification. Moses shows that idolatry is unwarranted.

11:29 וְהָיָ֗ה כִּ֤י יְבִֽיאֲךָ֙ יְהוָ֣ה אֱלֹהֶ֔יךָ אֶל־הָאָ֕רֶץ אֲשֶׁר־אַתָּ֥ה בָא־שָׁ֖מָּה לְרִשְׁתָּ֑הּ וְנָתַתָּ֤ה אֶת־הַבְּרָכָה֙ עַל־הַ֣ר גְּרִזִ֔ים וְאֶת־הַקְּלָלָ֖ה עַל־הַ֥ר עֵיבָֽל׃

ND. A temporal protasis in future time with a *yiqtol* (v. 29a) is followed by injunctive temporal apodosis with a modal *qatal* (v. 29b). HD. The assumption is that they will enter the land. They are to hold a ceremony when they do, to highlight the two choices facing them (cf. on 1:1-5).

וְהָיָ֗ה. Qatal (modal) 3ms Qal √היה. והיה here anchors discourse time in the future (see on 6:12).

כִּ֤י יְבִֽיאֲךָ֙ יְהוָ֣ה אֱלֹהֶ֔יךָ אֶל־הָאָ֕רֶץ. *Yiqtol* 3ms Hiph √בוא with 2ms pronominal suffix. See on 6:12 for the identical phrase.

אֲשֶׁר־אַתָּ֥ה בָא־שָׁ֖מָּה לְרִשְׁתָּ֑הּ. See on 7:1 for the identical phrase (also 11:10). Restrictive relative clause with **head** הארץ.

וְנָתַתָּ֤ה אֶת־הַבְּרָכָה֙ עַל־הַ֣ר גְּרִזִ֔ים וְאֶת־הַקְּלָלָ֖ה עַל־הַ֥ר עֵיבָֽל׃. *Qatal* (modal) 2ms Qal √נתן. The 2ms *qatal* of √נתן more frequently is found with ending תָּה- than without the ה (תָּ-). Probably this is due to "orthographic compensation" because of the assimilation of the final root letter, ן (GKC §66h; cf. GKC §44g). Temporal apodosis. ו + modal *qatal* often introduces a temporal (or conditional) apodosis (GKC §112ff; JM §176f). על־הר עיבל and על־הר גרזים are oblique complements. Both have construct NPs as the object of the preposition על. The absolute specifies the name of the mountain (cf. GKC §128k; WO §9.5.3h).

11:30 הֲלֹא־הֵ֜מָּה בְּעֵ֣בֶר הַיַּרְדֵּ֗ן אַחֲרֵי֙ דֶּ֚רֶךְ מְב֣וֹא הַשֶּׁ֔מֶשׁ בְּאֶ֙רֶץ֙ הַֽכְּנַעֲנִ֔י הַיֹּשֵׁ֖ב בָּעֲרָבָ֑ה מ֚וּל הַגִּלְגָּ֔ל אֵ֖צֶל אֵלוֹנֵ֥י מֹרֶֽה׃

D2. ED. The **asyndesis** marks this as a parenthetical comment giving geographical data about the two mountains mentioned in v. 29. The geographical issues vex commentators here (see McConville, 196; Nelson, 141 for concise summaries).

הֲלֹא־הֵ֜מָּה בְּעֵ֣בֶר הַיַּרְדֵּ֗ן אַחֲרֵי֙ דֶּ֚רֶךְ מְב֣וֹא הַשֶּׁ֔מֶשׁ. Asyndetic **null-copula** clause with PP predicate בעבר הירדן. ED. The **asyndesis** marks this clause out as an almost parenthetical commentary on the previous verse. הלא is probably not introducing a rhetorical question, but is the presentative clausal adverb (see on 3:11). For בעבר הירדן, see on 1:1.

אַחֲרֵי֙ דֶּ֚רֶךְ מְב֣וֹא הַשֶּׁ֔מֶשׁ. Adjunct construct PP. For the directional sense of אחרי, "to the west of" (cf. "behind"), see WHS §359. דרך מבוא השמש is construct NP, the object of the preposition אחרי; it comprises דרך as the first construct, "the way of/to" (see on 1:2), and the phrase מבוא השמש, "the setting of the sun" (cf. Josh 1:4), hence "the road to the west," "the western road."

בְּאֶ֙רֶץ֙ הַֽכְּנַעֲנִ֔י. Adjunct construct PP. The presence of the article on the gentilic adjective, כנעני, indicates the whole group is meant (see on האמרי in 1:4; cf. 1:7).

הַיֹּשֵׁ֖ב בָּעֲרָבָ֑ה. Ptcp ms Qal √ישב, with the relative use of the article (see on 1:30). בערבה (see on 1:1) is oblique complement PP with √ישב.

מ֚וּל הַגִּלְגָּ֔ל אֵ֖צֶל אֵלוֹנֵ֥י מֹרֶֽה׃. Adjunct PPs. For מול, "opposite," see on 1:1 (cf. 3:29). The presence of the article with הגלגל indicates that it was not originally a proper noun, but the name of a place ("the circle"?) that has become a proper name (cf. GKC §125d, e; WO §13.6a; JM §137b). אלוני מרה is construct NP object of the preposition אצל.

11:31 כִּ֤י אַתֶּם֙ עֹבְרִ֣ים אֶת־הַיַּרְדֵּ֔ן לָבֹא֙ לָרֶ֣שֶׁת אֶת־הָאָ֔רֶץ אֲשֶׁר־יְהוָ֥ה אֱלֹהֵיכֶ֖ם נֹתֵ֣ן לָכֶ֑ם וִֽירִשְׁתֶּ֥ם אֹתָ֖הּ וִֽישַׁבְתֶּם־בָּֽהּ׃

D2. A causal clause with participial predicate indicates imminent action. It is followed (v. 31b) by two modal *qatals* that continue the narrative action of the causal clause: "Because you are crossing . . . and will possess . . . and will live. . . ."

כִּי אַתֶּם עֹבְרִים אֶת־הַיַּרְדֵּן. Ptcp mp Qal √עבר. For the almost identical phrase and for √עבר followed by לבא לרשת, see on 9:1. כי here introduces a causal clause (Weinfeld, 453; cf. LXX γάρ), not a temporal one (Tigay 1996: 118; Nelson, 141), because there is no finite verb (see on 8:7).

לָבֹא לָרֶשֶׁת אֶת־הָאָרֶץ. Inf constr Qal √בוא and √ירש, both with preposition ל. See on 9:1 for both verbs. Here it is (the more usual) הארץ not גוים that is the accusative complement.

אֲשֶׁר־יְהוָה אֱלֹהֵיכֶם נֹתֵן לָכֶם. Ptcp ms Qal √נתן. Restrictive relative clause, with **head** הארץ. For the clausal syntax, see on 1:20.

וִירִשְׁתֶּם אֹתָהּ וִישַׁבְתֶּם־בָּהּ. *Qatal* (modal) 2mp Qal √ירש and Qal √ישב. For the vocalization of וירשתם, see on 4:1. These modal *qatals* continue the causal clause, with the expectation of an imminent possession and living in the land (cf. 4:22).

11:32 וּשְׁמַרְתֶּם לַעֲשׂוֹת אֵת כָּל־הַחֻקִּים וְאֶת־הַמִּשְׁפָּטִים
אֲשֶׁר אָנֹכִי נֹתֵן לִפְנֵיכֶם הַיּוֹם:

D2. HD. Building on the causal clause (v. 31), Moses concludes in the causal apodosis with the characteristic call to "keep by doing" what he is setting before them "today" in the plains of Moab.

וּשְׁמַרְתֶּם לַעֲשׂוֹת אֵת כָּל־הַחֻקִּים וְאֶת־הַמִּשְׁפָּטִים. *Qatal* (modal) 2mp Qal √שמר followed by inf constr Qal √עשה with preposition ל. HD. See on 5:1 for ושמרתם לעשות. When כי introduces a causal clause that is in "first position," often the apodosis begins with what Joüon-Muraoka term a "Waw of apodosis" (JM §170o). Because of the imminent entry, they should keep the statutes and commands Moses is giving.

אֲשֶׁר אָנֹכִי נֹתֵן לִפְנֵיכֶם הַיּוֹם:. See on 4:8 for the identical phrase.

GLOSSARY

This glossary is only for words that are found in **bold** in the handbook. It is not meant to be comprehensive. Terms that are very common and well understood are not explained at all in the book. Terms/concepts that are either fairly common or recur frequently in the handbook (or both) are included in the Linguistic Background section of the Introduction (§5); some may also appear below. If a term is neither in the glossary nor in the Linguistic Background section, you should look in the glossary in Waltke and O'Connor (WO), van der Merwe, Naudé and Kroeze (MNK) or Arnold and Choi (AC).

aphaeresis—the dropping out of an initial consonant (e.g., שבת, 1:6)
apocopation—shortening of a word form at the end (e.g., צו, 2:4)
asyndesis—see §5.3
by-form—a subsidiary or variant form of a word (e.g., ושננתם, 6:7)
casus pendens—"hanging case"; see on **extraposition**
cleft sentence—where "a single clause has been divided into two separate sections, each with its own verb, one of which appears in a dependent *wh*-clause (relative clause)" (Crystal, 75) (e.g., "it is he that you should fear," 6:13)
complementizer—"a function word that introduces a clause and allows it to be subcategorised as a noun phrase" (Holmstedt 2006: 9) (e.g., לאמר, 1:5)
deictic—points to something "near" within the mental map of the speaker (e.g., אלה, 1:1)
denominative—a verb form derived from a noun (e.g., האזין, 1:45)
discourse active—in a dialogue, the participants may not have every detail of the dialogue in their mind at a particular point. Those things which *are* in mind are said to be "discourse active."

ellipsis—omission of a part of speech from a clause or phrase (e.g., אעברה־נא, 3:25)

elliptical—economical or obscure mode of expression, where an element has been left out (e.g., 5:11: לא תשא את־שם־יהוה אלהיך לשוא)

extraposition (extraposed)—extraposition is the movement of a clausal constituent to a different part of the clause or even outside the clause (**casus pendens**) (e.g., על־פני העמים תחת כל־השמים אשר ישמעון 2:25)

focus—see §5.10

gerund (gerundial)—a verbal noun, "-ing," occupying the place of a noun in a clause (e.g., שבת, 1:6)

gerundive—a verbal adjective, expressing the desirability or necessity of the verbal action (e.g., נורא, 1:19)

hapax—a word that occurs once (e.g., √הון, 1:41)

head—the antecedent of a relative clause (e.g., . . . הארץ אשר, 4:1)

hendiadys—expressing one idea with two words (e.g., הברית והחסד, 7:9)

homonym—an identical root (e.g., √גור, 1:17)

inclusio—a literary device, whereby a section is framed or bracketed by a word or phrase (e.g., פנה and נסע in 1:7 and 2:1).

indirect speech act—one where there is "an indirect relationship" between the "structure" of the speech act and its "function" (Yule, 55) (e.g., וירשתם, 4:22)

indirect volitive—the expression of purpose or result through a sequence of verbs coordinated with ו, usually with a change of subject (e.g., נשלחה אנשים לפנינו ויחפרו־לנו את־הארץ, 1:22)

irrealis—see §5.8

litotes—rhetorical device, where a double negative yields an understatement amounting to a strong positive (e.g., לא במסכנת, 8:9)

merism—the use of parts/opposites to indicate the whole (e.g., כקטן כגדל, 1:17)

metonymy—a figure of speech that replaces the name of something with the name of another thing with which it is closely associated

null-copula—the absence of a copula (a form of the verb "to be") in a clause (e.g., אלה הדברים, 1:1)

null-head—the absence of an overt **head** (or antecedent) in a relative clause (e.g., עד אשר, 2:14)

null subject—pro-drop—the omission of the syntactic subject

paragogic—word-extending; it can be ן, at the end of certain verb forms (e.g., תשמעון, 1:17), ה, the so-called locative ה (e.g., ההרה, 1:24), or י (e.g., זולתי, 4:12)

paronomastic—the use of the infinitive absolute with a finite verb of the same root (e.g., שמור תשמרון, 6:17)

periphrasis (periphrastic)—the use of a longer way of expressing something rather than an inflected form (e.g., צדיקם, 4:8)

pro—instead of having an overt (see §5.4) personal pronoun subject, the **null subject pro** is usually found in the verb (e.g., לא תעשׂה, 5:14)

quotative frame—A "quotative frame" gives the "speech of the reporting speaker" that introduces the "quotation" itself, "the speech of the reported speaker" (Miller 1995: 156) (e.g., 1:5)

realis—see §5.8

resultative—the Piel of a fientive verb which occurs transitively in the Qal, "bringing about a state corresponding to the verbal meaning of the *Qal*" (WO §24.3b) (e.g., ינהג, 4:27)

syncopation—rejection of a consonant (often the article ה) in the middle of a word (e.g., בצר, 4:30)

topic—see §5.10

triggered inversion—a change in word order "triggered" for syntactic or pragmatic reasons (e.g., אשר דבר משה, 1:1)

tripartite nominal clause—a clause of three components where one of the components is a third-person independent personal pronoun (e.g., כי משפט לאלהים הוא, 1:17)

WORKS CITED

Andersen, Francis I. *The Hebrew Verbless Clause in the Pentateuch*. Nashville: Abingdon, 1970.
Arnold, Bill T. "The Love-Fear Antinomy in Deuteronomy 5–11." *Vetus Testamentum* 61 (2011): 551–69.
Austin, J. L. *How to Do Things with Words*. Edited by J. O. Urmson. Oxford: Oxford University Press, 1962.
Barr, James. "'Determination' and the Definite Article in Biblical Hebrew." *Journal of Semitic Studies* 34 (1989): 307–35.
Bauckham, Richard J. "Biblical Theology and the Problems of Monotheism." Pages 187–232 in *Out of Egypt: Biblical Theology and Biblical Interpretation*, edited by Craig Bartholomew, Mary Healy, Karl Möller, and Robin Parry. Scripture and Hermeneutics Series 5. Bletchley, U.K.: Paternoster, 2004.
Blau, Joshua. *Phonology and Morphology of Biblical Hebrew: An Introduction*. Linguistic Studies in Ancient West Semitic 2. Winona Lake, Ind.: Eisenbrauns, 2010.
Block, Daniel I. *Deuteronomy*. NIVAC. Grand Rapids: Zondervan, 2012.
———. "The Grace of Torah: The Mosaic Prescription for Life (Deut. 4:1-8; 6:20-25)." *Bibliotheca Sacra* 162 (2005): 3–22.
———. "How Many Is God? An Investigation Into the Meaning of Deuteronomy 6:4-5." *Journal of the Evangelical Theological Society* 47 (2004): 193–212.
Bruno, Christopher R. "A Note Pertaining to the Translation of Deut 6:4." *Vetus Testamentum* 59 (2009): 320–22.
Buth, Randall. "Word Order in the Verbless Clause: A Generative-Functional Approach." Pages 79–108 in *The Verbless Clause in Biblical Hebrew: Linguistic Approaches*, edited by Cynthia L. Miller. Linguistic Studies in Ancient West Semitic 1. Winona Lake, Ind.: Eisenbrauns, 1999.

Callaham, Scott N. *Modality and the Biblical Hebrew Infinitive Absolute*. Abhandlungen für die Kunde des Morgenlandes 71. Wiesbaden: Harrassowitz, 2010.

Carasik, Michael, ed. and trans. *The Rubin JPS Miqra'ot Gedolot: Deuteronomy*. The Commentators' Bible. Lincoln: University of Nebraska Press, 2015.

———. "To See a Sound: A Deuteronomic Rereading of Exodus 20:15." *Prooftexts* 19 (1999): 257–65.

Cassuto, Umberto. *A Commentary on the Book of Exodus*. Translated by Israel Abrahams. Publications of the Perry Foundation for Biblical Research in the Hebrew University of Jerusalem. Jerusalem: Magnes, 1967.

Christensen, Duane L. *Deuteronomy 1:1–21:9*. 2nd ed. Word Biblical Commentary 6A. Nashville: Nelson, 2001.

Conklin, Blane. *Oath Formulas in Biblical Hebrew*. Linguistic Studies in Ancient West Semitic 5. Winona Lake, Ind.: Eisenbrauns, 2011.

Cook, John A. "The Hebrew Participle and Stative in Typological Perspective." *Journal of Northwest Semitic Languages* 34 (2008): 1–19.

———. "The Semantics of Verbal Pragmatics: Clarifying the Roles of *Wayyiqtol* and *Weqatal* in Biblical Hebrew Prose." *Journal of Semitic Studies* 49 (2004): 247–73.

———. *Time and the Biblical Hebrew Verb: The Expression of Tense, Aspect, and Modality in Biblical Hebrew*. Linguistic Studies in Ancient West Semitic 7. Winona Lake, Ind.: Eisenbrauns, 2012.

Costecalde, Claude-Bernard, Henri Cazelles, and Pierre Grelot. "Sacré (et Sainteté)." Vol. 10, pages 1342–1483 in *Dictionnaire de la Bible: Supplément*, edited by L. Pirot, A. Robert, H. Cazelles, and André Feuillet. 12 vols. Paris: Letouzey, 1928–.

Craigie, Peter C. *The Book of Deuteronomy*. New International Commentary on the Old Testament. Grand Rapids: Eerdmans, 1976.

Crystal, David. *A Dictionary of Linguistics and Phonetics*. 5th ed. The Language Library. Oxford: Blackwell, 2003.

de Regt, Lénard J. *A Parametric Model for Syntactic Studies of a Textual Corpus, Demonstrated on the Hebrew of Deuteronomy 1–30*. 2 vols. Studia Semitica Neerlandica. Assen: Van Gorcum, 1988.

DeRouchie, Jason S. "Counting the Ten: An Investigation Into the Numbering of the Decalogue." Pages 93–126 in *For Our Good Always: Studies on the Message and Influence of Deuteronomy in Honor of Daniel I. Block*, edited by Jason S. DeRouchie, Jason Gile, and Kenneth J. Turner. Winona Lake, Ind.: Eisenbrauns, 2013.

———. *A Call to Covenant Love: Text, Grammar, and Literary Structure in Deuteronomy 5–11*. Gorgias Dissertations 30. Piscataway, N.J.: Gorgias, 2007.

Driver, S. R. *A Critical and Exegetical Commentary on Deuteronomy*. International Critical Commentary. Edinburgh: T&T Clark, 1895.

Dyk, J. W., and Eep Talstra. "Paradigmatic and Syntagmatic Features in Identifying Subject and Predicate in Nominal Clauses." Pages 133–85 in *The Verbless Clause in Biblical Hebrew: Linguistic Approaches*, edited by Cynthia L. Miller. Linguistic Studies in Ancient West Semitic 1. Winona Lake, Ind.: Eisenbrauns, 1999.

Eslinger, Lyle M. "Watering Egypt (Deuteronomy xi 10-11)." *Vetus Testamentum* 37 (1987): 85–90.

Fishbane, Michael. *Biblical Interpretation in Ancient Israel*. Oxford: Clarendon, 1985.

Frese, Daniel A. "A Land of Gates: Covenant Communities in the Book of Deuteronomy." *Vetus Testamentum* 65 (2015): 33–52.

Geller, Stephen A. "Fiery Wisdom: Logos and Lexis in Deuteronomy 4." *Prooftexts* 14 (1994): 103–39.

———. "Cleft Sentences with Pleonastic Pronoun: A Syntactic Construction of Biblical Hebrew and Some of Its Literary Uses." *Journal of the Ancient Near East Society* 20 (1991): 15–33.

Hawk, L. Daniel. *Joshua*. Berit Olam. Collegeville, Minn.: Liturgical Press, 2000.

Hillers, Delbert R. "Delocutive Verbs in Biblical Hebrew." *Journal of Biblical Literature* 86 (1967): 320–24.

Himmelfarb, Lea. "The Exegetical Role of the Paseq." *Sefarad* 58, no. 2 (1998): 243–60.

Hoftijzer, Jacob. *The Function and Use of the Imperfect Form with Nun Paragogicum in Classical Hebrew*. Studia Semitica Neerlandica 21. Assen: Van Gorcum, 1985.

Holmstedt, Robert D. "The Relative Clause in Biblical Hebrew: A Linguistic Analysis." Ph.D. diss. University of Wisconsin-Madison, 2002.

———. "The Story of Ancient Hebrew ʾăšer." *Ancient Near Eastern Studies* 43 (2006): 7–26.

———. "So-Called First Conjunct Agreement in Biblical Hebrew." Pages 105–29 in *Afroasiatic Studies in Memory of Robert Hetzron: Proceedings of the 35th Annual Meeting of the North American Conference on Afroasiatic Linguistics (NACAL 35)*, edited by Charles G. Häberl. Newcastle-upon-Tyne: Cambridge Scholars, 2009.

———. *Ruth: A Handbook on the Hebrew Text*. Baylor Handbook on the Hebrew Bible. Waco, Tex.: Baylor University Press, 2010.

———. "The Typological Classification of the Hebrew of Genesis: Subject-Verb or Verb-Subject?" *Journal of the Hebrew Scriptures* 11, no. 14 (2011).

Holmstedt, Robert D., and Andrew R. Jones. "The Pronoun in Tripartite Verbless Clauses in Biblical Hebrew: Resumption for Left-Dislocation or Pronominal Copula?" *Journal of Semitic Studies* 59 (2014): 53–89.

Janzen, J. Gerald. "On the Most Important Word in the Shema (Deuteronomy VI, 4-5)." *Vetus Testamentum* 37 (1987): 280–300.

Joosten, Jan. *The Verbal System of Biblical Hebrew: A New Synthesis Elaborated on the Basis of Classical Prose*. Jerusalem Biblical Studies 10. Jerusalem: Simor, 2012.

Gemser, B. "*Beʿēber hajjardēn*: In Jordan's Borderland." *Vetus Testamentum* 2 (1952): 349–55.

Goudoever, Jan von. "The Liturgical Significance of the Date in Dt 1, 3." Pages 145–48 in *Das Deuteronomium: Entstehung, Gestalt und Botschaft*. Edited by Norbert Lohfink. Bibliotheca Ephemeridum Theologicarum Lovaniensium 68. Leuven: Leuven University Press, 1985.

Heller, Roy L. *Narrative Structure and Discourse Constellations: An Analysis of Clause Function in Biblical Hebrew Prose*. Harvard Semitic Studies 55. Winona Lake, Ind.: Eisenbrauns, 2004.

Kraut, Judah. "Deciphering the Shema: Staircase Parallelism and the Syntax of Deuteronomy 6:4." *Vetus Testamentum* 61 (2011): 582–602.

Kreuzer, Siegfried. "Zur Bedeutung und Etymologie von *hištaḥawah/yštḥwy*." *Vetus Testamentum* 35 (1985): 39–60.

Lambdin, Thomas O. *Introduction to Biblical Hebrew*. London: Darton, Longman & Todd, 1973.

Lapsley, Jacqueline E. "Feeling Our Way: Love for God in Deuteronomy." *Catholic Biblical Quarterly* 65 (2003): 350–69.

van Leeuwen, Raymond C. "On the Structure and Sense of Deuteronomy 8." *Proceedings: Eastern Great Lakes and Midwest Biblical Societies* 4 (1984): 237–49.

———. "What Comes Out of God's Mouth: Theological Wordplay in Deuteronomy 8." *Catholic Biblical Quarterly* 47 (1985): 55–57.

Levenson, Jon D. "Who Inserted the Book of the Torah?" *Harvard Theological Review* 68 (1975): 203–33.

Levinsohn, Stephen H., and Robert A. Dooley. *Analyzing Discourse: A Manual of Basic Concepts*. Dallas, Tex.: SIL International, 2001.

Lindquist, Maria. "King Og's Iron Bed." *Catholic Biblical Quarterly* 73 (2011): 477–92.

Lohfink, Norbert. "Deuteronomy 6:24: לְחַיֹּתֵנוּ 'To Maintain Us'." Pages 111–19 in *Shaʿarei Talmon: Studies in the Bible, Qumran, and the*

Ancient Near East Presented to Shemaryahu Talmon, edited by Michael Fishbane and Emanuel Tov. Winona Lake, Ind.: Eisenbrauns, 1992.

Longacre, Robert E. *Joseph: A Story of Divine Providence: A Text Theoretical and Textlinguistic Analysis of Genesis 37 and 39–48*. Winona Lake, Ind.: Eisenbrauns, 1989.

Lowery, Kirk E. "Relative Definiteness and the Verbal Clause." Pages 251–72 in *The Verbless Clause in Biblical Hebrew: Linguistic Approaches*, edited by Cynthia L. Miller. Linguistic Studies in Ancient West Semitic 1. Winona Lake, Ind.: Eisenbrauns, 1999.

Lundbom, Jack R. *Deuteronomy: A Commentary*. Grand Rapids: Eerdmans, 2013.

MacDonald, Nathan. "The Literary Criticism and Rhetorical Logic of Deuteronomy i-iv." *Vetus Testamentum* 56 (2006): 203–24.

———. *Deuteronomy and the Meaning of 'Monotheism'*. Forschungen zum Alten Testament 2/1. Tübingen: Mohr Siebeck, 2003.

Mayes, A. D. H. "Deuteronomy 4 and the Literary Criticism of Deuteronomy." *Journal of Biblical Literature* 100 (1981): 23–51.

———. *Deuteronomy*. NCBC. London: Marshall, Morgan & Scott, 1979.

McBride, S. Dean, Jr. "The Yoke of the Kingdom: An Exposition of Deuteronomy 6:4-5." *Interpretation* 27 (1973): 273–306.

McConville, J. Gordon. *Deuteronomy*. Apollos Old Testament Commentary 5. Leicester: Apollos, 2002.

McKay, J. W. "Man's Love for God in Deuteronomy and the Father/Teacher—Son/Pupil Relationship." *Vetus Testamentum* 22 (1972): 426–35.

Meek, Theophile J. "Old Testament Notes." *Journal of Biblical Literature* 67 (1948): 233–39.

Meier, Samuel A. *Speaking of Speaking: Marking Direct Discourse in the Hebrew Bible*. Supplements to Vetus Testamentum 46. Leiden: Brill, 1992.

Merrill, Eugene H. *Deuteronomy*. New American Commentary 5. Nashville: Broadman, 1994.

Miller, Cynthia L. "Pivotal Issues in Analyzing the Verbless Clause." Pages 3–17 in *The Verbless Clause in Biblical Hebrew: Linguistic Approaches*, edited by Cynthia L. Miller. Linguistic Studies in Ancient West Semitic 1. Winona Lake, Ind.: Eisenbrauns, 1999.

———. *The Representation of Speech in Biblical Hebrew Narrative: A Linguistic Analysis*. Harvard Semitic Monographs 55. Atlanta, Ga.: Scholars Press, 1996.

———. "Discourse Functions of Quotative Frames in Biblical Hebrew Narrative." Pages 155–82 in *Discourse Analysis of Biblical Literature: What*

It Is and What It Offers. Edited by Walter Bodine. Society of Biblical Literature Semeia Studies. Atlanta, Ga.: Scholars Press, 1995.

Miller-Naudé, Cynthia L., and Christo H. J. van der Merwe. "הִנֵּה and Mirativity in Biblical Hebrew." *Hebrew Studies* 52 (2011): 53–81.

Moberly, R. W. L. "Toward an Interpretation of the Shema." Pages 124–44 in *Theological Exegesis: Essays in Honor of Brevard A. Childs*, edited by Christopher R. Seitz and Kathryn Greene-McCreight. Grand Rapids: Eerdmans, 1999.

———. "Yahweh Is One: The Translation of the Shema." Pages 209–15 in *Studies in the Pentateuch*, edited by J. A. Emerton. Supplements to Vetus Testamentum 41. Leiden: Brill, 1990.

Moran, William L. "The Ancient Near Eastern Background of the Love of God in Deuteronomy." *Catholic Biblical Quarterly* 25 (1963a): 77–87.

———. "The End of the Unholy War and the Anti-Exodus." *Biblica* 44 (1963b): 333–42.

Moshavi, Adina. "Can a Positive Rhetorical Question Have a Positive Answer in the Bible?" *Journal of Semitic Studies* 56, no. 2 (2011a): 253–73.

———. "Rhetorical Question or Assertion? The Pragmatics of הֲלֹא in Biblical Hebrew." *Journal of the Ancient Near Eastern Society* 32 (2011b): 91–105.

———. *Word Order in the Biblical Hebrew Finite Clause. A Syntactic and Pragmatic Analysis of Preposing.* Linguistic Studies in Ancient West Semitic 4. Winona Lake, Ind.: Eisenbrauns, 2010.

———. "Syntactic Evidence for a Clausal Adverb הלא in Biblical Hebrew." *Journal of Northwest Semitic Languages* 33, no. 2 (2007): 51–67.

Muraoka, Takamitsu. "The Tripartite Nominal Clause Revisited." Pages 187–214 in *The Verbless Clause in Biblical Hebrew: Linguistic Approaches*, edited by Cynthia L. Miller. Linguistic Studies in Ancient West Semitic 1. Winona Lake, Ind.: Eisenbrauns, 1999.

———. *Emphatic Words and Structures in Biblical Hebrew.* Jerusalem: Magnes, 1985.

Muraoka, Takamitsu, and M. Malessa. "A Deuteronomistic Formula." *Vetus Testamentum* 52 (2002): 548–51.

Nelson, Richard D. *Deuteronomy*. Old Testament Library. Louisville, Ky.: Westminster John Knox, 2002.

Nicol, George G. "Watering Egypt (Deuteronomy xi 10–11) Again." *Vetus Testamentum* 38 (1988): 347–48.

O'Connell, Robert H. "Deuteronomy VIII 1-20: Asymmetrical Concentricity and the Rhetoric of Providence." *Vetus Testamentum* 40 (1990): 437–52.

Olson, Dennis T. *Deuteronomy and the Death of Moses: A Theological Reading*. Overtures to Biblical Theology. Minneapolis: Fortress, 1994.
von Rad, Gerhard. *Deuteronomy*. Translated by Dorothea Barton. Old Testament Library. London: SCM Press, 1966.
Revell, E. J. "The Two Forms of First Person Singular Pronoun in Biblical Hebrew: Redundancy or Expressive Contrast?" *Journal of Semitic Studies* 40 (1995): 199–217.
———. "The Conditioning of Stress Position in Waw Consecutive Perfect Forms in Biblical Hebrew." *Hebrew Annual Review* 9 (1985): 277–300.
Robar, Elizabeth. *The Verb and the Paragraph in Biblical Hebrew: A Cognitive-Linguistic Approach*. Studies in Semitic Languages and Linguistics 78. Leiden: Brill, 2015.
Robson, James E. *Honey from the Rock: Deuteronomy for the People of God*. Nottingham: Apollos, 2013.
Sarna, Nahum M. "Interchange of the Prepositions *beth* and *min* in Biblical Hebrew." *Journal of Biblical Literature* 78 (1959): 310–16.
Schüle, Andreas. "'Denn er ist wie Du': Zu Übersetzung und Verständnis des alttestamentlichen Liebesgebotes Lev 19,18." *Zeitschrift für die Alttestamentliche Wissenschaft* 113 (2001): 515–34.
Tigay, Jeffrey H. *Deuteronomy*. JPS Torah Commentary. New York: Jewish Publication Society, 1996.
———. "On the Meaning of *Ṭ(W)ṬPT*." *Journal of Biblical Literature* 101 (1982): 321–31.
Tov, Emanuel. *Textual Criticism and the Hebrew Bible*. 3rd ed. Minneapolis: Fortress, 2012.
Walton, John H. "The Object Lesson of Jonah 4:5-7 and the Purpose of the Book of Jonah." *Bulletin of Biblical Research* 2 (1992): 47–57.
Weinfeld, Moshe. *Deuteronomy 1–11*. Anchor Bible 5. New York: Doubleday, 1991.
Wickes, W. *A Treatise on the Accentuation of the Twenty-One So-Called Prose Books of the Old Testament*. Oxford: Clarendon, 1887.
Wright, Christopher J. H. *Deuteronomy*. New International Biblical Commentary. Peabody, Mass.: Hendrickson, 1996.
Yeivin, Israel. *Introduction to the Tiberian Masorah*. Edited and translated by E. J. Revell. Masoretic Studies 5. Missoula, Mont.: Scholars Press, 1980.
Yule, George. *Pragmatics*. Oxford: Oxford University Press, 1996.
Zevit, Ziony. *The Anterior Construction in Classical Hebrew*. Society of Biblical Literature Monograph Series 50. Atlanta: Scholars Press, 1998.
Zimmerli, Walther. "I Am Yahweh." Pages 1–28 in idem, *I Am Yahweh*, edited by Walter Brueggemann, translated by Douglas W. Stott. Atlanta: John Knox, 1982.

AUTHOR INDEX

Entries with more than 100 occurrences have *passim* ("everywhere")

AC, 37, 48, 52, 62, 70, 90, 116, 120, 124–25, 127, 133, 135, 139–40, 144, 153–54, 157, 169, 181, 200, 212, 217, 219, 226, 233, 238, 241, 245–46, 271, 278, 285, 295, 297, 299, 308, 321, 324, 330, 335, 337, 343, 350, 355
Andersen, 32
Arnold, 190
Austin, 26, 86

Barr, 49, 120
Bauckham, 169
BDB, 70, 110, 124, 149, 155, 172, 315, 322
BHQ, 19, 44, 66, 74, 94–95, 109, 112, 126, 150, 159, 168, 171, 188, 190, 195, 213, 242, 262, 264, 272, 302, 312, 340
BHS, 185, 262
Blau, 56, 62, 204, 297–300
Block, 101, 214, 230, 269, 328, 337, 346
Bruno, 214
Buth, 8, 32, 69, 121, 280

Callaham, 5, 34, 156

Carasik, 62, 137
Cassuto, 188
CDCH, 149, 155, 158
Christensen, 11
Choi, 355
Conklin, 55
Cook, 3, 16, 19, 26, 34, 41, 64, 76, 86, 93, 106, 120, 151, 164, 172, 219, 266, 277, 288–89, 339
Costecalde, 237
Craigie, 18, 56, 123, 142, 177, 181, 194–95, 202, 210, 219, 266
Crystal, 355

de Regt, 4–5
DeRouchie, 4, 7, 175, 180–81, 183–84, 207, 237, 261, 266, 291, 312, 328, 345
DHS, 220, 225
Dooley, 9
Driver, 13–14, 29, 66, 88, 94, 103, 107, 109, 111–13, 115, 117, 119, 146, 159, 160, 162–64, 167–68, 174–76, 214–15, 217, 246, 252, 255–56, 266, 272, 282, 289–90, 294, 303, 328, 332, 336–37
Dyk, 135, 319

Eslinger, 336

Fishbane, 147
Frese, 193, 217

Geller, 121, 127, 132, 137
GKC, *passim*
Gemser, 14
Goudoever, von, 16

HALOT, 23, 29, 53, 62, 66–67, 76, 87, 98, 124, 126, 134, 149, 155, 158, 172, 188–89, 195, 205, 216, 223, 235, 246, 252, 255, 277, 296, 313, 328, 341
Hawk, 13
Heller, 5, 16
Hillers, 58, 127
Himmelfarb, 119
Hoftijzer, 35
Holmstedt, 6, 8–9, 12, 36, 49, 51, 77, 84, 88, 95, 120, 123, 139, 140, 154, 166, 171–72, 176, 192, 200, 275, 288, 311, 314, 318, 322, 330, 332, 335, 350, 355

Janzen, 214
JM, *passim*
Joosten, 3

Kraut, 214
Kreuzer, 149
Kroeze, 355

Lambdin, 42
Lapsley, 190
Leeuwen, van, 258
Levenson, 128
Levinsohn, 9
Lindquist, 109
Lohfink, 229
Longacre, 5
Lowery, 135, 319

Lundbom, 77, 79, 101, 162, 167–69, 174, 185–86, 188, 210, 216, 230, 235, 253, 266–67, 269, 282–83, 312, 314, 322, 325–26, 328, 337, 340, 342, 345

MacDonald, 167, 214
Malessa, 135
Mayes, 24, 128, 161, 185, 265
McBride, 214
McConville, 11–12, 44, 159, 167, 201, 216, 222, 235, 252–53, 265, 269, 301, 348, 352
McKay, 190
Meek, 341
Meier, 21
Merrill, 301
Merwe, van der, 28, 109, 293, 296, 355
Miller, 28, 61, 109, 214, 293, 296, 357
MNK, 14, 30, 48, 50, 52, 90, 129, 140, 150, 154–55, 173, 182, 214, 217, 219, 239, 241, 252, 255, 264, 290, 301, 320–21, 326, 350, 355
Moberly, 214
Moran, 65, 190
Moshavi, 71, 91, 109, 163, 181, 234, 236, 272, 290, 321
Muraoka, 36, 48, 121, 135, 168, 220, 282, 353

Naudé, 28, 109, 293, 296, 355
Nelson, 11, 13, 17, 19, 46, 62–63, 82–83, 92, 94, 101, 112, 114, 123, 126, 128, 131, 154, 160, 167, 169, 185, 188, 195, 215, 217, 235, 241, 253, 265–66, 269, 275, 282, 284, 320, 325, 328, 348, 352–53
Nicol, 336

O'Connell, 258
O'Connor, 355
Olson, 16, 122, 248–49, 258, 279

Rad, von, 169, 174
Revell, 93, 130
Robar, 3
Robson, 29, 50, 128, 132, 134, 137, 230, 248, 258, 279

Sarna, 65
Schüle, 193

Talstra, 135, 319
Tigay, 33, 41–42, 44, 62, 65, 91, 98, 110, 113, 115, 117, 136, 142, 149, 172, 177, 183–85, 190, 213, 216–217, 229–30, 253, 255, 266, 269, 274, 296, 321–22, 328–29, 331–32, 337, 340, 353
Tov, 73

Walton, 52
Weinfeld, 13–14, 17, 19–20, 41–42, 53, 62, 78, 88, 101, 109, 112, 114–15, 117, 123, 126, 128–29, 131–32, 134, 136, 142, 149, 154, 156, 159–60, 163–64, 172–75, 179, 181, 183, 187–88, 192, 196, 207, 213–16, 230, 235, 237, 241–42, 251–53, 255, 265, 267–69, 274–75, 282, 294, 314, 328, 331–32, 340, 342, 345, 350, 353
WHS, 24, 44, 47, 50, 52, 55, 65, 70, 75, 85, 125, 131–32, 146, 150–51, 154, 165, 167, 171–73, 181, 186, 192, 206–7, 212, 219, 222, 227–29, 236, 239–42, 257, 266, 273, 284, 287–89, 292–94, 296–301, 303–4, 308, 313, 315, 318, 320–21, 323–26, 336–37, 343, 350, 352
Wickes, 119
WO, *passim*
Wright, 16, 164, 278
WS, 17, 141, 154–55, 163, 192

Yeivin, 339
Yule, 9, 356

Zevit, 314
Zimmerli, 185

SUBJECT INDEX

Entries with more than 100 occurrences have *passim*
("everywhere")

accusative, 3; adverbial, 34, 72, 75, 100, 117, 135, 157, 191, 282, 290, 293, 296, 314; attributive, of state, 164, 188, 203, 212, 241–42, 267, 291, 322–23; cognate, 88, 255, 298, 335; complement, *passim*; double, 39, 53, 58, 70, 76, 82, 123, 127, 133–34, 140, 144, 151, 169, 200, 209, 262–63, 276, 287, 336, 343; indirect, 70, 75, 151, 164, 169, 181, 203, 212, 267, 291, 302; internal, 199, 255, 298; motion toward, 90; predicative, 157, 181

adjective: attributive, 31, 39, 48, 49, 86, 111, 118, 123–24, 133, 135, 154, 164–65, 168, 188, 192, 202, 212, 215, 253, 282, 291, 300, 322, 347; demonstrative, 112; gentilic, 19, 24–25, 47, 64, 86, 104, 110–11, 113, 174, 233, 312, 352; predicative, 19, 32, 48–49, 85, 120, 227, 273, 276, 282; substantive (substantival), 19, 36, 86, 104, 111, 113, 133, 147, 172, 189, 224, 233, 241–42, 247, 252, 288, 325

adverb: item, 48, 57, 71, 102, 108, 119, 180, 239, 262, 268, 284–85, 298–99, 320, 329; locative, 49, 57, 59, 120–21, 134, 157–58, 170, 172, 177, 179, 311; restrictive, 91, 135, 138, 320; temporal, 72, 77, 141, 159, 173, 211, 261, 264, 317, 337

apposition, *passim*

anaphora, 278, 324

anterior, 56, 269, 314

apocopation, 16, 33, 69, 75, 87, 95, 116, 126, 185, 294–95, 304, 309, 355

apodosis, 8; causal, 167–68, 353; conditional, 159, 201, 202, 229–30, 249–50, 277–78, 340, 344–47; imperatival, 218; temporal, 80–81, 155–60, 202, 221, 227, 231, 233, 265–66, 269, 271, 273, 289–90, 300–301, 340, 351; waw of apodosis, 167–68, 227, 245, 353

asseverative, 135, 162, 328, 345

asyndesis (asyndetic), *passim*

by-form, 64, 74, 94, 216, 255, 355

369

cardinal (number), 17, 29
casus pendens: *see* **extraposition**
cataphora (cataphoric), 236
cleft sentence, 36, 110, 121, 355
clause: adversative, 157, 181, 236, 263, 284–85, 318, 332; causal, 8, 47, 62–63, 101, 123, 161, 167–68, 170, 219, 244–45, 352–53; circumstantial, 78, 141, 173, 182, 200, 283–84, 289–91, 295, 297, 306, 309; comparative, 30, 39–40, 51, 65, 67, 77, 79–80, 84, 91–92, 101, 105, 133–34, 164, 191, 193–94, 208, 223, 225, 230, 264, 278, 311, 314; conditional, 8, 148, 154–55, 158–59, 201–2, 219, 221, 226–27, 229–30, 249–50, 272, 277–78, 339–40, 344–47, 349, 350–51; disjunctive, 6, 45–46, 63, 65, 75, 77, 92, 105, 107, 141, 143, 150, 236, 311; exceptive, 108, 119, 126; explanatory, 7, 35–36, 58, 70, 72, 75, 82, 92–93, 101, 108, 112, 121, 125–27, 135–36, 142, 145, 151, 154, 160, 162, 166, 175, 182, 188, 190, 202, 219, 222–23, 235–39, 248, 253, 256–58, 265–66, 269, 285–86, 292, 298, 303, 322–24, 328, 335, 345; **null-copula**, *passim*; purpose, 88, 92–93, 140, 170–71, 192–95, 206, 209, 211–12, 224–25, 260, 333–34, 344; purpose (negative), 63, 139, 153, 218, 221–23, 254, 256–57, 271–72, 275, 304–5, 340–41; relative (non-restrictive), 8, 19, 40, 57–59, 69, 84–85, 92, 97, 110, 135, 149, 176, 185, 221, 263, 275, 281, 292, 306, 325, 335, 351; relative (restrictive), *passim*; restrictive, 96–98, 108, 117; result, 79, 90–91, 129–30, 155, 157, 193, 204, 209, 225, 228, 238, 260–61, 321, 323, 341–42, 356; **tripartite** nominal, 36, 121, 154, 166, 170, 214, 241, 282, 314, 322, 335, 357
cognate: accusative (*see* accusative, cognate); genitive (*see* genitive, cognate); language, 149, 216; verb, 156, 224, 233, 250, 258, 277, 339, 345
cohortative, 31, 41–42, 90–91, 124, 140, 207, 294
collocation, 88
comparative: clause (*see* clause, comparative); *min*, 48, 98, 169, 233, 246, 250, 346; phrase, 29, 75–76, 93, 118, 123, 136–37, 163, 169, 193, 203, 258, 277–78, 291, 308, 310, 314, 321, 326, 335–36, 344; superlative (*see* superlative)
compensatory lengthening, 15, 292
complementizer, 21, 27, 42, 51, 54, 68, 81, 89, 116, 118, 120, 122–23, 132, 140, 156, 170, 182, 193, 201, 219, 226, 241, 263–64, 276, 282–83, 285, 288, 293, 301, 327–32, 350, 355
compound preposition, 147, 156, 255, 294, 296, 315, 318, 324, 329, 346
coordination (coordinate), 6–7, 40, 42, 63, 140, 160, 200, 206, 248, 292, 338

dagesh forte, 16, 18, 32, 43–44, 65, 86, 95, 106, 167, 230, 234, 273, 299, 308, 332
dagesh lene, 17, 25
defective (verb), 28–29, 125, 131, 171, 209, 229, 298, 236
defective writing, defectively (cf. *plene*), 17–18, 27, 77, 117, 179, 194, 211, 248, 300
deictic (deixis), 12, 28, 109, 293, 296, 325, 355
demonstrative, 12, 21, 28, 39, 72, 103, 112, 120, 126, 134, 152, 173, 202, 206, 236, 251, 254, 278, 292, 325, 343

Subject Index

denominative, 44, 66, 355
directional *heh*: *see* paragogic [*heh*]
discourse active, 9, 58–59, 61–62, 76, 82–83, 94, 96, 100, 108, 139, 150, 156, 227, 229, 268, 292–93, 314, 330, 355
domains (of discourse), 3–5, 21–22, 178
dual, 104

ellipsis, 17, 109, 124, 243, 320, 328, 338, 356
extraposition, 9, 36, 49, 57–59, 84, 88, 121, 132, 154, 166, 170, 214, 241, 247, 275, 282, 309, 314, 322, 335, 355

focus (fronting), *passim*
fronting: *see* **focus** and **topic**

genitive, 3, 103, 137, 189, 245, 267, 274, 347; adjectival, 78, 81, 115, 117, 143, 147, 150, 329, 196, 238, 267, 274, 286, 296, 308, 329; adverbial, 212, 267, 323, 340; agency, (*see* genitive, subjective); appositional, 157, 192; association, 43, 86, 114; attributive (*see* genitive, adjectival); cognate, 320, 322; objective, 87–88, 150, 161, 189, 212, 241, 323, 340, 348; species, 191; subjective, 47, 189, 240, 301, 305–6, 329; superlative (*see* genitive, cognate)
gentilic (*see* adjective, gentilic)
gerund (gerundial), 23, 68, 79, 137, 168, 180, 191, 211–12, 225, 243, 260, 265, 271, 297, 318, 323, 343, 351, 356
gerundive, 39, 180, 253, 322, 356

hapax, 62, 70, 109, 268, 304, 356
hendiadys, 93, 241, 245, 303, 306, 356
homonym, 36, 64, 71, 94, 109, 124, 155, 356

inclusio, 20, 26, 67, 105, 194, 230, 269, 286, 326, 330, 342, 348, 356
indirect volitive, 31, 42, 207, 294, 308–9, 356
interrogative (cf. question), 6, 30, 42, 48, 109, 123, 136, 163–65, 202, 226, 250, 262, 318

jussive, 16, 29–30, 35, 41–42, 70, 75, 82, 101, 125, 185, 187, 248, 283, 287, 303–4, 315

litotes, 73, 268, 356
locative *heh*: *see* **paragogic** [*heh*]

marked (cf. unmarked), 8, 32, 59, 61, 164
merism, 36, 123, 170, 216–17, 267, 319, 356
metonymy, 46, 67, 92, 102, 139, 168, 192, 215, 217, 252, 299, 305, 356

oath, 54–59
ordinal, 17, 297

paragogic [*heh*], 43, 356
paragogic [*nun*], 17, 37, 41, 49, 88, 135, 140–41, 146, 156, 158, 194, 200, 209, 211–12, 222, 224, 236, 244, 256, 260, 263, 272, 275, 278–79, 345, 356
paragogic [*yod*], 55, 142, 151, 271, 356
paronomastic infinitive absolute, 155–57, 224, 233, 250, 258, 277, 339, 345, 357
particle, 21, 28, 30, 34, 48, 72, 76, 82, 109, 224, 250, 293, 296, 318, 337, 349–50
partitive: *bet*, 55; *min*, 44, 70, 75, 82, 108, 110, 114, 131, 173, 222, 239, 321
performative, 26, 86, 133, 155–56, 277–78
periphrasis (**periphrastic**), 137, 288, 357

plene, 19, 117, 175, 188, 248
pleonasm (pleonastic), 125, 163, 180, 202, 288, 337
predicate, 7–8, 12–13; adjectival, 141, 214, 250, 288; adverbial, 163, 177, 206, 326, 332, 335, 337; participial, 49, 81, 120, 202, 246, 264, 278, 284–85, 288–89, 318, 349, 352; substantival (or nominal), 78, 135, 175, 192, 210, 214, 223, 276, 282, 306, 322, 325, 337
protasis, 8; conditional, 8, 55, 154–55, 158–59, 201–2, 227, 229–30, 249–50, 277–78, 339, 344–45, 349–50; temporal, 8, 80, 154–56, 159–60, 217–18, 220–21, 226–27, 232–33, 265–66, 269, 271–72, 289, 300, 351
purpose; clause (*see* clause, purpose); phrase, 53, 64, 93–94, 140–41, 165–69, 172, 228, 261, 263, 280–81, 285, 290, 306, 312–13, 315, 319

qere-ketiv, 27, 95, 123, 189–190, 241–42, 248, 262, 298, 336
question: indirect, 262; rhetorical, 30, 109, 128, 138, 161–63, 165–66, 202, 317–18, 352

resumption/resumptive: pronoun, 36, 42, 49, 51, 53, 56–57, 59, 66, 84, 121, 123, 132, 134, 149, 154, 166, 214, 247, 251–52, 268, 274, 282, 288, 312, 324, 335, 337, 347–48; adverb, 51, 66, 121, 134, 157, 274, 305, 335

stative (verb), 47, 59, 133, 141, 173, 182, 220, 240, 252, 298, 323–24, 346
superlative, 239, 320, 322; relative/comparative superlative, 36, 320, 322
syncopation, 159, 200, 223, 229, 357

syndesis (syndetic), 6, 183, 197, 209–10

topic (fronting), 9, 20, 29, 36–37, 49, 57–61, 69, 71–73, 76–77, 83–84, 91, 96, 103, 108, 132, 139, 150, 154, 166, 170, 201, 207, 214, 234, 236, 241, 256, 268, 272, 280–82, 289–90, 300, 307, 311–12, 314, 317, 321, 335, 342, 357
triggered inversion, 9, 12, 30, 39–40, 51, 58, 65, 67, 72, 77, 79–80, 84, 92–93, 101, 108, 118, 120, 127, 130, 134, 160, 164, 176, 191, 202, 223, 236–37, 248, 251, 253, 257, 261, 264, 275, 281, 286, 292, 303, 314, 324, 341, 357

unmarked (cf. marked), 8, 22, 28, 48, 69, 72, 81, 83, 85, 107, 108, 113, 116, 118, 120, 134, 137, 141, 151, 175, 177, 179–80, 182, 210, 223, 239, 252–53, 264–65, 268, 272, 276, 278, 280, 306, 309, 325, 337, 349

volitive, indirect: *see* **indirect volitive**

word order (cf. **triggered inversion**), 8, 357; S–P, 12, 22, 28, 32, 40, 48, 69, 72, 76, 81, 83, 85, 107, 108, 113, 116, 118, 120, 130, 134, 137, 141, 151, 154, 175, 177, 179–80, 182, 184, 210, 223, 236, 239, 251–52, 264–65, 268, 272, 276, 278, 282, 306, 309, 325, 337, 347, 349; P–S, 12, 15, 23, 30, 32, 36, 39–40, 44, 51, 65, 68, 77, 79–80, 84, 92, 109, 130, 134–35, 154, 161, 164, 191, 202, 223, 236–37, 248, 250–51, 257, 261, 264, 275, 286, 293, 303, 312, 314, 335; X–P–S, 20, 120, 236, 239–40, 251, 335; X–S–P, 32, 121, 284–85